CRIME
PREVENTION

Edited by

David A. Mackey
Professor
Department of Criminal Justice
Plymouth State University
Plymouth, NH

Kristine Levan
Assistant Professor
Department of Criminal Justice
Plymouth State University
Plymouth, NH

JONES & BARTLETT
LEARNING

World Headquarters
Jones & Bartlett Learning
5 Wall Street
Burlington, MA 01803
978-443-5000
info@jblearning.com
www.jblearning.com

Jones & Bartlett Learning books and products are available through most bookstores and online booksellers. To contact Jones & Bartlett Learning directly, call 800-832-0034, fax 978-443-8000, or visit our website, www.jblearning.com.

Production Credits:
Publisher: Cathleen Sether
Acquisitions Editor: Sean Connelly
Editorial Assistant: Caitlin Murphy
Director of Production: Amy Rose
Production Assistant: Alyssa Lawrence
Marketing Manager: Lindsay White
Project Management Services: DataStream Content Solutions, LLC
Rights and Permissions Manager: Katherine Crighton
Permissions Supervisor: Toby Leith
Rights and Photo Research Supervisor: Anna Genoese
Cover Design: Kristin E. Parker
Cover Image: © B.G. Smith/Shutterstock, Inc.
Printing and Binding: Malloy, Inc.
Cover Printing: Malloy, Inc.

Some images in this book feature models. These models do not necessarily endorse, represent, or participate in the activities represented in the images.

Library of Congress Cataloging-in-Publication Data
Mackey, David A.
  Crime prevention / David A. Mackey and Kristine Levan.
     p. cm.
  Includes index.
  ISBN 978-1-4496-1593-2 (pbk.)—ISBN 1-4496-1593-7 (pbk.)
1. Crime prevention.   I. Levan, Kristine.   II. Title.
  HV7431.M24 2013
  364.4—dc23
                              2011048036

6048
Printed in the United States of America
15 14 13 12 11   10 9 8 7 6 5 4 3 2 1

Dedication

To my parents Garry and Dotti, and to Nick my partner and best friend.

KL

To my wife Lisa and my sons Ryan and Tyler.

DM

Contents

Contents

Preface

This work seeks to contribute to the growing body of literature that examines crime prevention rooted in the medical model tradition of primary, secondary, and tertiary prevention. This book was written out of a desire to generate a collective work on crime prevention, including a merging of theory and practice. Moreover, we share an interest in evidence-based practices in criminal justice. It seems practical and sensible to provide information to students and practitioners alike on various crime prevention practices and their effectiveness.

As criminal justice educators, we discuss programs, policies, and tactics intended to have a positive impact on the reduction or prevention of crime. Some students have not yet developed a critical appreciation for examining society's efforts to address crime and criminal victimization by their acceptance of current efforts as effective approaches. Other students question why we, as a society, continue to use programs that fall short of their intended outcomes. Likewise, students may question the wisdom of favoring solutions geared toward short-term impacts at the expense of long-term efforts that have the potential to both improve outcomes and be more cost effective. This work seeks to bridge the gap of preexisting knowledge of students by providing a comprehensive discussion of a range of crime prevention topics incorporating a theoretical foundation, previous research, as well as policy analysis.

Crime prevention is an important topic, both in American society and worldwide. As researchers, we know that there is no short supply of opportunities to commit various types of crimes. As such, in order to reduce the likelihood that we, or others in society, will become victims of crime, it seems necessary that we become knowledgeable on topics related to crime prevention. Selections for this volume reflect a range of interests and applications for crime prevention. Both traditional and emerging areas of crime prevention are reflected throughout this volume, ranging from family/schools, guns, policing, sentencing, and correctional programs to technology, surveillance, and specific efforts to protect more vulnerable populations. These selections are included in this volume to provide the reader with insights into cross-cultural crime prevention. The purpose of their inclusion is to provide the reader with a level of understanding of traditionally low-crime societies. As the editors and contributing authors of this crime prevention textbook, we sought other contributing authors who were experts in their specialized sub-fields of criminal justice and criminology. We are very excited to bring this information to the reader, and have provided chapters on current topics of interest in the field of crime prevention. In particular, we acknowledge the change in direction that crime prevention has taken in light of modern factors, such as an increased awareness of terrorism and increases in technological capabilities.

Acknowledgments

The editors would like to thank the authors of the chapters: Timothy Austin, Dhruba J. Bora, Hank J. Brightman, George Burruss, Michael Bush, Kevin M. Cieplowski, Kimberly A. DeTardo-Bora, Steven Downing, Rod K. Brunson, Nicholas Corsaro, Jessica L. Deaton, Seungmug Lee, Danielle McDonald, Edmund F. McGarrell, Katherine Polzer, Eric S. See, Tony Smith, Jason Scott, Victoria M. Time, Patricia B. Wagner, and Harry J. Wilson. We are thankful to share their expertise. Without exception, it was a pleasure to work with these authors. Some we have known for some time while others we consider new friends.

Appreciation and acknowledgment also goes out to the administration of Plymouth State University. David Mackey had the benefit of being on sabbatical during this project. We would also like to thank Sean Connelly and Caitlin Murphy, our editors at Jones & Bartlett Learning, and Cherie Andrews, our project manager from DSCS, who provided outstanding support for the project.

We would like to acknowledge the following individuals for reviewing the text:

Joshua R. Battin, *Mansfield University of Pennsylvania*
Robert A. Brooks, *Worcester State College*
Daniel R. Lee, *Indiana University of Pennsylvania*
Christopher M. Sedelmaier, *University of New Haven*
Martha L. Shockey-Eckles, *Saint Louis University*
Mahendra Singh, *Grambling State University*

List of Contributors

Timothy Austin, *Indiana University of Pennsylvania*
Dhruba J. Bora, *Marshall University*
Hank J. Brightman, *United States Naval War College*
Rod K. Brunson, *Southern Illinois University—Carbondale*
George W. Burruss, *Southern Illinois University—Carbondale*
Michael Bush, *Northern Kentucky University*
Kevin Cieplowski, *Ohio Northern University*
Nicholas Corsaro, *Southern Illinois University—Carbondale*
Jessica L. Deaton, *Southern Illinois University—Carbondale*
Kimberly A. DeTardo-Bora, *Marshall University*
Steven Downing, *University of Ontario Institute of Technology*
Seungmug Lee, *Western Illinois University*
Kristine Levan, *Plymouth State University*
David A. Mackey, *Plymouth State University*
Danielle McDonald, *Northern Kentucky University*
Edmund F. McGarrell, *Michigan State University*
Katherine Polzer, *Texas Christian University*
Jason Scott, *Rochester Institute of Technology*
Eric S. See, *Methodist University*
Tony R. Smith, *Rochester Institute of Technology*
Victoria M. Time, *Old Dominion University*
Patricia B. Wagner, *Youngstown State University*
Harry J. Wilson, *Ohio Northern University*

CHAPTER 1

Introduction to Crime Prevention

David A. Mackey
Plymouth State University

INTRODUCTION

On Sunday, October 4, 2009, the peaceful tranquility of Mont Vernon, New Hampshire, was shattered after police responded to an open 911 call with no one on the telephone line. Initial news reports indicated that 42-year-old Kimberly Cates had been murdered and her 11-year-old daughter severely injured during the course of an early morning home invasion. The mother and daughter had been attacked with a machete during a burglary-turned-murder. Tips immediately began to surface, leading the police to investigate four local youths: Steven Spader, Christopher Gribble, William Marks, and Quinn Glover. According to the police affidavit (State of New Hampshire, 2009), Gribble stabbed Jamie Cates in the right lung and then tried to stab her in the heart through her back. Steven Spader mortally wounded Kimberly Cates. The four assailants intended to kill both mother and daughter to eliminate witnesses to the crime.

Steven Spader was the first of the four individuals to stand trial for the murder. On his 19th birthday, Spader received a sentence of life in prison for the murder of Kimberly Cates. With media cameras capturing the moment, Spader asked his attorney if the jury would sing "Happy Birthday" to him (WMUR-TV, 2010). In a separate trial, Christopher Gribble received a life sentence following his unsuccessful attempt to use the insanity defense. As for the other defendants, Quinn Glover would be sentenced to 20–40 years in prison for burglary, burglary conspiracy, and robbery, and William Marks received a 30–60-year sentence for first-degree assault, burglary conspiracy, and murder conspiracy. Autumn Savoy, a fifth suspect subsequently arrested for hiding evidence and providing alibis for the other four, received a 5–12-year prison sentence and a suspended 3.5–7-year term after his release when he pled guilty to conspiracy to hinder apprehension and two counts of hindering apprehension (Associated Press, 2011).

The Mont Vernon murders shattered the tranquility of the local area. Residents unaccustomed to crime faced a range of emotions, from shock and fear to anger. Some communities experience crime, whether property, violent, or so-called victimless crimes, on a regular basis, and criminal activities and violence often follow a familiar pattern. According to the Federal Bureau of Investigation's annual crime statistics for New Hampshire (Federal Bureau of Investigation, 2009a), Kimberly and Jamie Cates were the victims of Mont Vernon's only two violent crimes in the entire year. Mont Vernon, a town of just over 2,400 people, is located in the safest state in the nation, according to the FBI's Uniform Crime Reports.

COSTS OF CRIME

The costs of crime to society are staggering, despite the fact that the United States has experienced a substantial decline in the overall amount of crime since 1990. The FBI notes that from 2000 to 2009, the nation's violent crime rate dropped 15.2% (Federal Bureau of Investigation, 2009b) and declined 40% from 1990 to 2009 (Federal Bureau of Investigation, 2009c). Results from the 2009 National Crime Victimization Survey (NCVS) indicate that criminal victimization is at a historic low point since the inception of this victimization measurement survey (Truman & Rand, 2010). Results from the NCVS indicated specific declines of 39% from 2000 to 2009 for the rate of violent crime and a decline of 29% for the rate of property crime (see **Table 1-1**). Nevertheless, crime prevention remains a central issue for the criminal justice system as well as society as a whole. In 2009, the Uniform Crime Reports index of offenses (Federal Bureau of Investigation, 2009c) indicated that more than 1.3 million violent crimes and 9.3 million property crimes have been reported.

Although these decreases in crime might imply that the costs of criminal justice have decreased proportionately, such is not the case. Data from 2007 (Bureau of Justice Statistics, 2011) show

TABLE 1-1 Rates of Criminal Victimization and Percentage Change, by Type of Crime, Between 2000 and 2009

Type of Crime	Victimization Rates		Percentage Change
	2000	2009	2000–2009
Violent crime	27.9	17.1	−38.7*
Rape/sexual assault	1.2	0.5	−56.9*
Robbery	3.2	2.1	−34.9*
Assault	23.5	14.5	−38.3*
Aggravated	5.7	3.2	−43.1*
Simple	17.8	11.3	−36.8*
Personal theft	1.2	0.5	−56.6*
Property crime	178.1	127.4	−28.5*
Household burglary	31.8	25.6	−19.4*
Motor vehicle theft	8.6	6.0	−30.5*
Theft	137.7	95.7	−30.5*

Note. The total population age 12 or older was 226,804,610 in 2000 and 254,105,610 in 2009. The total number of households in 2000 was 108,352,960 and 122,327,660 in 2009. An asterisk (*) indicates that difference is significant at the 95%-confidence level. Victimization rates are per 1,000 persons age 12 or older for violent crime or per 1,000 households for property crime. Differences between the annual rates shown do not take into account changes that may have occurred during interim years. Percent change calculated on unrounded estimates. Violent crime excludes murder because the NCVS is based on interviews with victims and therefore cannot measure murder. Personal theft includes pocket picking, completed purse snatching, and attempted purse snatching.

Adapted from: Truman, J. L., & M. R. Rand, 2010. Criminal Victimization, 2009. Bureau of Justice Statistics, U.S. Department of Justice, p. 2. Retrieved from http://bjs.ojp.usdoj.gov/content/pub/pdf/cv09.pdf.

that the United States annually spent an estimated $230 billion on criminal justice. This figure includes only costs associated with police, courts, and corrections; vast additional funds go toward homeland security. In addition to the costs of criminal justice at the federal, state, county, and local levels, there are costs borne by the victim, whether the victim is an individual or a business entity. Some monetary aspects of criminal victimization are more easily counted than others. For instance, Maguire (2003) notes the average loss in 2002 for a robbery was $1,281, for a purse snatching, $332, and for a bicycle theft, $257. The costs of crime are both direct and indirect and include money spent on private security and loss prevention, alarm monitoring, medical costs, lost wages/lost work days, stolen property, increased security or target hardening measures, and increased product costs due to shoplifting and pilferage. Other costs include incarceration and those that are more difficult to quantify, such as the associated impact on prisoners' families and children, subsequent public assistance for those families, and even lost tax revenue that might have been generated had individuals been working instead of serving time.

Society bears the costs of crime and crime prevention in both the public and the private sectors. In fact, private security now accounts for more spending and more personnel than traditional public policing. The U.S. Bureau of Labor Statistics (2011) notes that there were approximately 884,000 persons employed as police or detectives in 2008, while private security employed 1.1 million individuals. This gap favoring private sector security is projected to increase even further. The Bureau of Labor Statistics notes that while the number of policing jobs is expected to increase 10% by 2018, private security jobs are expected to increase by 14% during the same period (U.S. Bureau of Labor Statistics, 2011). As these statistics suggest, crime prevention efforts benefit when private security and public law enforcement agencies collaborate. For instance, the Law Enforcement–Private Security Consortium (2009) emphasizes collaboration in the areas of homeland security, infrastructure protection, special event security, transportation security, and financial crime investigation. Collaboration in these areas provides both public and private sector crime prevention entities with additional resources and deeper knowledge of specific areas, such as power-generating facilities, manufacturing plants, and even schools. The consortium also notes specific examples of collaboration in which private security provides law enforcement with access to closed-circuit television capabilities, thereby expanding the resources available to law enforcement without forcing taxpayers to support the purchase, installation, and maintenance of such security tools.

THEORETICAL FOUNDATIONS OF CRIME PREVENTION

Several theoretical models, drawn from both the public health field and criminology, are directly applicable to the prevention of crime. By applying these theoretical models, researchers and policy makers can plan and implement intervention programs, that is, programs to prevent crime. Having a sound theoretical model helps researchers evaluate such programs and determine the impact of the intervention on the targeted problem. Farrington (2000) notes the recent trend of identifying key variables for delinquency prevention during the course of longitudinal studies that policy makers can then use when implementing delinquency prevention programs. Ideally, this connection would produce a synergy of policy implementation and delivery, which can then be tested empirically. Information from those tests can then help officials improve the intervention program.

Public Health Model

Until recently, criminal justice policy focused on reacting to criminal events. This traditional approach relied heavily on the police responding to calls for service or reports of suspected criminal activity. With this type of reactive policy approach in place, society can assess police effectiveness on the basis of number calls for service, reported crime rates, clearance rates, and similar measures. Recently, however, the criminal justice system has shifted its emphasis to the public health model, or the medical model. To illustrate the medical model, consider approaches to prevent individuals from suffering heart attacks. Would it be wise for society's main response to the dangers of heart attacks to be a solely reactive focus on advancing emergency room technology to respond to heart attack victims? Individuals would also benefit from proactive lifestyle changes to reduce their risk of heart trouble. Heart-healthy lifestyle changes may include diet, exercise, and smoking cessation (Farrington, 2000). In addition, individuals who are at increased risk of a heart attack may start a risk-mitigation regimen of medications as well as additional lifestyle modifications.

The public health model, when applied to criminal behavior, emphasizes three interrelated and coordinated approaches for reducing the both the incidence and seriousness of criminal behavior: primary prevention, secondary prevention, and tertiary prevention. Primary prevention seeks to strengthen *resiliency factors*, which are factors associated with avoiding criminal behavior, and to reduce *risk factors*, which are factors that increase an individual's propensity to engage in crime (Shader, 2003). Farrington (2000) notes that some may view protective factors and risk factors as opposite ends of a continuum for the same variable, but such a view is not accurate because some variables have a nonlinear relationship to delinquency. Farrington points out that statistical analysis has allowed researchers to compute an odds ratio to determine the relative impact of such factors on offending patterns. This calculation would be a critical tool for performing a cost-benefit analysis of various types of interventions. Armed with such information, communities can then implement interventions that target factors more selectively and also emphasize those interventions targeting factors with the greatest cost-savings potential.

Primary prevention typically focuses on proactive and preventative efforts well before the onset of crime. Primary prevention strategies in the area of juvenile delinquency include prenatal programs, parenting programs, and preschool programs with delinquency prevention potential (Regoli, Hewitt, & DeLisi, 2010). For example, prenatal programs focus resources on improving the physical well-being of the mother. These efforts seek to avoid or minimize negative factors for the baby such as low birthweight, neurological impairments, and exposure to environmental toxins associated with developmental and educational impairments. All of these negative factors are linked to poor school achievement, which, years down the road, could lead to a higher likelihood of involvement in delinquency.

Secondary prevention focuses on individuals and settings considered to be at an increased risk for continuation of delinquency. As Regoli, Hewitt, and DeLisi (2010) note, the focus of secondary prevention is to reduce the prevalence, seriousness, or duration of delinquent involvement. Secondary prevention programs target a narrower population than primary prevention programs. These individuals are at risk for offending, but have not engaged in serious, chronic delinquency. Farrington (2000) identified nine criminality risk factors for boys aged 8 to 10 in separate studies conducted in London and Pittsburgh 3 decades apart. The nine variables were "hyperactivity, poor concentration, low achievement, an antisocial father, large family size, low family income, a broken family, poor parental supervision, and parental disharmony" (p. 5). To counter these and similar risk factors, between 1995 and 1999 the Juvenile Mentoring Program (JUMP) funded 164 mentoring programs serving approximately 7,500 youths (Novotney, Mertinko, Lange, & Kelly Baker, 2000). The average age for juveniles starting the program was 12, and about 75% of the boys served by the program had problems in school identified as behavioral issues, poor grades, or truancy.

Tertiary prevention seeks to prevent further crime and delinquency by those who are already under the control of the justice system. Rehabilitative efforts are the focus of tertiary crime prevention, and they address risk and protective factors as well as isolating individuals from dangerous situations through programs like boot camps, drug and alcohol treatment programs, and educational programs. Historically, programs such as Scared Straight targeted youths whom teachers, parents, and juvenile probation officers believed were likely to engage in more serious delinquency if not be diverted from their current life trajectory. The Scared Straight approach gained popularity after the release of *Scared Straight* (1978), a TV documentary narrated by Peter Falk that showcased a confrontational juvenile awareness program led by long-term adult prisoners at what was then Rahway State Prison in New Jersey. To deter youths from crime, the Scared Straight program delivered graphic information about life inside prison and employed verbal harassment, homosexual taunts, threatened violence, and not-so-subtle intimidation on the part of the adult prisoners. A study by Finckenauer, Gavin, Hovland, and Storvoll (1999) indicated that the youths who participated in Scared Straight had worse outcomes in terms of delinquency than did their counterparts in the control group. More recently, Klenowski, Bell, and Dodson (2010) examined the research on juvenile awareness programs, including Scared Straight and similar ones. They identified eight studies of sufficient rigor, based on the requirements of experimental designs (discussed below), to include in their analysis. They conclude that juvenile awareness programs are not effective in deterring juveniles from delinquency and crime. Research on the Rahway program specifically, as well as some other studies, indicates that youths who participate in the Scared Straight program have worse outcomes than their peers who do not attend the program. Klenowski, Bell, and Dodson note that these programs typically do not include a rehabilitation component, and others contend that one Scared Straight-style encounter may be insufficient to deter youths from crime.

Rational Choice Theory

The contemporary criminal justice system, which has defined laws to deter crime and sentencing guidelines to punish crime, operates on the principles of rational choice theory. Dating back to the late 18th century, the concept of rational choice suggests that all human decisions are based on calculated self-interest. Jeremy Bentham's *Introduction to the Principles of Morals and Legislation* (1781/1948) used the term utilitarianism to identify the concept. In Bentham's view, humans judge actions according to the amount of happiness produced and will act in ways to produce the greatest level of happiness for themselves. In the same way, rational choice theorists believe that individuals have free will and can choose to engage in either criminal or noncriminal behaviors. Rational choice theory thus leads into deterrence theory, or the idea that, when the personal costs of engaging in crime outweigh the expected gains, an individual will choose not to commit a crime; the threatened punishment has thus deterred the crime (Pratt, Cullen, Blevins, Daigle, & Madensen, 2006). In this view, society needs swift, certain, and severe sanctions for criminal behavior so that individuals will choose not to engage in crime. Proponents of this view note that deterrence offers a fairly straightforward solution to the problem of crime: increasing the likelihood of detecting crime and increasing the punishments associated with specific criminal behaviors. Deterrence comes in two forms: general and specific. General deterrence seeks to prevent crime among the general population by passing laws prohibiting various acts. Specific deterrence seeks to prevent those who have already committed a crime from engaging in further criminal activity. In theory, those individuals would not commit another offense because they have experienced the unpleasant aspects of punishment. Deterrence theory has a commonsense appeal; most people find it reasonable because they themselves seek to avoid unpleasant and painful experiences. Pratt et al. (2006) contend that the focus of deterrence is at the individual level, specifically, an individual's perception of the likelihood that he or she, having committed a crime, will be apprehended and the sanction imposed.

Deterrence theory focuses heavily on the response by the formal legal and judicial system, and, as such, society does not gain the advantage of informal social control, shaming, and types of sanctioning that are not aspects of the legal or judicial system (Pratt et al., 2006). Some researchers contend that these informal controls have much more influence on the individual than do formal controls. The work of Braithwaite (1989) best illustrates the concept of reintegrative shaming. With this approach, society attempts to reintegrate the offender into the community rather than positioning such individuals to face what may amount to permanent outcast status.

Routine Activity Theory

In 1979, Cohen and Felson conceptualized routine activity theory, which is a relatively straightforward theoretical explanation for crime, although its significant utility lies in its application for crime prevention. The theory suggests that a crime is more likely to take place when three factors converge in time and place: a potential victim is present, a motivated or likely offender is also present, and capable guardians are absent. Simply stated, routine activity theory assumes a crime is more likely to take place when a motivated offender encounters a suitable target and no one is around to stop a criminal act. This theory has links to rational choice theory, since it presumes that offenders engage in a decision-making process (choosing whether to engage in crime) but in a very specific context. In routine activity theory, an individual's propensity to commit a crime remains, but what varies is the specific risk undertaken by committing the criminal act. The key component of the theory is the idea that crime can be controlled by manipulating the opportunity for crime. Opportunities for crime decrease with increasing supervision, and Felson (2002) notes that supervision can be performed either directly or indirectly. For instance, *place managers* are responsible for supervision in specific locations; examples of place managers include homeowners, teachers, bouncers, and police officers. *Handlers* provide additional supervision for those at risk of becoming an offender, while *guardians* provide supervision for potential victims; a mentor would be an example of both a handler and a guardian. With recourse to routine activity theory, one can gain a better understanding of how and why property crime and predatory violent crime vary in frequency depending on the time and place. In *Crime and Everyday Life*, Felson (2002) states that "settings vary moment to moment in their degree of temptation or control—the cues they emit—hence the degree of choice they provide. Constraints on individuals shift quickly as events unfold" (p. 41).

Environmental Criminology

Brantingham and Brantingham (1991) have elaborated an environmental theory of criminology. A fundamental starting point in their theoretical orientation is a focus on the role of space and place in the criminal event rather than on the motivations of particular offenders. They contend that patterns of criminality are a reflection of street networks, mass transit, business, and residential areas. Environmental criminology has its roots in efforts to map crime in France in the early 1800s, and most students of criminology are familiar with a study of the spatial distribution of crime by

Shaw and McKay (1969). Brantingham and Brantingham (1991) posit a number of propositions about crime and the physical environment. For example, they contend that motivated offenders use cues in the environment to compare potential victims in the physical setting to their template of a "good victim." They also argue that criminal events usually occur a short distance from an offender's home but that, with the exception of homicide, little crime occurs in the *immediate* vicinity of an offender's home. Thus, there is a peak in offending as one moves away from the home, and then a decline as one moves farther away from the home; this peak area for offenses roughly corresponds with the perception of the highest risk of getting caught and the offender's knowledge and familiarity with the area. A person's noncriminal activities take place across a wider area, termed the *awareness space*, and an offender's knowledge of that wider awareness space influences selection of an *action space*, where the offender considers the risk of apprehension to be. Brantingham and Brantingham contend that places connected to home, work, recreation, and other pursuits as well as the mode of transportation between locations (e.g., bus, subway, motor vehicle, or walking) influence the formation of an offender's awareness space. The physical distribution of potential offenders, business/commercial establishments, recreational opportunities, and other entities will reflect differences in the overall distribution of crime in a city. The authors point out that older cities with a concentric zone pattern, akin to the concentric zone maps used by Shaw and McKay (1969), will have markedly different distributions of crime than cities with a more mosaic pattern of development (Brantingham & Brantingham, 1991). Fringe areas adjacent to urban centers may attempt to lure businesses with tax incentives, reduced land prices, and better access to highways, but routine activity theory suggests that the movement of work and recreation opportunities to the fringe areas of cities will result in an increase in crime in those areas.

Situational Crime Prevention

While deterrence theory still continues to have significant influence on criminal law and policy, several variants of rational choice theory have generated a great deal of attention among scholars and professionals in the area of crime prevention. One such variant is situational crime prevention, which applies rational choice theory tenets to very specific situations in which crime may occur. In effect, situational crime prevention efforts seek to increase the risks associated with specific criminal acts and/or to decrease the rewards associated with the offense (Clark, 1995). This type of crime prevention may emphasize increasing the effort required to commit the offense, increasing the risk of detection, reducing the gains associated with the crime, reducing the provocations that may escalate a course of action, and remove excuses for offending (Center for Problem-Oriented Policing, 2011).

These types of crime prevention efforts have been formalized by Crowe (1991) as principles of crime prevention through environmental design (CPTED). CPTED employs the interconnected strategies of natural access control, natural surveillance, and territorial reinforcement. These strategies seek to reduce opportunities for crime and to increase the risks of detection for offenders. CPTED thus seeks to effectively arrange the physical environment, whether it is a neighborhood, a park, or a building, such as a school, to simultaneously give legitimate users more efficient access to the space and to let potential offenders know that risks and rewards are not in their favor in the particular location. Rather than relying on mechanical restraints or equipment, CPTED seeks to take advantage of the designed layout. Crowe (1991, pp. 106–107) lists nine major CPTED strategies: (1) providing clear border definition of controlled space; (2) providing clearly marked transitional zones; (3) relocating gathering areas; (4) placing safe activities in unsafe locations; (5) placing unsafe activities in safe locations; (6) redesignating the use of space to provide natural barriers; (7) improving the scheduled uses of space; (8) redesigning or revamping space to increase the perception of natural surveillance; and (9) overcoming distance and isolation.

To illustrate these strategic uses of CPTED, Crowe (1991) provides numerous recommendations for redesigning urban space, including fewer one-way streets, on-street rather than garage or ramp parking, and wider sidewalks. These alterations to urban space and design are intended to reduce the intensity of traffic flow, divert through traffic to other routes, provide more space for pedestrians, and give local merchants a sidewalk presence. Also relating to the manipulation of the physical environment to alter human behavior are the techniques known as *chunking* and *channeling* (Felson et al., 1996). Chunking is the division of a larger physical space into smaller areas, and channeling refers to directing the flow of individuals into specified pathways.

Crowe (1991) notes that CPTED can be used in very narrow applications, such as school restrooms. Traditionally, school architects placed restrooms in more remote areas of a building due to economic considerations and cultural sensitivity; restrooms were usually not located adjacent to more prime locations. Double-door trap designs, which create an enclosed vestibule between the exterior entry door and the interior entry door, were intended to isolate the sights, sounds, and smells of the restroom. The result was that unconventional users of the restroom space were rewarded with a location that was geographically and socially more isolated from other settings and where the extra door provided offenders with a warning interval. Conventional users might avoid the restrooms due to fear of the unconventional users' behavior and the desire to avoid unpleasant encounters. This situation would reinforce the unconventional users' territorial control over the space. Crowe advocates using a maze entry design for restrooms and placing them in more centralized locations.

Convenience stores offer their own set of CPTED challenges. According to Crowe (1991), the placement of the cashier station is a critical feature for loss prevention and robbery prevention. The cashier should have the ability to observe gas pumps, parking, and the approach to the store entrance and also have adequate lines of sight within the store. Access to the sides of the building should be limited to prevent undetected approaches to the store. For maximum visibility, windows should be unobstructed and not covered with advertisements or blocked by product displays.

The design and layout of communities and neighborhoods can have a profound impact on social problems and resident satisfaction. Poorly designed roadway systems and traffic flow may lead commuters to use residential streets to avoid congestion, thus funneling vehicles onto what should have been quiet, safe residential streets. In such cases, decorative barriers have been used with some degree of success to close through access to some residential streets. Traffic would thus be limited to residents of the area, and natural surveillance over public behavior, including children playing and vehicles in the area, would be increased as residents would have a clearer sense of who belonged in the area and who did not.

Situational crime prevention techniques can draw upon the concepts of familiarity with physical space, easy access, sense of ownership, and risk of detection, which constitute the core principles of *defensible space*, a concept often attributed to Oscar Newman (1996), who argues that defensible space relies on resident self-help and reinforcement of territorial boundaries. The defensible space concept arose from the failure of the Pruitt-Igoe housing project in St. Louis, Missouri. Constructed in the mid-1950s, the high-rise complex had more than 2,700 residential units. After it opened, conditions deteriorated rapidly, culminating in the demolition of the units 10 years later. The architects had designed the modernist complex to have ample public space between the high-rise buildings as well as common areas for laundry and recreation in each building. However, no one took responsibility for the public areas, and, as a result, they became run down, littered, uninviting, and eventually unusable. Residents perceived fundamental differences between the private space in their own units and the public spaces. In Newman's analysis of the defensible space concept as applied in the Clason Point housing project in the Bronx, he states that "the smaller the number of families that share an area, the greater the felt responsibility for maintaining and securing it, and the easier it is for people to agree on mutually acceptable rules for using it" (Newman, 1996, p. 78). Alternatives exist for assigning space. Newman notes that fencing, landscaping, and hardscape can be used to allocate space to particular units. Space is more likely to be maintained when a clear sense of territoriality is maintained.

Another good example of defensible space is Newman's (1996) case study of the Five Oaks neighborhood in Dayton, Ohio. As Five Oaks began to decline, officials brought in Newman to consult on efforts to reclaim the neighborhood. Originally a stable neighborhood of owner-occupied housing, Five Oaks transitioned to an area dominated by rental units, unauthorized multifamily units, absentee landlords, declining home prices, and an overabundance of houses for sale. Rental unit vacancies were extensive, averaging between 10 and 29%. Some landlords were inclined to rent to drug dealers because they paid their rent and were not demanding upgrades to their units. As he began his consulting work, Newman noted the presence of social disorder as well, including drug sales and prostitution.

The situation called for a systemic response, and for his part Newman (1996) designed a system of mini-neighborhoods. In a series of community meetings, residents helped identify the mini-neighborhoods, which broke up a grid street design by creating numerous cul-de-sacs. The new neighborhood street patterns involved the use of ornamental gates with the appearance of wrought iron; these would be used to block roads. The gates created a street pattern similar to a tic-tac-toe square, with seven of the eight streets closed off with gates. Another design involved having one horizontal street with two vertical cross streets, with five of the six roadways closed off with gates. The only open road had a portal constructed to signify the start of the neighborhood. Some accommodations were made for emergency vehicles, snow removal, moving vans, and garbage collection. Garbage trucks, for instance, were too big to turn around at a gate because technically there was no cul-de-sac circle, and backing the trucks down the roads was deemed unsafe.

Newman's (1996) plan called for more than just gated neighborhoods. It also specified increased law enforcement efforts to apprehend street-level drug dealers. Another major focus of his plan was a coordinated program to encourage homeownership in the neighborhood. Homeowners, in theory, should have a greater stake in the mini-community and a personal identification with the neighborhood. Code enforcement was also used to provide additional incentive to landlords to bring their properties in line with building and safety codes. Newman notes a degree of success with the Five Oaks plan. Violence in the area decreased 50%, overall traffic flow was reduced by more than one-third, and two-thirds of the residents indicated that the neighborhood was a better place to live.

RESEARCH DESIGNS

Readers should have some familiarity with research methodologies used in subsequent chapters, so what follows is a brief introduction to important concepts, terms, and practices.

Crime prevention efforts involve social, political, legal, and economic choices. Implementing a program or an initiative requires the expenditure of resources and thus subjects individuals to additional burdens. Ideally, the selection of particular crime prevention strategies should be based on a review of programs using objective evaluation measures. Objective evaluation adheres to the principles of the scientific method. Farrington (2000) notes that not all scientific research is of equal validity, due in part to the research design utilized. There are numerous examples of programs implemented that did not work as originally intended. Despite its popularity, the Drug Abuse Resistance Education program (Project DARE), with its earlier curriculum, suffered from fairly disappointing evaluation results (Rosenbaum & Hanson, 1998). Research noted that suburban youths who completed the program actually used more drugs and liked police officers less than the youths who did not participate in the program.

Experimental Designs

Experimental designs are some of the more rigorous methods of scientific inquiry because they allow researchers to make statements about cause-and-effect relationships; without experimental designs, scientists merely observe, making their statement of findings simply a description of what they observe. The classic experimental design consists of four major components: (1) independent and dependent variables, (2) experimental and control groups, (3) pretesting and posttesting, and (4) randomization or equivalence of the experimental and control group (Hagan, 2010). The independent variable is considered the causal agent, while the dependent variable is considered the outcome in the experimental design. In setting up an experimental design, the researcher controls or manipulates the independent variable to determine its effect, and the nature of its effect, if any, on the outcome—the dependent variable. For example, Clark (2002) provides a succinct set of recommendations to address shoplifting in retail stores. Measures such as strategic placement of mirrors, keeping expensive items in controlled-access locations, and moving products away from exits may lower the incidence of shoplifting. In a hypothetical study, those store design changes would be the independent variables, and a measure of product loss attributed to shoplifting would be the dependent variable.

The second major component of an experimental design consists of the experimental group, which is exposed to changes in the independent variable or stimulus, and the control group, which is not exposed to the changes in the stimulus. Without a control group, the research would not be able to determine whether changes in the dependent variable are the result of the manipulation of the independent variable or other factors. For instance, people may alter their behavior if they know they are being observed, which is a finding derived from the Hawthorne study. This study sought to examine factors that might increase worker productivity in a wiring room in a Western Electric assembly plant in Hawthorne, Illinois, in the 1920s. Researchers manipulated lighting levels, the timing of break periods, and other environmental factors, each resulting in increased worker performance. Eventually, the researchers determined that regardless of the stimulus intervention, productivity improved, ostensibly because workers liked the attention provided by the research. This finding spurred businesses to transition from scientific management to produce efficient workflows (a concept known as Taylorism) to the human relations model of management, which focuses on employee motivation and recognition.

For the third component of an experimental design, the pretest determines the nature of the dependent variable prior to exposure to or manipulation of the independent variable. After the introduction of the independent variable, or stimulus, the dependent variable is then measured again. Differences in the dependent variable would be attributed to the effect or influence of the independent variable, although some complicating factors, described more fully below, may come into play. The pretest provides a baseline for the dependent variable. For example, a student may score very well on an exam in an introductory criminal justice course. The exam grade provides only a baseline measure; it does not distinguish between the information the student learned in the course and the information that student may have learned over many years of employment in the criminal justice field.

The fourth and final required component of an experimental design consists of randomization and the equivalence of groups. Equivalence means that one uses a random process to assign people to one of the design categories (the experimental or control groups). Equivalence does not mean that the allocation of individuals to each group is a haphazard process; it means that the researcher ensures that every eligible person or group has the same probability of receiving any level of the independent variable (treatment). This equivalent allocation process ensures that differences in outcomes (based on measures of dependent variable levels) are attributable to variations in the treatment condition (independent variable) and not to preexisting differences between groups.

Reliability and validity are concerns for any type of design methodology. Reliability refers to consistency in the measurement of the variable. Validity is the extent to which a specific measurement of a variable actually measures what it is supposed to measure. Each experimental research design, in general, should address reliability and validity concerns, and each project will have its own unique threats to reliability and validity. Recall that differences in the outcomes of the control group versus the experimental or treatment groups are supposed to be attributable to the effect of the independent variable. In any particular research design, however, other forces or factors may influence the outcome of the study. The intervention of those outside forces or factors threatens the validity of any apparent cause-and-effect relationships between the independent variable and the dependent variable. These threats to a study design's internal validity are numerous and may include such things as history, maturation, testing, instrumentation, statistical regression, selection bias, experimental mortality, and selection–maturation interaction (Hagan, 2010).

Threats to a Study's Internal Validity

In the context of threats to the validity of an experimental design, *history* is a threat when an observed effect might be due to an event that takes place after the pretest and before the posttest and is beyond the realm of influence or control of the research design. In much laboratory-based experimental research, the history threat is controlled by insulating participants from outside influences (e.g., by locating participants in a quiet and controlled lab setting), by making sure there is only a brief window of time between the pretest and the posttest, or by choosing dependent variables that cannot plausibly be affected by outside forces (e.g., such as with lab-based psychology experiments).

Maturation is a threat to a study's validity when an observed effect might be due to the participants growing older, wiser, stronger, or more experienced during the lag time between the pretest and posttest. Thus, the threat of maturation must be addressed and accounted for in experimental designs, particularly for those with long time horizons, like studies involving juvenile offenders. One of the more stable patterns in criminology is the age-crime curve, which shows that violent crimes and property offenses reach their peak in a person's late teen years (Laub & Sampson, 1993). Experimental designs examining the impact of a program or intervention for juvenile offenders should consider the aging out process in addition to the impact, if any, of the program.

Testing is a threat to research design validity when the differences between the pretest and the posttest can be attributed to participants' familiarity with the test used as the dependent variable. For example, study participants may enhance their performance on later tests if they remember test items or patterns from earlier testing sessions. A related problem is that participants might guess what the research is seeking to test and then craft their responses to fit their own hypothesis for what the study is seeking to determine.

Instrumentation is a threat to validity when an effect may be attributable to a change in the measuring instrument between the pretest and posttest and not to the treatment's differential impact at each time interval. Thus, the testing threat to internal validity exists when people become more experienced between the pretest and posttest, while the instrumentation threat exists when there is a change in the measuring method or tool at different points in time.

A related threat to internal validity is *statistical regression* (Hagan, 2010), which exists because there is a tendency for groups or people at the extremes of a distribution to move toward the middle of the distribution (in statistical terms, the mean or average). Thus, the change measured in a group over time may be attributable to the fact that some participants at the beginning of the study were exhibiting extremes of behavior and during the study they modified their behavior so that it was more in line with the group average. For example, studies show that juveniles and adults who commit offenses at extremely high rates will eventually reduce their offense rate. There are numerous reasons for this tendency. The individual may be incarcerated for a period of time (with increasing probability for longer periods of incarceration); high-rate offenders may be using alcohol, drugs, and tobacco, resulting in poorer health; and lower education levels combined with high-risk activities are likely to take a physical toll on the individual.

The composition of the study participant groups may also introduce the threat of *selection bias* to internal validity. Selection bias occurs when the control group is not equivalent to the comparison group in some key respects. Traditionally, individuals who readily volunteer for participation in a study may have some fundamental personal differences in comparison to those individuals not so eager. Participants who drop out, cannot be located, or even die during the study (as in the case of long-term research) may differ in key respects from those who complete the study. This phenomenon is known as *experimental mortality*, and to address this threat to a study's validity it would be critical to determine in what ways the group no longer in the study is different from the participants remaining and whether these differences are associated with the outcome variable. For instance, Laub and Sampson (2003) note that mortality and incarceration have an obvious impact on the continuity of criminal offending, and offenders have a lower life expectancy than do nonoffenders. In their reanalysis, this phenomenon resulted in 50% of their delinquent sample being dead by age 70 compared to less than 30% of the nonoffenders in the study. This trend began early; by age 32, the offenders had a mortality rate that was double that of the nonoffenders. The period of time that individuals are at risk for offending is thus a key factor in experimental design.

A good experimental design requires the isolation of the stimulus to the treatment group; thus, only the experimental group should receive the intervention. The threat to internal validity when the stimulus is not contained or when there is sufficient interaction between the experimental and control groups such that the stimulus is no longer confined to the experimental group is known as *imitation* or *diffusion of treatment*. In effect, the control group has become contaminated to some degree. A related threat to internal validity is *compensatory rivalry*, in which the control group wants the same treatment the experimental group is receiving because that treatment is viewed as desirable. The experimental treatment may create among participants the perception of an inequality as a result of the experiment. Thus, compensatory rivalry is a rivalry between the control group and the experimental group as a result of this perceived inequity. The control group, as the underdog, may be motivated to reduce or reverse the expected difference due to a competitive spirit. The opposite response—a sense of resignation due to feelings of inadequacy or frustration—would result in *demoralization*, also a threat to internal validity.

One of the purposes of an experimental design is to make a cause-and-effect determination as to the power and influence of the tested independent variables on the dependent variable. Researchers seek to control or limit the ability of outside factors or forces to influence the dependent variable. In some situations, it may be difficult to specify the influence of a specific independent variable when multiple treatments are included in the design. The result is a threat to external validity known as *multiple treatment interferences* or *multiple treatment effects*. In crime prevention studies, there are a number of research examples to illustrate the issue of multiple treatment effects.

Threats to a Study's External Validity

An experimental design's validity may also face external challenges. If a study has external validity, then the results can be generalized to other places and times. Certain factors may limit this generalizability. An example of such a factor is the *interaction of selection and treatment*, which addresses the question of whether the results can be generalized beyond the groups or participants in the original study. Findings of a study using particular participants may be limited to similar groups based on such factors as race, social class, geography, age, or sex.

Likewise, the *interaction of setting and treatment* may limit the generalizability of the findings (Hagan, 2010). Research conducted in a specific type of setting may yield information that is not applicable to other groups in other settings. For instance, there is much research conducted in which all of the study participants are college undergraduates, but researchers must then ask themselves to what extent college students differ from the larger population.

The *interaction of history and treatment* refers to the impact that the past and future can have on particular causal relationships. Thus, particular issues may be unique to a particular time period. For example, Laub and Sampson (1993) analyzed data from a large group of individuals who participated in a long-term study. Members of this research study group lived during the Great Depression, served in World War II, and experienced the postwar economic period. This group faced a unique set of challenges that also provided a unique set of opportunities for young men from lower economic status groups. For instance, military service in World War II provided these men with geographic mobility, GI Bill educational opportunities, and enhanced employment opportunities. Those benefits also effectively removed them from neighborhood environments that may have nurtured criminal activity.

From Research Methodology to Theoretical Models

There are several theoretical models that may suggest new approaches to preventing crime. A sound theoretical model buttresses an effective research methodology and vice versa. The work of Sherman and Weisburd (1995) illustrates this connection. The pair conducted an experiment measuring the impact of increased police presence on activity in crime hotspots. Their study built on the foundation of the Kansas City Patrol Study, which found no difference in crime levels, or other key outcomes, based on levels of police patrol. The Sherman and Weisburd study also underscores and reinforces a key notion in the field of crime prevention research: the importance of rigorous replication studies.

Despite the fact that law enforcement agencies, in traditional terms, *react* to crime, their involvement in *preventing* crime has been evident since the inception of actual police departments.

Many researchers contend that Sir Robert Peel envisioned crime prevention as a primary mission of the entity he established: the London Metropolitan Police Department. Peel's nine principles of policing begin with that very assertion:

- The basic mission for which the police exist is to prevent crime and disorder.
- The ability of the police to perform their duties is dependent upon the public approval of police actions.
- Police must secure the willing cooperation of the public in voluntary observation of the law to be able to secure and maintain the respect of the public.
- The degree of cooperation of the public that can be secured diminishes proportionately to the necessity of the use of physical force.
- Police seek and preserve public favor not by catering to public opinion, but by constantly demonstrating absolute impartial service to the law.
- Police use physical force to the extent necessary to secure observance of the law or to restore order only when the exercise of persuasion, advice, and warning is found to be insufficient.
- Police, at all times, should maintain a relationship with the public that gives reality to the historic tradition that the police are the public and the public are the police; the police being only members of the public who are paid to give full-time attention to duties which are incumbent upon every citizen in the interests of community welfare and existence.
- Police should always direct their action strictly towards their functions, and never appear to usurp the powers of the judiciary.
- The test of police efficiency is the absence of crime and disorder, not the visible evidence of police action in dealing with it. (Nazemi, 2009)

According to this historical perspective, police agencies should ideally prevent crime from happening rather than merely react to crime after it occurs. The concept of crime prevention makes intuitive sense if one follows the precepts of utilitarianism, the philosophy in which one seeks the greatest possible good for the largest number of people. A primary crime prevention technique used by the police is preventive patrol. Police departments have employed this tactic since the formation of early police departments right up to today. O. W. Wilson, a leading police professionalism advocate of the early 1900s, stressed the need for an omnipresence of police on patrol (Kelling & Coles, 1996, p. 78). There have of course been many technological advances in patrolling since then, such as those described in Chapter 3 by Smith and Scott. In the first half of the 20th century, police officers were able to begin motorized patrols and radio dispatching for calls for service. Kelling and Coles note that between calls for service, police would patrol public areas and remain on alert for possible crimes in the area. This patrolling activity was intended to create the perception among the public that the police were everywhere, essentially an omnipresence in the community, which would theoretically deter would-be criminals. The emphasis on preventive patrol remained largely untested and unchallenged for decades, until the Kansas City Patrol Study appeared. That research represents a landmark effort to assess the effectiveness of preventive patrol (Kelling, Pate, Dieckman, & Brown, 1974).

Experimental Design Examples in Policing Research

Aware of two key shortcomings in the Kansas City Patrol Study, Sherman and Weisburd (1995) determined that the famous study's experimental design created a built-in bias toward the finding that preventive patrols had no effect on crime. They noted that this bias derived from the fact that the Kansas City study involved only 15 precincts, a rather small sample. Conversely, many studies, such as surveys with very large samples, have a built-in bias toward the finding of statistically significant differences, although the true nature of that difference is rather small. The other shortcoming of the Kansas City study was that it covered a rather large geographic area, and Sherman and Weisburd note that it was difficult to determine the level of police presence at any specific location. For their own study of police patrolling, Sherman and Weisburd (1995) focused on 110 crime hotspots in the city of Minneapolis, Minnesota. These locations, generating nearly 11% of the total calls for service in the city, were narrowly defined clusters of addresses. These clusters, however, did not include hotels, schools, commercial buildings, or areas that may have overlapped with other hotspots. The researchers randomly divided the 110 locations into an experimental group and a control group. In the year prior to the study, the experimental group logged about 19,322 total calls for service and the control group logged 19,693 calls for service. For the experimental group locations, the researchers requested 3 hours' worth of total police presence between the hours of 11:00 PM and 3:00 AM, a period corresponding to the highest distribution of calls for service (the actual policing hours did not reach the target goal of 3 hours, however). The experimental group did receive roughly double the amount of police presence that the control group received, as measured by observers on the research team and in police logs. Police activity during this directed patrol assignment was not defined, so the officers engaged in a variety of activities. The research intent was merely for officers to stay at the hotspot for a relatively short period of time but to return to it as frequently as possible.

Sherman and Weisburd (1995) report that using directed police patrols in crime hotspots produced a modest deterrent effect. They describe the impact as a microdeterrence effect since the impact had a small geographic application and the displacement of crime was not tested. Displacement of crime refers to the movement of crime from one location (in this case, the physical area receiving a fairly significant level of police presence) to another area. In effect, there is a potential for motivated offenders to seek criminal opportunities in other areas where there is less official supervision and police presence. Sherman and Weisburd note that the optimal length of police presence in the directed patrol is about 12 minutes and that the directed patrol had a noticeable impact on social disorder, which includes activities such as prostitution and public drinking. Their results indicated that social disorder was present in 1 of every 50 encounters on the street in the experimental group, while in the control group, social disorder was present in 1 of every 25 encounters.

Braga and Bond (2008) prepared an experimental design to examine how a strategy for policing social disorder might affect crime rates in Lowell, Massachusetts. The policing strategy they tested drew elements from the so-called SARA model (scanning, analysis, response, and assessment). They analyzed crime and calls for service in Lowell and found 34 hotspots. Hotspots were matched and randomly assigned to either the control group or the experimental group. These hotspots, although constituting only 2.7% of the total area of the city, accounted for 23.5% of all police calls, 29.3% of the violent crimes, 25.1% of property crimes, and nearly 20% of the disorder-related calls. The researchers measured displacement of crime by using a two-block catchment area for data comparison.

As part of the study, Braga and Bond (2008) conducted monthly meetings with the police captains responsible for patrols in the experimental group of hotspots. A variety of strategies for policing disorder were implemented based on the characteristics and the specific nature of the problems associated with the hotspot. The researchers note that 4.4 strategies on average were used at each hotspot in the experimental group, with 2 to 8 interventions for each location. These interventions included improving street lighting, securing vacant lots, doing code inspections, employing stop-and-frisk procedures, and increasing youth recreation opportunities. The locations of the control group hotspots were not revealed to the police captains charged with reducing the crime rate at the experimental group hotspots; although some hotspots in the control group did receive additional interventions, none was considered long term.

Braga and Bond (2008) collected data on calls for service as one outcome measure. In addition, the researchers made systematic observations of the patterns of street activity and took standardized photographs of each hotspot. They then coded the amount and type of physical disorder at each location. The researchers also personally observed each of the hotspots to record the number of incidents of social disorder. The experimental group and the control group yielded fairly large and statistically significant differences. Specifically, the researchers reported that the experimental group saw a 19.8% decrease in total calls for service, a 41.8% drop in robbery calls, and a 35.5% reduction in burglary calls. Interventions also eliminated social disorder in 15 of the 17 hotspots and physical disorder in 13 of 17 hotspots. Although there was some displacement of crime and disorder to the immediate catchment areas, the amount was not statistically significant. Based on their study results, Braga and Bond (2008) advocate situational crime prevention strategies that focus on removing motivated offenders from specific locations and increasing the perceived risks of offending.

Case Studies

In addition to experimental designs, researchers may use other methods to develop and examine crime prevention strategies. In some situations, experimental designs, although considered the most desirable technique for determining cause-and-effect relationships, are not practical or cannot be used at all. In such situations, researchers studying crime prevention may employ case studies to document policing procedures and determine which theoretical models underlie those procedures. Berg (2009) describes the case study method as a weaker sister of other social science methodologies but contends that the advantage of case studies is that they provide in-depth, extensive information about a particular event, situation, or group.

One of the better known case studies in the field of crime prevention research involves efforts to identify and respond to crime and disorder at New York City's Port Authority Bus Terminal, the size and complexity of which made it impossible to use an experimental design. The team conducting the Port Authority case study (Felson et al., 1996) identified numerous problems at the transit facility, particularly disorderly activity, which rose to the level of impeding legitimate transportation functions.

According to Felson et al. (1996), the bus terminal averaged 174,000 passengers a week, more than 6,800 buses used the facility each day, and more than 200 gates were in use for loading and unloading buses. The levels of disorder and crime in the bus terminal were also due in part to its proximity to Times Square. The facility underwent numerous design and operational changes to reduce opportunities for crime and crime attractors within the facility (Felson et al., 1996). At the time of the implementation of these changes at the bus terminal, Times Square had a reputation for drug distribution, prostitution, and street hustling. The transit facility was described as "a grim gauntlet for bus passengers dodging beggars, drunks, thieves, and destitute drug addicts" (Manegold, 1992, p. 1, as cited in Felson et al. 1996, p. 10).

The Port Authority terminal, Times Square, and adjacent areas had many interconnected problems. For example, in the early 1990s, before the advent of cell phones, travelers had to rely on public telephones, but in the bus terminal many of the banks of public telephones had been co-opted by criminal entrepreneurs who charged a flat rate for unlimited international calling. People wanting to use the telephones for legitimate purposes faced threats from these scam operators. In addition, homeless individuals, as well as those transients technically with a place to live but who spent part of their day at the bus terminal, constituted a major obstacle to the efficient operation of the facility. Hundreds of persons thus lived within the facility. The problem of having a homeless community living in the terminal made headlines when a five-gallon drum of human waste fell from above a bus gate and when transients made homes above the removable ceiling tiles in the facility's restrooms. Officers with the Port Authority Police Department could do little in response to the issue of loitering within the facility because then-recent New York court cases protected transients from ejection from public places (a later case stripped panhandling of any constitutional protection). In addition, police did not consider transients' loitering and panhandling to be important or worthy targets of police work. The Port Authority Police Department did not ignore these more minor issues, however; in conjunction with a social service agency, Project Renewal, the department instituted a "refer-or-arrest" policy in which transients would be given a choice to move along, be arrested, or be referred to the social service agency. In addition, Port Authority officers received additional training for dealing with transients' issues. Other major problems for police focus were prostitution and the sale and use of drugs. Prostitutes and drug dealers plied their trade in many areas, some open, some hidden within the facility. Fear among travelers and members of the bus terminal's business community (those who rented retail space within the facility) faced high levels of social disorder and crime, especially robbery, pickpocketing, theft of luggage and other items, and assault.

The strategic interventions selected to transform the Port Authority Bus Terminal were designed to make the facility easier to navigate from the perspective of its travelers (Felson et al., 1996). Of particular note here is the role of physical changes to the facility and their impact on the activities within the building. Crime prevention through environmental design (CPTED) was the dominant theoretical model at the time, and a key focus in the project was on improving the flow of people through the facility and eliminating the nooks and crannies within the facility (Felson et al., 1996). These niches often teemed with loitering transients or other undesirable activity. Loitering and various other undesirable activities were perceived as crime attractors, as well as obstacles for maintenance staff trying to perform their duties. The CPTED plan emphasized increasing and improving retail space within the facility. The renovations removed physical niches, and in some cases minor construction created new retail spaces for rent-paying tenants, who provided both revenue to the facility as well as natural surveillance in a particular area. Physical redesign made storefronts more appealing to the thousands of commuters and also removed features that attracted crime and disorder to the location. The physical changes to the restrooms clearly highlight the application of situational crime prevention strategies. These changes included closing off smaller restrooms, changing ceiling tiles, replacing old stall doors with a new model allowing a visual inspection of how many feet were in a stall at one time, and replacing larger sinks with smaller size units (see Felson et al., 1996, p. 28, for the complete list of restroom changes). Similar efforts to eliminate loitering included replacing benches in the terminal's waiting areas with plastic flip seats that prevent someone from lying across several chairs. In addition to the facility's reputation for crime, the overall appearance of the facility was grim and did nothing to counter negative public perceptions. Thus, the efforts to transform the facility included new procedures for cleaning the floors, improved lighting, glass block for walls, and sealing off little-used stairways.

Felson et al. (1996) note several positive findings involving data collected before, during, and after the physical renovations and policing reforms at the bus terminal. They report that satisfaction levels increased, complaints about social problems declined, revenues/sales increased, and the number of actual crimes reported decreased. The researchers do point out however, that there were some drawbacks of the case study: it was retrospective in its approach, multiple treatments were implemented simultaneously, and it did not utilize an experimental design. Despite these drawbacks, this case study does identify numerous environmental and physical changes that reduce crime and disorder and that may be applicable to other venues.

Another noteworthy case study involves crime prevention efforts in the Metro subway system (La Vigne, 2006), which began operating in Washington, DC, in 1976. The researcher who conducted this case study notes three key features of the Metro's crime prevention system: its architectural design, the management's rigid maintenance policies, and stringent rule enforcement. Each of these features has been linked to the system's relatively low crime rate. When the Metro's planners were designing the system, they were able to take advantage of lessons learned from numerous older systems. They integrated both aesthetics and physical security measures (i.e., target hardening approaches) into the system's design, such as uniform platform length to accommodate the entire span of the train so that no cars are left without direct access to the platform. Designers opted for long escalators rather than stairways for the descent into the transit stations so as to avoid blind corners, which may attract potential offenders, and landings, which may attract transients. Transit police enforce rules that enhance quality of life in the system; there are prohibitions against eating, drinking, and playing loud music. Maintenance policies require that graffiti be reported and removed immediately and that lighting problems be corrected without delay. La Vigne (2006) compared the Metro's crime rate to that of three other subway systems, as well as to the census tracts above its stations. Results indicated that Metro riders experienced lower crime rates than did riders of the other three systems studied. In addition, La Vigne notes that Metro crime rates do not vary station to station, whereas the crime rates for the aboveground census tracts do show variation.

SAMPLE TOOLS IN CRIME PREVENTION THROUGH DESIGN

Street Lighting

In their review of theory and research on street lighting and crime, Farrington and Welsh (2007) mention multiple theoretical models promoting the use of lighting to deter crime. They also point to an array of street lighting research findings indicating everything from a positive impact on crime prevention to a negative one, with much of the work prior to 1990 indicating that lighting did not prevent crime. According to these researchers, improved street lighting is a component of CPTED that specifically increases the risk of detection for offenders. Improved lighting can also be one aspect of a community reinvestment program. Similarly, improved lighting may allow the conventional population (i.e., law-abiding nonoffenders) to increase their use of urban spaces at night. Improved lighting may thus be used to exert social control over a particular place during nighttime hours. However, improved street lighting could actually increase crime because more people may be out at night, thus increasing the opportunity for criminal victimizations.

Farrington and Welsh (2007) identified 13 studies of street lighting that met the criteria for inclusion in their analysis. All of those studies utilized an experimental design of street lighting and crime that had at least 20 crimes in its pretest, but the studies did vary in terms of the qualifiers used to describe the level of improved lighting. Ideally, such studies should have three geographic areas: the experimental area, the control area, and an area adjacent to the experimental area for determining whether crime was displaced from the experimental area because of its increased lighting, to a less well lit area nearby. Repetto (1976, as cited in Farrington & Welsh, 2007, p. 214) has written that five types of crime displacement (also known as diffusion) are possible: temporal (crime is delayed to another time), tactical (offenders shift to a different method), target (offenders choose a different victim), territorial (offenders move to a different place), and functional (offenders choose to perpetrate a different type of crime). Although improved lighting may displace crime to an adjacent area, another possible outcome is that crime also decreases in the adjacent area due to the diffused benefits of lighting. In other words, the positive effects in one area may spill over into nearby areas.

Based on the results of the 13 studies examined by Farrington and Welsh (2007), improved street lighting reduced crime by about 20% in the experimental areas compared to the control areas. Eight of the 13 locations studied were in the United States, and the researchers note that four studies indicated that better lighting had a positive impact on crime (i.e., it reduced crime rates), while four studies showed no difference in crime between the experimental areas with improved lighting and the control areas. The five studies conducted in Britain showed that lighting had a greater impact; those studies noted that crime decreased 29% in the experimental groups. Interestingly, the reduced crime rates are based on comparisons of day and night crime rates rather than just nighttime crime rates. Farrington and Welsh note that this overall reduction in crime both day and night, not just at night when street lighting becomes a factor, may reflect increased community involvement and community pride rather than simply the deterrence effect of improved lighting.

Closed-Circuit Television

Many crime prevention professionals consider closed-circuit television (CCTV) a promising approach for deterring criminal activity in public places as well as for identifying individuals who commit crimes in areas with surveillance cameras. Technology associated with CCTV has become less expensive, improved in quality, and gained a certain level of social acceptability. Welsh and Farrington (2009) note that, despite a tremendous increase in the deployment of CCTV, its use presents several problems. CCTV is not cost effective, and monitoring the images produces boredom to the point that, after the initial novelty of CCTV wears off and the perceived threat level diminishes, monitoring of the images is reduced.

To address the shortcomings of CCTV and to take advantage of the public's voyeuristic tendencies, one company, Internet Eyes®, has created a unique business model in which businesses subscribe to a service that webcasts their CCTV feeds. Subscribers who have registered for access to the video feeds then monitor the webcasts and watch for suspected violations, which are reported to the monitoring station. The subscribing business then receives an alert so that it can take action. The company's website is http://interneteyes.co.uk/.

Opera Solutions

To prevent more sophisticated types of crimes, such as financial fraud, one company uses advanced analytics and data management capabilities to assist private firms and public agencies in managing their data for decision-making functions. Opera Solutions helps companies and government entities minimize risk associated with credit and lending practices. Major companies, such as Google, use similar technology to provide recommendations customized for each user based on patterns of similar users (Opera Solutions, 2010). Opera Solutions developed a tool called Matrix Factorization Singular Value Decomposition (SVD) to categorize individuals based on their characteristics compared to known consumer habits (Opera Solutions, 2009). In a sense, this type of modeling that predicts people's behavior might be termed "economic profiling."

Companies can use the data generated by prediction tools like the one developed by Opera Solutions to identify patterns associated with something called "bust-out fraud." Opera Solutions describes a bust-out fraud scenario as a situation that occurs when credit card holders buy many items within a short period of time and reach their maximum credit limit without the intention of paying the credit card company (Opera Solutions, 2009). Individuals engaged in bust-out fraud then sell the recently purchased items for cash. The credit card company is unable to recover payment for the goods sold, and the associated losses are passed on to consumers. Opera Solutions uses nonlinear modeling techniques to compare patterns of previous bust-out fraud cases to the purchasing patterns of current card holders. Their intent is to provide credit card companies with the tools and information needed to take precautions and minimize the financial losses associated with this type of crime. For the financial services industry, Opera Solutions offers analytic techniques for identifying prospective customers. As relationships between the financial entity and customer progress, Opera Solutions seeks to predict customer behavior in an effort to maximize profits through service delivery while attempting to minimize the risk of financial losses associated with specific individuals. The type of analytic modeling information provided by a company like Opera Solutions enables companies to detect potential fraud or an impending default on a loan. There are numerous other applications for analytic modeling technology in crime prevention efforts. Although not as robust as the models described previously, analytic tools have been used to develop instruments such as offender risk needs assessments. Such tools have many possible applications, including homeland security, securities code enforcement, public assistance claims, and medical claims.

LEGISLATIVE EFFORTS AND CRIME PREVENTION

While much of the focus of crime prevention centers on law enforcement activities and public awareness, preventing crime can also be a stated goal of corrections programs, legislation, and the courts. Sentencing and parole policies are important factors in crime prevention because they determine the criteria for releasing offenders, who may or may not return to criminal pursuits. For instance, the state of New Hampshire (2010) passed Senate Bill 500, which called for changes in the probation, parole, and sentencing of certain offenders in an effort to increase public safety, strengthen community supervision, and reduce recidivism. The legislation noted that nearly 60% of admissions to the state prison system in New Hampshire were because of probation and parole revocations. Another concern the legislation noted was that about 16% of the state's prison population had served their entire sentences and were released into the community without any correctional supervision. A key provision of this legislation requires each state prisoner to have at least 9 months of postrelease supervision, with the exception of those prisoners who are the subject of a pending petition for civil commitment. A controversial aspect of the legislation concerned parole revocation decisions. Under the new legislation, if a parolee violates conditional release criteria and is to be returned to prison, he or she would serve a maximum of 3 months and then be released on parole once again. The intent of the legislation was to enhance community-based sanctions, controls, and supervision using resources that would otherwise have been spent on incarceration costs.

Community-based crime prevention efforts often involve preventing drug crimes through nuisance abatement programs, which employ civil remedies and procedures to resolve drug-related cases. There are numerous models for these programs, but they typically begin with a process that involves producing initial documentation of the problem. This initial step may be the result of undercover officers buying drugs or making an arrest for a drug-related offense at a particular location. The city would notify the landowner at that location about the nature of the nuisance and identify what steps the landowner should take to remedy the situation. In their examination of community-based efforts at drug prevention through nuisance abatement programs, Davis and Lurigio (1996) note that the majority of problematic situations were resolved after the city identified nuisance issues in written communication to a landowner and the landowner subsequently took action to remedy the situation. Most often this remedy involved the eviction of tenants.

Nuisance abatement programs may incorporate a variety of sanctions, for example, building code enforcement. Although cities can implement a variety of ordinances as part of nuisance abatement programs, landowners must cooperate if the program is to be successful. If landlords fail to take satisfactory actions, the city could in many cases seize the property and sell it at auction. During the process, tenants may be evicted, buildings padlocked, and landlords denied rental income as long as the owner remains in noncompliance. In some programs, proceeds would go to any mortgage lien holder and then to the city to fund the program; the owner would not receive any funds from the sale.

In a study of how effectively nuisance abatement programs operated in practice, Davis and Lurigio (1996) considered a building in Milwaukee, Wisconsin that, with only 36 rental units, generated 164 arrests over a 2-year period. When the city attempted to compel the owner to make required changes, a legal battle ensued. Before the case could be resolved, the building burned. However, most of the Milwaukee cases Davis and Lurigio studied did not require action beyond the city's letter asking the landlord to make required changes. They do note, however, that fairness in the nuisance abatement procedures is critical and that eviction proceedings will affect not only the targeted nuisance but also law-abiding families.

McCabe (2008) examines the influence of nuisance abatement closings, drug arrests, and marijuana arrests on the rates of serious crime in the borough of Queens, New York, from 1995 to 2000. The theoretical context for McCabe's study was Kelling and Wilson's (1982) broken windows theory. The theory contends that signs of social and physical disorder, such as broken windows, will lead to greater amounts of disorder as well as contribute to a downward spiral of informal social control in the area. The geographic area with visible signs of disorder will become a magnet for more serious offenders, causing more conventional users of the area to alter their behavior even more. Advocates of the broken windows theory contend that authorities should employ zero tolerance policing and order maintenance strategies to improve neighborhood quality of life.

According to McCabe (2008), New York law permits nuisance abatement by allowing the city to seek a court declaration closing a specific building for 1 year. The threshold to determine whether a nuisance exists in a specific location is three arrests for violations of the drug laws or marijuana offenses on three different dates at the location within 1 year. The justification for the law is that such nuisances interfere with the public's interest in maintaining the quality of life, tone of commerce, and property values and that they have a negative impact on public health. While McCabe (2008) points to significant declines in the overall crime rate between 1995 and 2000, McCabe was also interested in determining the individual contribution of several variables to the decline and used statistical analysis to determine the impact of demographic variables such as poverty, unemployment, and demographics in specific police precincts in Queens.

McCabe (2008) reports that demographic and social variables such as poverty and unemployment were not associated with the crime rate reduction in Queens. Arrests for violations of drug laws, however, were positively associated with arrests for serious crimes such that an increase in serious drug arrests correlated with an increase in arrests for seven of the eight offense categories in Part I of the FBI's Uniform Crime Reporting handbook (arson was the exception). Arrests for marijuana violations were negatively associated with the serious crime rate. Closings of buildings for nuisance abatement purposes were strongly correlated with a reduction of serious crime. McCabe's interpretation of these findings suggests that the threat of arrest did not deter drug offenders, who continued to seek out sources of revenue to buy drugs, thus generating street crime. Marijuana users, on the other hand, were more integrated into mainstream society and were deterred by the threat of arrest. Nuisance abatement closures of buildings linked to drug sales disrupted users' drug-seeking behavior. McCabe (2008) cautions that particular situations may have impacted the findings. For example, during the study period the nature of the city's drug problem was evolving as crack cocaine use declined, and being arrested for drugs had more of an impact on some persons than on others.

Due to the complicated web of legal issues surrounding nuisance abatement, the Office of the Attorney General for Texas provides law enforcement agencies with a manual of instruction on proper use of the state's nuisance abatement laws (Abbott, 2005). Authority for nuisance abatement in Texas is based on two sources: the Texas Civil Practice & Remedies Code and the Texas Alcoholic Beverage Code. Nuisance abatement can be used to remedy problematic situations caused by such things as drug-related activities, gang activity, and alcohol violations. The process emphasizes remedies short of closure of the property, payment of fines, or jail time. Another emphasis is the need for accurate information concerning the nuisance activities; such information may include arrest reports, testimonials, and photographs documenting the condition of the property. Documentation of, for example, six arrests for similar types of behavior within a year at one location may constitute a nuisance under the Texas statutes (Abbott, 2005). When a law enforcement agency has gathered the proper documentation of a nuisance, it sends a written notice to the property owner to arrange a meeting in which the two parties discuss the nature of the allegations and a set of recommendations for compliance. Ideally, the owner takes the necessary steps to bring the property into compliance. If the owner does not take the necessary steps, the building may be closed for up to 1 year or a bond posted to keep the building open. Law enforcement would investigate further to determine whether the nuisance activities continue.

CONCLUSION

According to the authors of *Preventing Crime: What Works, What Doesn't, What's Promising* (Sherman et al., 1998), most crime prevention evaluation studies have not been evaluated with sufficient rigor to make possible any definitive statements about their value. The work of Sherman et al. highlights federal funding initiatives that have provided resources for crime prevention programs to deliver services yet have not paid sufficient attention to analysis of the effectiveness of those programs and services. The researchers' emphasis on using scientific principles to evaluate programs lends greater objectivity to the evaluation process, which means that their findings have greater value, whether the impact of those findings is positive or negative. Their work also inaugurated a standard metric, the five-point Maryland Scale of Scientific Methods (MSSM), for evaluating the quality of experimental designs addressing similar populations or problems. According to the Maryland Scale, level 5 studies were the most scientifically rigorous and level 1 studies, the weakest. For a study to have level 3 quality, the design must have an experimental group and a control group. Thus, a level 3 study is rigorous enough to determine whether an intervention program is or is not working because the difference in outcome between the two groups indicates the effectiveness or impact of the program.

Sherman et al. (1998) identified numerous initiatives that were reported to be working to prevent crime and delinquency and that were supported by available evidence. Many of these programs will be discussed in subsequent chapters. Among the programs they identified as working effectively were nurse visits to homes with infants, reinforcement of positive behaviors in school, nuisance abatement, hotspot policing, and prison-based drug treatment. They also identified examples of programs that, based on outcome evaluations, were not working as intended. These included gun buy-back programs, Project DARE, Scared Straight, and storefront police offices. As society deals with shifting demographic and economic dynamics, there is increasing emphasis on more rigorous evaluation of all manner of programs, especially those supported by tax dollars. More rigorous assessment of programs serves multiple positive objectives, not least among them the opportunity to ensure that scarce resources are not wasted on programs that do not work as intended.

CRIME PREVENTION AND YOUTH

Society is becoming ever more proactive when it comes to crime. Most entities, whether businesses, religious groups, or schools, now undertake some sort of crime prevention effort. Schools, for example, once focused primarily on fire safety, customarily conducting fire drills. Many schools now have security plans and prepared responses for a variety of hazardous situations, including criminal behavior.

The Boy Scouts of America have merit badges related to crime prevention and emergency preparedness.

BOX 1-1 Crime Prevention Merit Badge

1. Discuss the role and value of laws in society with regard to crime and crime prevention. Include in your discussion the definitions of "crime" and "crime prevention."
2. Prepare a notebook of newspaper and other clippings that addresses crime and crime prevention efforts in your community.
3. Discuss the following with your counselor:
   a. The role of citizens, including youth, in crime prevention
   b. Gangs and their impact on the community
   c. When and how to report a crime

(continues)

4. After doing EACH of the following, discuss with your counselor what you have learned.
   a. Inspect your neighborhood for opportunities that may lead to crime. Learn how to do a crime prevention survey.
   b. Using the checklist in this *(the merit badge)* pamphlet, conduct a security survey of your home and discuss the results with your family.
5. Teach your family or patrol members how to protect themselves from crime at home, at school, in your community, and while traveling.
6. Help raise awareness about one school safety issue facing students by doing ONE of the following:
   a. Create a poster for display on a school bulletin board.
   b. With permission from school officials, create a page long public service announcement that could be read over the public address system at school or posted on the school's website.
   c. Make a presentation to a group such as a Cub Scout den that addresses the issue.
7. Do ONE of the following:
   a. Assist in the planning and organization of a crime prevention program in your community such as Neighborhood Watch, Community Watch, or Crime Stoppers. Explain how this program can benefit your neighborhood.
   b. With your parent's and counselor's approval, visit a jail or detention facility or a criminal court hearing. Discuss your experience with your counselor.
8. Discuss the following with your counselor:
   a. How drug abuse awareness programs, such as "Drugs: A Deadly Game," help prevent crime
   b. Why alcohol, tobacco, and marijuana are sometimes called "gateway drugs" and how "gateway drugs" can lead to the use of other drugs
   c. Three resources in your city where a person with a drug problem or drug-related problem can go for help
   d. How the illegal sale and use of drugs lead to other crimes
   e. How to recognize child abuse
   f. The three R's of Youth Protection
9. Discuss the following with your counselor:
   a. The role of a sheriff's or police department in crime prevention.
   b. The purpose and operation of agencies in your community that help law enforcement personnel prevent crime, and how those agencies function during emergency situations.
   c. Explain the role private security plays in crime prevention.
10. Choose a career in the crime prevention or security industry that interests you. Describe the level of education required and responsibilities of a person in that position. Tell why this position interests you.

Source: U.S. Scouting Service Project, retrieved from http://usscouts.org/mb/mb131.asp

---

BOX 1-2 Emergency Preparedness Merit Badge

1. Earn the First Aid Merit Badge.
2. Do the following: Discuss with your counselor the aspects of emergency preparedness:
   a. **Prepare** for emergency situations
   b. **Respond** to emergency situations
   c. **Recover** from emergency situations
   d. **Mitigate and prevent** emergency situations

3. Make a chart that demonstrates your understanding of each of the aspects of emergency preparedness in requirement 2a (prepare, respond, recover, mitigate) with regard to 10 of the situations listed below. **You must use situations 1, 2, 3, 4, and 5 below in boldface** but you may choose any other five listed here for a total of 10 situations. Discuss this chart with your counselor.
   a. **Home kitchen fire**
   b. **Home basement/storage room/garage fire**
   c. **Explosion in the home**
   d. **Automobile accident**
   e. **Food-borne disease (food poisoning)**
   f. Fire or explosion in a public place
   g. Vehicle stalled in the desert
   h. Vehicle trapped in a blizzard
   i. Flash flooding in town or in the country
   j. Mountain/backcountry accident
   k. Boating accident
   l. Gas leak in a home or a building
   m. Tornado or hurricane
   n. Major flood
   o. Nuclear power plant emergency
   p. Avalanche
   q. Violence in a public place
4. Meet with and teach your family how to get or build a kit, make a plan, and be informed for the situations on the chart you created for requirement 2b. Complete a family plan. Then meet with your counselor and report on your family meeting, discuss their responses, and share your family plan.
5. Show how you could safely save a person from the following:
   a. Touching a live household electric wire
   b. A room filled with carbon monoxide
   c. Clothes on fire
   d. Drowning using nonswimming rescues (including accidents on ice)
6. Show three ways of attracting and communicating with rescue planes/aircraft.
7. With another person, show a good way to transport an injured person out of a remote and/or rugged area, conserving the energy of rescuers while ensuring the well-being and protection of the injured person.
8. Do the following: Tell the things a group of Scouts should be prepared to do, the training they need, and the safety precautions they should take for the following emergency services:
   a. Crowd and traffic control
   b. Messenger service and communication
   c. Collection and distribution services
   d. Group feeding, shelter, and sanitation
9. Identify the government or community agencies that normally handle and prepare for the emergency services listed under 8, and explain to your counselor how a group of Scouts could volunteer to help in the event of these types of emergencies.
   a. Find out who is your community's emergency management director and learn what this person does to **prepare, respond to, recover from,** and **mitigate and prevent** emergency situations in your community. Discuss this information with your counselor and apply what you discover to the chart you created for requirement 2b.
10. Take part in an emergency service project, either a real one or a practice drill, with a Scouting unit or a community agency. Do the following:
    a. Prepare a written plan for mobilizing your troop when needed to do emergency service. If there is already a plan, explain it. Tell your part in making it work.
    b. Take part in at least one troop mobilization. Before the exercise, describe your part to your counselor. Afterward, conduct an "after-action" lesson, discussing what you learned during the exercise that required changes or adjustments to the plan.

(continues)

c. Prepare a personal emergency service pack for a mobilization call. Prepare a family kit (suitcase or waterproof box) for use by your family in case an emergency evacuation is needed. Explain the needs and uses of the contents.

11. Do ONE of the following:
   a. Using a safety checklist approved by your counselor, inspect your home for potential hazards. Explain the hazards you find and how they can be corrected.
   b. Review or develop a plan of escape for your family in case of fire in your home.
   c. Develop an accident prevention program for five family activities outside the home (such as taking a picnic or seeing a movie) that includes an analysis of possible hazards, a proposed plan to correct those hazards, and the reasons for the corrections you propose.

Source: U.S. Scouting Service Project, retrieved from http://usscouts.org/usscouts/mb/mb006.asp

INTERNET RESOURCES FOR CRIME PREVENTION

National Crime Prevention Council
> http://www.ncpc.org/

Home Office
> http://www.homeoffice.gov.uk/

Bureau of Justice Statistics
> http://bjs.ojp.usdoj.gov/

The CPTED Page
> http://www.thecptedpage.wsu.edu/

Center for Problem-Oriented Policing
> http://www.popcenter.org/

Office of National Drug Control Policy
> http://www.whitehousedrugpolicy.gov/

Office of Juvenile Justice and Delinquency Prevention
> http://www.ojjdp.gov/

KEY TERMS

Crime prevention through environmental design
Nuisance abatement
Routine activity theory
Situational crime prevention
Experimental design
Crime hotspots

DISCUSSION QUESTIONS

1. In your view, what factors have contributed to the decline in the crime rate?
2. Describe how a college or university town could use nuisance abatement to control nuisance properties near campus.

3. Why have some programs endured even though research findings indicate that they do not work as intended?
4. Discuss the application of situational crime prevention principles to a college or university.

REFERENCES

Abbott, G. (2005). *Nuisance abatement manual* (14th ed.). Criminal Law Enforcement Division, Office of the Attorney General for the State of Texas. Retrieved from https://www.oag.state.tx.us/ag_publications/pdfs/2005nuisance.pdf.

Associated Press. (2011). Final man gets 5–12 in NH burglary killing. My Fox Boston. Retrieved from http://www.myfoxboston.com/dpp/news/crime_files/crime_watch/final-man-gets-5-12-in-nh-burglary-killing-25-apx-20110427.

Bentham, J. (1948). *The principles of morals and legislation*. New York, NY: Hafner Publishing Co.

Berg, B. (2009). *Qualitative research methods for the social sciences* (7th ed.). Boston, MA: Allyn & Bacon.

Braga, A. A., & Bond, B. J. (2008). Policing crime and disorder hot spots: A randomized controlled trial. *Criminology, 46*(3), 577–607.

Braithwaite, J. (1989). *Crime, shame, and reintegration*. Cambridge, UK: Cambridge University Press.

Brantingham, P. L., & Brantingham, P. J. (1991). Notes on the geometry of crime. In P. L. Brantingham & P. J. Brantingham (Eds.), *Environmental criminology* (pp. 27–54). Prospect Heights, IL: Waveland Press.

Bureau of Justice Statistics. (2011). Employment and expenditure. Retrieved from http://bjs.ojp.usdoj.gov/index.cfm?ty=tp&tid=5#pubs.

Center for Problem-Oriented Policing. (2011). Twenty five techniques of situational [crime] prevention. Retrieved from http://www.popcenter.org/25techniques/.

Clark, R. V. (1995). Situational crime prevention. In M. Tonry and D. P. Farrington (Eds.), *Building a safer society: Strategic approaches to crime prevention* (pp. 91–150). Chicago: University of Chicago Press.

Clark, R. V. (2002). Shoplifting: Guide no. 11; The problem of shoplifting. Center for Problem-Oriented Policing. Retrieved from http://www.popcenter.org/problems/shoplifting.

Cohen, L. E., & Felson M. (1979). Social change and crime rate trends: A routine activity approach. *American Sociological Review, 44*, 588–605.

Crowe, T. D. (1991). *Crime prevention through environmental design: Applications of architectural design and space management concepts*. Boston, MA: Butterworth-Heinemann.

Davis, R. C., & Lurigio, A. J. (1996). *Fighting back: Neighborhood antidrug strategies*. Thousand Oaks, CA: Sage Publications.

Farrington, D. P. (2000). Explaining and preventing crime: The globalization of knowledge; The American Society of Criminology 1999 presidential address. *Criminology, 38*(1), 1–24.

Farrington, D. P., & Welsh, B. C. (2007). Improved street lighting. In B. C. Welsh & D. P. Farrington (Eds.), *Preventing crime: What works for children, offenders, victims, and places* (pp. 209–224). New York, NY: Springer.

Federal Bureau of Investigation. (2009a). Crime in the United States: Table 8, New Hampshire, Offenses known to law enforcement, by state by city, 2009. Retrieved from http://www2.fbi.gov/ucr/cius2009/data/table_08_nh.html.

Federal Bureau of Investigation. (2009b). Crime in the United States: Table 1A, Crime in the United States, Percent change in volume and rate per 100,000 inhabitants for 2 years, 5 years, and 10 years. Retrieved from http://www2.fbi.gov/ucr/cius2009/data/table_01a.html.

Federal Bureau of Investigation. (2009c). Crime in the United States: Table 1, Crime in the United States, by volume and rate per 100,000 inhabitants, 1990–2009. Retrieved http://www2.fbi.gov/ucr/cius2009/data/table_01.html.

Felson, M. (2002). *Crime and everyday life* (3rd ed.). Thousand Oaks, CA: Sage Publications.

Felson, M., Belanger, M. E., Bichler, G. M., Bruzinski, C. D., Campbell, G. S., . . . Williams, L. M. (1996). Redesigning hell: Preventing crime and disorder at the Port Authority Bus Terminal. In R. V. Clarke (Ed.), *Preventing mass transit crime* (pp. 5–92). Monsey, NY: Criminal Justice Press.

Finckenauer, J. O., Gavin, P. W., Hovland, A., & Storvoll, E. (1999). *Scared Straight: The panacea phenomenon revisited*. Prospect Heights, IL: Waveland Press.

Hagan, F. E. (2010). *Research methods in criminal justice and criminology* (8th ed.). Upper Saddle River, NJ: Prentice Hall.

Kelling, G., & Coles, C. (1996). *Fixing broken windows: Restoring order and reducing crime in our communities*. New York, NY: Free Press.

Kelling, G., L., Pate, D., Dieckman, D., & Brown, C. E. (1974). The Kansas City Preventive Patrol Experiment: A Summary Report. Washington, DC : Police Foundation. Retrieved from http://www.policefoundation.org/pdf/kcppe.pdf.

Kelling, G. L., & Wilson, J. Q. (1982, March). Broken windows: The police and neighborhood safety. *The Atlantic*. Retrieved from http://www.theatlantic.com/magazine/archive/1982/03/broken-windows/4465/.

Klenowski, P. M., Bell, K. J., & Dodson, K. D. (2010). An empirical examination of juvenile awareness programs in the United States: Can juveniles be "Scared Straight"? *Journal of Offender Rehabilitation, 49*, 254–272.

La Vigne, N. G. (2006). Safe transport: Security by design on the Washington Metro. In R. V. Clark (Ed.), *Preventing mass transit crime* (pp. 163–197). Monsey, NY: Criminal Justice Press.

Laub, J. H., & Sampson, R. J. (2003). *Shared beginnings, divergent lives: Delinquent boys to age 70*. Cambridge, MA: Harvard University Press.

Law Enforcement–Private Security Consortium. (2009). Operation Partnership: Trends and practices in law enforcement and private security collaboration. Office of Community Orientated Policing Services, U.S. Department of Justice. Retrieved from http://www.ilj.org/publications/docs/Operation_Partnership_Private_Security.pdf.

Maguire, K. (2003). Sourcebook of criminal justice statistics (Table 3.111). Retrieved from http://www.albany.edu/sourcebook/pdf/t3111.pdf.

McCabe, J. E. (2008). What works in policing? The relationship between drug enforcement and serious crime. *Police Quarterly, 11*(3), 289–314.

Nazemi, S. (2009). Sir Robert Peel's nine principals [*sic*] of policing. Retrieved from http://www.lacp.org/2009-Articles-Main/062609-Peels9Principals-SandyNazemi.htm.

New Hampshire. (2010). Senate Bill 500. Retrieved from http://www.nhliberty.org/bills/view/2010/SB500.

Newman, O. (1996). *Creating defensible space*. Washington, DC: Office of Policy Development and Research, U.S. Department of Housing and Urban Development. Retrieved from http://www.huduser.org/publications/pdf/def.pdf.

Novotney, L. C., Mertinko, E., Lange, J., & Kelly Baker, T. (2000). Juvenile Mentoring Program: A progress review. Office of Juvenile Justice and Delinquency Prevention, Office of Justice Programs, U.S. Department of Justice. Retrieved from http://www.ncjrs.gov/pdffiles1/ojjdp/182209.pdf.

Opera Solutions. (2009). Transformative analytics: The next level in predicting and shaping consumer behavior. Retrieved from http://www.operasolutions.com/news_whitepaper_downloads_form.html.

Opera Solutions. (2010). About us. Retrieved from http://www.operasolutions.com/about.html

Pratt, T. C., Cullen, F. T., Blevins, K. R., Daigle, L. E., & Madensen, T. D. (2006). The empirical status of deterrence theory: A meta-analysis. In F. T. Cullen, J. P. Wright, & K. R. Blevins (Eds.), *Taking stock: The status of criminological theory* (pp. 367–395). New Brunswick, NJ: Transaction Publishers.

Regoli, R. M., Hewitt, J. D., & DeLisi, M. (2010). *Delinquency in society* (8th ed.). Sudbury, MA: Jones and Bartlett Publishing.

Rosenbaum, D. P., & Hanson, G. S. (1998). Assessing the effects of school-based drug education: A six-year multilevel analysis of Project D.A.R.E. *Journal of Research in Crime and Delinquency, 35*(4), 381–412.

Shader, M. (2003). Risk factors for delinquency: An overview (NCJ 207540). Washington, DC: Office of Juvenile Justice and Delinquency Prevention, Office of Justice Programs, U.S. Department of Justice. Retrieved from http://www.ncjrs.gov/pdffiles1/ojjdp/frd030127.pdf.

Shaw, C. R., & McKay, H. D. (1969). *Juvenile delinquency and urban areas* (Rev. ed.). Chicago, IL: University of Chicago Press.

Sherman, L. W., Gottfredson, D. C., MacKenzie, D. L., Eck, J., Reuter, P., & Bushway, S. (1998). Preventing crime: What works, what doesn't, what's promising. National Institute of Justice, U.S. Department of Justice. Retrieved from http://www.ncjrs.gov/pdffiles/171676.pdf.

Sherman, L. W., & Weisburd, D. (1995). General deterrent effects of police patrol in crime "hot spots": A randomized controlled trial. *Justice Quarterly, 12*(4), 625–648.

State of New Hampshire. (2009). Gerstein affidavit. Retrieved from http://www.wmur.com/download/2010/1012/25368504.pdf.

Truman, J. L., & Rand, M. R. (2010). Criminal victimization, 2009. Bureau of Justice Statistics, U.S. Department of Justice. Retrieved from http://bjs.ojp.usdoj.gov/content/pub/pdf/cv09.pdf.

U.S. Bureau of Labor Statistics. Office of Occupational Statistics and Employment Projections. (2011). *Occupational outlook handbook 2010–2011 Edition.* Retrieved from http://www.bls.gov/oco/.

U.S. Scouting Service Project. (2006). Crime prevention. Retrieved from http://usscouts.org/mb/mb131.asp.

U.S. Scouting Service Project. (2008). Emergency preparedness. Retrieved from http://usscouts.org/usscouts/mb/mb006.asp.

Welsh, B. C., & Farrington, D. P. (2009). *Making public places safer: Surveillance and crime prevention.* New York, NY: Oxford University Press.

WMUR-TV (2010, November 9). Spader: "Think jury will sing happy birthday to me?" Retrieved from http://www.wmur.com/video/25687158/detail.html.

CHAPTER 2

Primary Interventions: Crime Prevention in the Family and Schools

David A. Mackey
Plymouth State University

INTRODUCTION

Early intervention programs designed to reduce crime rates have shown promising results in studies conducted over the past few decades. Primary prevention programs have gained attention because of their effectiveness in reducing social problems as well as their potential to save taxpayer dollars (Farrington, 2000; Karoly et al., 1998; Welsh & Piquero, 2012). The main objective of early, placed-based delinquency prevention programs is to prevent not only juvenile delinquency but also adult criminality by reducing the prevalence of *risk factors* associated with delinquent behavior and strengthening *protective factors* that insulate youths from situations that may favor the development of delinquent behavior (Farrington, 2000; Shader, 2003). Reducing the prevalence of risk factors should have an impact on the frequency and seriousness of delinquent offending. With this approach, the incidence of crime should decrease, thus providing benefits for society, potential crime victims, and even potential offenders. Two critical social institutions provide the setting for such programs: the family and the school. This chapter first discusses family-based crime prevention initiatives and then describes school-based programs.

There is a common assumption that family training programs and school-based initiatives such as Project DARE (a drug abuse and resistance education program) will have a positive impact on youth development and will promote prosocial outcomes; however, evaluations of such programs show that this assumption may be overly optimistic. The sometimes disappointing results of these program evaluations underscore the need for a strong evaluation design that will determine whether or not a program works as intended. McCord (2007) notes that program outcomes may fall along a continuum, from intended positive outcomes to unintended negative outcomes. In this sense, a program may not only fail to produce a positive outcome but also yield negative outcomes. In other words, an intervention may produce more harm than good. For example, the Cambridge Somerville Youth Study program had good intentions, a theoretical model, and a sound implementation plan, but long-term evaluation results indicated that the program did more harm than good for its participants (McCord, 2003, as cited in McCord, 2007). Likewise, an evaluation of Project DARE indicated that students who completed the program used drugs more and disliked the police more than did their counterparts who did not participate in DARE (Rosenbaum & Hanson, 1998).

FAMILY-BASED CRIME PREVENTION

Society offers few occupations that may be taken up without any training or experience, but becoming a parent is the obvious exception. Families, and particularly parents, play a major role in the socialization and development of children (Farrington & Welsh, 2007; Welsh & Piquero, 2012). Parents have the primary role in the physical, mental, and social development of the child, but how well they perform that role and how well their families function should not necessarily be viewed as a dichotomy of either good or bad. A more apt assessment scale would be a continuum. Between good and bad, the family environment shapes not only a child's early development within the family but also his or her trajectory in life. Positive early experiences in a loving, supportive family that provide developmentally appropriate challenges improve a child's trajectory from infancy to adulthood. Conversely, a family environment marked by parental discord, parental violence, parental criminality, alcohol and drug abuse, physical and emotional abuse, apathy or indifference toward children, and inadequate supervision of children has a negative impact on the social trajectory of young family members.

Since there are no educational prerequisites for parenthood, how does a parent develop his or her parenting style and repertoire of parenting skills? Since most new parents have only their own experience as the children of parents, educational and support services offer a means of filling this critical need for parenting skills that will encourage positive development. Early parenting programs can have multiple connected goals. Some have a delinquency prevention component that begins very early; efforts to prevent teen pregnancy constitute one example, because being born to a teenage mother increases the risk that a child will later engage in delinquent behavior. Likewise, home visitation programs seek to improve parenting skills and expose expecting or new parents to community resources that will support their efforts. Teen pregnancy prevention and home visitation programs fall under the heading of "primary prevention" of delinquency. Unlike these primary prevention programs that focus on early family situations or even forestalling family formation, secondary prevention programs focus on youth who are seen as at-risk for offending, and tertiary programs seek to prevent first-time offenders from committing subsequent offenses. Thus, primary prevention programs seek to strengthen protective factors and minimize risk factors among a broad population.

As noted above, primary prevention programs offer potential benefits not only for individuals but for society as a whole. Preventing crime means that taxpayers potentially see reduced spending on criminal justice activities and social services. Consumers might even see lower insurance costs. Victims may also avoid experiencing loss and possible harm. Primary prevention efforts might raise some political concerns, however, perhaps by giving the appearance that society is being soft on crime; such programs emphasize a shift from formal control, such as the incarceration of individuals, to a more sustainable social structure. Society spends vast sums of money responding to crime after the fact, but primary prevention programs have the potential to divert some individuals from a life of crime and thus to save taxpayer money in the long run. Welsh and Piquero (2012) note that the long-term financial savings generated by primary prevention programs theoretically allow society to pay for those programs by saving money that otherwise would have been spent responding to crime.

One of the drawbacks of programs that seek to prevent delinquency is that the results of the program, whether positive, negative, or statistically insignificant, would not be available for 10–15 years or more. With such long time horizons, especially compared to the types of programs—such as juvenile drug court initiatives—that McDonald and Bush discuss in Chapter 12 of this volume, these programs may not hold much appeal for key decision makers, who often have much shorter time horizons in which to measure success or failure.

Risk Factors

The criminal justice field has borrowed the terminology and philosophy of the public health approach most commonly identified with a medical model of prevention (Farrington, 2000), specifically with the emphasis on risk and protective factors. Shader (2003) notes that the presence of multiple risk factors in a family setting increases the likelihood that a youth will engage in delinquent acts. Specific risk factors that have been correlated with delinquency include inadequate prenatal nutrition, prenatal drug use; family resources/poverty; poor parental supervision of children; harsh, lax, or indifferent discipline; poor parent–child attachment; and parental deviance (Farrington & Welsh, 2007; Sampson & Laub, 1993; Shader, 2003; Welsh & Piquero, 2012).

Prenatal drug, tobacco, and alcohol use. A high-risk mother is one who has a child or is pregnant with a child while experiencing one of the following disadvantages: no employment/low socioeconomic status, low education level, no marital partner, a history of drug or alcohol abuse, or a history of physical or sexual abuse. Drug use by expectant mothers can have a profound impact on the future of an unborn child. Feldman, Minkoff, McCalla, and Salwen (1992) analyzed drug tests conducted on urine samples from 1,111 inner city pregnant women who later gave birth in a city hospital in New York City. Their results indicated that 14% of the women tested positive for drugs. In addition, the majority (70%) of the drug users also smoked cigarettes. Based on these findings, they concluded that 20–30% of premature deliveries were due to drug use by the mother, and smoking cigarettes contributed to these premature births. Likewise, in a telephone survey of 1,550 white women ages 20–44 in 1986, only 39% of smokers quit smoking while pregnant, either when they found out they were pregnant or shortly into their pregnancy (Fingerhut, Kleinman, & Kendrick, 1990). That study also found that women with fewer than 12 years of education were five times more likely to smoke but were only one-fourth as likely to quit smoking during their pregnancy. Younger and unmarried women were also more likely to smoke compared to women who were older or married. It is reasonable to conclude that drug education and smoking cessation programs can be more fully integrated into parenting education programs so that expectant mothers have additional opportunities to learn about the impact drugs have on an unborn child.

Low birthweight babies. According to the March of Dimes (2010), babies born weighing less than 5 pounds, 8 ounces, are considered low birthweight, and nearly 1 in 12 babies born in the United States each year is considered low birthweight. Probable causes include expectant mothers' poor health habits such as smoking, lack of proper nutrition, and lack of adequate health care. Underweight newborns are much more likely to have developmental, educational, medical, and behavioral issues later in life. For instance, low birthweight may impede age-appropriate development, which negatively impacts school performance, and strong performance in school is a strong insulator from delinquency. Therefore, low birthweight would not be seen as a direct cause of delinquency but as a factor associated with the development of additional risk factors. Efforts to reduce the incidence of at-risk babies might include improving the quality of pregnancies or responding to the social problems associated with risk factors for low birthweight babies, such as prenatal smoking or lack of health care.

Teen mothers. Many programs have focused on reducing the incidence of teenage parenthood not because of the moral aspect of the issue but because teenage mothers are at additional risk for child poverty and dependency on public assistance. Waller, Brown, and Whittle (1999,

p. 468) state that "an early pregnancy is typically just one more constricting factor in a life path full of social and economic obstacles." While teen births have been trending downward, there were still 434,758 births for mothers aged 15–19 years recorded in 2008 (Centers for Disease Control and Prevention, 2010a). Also, about 70% of teen births are to unwed mothers. The at-risk status for teen mothers is correlated with higher unemployment rates, lower levels of education, and a higher percentage of low birthweight infants (Nguyen, Carson, Parris, & Place, 2003). Teen mothers often face additional pressures due to limited economic circumstances. In addition, teen mothers are more likely to have experienced sexual abuse than are older mothers because there is a greater likelihood that the pregnancy resulted from intercourse with an older male, which raises the question of whether or not the encounter was consensual (Waller, Brown, & Whittle, 1999). Young mothers are also at a higher risk for stress, social isolation, and substance abuse, leading to a greater incidence of child abuse and child neglect (Nguyen, Carson, Parris, & Place, 2003). In addition to suffering more abuse and neglect, the children born to teen mothers also have greater health and medical risks than children of the average adult mother. Teen mothers are more likely to face the economic disadvantages of single parenthood, have limited education, and poor parenting skills, all of which may lead to later problems for both the mother and child.

Waller, Brown, and Whittle (1999, p. 467) claim that, despite considerable policy focus on the issue and many educational programs designed to prevent unwanted pregnancies among teenagers, once a teen becomes pregnant, she is "dropped from the world agenda." They propose a cost-effective alternative approach to these "top-down" measures: a community-based mentoring program. In their view, teen pregnancy is not a cause of poverty but a symptom of a series of social problems illustrated by economic and social hardships. Waller, Brown, and Whittle contend that most adult figures in a pregnant teenager's life—parents, relatives, teachers, clergy—judge and reject them. These authors propose that each teen mother have a mentor to provide guidance and, more importantly, social support. They contend that "many of the risk factors associated with early pregnancy and child maltreatment may be significantly altered by the social support that mentoring relationships provide" (Waller, Brown, & Whittle, 1999, p. 471). The mentor should encourage prenatal and postnatal care, as well as urge the young mother to continue her education and thus break the cycle of poverty. They detail appropriate training for mentors, which would include teaching them techniques to develop rapport and basic education regarding child development, family violence, and pregnancy issues. Their evaluation strategy focuses on outcomes for both the youth and the mother.

Home Visitation Programs

Home visitation programs have been promoted as a promising means of preventing negative health and developmental issues for the children of program participants (Olds & Korfmacher, 1998). These programs seek to equip participating mothers with life skills that will help families—both parents and children—have more positive life course trajectories. Program objectives include improving multiple positive outcomes, such as better health, better education, and employment success. A common form of the program involves a professional, such as a nurse or social worker, entering the home to provide structured training and education over a substantial period of time, perhaps from early in the mother's pregnancy until the child is of preschool age. The professionals who work with the mothers receive training in various areas, which include not only service delivery but also honing the communication skills necessary to develop rapport with the mother. Typical home visitation programs also supply the mother with information on child development, educating her as to what kinds of behaviors and skills to expect of children at various ages. In addition, a home visitation program can include the provision of assistance or resources such as transportation for medical checkups, parenting classes, and social/educational learning groups for the children.

The Elmira Study

Among these home visitation training programs is the Elmira Parent/Early Infancy Project, considered by some to be a landmark program. It is one of the first programs to support the view that home visitation can be an effective means of preventing child abuse and neglect. Its goals are to improve the outcome of the pregnancy, to improve the quality of child care that parents provide, and to improve the woman's own life course development (Olds et al., 1997). The Elmira Project is of particular interest because the original controlled experimental design included 15 years of follow up on the participants, thus generating valuable long-range data.

Between 1978 and 1980, 400 women in Elmira, New York, volunteered to participate in the program. Each of them was less than 30 weeks' pregnant with her first child (Olds et al., 1997). The majority of the women were considered high risk because of some preexisting circumstance, such as economic disadvantage, young age, and/or status as a single parent. In the sample, 85% of the participating pregnant women had at least one risk characteristic. Specifically, 48% of the participants were younger than 19 years old, 62% were unmarried, 59% were from households classified as having low socioeconomic status, and 11% were African American (Olds et al., 1997).

There were four groups in the experimental design: two control groups and two treatment groups. Each of the children in the four control groups received screening for developmental and sensory problems at 12 months and 24 months of age, with subsequent referral for additional assistance if warranted. This screening was given to all groups. The first control group (group 1) received no additional screening, training, or treatment. The second control group (group 2) received, in addition to the screening, transportation vouchers enabling participants to have regular prenatal exams by a physician as well as well-child pediatric medical care through age 2. Researchers eventually combined groups 1 and 2 for the subsequent analysis. Group 3 received the developmental screening plus free transportation vouchers and home visits from a nurse every 2 weeks during the mother's pregnancy. Group 4 received the developmental screening as well as home visits from a nurse not only during the mother's pregnancy but also, at a reduced frequency, during the first 2 years of the child's life (Olds et al., 1998).

The researchers noted positive results for the group that had home visits through the child's 2nd year, and the 13-year follow up provided data enabling the researchers to determine whether there were more lasting positive impacts of the program. According to Olds et al. (1997), visiting nurses sought to develop a close working relationship with the mother as well as any other family members present. The nurses helped expectant mothers to set manageable goals and develop problem-solving skills in an effort to improve their education and employment status as well as the overall family dynamic. The goal-setting effort focused on short-term achievability—goals that could be accomplished between visits—to help build the mother's self-confidence. Out of the 400 women who participated in the original home visitation program, 324 were eligible for a follow-up study and agreed to participate in that study, conducted when the children were 15 years old. Researchers asked the mothers to complete a life history calendar designed to help them recall major life events of the previous 13 years, such as births, marriages, divorces, employment, and residential moves. The follow-up study also called for the women to estimate the number of months they received any Medicaid and food stamp assistance and any contact with the criminal justice system (Olds et al., 1997). Researchers also asked participating mothers about alcohol and drug use and, with the subjects' consent, examined child protective service records on the youth.

The researchers then compared results from the two groups (combined control groups 1 and 2 and treatment group 4). Results of the follow-up study showed that women whom the nurses visited up to the child's 2nd birthday had fewer subsequent pregnancies, used food stamps for fewer months, were arrested fewer times, had fewer instances of substance abuse, and were cited for fewer instances of child abuse/neglect (Olds et al., 1997). The researchers also note that the finding of fewer instances of child abuse/neglect is noteworthy, considering that the group receiving nurse visits was under a higher level of supervision; the regular presence of visiting nurses in the home should, in theory, result in higher detection of certain behaviors. Karoly et al. (1998) note that the Elmira Project produced substantial cost savings; they estimate savings of just over $18,000, although the actual lifetime total would likely be higher since this calculation considered only the youths' first 15 years of life.

Researchers also examined the nature and extent of differences in antisocial behavior among juveniles in the program during the 15-year follow-up (Olds et al., 1998). Data included both self-reports and comparisons with official records from social service agencies, police departments, and the schools. The children of group 4 (which received regular nurse visits until age 2) reported more stops by the police but did have fewer arrests, convictions, and violations of probation (Olds et al., 1998). The children in group 4 also had fewer sexual partners, smoked fewer cigarettes per day, reported fewer incidents of running away, and consumed alcohol on fewer days during the 6-month period prior to the interview. The children in group 3 of the design (nurse visits only during pregnancy) did not have as many positive results as the youths in group 4, which would seem to indicate the importance of home visitation after the child is born, not just during the mother's pregnancy. With the exception of illegal drug use, group 4 showed more pronounced positive results for youths of lower socioeconomic status (SES) backgrounds, which may indicate additional benefits of the home visits for particular populations.

The original Elmira Project participants were later subject to an additional analysis, this time to find out if domestic violence would decrease the effectiveness of home visitation in preventing child abuse and neglect (Eckenrode et al., 2000). Researchers offer several reasons why children who live in households with domestic violence could be at risk for abuse or neglect. For example, while male abusers may be the cause of some neglect, mothers who are in a violent relationship may lash out violently and, due to mental impairments, may have reduced capacity to respond to their children. Children who witness domestic violence may exhibit behavioral problems, which can make them more challenging to parent. Just under half of the mothers in the Elmira study had experienced some form of domestic violence since the birth of their child (Eckenrode et al., 2000). The follow-up study findings showed that families who received home visitation during the mother's pregnancy and the child's infancy (group 4) had significantly fewer child maltreatment reports involving the mother as the perpetrator, but that the beneficial effects of the nurse visits decreased as the level of domestic violence increased. Interestingly, home visitation did not have an impact on the amount of domestic violence. Results indicate that additional resources and supervision may be warranted in family situations in which the mothers are at risk for domestic violence.

With numerous early intervention programs available, questions remain as to the effectiveness of various models. Nguyen, Carson, Parris, and Place (2003) report results from an experimental design comparing the Nursing–Family Partnership model to the Public Health Field Nursing (PHFN) Program for a sample of Hispanic teens. The expectant mothers in the control group received only three visits from a traditional public health field nurse in the PHFN Program. The intervention group received weekly home visits for the first 4 weeks after they entered the program (during pregnancy), visits every other week until delivery, weekly visits for the first 6 weeks after delivery, visits every other week until the child was 20 months old, and monthly visits until the child was 24 months old. The home visits by public health nurses with advanced training in the Nursing–Family Partnership model were 60–90 minutes in duration and focused on a range of topics, including maternal and child health, child development, family dynamics, and information about existing health and human service agencies. Both groups experienced positive results with respect to premature births, which occurred at a rate of less than half of the state's average. The mothers in the Nurse–Family Partnership group had a lower percentage of low birthweight babies compared to the control group. Although the authors note fairly favorable results, roughly 22% of the mothers effectively dropped out of the program by missing an excessive number of appointments or because of other factors related to the fact that this population tended to have significant residential instability. The research findings also stress the importance of cooperation and sustained interest on the part of the expectant mother as well as the difficulties in successfully working with at-risk mothers who can easily drop out or fail to meet program requirements.

Ammerman et al. (2006) share this concern about the active engagement of program participants. They studied the impact of the home visitation program on 515 first-time teen mothers taking part in Healthy Families America. About 32% of the 515 mothers ended their participation by the first month, which, the authors note, was prior to the establishment of a strong rapport between the mother and the home visitor. The authors offer a number of reasons why women might drop out of the program: inexperience in making or inability to schedule appointments, a perception of duplication in program services, lack of rapport with the visiting professional, moving out of the area, and even a lack of privacy during the visit because of living arrangements. Many mothers might consider the home visits redundant due to the nature of the information being conveyed. Ammerman et al. (2006) contend that it is critical that the home visitor keep the visits engaging, with each visit including new material that evolves as the child grows. In addition, there must be a continuity of professionals to maintain a rapport between the mother and the visiting nurse. The researchers note that among the variables that seemed to predict more sustained involvement with the home visitation program included the mother being white, a history of criminal behavior, mental illness, or substance abuse, lower levels of social support, and multiple stressors.

A 2009 study using data collected from 806 at-risk, first-time mothers enrolled in a home visitation program addressed the mental health issues of participating mothers. Researchers collected data on self-reported depression symptoms at enrollment and again 9 months later (Ammerman et al., 2009). Their findings indicate that 45.3% of mothers had experienced clinically elevated depression symptoms at some point in the first 9 months of their home visitation program. Of particular interest, 74% had experienced an interpersonal trauma prior to beginning the home visitation program. More than half of the expecting mothers were clinically depressed at the start of their participation but were no longer depressed at the nine-month interval. This study also showed higher rates of depression among African American mothers. Mothers with self-reported depression may find it more difficult to participate in an extended home visitation program, and simultaneously treat their depression. Adding to this challenge is the likelihood that participants who present symptoms of clinical depression may also have some coexisting mental disorders. Because of the apparent prevalence of depression and other mental health issues among at-risk mothers, effective home visitation programs should integrate mental health screening and service referral.

Hammond-Ratzlaff and Fulton (2001) discuss the knowledge that mothers gain when they participate in home visitation programs. Previous studies have noted that mothers who participate in home visitation programs expand their knowledge in many areas, including childbirth, child care, social support services, home safety, and health awareness. Children of these mothers also experience positive outcomes, such as fewer emergency room visits and fewer behavioral problems in schools. Hammond-Ratzlaff and Fulton found that the 47 mothers in the program they studied also increased their knowledge of child development.

Perry Preschool Project

One early intervention program aimed at preschool age children is the High/Scope Perry Preschool Project, which has been in operation for 40 years (Parks, 2000). The program began with an experimental design involving random assignment of 123 high-risk youths. Youths were matched based on gender, age, IQ, and SES. One group participated in the program while the other became the control group. The experimental group attended a daily preschool program Monday through Friday that focused on cognitive development, such as enhanced thinking and reasoning abilities. In addition, the school staff made weekly home visits. Program enrollment was for 2 years. By age 19, members of the experimental group had experienced fewer arrests than the control group (31% compared to 51% of the control group), and by age 27, the experimental group had half as many arrests on average relative to the control group. The control group also had a higher percentage of frequent offenders, defined as five or more arrests, than did the experimental group (35% compared to 7%). Parks (2000) notes that more than 70% of the experimental group graduated from high school, while only 54% of the control group graduated. The cost benefits of the program were estimated to be just over $88,000 (including savings to crime victims) per youth in the program or a savings of $7.16 for every dollar spent on the program.

Incredible Years Training Series

The Incredible Years Training Series is designed to identify and reduce behavioral problems among children 2–10 years old (Webster-Stratton, 2000). The program uses video modeling, discussion, and rehearsal intervention techniques to increase the competence of adults, such as parents and teachers, who work in various capacities with youths. There are five programs in the series, each based on the age of the youth and the program target audience: (1) Incredible Years BASIC Parent Training, (2) Incredible Years ADVANCED Parent Training, (3) Incredible Years EDUCATION Parent Training, (4) Incredible Years Teacher Training, and (5) Incredible Years Child Training. The BASIC program, based on social learning theory, is for parents. It lasts 12 weeks and presents various scenarios in video format. Discussion follows the scenario presentations so that parents can begin to develop a repertoire of response options appropriate to a variety of family situations. The ADVANCED program, also for parents, emphasizes the building of interpersonal skills, such as communication and problem-solving techniques. The EDUCATION program teaches parents techniques to strengthen their role in their child's educational experience, such as supporting homework efforts and encouraging children to read. The Teacher Training program similarly emphasizes the role of positive techniques, such as incentives, praise, and rewards. The Child Training program reinforces positive social skills and behaviors for the child to model, such as conflict resolution techniques. According to Webster-Stratton (2000), one of the main goals of the program is the development of social competence skills, which serve as a protective factor for youths. The Incredible Years Training Series seeks to minimize a focus on negative reinforcement and emphasize a more proactive and positive manner of supervision and discipline.

The BASIC program teaches parents how to play with their children and to recognize the importance of children's play for their development. It also emphasizes the importance of play in minimizing disruptions caused by a child's boredom. Another important aspect of the program deals with how and when parents should praise and reward children. Webster-Stratton (2000) describes effective parental praise as an art requiring finesse. For example, parents must avoid praising only "perfect" behavior. Similar insights are brought to bear on developing an effective reward system, one in which parents understand the difference between rewards and bribes. In addition to teaching parents how to provide positive reinforcement and suitable alternatives, the program's training objectives include helping youths to accept limits and showing parents how to handle children's noncompliance with rules and limits, including what penalties, such as "time out," are appropriate.

The Incredible Years programs for parents are designed to be delivered by one or two leaders guiding the activities of a group of 12 to 14 parents. Webster-Stratton (2000) notes that the program format consists of approximately 15% teaching, 25% video presentation, and 60% discussion. The videos show parents interacting in positive ways with their children and lead to an opportunity for structured discussion within the group. The Incredible Years programs also integrate role-playing activities to complement scenarios depicted in the videos. Webster-Stratton notes that experimental designs testing the effectiveness of the program have shown positive results in three key areas: parents' social competence, positive methods of discipline, and child management skills.

SCHOOL-BASED CRIME PREVENTION

Once children reach school age, they spend a considerable amount of time away from the direct supervision of their parents. The school, much like the family, is the focus of several contemporary theories in criminology. For instance, Hirschi's (1969) social control theory emphasizes a youth's attachment to and involvement in school. Youths who have better grades, more attachment to school, and see value in education are less likely to be delinquent. Agnew's (1992) general strain theory identifies a number of sources of strain in youths, including failure to achieve positively valued goals, the removal of positively valued stimuli, and the presence of negative stimuli, all of which may occur in a typical school setting. Negative outcomes are likely if youths cannot respond to strain using prosocial mechanisms. Typical school settings also lend themselves to situational crime prevention. While attending school, youths are sometimes under fairly close supervision, such as while in a classroom; at other times, there is much less direct supervision of youths, such as in restrooms, locker rooms, hallways, and stairwells.

Youths experience a much higher rate of victimization than do other age groups. In 2008, youths 12–15 years old were victimized at a rate of 42.2 per 1,000 individuals, while individuals 65 and older had a victimization rate of 3.1 per 1,000 (Rand & Truman, 2010). In addition, youths commit a disproportionate number of offenses. Schools present a situation where likely offenders and potential victims interact with one another under varying degrees of supervision.

There are a number of excellent sources of data on violence, drugs, and weapons in schools. For instance, the Youth Risk Behavior Surveillance System (YRBSS), administered biannually since 1991 by the Centers for Disease Control and Prevention (CDC), monitors specific health-related risk behaviors among youth. In the YRBSS, there are six key areas of health-related risk behaviors: (1) behaviors that contribute to unintentional injuries and violence; (2) tobacco use; (3) alcohol and other drug use; (4) sexual behaviors that contribute to unintended pregnancy and sexually transmitted diseases (STDs), including human immunodeficiency virus (HIV) infection; (5) unhealthy dietary behaviors; and (6) physical inactivity (Centers for Disease Control and Prevention, 2010b). The YRBSS is a school-based survey administered on the national, state, and district level for students in grades 9–12. Some noteworthy results from the 2009 YRBSS for all high school students include the following: 17.5% of students had carried a weapon (e.g., a gun, knife, or club) on at least 1 day during the 30 days before the survey; 19.9% of students had been bullied on school property during the 12 months before the survey; 26.1% of students nationwide had felt so sad or hopeless almost every day for 2 or more weeks in a row that they stopped doing some usual activities; 24.2% of students had had five or more drinks of alcohol in a row (i.e., within a couple of hours) on at least one day during the 30 days before the survey; and 20.8% of students had used marijuana one or more times during the 30 days before the survey.

Crime in Schools

The first national study of school crime was a National Institute of Education 1978 study based on a national sample of 4,014 principals, 23,895 teachers, and 31,373 students. Results indicated that more than 280,000 secondary school students were physically attacked each month and that 8% of junior high and 4% senior high students skipped school due to fear of victimization (cited in Toby, 1983). Less than 1% of the high school students reported being robbed and less than 2% reported being assaulted during the previous month (Toby, 1995).

Another data source for school crime statistics is the National Crime Victimization Survey/ School Crime Supplement (NCVS/SCS). Robers, Zhang, Truman, and Snyder (2010) note that between July 1, 2008, and June 30, 2009, there were 38 school-associated violent deaths. In 2008 alone, 1.2 million criminal victimizations occurred in school settings. This total was roughly split between property crimes and violent crimes. It is interesting to note that the risk of violent victimization for youths was higher away from school than in school. The authors note that about one-third of all students between 12 and 18 years of age reported being bullied at least once at school in the previous year.

As society contends with the negative impacts of numerous high-profile shootings in school settings, communities have taken a critical look at creating and maintaining a positive school climate. For instance, some states such as California, have declared that students have the state constitutional right to attend schools that are safe, secure, and conducive to learning. Michigan granted students the right to transfer from schools that have been deemed persistently dangerous. A constitutional right to attend safe schools potentially makes schools liable for failing to protect students from foreseeable harms. These harms can include the presence of gangs, weapons, bullying, or sexual harassment. The Obama administration elevated the prevention of bullying in schools to a national issue.

There are two fairly broad approaches to school crime and disorder; one approach relies on more formal social control within the school, and the second approach emphasizes informal social control. A number of schools have opted for the formal approach, utilizing such techniques as perimeter security (fences), secured parking areas, closed-circuit television, security guards, uniformed police officers, anonymous tip lines for students to report crimes, metal detectors, removal of all lockers, limiting access to open doors/windows, transparent book bags, Kevlar backpacks, desks bolted to the floor, panic buttons and telephones in the classrooms, drug testing for students involved in extracurricular activities, identification tags or badges, glass block instead of cinderblock walls to allow surveillance, restroom monitoring by staff, random visits by drug dogs, controlled visitor access to the school, and bans on offensive clothing. Other approaches have emphasized high expectations for performance, positive school climate, increased homework, specialized programs such as conflict resolution, improving student awareness of civic duties and responsibilities, a sense of mission regarding education, the use of place managers to watch over specific areas of the school (shops, gyms, locker rooms, stairs, hallways, and restrooms), handlers for high-risk youths (emphasizing both mentoring and surveillance of potential offenders), and guardians (similar to handlers but focusing on potential victims).

Contemporary schools have a complex mission. Their objectives can include providing proper socialization for students, setting educational objectives, making sure that students master material in order to meet standardized test requirements, providing skills that will prepare students to enter the workforce, academically preparing students to enter college, and providing students with the life skills and social skills needed in order to be active and engaged citizens. School administrators have contemplated enacting a number of policies intended to improve safety and order, but such measures can negatively impact the learning environment, such as the potential for zero-tolerance policies. Many structural and procedural changes can make school seem more like a prison than a place for learning, growth, and dialogue. Some individuals contend that schools should enact measures that advance the learning process, provide students with adequate information about what is expected of them, and enforce rules in a fair and systematic manner.

As research on school experiences and delinquency has shown, what happens to students in school can lead to misbehavior, including delinquency. Factors such as personality, self-control, intelligence, social class, family factors, school characteristics, and community context also play a role. Agnew (2009, p. 241) states that "many juveniles do poorly in school and come to dislike or even hate school. School then becomes a source of strain for them, it exercises little control over them, and it provides a context for associating with other dissatisfied, often delinquent, juveniles." Agnew notes that delinquents are more likely to perform poorly in school (reflected in poor grades and lower academic tracks), be less involved in school activities, have lower attachment to school, have poor relations with teachers (reflected in weak rapport and confrontational attitudes), have lower educational goals, and have higher rates of misbehavior in school.

Some states changed their compulsory education laws in an effort to extend educational opportunities for all students. For example, the New Hampshire state legislature raised the maximum age for compulsory education from 16 to 18. Reports indicate that the annual dropout rate decreased to 0.97% in 2009–2010 (WMUR-TV, 2011). Taking an alternative view, Toby (1995) contends that schools have a "stay-in" problem rather than a "dropout" problem. One of the factors contributing to school disorder, Toby argues, is that schools must deal with the presence of students who have little if any interest in learning and who create distractions for other students.

While serious crime and violence do occur in schools, the majority of criminal acts in school are relatively minor in nature. Most schools do not have problems with weapons, violence, and crime. Toby (1983) contends that serious violent crimes in schools are like a flood or tornado in a typical community; they are difficult to predict and tough to stop. Agnew (2009) notes that delinquency tends to be lower in small schools with good resources, good discipline (e.g., clear rules that are enforced consistently and fairly but are not overly punitive), opportunities for student success and accomplishment, high expectations for all students, a pleasant learning environment, and good cooperation between administrators and teachers. Many of the characteristics of a positive school climate are similar to those of a positive family environment. Large schools where students can remain aloof from activities and anonymous to overwhelmed teachers tend to have a higher incidence of school disorder and crime. Schools that maintain a tight focus on academic standards and achievement have less disorder.

Historical Trends in School Order and Discipline

Toby (1995) contends that formal and informal control within schools has weakened over time. In the past, for better or worse, the authority of many principals was similar to that of a pre-1950 prison warden. Both types of administrators—prison wardens and school principals—had wide authority and discretion in their respective institutions. The courts and communities were reluctant to get involved in the internal matters of schools (or prisons). Principals have seen their authority weakened, in part due to court cases granting due process rights to students in school, thus limiting the authority of principals. Toby notes that, in addition to the decline in the authority of principals, parental support for schools and teachers has decreased, as has the overall structure of the school day and curriculum. These three factors mean that teachers have less authority in the classroom. According to Toby, less teacher authority leads to less control in the classroom, which is associated with lower student performance. Less control in the classroom means that there may be greater opportunities for student misbehavior, such as cutting class, arriving late, and failing to complete assignments. Lower standards lead to weak academic skills. The complete picture is one of a critical mass of uninterested students in a vicious cycle of decreasing involvement. For example, students are given less homework on a regular basis because students who are out of school will not get the assignment, and of those who do get the assignment, some will be absent the next day. Students do minimal amounts of homework and are not reading on a regular basis. There are also a number of "internal dropouts"—students who are technically still enrolled but may skip days or blocks of time on a regular basis and who receive bad grades, have little motivation to improve, and have no stake in conforming to school rules.

Toby (1995) contends that there is a norm for high expectations of good grades (honor roll grades) that does match the true performance of students. International comparisons of performance on standardized tests demonstrate a wide gap in academic outcomes between students in the United States and those in other nations. The Organisation for Economic Co-operation and Development (OECD) provided literacy data for 15-year-old students in the areas of mathematics, reading, and science for 30 participating countries in 2006. The United States ranked 25th out of the 30 nations for the mathematics literacy average and 10th out of the 30 nations in science literacy (National Center for Educational Statistics, 2010). Toby describes this condition as the hoax of learning: students get fewer assignments and do less work but continue to receive the reward of good grades. In schools where this downward cycle gains momentum, students and teachers often leave that particular school setting for another school if they have the opportunity to do so. This situation siphons off the most motivated and capable teachers and students, thus perpetuating the cycle. He advocates an end to social promotion, lowering of the minimum age for compulsory education, and allowing young adults who have dropped out sometime in the past to resume their education in a controlled environment rather than rely on the self-motivation needed for nighttime GED classes. Toby (1995) also contends that interrupting the cycle requires that school be more academically challenging. However, this move might lead students who have little interest in serious school work to drop out.

Student Rights

Students have the right to a public education. In fact, with compulsory education laws, they must attend school until they reach a certain age, which varies by state. However, students who remain in school also need to conduct themselves in a manner that does not interfere with the right of other students to receive an education. The Supreme Court of the United States recognizes that school officials have inherent authority over students and that this authority is necessary in order to maintain an environment conducive to learning. The existence of this authority need not be expressly stated in school manuals, but the courts have recognized it in the concept of "*in loco parentis*," meaning "to stand in the place of parents." Teachers and school administrators thus have authority over youths while they are at school and must ensure an appropriate level of discipline and civility to maintain an environment conducive to learning.

Although the *in loco parentis* concept governing the exercise of authority in the schools is fairly straightforward, complexities arise when it comes to defining the balance between the administration's ability to make and enforce rules and students' ability to enjoy their constitutional rights, such as freedom from unreasonable searches and seizures, free speech, and due process. For example, in a landmark school rights case, Justice Abe Fortas (*Tinker v. Des Moines Independent Community School District*, 1969) stated, "It can hardly be argued that either students or teachers shed their constitutional rights to freedom of speech or expression at the schoolhouse gate." He went on to state that, "in our system, state-operated schools may not be enclaves of totalitarianism. School officials do not possess absolute authority over their students. Students in school, as well as out of school, are 'persons' under our Constitution. They are possessed of fundamental rights which the State must respect, just as they themselves must respect their obligations to the State."

Student Privacy Interests

Searching students suspected of possessing contraband, drugs, or weapons is one tactic administrators may employ to minimize crime in school and to enforce school rules. To what extent does the Fourth Amendment, which protects individuals from unreasonable searches and seizures, apply to students? Under what circumstances can school officials conduct searches of students, their belongings, or even their vehicles in the school parking lot? An increasingly prominent issue has been the desire of school officials to discipline students for infractions of school rules during nonschool hours or away from school property.

New Jersey v. T.L.O. (1985). "T.L.O." was a 14-year-old female freshman who was smoking cigarettes in the restroom when a teacher caught her in the act. The teacher took her to the principal's office, and upon questioning by the vice principal, she claimed that she did not smoke. A school official searched her purse to recover the remaining cigarettes. The school official found marijuana, rolling papers, a list of names of students who owed her money, a pipe, and a letter she had written to a friend describing her activities selling marijuana at school. School officials notified the police, and the student was later adjudicated delinquent. The decision was eventually overturned by the New Jersey Supreme Court, and the case reached the Supreme Court of the United States. The case featured several issues of key importance. In the majority opinion written by Justice Byron White (*New Jersey v. T.L.O.*, 1985), he noted that the Constitution protects students against unreasonable searches and seizures. The Court noted that the search of T.L.O.'s purse to discover whether school rules were being violated was reasonable at the inception of the search. The search must be justified when it begins; it cannot be justified retroactively, based on what is found or recovered during the search. Of particular importance was the Court's statement that school officials are not held to the same standard as police—the probable cause standard—when conducting a search, and they are not required to obtain a warrant. Her later adjudication and the resulting declaration of delinquency rested on the evidence school officials seized. In its decision, the Court noted that a search of a student by a school official is "justified at its inception when there are reasonable grounds for suspecting that the search will turn up evidence that the student has violated or is violating either the law or the rules of the school. Such a search will be permissible in its scope when the measures adopted are reasonably related to the objectives of the search and not excessively intrusive in light of the age and sex of the student and the nature of the infraction" (*New Jersey v. T.L.O.*, 1985, p. 469 U.S. 343).

Strip searches. The issue of searching students for contraband that school officials believe will negatively affect school safety and detract from the learning environment reappeared with the controversy surrounding the strip search of a 13-year-old female student, Savana Redding, with the intent to uncover prescription ibuprofen (*Safford Unified School District #1 et al. v. Redding*, 2009). A key principle came into play in the controversy over whether the strip search was reasonable given the nature of the infraction and the age and gender of the student. Prior to the search, the principal was aware that another student had become ill after taking another person's prescription drugs and that yet another student claimed to have gotten a pill from Savana. During a search of her person, the student who provided Savana's name to the principal was caught with a blue pill (later determined to be naproxen), several white pills, and a razor blade. The principal searched Savana's backpack and did not find any pills. In the presence of the school nurse, Savana was asked to pull her bra and underwear away from her body, and no pills were found to be concealed. In the majority opinion, Justice David Souter noted that the intrusiveness of the search was not justified given the circumstances. While not creating a prohibition on the use of strip searches, the decision does provide some guidance in terms of when searches would be appropriate in maintaining a safe and secure environment.

School lockers. Do students have a reasonable expectation of privacy in their school lockers? By their nature, school lockers are no doubt perceived as providing some level of privacy and security for students. After all, students may be assigned individual lockers, which do not permit contents to be examined from the outside, and students may be provided with a key or combination lock. These factors can create a reasonable expectation of privacy on the part of students. With a widely perceived expectation of privacy because of the very nature of school lockers, it stands to reason that schools should communicate to students an understanding of the actual level of privacy they can expect with regard to their school lockers. An interesting example of such communication is the Milwaukee Public Schools locker policy, which clarifies the "reasonable expectation of privacy" with an "expressed understanding to the contrary." The policy states,

> *School lockers are the property of Milwaukee Public Schools. At no time does the Milwaukee Public School District relinquish its exclusive control of lockers provided for the convenience of students. School authorities for any reason may conduct periodic general inspections of lockers at any time, without notice, without student consent, and without a search warrant. (Van Hollen, 2007, p. 6)*

An effective policy communication such as the Milwaukee example would ideally be distributed to students and parents as part of the student handbook outlining rights and responsibilities of students.

Metal detectors. In *People v. Dukes* (1992), the New York Criminal Court upheld the use of a walk-through metal detector at a high school. In justifying the need for metal detectors, the school provided documentation that it had confiscated more than 2,000 weapons during a specified time period. The Supreme Court ruled that although individuals have a reasonable expectation of privacy in their persons and effects and are also protected against unreasonable searches and seizures, the government has a legitimate interest in maintaining a safe, orderly, and disciplined environment in schools. As a practical matter though, very few schools utilize metal detectors. They are expensive to operate due to equipment costs, the hiring of personnel to run the machine, training for those personnel, supervision for those personnel, gender and sensitivity issues, and the costs of making the physical setting conducive to the operation. Schools traditionally have many doors and windows because of the long-held view that the greatest danger facing a school is fire and that students need to be able to exit in a hurry. Many points of entry are not conducive to the installation and operation of metal detectors. Furthermore, individuals may bring weapons into the school through windows or side entries and then stash them in drop ceilings, restrooms, lockers, classrooms, and libraries.

Drug dogs. In *United States v. Place* (1983), the Supreme Court of the United States ruled that a search with a drug dog does not necessarily amount to a search under the Fourth Amendment. In the *Place* case, Drug Enforcement Administration agents seized luggage from a passenger when he arrived at LaGuardia Airport and took it to Kennedy Airport, where there was a drug dog. Ninety minutes after agents seized the passenger's luggage, a canine sniff detected the presence of drugs, and agents obtained a warrant to open the luggage, revealing drugs. The Court ruled that the 90-minute seizure was unreasonable, especially since officials knew when the passenger's flight was arriving from Miami, where he had originally raised suspicion. However, the Court did note that the use of a drug dog can be very intrusive and can affect the dignity of those individuals who are searched, especially children.

Drug testing. Drugs in school pose a number of concerns for both students and school officials. The negative impact of drugs can include debasing the school environment and students' health as well as promoting intimidation and the involvement of gangs. Schools face multiple challenges and options when attempting to reduce the presence of drugs in schools and students' drug use in general. One response is to implement drug testing for segments of the student population. In the first of two significant cases involving drug testing for students, the Supreme Court was asked to address whether drug testing for student athletes was reasonable. In *Vernonia School District v. Acton* (1995), the Court upheld the use of drug testing for student athletes as a condition of their participation in school-sponsored athletics. The Court reasoned that the testing procedure outlined in this particular case met a clear, narrowly defined purpose, was objectively administered, and provided student athletes with an appropriate level of due process protection. The school district's policy of testing stated that circumstances must demonstrate a compelling need for drug testing; the program must have clearly defined goals and be limited in scope; the school district must have already attempted less intrusive methods; personnel who administer the program must have limits to their discretion (i.e., who gets tested and why); and the drug test must be used to investigate violations of school rules rather than to seek evidence of criminal activity. The Court also recognized that student athletes have a lower expectation of privacy than do other students since they already undergo physical exams, have a somewhat public image, and interact in a locker room environment.

The Court would later expand the scope of permissible drug testing in public schools with its decision in *Board of Education of Independent School District No. 92 of Pottawatomie County et al. v. Earls et al.* (2002). In this case, the school district's policy required all middle and high school students to consent to drug testing in order to participate in any extracurricular activity, such as athletics, Future Farmers of America, or the band, but school officials used the drug test results to determine the student's eligibility to participate in extracurricular activities and not as part of a criminal investigation against the student.

Free speech. Students' right to free speech presents a contemporary challenge for some school districts. In the wake of rapid technology change, controversy has centered on the ability of schools to address web- and cell phone–based bullying and harassment, but two court cases addressing more basic free speech issues are worth noting in addition to one in which new technology takes center stage. The Supreme Court upheld students' free speech rights in *Tinker v. Des Moines Independent Community School District* (1969). The case involved students wearing black arm bands in school to protest U.S. involvement in Vietnam. A teacher told the students to remove the arm bands and cited a recently enacted school policy that prohibited wearing them. In the majority opinion, Justice Fortas stated that, "in our system, undifferentiated fear or apprehension of disturbance is not enough to overcome the right to freedom of expression" (*Tinker v. Des Moines Independent Community School District*, 1969, para. 13). The Court ruled that schools can limit any speech, whether active or passive, that substantially interferes with the learning environment and not just speech that some may find offensive or unpopular. The Supreme Court ruled in favor of the students in the *Tinker* case, citing students' free speech rights. The Court later sided with the school in limiting active speech by students in *Bethel School District No. 403 v. Fraser* (1986). The case arose as the result of a speech delivered in front of about 600 14-year-olds by a student whose name had been on a list of potential graduation speakers. One part of the speech (quoted here from Justice Brennan's concurring opinion, para. 1) in particular led the school to suspend the student and remove his name from the list of potential graduation speakers:

> *I know a man who is firm—he's firm in his pants, he's firm in his shirt, his character is firm—but most . . . of all, his belief in you, the students of Bethel, is firm. Jeff Kuhlman is a man who takes his point and pounds it in. If necessary, he'll take an issue and nail it to the wall. He doesn't attack things in spurts—he drives hard, pushing and pushing until finally—he succeeds. Jeff is a man who will go to the very end—even the climax, for each and every one of you. So vote for Jeff for A. S. B. vice-president—he'll never come between you and the best our high school can be.*

Siding with the school's interest in banning speech considered vulgar and offensive, the Court upheld the school's decision.

A more recent case, popularly known as "Bong hits for Jesus," addressed the issue of whether a school can limit student speech that occurs off campus. Prior to the beginning of the 2002 Winter Olympics, in conjunction with a school-sanctioned event, school officials allowed students to watch the Olympic torch relay as it passed in front of the school during the day on its way to Utah. Officials allowed students to watch the event from either side of the street. As the torch and the trailing camera crews neared, students unfurled a 14-foot banner that read "BONG HiTS 4 JESUS." The school principal demanded that the banner be lowered. Later, the principal suspended a student for 10 days for violating the school's policy against advocating the use of illegal substances (*Morse et al. v. Frederick*, 2007).

Students face new forms of harassment and bullying via social networking websites and text messaging, and school officials are grappling with ways to address such abuse. In some student bullying cases, either the perpetrators' actions or school administrators' inadequate responses may violate federal antidiscrimination laws (Ali, 2010). Federal statutes would be triggered if harassment is based on race, color, national origin, sex, or disability and is considered serious enough to create a hostile environment. Ali (2010, pp. 2–3) notes that, "if an investigation reveals that discriminatory harassment has occurred, a school must take prompt and effective steps reasonably calculated to end the harassment, eliminate any hostile environment and its effects, and prevent the harassment from recurring." Additional due process considerations apply for situations involving bullying based on disabilities. Among the scenarios outlined in the U.S. Department of Education memo

(Ali, 2010) depicting a school's failure to recognize civil rights violations, one included a situation in which students posted bullying comments on social networking websites.

New Hampshire is one state that has amended its school safety laws to incorporate protections against cyber-bullying. The relevant section of New Hampshire's Revised Statutes states in part,

> (a) *"Bullying" means a single significant incident or a pattern of incidents involving a written, verbal, or electronic communication, or a physical act or gesture, or any combination thereof, directed at another pupil which:*
>   (1) *Physically harms a pupil or damages the pupil's property;*
>   (2) *Causes emotional distress to a pupil;*
>   (3) *Interferes with a pupil's educational opportunities;*
>   (4) *Creates a hostile educational environment; or*
>   (5) *Substantially disrupts the orderly operation of the school.*
> (b) *"Bullying" shall include actions motivated by an imbalance of power based on a pupil's actual or perceived personal characteristics, behaviors, or beliefs, or motivated by the pupil's association with another person and based on the other person's characteristics, behaviors, or beliefs. (Title XV Education, 2010)*

Key provisions of the law protect youths from cyber-bullying, which can originate off campus, and identify five conditions that would trigger action under the law, including the potential to disrupt the orderly operation of the school. Federal appeals courts have been split as to whether school officials have constitutional authority to limit and discipline students for conduct some people may consider off-campus protected speech.

Due Process Considerations

Schools face several limitations when it comes to disciplining students. As noted above, school principals historically had power and authority very much like those of prison wardens; they could administer a range of punishments without review and appeal. Society gave both principals and wardens considerable power and discretion in running their institutions, and they performed their duties without much public oversight or court involvement. In the 1960s, this situation began to change as a number of court cases introduced due process, or the idea of fundamental fairness, into school discipline proceedings. These cases focused on reducing the arbitrary nature of decision making, thus replacing individual authority with substantive rules and documented procedures to follow. According to the documentation for *Goss v. Lopez* (1975), a student named Lopez received a 10-day suspension for allegedly taking part in a disturbance in the school cafeteria. He was one of 75 students suspended for 10 days without a hearing, without any presentation of evidence or testimony alleging the nature of the evidence for a violation of school rules, and without recourse to an appeal. The case eventually reached the Supreme Court of the United States, which ruled that the suspension was unconstitutional since the school had not held any sort of hearing to consider evidence or testimony.

Corporal punishment in schools refers to the infliction of physical punishments as a penalty for violating a school rule. Can and should schools use corporal punishment, such as paddling, to deter students from violating school rules? The Supreme Court has ruled that school administrators' use of corporal punishment against students does not violate the Constitution (*Ingraham v. Wright*, 1977). About 20 states have legislation authorizing the use of corporal punishment in schools, but some school districts and individual schools in states that do not have laws prohibiting corporal punishment do not allow it within their own jurisdictions. Of the states that allow corporal punishment in schools, the majority of instances of its use are reported in Texas, Mississippi, and Alabama (Center for Effective Discipline, 2010). An interesting news report on the use of corporal punishment in schools is available at http://cnettv.cnet.com/corporal-punishment-schools/9742-1_53-50048181.html.

School Climate

Even before the advent of high-tech bullying, the National School Safety Center (NSSC) stated that "the days when student-related school problems consisted mostly of a few playground squabbles and some kids playing hooky are long gone" (quoted in Greenbaum & Turner, 1990, p. 2). Such nostalgic views of school disorder have grown increasingly dim as numerous high-profile incidents of serious school violence and shootings have occurred. While society may tend to focus its attention on the more dramatic incidents, we may inadvertently downplay the significance of the more common and routine occurrences that may not be physical in nature but that amount to emotional abuse. While more extreme forms of violence dominate the headlines, it is the minor events that affect the majority of students at some point in their academic careers and some students on a regular basis. Bullying, harassment, and minor victimizations can have a negative impact on the learning environment and are often seen as a public health concern, because an unstable school environment affects the personal well-being and development of the victim. For example, a rash of suicides by individuals who had suffered continual harassment by peers led to a growing focus on the prevention of bullying.

Data from a study addressing the issue of violence and disorder in three high schools in a northeastern state are presented below. The research problem analyzed the relationship between students' perceptions of their school's general climate and their experiences of victimization within the school. The idea of school climate, as utilized in this study, involved students' perception of the quality of their school's social atmosphere and learning environment. Perceptions of school climate included how students at each school viewed the educational process, what social value they obtained from the education they were receiving, their impressions of the school's atmosphere, and the nature of their experiences within the school. In their review of school-based crime prevention, Gottfredson, Wilson, and Skroban Najaka (2006) note the importance of school climate as an indication of the expected level of order within the school. In their view, the clarity of rules and expectations for behavior promote a collective sense of identity.

Hurbanis and Walters (as cited in Odell-Gonder & Hymes, 1994, p. 12) developed four dimensions of school climate: academic, social, physical, and affective. The academic dimension pertains to students' perceptions of instructional norms, beliefs, and practices of the school, such as the emphasis on academic pursuits, expectations for the quality of student work, and the quality of the monitoring of student progress. According to the Office of Educational Research and Improvement (1993; see also McDermott, 1980), having a positive school climate involves, at the minimum, having a clear sense of mission, with emphasis on high academic standards and clear expectations for behavior. Schools focusing on academic achievement provide their students and faculty with a common bond and a shared sense of purpose. A central condition of the academic dimension is the perception of safety and order, specifically, how a secure and orderly environment enhances the ability of students and teachers to concentrate on academic efforts. According to Hurbanis and Walters (as cited in Odell-Gonder & Hymes, 1994, p. 12), the social dimension includes the types and quality of the communication among individuals in the school, whether between students and teachers or among students themselves. In a positive school climate, students have input on school rules and are more likely to view the rule enforcement process as being fair. Increased involvement and investment by students are likely to produce an increase in attachment and belief in the process. Hurbanis and Walters note that the physical dimension addresses students' perception of the school's physical environment, including the level of maintenance and overall condition of the school. The emphasis is not on whether the school building is new or old but whether the environment is clean and maintained to an appropriate level, resulting in a sense of ownership by staff and students. The affective dimension pertains to the feelings and attitudes shared by the students of the school or the existence of a shared system of values and beliefs. The behaviors or attitudes prevalent when values are shared suggest that students have a sense of belonging to and identification with their school. This affective dimension encompasses the behavioral manifestations of a positive school climate, such as trust, rapport, and respect.

Furlong, Morrison, and Clontz (1991) also identify four dimensions of school climate: student and staff characteristics, physical environment, social environment, and cultural characteristics. Student and staff characteristics involve the diversity of viewpoints, experiences, and expertise in the school. The physical environment reflects the extent of physical and social disorder within the school. The social environment comprises classroom structure and the level of student participation. The curriculum, included as a component of the social dimension, favors student cooperation in meeting learning objectives rather than conflict and competition among students. Cultural characteristics address affiliation and bonding, traditions of high behavioral and academic expectations, and the opportunity for growth and recognition for positive activities.

In the data from the study of high school violence and disorder presented here, the three northeastern U.S. high schools are identified by pseudonymous community names: Ashton, Westville, and Mayville. Each of the high schools is the only academically oriented public secondary school in its community. The majority of school-aged youths in each community attend the local public school. Ashton was described as an economically developed suburb having 30,000 residents, Westville as an urban center with 70,000 residents, and Mayville as a growth community with 9,000 residents (**Table 2-1**). Each of the three schools has experienced some recent change in its student population due to changes in the demographics of the community. Westville's high school graduating class size decreased about 3% in the few years before the study, while Ashton's graduating class size decreased more than 20%, and Mayville's increased more than 36%. The racial and ethnic characteristics of the three schools are listed in **Table 2-2**. Parental consent for the study was arranged by having the parent(s) or guardian sign and return a consent form that explained the purpose of the study. On the day of the survey, students who received parental consent received the survey instrument. Students who did not have parental consent, who did not wish to participate

TABLE 2-1 Demographic Distribution in Participating Communities

School	Town population	School population	Sample count	Percentage of sample
Ashton	30,000	1,500	190	34.6
Mayville	9,000	400	80	14.6
Westville	75,000	2,000	279	50.8

TABLE 2-2 Demographic Distribution of Student Sample

Demographic	Number	Percentage of total
Gender		
Female	283	51.8
Male	263	48.2
Grade		
9	160	29.4
10	79	14.5
11	163	30.0
12	142	26.1
Race/ethnicity		
White	379	69.5
Black	51	9.4
Asian	45	8.3
Hispanic	32	5.9
Other	38	6.9

after reading the informed consent statement, or who arrived at that conclusion after beginning the instrument were told to use the block of time as study time.

Victimization. The study assessed victimization levels by asking students to enumerate their experiences as targets of a number of behaviors, including theft without contact, verbal and nonverbal harassment, robbery, aggravated assault and battery, and gang victimization (**Table 2-3**). The range of experiences suggested in the survey may more fully capture the extent of victimization than would a single item. The National Institute of Education study (Toby, 1983), employed similar survey items, as did the National Crime Victimization Survey and Williams, Winfree, and Clinton (1989). See **Box 2-1** for questions posed to students in order to measure victimization.

TABLE 2-3 Victimization Experiences for Student Sample (percentage in parentheses)

	Victimization experience	
Nature of victimization	**No**	**Yes**
Nonverbal abuse	379 (70.7)	157 (29.3)
Verbal abuse	358 (66.1)	184 (33.9)
Theft	385 (72.1)	149 (27.9)
Robbery	510 (96.2)	20 (3.8)
Assault	493 (92.7)	39 (7.3)
Aggravated assault	513 (95.7)	23 (4.3)
Gang related	533 (98.2)	10 (1.8)

BOX 2-1 Victimization Items

1. Since the start of this school year, has anything been stolen from you while you were at school and were not around it?
2. So far this school year, has anything been stolen or taken from you by force, threats, or intimidation while you were in school or on the way to or from school?
3. So far this school year, have you been physically attacked or assaulted in school or on the way to or from school?
4. During this school year, how many times has someone threatened or injured you with a weapon, such as a gun, knife, or club, while in school or on school grounds?
5. During this school year, have you been the victim of verbal abuse, such as racial or ethnic slurs, profanity, or sexual comments, while in school or on school grounds?
6. During this school year, have you been the victim of nonverbal abuse, such as obscene gestures, while in school or on school grounds?
7. Have you been assaulted or threatened by "gangs" while in school?

School climate results. Out of the 690 consent forms sent home with students, a total of 549 completed surveys were collected. Overall, there was a 79.5% response rate based on the number of consent forms collected with affirmative parental consent as well as the number of students who were absent the day the survey was administered. In Mayville, of the 90 consent forms distributed to students, 80 surveys (89%) were collected. In Ashton, 300 consent forms were distributed and 190 surveys (63%) collected. In Westville, 300 consent forms were distributed and 279 surveys (93%) collected. The sample was 48% male and 52% female. There was roughly equal representation among 9th–12th graders, although slightly fewer 10th graders participated. Two hundred students (36.4%) reported that they had moved at least once during the last 5 years.

More than half of the sample reported experiencing at least one of the seven types of victimization. A sizable number of students reported experiencing verbal victimization (34%) and nonverbal victimization (29%). In addition, more than 19% of the sample experienced repeated incidents of nonverbal victimization, and more than 25% of the sample experienced repeated incidents of verbal victimization. Theft victimizations were fairly common (28%) among students in the sample. Students were asked to identify the most recent item stolen if they had been the victim of theft while in school, and 141 of the 149 students who reported a theft specified an item. Some items students listed as being stolen were of the type one would expect, while other items were somewhat unusual and others were very unusual. Fifty students reported having money, purses, and wallets stolen; other stolen items of note included jewelry, cellular phones, electronic devices, and even a bong. Almost 40% of the students who had experienced a theft in school did not report the incident to parents, teachers, administrators, police, or anyone else. Victimizations of greater severity were less common among the sample. Ten students (1.8%) reported experiencing a gang-related victimization. Twenty students (3.8%) reported experiencing a robbery. Thirty-nine (7.1%) students experienced simple assault, and 23 students (4.2%) experienced at least one incident of aggravated assault in school (see Table 2-3).

School climate was operationalized as a 23-item scale utilizing a fixed-choice response format (see **Box 2-2** for school climate items). Students were asked to respond to each statement by placing a vertical slash mark through a 10-centimeter line to represent their degree of agreement

---

BOX 2-2 School Climate Items

1. In general, I like school.
2. Getting good grades is important to me personally.
3. I try hard in school.
4. I care what teachers think of me.
5. Getting good grades in school will help me get a good job.
6. Doing homework and studying are important to me.
7. Faculty members at this school believe every student can achieve success.
8. Faculty and students demonstrate pride in being a member of this school.
9. If I had a child my age, I would want them to go to this school.
10. If I had the chance, I would have left this school for something better.
11. There are always enough staff in the hallways to make sure no one gets hurt or so that things don't get out of hand.
12. Punishment for violations at this school is fair, so that no one gets special treatment or gets away with anything.
13. The quality of education I receive at this school matches what I think my needs are for the future.
14. I feel teachers, administrators, and staff really do care about my education and my future.
15. Most people get by at this school without even trying.
16. Everyone here takes pride in keeping the school clean.
17. The school is always well maintained.
18. When things are broken at this school, it's a long time before they're fixed.
19. This school places great emphasis on academic achievement.
20. Even slackers get good grades here.
21. Most of the class time here is spent on things other than learning.
22. Teachers don't really care if we learn anything or not because they get paid anyway.
23. Teachers here spend time only on the kids they think want to learn.

---

with each statement. The range for each individual item ranges from 0 to 10, thus allowing for 11 possible responses for each item and producing an actual range of 0 to 214 (for additional information on the use of the 10-centimeter line as a rating scale, see Gibbs & Giever, 1994; Mackey & Courtright, 2000; Mackey, Courtright, & Packard, 2006). Similar school climate items have been used by Anderson (1982), Cernkovich and Giordano (1992), Jenkins (1992), and the Office of Educational Research and Improvement (1993). Six scale items were reverse coded to produce a consistent interpretation of the scale. The recoded items were originally phrased so that a score of 10 would indicate a negative school climate and thus provide a sense of balance in the questionnaire. The reliability of the school climate scale was determined by assessing the extent of internal consistency among the items in the scale using Cronbach's alpha. Alpha for the scale was .86, which is above the minimal level for internal consistency.

An analysis was conducted examining the extent of differences in students' perceptions of school climate and their reported victimization experiences (**Table 2-4**). Students who reported experiencing an episode of victimization in school perceived a lower-quality school climate than

TABLE 2-4 T-Tests Examining the Relationship Between Students' Perceptions of the School Climate and Their Victimization Experiences

Victimization	n	Mean	SD	SE of mean	t	p
Nonverbal abuse						
No	379	135.41	32.58	1.67	4.91	.00
Yes	157	120.06	33.86	2.70		
Verbal abuse						
No	357	136.78	33.05	1.75	5.74	.00
Yes	184	119.72	32.23	2.38		
Theft						
No	384	113.39	32.97	1.68	2.64	.00
Yes	149	124.28	36.83	3.02		
Robbery						
No	509	132.06	33.47	1.48	3.44	.00
Yes	20	105.85	32.20	7.20		
Assault						
No	492	132.79	33.09	1.49	3.67	.00
Yes	39	112.46	35.78	5.73		
Aggravated assault						
No	512	132.85	33.26	1.47	4.79	.00
Yes	23	99.13	27.95	5.83		
Gang related						
No	532	131.73	33.60	1.46	4.83	.00
Yes	10	80.10	24.88	7.87		

their peers who did not report victimization. This pattern held constant across all seven types of victimization.

Students were asked to rate their perception of safety in eight specific places in school such as classrooms, cafeteria, student restrooms, hallways, stairways, locker rooms, gym, and parking lot. The operationalization of perception of safety utilized the work of Williams, Winfree, and Clinton (1989). For each item, the response category ranged from completely unsafe to completely safe on a 10-centimeter line. The range for this scale was from 0 to 80. Students were also asked whether they avoided the location due to fear or apprehension. Toby's (1995) emphasis on the importance of order, safety, and informal control present in school has some level of support from the findings presented here. The mean score for the perception of safety scale, with the sum of the perceptions of safety for eight locations (classrooms, cafeteria, restrooms, hallways, stairways, locker rooms, gym, and parking lot), was 52.2, with a maximum score of 80. Six of the eight locations had mean scores above 6.3. Restrooms and the parking lot had the lowest scores for students' perception of safety. The mean perception of safety score for student restrooms was 5.4. In particular, 164 students (24.4%) rated the safety of restrooms with scores of 3 or lower, with the maximum being a score of 10. Students who reported avoiding restrooms at school due to fear of victimization had a lower rating of the perception of safety than students who did not avoid restrooms at school. Students who reported never having avoided restrooms had a mean score of 5.7, whereas students who avoided restrooms had a score of 3.1. The mean perception of safety score for the parking lot was 5.7, with 144 students rating the level of safety in that location as a 3 or lower.

These results indicate support for the role of teachers in preventing victimization and improving the perception of safety. There was a .28 correlation between school climate item 19 ("There are always enough staff in the hallways to make sure no one gets hurt or so that things don't get out of hand") and the perception of safety scale. There was also strong positive correlation (.44) between school climate item 31 ("If I were to imagine the safest school environment, this school would rank near the top") and the safety scale.

Students experiencing an episode of victimization had lower overall ratings of the school climate than youths who were not victimized. The causal order of the relationship is certainly a point open to discussion, and a number of interpretations of the relationship are possible. For example, students who are victimized at school may withdraw from the setting and therefore have diminished expectations for the value of education, their connectedness with teachers, and a shared positive culture. In addition, isolated students may be easier targets for victimization by their peers. Regardless of the causal order, strengthening the positive dimensions of school climate (a shared sense of norms for behavior, collective identity, meaningfulness of the educational experience, and positive relations in the school) as well as reducing victimization in schools would maximize a student's educational opportunity, which is a protective factor, and would in some states fulfill the obligation to provide safe and disciplined schools.

A basic component of school climate is the degree of order and discipline present in the school. Aside from the liability concerns raised by its absence, discipline contributes to the safety of students and staff and ensures an environment conducive to learning (Gaustad, 1992). Commenting on acceptable levels of discipline, Leriche (1992, p. 77) states, "This is an absolute necessity because if order is not maintained, chaos results, and no positive learning ensues when anarchy reigns." Discipline is a key element of both a positive school climate and a safe school, and maintaining it requires perfecting a delicate balance. Kadel and Follman (1993, p. 21) contend that, to maintain a safe and secure educational environment, schools must balance the coercive and negative aspects of power against the generally more permissive and open qualities associated with learning. This balancing process involves examining the role of discipline in relation to the school's two objectives of preventing violence and promoting educational achievement.

As the Office of Educational Research and Improvement (1993, p. 2) has reported, "The best way to reduce youth violence is by creating an atmosphere that encourages students to focus their energies on learning." A basic point in maintaining a degree of order is maintaining a set structure for the class. In this sense, classroom procedures should be clear and consistent; there should be smooth transitions from one activity to another; and rules should be clear and evenly enforced (Goldstein et al., 1995, pp. 10–11). Discipline, student effort, and school climate, according to Toby (1995), are all linked together, and a school climate that is tense can send student discipline and effort into a downward spiral. As the number of uninterested and unmotivated students increases, teacher burnout also increases (Toby, 1983, p. 28). Teachers may be less motivated or become less likely to confront student misbehavior in halls, classrooms, and common areas. The work of Felson

(1995) can provide a relevant framework for specific policy recommendations based on social control theory. Felson bases his approach to reducing crime and victimization in schools on what he calls the two-step control theory. The first step is to attach a "handler" to the particular at-risk youth. The handler serves as a mentor or friend—either formally or informally—who can exert control or influence over the youth, using persuasion and resorting to more coercive or formal methods of control only when absolutely necessary. Felson notes that delinquency or victimization is likely when someone can evade the social rules of a particular setting by not being recognized. In this sense, informal control increases when an individual has a sense of being known and identified by individuals in the setting, thus extending the influence of the handler to other individuals.

Other strategies that can reduce victimization and the perception of fear in specific locations in school include the use of place managers (Felson, 1995). Place managers are responsible for specific locations within the school setting rather than, like the handler, being responsible for guarding potential victims or controlling potentially motivated offenders. For the three schools participating in the study described here, the locations where place managers would provide the greatest impact based on students' survey responses, include the parking lot, restrooms, and locker rooms. These specific locations tend to have less structured surveillance than other places within the school. Any area of the school setting with a lower level of adult supervision will expose students to potentially motivated offenders. Improving school climate can reduce the incidence and prevalence of minor delinquency by increasing the bond between students and the school.

SUMMARY

Primary prevention programs seek to strengthen protective factors and to disrupt the development of risk factors among a broad population. Effective primary prevention programs offer substantial social and financial benefits to society, including reduced crime and victimization and reduced costs for both adjudicating offenders and dealing with the wide variety of damage to life trajectory that may result from victimization. Such programs also provide numerous benefits for would-be offenders, who may experience more positive outcomes in education, employment, and personal relations as well as not experiencing the negatives of entering the criminal justice system. Family-based programs, such as home visitation and parent training programs, have demonstrated a degree of success with respect to preventing future delinquency. These programs have demonstrated their cost-effectiveness as well. Because young people spend a significant amount of time in schools and interact so closely with their peers, educational administrators face numerous challenges in their efforts to maintain a safe, secure environment that is conducive to learning. Schools must balance student rights against safety concerns, and numerous court decisions provide teachers and administrators with information upon which to base their disciplinary policies and actions.

Numerous concerns related to primary prevention remain, however. Only some of the individuals targeted in primary prevention programs would actually go on to have extensive delinquent careers, which means that people who would not go on to extensive criminal careers are subjected to intervention programs. Bearing that criticism in mind, researchers must conduct solid evaluation studies to determine the effectiveness of primary programs. In doing so, they must assess the external validity of the research design, because a program that may be effective in one type of community and perhaps for a particular time period may not be effective in other geographic or temporal settings.

KEY TERMS

Risk factors
Protective factors
Elmira Parent/Early Infancy Project
Perry Preschool Project
Incredible Years Training Program
Bullying
Youth Risk Behavior Surveillance System (YRBSS)
School climate

DISCUSSION QUESTIONS

1. Can the state impose behavioral restrictions, such as prohibitions on smoking and alcohol use, on pregnant women to protect unborn children?
2. Are there circumstances when the state should compel participation in a parent training program?
3. Is it a reasonable expectation that all students should graduate from high school?
4. What are ways in which a school can promote a positive school climate?
5. Should schools have the authority to punish student bullying and harassment that occurs away from school grounds?

REFERENCES

Agnew, R. (1992). Foundation for a general strain theory of crime and delinquency. *Criminology*, *30*(1), 47–87.

Agnew, R. (2009). *Juvenile delinquency: Causes and control* (3rd ed.). New York, NY: Oxford University Press.

Ali, R. (2010, October 26). Open letter to educators from the assistant U.S. secretary for civil rights regarding bullying in schools. Retrieved from http://www2.ed.gov/about/offices/list/ocr/letters/colleague-201010.pdf.

Ammerman, R., Putnam, F. W., Altaye, M., Chen, L., Holleb, L. J., Stevens, J., . . . Van Ginkel, J. B. (2009). Changes in depressive symptoms in first time mothers in home visitation. *Child Abuse & Neglect*, *33*(3), 127–138.

Ammerman, R., Stevens, J., Putnam, F. W., Altaye, M., Hulsmann, J. E., Lehmkuhl, H. D., . . . Van Ginkel, J. B. (2006). Predictors of early engagement in home visitation. *Journal of Family Violence*, *21*(2), 105–115.

Anderson, C. S. (1982). The search for school climate: A review of the research. *Review of Educational Research*, *52*(3), 368–420.

Bethel School District No. 403 v. Fraser, 478 U.S. 675 (1986). Retrieved from http://laws.findlaw.com/us/478/675.html.

Board of Education of Independent School District No. 92 of Pottawatomie County et al. v. Earls et al, No. 01-332 (2002). Retrieved from http://laws.findlaw.com/us/000/01-332.html.

Center for Effective Discipline. (2010). U.S.: Corporal punishment and paddling statistics by state and race. Retrieved from http://www.stophitting.com/index.php?page=statesbanning.

Centers for Disease Control and Prevention (2010a). Teen births. Retrieved from http://www.cdc.gov/nchs/fastats/teenbrth.htm.

Centers for Disease Control and Prevention (2010b). Youth risk behavior surveillance: United States, 2009. *Morbidity and Mortality Weekly Report*, *59*(SS-5). Retrieved from http://www.cdc.gov/mmwr/pdf/ss/ss5905.pdf.

Cernkovich, S. A., & Giordano, P. C. (1992). School bonding, race, and delinquency. *Criminology*, *30*(2), 261–291.

Eckenrode, J., Ganzel, B., Henderson, C. R., Jr., Smith, E., Olds, D. L., Powers, J., . . . Sidora, K. (2000). Preventing child abuse and neglect with a program of home visitation. *Journal of the American Medical Association, 284*(11), 1385–1391.

Farrington, D. P. (2000). Explaining and preventing crime: The globalization of knowledge; The American Society of Criminology 1999 presidential address. *Criminology, 38*(1), 1–24.

Farrington, D. P., & Welsh, B. C. (2007). *Saving children from a life of crime: Early risk factors and effective interventions.* New York, NY: Oxford University Press.

Feldman, J. G., Minkoff, H. L., McCalla, S., & Salwen, M. (1992). A cohort study of the impact of perinatal drug use on prematurity in an inner-city population. *American Journal of Public Health, 82*(5), 726–728.

Felson, M. (1995). Those who discourage crime. *Crime Prevention Studies, 4*, 53–66.

Fingerhut, L. A., Kleinman, J. C., & Kendrick, J. S. (1990). Smoking before, during, or after pregnancy. *American Journal of Public Health, 80*(5), 541–544.

Furlong, M., Morrison, R., & Clontz, D. (1991). Broadening the scope of school safety. *School Safety: National School Safety Center News Journal, spring*, 8–11.

Gaustad, J. (1992). *School discipline* (ERIC Digest, No. 78, Report EDO-EA-92-11). Eugene, OR: ERIC Clearinghouse on Educational Management, University of Oregon.

Gibbs, J. J., & Giever, D. (1995). Self-control and its manifestations among university students: An empirical test of Gottfredson and Hirschi's general theory. *Justice Quarterly, 22*(2), 231–255.

Goldstein, A. P., Palumbo, J., Striepling, S., & Voutsinas, A. M. (1995). *Break it up: A teacher's guide to managing student aggression.* Champaign, IL: Research Press.

Goss v. Lopez, 419 U.S. 565 (1975). Retrieved from http://laws.findlaw.com/us/419/565.html.

Gottfredson, D. C., Wilson, D. B., & Skroban Najaka, S. (2006). School-based crime prevention. In L. W. Sherman, D. P. Farrington, B. C. Welsh, & D. L. Mackenzie (Eds.), *Evidence-based crime prevention* (Revised ed.). New York, NY: Routledge.

Greenbaum, S., & Turner, B. (1990). *School safety overview* (NSSC Resource Paper). Malibu, CA: National School Safety Center.

Hammond-Ratzlaff, A., & Fulton, A. (2001). Knowledge gained by mothers enrolled in a home visitation program. *Adolescence, 36*(3), 435–442.

Hirschi, T. (1969). *Causes of delinquency.* Berkeley, CA: University of California Press.

Ingraham v. Wright, 430 U.S. 651 (1977). Retrieved from http://laws.findlaw.com/us/430/651.html.

Jenkins, P. H. (1992). School delinquency and belief in school rules. Washington, DC: Office of Juvenile Justice and Delinquency Prevention, U.S. Department of Justice.

Kadel, S., & Follman, J. (1993). *Reducing school violence in Florida: Usable research, hot topics.* Palatka, FL: Southeastern Regional Vision for Education.

Karoly, L. A., Greenwood, P. W., Everingham, S. S., Hoube, J., Kilburn, M. R., Rydell, C. P., . . . Chiesa, J. (1998). *Investing in our children: What we know and don't know about the costs and benefits of early childhood interventions.* Santa Monica, CA: RAND Corporation. Retrieved from http://www.rand.org/pubs/monograph_reports/MR898.

Leriche, L. (1992). The sociology of classroom discipline. *The High School Journal, 75*(2), 77–89.

Mackey, D. A., & Courtright, K. E. (2000). Assessing punitiveness among college students: A comparison of criminal justice majors with other majors. *The Justice Professional, 12*, 423–441.

Mackey, D. A., Courtright, K. E., & Packard, S. H. (2006). Testing the rehabilitative ideal among college students. *Criminal Justice Studies: A Critical Journal of Crime, Law, and Society, 19*(2), 153–170.

March of Dimes. (2010). March of Dimes: Medical resources. Retrieved from http://www.marchofdimes.com/professionals/medicalresources_lowbirthweight.html.

McCord, J. (2007). *Crime and family: Selected essays of Joan McCord.* Philadelphia, PA: Temple University Press.

McDermott, J. (1980). High anxiety: Fear of crime in secondary schools. *Contemporary Education, 52*, 18–23.

Morse et al. v. Frederick, No. 06-278. (2007). Retrieved from http://laws.findlaw.com/us/000/06-278.html.

National Center for Educational Statistics. (2010). Average mathematics literacy, reading literacy, and science literacy scores of 15-year-old students, by sex and country: 2006. Retrieved from http://nces.ed.gov/programs/digest/d09/tables/dt09_402.asp.

New Jersey v. T. L. O., 469 U.S. 325 (1985). Retrieved from http://laws.findlaw.com/us/469/325.html.

Nguyen, J. D., Carson, M. L., Parris, K. M., & Place, P. (2003). A comparison pilot study of public health field nursing home visitation program interventions for pregnant Hispanic adolescents. *Public Health Nursing, 20*(5), 412–148.

Odell-Gonder, P., & Hymes, D. (1994). *Improving school climate and culture* (AASA Critical Issues Report No. 27). Arlington, VA: American Association of School Administrators.

Office of Educational Research and Improvement. (1993). *Reaching the goals: Goal 6—safe, disciplined, and drug-free schools* (Paper Prepared by the Goal 6 Workgroup).Washington, DC: Programs for the Improvement of Practice.

Olds, D., Eckenrode, J., Henderson, C. R., Jr., Kitzman, H., Powers, J., Cole, R., . . . Luckey, D. (1997). Long-term effects of home visitation on maternal life course and child abuse and neglect. *Journal of the American Medical Association, 278*(8), 637–643.

Olds, D., Henderson, C. R., Jr., Cole, R., Eckenrode, J., Kitzman, H., Luckey, D., . . . Powers, J. (1998). Long-term effects of nurse home visitation on children's criminal and anti-social behavior. *Journal of the American Medical Association, 280*(14), 1239–1243.

Olds, D., & Korfmacher, J. (1998). Findings from a program of research on prenatal and early childhood home visitation: Special issue introduction. *Journal of Community Psychology, 26*(1), 1–3.

Parks, G. (2000). *The High/Scope Perry Preschool Project* (NCJ 181725). Washington, DC: U.S. Department of Justice, Office of Justice Programs, Office of Juvenile Justice and Delinquency Prevention.

People v. Dukes, 580 NY2d 850, NY Crim. Ct. (1992). Retrieved from http://ny.findacase.com/research/wfrmDocViewer.aspx/xq/fac.19920131_0041269.NY.htm/qx.

Rand, M., & Truman, J. (2010). *Criminal victimization, 2009* (NCJ 231327). Retrieved from http://bjs.ojp.usdoj.gov/index.cfm?ty=pbdetail&iid=2217.

Robers, S., Zhang, J., Truman, J., & T. D. Snyder. (2010). *Indicators of school crime and safety: 2010* (NCES 2011-002/NCJ 230812). Washington, DC: National Center for Education Statistics, U.S. Department of Education, and Bureau of Justice Statistics, Office of Justice Programs, U.S. Department of Justice. Retrieved from http://bjs.ojp.usdoj.gov/content/pub/pdf/iscs10.pdf.

Rosenbaum, D. P., & Hanson, G. S. (1998). Assessing the effects of school-based drug education: A six-year multilevel analysis of Project D.A.R.E. *Journal of Research in Crime and Delinquency, 35*(4), 381–412.

Safford Unified School District #1 et al. v. Redding, No. 08-479. (2009). Retrieved from http://laws.findlaw.com/us/000/08-479.html

Sampson, R. J., & Laub, J. H. (1993). *Crime in the making: Pathways and turning points through life.* Cambridge, MA: Harvard University Press.

Shader, M. (2003). *Risk factors for delinquency: An overview* (NCJ 207540). Washington, DC: Office of Juvenile Justice and Delinquency Prevention, Office of Justice Programs, U.S. Department of Justice. Retrieved from http://www.ncjrs.gov/pdffiles1/ojjdp/frd030127.pdf.

Tinker v. Des Moines Independent Community School District, No. 21, 383 F.2d 988 (1969). Retrieved from http://laws.findlaw.com/us/393/503.html.

Title XV Education, N.H. Stat., RSA chap. 193-F: Pupil safety and violence prevention, §193-F:3 (2010). Retrieved from http://www.gencourt.state.nh.us/rsa/html/XV/193-F/193-F-3.htm.

Toby, J. (1983). Violence in schools. In M. H. Tonry & N. Morris (Eds.), *Crime and justice: An annual review of research* (Vol. 4, pp. 1–47). Chicago, IL: University of Chicago Press.

Toby, J. (1995). The schools. In J. Q. Wilson & J. Petersilia (Eds.), *Crime* (pp. 141–170). San Francisco, CA: Institute for Contemporary Studies.

United States v. Place, 462 U.S. 696 (1983). Retrieved from http://laws.findlaw.com/us/462/696.html.

Van Hollen, J. B. (2007). *Safe schools legal resource manual.* Madison, WI: Wisconsin Department of Justice. Retrieved from http://www.doj.state.wi.us/docs/safeschoolmanual.pdf.

Vernonia School District 47J v. Acton, No. 94-590 (1995). Retrieved from http://laws.findlaw.com/us/000/u10263.html.

Waller, M., Brown, B., & Whittle, B. (1999). Mentoring as a bridge to positive outcomes for teen mothers and their children. *Child & Adolescent Social Work Journal, 16*(6), 467–480.

Webster-Stratton, C. (2000). The Incredible Years Training Series. Washington, DC: U.S. Department of Justice, Office of Justice Programs, Office of Juvenile Justice and Delinquency Prevention. Retrieved from http://www.ncjrs.gov/pdffiles1/ojjdp/173422.pdf.

Welsh, B. C., & Piquero, A. R. (2012). Investing where it counts: Preventing delinquency and crime with early family-based programs. In R. Rosenfeld, K. Quinet, & C. Garcia (Eds.), *Contemporary issues in criminological theory and research: The role of social institutions* (2nd ed., pp. 13–28). Belmont, CA: Wadsworth/Cengage Learning.

Williams, L. E., Winfree, L. T., & Clinton, L. (1989). Trouble in the schoolhouse: New views on victimization, fear of crime, and teacher perceptions of the workplace. *Violence and Victims, 4*(1), 27–44.

WMUR-TV. (2011). NH dropout rate falls below 1 percent: Governor says rate has fallen 61 percent since 2007–2008 school year. Retrieved from http://www.wmur.com/education/27121902/detail.html.

CHAPTER 3

Policing and Crime Prevention

Tony R. Smith and Jason Scott*
Rochester Institute of Technology

INTRODUCTION

It is easy to conceive of a crime prevention role for the police because historically the concept of crime prevention was central to the founding mission and orientation of policing. In response to the crime, riots, and disorder associated with the rapid urbanization and industrialization of London, England, 19th-century reformers began advocating for the creation of an organized public police force. Due to the leadership of England's home secretary, Sir Robert Peel, Parliament passed the Metropolitan Police Act in 1829, effectively creating the first modern police force. Peel advocated for this form of policing based on his belief that the visible presence of uniformed officers, assigned to fixed areas of responsibility, or "beats," would be sufficient to prevent criminal and disorderly behavior. American cities that were experiencing the same challenges of crime and disorder quickly adopted public police structures modeled after London's. While there were some differences in the size, scope, and organization of the early police departments of Boston, Philadelphia, and New York, they shared that common central mission of crime prevention accomplished through visible patrol (Lane, 1975; Walker, 1998). While crime prevention has remained central to the mission of the police since the mid-19th century, the strategies used to accomplish crime prevention have changed. Some of these changes have come about with the advent of new technologies; other strategies have been promoted by research and evaluation, while other changes in crime prevention have been due to new theoretical perspectives explaining crime and criminality. This chapter begins by quickly highlighting the changing strategies the police have used to accomplish this crime prevention mission. Following that introduction these various crime prevention activities will be discussed in more detail with special attention to the theoretical underpinnings of each strategy and a review of the research evaluating the effectiveness of these approaches.

HISTORY OF LAW ENFORCEMENT CRIME PREVENTION STRATEGIES

The earliest and longest-standing police strategy designed to accomplish crime prevention is the general use of random patrol. The use of patrol for crime prevention purposes can be traced to the

---

*Both authors contributed equally to this chapter.

early principles of Sir Robert Peel and was further supported by mid-20th-century professional police management experts who explained that the purpose of patrol was to create "an impression of omnipresence" (Wilson, 1977, p. 320). Initially police patrol was accomplished on foot and was later replaced by the use of the automobile. More recently, police patrol has come full circle as departments are encouraging some officers to leave their vehicles and return to foot patrols to accomplish their crime prevention mission (Wilson & Kelling, 1982). Regardless of the approach, the practice of random patrol has been supported by the belief that the visible and, at the same time, unpredictable presence of the patrol officer deters crime in public places.

The increased reliance on the automobile, the two-way radio, and telephone-based emergency communication systems during the 1950s and 1960s created a new crime prevention strategy to complement general random patrol—rapid response to telephone and 911 dispatched emergencies. While more reactive by definition, this practice is supported as a crime prevention strategy by the belief that by rapidly responding to crimes in progress, officers can, through successful interception, reduce the harm caused by these incidents. Additional crime prevention benefits are believed to be derived from the deterrent effect of having potential criminals fear detection due to these increasingly rapid response capabilities of the police (Sherman, Gottfredson, MacKenzie, Eck, Reuter, & Bushway, 1997). The combined use of general random patrol and rapid response to crimes in progress represented the predominant crime prevention activity of the police prior to the 1980s. However, the continued reliance on these early crime prevention strategies was challenged by research that began to question the assumptions behind these law enforcement tactics as well as new demands for community engagement in the crime prevention efforts of cities and police departments.

By the 1970s and 1980s police departments began to broaden their crime prevention focus beyond random patrol for a number of reasons. First, research began to emerge during this period that questioned the efficacy of early patrol and rapid response-based crime prevention efforts (Kelling, Pate, Dieckman, & Brown, 1974; Pate, Ferrara, Bowers, & Lorence, 1976). This research will be discussed in more detail later in this chapter, but it is important to note that the findings from this research began to signal a need for police administrators to think about more effective

---

BOX 3-1 New Police Instructions

Early principles of crime prevention were communicated to early police officers in London through a *General Instructions* handbook. These instructions were also communicated to the public through their publication in the daily newspaper, *The Times,* on September 25, 1829. A concern for crime prevention was a central component of these instructions, which begin as follows:

> It should be understood at the outset, that the object to be obtained is "the prevention of crime." To this great end every effort of the police is to be directed. The security of person and property, the preservation of public tranquility, and all the other objects of a police establishment will thus be better effected than by the detection and punishment of the offender after he has committed the crime. (New Police Instructions, *1829*)

For a more detailed discussion of the treatment of Sir Robert Peel's principles in modern policing textbooks, see Lentz and Chaires (2007).

ways of preventing crime and more efficient means of managing and deploying resources. Second, it became clear that a strict concern for traditional crime (e.g., homicide, assault, robbery, burglary), which was often the focus of these early crime prevention activities, had come at the expense of attention to other problems that the police considered less serious. Police departments began to discover that citizens were frequently more concerned with eliminating the very visible signs of physical and social disorder (e.g., graffiti, prostitution markets, drug dealing, and drunk and disorderly persons) that plagued their communities (Skogan, 1990). Furthermore, critics argued that the traditional "patrol and respond" strategy limited the ability of officers and departments to appreciate and work to solve the underlying problems connecting criminal incidents (Goldstein, 1979). Finally, it became apparent that the police were ill equipped to deal with crime and neighborhood disorder problems alone. The early crime prevention approaches encouraged the police to view themselves as experts over a narrow range of legal problems; however, the range of problems with which the police were dealing was neither narrow nor strictly legal. In addition, the police, as well as federal criminal justice officials, began to realize that their crime prevention efforts were limited without the broad support of community members and other nongovernmental organizations. For example, in the early 1970s the Law Enforcement Assistance Administration (LEAA) appointed the National Advisory Commission on Criminal Justice Standards and Goals with the task of developing suggestions for the effective prevention and control of crime. One of the final reports of this commission contained a clear recommendation for greater involvement and engagement of the public in crime prevention activities: "Every police agency should immediately establish programs that encourage members of the public to take an active role in preventing crime ..." (National Advisory Commission on Criminal Justice Standards and Goals, 1973, p. 66). Therefore, the more modern crime prevention approaches of the police that have emerged since the 1970s have placed greater emphasis on the shared responsibility of the police and the public for social control.

Modern crime prevention techniques that have developed within policing can be roughly organized within the categories of: (1) community policing, (2) problem-oriented policing, and (3) intelligence-led policing. While there is a lot of variety that exists in the specific activities contained in each of these three broad categories, they all share a number of common beliefs or assumptions. First, it is assumed that the police role in crime prevention is most effective when the police are specific and deliberate about the target area or problem being addressed (Weisburd & Eck, 2004). This can be seen in problem-oriented policing where the careful analysis of the crime problem in question leads to specifically tailored responses. This belief can also be seen in the intelligence-led practice of proactive patrols directed at identified geographic or temporal "hotspots" of crime. This principle of specificity, or what David Bayley has referred to as "determined crime prevention," (Bayley, 1994, p. 124) is in contrast to early approaches, which relied on the general presence or deployment of police resources. Second, as mentioned previously, these modern crime prevention activities provide a new role for the public. The early approaches viewed the public as an important source of information to guide the crime prevention efforts of the police. However, some have pointed out that using citizens simply as the "eyes and the ears" for the police limits the crime prevention potential contained in these collaborations (Buerger, 1994). As the collaboration between police and citizens has evolved, there has been a growing emphasis on the need to use these interactions as a vehicle to indirectly prevent crime through the building and strengthening of communities (Correia, 2000; Scott, 2002). In this way, it is believed that the police can contribute to crime prevention by strengthening informal mechanisms contained within communities that independently help control and prevent crime. We now turn our attention to a discussion of the early crime prevention approaches that have been adopted by the police.

EARLY PREVENTION APPROACHES

The belief that the police can prevent crime through their uniformed patrol presence represents the backbone of early crime prevention orientation. Initially this patrol activity was carried out on foot. The advent of the automobile led to the increased reliance on motorized patrols. Technological advancements in communications after World War II led to the increased reliance on two-way radio and telephone as prompts to dispatch these motorized patrol units. As a result, the primary crime prevention activity of the police that emerged in the middle of the 20th century was the random patrol of uniformed and motorized units responding to citizen-directed emergencies. This activity was justified as a crime prevention activity based on a number of assumptions. First, O. W. Wilson, one of the earliest advocates of motorized patrols, argued that the unpredictability of random mobile patrol vehicles produced the perception of an omnipresent police force (Wilson, 1977). According to the random preventive patrol hypothesis, crime could be prevented to the extent that the police could increase the perception of an active and all encompassing police patrol presence. This was consistent with the popular view of criminals as rational beings who would alter their behavior or be deterred by factors that increased the risk of their detection. Further, the ability to rapidly deploy police vehicles through telephone-generated dispatch was believed to increase the opportunity to intercept criminal acts in progress. In much the same way that the visible presence of police patrols was believed to prevent or deter crime, the threat of an easily hailed and rapidly responding police force was expected to discourage criminal activity. These assumptions went largely untested until research emerged in the 1970s that began to question whether the practice of patrol and rapid response actually contributed to crime prevention. For example, early social scientific research involving the observation of the police found that patrol units were only infrequently dispatched to traditional crime-related problems and, in those cases, frequently did not have an opportunity to intercept a crime in progress (Reiss, 1971). As a result of these early findings, follow-up research and experiments conducted in the mid-to-late 1970s began to directly test the crime prevention value of random police patrols and the rapid response of motorized patrols to crimes in progress. This research is summarized and discussed in the next section.

Random Motorized Patrol and Rapid Response

The earliest and most widely cited test of the crime prevention impact of random police patrols was conducted in Kansas City, Missouri (Kelling, Pate, Dieckmand, & Brown, 1974). For one year between 1972 and 1973, a select number of patrol beats were divided into three different patrol conditions. Some beats, defined as a "controls," received no change in police patrol presence. Two categories of patrol beats were defined as the experimental conditions. The first group of experimental beats, referred to as "reactive" beats, received no preventive patrol presence. On these beats, police units responded to dispatched calls in the geographically defined areas but provided no additional preventive patrol presence. The final group of beats, referred to as "proactive" beats, received an elevated police patrol presence two to three times the norm. Outcome measures of reported crime and household surveys measuring citizen victimization, fear of crime, and satisfaction with the police were collected to assess the impact of the patrol experiment. The preventive patrol hypothesis predicts that crime rates and citizen fear of crime should increase in the "reactive" beats and decrease in the "proactive" beats. In other words, both potential suspects and victims of crime are believed to be sensitive to the changes in the visible presence of police patrol and are expected to conform their behavior appropriately.

BOX 3-2 Schematic Representation of the 15-Beat Kansas City Preventive Patrol Experiment

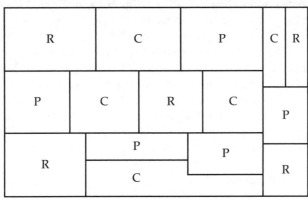

P = Proactive   C = Control   R = Reactive

This diagram was included in the Police Foundation report summarizing the Kansas City Preventive Patrol Experiment (Kelling et al., 1974). This schematic reflects the distribution of the three experimental conditions (*proactive, control,* and *reactive*) across the 15 beats included in the experiment.

Source: Kelling, G. L., Pate T., Dieckman, D., & Brown, C. E. (1974). *The Kansas City preventive patrol experiment: A summary report.* Washington, D.C. Police Foundation. Reprinted with permission of the Police Foundation. www.policefoundation.org/pdf/kcppe.pdf

The results of this experiment showed no statistically significant differences in crime across the various patrol beats and therefore failed to support the preventive patrol hypothesis. Importantly, public crimes like burglary, auto theft, vandalism, robbery, and others believed to be especially susceptible to a visible police patrol presence, were unrelated to the different levels of patrol. This research also found that citizen fear of crime and satisfaction with the police was unrelated to the intensity of police patrols in their neighborhoods. It is important to note that the Kansas City preventive patrol experiment has been criticized on a number of grounds. First, some have questioned whether the experiment actually established the appropriate differences in patrol dosage across the three categories of beats (Larson, 1975). If police officers failed to follow the experimental patrol assignments, the lack of fidelity to the experimental conditions could help explain these null findings. Others have questioned the experiment on the grounds that the patrol dosages were not assigned to these beats randomly (Farrington, 1982). Despite these criticisms, the Kansas City experiment represents one of the earliest attempts to measure the preventive value of visible police patrols. Further, the results that emerged from the Kansas City study caused individuals to question the longstanding hypothesis that routine motorized patrol has a deterrent effect on crime.

Some early advocates of motorized patrols argued that the ability of the police to rapidly respond to dispatched emergencies should enhance the deterrent capabilities of random patrol. The belief that the length of police travel time is related to their ability to apprehend suspects has been tested in a number of studies. One of the earliest studies to investigate response time was sponsored by the National Institute of Justice (NIJ) and also took place in Kansas City, Missouri (Kansas City, 1977). For 10 months in 1975 the police department recorded the length of time it took for police patrol units to respond to dispatched calls for service and crimes in progress. The study used 69 patrol beats, all selected for their high rates of robbery and assault, because these were the types of "in-progress" crimes expected to be most readily intercepted by rapid police response. Using police dispatch records, the study divided the total police "response time" into three separate phases. The first phase consisted of the amount of time it took the complainant or victim to call the police after they had been victimized. The second phase consisted of the time it took for dispatch operators to process the call and alert the patrol unit. Finally, the third phase consisted of the time from the patrol receipt of the dispatch to the arrival of the patrol unit at the scene. This third "travel time" phase is the most important from the police perspective because it is the one area that patrol officers arguably have the most control over and is central to the rapid response philosophy adopted by many police departments. The Kansas City response time study found that the longest response phase was the first, or the length of time it took crime victims to call 911. The analysis found that for crimes involving direct contact between a victim and an offender, such as robbery or assault, it took victims an average of 41 minutes to call the police. For that reason, the study also concluded that there was no relationship between the time it took for officers to travel to the crime scene and their ability to apprehend suspects (Kansas City, 1977). In other words, the total response time was so heavily dependent upon victim behavior that the speed with which patrol units responded after they had been dispatched was negligible.

Several years later these findings were supported by research conducted by Spelman and Brown (1981) who investigated crime victim reporting behavior in four different cities. This study essentially replicated the portion of the Kansas City study that measured the length of time it took crime victims to call the police or 911. This research drew a number of conclusions that were consistent with the original findings in Kansas City. First, the study found that the majority (75%) of crimes reported to the police are discovered by victims long after the fact and do not involve any direct contact with a perpetrator. These include crimes like burglary, vandalism, and motor vehicle theft. Crimes involving victim–suspect direct contact were significantly less common, and on average it took victims 5 or more minutes after the crime was completed to report the crime to police or 911 dispatchers (Spelman & Brown, 1981). This research reinforced the importance of crime victim behavior in the police response equation and further called into question the crime prevention capacity that was supposedly built into the rapid response capabilities of motorized police patrol.

Foot Patrol

By the late 1970s many police departments had begun experimenting with foot patrols as an alternative to motorized patrols. Removing officers from their vehicles and having them patrol on foot was consistent with an increased concern with community engagement that many police departments were adopting. Building on the Kansas City preventive patrol experiment, some researchers began to wonder whether foot patrols might provide a more visible police presence and contribute to crime prevention in ways that random motorized patrols could not. In this way, foot patrol can also be viewed as an additional patrol tactic to help accomplish the traditional goals of promoting a visible law enforcement presence that is detached or separate from the goals of community engagement (Cordner, 1994).

Early evaluations of foot patrols tended to produce contradictory findings. For example, one study of foot patrol in Fort Worth, Texas found that foot patrol in a high-crime neighborhood was related to lower rates of reported crime and an increase in citizen satisfaction (Pendland & Gay, 1972). Other evaluations in Virginia and California found that foot patrol, while popular with and supported by the public, was unrelated to crime (Kinney, 1979; Resource Planning Corporation, 1975). Two additional and widely cited studies added to the contradictory findings. These studies took place in Newark, New Jersey (Pate, 1986; Police Foundation, 1981) and Flint, Michigan (Trojanowicz, 1986).

The Newark Foot Patrol experiment was conducted by the Police Foundation and relied on data from a state-sponsored program designed to enhance crime prevention through the support of visible foot patrols. The design of the experiment allowed researchers to compare the impact of retaining, adding, and eliminating foot patrols over an extended period of time. The Newark experiment relied on a survey of households and nonresidential establishments (e.g., businesses), as well as official reported crime, to measure the impact of foot patrols. The results indicated that residents were aware of the presence of foot patrols and that the presence of foot patrols was significantly related to improvements in resident perceptions of crime and disorder problems. The presence of foot patrols was also shown to be positively related to ratings of satisfaction with police service. However, the study also found that the addition or removal of foot patrols was unrelated to self-reported victimization, the likelihood that residents would report crime, or actual crimes reported to the police (Pate, 1986; Police Foundation, 1981). In other words, while foot patrol made residents feel better about their neighborhood and the police, they did not appear to directly contribute to crime prevention in Newark.

A similar study of foot patrol was conducted in Flint, Michigan beginning in the late 1970s. The Neighborhood Foot Patrol Program (NFPP) operated in 14 neighborhoods between 1979 and 1982. The use of foot patrol and the research design in Flint differed from that in Newark in a number of ways. First, in Flint there appeared to be a more deliberate attempt to use foot patrol officers to engage and organize citizens. According to Robert Trojanowicz, director of the research team that conducted the evaluation of the NFPP, "The Flint foot patrol officers were not expected to be just security officers, 'shaking doors' and deterring criminal activities by their mere presence in uniform ... foot patrol officers in the Flint program were expected to function as catalytic agents of community organization. They were expected to encourage citizens to work together—in neighborhood associations, citizen watch groups, or some other form of organization—for their mutual support and protection" (Trojanowicz, 1986, p. 160). This difference in engagement is significant because it reflects one of the earliest integrations of foot patrol into the newly emerging philosophy of community policing. The foot patrol program and research in Flint also differed in that the program changed and was modified based on an attempt to make ongoing improvements. Some of these changes were precipitated by feedback from police officers and the research staff. Additional changes were motivated by political pressure to expand the program beyond the original 14 patrol areas. While the dynamic nature of this research study no doubt improved some of the outcomes, it provided challenges for the evaluation of the program. For example, researchers had intended to identify 14 neighborhoods not receiving foot patrol to serve as comparable control areas. However, as foot patrols grew in popularity, the city was forced to extend the program, making it increasingly difficult to identify the appropriate number of comparison areas (Trojanowicz, 1986). Despite these challenges, the Flint study deepened our understanding of the crime prevention capabilities of foot patrol.

The research team in Flint relied on a number of sources of data to evaluate the success of the foot patrol program. These included surveys of neighborhood residents, community leaders, and police personnel. Data on reported crime and police calls for service were collected for 1978, the year before the foot patrol program began, and for the three years in which it was in full operation. The results from the citizen surveys confirmed the findings from the Newark study. First, there was clear evidence that citizens were aware of the program. The majority of citizens surveyed reported that they had either seen or had personal contact with a foot patrol officer during the study period. Almost two-thirds of residents surveyed reported that the foot patrol officers had encouraged them to report crime and become more involved in community crime prevention efforts. Second, citizens reported improved satisfaction with the police and improvements in perceptions of public safety that increased with each year of the 3-year foot patrol program. Finally, in the 3rd year of the program citizens were asked to compare the effectiveness of foot patrol versus motor patrol officers across a number of patrol function activities. Citizens rated foot patrol officers as substantially more effective in their ability to: (1) prevent crime, (2) encourage citizen self-protection, (3) work with juveniles, and (4) follow up on complaints (Trojanowicz, 1986).

Unlike the Newark foot patrol study, the results in Flint suggested that there was a relationship between the presence of foot patrol officers and reductions in crime. Comparing the preprogram (1978) level of crime to the volume of crime reported in the 3rd year (1981) of the program, the research team found that crime had declined close to 9% in the 14 foot patrol areas. In comparison, citywide reported crime increased by 10% during the same period of time. The two exceptions to this pattern were for the criminal categories of robbery and burglary. Robbery and burglary increased in the target foot patrol area and for the city as a whole during the study period. According to the research team: "The foot patrol was less effective in reducing these serious crimes, because most of these offenses took place at night, when the officers on foot were not working" (Trojanowicz, 1986, p. 167). Additional evidence of the crime prevention impact of foot patrol in Flint can be seen in the analysis of police call-for-service data. During the course of the study, calls for police service decreased by 43% from the 1978 prestudy year to 1981, the 3rd year of foot patrol implementation.

While the Flint foot patrol study was limited by the fact that it did not utilize comparable control areas, this study added to the knowledge about foot patrol in at least two important ways. First, the Flint study provided support for the use of foot patrol as a means to encourage greater police–community engagement. A large proportion of residents reported that they were aware of the program, were satisfied with the addition of foot patrol officers, and believed that the foot patrol officers encouraged them to take part in community crime prevention efforts. Second, the Flint study demonstrated the crime prevention value of foot patrol. While it is not entirely clear what mechanism was responsible for the improvements in public safety, the design of the foot patrol program in Flint intentionally emphasized the importance of community engagement and organization. A more recent implementation of foot patrol in Lexington, Kentucky suggests that the simple visible presence of foot patrol in selected high crime areas may further serve this crime prevention function.

In the early 1990s the city of Lexington utilized foot patrols to help maintain and reinforce an aggressive police crackdown that occurred at a public housing site. The initial police crackdown lasted from May to December 1990 and was designed to address the high crime and open-air drug dealing that was occurring in and around the Bluegrass-Aspendale public housing site. Following the crackdown, the police department implemented overtime foot patrols deployed in two-officer units. The foot patrols operated from 2:00 PM to 2:00 AM for all of 1991. Foot patrols were continued in 1992 but at a reduced level. Unlike the use of foot patrol in Flint, the Lexington patrols were not designed to meet the community-oriented goals of improved police–citizen relationships or general community building. Rather, the Lexington program was more narrowly focused on reinforcing the visible police presence that had been established by the aggressive crackdown during the preceding months (Cordner, 1994).

The success of the foot patrol program was evaluated using police call-for-service data for a 48-month period from 1989 to 1992. Calls for service in 1989, before the crackdown and foot patrols, were compared to calls for service in 1991 and 1992, the years after the program was initiated. In addition, citywide police call-for-service data were used as a comparison. Interviews with police and housing officials suggested that the crackdown and reinforcement of foot patrol officers reduced the level of drug dealing and increased the legitimate use of public spaces (e.g., sidewalks and parks) by residents. The analysis of police data indicated a reduction in calls for service in 1991. This was true for three out of four categories of calls, and this pattern of improvement was not seen in the city as a whole. However, by 1992 the calls for service increased substantially and returned to levels substantially higher than the preintervention year. The evaluation also concluded that while there was some evidence that foot patrols were associated with reduced calls for police service, the independent effects of the number of occupied housing units and the role of seasonality (i.e., summer versus winter months) were more powerful in explaining changes in calls for service (Cordner, 1994). Therefore, it appears that the targeted use of foot patrols to supplement aggressive police crackdowns in high-crime neighborhoods can produce short-term improvements in public order. It remains to be seen how those short-term improvements can be sustained.

Summary—Early Prevention Approaches

In summary, the early crime prevention efforts of the police have produced mixed results. There is little evidence supporting the crime prevention value of random motorized patrol. Evaluations have failed to demonstrate that citizens notice deliberate changes in police patrol presence and have not found a relationship between variations in the level of patrol presence and rates of crime. In addition, the combined use of motorized patrol with rapid police response has not been supported as an effective crime prevention strategy. Research has shown that citizens generally take too long to alert the police to a crime-in-progress. As a result, the rapid response efforts of the police do not intercept a large enough proportion of in-progress crimes to serve as an effective crime prevention tool. The evaluations of the use of foot patrol also have produced mixed results. In comparison to the evaluations of motorized patrol, evaluations of foot patrol have demonstrated that citizens *are* aware of the addition and removal of foot patrol officers from communities. Furthermore, there is strong evidence that the addition of foot patrol is associated with increased levels of public satisfaction with the police. In response to foot patrols, citizens have reported perceived improvements to public safety and lower levels of fear of crime. The research evaluating the actual crime prevention value of foot patrol has been inconclusive. Some studies have failed to find any connection between the implementation of foot patrols and lower rates of reported crime or calls for police service. Other research has found that foot patrols have produced a modest and short-term crime prevention impact when measured by these same outcomes. We now turn our attention to a description of some more modern crime prevention approaches that have been adopted by the police. These approaches include community policing, problem-oriented policing, and intelligence-led policing.

MODERN PREVENTION APPROACHES

The early crime prevention approaches that we have just described shared a number of characteristics. First, they relied heavily on the simple presence of general motorized and foot patrol units to generate crime prevention. Second, these early crime prevention strategies tended to focus their efforts on the general prevention of crime rather than a focus on specific target areas, individuals, or types of problems. Finally, with the exception of some of the more community-oriented applications of foot patrol (e.g., Flint's foot patrol described in Trojanowicz, 1986), most of these approaches tended to provide a limited role for community engagement in their crime prevention efforts. In general, the modern prevention approaches that we will describe in the following sections differ with regard to all three of these characteristics. For instance, rather than relying on the mere presence of the police, these strategies have placed a greater emphasis on the more intentional or deliberate crime prevention activity of officers and departments. Furthermore, the modern prevention approaches are more focused on specific targets. Sometimes these targets are locations (e.g., hotspots of criminal activity) while other times they are designed to address specific crime problems (e.g., daytime residential burglaries). Finally, many of these modern crime prevention activities provide a greater role for community engagement. Rather than viewing the public as simply a "consumer" of public safety, these strategies view the public as a partner and "co-producer" of social control leading to greater public safety (Rosenbaum, Lurigio, & Davis, 1998). The strategies of community policing, problem-oriented policing, and intelligence-led policing are generally consistent with at least one or more of these characteristics.

Community Policing

Community policing has become such a universally popular and accepted practice that it would be difficult to find a police executive not claiming to be engaged in some aspect of this reform. The challenge with community policing is that it has frequently been subjected to multiple and imprecise definitions (Bayley, 1988; Maguire & Mastrofski, 2000; Mastrofski, 1988). Despite these definitional challenges, a number of critical features and goals, especially as they relate to crime prevention, appear to be central to community policing. According to Lorie Fridell, "The goals of community policing are to reduce crime and disorder, promote citizens' quality of life in communities, reduce fear of crime and improve police-citizen relations" (Fridell, 2004, p. 4). A number of different conceptual models have been developed that have attempted to explain how community policing can strategically accomplish these new goals.

Looking across these models there appear to be at least four common elements of community policing that can be identified (Scott, 2002). One common theme is that of organizational change. These changes are most typically reflected in decentralization and the recognition of the unique character of neighborhood issues and problems (Bayley, 1994; Cordner, 2000; Skogan & Hartnett, 1997). Consistent with this theme, there are a variety of policies that serve to increase interactions between police and residents and improve the general accessibility of the police. These policies include the creation of storefront presences or substations, foot and bike patrols, the alignment of police beats that are consistent with neighborhood boundaries, and the permanent beat assignment of officers. The second element represents a commitment to problem solving. This appears to be such a central component that it is almost difficult to find a description of community policing that does not, in some way, offer a description of problem analysis and implementation of solutions to address neighborhood problems. In this way, problem-oriented policing, which we will discuss after community policing, represents a subset of community policing activity (Skogan et al., 2000). Another common theme reflects a redefinition of the role of residents in public safety and crime control. This component stresses the importance of community partnership and collaboration between police and residents. This approach can involve improved information sharing between police and residents or the involvement of residents in joint police–citizen patrols. Importantly, these models note that these partnerships are typically directly linked to the problem-solving processes described previously (Bayley, 1994; Skogan & Hartnett, 1997). Finally, although some have noted that community policing represents a reform that leads to optimism concerning the ability of the police to control crime and improve the quality of residential life, at least one common element of community policing appears to suggest that this optimism should remain guarded. This guardedness is reflected in the fact that a number of these conceptual models include a component that recognizes the limitations the police have in terms of their ability to control crime and uphold community norms. Several have argued that a key element of community policing involves attempts made by the police to mobilize and empower residents to enhance their collective sense of responsibility and thereby address issues on their own (Bayley, 1994; Skogan & Hartnett, 1997). The involvement of the police in crime-prevention training, community meetings, local social events, and citizen patrols represents activities the police may engage in to generate collective efforts among residents. We now turn our attention to the research evaluating the crime prevention potential contained in a number of these community policing strategies.

Neighborhood Watch

The use of Neighborhood Watch (also referred to as "Block Watch") represents one of the earliest and most readily cited community policing strategies. This strategy involves a process whereby residents meet with one another and the police to share crime prevention tips and make arrangements for the collective surveillance of the neighborhood. This process frequently involves agreements to watch one another's homes when residents are away or to generally be on the "look-out" for suspicious activity. National household surveys suggest that this type of neighborhood-based home surveillance activity increased substantially in the United States during the 1980s (O'Keefe, Rosenbaum, Lavrakas, Reid, & Botta, 1996). Neighborhood Watch is expected to reduce or prevent crime through two main mechanisms. First, because watch-type strategies bring residents together, the collective nature of this activity is believed to foster relationships, improve social cohesion, and reduce fear of crime within neighborhoods (Rosenbaum, 1987). Therefore, these programs may indirectly prevent crime through their influence on the social organization of the neighborhood. Second, by asking residents to be the additional "eyes and ears" for the police, criminal opportunities are expected to decrease (Rosenbaum, Lurigio, & Davis, 1998). In addition, these programs frequently include visible signs or markers denoting the neighborhood as a "watch" community. The combined effect of surveillance and message sending is expected to serve as a deterrent.

There have been a number of important evaluations of Neighborhood Watch programs. These include programs in Chicago (Rosenbaum, Lewis, & Grant, 1985), Minneapolis (Pate, McPherson, & Silloway, 1987), and Seattle (Cirel, Evans, McGillis, & Whitcomb, 1977). In a comprehensive review of these evaluations, Dennis Rosenbaum and his colleagues contend that the results are generally not supportive of the hypothesized crime prevention benefit of Neighborhood Watch (Rosenbaum et al., 1998). While these programs were able to increase residents' awareness and participation, they failed to generate the expected crime prevention benefits. Crime rates did not decrease, and in some instances actually increased. Residents' fear of crime did not decrease, but, contrary to expectations, actually increased in some locations. This finding is consistent with other research that has suggested that fear of crime can actually be enhanced when residents meet to discuss crime and their experiences of victimization (Rosenbaum, Lewis, & Grant, 1985; Skogan, 1990). Some have observed that developing watch-type activities is especially difficult in communities where crime prevention programs are needed most; low-income, high-crime urban neighborhoods (Rosenbaum, 1987). In these communities the high levels of fear, low levels of social cohesion, and historically poor relationships with the police may be too much for the Neighborhood Watch program to overcome. As a result, Neighborhood Watch is more frequently successful at gaining support and resident participation in middle-class communities that have substantially less serious crime problems to begin with.

Citizen Patrols

An additional strategy frequently employed within a community policing framework is the use of citizen patrols. These patrols represent an active mobile presence of residents within communities. Like police patrols, citizen patrols have been implemented on foot, on bicycle, and in motorized vehicles. They are most commonly organized as a local neighborhood group although there are other examples of citizen patrols that are citywide or national in scope. For example, the Guardian Angels is a national group that has been employed across multiple U.S. cities (Pennell, Curtis, & Henderson, 1985). There is a substantial amount of similarity between Neighborhood Watch and citizen patrols in terms of their rationale, use, and evaluation results. First, citizen patrols are frequently associated with Neighborhood Watch. One national survey of Neighborhood Watch programs found that 12 percent had a mobile citizen patrol component to them (Garofalo & McLeod, 1986). Second, citizen patrols have been developed with the goal of reducing criminal opportunities by providing increased surveillance and by directing the attention of the police to problem areas. This is very similar to the goals and rationales of Neighborhood Watch programs. Finally, like Neighborhood Watch, citizen patrols have been more readily adopted in middle-class communities that have high levels of homeownership. In these communities the citizen patrols tend to be concerned with general crime prevention or, as is frequently the case with Neighborhood Watch, focused on reducing opportunities for residential burglary. Citizen patrols in high-crime urban communities have generally struggled to develop the same level of participation. However, since the mid-1980s there has been an increased use of citizen patrols in inner-city neighborhoods where they have been used as a tool to deal with open-air drug markets and known drug houses (Davis, Smith, Lurigio, & Skogan, 1991) as well as public housing complexes (Popkin et al., 1996). One way that citizen patrols differ from one another is the extent to which the activity of the residents is integrated into the broader crime prevention efforts of the local police department. There has been reluctance to support citizen patrols on the part of some police executives who fear that these efforts may lead to vigilantism or, if citizens were to intervene in a crime in progress, might jeopardize the safety of those involved (Rosenbaum et al., 1998). As a result, some police departments have distanced themselves from particular citizen patrols. In other locations citizen patrols have been carefully integrated into the broader community policing strategy. Some of these areas have employed detailed training for citizen participants, paired citizens with police officers, provided mobile phones for citizens, and implemented written reporting procedures (Rosenbaum & Kaminska, 1997; Skogan & Rosenbaum, 1997).

Unfortunately there have been very few evaluations of citizen patrols. One of the challenges associated with evaluating this approach is that it is frequently implemented as a component of some larger community policing initiative. This layered approach makes it difficult to isolate the independent effect of the citizen patrol intervention from the effect of the comprehensive community policing program (Weisburd & Eck, 2004). There have been two evaluations of general citizen patrols that provide modest support for the crime prevention value of this strategy. However, according to one review, the findings from these studies should be viewed with caution due to limitations associated with the research design (Rosenbaum et al., 1998). An evaluation of a walking citizen patrol in Columbus, Ohio found that this intervention was associated with a reduction in burglary and automobile theft (Latessa & Allen, 1980). An additional evaluation examined the impact of the highly publicized Guardian Angels. The study took place in San Diego and found that the Guardian Angels patrols were not associated with a change in violent crime rates. There was evidence of a short-term decline in property crime during a period of time when the patrols were most visible (Pennell et al., 1985). In addition to these two studies, there has been at least one comprehensive evaluation of citizen patrols directed to intervene in active drug markets (Davis et al., 1991). In this evaluation, Davis and his colleagues examined four citizen patrols and compared them with four comparison neighborhoods in the same city. In each location residents were surveyed and asked questions about their perceptions of neighborhood problems, fear of crime, social cohesion, and satisfaction with the neighborhood. Before the citizen patrols were enacted there were very few differences between the target and comparison neighborhoods. However, after the implementation of the anti-drug citizen patrol program residents in the target neighborhoods reported lower levels of fear, improvements in social cohesion among residents, increased satisfaction with the neighborhood, and perceived reductions in physical decay. These same changes were not observed in the comparison neighborhoods (Davis et al., 1991). Taken as a whole, these findings suggest that citizen patrols do hold some limited crime prevention potential. Citizen patrols directed at specific targets (e.g., active drug markets) have shown greater potential than general patrols. Consistent with the findings from the evaluations of Neighborhood Watch, one of the challenges associated with citizen patrols is the ability to generate the sustained participation of residents who are broadly representative of their neighborhoods.

Information Sharing

A variety of activities within community policing have been designed to enhance the sharing of information between police and residents. Many of these approaches represent efforts made by the police to increase their accessibility to residents. These strategies include the opening of neighborhood storefront stations, community meetings, and newsletters. The sharing of information is expected to enhance crime prevention in at least two ways. First, these efforts provide opportunities for the police to share crime prevention information with residents and alert them to emerging criminal activity within neighborhoods. It is expected that residents can use this information to better protect themselves from criminal victimization, or it might motivate residents to become involved in joint police–community responses to these problems (Lavrakas, 1986). The second crime prevention mechanism involves the valuable information that residents can provide to the police. Residents are frequently an excellent source of information regarding new emerging problems and locations within neighborhoods that the police may not yet be familiar with. Frequently this information can be used as the initial step in the joint police–community problem-solving process that is central to problem-oriented policing. Therefore, these strategies may hold potential as a crime prevention tool to the extent that they open up better avenues of communication between residents and the police. We now turn our attention to a number of evaluations of these information sharing strategies.

Like much of the research that we have previously discussed, the evaluations of testing for the crime prevention value of information sharing have garnered mixed results and do not reflect strong support for community policing. These strategies have been implemented broadly in the United States but some of the more detailed evaluations have taken place in Houston, Madison, Newark, and Chicago. The two approaches that have consistently shown limited-to-no crime prevention value include the use of police storefront stations and the use of anticrime newsletters. In contrast, research evaluating the use of community meetings has recently shown that this strategy has the potential to produce greater success in terms of crime prevention.

One of the earliest and most careful evaluations of the storefront police station approach was carried out in Houston and conducted by the Police Foundation (Skogan & Wycoff, 1986). This storefront office was staffed by police personnel between the fall of 1983 through the summer of 1984 and was typically open during daytime and evening hours. In addition to simply staffing the station, station officers also developed a number of programs (e.g., newsletters and community meetings) that provided additional avenues of communication with the community. Researchers conducted both residential and nonresidential (e.g., business owners) surveys 3 months before and 9 months after the development of the storefront station. To help better ascertain the impact of the storefront police station, similar surveys were conducted in a comparison neighborhood that did not receive any change in police service. The evaluation concluded that the storefront station contributed to reductions in residents' fear of crime as well as perceptions of crime and other forms of social disorder in the neighborhood. However, the establishment of the police storefront station did not produce any changes in the actual levels of personal or property crime victimizations (Skogan & Wycoff, 1986). These findings were confirmed in a study of a storefront police station that was opened in Birmingham, Alabama and designed to address the violence associated with an active drug market. After the storefront station was established, residents reported lower levels of fear of crime. However, the development of the station was not associated with reductions in actual crime or in drug availability (Uchida, Forst, & Annan, 1992).

Two of the more well-known studies of police anticrime newsletters were conducted in Newark, New Jersey and Houston, Texas as part of a federally sponsored "fear reduction" project. This project was evaluated by the Police Foundation (Pate, Lavrakas, Wycoff, Skogan, & Sherman, 1985). A third study of police newsletters was conducted in Evanston, Illinois. All three of these programs shared a number of characteristics and are summarized in a review written by Paul Lavrakas (Lavrakas, 1986). These newsletters were designed as a means to generate citizen interest in personal safety and crime prevention activities involving the police. At the same time these evaluations were designed to test the possibility that sharing crime information might generate or amplify residents' fear of crime. To test this, two versions of the newsletters were distributed in selected neighborhoods in each of the three cities. One version of the newsletter simply provided information to residents about how they could protect themselves or assist the police. The second version of the newsletter supplemented this general crime prevention information with crime statistics specific to that neighborhood. There were a number of common findings across all three of these cities. Residents generally reported that they liked receiving the newsletters and found them valuable. In addition, there was no consistent evidence that either version of the newsletter contributed to higher levels of fear of crime. The one exception to this general finding was in Houston where exposure to the newsletter supplemented with crime statistics was associated with an increase in fear of property crime (Pate et al., 1985). Importantly however, these evaluations did not produce overwhelming evidence to support the crime prevention value of the newsletters. In none of the cities was there any evidence that the newsletters were associated with lower rates of reported victimization. In addition, in two of the three cities (Newark and Houston) there was no association between receiving the newsletter and actual crime prevention steps residents reported taking (Lavrakas, 1986).

A final approach to increase the transfer of information between police and residents is the use of public community meetings. Community meetings provide a venue for the police to share crime prevention information, for residents to voice concerns, and for the police and residents to collaborate on issues of public safety and general neighborhood improvements. One of the earliest and most widely published evaluations of the community meeting approach was associated with an experimental community policing effort that took place in Madison, Wisconsin (Wycoff & Skogan, 1993). In 1987 Madison developed an Experimental Police District (EPD) that was designed to test the value of community policing implementation. In addition to representing innovation in organization and management practices, the EPD provided a decentralized approach that put a strong emphasis on the use of community meetings. During the experimental period there was evidence that community meetings were frequently used by the police and community members to discuss crime and other problems residents were experiencing. In one instance the local neighborhood association coordinated with EPD officers to address concerns about speeding and traffic enforcement. The evaluation of the EPD community meetings was conducted using a quasi-experimental design that relied on citizen surveys of residents before the EPD station opened and 2 years later. Similar surveys of residents in the rest of the city served as a comparison. The evaluation produced mixed results. There was evidence that the presence of the EPD was associated with an increase in citizens reporting that they had attended a community meeting in which an officer was present. In addition, there was an increase in the perception that the police were working with citizens to solve problems. While the surveys also indicated that residents felt that some crime problems (e.g., robbery) had improved, there was no evidence of a relationship between actual criminal victimization and the increased use of community meetings (Wycoff & Skogan, 1993).

In contrast to the limited support for the crime prevention value of community meetings that came out of the Madison evaluation, recent research by Wesley Skogan and his colleagues at the Institute for Policy Research at Northwestern University is more positive. Since the early 1990s Skogan and his colleagues have been evaluating a community policing model in Chicago know as CAPS (Chicago Alternative Policing Strategy). Neighborhood or "beat" meetings represent one

BOX 3-3 CLEARpath

Increasingly, police departments are relying on Internet technology as a means to interact and share information with the public. To support CAPS, the Chicago Police Department has launched the following website: https://portal.chicagopolice.org/portal/page/portal/ClearPath

CLEARpath not only provides background information describing opportunities to get involved in CAPS, but it also provides avenues for citizens to

- Register their private closed-circuit security cameras for coordinated police use
- Report and check on the status of a community concern
- Compliment or make a complaint about a police officer

CRITICAL THINKING QUESTIONS
1. What are the potential strengths and limitations associated with Web-based communication strategies like CLEARpath?
2. Research evaluating traditional anticrime newsletters has failed to find support for their crime prevention value. What reasons exist to believe that the modern use of websites like CLEARpath, offer additional crime prevention value over these traditional newsletters?

of the key features of CAPS. One of the distinguishing characteristics of these Chicago beat meetings is their strong problem-oriented focus (Skogan & Hartnett, 1997; Skogan et al., 2000). Rather than simply providing an opportunity for the police to share crime prevention tips or for residents to complain about problems they are experiencing, police and residents were trained to use these meetings to carefully identify and analyze problems. In addition, these meetings then move the process along to the development of solutions that police and community members can implement jointly. We will discuss this problem-oriented model in more detail in subsequent sections of this chapter. For now it is important to note that these focused efforts in Chicago have been associated with improvements in crime and victimization (Skogan & Hartnett, 1997). The findings in Chicago are also notable because some of the most active and successful examples of problem solving have come out of neighborhoods characterized by high crime, low socioeconomic status (SES), and low levels of social and political capacity (Skogan et al., 2000). We now turn our attention to a more detailed discussion of problem-oriented aspects of policing like those used in Chicago.

Problem-Oriented Policing (POP)

A primary objective of community-oriented policing is to forge partnerships with private citizens, businesses, community organizations, and local government agencies to collectively address a wide range of problems that have impacted a community's quality of life. In contrast to the traditional model of policing where citizens have a narrowly defined role—simply reporting crimes to the authorities—the community-oriented policing model embraces the notion that the public should not only help identify problems and their underlying causes but can also be instrumental in providing solutions and, in many instances, be active participants in strategies to reduce or eliminate a problem. This last point underscores a very fine distinction between community-oriented and problem-oriented policing. Although citizen participation is a core feature of community-oriented policing, it is not absolutely required to remedy a troublesome situation under the problem-oriented model (Lab, 2010). In this sense, "problem-oriented policing relies on and supports community policing, but it is not synonymous with community police" (Eck & Spelman, 1987b, p. 46).

Background

In his seminal piece "Improving Police: A Problem-Oriented Approach," Herman Goldstein (1979) inspired the development of an intellectual framework for a problem-oriented strategy that has since been adopted in various forms by numerous law enforcement agencies in the United States and abroad. Based on his extensive work with the American Bar Foundation and the Chicago Police Department, Goldstein observed that a preoccupation with improving the efficient administration of law enforcement organizations (e.g., management, recruitment, staffing, training, etc.) during the professionalization era produced a "means over ends" syndrome where police administrators had lost sight of the substantive outcome of their work. While the smooth management of law enforcement agencies is clearly a desirable organizational goal, it should never be confused with the end product of policing: reducing crime, disorder, and fear in the community. With a renewed focus on the substantive outcome of police work, Herman Goldstein persuasively argued that the traditional reactive approach to handling problems in the community—incident-driven policing—was ineffective because the tactic fails to adequately address the underlying cause of a problem. Employing a medical analogy to understand the reactive incident-based strategy, law enforcement had simply reacted to the symptoms by providing temporary measures of relief—

arrests for example—but had not treated the cause(s) of the illness. As a result, the symptoms were bound to return again because the illness had not been properly treated. Addressing this shortcoming, Goldstein proposes a proactive model of policing that encourages law enforcement to become problem solvers who address underlying factors that give rise to these community concerns in the first place. The problem-solving model also fully embraces research to identify and understand the root causes of problems as well as to evaluate the effectiveness of experimental solutions that have been implemented. In the spirit of innovative thinking, the new model of policing emphasizes the idea that law enforcement agencies should seek out a broad range of solutions that extend beyond traditional criminal justice responses by engaging community organizations, public agencies, and the private sector in crime prevention efforts (Goldstein, 2001). It is with this backdrop in mind that we now turn to a popular approach for analyzing and responding to community concerns—the SARA problem-solving model.

The SARA Model

Scanning stage. SARA is an acronym representing the four chronological stages of a systematic problem-solving process: Scanning, Analysis, Response, and Assessment (The Sara Model, n.d.). The first stage, *scanning*, seeks to identify and understand the nature and scope of a significant problem in the community. This fact-finding mission requires gathering information from a wide variety of sources including, but not limited to, law enforcement records such as police reports and calls-for-service. Receiving input from the community can be achieved in a number of different ways—for example, by administering household or merchant surveys, holding community meetings, following media coverage and editorials, and reviewing letters of complaint published in local newspapers or correspondences received by the department (U.S. Department of Justice, 2010, p. 7). These exploratory data mining efforts may identify clusters of related or repeated incidents that point to four possible categories of problems (The Problem Analysis Triangle, n.d.):

- *Behavior*. Certain behavior(s) is (are) common to the incidents. For example, making excessive noise, robbing people or businesses, driving under the influence, crashing vehicles, dealing drugs, stealing cars. There are many different behaviors that might constitute problems.
- *Place*. Certain places can be common to incidents. Incidents involving one or more problem behaviors may occur at, for example, a street corner, a house, a business, a park, a neighborhood, or a school. Some incidents occur in abstract places such as cyberspace, on the telephone, or through other information networks.
- *Persons*. Certain individuals or groups of people can be common to incidents. These people could be either offenders or victims. Incidents involving one or more behaviors, occurring in one or more places may be attributed to, for example, a youth gang, a lone person, a group of prostitutes, a group of chronic inebriates, or a property owner. Or incidents may be causing harm to, for example, residents of a neighborhood, senior citizens, young children, or a lone individual.
- *Time*. Certain times can be common to incidents. Incidents involving one or more behaviors, in one or more places, caused by or affecting one or more people may happen at, for example, traffic rush hour, bar closing time, the holiday shopping season, or during an annual festival.

Analysis stage. After a potential problem has been identified during the scanning phase, the next logical step, *analysis*, is undertaken in an attempt to isolate the factors that may contribute to, facilitate, or otherwise causes the disturbance. Intimately understanding the nature of the problem is critically important in fashioning a new intervention strategy or employing or modifying remedies that might have been used elsewhere or in the past. Miscalculations made at this stage will render interventions, shaped in the next stage of the SARA model, ineffective as the solution will not specifically address the underlying causes of the problem. For example, the crime of arson has many different motivations including vandalism, pyromania, insurance fraud, and intimidation or terrorism along with modus operandi that might require fundamentally different solutions.

To assist problem solvers with this phase of the problem-solving process, a Problem Analysis Triangle (PAT) is often utilized to introduce structure into the investigation. The sides of the triangle consist of three central ingredients of routine activities theory that converge in time and space to produce opportunities to commit crime—victim, offender, and target or location. The advantage of examining a problem from all sides of the crime triangle allows problem solvers to formulate a comprehensive plan of action that should deflect offenders, attack conditions that are conducive to crime in a location, and protect at-risk populations of the community (U.S. Department of Justice, 2010, p. 1).

Response stage. In the third stage of the SARA model, *response*, problem solvers carefully develop and implement remedies to deal with the problem that, ideally, addresses the underlying causes of at least two sides of the problem triangle identified during the analysis phase. It is important to note that traditional law enforcement approaches to a crime problem, such as crackdowns or increased police presence for example, are not the only means available to address a community concern. Problem solvers are encouraged to "think outside of the box" and consider nontraditional responses for handling problems that go beyond the simple enforcement of criminal codes to include, for example, civil remedies (Mazerolle & Roehl, 1998) or other nonlegal solutions. Moreover, these interventions can involve other government agencies and the private sector in a collective effort to address problems.

One approach to addressing problems involves the use of situational crime prevention techniques where problem solvers develop remedies that, broadly conceptualized, attempt to increase the amount of effort needed to attempt a crime, increase the perceived and real risk of apprehension, reduce the rewards gained by an offense, reduce factors that may incite crime, and reduce excuses for offending behavior. The popularity of situational crime prevention techniques warrants further discussion and is presented in greater detail in a subsequent section of this chapter.

Assessment stage. The final stage of the problem-solving process, *assessment*, involves two types of evaluations—a process evaluation and an outcome evaluation. A process evaluation is conducted to determine whether the proposed solution was implemented as it was originally designed or conceived. This is particularly important if the assessment finds the intervention to be ineffective at reducing or eliminating a problem. Without a process evaluation, the failure may erroneously be attributed to a shortcoming of the intervention when, in fact, the crime reduction strategy was never given a genuine opportunity to address a problem in the first place.

The second type of assessment, an outcome evaluation, is an empirical attempt to determine the impact control efforts have had on the targeted problem. Oftentimes this involves a comparison of outcome data taken prior to and after an intervention has been instituted. Although the complete elimination of a problem is a desirable outcome, it is not the only way to determine whether the strategy was successful or not. A positive intervention may also include (Eck & Spelman, 1987a, p. 49): (1) a decrease in the number of incidents, (2) a reduction in harm produced by the problem,

(3) an improved response to the problem such as lower cost, and (4) shifting responsibility of the problem to others who are better equipped to address it.

In terms of gauging an intervention effect, once again problem solvers are encouraged to think creatively about the outcome measures used to measure effectiveness. Consistent with the creative mindset, problem solvers can employ traditional measures, such as calls for service and citizen complaints, as well as nontraditional outcome measures in their assessments. For example, the number of drug arrests at a local park overtaken by drug dealers might tell us nothing more than that police activity has increased in this area. Using this traditional measure of police effectiveness, number of arrests, we may never really know if the park is now safe for the community to enjoy simply because drug enforcement has increased. In this instance, perhaps counting the number of visitors to the park prior to and after the intervention was implemented could provide additional evidence to determine whether the solution is effective.

It should also be noted that assessment is an ongoing process, constantly gauging short- and long-term effects of the intervention as well as identifying weaknesses in the plan that may require adjustments to existing components or the addition of another stopgap measure to augment the original strategy. Additionally, evaluators are charged with the task of routinely monitoring for the presence of a displacement effect. Displacement can be divided into two general types: benign and malign (Barr & Pease, 1990). Benign displacement, as the name implies, is beneficial to the community with respect to harm reduction. Offenders may consider committing less serious criminal activities in lieu of a more serious crime that has been targeted by the police; for example, armed robbers now engage in another type of crime such as auto theft. On the other hand, malign displacement creates intolerable effects that may produce detrimental outcomes that are much more harmful than the crime originally targeted for elimination; for example, car thieves are now engaging in potentially more harmful crimes such as carjacking. The examples just mentioned represent a specific type of displacement—*offense displacement*—conceptualized by Reppetto (1976), where an offender switches from one type of crime to another. In addition to changes in the types of offenses committed, displacement can shift crime to different times of the day (*temporal displacement*), locations (*spatial displacement*), or victims (*target displacement*), or change the offender's modus operandi (*tactical displacement*). A sixth type of displacement—*offender displacement*—was introduced by Barr and Pease (1990) and represents a situation where an offender desists from crime, willingly or unwillingly, but is replaced by another motivated individual. An offender who gives up dealing drugs, for example, might be replaced by another individual willing to take on the risks associated with the narcotics trade.

Finally, it is worth mentioning that some interventions may produce the complete opposite or reverse of a displacement effect, a *diffusion of benefits* (Poyner, 1988), where reductions in crime or disorder benefit people, places, or objects not directly targeted by prevention efforts. The phenomenon is also referred to as a "spillover effect" (Baker & Wolfer, 2003), "halo effect" (Scherdin, 1986), "free bonus effect" (Sherman, 1990), or "free-rider effect" (Miethe, 1991) and is thought to be caused by increasing the real or perceived risk of apprehension or decreasing the incentive to commit a crime by increasing the effort required and reducing the rewards (Clarke & Weisburd, 1994).

The problem-solving approach encourages experimentation with various prevention strategies to deal with crime and disorder. Planned responses, however, do not operate within a vacuum, uninfluenced by criminological thought. We now turn our attention to a popular criminological paradigm that often guides problem solvers in their efforts to devise a response to crime and disorder in their communities.

Opportunity Makes the Thief

Felson and Clarke (1998, p. 1) argue that "individual behavior is a product of an interaction between the person and the setting." Much of criminology, however, has devoted its energy toward understanding variations in individual proclivities towards criminality (remote causes) and has largely ignored the second element, the criminogenic setting (immediate causes), which "translate(s) criminal inclinations into action." In other words, expressions of the propensity to commit crime are structured by environmental conditions. If the milieu does not provide a tempting opportunity to commit a crime, criminal propensities are irrelevant. Therefore, the opportunity becomes a necessary causal condition for crime to occur.

Given the importance of opportunity in explaining crime, a number of theories—routine activities, crime pattern, rational choice—have incorporated the concept that "easy or tempting opportunities entice people into criminal action" (Felson & Clarke, 1998, p. 2). Furthermore, the idea that opportunities play a role in criminal conduct is intuitively appealing to law enforcement because it is readily amenable to the development of practical strategies to treat an immediate cause of crime. Considering the weight of opportunity in the crime equation, Felson & Clarke (1998, pp. v–vi) offer ten principles of crime opportunity to steer problem solvers into thinking about ways to respond to crime:

1. *Opportunities play a role in causing all crime.* Early explorations of opportunity as a causal factor had mistakenly been interpreted to mean that opportunity was limited to explaining common acquisitive crimes such as theft. The extant literature, however, illustrates how opportunity can logically account for all classes of crime—property, violent, victimless, and white collar offenses—and is therefore amenable to opportunity reduction techniques (Felson & Clarke, 1998, pp. 9–12).

2. *Crime opportunities are highly specific.* A global opportunity factor may not exist that can explain the entire universe of crimes. Similarly, opportunities may vary by crimes within the same legal category such as bank robbery or car theft. This is exactly why the utility of analyzing crimes as a violation of existing legal codes is not very helpful for crime reduction purposes. Instead, it is much better to think of criminal opportunities as varying by setting and motivation. In the case of bank robberies, for example, different modus operandi for those committing an "inside job" as compared to ordinary "stickups" exists that may require very different prevention strategies. In the case of car thefts, opportunity patterns may be different for those who steal cars to joyride, strip the automobile for their parts, or sell the entire vehicle to foreign markets (Felson & Clarke, 1998, pp. 13–14). This point drives home the importance of developing responses that are tailored to a specific situation.

3. *Crime opportunities are concentrated in time and space.* Criminal victimization does occur at random but has distinct temporal and spatial patterns that reflect differences in opportunities. Residential burglaries, for example, are attractive during the daytime hours because homes are likely to be unoccupied, thereby reducing the chances of being apprehended or hurt during a chance encounter with a homeowner. As discussed in a previous section of this chapter, "hotspots" demonstrate the idea that certain spaces can generate opportunities and attract criminal elements to a particular location (Felson & Clarke, 1998, pp. 14–15).

4. *Crime opportunities depend on everyday movements of activity.* Routine movements of everyday life based on work, school and recreation patterns can create opportunities for offenders.

"If vendors of snacks and drinks seek crowds, so do pickpockets, luggage thieves, and bag snatchers. Other offenders pay closer attention to the absence of people … the flow of workers home at night and on weekends produces a counter flow a few hours later of commercial and industrial burglars to take advantage of the situation" (Felson & Clarke, 1998, p. 16).

5. *One crime produces opportunities for another.* Crime begets crime in several different ways (Felson & Clarke, 1998, pp. *vi*, 17–19):
   - Blowing illegal gains on drugs or prostitutes
   - Repeating the offense later against the same victim or target
   - Spending time with co-offenders, who lead them into more crime
   - Spending time with dangerous people, who then victimize them
   - Spending more time in dangerous settings at dangerous hours
   - Provoking others to attack them
   - Developing expensive drug dependencies, thus leading to criminal acts
   - Impairing judgment through substance abuse, and then taking more risks
   - Creating "broken windows" environments where the perception of a breakdown of social controls invites offenders to the location
   - Being a victim of crime may justify committing one to make up for the loss (e.g., having a bike stolen and then stealing another's to compensate)

6. *Some products offer more tempting crime opportunities.* Some targets, also known as "hot products," are more attractive to offenders than other targets, particularly if the commodity has VIVA properties: the item has value, is portable (inertia), visible, and accessible (Felson & Clarke, 1998, pp. 19–20).

7. *Social and technological changes produce new crime opportunities.* Consumer products can experience life cycles—innovation, growth, mass market, and saturation—that predictably determine the likelihood that a product will be stolen. During the innovation stage, the product is expensive and appeals only to a small segment of consumers. From an offender's perspective, why take the risk when the product may not be easily fenced? During the growth and mass market phases, thefts will increase as the demand for such a product increases among the general population. During the saturation phase, thefts will decrease as the price drops to a level where most can afford the product, thereby removing any incentive to steal it (Felson & Clarke, 1998, pp. 22–23). Hand calculators, for example, were once expensive and in great demand but have become more affordable over time and currently so ubiquitous that they are now infrequently stolen.

8. *Crime can be prevented by reducing opportunities.* "If it were not true that reducing opportunities helps prevent crime, no-one would bother to take routine precautions such as locking their cars and houses, keeping their money in safe places, counseling their children to avoid strangers, and watching the neighbors' home when they are away" (Felson & Clarke, 1998, p. 23). Situational crime prevention techniques, discussed in the next section of this chapter, are particularly well-suited to addressing opportunities that give rise to crime.

9. *Reducing opportunities does not usually displace crime.* While displacement may diminish efforts at reducing crime, it is not a certainty that displacement will occur. Additionally, much evidence suggests that when displacement occurs it does not necessarily offset the gains of crime reduction efforts (Felson & Clarke, 1998, p. 28).

10. *Focused opportunity reduction can produce wider declines in crime.* As discussed in a previous section of this chapter, "diffusion of benefits" may be an unexpected dividend of crime

reduction efforts as offenders overestimate the reach of prevention efforts and "believe the measures have been implemented more widely than they really have, and that the effort needed to commit crime or the risks incurred have been increased for a wider range of places, times or targets than in fact is the case" (Felson & Clarke, 1998, p. 31).

Situational Crime Prevention Techniques

Ronald V. Clarke (1997), a pioneer in the area of crime prevention, defines situational prevention as "opportunity-reducing measures that (1) are directed at highly specific forms of crime, (2) involve the management, design or manipulation of the immediate environment in as systematic and permanent as possible, (3) make crime more difficult and risky, or less rewarding and excusable as judged by a wide range of offenders" (p. 4). Over the years, the situational crime prevention typology has expanded considerably and currently includes 25 techniques within 5 categories: increasing effort, increasing risk, reducing rewards, reducing provocations, and removing excuses.

Increase the effort. Making criminal opportunities difficult to execute may discourage offenders and is accomplished by target hardening, access control, screening exits, deflecting offenders, and controlling tools or weapons. *Target hardening* employs the use of physical barriers, such as locks or screens, to increase the difficulty of carrying off a crime. *Access control* prevents unauthorized persons from entering areas in which they do not belong and may provide an opportunity to examine objects brought into the environment (e.g., baggage screening procedures at airports). *Screening exits* prevents individuals from leaving a facility without paying for merchandise or services provided (e.g., electronic merchandise tags). *Deflecting offenders* employs techniques that avert offenders away from crime targets or provide alternatives to illegal behavior. Road closures, for example, prevent "johns" from cruising an area looking for street prostitutes. *Controlling tools or weapons* that make crime easier or possible to commit is the final subtype of the increasing effort category. For example, restricting sales of large quantities of products containing pseudoephedrine makes it difficult to manufacture methamphetamine on a large scale or on a frequent basis.

Increase the risk. Increasing the risk of detection, resistance, and apprehension is accomplished by extending guardianship, assisting natural surveillance, reducing anonymity, utilizing place managers, and strengthening formal surveillance. *Extending guardianship* involves taking precautionary measures to increase protection of persons or property. For example, leaving a light on at home while away is a signal of occupancy and may reduce the likelihood of burglary. *Assisting natural surveillance* entails enhancing the incidental ability for an environment to be observed by anyone without visual obstruction. Improved street lighting, for example, removes the refuge that darkness provides to offenders lying in wait. *Reducing anonymity*, as the name suggests, is based on the idea that people are less likely to commit a crime if they are easily identified. "How's my driving?" bumper stickers, for example, may reduce aggressive driving. *Utilizing place managers* takes advantage of employees who naturally monitor the work environment. Their presence alone may act as a deterrent. Convenience store robberies, for example, are significantly reduced if two clerks are on duty (Hunter & Jeffery, 1997). Finally, *strengthening formal surveillance* adds more security professionals—e.g., police and security guards—to the environment or provides technology, such as burglar alarms, to assist them in their crime prevention efforts.

Reduce the rewards. Eliminating or reducing the benefits of a crime is accomplished by concealing targets, removing targets, identifying property, disrupting markets, and denying benefits. *Concealing targets* may reduce the temptation to commit a crime (e.g., gender neutral phone listings may prevent obscene phone calls targeting females). *Removing targets* eliminates the opportunity for theft or violence. For example, domestic violence shelters remove the victim from her abuser. *Identifying property* reduces the attractiveness of targets because offenders risk certain prosecution for marked items that have been reported as stolen. *Disrupting markets* reduces the benefits to offenders who are interested in converting stolen items into currency. Carefully monitoring pawn shop transactions, for example, may decrease the ability to fence stolen goods. *Denying benefits* eliminates the ability to directly enjoy the crime (e.g., exploding ink tags ruins garments when tampered with).

Reduce Provocations. Eliminating noxious stimuli from the environment can be accomplished by reducing frustrations and stress, avoiding disputes, reducing emotional arousal, neutralizing peer pressure, and discouraging imitation. *Reducing frustrations and stress* in an environment can decrease a powerful emotional state, anger, and the likelihood of violence. Ample seating, for example, may reduce agitation associated with discomfort. *Avoiding disputes* is an attempt to reduce conflict. Fixed taxi fares, for example, eliminate arguments between passengers and cab drivers. *Reducing emotional arousal* can counteract feelings that may incite illegal behavior. Preventing pedophiles from having contact with children suppresses, at least for the moment, their unhealthy sexual desires. *Neutralizing peer pressure* is self-explanatory and can be accomplished, for example, with public service announcement such as "friends don't let friends drive drunk" and "drink responsibly" campaigns. Finally, *discouraging imitation* attempts to eliminate copycat crimes by, for example, withholding details about how crimes were committed in broadcast or print media or quickly removing signs of vandalism.

Remove excuses. Rationalization of criminal behavior can be neutralized by setting rules, posting instructions, alerting conscience, assisting compliance, and controlling drugs and alcohol. *Setting rules* explicitly establishes conduct expectations, reduces potential conflict, and promotes compliance with regulations. For example, requiring fishing licenses to be worn by outdoorsmen may decrease the number of anglers that intentionally fish without a license. *Posting instructions* removes excuses, such as ignorance of the law, for unacceptable behavior (e.g., "no parking," "don't feed the animals," or "no trespassing"). *Alerting conscience* makes an offender temporarily reconsider his or her behavior if he or she is contemplating or is engaged in an illegal act. Signs such as "shoplifting is stealing" and roadside speed displays that flash when motorists are driving above the posted speed limit are a few examples of this prevention strategy. *Assisting compliance* makes it easier for citizens to abide by the rules. Providing ample public restrooms, for example, can cut down on public urination. Finally, *controlling drugs and alcohol* is based on the idea that these substances facilitate crime and incivility by lowering inhibitions and impairing judgment. Regulating the sale of alcohol at sporting events (e.g., serving size, number of beverages that can be purchased per transaction, or cutting off sales at half-time) has become routine for many venues over concerns with drunk driving.

Evaluations of POP

As a testament to the popularity of the problem-oriented policing approach, there are well over 100 evaluations found in the research literature, with much evidence to suggest that POP outcomes are, overall, generally positive and moderately effective in reducing crime and disorder (Weisburd & Eck, 2004; Weisburd, Telep, Hinkle, & Eck, 2008). While an exhaustive review of the evaluation literature is not possible, three methodologically rigorous studies examining the impact of POP interventions on a wide range of problems—alcohol use, drug use, vandalism, violent crime, and disorder—are presented in the following sections.

Violent Hotspots in Jersey City

Using a crime mapping approach to scan for problems, Anthony Braga and his colleagues (1999) identified several locations in Jersey City, New Jersey that experienced abnormally high levels of violent crime, such as robbery, bar fights, carjacking, and street fighting. Twenty-four violent hotspots were paired together with one area in each pair randomly selected to receive POP treatment, while the nontreatment (control) group experienced routine patrol presence. All troubled areas were analyzed using existing crime data supplemented with interviews and residential surveys. Based on the results from the analysis phase, solutions were tailored for each area using an array of strategies, including: "(1) aggressive order maintenance, (2) drug enforcement, (3) requiring store owners to clean store fronts, (4) removing trash, (5) increased lighting, (6) housing code enforcement, (7) erecting fences around vacant lots, (8) cleaning vacant lots, (9) boarding and fencing abandoned buildings, (10) hanging signs explaining rules such as '*No Drinking,*' (11) video surveillance, (12) evicting troublesome tenants, (13) improving building security by adding locks, (14) disseminate crime prevention literature, (15) conducting code investigations of taverns, (16) parking enforcement, (17) razing abandoned buildings, (18) adding trash receptacles, (19) opening vacant lot for youth recreation, (20) graffiti removal, (21) directed patrol after school hours, (22) helping homeless find shelter and substance abuse treatment, (23) discouraging loitering, and (24) removing guns" (Braga, Weisburd, Waring, Mazerolle, Spelman, & Gajewski, 1999, p. 554).

Comparing crime incident reports and emergency calls for service 6 months prior to and after the POP intervention, the study reported significant reductions for the treatment groups as compared to the control groups in terms of total criminal incidents and calls for service. Additionally, there were statistically significant decreases for calls related to street fighting, property offenses, and narcotics, as well as the incidence of robberies and property offenses. Signs of social disorder, such as public drinking or loitering, and physical disorder, such as trash, graffiti, and broken windows, decreased for 10 of the 11 treatment areas (one was excluded because the data were not properly collected). With respect to displacement the study found that most of the crimes analyzed, except for property offenses, were not displaced into surrounding areas and that a diffusion of benefits was reported for disorder calls and assault incidents.

Drug and Disorder Problems in Oakland

Mazerolle, Price and Roehl (2000) conducted a randomized experiment evaluating the Oakland Police Department's Beat Health Unit, a program designed to alleviate drug and disorder issues. The Beat Health Unit uses civil remedies to coerce property owners to clean up nuisance locations that have come to their attention because of a high number of emergency calls, narcotics arrests, or complaints made by community groups. Nuisance locations are evaluated by the Beat Health Team and other city officials to identify problems and to work with place managers to make positive changes such as cleaning up or fixing properties and enhancing security. The study identified 100 sites referred to the Beat Unit and randomly selected half of the locations to receive the Beat Health intervention with the remaining sites receiving routine patrol coverage.

Calls for service for violent, property, drug, and disorder offenses were analyzed 12 months prior to the intervention, during the intervention period (a 5.5-month period), and 12 months after the intervention. The study found significant decreases between the experimental and control group with respect to calls related to drugs but no intervention effect for other crimes examined for residential locations. As for changes in commercial locations, the investigation did report a significantly lower number of calls related to disorder, but no other intervention effects were reported.

Regarding visible signs of disorder, observational data did evidence a decrease in males selling drugs and increases in civil interactions in the experimental locations (Mazerolle, Price, & Roehl, 2000, pp. 230–231). In terms of spatial displacement, commercial sites did evidence an increase in drug calls in surrounding areas but it was much more pronounced in commercial sites in the control group, highlighting the deleterious impact that a patrol-only strategy has on drug crimes. Finally, the investigation reported "a positive diffusion of crime control benefits beyond the residential experimental sites" (Mazerolle, Price, & Roehl, 2000, p. 234).

Park Vandalism and Substance Use in Suburban Pennsylvania

Baker and Wolfer (2003) evaluated the impact of interventions designed to respond to vandalism, drug, and alcohol use in a public park located in a small suburban town in Pennsylvania. During the scanning and analysis phase, officers made careful observations of the park and noted that many overgrown bushes obstructed natural surveillance and provided refuge for offenders to hide. Fences had also been cut to provide escape routes if law enforcement presence was detected. Also, surveys and crime maps identified hotspots where most of the problems were occurring. In response, the officers decided to abandon random patrols in favor of proactive patrols of hotspot areas and instituted a variety of situational crime prevention tactics—e.g., pruning or removing overgrown vegetation, installing closed-circuit surveillance cameras, improving lighting, repairing fences, limiting access at night, posting signs reminding park users of park rules and regulations, and removing pay phones suspected of being used by drug dealers. Additionally, the officers vigorously enforced juvenile curfew and public drinking laws and increased their communications with community residents with monthly meetings and the publication of a crime newsletter.

A quasi-experimental study was conducted to evaluate the impact of the POP intervention. Questionnaires were administered to a large random sample of citizens residing by the park, the target group, and compared to a large random sample of citizens residing elsewhere, the nonequivalent comparison group. Surveys administered prior to the POP intervention found significant differences between the target and comparison group in terms of fear of the park during daytime and evening hours. The postintervention data found a significant difference between the two groups, but now the target group was more likely to feel safe in the park during the day than the comparison group. There were no differences in fear between the two groups for evening hours. In terms of criminal victimization, the target group reported significant reductions in vandalism, breaking and entering, property theft, and witnessing drunk and disorderly persons harassing citizens after the intervention. Finally, the authors suggested that displacement to a coffee shop in the downtown area may have taken place as a result of the intervention but did not conduct any tests of statistical significance.

BOX 3-4 Learn More About Problem-Oriented Policing

The Center for Problem-Oriented Policing is a nonprofit organization that has won many awards for the content and design of their website. The website offers a variety of practical guidance on responding to a wide array of problems, case studies employing the SARA model, and interactive problem-solving tools such as the Problem Analysis Module (PAM). Visit www.popcenter.org to learn more about problem-solving approaches to crime and disorder.

Intelligence-Led Policing: Proactive Directed Patrols of Hotspots

Early in this chapter we discussed the research evaluating the crime prevention value of random patrol. One of the strongest and most consistent findings in policing crime prevention literature is that the general random presence of patrol officers does not serve as an effective crime prevention tool. However, in contrast, the development of deployment strategies that focus police patrol resources on specific targets do appear to hold more crime prevention potential. In the following section we discuss why this new intelligence-led practice of proactive directed patrols has increased since the 1990s and we review some of the research evaluating the crime prevention value of this approach.

There have been at least two major contributing factors to the increased use of proactive directed patrols by police departments. These factors include the increased popularity of the "broken windows" hypothesis for explaining the escalation of urban disorder and crime, and the increased reliance on technology for a more efficient deployment of police resources. The broken windows hypothesis was established in a landmark article written by James Q. Wilson and George Kelling (1982). Wilson and Kelling argued that local forms of disorder and incivilities, however minor, if not addressed will lead to more serious crime. These incivilities can take the form of social (e.g., public intoxication, open-air drug markets, and loud parties) or physical (e.g., litter, graffiti, and abandoned buildings) disorder. Lack of attention to these problems, either by the police or residents, can communicate the message that "no one cares," thereby inviting additional disorder and more serious crime. Additional increases in disorder may increase residents' fear of crime to the point where they become more withdrawn and isolated and less likely to take collective actions to make improvements to public safety. This belief caused Wilson and Kelling and others to advocate for the aggressive enforcement of less serious crime and informal community norms by the police. This has been referred to as aggressive order maintenance policing and is consistent with the use of proactive directed patrols that evolved in the 1990s. A second factor contributing to the increased presence of proactive directed police patrols is technological advancements that aid police departments in identifying concentrations of crime and disorder. The use of computer mapping software (GIS) and spatial crime analysis within police departments has assisted in the identification of locations where there is as strong intersection between both traditional predatory street crime (e.g., robbery) and disorder (e.g., calls for police service to address drug dealing). The rationale supporting the identification and targeting of these "hotspots" is based on the perceived failure of the general random patrol approach that drew criticism based on the results of the Kansas City Patrol Experiment (Kelling et al., 1974). Specifically, that criticism lies in the belief that general random patrol spreads police resources too thin and devotes too many patrol units to areas generally not affected by crime. In contrast, the directed patrol hypothesis argues that a proactive patrol strategy that is directed at known problem locations is a more effective and efficient use of police resources

---

BOX 3-5 Learn More About Hotspot Policing

The National Institute of Justice (NIJ) has developed a website to help law enforcement find the resources to identify, predict, and respond to hotspots. Visit www.nij.gov/nij/topics/law-enforcement/strategies/hot-spot-policing/welcome.htm to learn more about hotspot policing and download free geospatial tools for crime mapping.

(Buerger, Cohn, & Petrosino, 2000). There is growing evidence supporting the proactive use of patrol resources directed at problem locations.

There have been a number of important studies investigating the crime prevention benefit of concentrating police resources at hotspots. One of the first tests of the directed patrol hypothesis came shortly after the publication of the original Kansas City Patrol Experiment. In response to an increase in crime occurring in the New York City subway system, the number of officers employed by the Transit Authority Police Force was nearly tripled. In addition, resources were directed to provide additional patrols on trains and subway stations during the night. The evaluation of this study found that a substantial reduction in felony crime was associated with this increase in directed patrols (Chaiken, Lawless, & Stevenson, 1975). One of the largest implementations and tests of the directed patrol hypothesis took place in Minneapolis. There were a total of 110 hotspot street corner intersections that were identified, and half of these locations received increased patrols, especially during peak periods or "hot times." The evaluation utilized the other 55 hotspot locations as a control group, and these areas did not receive increased directed patrols. The research utilized both police call-for-service data and the observations of street corner disorder assessed by trained observers. The evaluators were able to determine that the directed patrols were associated with modest improvements in crime prevention as measured by calls for service, and substantial improvements in the reduction of disorder as measured by the trained observers (Sherman & Weisburd, 1995). Recently there has been an increased use of proactive directed patroling to address hotspots of drug activity. Operation Safe Streets was implemented in Philadelphia in 2002 and involved the placement of patrol officers in approximately 200 high drug activity locations on a continuous basis. The evaluation of this program suggests that the strategic placement of these officers was not associated with a citywide impact on drug crime or violent crime. However, when analyzing the specific target locations over time there was evidence of a deterrent effect for both drug crime and violent crime (Lawton, Taylor, & Luongo, 2005). Finally, an important trend within directed patrol that has increased recently is the integration of problem-solving approaches with the proactive patrol activity. These approaches frequently blend aggressive forms of directed patrol with situational crime prevention and other problem-oriented approaches. Results from two evaluations in Lowell, Massachusetts (Braga & Bond, 2008) and Jersey City, New Jersey (Braga, Weisburd, Waring, Mazerolle, Spelman, & Gajewski, 1999) suggest that these represent some of the most promising modern approaches to crime prevention. The targeted patrol approach and comprehensive problem-solving strategy in these cities were associated with significant improvements in the reduction of crime, drug sales, and general neighborhood disorder.

BOX 3-6 What Works in Policing?

What policing strategies work? The new climate in policing is grounded in evidence-based practices. However, there is great difficulty sorting through hundreds of evaluations, varying in methodological rigor, to determine which activities are found to be scientifically effective. The Center for Evidence-Based Crime Policy at George Mason University has created an online research-to-practice visual tool to assist law enforcement in their crime prevention efforts. The matrix organizes research along three dimensions: (1) level of proactivity, (2) specific or general focus, and (3) type or scope of target. Visit http://gemini.gmu.edu/cebcp/Matrix/index.html to learn more.

SUMMARY

Policing is a grand social experiment that has consistently demonstrated a willingness to consider new strategies and jettison ineffective practices. History shows us that crime prevention has been a central mission of law enforcement since the very first public police force was organized in London nearly 2 centuries ago. Major shifts in policing strategies in the past 40 years—community-oriented, problem-oriented, and intelligence-led policing—have shown great promise and are a testament to the idea that policing is amenable to experimentation and scientific evaluation. What the future will hold for policing is uncertain, but we can be confident that law enforcement will continue to test new ideas in order to fulfill its crime prevention mission.

KEY TERMS

Preventive patrol
Foot patrol
Community policing
Proactive patrol of hotspots
"Means over ends" syndrome
Incident-driven policing
SARA model
Problem Analysis Triangle (PAT)
Situational crime prevention
Process and outcome evaluation
Displacement effect
    Benign and malign
    Offense, temporal, spatial, target, tactical, offender
Diffusion of benefits
Principles of crime opportunity
Routine activities theory
Problem types
    Behavior, place, persons, time

DISCUSSION QUESTIONS

1. What does the Kansas City Preventive Patrol Experiment suggest about the ability of the police to prevent crime through their traditional motorized presence?
2. In what important ways do modern crime prevention strategies (e.g., problem-oriented policing) employed by the police differ from the more traditional approaches (e.g., motorized preventive patrol)?
3. How did the use of foot patrol in Flint and Lexington differ from the use of foot patrol in Newark? How might these differences help us explain the disparate crime prevention outcomes reported in these evaluations?
4. What are the five broad typological categories of situational crime prevention techniques?
5. What are the three sides of the problem analysis triangle (PAT)?
6. What are the four problem types that the SARA model attempts to identify during the scanning phase?

REFERENCES

Baker, T. E., & Wolfer, L. (2003). The crime triangle: Alcohol, drug use, and vandalism. *Police Practice and Research: An International Journal, 4*(1), 47–61.

Barr, R., & Pease, K. (1990). Crime placement, displacement, and deflection. In M. Tonry & N. Morris (Eds.), *Crime and justice: A review of research* (Vol. 12, pp. 277–318). Chicago, IL: University of Chicago Press.

Bayley, D. H. (1988). Community policing: A report from the devil's advocate. In J. R. Greene & S. D. Mastrofski, (Eds.), *Community policing: Rhetoric or reality?* (pp. 225–238). New York, NY: Praeger.

Bayley, D. H. (1994). *Police for the future.* New York, NY: Oxford University Press.

Braga, A. A., & Bond, B. J. (2008). Policing crime and disorder hot spots: A randomized, controlled trial. *Criminology, 46,* 577–607.

Braga, A. A., Weisburd, D. L., Waring, E. J., Mazerolle, L. G., Spelman, W., & Gajewski, F. (1999). Problem-oriented policing in violent crime places: A randomized controlled experiment. *Criminology, 37*(3), 541–580.

Buerger, M. E. (1994). The limits of community. In D. P. Rosenbaum (Ed.), *The challenge of community policing: Testing the promises* (pp. 270–273). Thousand Oaks, CA: Sage Publications.

Buerger, M. E., Cohn, E. G., & Petrosino, A. J. (2000). Defining the hot spots of crime: Operationalizing theoretical concepts for field research. In R. W. Glensor, M. E. Correia, & K. J. Peak (Eds.), *Policing communities: Understanding crime and solving problems* (pp. 138–150). Los Angeles, CA: Roxbury Publishing Company.

Chaiken, J. M., Lawless, M., & Stevenson, K. (1975). The impact of police activity on crime: Robberies on the New York City Subway System. *Urban Analysis, 3,* 173–205.

Cirel, P., Evans, P., McGillis, D., & Whitcomb, D. (1977). *Community crime prevention program in Seattle: An exemplary project.* Washington, DC: U.S. Department of Justice, National Institute of Justice.

Clarke, R. V. (1997). *Situational crime prevention: Successful case studies* (2nd ed.). Monsey, NY: Criminal Justice Press.

Clarke, R. V., & Weisburd, D. (1994). Diffusion of crime control benefits: Observations on the reverse of displacement. In R. V. Clarke (Ed.), *Crime prevention studies* (Vol. 2, pp. 165–182). Monsey, NY: Criminal Justice Press.

Cordner, G. W. (1994). Foot patrol without community policing: Law and order in public housing. In D. P. Rosenbaum (Ed.), *The challenge of community policing: Testing the promises* (pp. 182–191). Thousand Oaks, CA: Sage Publications.

Cordner, G. W. (2000). Community policing: Elements and effects. In G. P. Alpert & A. R. Piquero (Eds.), *Community policing: Contemporary readings* (2nd ed. pp. 45–62). Prospect Heights, IL: Waveland.

Cornish, D. B., & Clarke, R. V. (2003). Opportunities, precipitators, and criminal decisions: A reply to Wortley's critique of situational crime prevention. In M. J. Smith & D. B. Cornish (Eds.), *Theory for practice in Situational Crime Prevention.* Monsey, NY: Criminal Justice Press.

Correia, M. E. (2000). Social capital and sense of community building: Building social cohesion. In R. W. Glensor, M. E. Correia, & K. J. Peak (Eds.), *Policing communities: Understanding crime and solving problems* (pp. 75–82). Los Angeles, CA: Roxbury Publishing Company.

Davis, R. C., Smith, B. E., Lurigio, A. J., & Skogan, W. G. (1991). *Community response to crack: Grassroots anti-drug programs.* Report of the Victim Services Agency, New York, to the National Institute of Justice.

Eck, J. E., & Spelman, W. (1987a). *Problem solving: Problem-oriented policing in Newport News.* Washington, DC: Police Executive Research Forum.

Eck, J. E., & Spelman, W. (1987b). Who ya gonna call? The police as problem-busters. *Crime & Delinquency, 33*(1), 31–52.

Felson, M., & Clarke, R. V. (1998). *Opportunity makes the thief: Practical theory for crime prevention.* London, England: Home Office, Policing and Reducing Crime Unit.

Farrington, D. P. (1982). Randomized experiments on crime and justice. In M. Tonry. & N. Morris (Eds.), *Crime and justice: An annual review of research.* Chicago, IL: University of Chicago Press.

Fridell, Lorie (1994). The defining characteristics of community policing. In L. Fridell & M. A. Wycoff (Eds.), *Community policing: The past, present, and future* (pp. 3–12). Washington, DC: Police Executive Research Forum.

Garofalo, J., & McLeod, M. (1986). *Improving the effectiveness and utilization of Neighborhood Watch programs*. Draft final report to the National Institute of Justice. Albany, NY: State University of New York at Albany, Hindelang Criminal Justice Research Center.

Goldstein, H. (1979). Improving police: A problem-oriented approach. *Crime & Delinquency, 25*(2), 236–258.

Goldstein, H. (2001). *What is POP?* Retrieved from http://www.popcenter.org/about/?p=whatiscpop

Hunter, R. D., & Jeffery, C. R. (1997). Preventing convenience store robbery through environmental design. In R. V. Clarke (Ed.), *Situational crime prevention: Successful case studies* (2nd ed., pp. 191–199). Monsey, NY: Criminal Justice Press.

Kansas City Missouri Police Department (1977). Police Response Time Analysis.

Kelling, G. L., Pate, A. M., Dieckman, D., & Brown, C. (1974). *The Kansas City preventive patrol experiment: A technical report*. Washington, DC: Police Foundation.

Kinney, J. A. (1979, November). *Isla Vista foot patrol*. Paper presented at the annual meeting of the American Society of Criminology, Philadelphia, PA.

Lab, S. P. (2010). *Crime prevention: Approaches, practices and evaluations* (7th ed.). Cincinnati, OH: Anderson Publishing.

Lane, R. (1975). *Policing the city: Boston, 1822–1885*. New York, NY: Atheneum.

Larson, R. (1975). What happened to patrol operations in Kansas City? *Journal of Criminal Justice, 3*, 299–330.

Latessa, E., & Allen, H. (1980). Using citizens to prevent crime: An example of deterrence and community involvement. *Journal of Police Science and Administration, 8*(1), 69–74.

Lavrakas, P. J. (1986). Evaluating police-community anticrime newsletters: The Evanston, Houston, and Newark field studies. In D. P. Rosenbaum (Ed.), *Community crime prevention: Does it work?* (pp. 269–291). Beverly Hills, CA: Sage Publications.

Lawton, B. A., Taylor, R. B., & Luongo, A. J. (2005). Police officers on drug corners in Philadelphia, drug crime, and violent crime: Intended, diffusion, and displacement impacts. *Justice Quarterly, 22*, 427–451.

Lentz, S. A., & Chaires, R. H. (2007). The invention of Peel's principles: A study of policing "textbook" history. *Journal of Criminal Justice, 35*(1), 69–79.

Maguire, E. R., & Mastrofski, S. D. (2000). Patterns of community policing in the United States. *Police Quarterly, 3*(1), 4–45.

Mastrofski, S. D. (1988). Community policing as reform: A cautionary tale. In J. R. Greene & S. D. Mastrofski (Eds.), *Community policing: Rhetoric or reality?* (pp. 47–68). New York, NY: Praeger.

Mazerolle, L. G., Price, J. F., & Roehl, J. (2000). Civil remedies and drug control: A randomized field trial in Oakland, California. *Evaluation Review, 24*(2), 212–241.

Mazerolle, L. G., & Roehl, J. (Eds.). (1998). *Civil remedies and crime prevention* (Vol. 9). Boulder, CO: Lynne Rienner.

Miethe, T. D. (1991). Citizen-based crime control activity and victimization risks: An examination of displacement and free-rider effects. *Criminology, 29*(3), 419–439.

National Advisory Commission on Criminal Justice Standards and Goals. (1973). *Police*. Washington, DC: Government Printing Office.

New Police Instructions (1829, September 25). *The Times*.

O'Keefe, G. J., Rosenbaum, D. P., Lavrakas, P. J., Reid, K., & Botta, R. A. (1996). *Take a bite out of crime: The impact of a national prevention campaign*. Newbury Park, CA: Sage.

Pate, A. M. (1986). Experimenting with foot patrol: The Newark experience. In D. P. Rosenbaum (Ed.), *Community crime prevention: Does it work?* (pp. 137–156). Beverly Hills, CA: Sage Publications.

Pate, A. M., Lavrakas, P. J., Wycoff, M. A., Skogan, W. G., & Sherman, L. W. (1985). *Neighborhood police newsletters: Technical report*. Washington, DC: Police Foundation.

Pate, A. M., McPherson, M., & Silloway, G. (Eds.) (1987). *The Minneapolis community crime prevention experiment*. Draft evaluation report. Washington, DC: Police Foundation.

Pate, T., Ferrara, A., Bowers, R. A., & Lorence, J. (1976). *Police response time: Its determinants and effects*. Washington, DC: Police Foundation.

Pendland, M. B., & Gay, W. G. (1972). Foot patrols: The Fort Worth experience. *Police Chief, 39*(4), 46–48.

Pennell, S., Curtis, C., & Henderson, J. (1985). *Guardian Angels: An assessment of citizen responses to crime* (Vol. 2). Technical report to the National Institute of Justice. San Diego, CA: San Diego Association of Governments.

Police Foundation (1981). *The Newark foot patrol experiment.* Washington, DC: Police Foundation.

Popkin, S. J., Gwiasda, V. E., Amendolia, J. M., Anderson, A. A., Hanson, G., Johnson, W. A., Martel, E., Olson, L. M., & Rosenbaum, D. P. (1996). *The hidden war: The battle to control crime in Chicago's public housing.* Final Report. Washington, DC: U.S. Department of Justice, National Institute of Justice.

Poyner, B. (1988). Video cameras and bus vandalism. *Security Administration, 11*(2), 44–51.

Reiss, A. (1971). *The police and the public.* New Haven, CT: Yale University Press.

Reppetto, T. (1976). Crime prevention and the displacement phenomenon. *Crime and Delinquency, 22,* 166–177.

Resource Planning Corporation (1975). *A survey of households and building establishments in foot patrol, scooter patrol, and control areas in Arlington County, VA.* Unpublished manuscript.

Rosenbaum, D. P. (1987). The theory and research behind Neighborhood Watch: Is it a sound fear and crime reduction strategy? *Crime and Delinquency, 33,* 103–134.

Rosenbaum, D. P., & Kaminska, S. J. (1997). *Salt Lake City's Comprehensive Communities Program: A case study.* Cambridge, MA: BOTEC Analysis Corporation.

Rosenbaum, D. P., Lewis, D. A., & Grant, J. A. (1985). *The impact of community crime prevention programs in Chicago: Can neighborhood organizations make a difference?* Evanston, IL: Northwestern University, Center for Urban Affairs and Policy Research.

Rosenbaum, D. P., Lurigio, A. J., & Davis, R. C. (1998). *The prevention of crime: Social and situational strategies.* Belmont, CA: West/Wadsworth.

Scherdin, M. J. (1986). The halo effect: Psychological deterrence of electronic security systems. *Information Technology and Libraries, 5*(3), 232–235.

Scott, J. D. (2002). Assessing the relationship between police-community coproduction and neighborhood-level social capital. *Journal of Contemporary Criminal Justice, 18,* 147–166.

Sherman, L. (1990). Police crackdowns: Initial and residual deterrence. In M. Tonry & N. Morris (Eds.), *Crime and justice: A review of research* (Vol. 12, pp. 1–48). Chicago, IL: University of Chicago Press.

Sherman, L. W., Gottfredson, D., MacKenzie, D., Eck, J., Reuter, P., & Bushway, S. (1997). *Preventing crime: What works, what doesn't, what's promising?* Washington, DC: A Report to the United States Congress prepared for the National Institute of Justice, U.S. Department of Justice.

Sherman, L. W., & Weisburd, D. (1995). General deterrent effects of police patrol in "hot spots": A randomized, controlled trial. *Justice Quarterly, 12,* 625–648.

Skogan, W. G. (1990). *Disorder and decline: Crime and the spiral of decay in American neighborhoods.* Los Angeles, CA: University of California Press.

Skogan, W. G., & Hartnett, S. M. (1997). *Community policing, Chicago style.* New York, NY: Oxford University Press.

Skogan, W. G., Hartnett, S. M., DuBois, J., Comey, J. T., Kaiser, M., & Lovig, J. H. (2000). *Problem solving in practice: Implementing community policing in Chicago* (Research report). Washington, DC: National Institute of Justice, U.S. Department of Justice.

Skogan, W. G., & Rosenbaum, D. P. (1997). *Fort Worth's Comprehensive Communities Program: A case study.* Cambridge, MA: BOTEC Analysis Corporation.

Skogan, W. G., & Wycoff, M. A. (1986). Storefront police offices: The Houston field test. In D. P. Rosenbaum (Ed.), *Community crime prevention: Does it work?* (pp. 179–199). Beverly Hills, CA: Sage Publications.

Spelman, W., & Brown, D. K. (1981). *Calling the police: A replication of the citizen reporting component of the Kansas City response time analysis.* Washington, DC: Police Executive Research Forum.

The Problem Analysis Triangle. (n.d.). Retrieved http://www.popcenter.org/about/?p=triangle.

The Sara Model. (n.d.). Retrieved from http://www.popcenter.org/about/?p=sara.

Trojanowicz, R. C. (1986). Evaluating a neighborhood foot patrol program: The Flint, Michigan project. In D. P. Rosenbaum (Ed.). *Community crime prevention: Does it work?* (pp. 157–178). Beverly Hills, CA: Sage Publications.

Uchida, C., Forst, B., & Annan, S. (1992). *Modern policing and the control of illegal drugs: Testing new strategies in two American cities* (Summary report). Washington, DC: National Institute of Justice; U.S. Department of Justice.

U.S. Department of Justice. (2010). *Problem-solving tips: A guide to reducing crime and disorder through problem-solving partnerships.* Washington, DC: Office of Community Oriented Policing Services.

Walker, S. (1998). *Popular justice: A history of American criminal justice.* New York, NY: Oxford University Press.

Weisburd, D., & Eck, J. E. (2004). What can police do to reduce crime, disorder, and fear? *The ANNALS of the American Academy of Political and Social Science, 593*(May), 42–65.

Weisburd, D., Telep, C., Hinkle, J., & Eck, J. (2008). *Effects of problem-oriented policing on crime and disorder.* Retrieved from http://www.ncjrs.gov/pdffiles1/nij/grants/224990.pdf.

Wilson, J. Q., & Kelling, G. (1982). Broken windows. *Atlantic Monthly, 249,* 29–38.

Wilson, O. W. (1977). *Police administration* (4th ed.). New York, NY: McGraw-Hill.

Wycoff, M. A., & Skogan, W. G. (1993). *Community policing in Madison: Quality from the inside out. An evaluation of implementation and impact* (Technical report). Washington, DC: Police Foundation.

CHAPTER 4

Guns and Crime: Crime Facilitation Versus Crime Prevention

Kristine Levan
Plymouth State University

INTRODUCTION

On April 16, 2007, Americans watched as events unfolded in the deadliest shooting incident by a lone gunman in the nation's history. Now known as the Virginia Tech massacre, the sequence of events included the deaths of 32 individuals, as well as injuries to many others. The shooter, Seung-Hui Cho, committed suicide shortly after committing these egregious acts. Many compared the mass shooting to the events that had occurred at Columbine High School just 8 years before, where 12 students and 1 teacher were killed by students Eric Harris and Dylan Klebold before they also killed themselves.

These extraordinary cases are the exception rather than the rule. Many gun-related crimes are those that simply involve the presence of a firearm that may actually never be discharged. When guns are used in commission of crimes, there is often a single victim, rather than multiple victims, as illustrated by the previous examples. However, high-profile cases such as these create a great deal of controversy over a variety of issues since these are the cases to which the public is most often exposed. In addition to raising concern over mental health issues, concerns over both gun availability and gun ownership have been brought to the forefront. Debate ensues over who is ultimately responsible for this type of tragedy. However, the primary concern for many is how to prevent atrocities such as these from occurring in the first place.

THE SCOPE OF FIREARM OWNERSHIP IN THE UNITED STATES

The United States leads modern developed countries in firearm ownership. Even though other countries have similar rates of violence, America is unique in its levels of lethal violence, in part due to the availability of guns (Zimring & Hawkins, 1997). For example, Japan, which has very stringent laws on firearms, has very low crime rates (Kaplan, 2007). In contrast, since banning handguns in 1997, England's crime rate has more than doubled (Malcolm, 2003). However, other countries such as Switzerland and Finland also have relatively high levels of gun ownership but correspondingly low levels of homicide (Lott, 2000; Kates & Mauser, 2007). Russia, which has relatively low levels of gun ownership, has extremely high murder rates, and in Luxembourg, where firearm ownership is practically nonexistent and handguns have been completely banned, homicide rates remain relatively high (Kates & Mauser, 2007).

American culture has been strongly associated with firearms throughout its history. In 1970, America was described as having a "gun culture" due to the long-held belief that guns are considered a necessity and a right granted to all Americans (Hofstadter, 1970). Attempts to curb firearm ownership are often met with great resistance for multiple reasons. Early U.S. settlers were dependent on firearms for survival and protection. Guns were necessary for hunting as well as for protection, and as settlers moved westward, they carried their firearms with them (Spitzer, 2007). Of course, it should be remembered that much of America's violent past has been romanticized and mythologized (Alvarez & Bachman, 2008; Riedel & Welsh, 2008). As quoted in Riedel and Welsh (2008, p. 36), one historian cites that "... nowhere in the Wild West, nor ever, did any two cowboys or anyone else stand in the middle of a street, revolvers strapped to their sides, and challenge each other to a fatal 'quick draw' contest" (Lane, 1997, p. 171).

Couple the historical involvement with firearms with America's desire and need for independence, and it seems likely that any attempt at government involvement in controlling firearms will be viewed as intrusive and invading on individual rights and civil liberties.

At any given time, there are more than 258 million firearms in circulation in the United States, 93 million of which are handguns (Braga & Pierce, 2005). Approximately 40% of households report ownership of at least one firearm (NRC, 2005, as cited in Riedel & Welsh, 2008). The primary sources used in determining the prevalence of firearm possession are survey data of individuals and firearm production data. However, this data does not present the whole spectrum of firearm ownership since it does not account for guns that were already in existence, some of which have made their way into the black market for firearms.

As with all survey data, some individuals may also not be truthful as to whether they currently own a firearm, nor as to how many firearms they currently own. As with most crime-related data, facts on gun ownership and gun usage are often based on a collaboration of various sources. For instance, the Uniform Crime Report (UCR), the National Incident Based Reporting System (NIBRS), and the National Crime Victimization Survey (NCVS) may be combined to allow for an understanding of the overall scope of firearm ownership and use in the United States.

The prevalence of reported firearm ownership is based on various factors. Geographically, there are far more firearms in the Southern states than in any other location within the United States (Cook & Ludwig, 1995). The frequency of firearm ownership among Southern residents is often linked to a culture of honor among them, especially for males (Cohen & Nisbett, 1994, as cited in Felson & Pare, 2010). This culture of honor dictates that males are expected to defend others, as well as themselves, against both perceived physical and verbal threats (Greenberg, 1997, as cited in Felson & Pare, 2010). Moreover, the Southern states have a historical reliance on vigilante justice (Chilton, 2004, as cited in Felson & Pare, 2010). Southern states developed formal law enforcement well after its development in the Northern states, leaving many Southern residents with a tendency toward self-reliance in dispute resolution (Courtright, 1996; Vandal, 2000, as cited in Felson & Pare, 2010)

These regional differences in firearms ownership and usage are complicated by the fact that those who reside in more rural locations are more likely to report owning a firearm than those who reside in either urban or suburban areas (Kleck, 1991; Cook & Ludwig, 1995). Additionally, sporting activities, such as hunting and sharpshooting, are far more prevalent among those who live in both Southern and rural locations, which may explain the pro-gun values that are common among these residents (Ellison, 1991, as cited in Felson & Pare, 2010).

Individual demographics can also explain a variance in reported firearm ownership. Closely related to the above differences between rural, urban, and suburban locations are the racial and gender differences in weapons carrying. There is an increased likelihood for whites to report owning a firearm when compared with African Americans. However, there has been scant research on inner-city youths residing in the Southern states (Spano, Freilich, & Bollard, 2002). This means that there may indeed be scores of firearms being carried illegally that are completely unaccounted for in both official statistics and research-based data.

Males are also significantly more likely to own a firearm than females (Cook, Moore, & Braga, 2002, as cited in Wyant & Taylor, 2007). This may be due to an increased propensity for males to be involved in hunting and sporting activities, to be employed in positions that require a firearm (such as a law enforcement officer), or because males are more likely to be drawn to firearms when considering options for self-defense and protection.

AMERICA'S GUN CULTURE

The debate in America continues as individuals remain divided over the right to own and carry a firearm. Those who oppose gun restrictions cite the Second Amendment's statement of "the right of the people to keep and bear arms" as a testament to an individual's right to own a firearm. More than three-quarters of Americans believe that the Second Amendment guarantees citizens the right to own a firearm, although many of those surveyed also believe that the government has the right to impose gun restrictions to some extent (CNN Poll, 2009). (For additional discussion on Second Amendment rights as they apply to other weapons, see **Box 4-1**.) Public opinion on gun control also has a tendency to fluctuate, depending on recent current events and perceptions of government imposition of restrictions on the individual's right to own firearms.

Those who endorse gun restrictions often state that owning and carrying a firearm is a privilege, not a right, and should be controlled to ensure that guns can generally be kept out of the hands of criminals. Still others hold that guns should be banned altogether, believing that they contribute to a great deal of crime and disorder in society. The important issue to note in the discussion in the following sections on the pro- and anti-gun cultures is that both refer exclusively to noncriminogenic populations. There are, of course, individuals who are pro-gun and are not characterized in the following description below but are proponents of firearms because of their personal intent to use them to commit crimes.

Pro-Gun Culture

Pro-gun advocates cite the potential protection of one's self, family, and home as a primary reason for arming citizens. Guns are also a necessity for certain types of activities, especially hunting. Advocates also explain that firearms are essential for certain professions, such as military and police forces.

It is important to note that political ideology often plays a role in an individual's stance on firearms. Those who belong to the pro-gun culture are typically conservative and Republican, although there are, of course notable exceptions to this generalization (Gimpel, 1998, as cited in Luna, 2002). Corresponding to this political ideology is the strong emphasis on the Second Amendment right to bear arms, in particular against a tyrannical government (Bogus, 1998, as cited in Luna, 2002). The greatest fear for those ascribing to the pro-gun culture would be an attempt by the government to

---

BOX 4-1 Second Amendment to the U.S. Constitution

The Second Amendment to the U.S. Constitution states: "A well regulated Militia, being necessary to the security of a free State, the right of the people to keep and bear Arms, shall not be infringed." This language has been up for much debate over the years. For instance, the meaning of the term "Militia" as used in the amendment may be taken in different ways. Do the individual people constitute a "Militia," or does it only apply to soldiers?

Recently, the arguments over the Second Amendment have extended beyond firearms to include other types of weapons, such as knives. Some locations are forgoing their previous bans on certain types of weapons. Individual cities in the state of Arizona have disallowed certain types of knives. For example, in Phoenix the only knives permitted to be carried are pocketknives, and in Tempe, no knives are considered legal (Lacey, 2010).

However, the state has now placed the discretion back to its state legislature, rather than leaving discretion to individual cities, which permits ownership and carrying of a wide range of knives. Knife advocates are now using the Second Amendment's guarantee as providing a constitutional basis to carry a knife. Others still fear that these weapons can be easily concealed and used to commit violent crime, and therefore should be banned (Lacey, 2010).

The knife arguments on both sides are interesting ones, and in many ways echo those on both sides of the debate on firearms. Will the nation see more states lift bans on various types of knives? As the debate over gun control continues, it is possible that debates over knife control may become more of a part of the controversy.

---

collectively disarm all the country's citizens, rendering them helpless against tyranny (Herz, 1995, as cited in Luna, 2002).

As stated previously, a great deal of support for a pro-gun culture emerges on a geographical basis, with those residing in the Southern and Western areas of the United States being more likely to own a firearm and/or ascribe to pro-gun values (Weisberg, 2002, as cited in Luna, 2002; Felson & Pare, 2010). Much of this pro-gun culture is derived from historical values of Western settlement, or due to the Southern subculture of violence. However, "pockets" of pro-gun culture also exist in small, rural towns throughout America (Brennan, Lizotte, & McDowall, 1993, as cited in Luna, 2002). These pro-gun subcultures may be a result of the sporting and hunting cultures and predominantly conservative values typically associated with these locations.

The organization that is most closely tied with pro-gun values is the National Rifle Association (NRA). The primary goal of the NRA is to maintain Second Amendment rights. As stated on the NRA website, "The most important benefit of NRA membership, however, is the defense of your Constitutional right to keep and bear arms" (Benefits of Membership, 2010). They promote the use of firearms for self-defense, hunting, and sporting activities and also promote firearm safety. The NRA continues to be ranked among the most powerful lobbying groups in the country (Alvarez & Bachman, 2008), and often endorses political candidates and contributes money to campaigns for candidates who support their position on firearms and firearm regulation.

Anti-Gun Culture

The anti-gun culture essentially counters the basic demographic and geographic correlates provided in the pro-gun culture discussion. Gun control advocates are more likely to belong to the

Democratic political party and/or be more liberal in their values than their pro-gun counterparts, and are more likely to reside in either the Northern or the Northeastern areas of the United States (Smith, 1980; Wright, 1988, as cited in Luna, 2002). Those who ascribe to this ideology have even been labeled as belonging to "cosmopolitan America" (Understanding Gun Control, 1972, as quoted in Luna, 2002, p. 88) since those in the ranks of doctors, lawyers, entertainers, and academics often belong to the anti-gun camp (Luna, 2002).

Although most of those who oppose guns acknowledge their purposes for events such as sports and hunting, they believe firearms essentially serve no other legitimate, noncriminogenic purpose (Luna, 2002). They often point to the high levels of firearm ownership in the country as the primary reason for the nation's relatively high homicide and violence rates. They also point out that African Americans are disproportionately more likely to be victims of firearm-related death (Black, 1983; Bogus, 1993; Hawkins, 1995, as cited in Luna, 2002), stating that firearms do more of a disservice to the African American community than to the white community.

One group that encompasses anti-gun ideals is the Coalition to Stop Gun Violence (CSGV). The CSGV actually comprises 48 organizations, including political action committees, child welfare advocacy groups, and social justice organizations. Their mission statement as listed on their website is "to secure freedom from gun violence through research, strategic engagement and effective policy advocacy" (CSGV, 2010). The CSGV remains interested and vigilant in issues relating to gun control and firearm safety.

PURPOSES OF FIREARMS

There are some marked differences between those who use their firearms for law-abiding behavior, such as self-protection or hunting, and those who own a firearm for purposes of committing crime. Recent evidence suggests that households in which individuals own firearms for sporting purposes are more likely to own more guns per household than those who own a firearm merely for protective self-defense purposes (Wyant & Taylor, 2007). This is likely because of the very different types of usage between these two groups of people. Those who use a gun for self-defense and home protection only require one working gun, and likely use their firearm on very rare occasions. In contrast, those who hunt may be more likely to own multiple firearms for various types of hunting, and may be more likely to use their guns on more frequent occasions because it is associated with their hobby.

As cited in the literature, there is a strong link between a fear of crime and gun ownership, which has been termed the "fear and loading" hypothesis (Lizotte, Bordua, & White, 1981; Wright, Rossi, & Daly, 1983, as cited in Watkins, Huebner, & Decker, 2008). As levels of fear increase, firearm ownership subsequently increases (Wright et al., 1983, as cited in Watklins et al., 2008), suggesting a pervasive need for individuals to protect themselves from potential victimization. The regional differences indicate that those in the Southern and Western areas of the United States are more likely to carry a firearm for self-protection than those who reside in the North (Felson & Pare, 2010).

An example of legislative support for self-defense is seen in the "castle doctrine," which has been enacted in many states. These laws provide additional freedom to individuals to protect themselves and, in some cases, their property from harm. All states with a castle law require that the individual who is using force to protect themselves must be legally allowed to be present in the location. Some states also do not require that individuals acting on behalf of the castle doctrine have a "duty to retreat," or an obligation to retreat and remove themselves from the present situation, if possible. The castle doctrine also provides protection against lawsuits from either the injured attackers or attackers' family members. For a discussion of recent controversies surrounding application of the castle doctrine in Texas, see **Box 4-2**.

But what about individuals who own illegal firearms or who primarily use them for criminal transactions? Similarly to law-abiding citizens, criminal offenders also cite fear of crime as a significant reason for gun ownership (Watkins et al., 2008). Offenders indicate that they have a need to possess and carry a firearm for protection against threats, especially during the commission of a crime, as well as to exact retribution against fellow offenders (Wright & Rossi, 1986; Jacobs & Wright, 2008). If an offender has had a violent crime committed again him, he is likely to resort to retributive justice against his attacker(s).

Ironically, one of the most frequently cited reasons for carrying a firearm into a criminal transaction is so that the offender would not have to harm the victim (Wright & Rossi, 1985). A victim may be less likely to resist or fight back against a perpetrator who is armed with a firearm when contrasted with other types of weapons, such as a knife. Victims understand the lethality of the weapon and the ease with which it can be used, and are therefore more likely to comply with less resistance.

Offenders may also carry a firearm into a situation without the initial intention of brandishing it. Rather, discretely arming themselves allows them to make demands of a victim. Their personal knowledge of their being armed gives them the advantage over the victims without the victims being made aware of this advantage. This allows the offender to be prepared for any situation, includ-

---

BOX 4-2 Castle Laws in Texas

On November 14, 2007, Joe Horn of Pasadena, Texas called 911 to report that his neighbor's home was being burglarized. He explained to the 911 operator of his intent to shoot the intruders. Against the operator's urgings, he proceeded to shoot the suspects as the operator listened on the telephone (Young, 2008).

Texas' castle doctrine, as enforced on September 1, 2007, protects individuals who use deadly force to protect their lives and property. It also extends this right for protection as long as you are in a location that you are allowed to be in and are not committing criminal activity. Individuals are allowed to use deadly force to prevent a suspect from fleeing, as long as the owner believes that it is the only way the property or land can be protected or recovered. It can also be used to prevent such crimes as robbery, arson, theft, or nighttime criminal mischief (Texas Penal Code, 2007).

Cases such as this one raise some interesting questions as to exactly how extensive the castle doctrine's reach is. Specifically, can the castle doctrine be used to justify deadly force if you are protecting the property of another individual? Is using deadly force to protect property, even if it is your own, excessive? By engaging in deadly force, are individuals making assumptions as to an individual's guilt, even though they have not been found guilty in a court of law?

"People don't get the death penalty for breaking and entering. Defending your family, defending yourself against someone who is armed is one thing. But now it's like we don't need to call the police anymore."

—Marsha McCartney,
member of the Brady Campaign to prevent gun violence (quoted in Young, 2008)

ing potentially high levels of victim resistance, without actually having to display the firearm to the victim until or if absolutely necessary to carry out their crime (Wright & Rossi, 1985).

Of course, not all offenders are equally likely to carry a firearm. Previously convicted criminal offenders who fear an impending arrest indicate that they are less likely to carry a firearm (Watkins et al., 2008). Offenders may know that there are potentially severe consequences for carrying an unlicensed gun, especially if they are currently on probation or parole. They may be less likely to carry a firearm for either self-protection or as a mechanism by which to commit a crime if they perceive an arrest is possible. This finding suggests that deterrence may work as a mechanism to prevent gun-related crime, as long as the offenders hold the belief that it is more certain that they will be discovered and caught by the authorities.

When examining criminal use of firearms in comparison with other forms of weapons, guns hold many advantages. For instance, a gun "psychologically distances the attacker from his victims" (Fox, Levin, & Quinet, 2008). This means it may be easier for an offender who is using a gun in comparison with a knife or other weapon that requires close contact, to fully separate themselves from the victim's psychological experiences involved in a crime. Many argue, as will be discussed further in this chapter (see discussion under The Gun–Crime Nexus), that victims who are approached by an offender with a gun may be less likely to sustain injuries than those who are victimized by a perpetrator with a knife. Because guns are viewed as more lethal, victims may feel less empowered when they are confronted with an attacker who is armed with a gun rather than a knife.

THE GUN–CRIME NEXUS

Much debate remains over the extent to which firearms are involved in criminal transactions. The involvement of firearms in crime is undisputable. However, some contend that much of this crime would have occurred regardless of the presence of a firearm. Still others posit that the presence of firearms may actually prevent a great deal of potential criminal activity. Although the prevalence of firearms and crime may be correlated, it may be problematic to state that one is causally influenced by the other. As previously stated, measures of gun ownership are highly flawed and do not consider the vast numbers of firearms that are completely unaccounted for by the government (Duggan, 2001).

Furthermore, crime rates may be impacted by many other factors aside from simple firearm ownership, such as the existing economic and social climates, social constructions of definitions of crime and numbers of individuals under the control of the criminal justice system. Examining the issue on an international level further illustrates this, as previously discussed. Varying levels of gun control contribute to varying levels of homicide, and not in a consistent direction. For example, if a nation has had no preexisting crime problem, the government may not feel it is necessary to impose strict firearms restrictions (Kates & Mauser, 2007). As such, the relationship between firearms and crime rates is much more complex than originally believed.

More Guns, More Crime

In the 1980s and 1990s, the United States experienced an increase in homicide rates. Approximately half of this increase was due solely to an increase in handgun homicides (Committee on Law and Justice, 2004). Although the rate of firearm use during a crime has been on the decline since 1993, guns do continue to play a role in criminal activities. Overall, approximately 20% of all violent crimes involve some type of weapon, and firearms are used in 7% of all violent crime. Although most rapes do not involve a firearm or other weapon, firearms are the most common weapon used in robberies. Almost half of all robberies (47%) involve a weapon of some sort, and in 26% of all robberies, the weapon used is a firearm (Truman & Rand, 2010). Although other weapons may be used in a robbery, if a gun is used, there is a significantly greater likelihood of a fatality occurring, thus escalating the incident to a homicide (Cook, 1987; Kleck & McElrath, 1991).

In at least two-thirds of all homicides, a firearm is involved (NRC, 2005, as cited in Riedel & Welsh, 2008). The involvement of a firearm is often circumstantial; murder may be seen as an outcome to a crime, rather than as the original intention. Most homicides are situational, beginning as an argument or simple assault, and escalating into a homicide (Luckenbill, 1977). The presence of a weapon, especially a firearm, is one situational feature that can escalate the incident to a homicide. The role of firearm availability in translating a nonfatal interaction into a homicide has been confirmed by inmates, who indicate that 90% of those who carry a weapon to the scene of their crime used it (Beck et al., 1993 as cited in Riedel & Welsh, 2008). As stated by Felson and Boba (2010), "Murder has two central features: a gun too near and a hospital too far" (p. 3). An argument or an assault is more likely to have a fatal outcome if a firearm is present and readily available (Hepburn & Hemenway, 2004).

Domestic violence is one crime that is particularly illustrative of this notion. Many people have a firearm in the house, often for purposes of self-protection. In the case of a domestic dispute, the presence of a firearm increases by three-fold the likelihood that a domestic altercation will escalate into a domestic homicide (Kellerman et al., 1993; Davies, 2008).

Those who fall victim to crimes committed by firearms are disproportionately young, African American males. Although African Americans comprise only 13% of the total population in the United States, they account for approximately half of all gun-related homicides. Since 1985, those 20 years of age or younger have experienced the highest risk of homicide victimization committed with a firearm (Perkins, 2003). While approximately 1 in 5 females are victims of firearm violence, 1 in 3 males are victimized in a transaction involving a firearm.

The vast differences in victimization rates between races are often attributed to the subculture of violence theory (Wolfang & Feracuti, 1967). Not only do African Americans have higher levels of victimization than their white counterparts, but they are also more likely to be commit offenses and be processed by the criminal justice system. Because African Americans are disproportionately more likely to live in communities that experience high levels of poverty, unemployment, and crime, they may be more likely to view violence, and particularly gun violence, as an acceptable means of dispute resolution. Income levels are highly correlated with various forms of crime, but individuals who reside in households with an annual income of $7,500 or less are more likely to be victimized by a firearm (Perkins, 2003).

These differences may also be explained by historical issues. African Americans have endured a long history of contending with less access to the legal system than whites (Black, 1983). This, coupled with gross levels of black oppression and racism (Hawkins, 1995), has potentially contributed to an increase in the levels of violence among the African American population in the United States.

When considering fatality rates, the type of weapon used to commit the crime is also important. There is considerable argument that if a gun is used during a criminal transaction, the likelihood of substantial injuries or fatalities increases (Roth, 1994). However, the counterargument claims that, when faced with a firearm rather than a less lethal weapon, such as a knife, the victim may be more likely to comply with the demands of the assailant (Kleck, 1991).

An interesting aspect of firearms and their involvement in crime is the various levels of lethality between different types of firearms. For example, firearms that can fire more rounds in a shorter span of time, such as automatic or semiautomatic weapons, may be more deadly than other types of guns, such as rifles, shotguns, and handguns. The first two types of firearms are used for the sole purpose of firing off multiple rounds in a short span of time, making it easier for offenders to kill multiple victims quickly (Alvarez & Bachman, 2008). An increase in the number of people killed at the scene of a crime increased during the 1980s as the number of semiautomatic weapons produced increased (McGonigal, 1993; Zawitz, 1995, as cited in Alvarez & Bachman, 2008). The ammunition itself has become more lethal as well. Some bullets are now designed to "mushroom" upon impact, and other bullets are filled with a soft lead that is designed to enlarge once it comes into contact with its target (Alvarez & Bachman, 2008).

The relationship between firearms and gang activity is also worth examining. Approximately 90% of all gang-related homicides involve a firearm, and gang-related homicides are more likely to involve a firearm than nongang-related homicides (Klein, 1995). The increase in gang activity is correlated with an increase in firearm-related violence, especially among juveniles. In general, juveniles have been found to be more likely than adults to both carry and fire a firearm. Juveniles also report owning multiple guns, with some studies reporting as many as 65% of juvenile gun own-ers owning at least three firearms (Wright, Sheley, & Smith, 1993; Sheley & Wright, 1994; Cook & Ludwig, 1995; Ruth & Rietz, 2003). Juveniles who are involved in gangs in particular, report that their gang membership and involvement is the primary reason for carrying a firearm (Watkins et al., 2008). The homicide victimization rate among gang members has been cited to be 60 times higher than for the general population (Wintemute, 2000). The correlation between juvenile gang membership and gun ownership peaked between 1985 and 1993, which has been primarily attrib-uted to the increase in the crack-cocaine market (Blumstein, 1998; Cork, 1999, as cited in Ruth & Reitz, 2003).

Juveniles involved in the crack-cocaine market quickly became more likely to carry firearms. Shortly after, even juveniles not involved with crack-cocaine began carrying weapons (Sheley & Wright, 1995; Hemenway et al., 1996). The end result of a small number of juveniles carrying guns became an epidemic since some began carrying for crime commission purposes, while others carried weapons for protection. Among young adults, when cocaine use decreases there is a subse-quent decline in societal level homicide rates, a condition that may also be correlated with firearms (Cerda et al., 2010). 1993 saw a significant increase in the gun-perpetrated homicide rate, as well as a tripling of juvenile arrests for gun-related violations of the law (Snyder, 1998).

More Guns, Less Crime

Many researchers have posited that an increase in firearms can actually lead to a decrease in crime (Kopel, 1996; Lott, 2000). Arming citizens makes them more able to defend themselves against of-fenders, making them less likely targets. These arguments are closely tied to deterrence and routine activities theory-related arguments of crime prevention. Offenders will be less likely to prey on innocent victims if the possibility exists that their crime will be unsuccessful or if there is a threat of retaliation from the victim (Kleck, 1991; Lott, 2000). These theorists may even fault recent changes to strengthen gun control, as discussed in the Firearm Legislation section of this chapter, for increases in crimes such as murder, assault, rape, burglary, and robbery (Lott, 2000). By keeping firearms out of the hands of the law-abiding, they believe that the government has placed potential victims at a significant disadvantage at the hands of the dangerous and armed offenders.

Moreover, from a routine activities perspective, those potential victims who arm themselves may be decreasing their likelihood of being a suitable target and increasing capable guardianship via the firearm (Cohen & Felson, 1979; Klepper & Nagin, 1989). This perspective is particularly pertinent when considering those who are less likely to be able to defend themselves without a firearm, such as those who are smaller in stature or the elderly. In this sense, Lott argues that firearms serve as "the great equalizer" for those who cannot serve as their own capable guardian in preventing crime.

Much of the "more guns, less crime" argument centers on the weapon being concealed (Kleck, 1991; Lott, 2000). The argument behind a citizenry with concealed firearms is that if the potential offenders do not have advanced knowledge of which potential victims are armed, they will be less likely to commit crimes on the population as a whole. Resting on the tenets of rational choice and deterrence theories, the logic behind this belief is that potential offenders will believe that there is an equal chance of their being unlikely to successfully complete a crime, regardless of the target. Thus, a few armed citizens would benefit the law-abiding citizens of society as a whole.

Recent changes to concealed carry laws hinge on the belief that arming the citizenry can subsequently reduce a potential offender's ability to victimize law-abiding citizens who do not carry weapons. Although a few states do not allow individuals to carry concealed weapons for any reason, other states leave it to the discretion of local agencies to determine eligibility for concealed permits. The latter group of states are those that have "may-issue" legislation, which means if certain requirements are met an individual may carry a concealed firearm. For example, Massachusetts restricts the type of firearm that can be concealed, limiting permission to shotguns and rifles (New Residents Overview, 2010), while Maryland allows concealed permits for certain types of carrier occupations, including business owners or retired police officers (General Licensing Division Application, 2010).

The vast majority of states in the country are considered "shall-issue" states. As of the date of this publication, this includes 37 states. These states allow anyone who applies and passes basic requirements as determined by the individual state, such as residency, background check, and minimum age, to obtain their concealed carry license. Shall-issue laws make it possible for individuals to not only have a firearm, but also to be able to carry it in an undisclosed manner among the general public. Coinciding with the arguments set forth by researchers such as John Lott, one argument behind shall-issue laws is that they allow for law-abiding citizens to protect themselves by leveling the playing field between potential victims and offenders. Not allowing individuals to conceal their weapons and use them for self-protection is essentially putting them at a disadvantage if they are placed in a situation where they have to face an armed offender.

In order to test the assumptions underlying shall-issue laws, researchers have asked inmates who have been convicted of a firearm-related offense to state their viewpoints on victimizing armed targets. The results were mixed. Some offenders indicated that they would be less likely to target those who they perceive might be armed. The majority of respondents, however, viewed shall-issue laws negatively. These inmates indicated that most offenders enter into a criminal transaction prepared for the possibility of an armed victim, so there will be little deterrent value associated with allowing law-abiding citizens to arm themselves. They also note another potential unintended consequence of shall-issue laws. By making it easier for potential targets to arm themselves, the number of legal guns in circulation increases. Although this may seem like more individuals will be able to defend themselves, increasing the number of guns in circulation will likely also increase the number of firearms on the black market since residential and commercial burglars may be more likely to seek out firearms to steal (Unnithan, Pogrebin, Stretesky, & Venor, 2008).

Concerns over potential criminals' knowledge of firearms in households were brought to the forefront in 2008 when a Memphis, Tennessee newspaper published an online database of all registered handgun holders. Their rationale was to publish the names so that potential criminals would be less likely to victimize that household. However, many critics, including the National Rifle Association, were concerned that the published information would lead to an increase in their victimization by making offenders aware of where the firearms might be more likely to be found (Locker, 2009, as cited in Acquisiti & Tucker, 2010). In comparing crime rates before and after the permit list was made publicly available, Acquisiti and Tucker (2010) found that crime rates in general did not fluctuate based on the publication of this information, and that publishing the names of those who were ultimately more likely to possess a firearm did not make them more likely targets. In support of deterrence theory, they did find that crimes decreased in the zip codes where there were greater numbers of gun permits.

The Role of Victim Resistance

The arguments for both camps center a great deal on the role that a potential victim may play in either preventing or facilitating crimes and injuries sustained during a crime. Many studies have been conducted that examine the role that carrying a firearm may play in comparison with other types of weapons.

Of particular interest is the finding that most victims who are in a situation where they brandish their weapon to prevent a crime never actually discharge it (Kleck & Gertz, 1995). This finding indicates that simply displaying the firearm may be enough to deter an offender from carrying out their intended crime. Arming potential victims with a firearm may empower them, giving them a sense of security and protection (Lott, 2000).

However, this sense of empowerment may be a false one, especially if the potential victims are not properly trained in the use of a firearm, or if they have the firearm taken away from them by their potential attacker. There are concerns that potential victims who are armed may be untrained or unprepared for the type of reaction time that may be necessary to administer a firearm for purposes of self-protection (Hemenway, Azrael, & Miller, 2000). Carrying a firearm may also lead some to venture into dangerous areas because of this sense of empowerment, making them more of a target than they would be if unarmed (Wilkinson & Fagan, 1996). There is also the issue of how great an opportunity the victim has to resist their assailant. The more suddenly that an attack occurs, the more likely an armed victim is to sustain injuries during an attack (Branas et al., 2009). This may render possession of a firearm by the victim useless for protection during a criminal transaction.

These findings counter other studies that indicate that armed victims are able to prevent both property loss and personal injury (Kleck & DeLone, 1993; Wells, 2002; Tark & Kleck, 2004). This situation may be more prevalent for some types of crimes, such as robberies, than for others, such as sexual assaults, especially considering the differences in frequency of firearm possession between males and females. Victims also do not frequently engage in the use of firearms as a self-protection measure (Hart & Miethe, 2009). Official statistics, such as those from the NCVS, are limited in measuring self-defense of potential victims because they focus on either completed or attempted crimes. The NCVS, which focuses specifically on victim experiences, lacks information on incidents where the offender was prevented from attempting the crime altogether because a firearm was present (Cook & Ludwig, 1998).

FIREARM LEGISLATION

Both state and federal legislation may be passed to address issues related to gun ownership. States are permitted to have different regulations than the federal government on possession, sale and licensing of firearms (Garland, 2010). This allows for geographical differences regarding varying views of guns and gun culture to be taken into account when considering state-level firearm legislation.

On a federal level, in 1968, the Gun Control Act was passed by the U.S. Congress. This act implemented several important nationwide restrictions on firearms. For example, it prohibited the sale of firearms across state lines as well as the importation of military weapons and inexpensive handguns from other countries. It also prohibited the sale of firearms to individuals who are deemed dangerous, such as those who have been convicted of a felony. The effectiveness of this portion of the act has been called into question since some believe that the type of felony that was committed should be considered when disarming citizens. Many felonies are nonviolent, and it seems impractical to enforce firearm restrictions against those who have not exhibited violence (Marshall, 2009). Furthermore, some also argue for a limitation on the length of time for this particular restriction in order to prevent individuals who were convicted of a crime many years ago from owning a firearm. For example, it may make little sense to prevent an elderly person from owning a gun for purposes of sport or self-protection because they committed a felony 40 years previously. Finally, many question whether an individual who commits a felony should lose their Second Amendment right to bear arms in the first place (Marshall, 2009).

Although the constitutionality of this piece of legislation was challenged in 1980 in *Lewis v. United States*, the Supreme Court upheld the right to prevent felons from possessing a firearm. In explaining the opinion of the court, Justice Blackmun wrote:

> *The federal gun laws, however, focus not on reliability, but on the mere fact of conviction, or even indictment, in order to keep firearms away from potentially dangerous persons. Congress' judgment that a convicted felon, even one whose conviction was allegedly uncounseled, is among the class of persons who should be disabled from dealing in or possessing firearms because of potential dangerousness is rational.*

The other important aspect of the Gun Control Act was to place the jurisdiction of firearms laws within the jurisdiction of the Bureau of Alcohol, Tobacco, and Firearms (ATF). Now called the Bureau of Alcohol, Tobacco, Firearms and Explosives, the ATF is a federal agency that is housed within the U.S. Department of Justice. The bureau serves a number of functions, but for the purposes of firearms regulation, they control the possession, sale, and transportation of firearms, as well as help to prevent and investigate crimes that are affiliated with firearms. To fulfill these duties, as well as numerous other functions, the ATF controls a budget, as of 2010, of over $1.1 billion (Congressional Budget Submission, 2009). Although the ATF was originally housed under the Department of Treasury, when the Homeland Security Act was signed into law in 2002, the bureau was transferred to the Department of Justice, and the name was also changed to include jurisdiction over "explosives."

The role of the ATF has remained fairly controversial throughout its existence. Many critics have requested the complete abolition of the ATF, including former President Ronald Reagan (Ruth & Reitz, 2003). The ATF has been faulted for trying to cover too much territory, as well as for having contradictory goals that prevent the bureau from being able to perform its job effectively. "The ATF is not a cohesive, rational, and focused organization, but an accident produced by a highly fragmented system obsessed with the dispersal of governmental authority" (Vizzard, 1997, as quoted in Ruth & Reitz, 2003, p. 183).

The Firearms Control Regulations Act of 1975 attempted to address many of the previously raised concerns by banning residents of Washington, DC from owning many types of firearms, including some types of semiautomatic and automatic weapons, as well as handguns. It also required that any firearms that were kept in an individual's residence must be locked, unloaded, and disassembled in order to prevent the firearm from being used unlawfully or from being accidentally discharged.

The constitutionality of the Firearms Control Regulations Act was called into question in 2008 in the landmark U.S. Supreme Court decision on *District of Columbia v. Heller*. The Court struck down some of the parameters required in the act, stating that they violated the Second Amendment by prohibiting homeowners from their entitled right to bear arms. Although the assault weapons ban remains intact, the handgun prohibition and the requirements to keep guns disassembled, unloaded, and locked were disallowed.

The Firearm Owners Protection Act of 1986 expanded on individual rights and worked against many of the regulations emerging from the Gun Control Act. For instance, it allowed interstate sales of certain types of firearms, such as long guns, which are primarily used for hunting. It also allowed for events such as gun shows to sell firearms with no restrictions, enabling those who may be potentially dangerous to still legally purchase a firearm.

Gun shows have been faulted for potentially providing a loophole for criminals to purchase a firearm because of a lack of restrictions on firearms dealers. The stipulations of the 1986 act were further strengthened by the passage of the Brady Bill in 1993, which continued to specifically exclude those vendors who sell their firearms at temporary events from conducting background checks on their customers. Just how expansive of an issue are gun shows? There are approximately 4,400 gun shows annually in the United States. For every gun show, there are an estimated 2,500 to 5,000 attendees (Ruth & Rietz, 2003). This means that as many as 12.5 million individuals may be attending gun shows every year.

Although federal legislation allows gun show vendors to circumvent requirements on background checks, it is at the discretion of the individual state to enforce stricter guidelines. Six states (California, Colorado, Illinois, New York, Oregon, and Rhode Island) require background checks on all firearms purchased at gun shows, while three states (Connecticut, Maryland, and Pennsylvania) require background checks on handguns that are purchased at gun shows. Hawaii, Iowa, Massachusetts, Michigan, New Jersey, North Carolina, and Nebraska require that individuals purchasing a handgun must obtain a permit and pass a background check. Florida requires that the counties conduct background checks on firearms purchased at gun shows. The remaining states do not currently address what has been called the "gun show loophole" in background checks for firearms.

A recent study has been conducted to investigate the extent to which firearm violence can be attributed to weapons purchased at gun shows, and finds no evidence to support a correlation between the two (Duggan, Hjalmarsson, & Jacob, 2008). However, other scholars have criticized this study methodology, stating that the researchers did not follow up the violent crime rates for a long enough time span after the gun shows since most violent crimes do not occur within the first few weeks after the purchase of a firearm (Crime Gun Trace Reports, 2000; Pierce, Braga, Hyatt, & Koper, 2004, as cited in Wintemute et al., 2010). Additionally, Duggan and his colleagues restrict their definitions of local gun-related crime to a radius of 25 miles or less from the gun show, when research indicates that as many as two-thirds of gun crimes occur outside the state or region where the firearm was purchased (Crime Gun Trace Reports, 2000, as cited in Wintemute et al., 2010). It may therefore be difficult to determine the extent to which the leniency shown to gun show vendors may contribute to violent crime.

Although the Firearm Owners Protection Act displayed some leniency compared to preexisting laws, such as in the case with gun shows, it also strengthened gun control. It expanded the banned category of weapons to include machine guns, and also expanded the list of who could no longer legally purchase a firearm. This list now includes those who received a dishonorable discharge from the military and illegal aliens.

One of the most sweeping pieces of legislation aimed at controlling the sale of legal firearms was passed in 1993. The Brady Handgun Violence Prevention Act, also known as the Brady Bill, is aimed at preventing the purchase of firearms by individuals who may use them for the purpose of crime commission. This law mandates a criminal background check on every individual applying to purchase a firearm. It also institutes a 5-day waiting period while this background check is being conducted. This waiting period simultaneously accomplished two goals. First, it intends to prevent those who have previously committed a crime from purchasing a firearm. It is also believed that those who wish to purchase a firearm for purposes of crime commission will have a cooling off period to rationally reconsider the consequences of their actions. It is important to note, however, that this prohibition does not apply to firearms sold at special events, such as gun shows, as stated by the Firearm Owners' Protections Act.

Shortly after passage of the Brady Bill, the Assault Weapons Ban and Law Enforcement Protection Act of 1994 was instituted. As the name indicates, it prohibits the sale, manufacture, importation, or possession of assault weapons by private citizens. It also banned all magazine clips that can hold more than 10 bullets. This act is applicable to all weapons sold after 1994 (the year of passage); however, in 2004 this ban expired.

The list of those considered dangerous individuals was again expanded in 1996 by the Lautenberg Amendment. This Amendment prohibits the sale of firearms to those convicted of domestic violence. One unintended consequence of this amendment was that it also prohibited some law enforcement officers who had been convicted of a domestic violence incident from owning a firearm (Garland, 2010).

Gun Storage and Child Safety Laws

Efforts to increase the safe storage of firearms may also decrease firearm usage. Appropriate storage with locking mechanisms can help prevent firearm thefts from occurring (research indicates that as many as 500,000 such thefts occur each year.) (Ludwig, 2005). They are considered an extremely valuable item with a high demand among burglars (Cook, Molliconi, & Cole, 1995). In Wright and Rossi's often-cited study (1985), 32% of respondents had stolen the firearm that they themselves used in their crime, 14% were certain that another individual had stolen the firearm that was used, and another 24% believed that the firearm had probably been stolen from the owner. This means that up to 70% of those included in the survey committed their crime with a stolen firearm (Ruth & Reitz, 2003). Considering the likelihood of a firearm being stolen during a residential burglary, it seems crucial that firearm owners take the necessary steps to ensure that their firearms are appropriately stored and locked to prevent these thefts.

Child Access Prevention (CAP) laws have been enacted by several states, and hold firearm owners criminally responsible if children gain access to their guns because they are not properly stored. Access to firearms by children may result in suicide, homicide, commission of any number of crimes, or the unintentional death of the child or his or her peers.

In order to test whether CAP laws have been successful in reducing unintentional firearm-related deaths among children, researchers have studied the rates of unintentional deaths occurring among children in each of the states with CAP laws. Their findings indicate that Florida's laws successfully reduced the number of deaths, but similar results were not seen in other states with CAP laws (Teret & Webster, 1999; Webster & Starnes, 2000). These differences experienced by Florida in comparison with the other states indicate that Florida may indeed be unique.

Florida was the first state to pass CAP laws, which means that the news coverage was likely extensive. Additionally, in comparison with the other states, Florida prescribes the harshest penalties for violation of the CAP laws. These two factors combined mean that there may be more of a deterrent effect experienced in Florida than in the other states (Webster & Starnes, 2000). Florida residents were more likely to be exposed to notification of the CAP laws, as well as the harsh penalties associated with not properly storing their firearm and making it accessible to a child.

The utility of proper storage with respect to preventing fatal accidents among children has been called into question. Gary Kleck (1997) explains that a majority of these incidents occur among adolescents and adults, not "children," as is often touted by the media. Moreover, he states that the number of these incidents is so infrequent that the storage issue bears little importance in terms of policy discussion or overall crime trends.

How effective is firearm legislation at keeping legal guns out of the hands of the criminal population? Early studies of the effects of the Brady Bill indicate that there were no significant differences shown between violence rates pre-Brady and post-Brady, with the notable exception of suicide rates for individuals age 55 and above (Ludwig & Cook, 2000, as cited in Riedel & Welsh, 2008). However, more recent studies indicate that since the passage of the Brady Act in 1994, over 1.9 million of the approximately 108 million applications have been denied. In 2009 alone, 1.4% of all firearm applications were denied at the federal, state and local levels, with the most common reason for denial being a felony conviction (Bowling, Frandsen, Lauver, Boutilier, & Adams, 2010). The decrease in the number of gun-related fatalities from domestic violence may also be attributed to the passage of the Brady Bill (Fox, et al., 2008). However, this decrease may also be due to other sociological factors, such as the increase in services for domestic violence victims or the increase in mandatory arrests. It should also be understood that very few domestic fatalities are carried out with a firearm, and only about six percent of those who are charged with a felony in a domestic violence situation used a firearm (Smith & Farole, 2009).

Current firearm legislation has been faulted for not having harsh enough penalties for gun dealers who violate existing protocol, and only one compliance inspection is required annually on firearm dealers (Webster, Vernick, & Bulzacchelli, 2009). The ATF states that they do not currently have the resources to inspect all firearms dealers. Therefore, they only target those dealers who have frequent violations or a large number of firearms that have been traced back to their establishment (Schwartz, 2007). It is also important to note that the federally mandated background checks only apply to licensed firearm dealers. As such, a private firearm owner can transfer possession of their firearm to another owner without completing the background check process.

Many argue that the existing firearm mandates are primarily keeping firearms out of the hands of law-abiding citizens, and that those who purchase guns legally are not the ones who are using them for crime commission. Gun control laws may ultimately do little to reduce crime, as is evidenced by some individual jurisdictions that have adopted very stringent firearm restrictions. For example, as noted, Washington, DC has very strict gun policies, yet 77% of their annual homicides involve a firearm, a number that exceeds the national average of about two-thirds of all homicides involving a firearm (Fox, Levin, & Quinet, 2008).

It is the individual who obtains firearms through alternate means who likely poses the greatest problem. Many believe that the increase in gun control does nothing to decrease crime (Moorhouse & Wanner, 2006). A majority of those who commit a firearm-related crime obtain their weapons either through an illegal source, through theft, or through friends or family members (Wright & Rossi, 1985; Harlow, 2001). Of the more than 260,000 firearms in circulation, only a fraction of those used in crime were legally obtained (Piquero, 2005). In all cases where firearms were confiscated for being instrumental to crime commission, 85% of those crimes were not committed by the original registered owner of the firearm (Bureau of Alcohol, Tobacco and Firearms, 2002).

Approximately half of all guns involved in a crime and recovered by police can be traced back to "straw" purchasers (ATF, 1999, as cited in Ruth & Reitz, 2003). A "straw" purchaser is an individual who meets the requirements to purchase a gun legally, but then sells the gun to an individual who cannot purchase their own firearm, often due to a felony conviction. To date no reliable way has been discovered to prevent "straw" purchasers from obtaining their firearms (Ruth & Reitz, 2003). As such, the disruption of illegal black markets is essential to curbing illegal gun activities.

FOCUSING ON ILLEGAL MARKETS AND CRIMINAL ACTIVITIES

Gun Tracing

Firearm manufacturers are now required to place serial numbers on all firearms. Serial numbers and other descriptive characteristics of a firearm can be used to trace the original purchaser. Therefore, if a gun is used in a crime, local law enforcement agencies and the ATF can contact the original firearm owner. Although the original owner is not typically the perpetrator of the crime (Bureau of Alcohol, Tobacco and Firearms, 2002), he or she can assist authorities by providing information such as whether the firearm was stolen from them, or if they are aware that a friend or family member has possession of the gun.

As the ATF began tracing firearms, one interesting fact that became apparent was that weapons previously used by law enforcement were quickly finding their way to the black market and being used in the commission of a crime. In 1999, more than 3,000 firearms that were once owned by police or other law enforcement agencies were tracked as being involved in a crime (O'Connell & Barrett, 1999). Shortly after this fact became clear, law enforcement agencies began destroying their used firearms rather than exchanging them for newer and more upgraded weaponry (Recycled, 1999, as cited in Ruth & Reitz, 2003).

Tracing resources seem to be vastly underused. Only about one-third of local law enforcement agencies regularly request a trace on a firearm that has been used in the commission of a crime (Johnson, 2007). Of all the firearms involved in the commission of a crime, less than one-fifth are actually traced by the ATF (Ruth & Reitz, 2003). In 2009, through the National Tracing Center, the ATF documented 343,746 firearm traces (ATF Fact Sheet, 2010). Additionally, serial numbers may be destroyed, rendering a firearm virtually untraceable (Ruth & Reitz, 2003).

Gun Buyback Programs

Gun buyback programs are one form of intervention that can be implemented at the community level. The goal of gun buyback programs is to keep illegal firearms off the street and out of the hands of potential offenders. Programs vary in the types of guns they will purchase, the amount of compensation provided for the guns, and the duration of the program.

One of the buyback programs that has been considered relatively successful was implemented in St. Louis, Missouri in 1991. Over the course of the program, approximately 7,500 firearms were collected. The compensation for each firearm was a gift certificate in the amount of either $25 or $50, depending on the type and condition of the firearm being exchanged (Welsh & Hoshi, 2002). Another widely known gun buyback program was implemented in Seattle, Washington in 1992. A total of 1,172 firearms were collected, of which 83% were in working condition (Callahan, Rivara, & Koepsell, 1994).

Despite the success of the number of firearms exchanged in these programs, they generally have little to no impact on gun-related violence. In the case of the Seattle program discussed above, the number of firearm-related injuries declined, but the number of both firearm-related crimes and deaths increased (Callahan et al., 1994). Three primary reasons have been cited for the failure of this type of program. First, the city hosting the buyback program may see no reduction in violence because individuals who reside outside the city can commute to the city to exchange their firearms. Second, the guns that are brought in to be sold can also be guns that were not used for crime commission. Rather, people may just bring in firearms that were being stored in their homes (Sherman, 1997). The end result may be a reduction in the total number of guns in individual households, but if many of these firearms were not used for crime commission, these programs could ultimately be ineffective in reducing crime rates (Romero, Wintemute, & Vernick, 1998). Finally, the cash paid out may be used to defray the cost of purchasing a new firearm, often one that is in better condition than the one turned in (Sherman, 1997).

Kansas City Gun Experiment

The Kansas City Gun Experiment was based on the ideas encompassed in routine activities theory. The idea is that by increasing patrols, the number of capable guardians would increase, thereby reducing the motivation of the potential offenders and the suitability of the potential targets. This rationale is that the focus needs to be on the inner-city neighborhoods that typically experience the greatest number of firearm-related crimes (Wilson, 1994; Sherman, Shaw, & Rogan, 1995).

Over the course of 29 weeks, during routine traffic stops and plain view searches, police officers increased the focus of searching for firearms in what they deemed their target area. This target location was an 80 by 10 block area. They also chose an area that was substantially similar in crime rates for their comparison beat (Sherman et. al., 1995)

The end result of the Kansas City Gun Experiment was a 65% increase in firearm seizures, as well as a 49% reduction in gun-related crime in Kansas City. Most notably, drive-by shootings dropped substantially in the target area, from seven incidents to only one. Moreover, neighborhood citizens who were within the target beat reported that they were much less fearful of crime. (Sherman et al., 1995).

Studies like this one indicate that more proactive police patrols may indeed be essential in reducing firearm-related crimes in areas that are considered to be at an increased risk for this type of offense. Many of our gun prevention measures have been focused on guns in general, such as purchasing restrictions, and not on guns that are used specifically for the intention of crime commission. Efforts such as these may be indicative of the positive effects that a proactive policing patrol could potentially have on preventing illegal activities perpetrated by firearms.

Boston Gun Project—Operation Ceasefire

A small percentage of offenders are responsible for a disproportionate amount of serious crime. For example, about 1% of the population contributes to 60% of homicides. Many of these offenders are known gang members who have prior convictions and/or arrests (McGarrell, Chermak, Wilson, & Corsaro, 2006; Davies, 2008). Findings like these provide the underpinnings for gun-focused interventions such as the Boston Gun Project—Operation Ceasefire.

In 1996, Operation Ceasefire also focused attention on interventions at the community level. This effort included multiple agencies and focused law enforcement efforts at targeting the illegal firearms market, in part through disrupting violence and gang-related activities. Multiple strategies were used to accomplish these goals, including specifically attacking drug markets and strictly monitoring probationers and parolees to ensure that they were abiding by their supervision restrictions.

These efforts were known as "pulling levers," and sent the message to gang members that they were targets of the efforts due to their involvement in various violent activities (Kennedy, 1997; Braga, Kennedy, Waring, & Piehl, 2001; McGarrell et al., 2006). Operation Ceasefire was considered a significant success for the city of Boston. Not only was there a decline in the number of firearm-related assaults, but there was also a 69% reduction in the number of homicides committed against the youth population (Braga, Kennedy, & Piehl, 1999). By disarming gang members and others who actively subscribe to violence as a means of dispute resolution, Operation Ceasefire may have successfully prevented potential acts of retaliation against rival gang members (Jacobs & Wright, 2006). Similar projects have been replicated in cities such as Indianapolis and Minneapolis with positive results (McGarrell et al., 2006; Davies, 2008).

Despite the successful outcome of this project, there are some issues that must be considered in order to understand whether it was truly successful in preventing violent crimes. Operation Ceasefire has been criticized for using too many strategies, making it difficult to know which strategy actually was successful (Reidel & Welsh, 2008). Was it the increased attention given to the parolees and probationers? Was it the increased attention given to gang members that deterred them from committing violent offenses? Was it the increase in policing? Also, understanding the success in a program such as this is dependent on having some form of a control group that does not employ tactics that are taken on by the experimental group (Riedel & Welsh, 2008). Comparing gang activity and violent crime rates in comparison cities in the same time frame is essential to understanding the true effect of these efforts.

Project Exile

In 1997, Project Exile was announced as an aggressive means to combat firearm-related crime in Richmond, Virginia. Under Project Exile any felon in possession of a firearm could be given a mandatory minimum sentence and prosecuted at the federal level. Although many states were already prosecuting firearm-related crimes with mandatory minimum sentences, federal level sentencing is much harsher and eliminates any judicial discretion that may provide for a more lenient sentence (O'Shea, 2007). Project Exile was seen as an aggressive means of both specific and general deterrence aimed at high-risk offenders, such as those with prior felony or domestic violence convictions.

Reviews of the results of Project Exile have been mixed. Some scholars indicate that it did not have a significant impact on the homicide rate in Richmond, and that the homicide decline that occurred was similar to other cities nationwide (Ludwig & Cook, 2003; Raphael & Ludwig, 2003). Using longitudinal data over a lengthier period of time, however, Rosenfeld, Fornango, and Baumer (2005) report a more significant decline in the homicide rate for Richmond (as cited in McGarrell et al., 2009)

Project Safe Neighborhoods

Legislation for Project Safe Neighborhoods (PSN) was closely modeled after Project Exile and was passed in 2001 under President Bush's tenure. There are four major tenets of PSN: (1) Those meeting particular criteria when committing their crimes would be given a mandatory minimum sentence of 5 years in prison. Some categories of individuals meeting these criteria include those who are previously convicted felons, those in possession of drugs at the time of their arrest, or those possessing a stolen gun. If an individual has been convicted of three violent crimes, this mandatory minimum sentence increases to 15 years in a federal prison. (2) A partnership would be established between local, state, and federal law enforcement agencies. (3) Community task forces would be created to propose new methods of decreasing gun violence in the community. (4) Every location participating in PSN would receive a $150,000 award and would hire an individual to oversee a public awareness campaign regarding firearms and crime (O'Shea, 2007; McGarrell et al., 2009).

The end results of the analysis of PSN strategies seem to indicate that locations engaging in PSN experienced decreased levels of violent crime. Most notably, even cities that only utilized increases in federal prosecution experienced reduced rates of violence (McGarrell et al., 2009). As all of the deterrence based strategies seem to indicate, aggressive policing, harsher sentences, and focused enforcement on those considered most "at risk" seems to be effective in reducing firearm-related criminal activities.

If the policies implemented from general firearm legislation such as the Brady Bill and the Firearm Owner Protection Act do not create decreasing rates of crimes perpetrated with firearms, it may be these targeted methods that must be relied upon. Ruth and Reitz (2003), therefore, may be accurate in their observation that gun control is not the answer. Rather, they point to efforts that focus on "crime gun regulation" and specifically address issues concerning those who use firearms primarily to perpetrate crimes, rather than those law-abiding citizens who rely on firearms for hunting, sport, or self-protection.

CONCLUSION

The complex relationship between firearms and crime is one that continues to perplex policymakers, criminal justice scholars, and the general public. The United States has made various types of efforts to control the situation. Some of these efforts focus specifically on the criminal population, while others focus on the firearm-carrying population at large. Many individuals and groups have strong opinions on the cause-and-effect relationship between guns and crime. There is no question that there is a relationship of some sort between the two, whether it is correlational or causal. Ultimately, though, we may be left with more questions than answers until more research can be undertaken that penetrates the complex nature of this relationship.

KEY TERMS

Gun Control Act of 1968
Firearm Owners Protection Act of 1986
Brady Handgun Violence Prevention Act of 1993
Assault Weapons Ban and Law Enforcement Protection Act of 2007
Lautenberg Amendment
Gun buyback programs
Boston Gun Project—Operation Ceasefire

DISCUSSION QUESTIONS

1. Explain why firearms may be more prevalent in the South than in other regions of the country.
2. Explain the arguments for how the Second Amendment is used to justify providing the right to carry a firearm. Explain the opposing side.
3. What are the differences in reasons for law-abiding citizens to carry a firearm versus those who intend on using a firearm for criminal purposes? What are the similarities?
4. Explain how guns can prevent crime, and how guns can promote crime.
5. How effective do you believe firearm legislation is at preventing criminals from acquiring a firearm?
6. Why are gun buyback programs generally ineffective?
7. Why do you think the Boston Gun Project has been successful?

REFERENCES

Acquisiti, A., & Tucker, C. (2010). Guns, privacy and crime. Paper presented at The Ninth Workshop on the Economics of International Security, Arlington, VA.

Alvarez, A., & Bachman, R. (2008). *Violence: The enduring problem*. Thousand Oaks, CA: Sage.

Beck, A., Gilliard, D., Greenfeld, L., Harlow, C., Hester, T., Jankowski, L., Snell, T., Stephan, J., & Morton, D. (1993). *Survey of state prison inmates, 1991* (NCJ-136949). Washington, DC: U.S. Department of Justice Programs, Bureau of Justice Statistics.

Benefits of Membership. (2010). National Rifle Association. Retrieved from http://www.nra.org/benefits.aspx.

Black, D. (1983). Crime as social control. *American Sociological Review 48*(1), 34–45.

Blumstein, A. (1998). Violence certainly is the problem—and especially with handguns. *University of Colorado Law Review, 69*, 960–965.

Bogus, C. T. (1993). Race, riots and guns. *Southern California Law Review, 66*, 1365–1383.

Bogus, C. T. (1998). The hidden history of the Second Amendment. *University of California at Davis Law Review, 309*, 386–390.

Bowling, M., Frandsen, R. J., Lauver, G. A., Boutilier, A. D., & Adams, D. B. (2010). *Background checks for firearm transfers, 2009—Statistical tables* (NCJ-231679). Washington, DC: U.S. Department of Justice, Bureau of Justice Statistics.

Braga, A. A., Kennedy, D. M., & Piehl, A. M. (1999). Problem-oriented policing and youth violence: An evaluation of the Boston Gun Project. Final report submitted to National Institute of Justice. Cambridge, MA: John F. Kennedy School of Government, Harvard University.

Braga, A. A., Kennedy, D. M., Waring, E. J., & Piehl, A. M. (2001). Problem-oriented policing, deterrence, and youth violence: An evaluation of Boston's Operation Ceasefire. *Journal of Research in Crime and Delinquency, 38*(3), 195–225.

Braga, A. A., & Pierce, G. L. (2005). Disrupting illegal firearms markets in Boston: The effects of Operation Ceasefire on the supply of new handguns to criminals. *Criminology and Public Policy, 4*(4), 717–748.

Branas, C. C., Richmond, T. S., Culhane, D. P., Ten Have, T. R., & Wiebe, D. J. (2009). Investigating the link between gun possession and gun assault. *American Journal of Public Health, 99*(11), 2034–2040.

Brennan, P. G., Lizotte, A. J., & McDowall, D. (1993). Guns, Southernness, and gun control. *Journal of Quantitative Criminology, 9*, 289–307.

Bureaus of Alcohol, Tobacco and Firearms (ATF). (1999). The youth crime gun interdiction inititative—crime gun trace analysis report: The illegal youth firearms markets in twenty-seven communities. Washington, DC: U.S. Department of the Treasury.

Bureau of Alcohol, Tobacco and Firearms (ATF). (2002). Crime gun trace reports (2000): The youth gun interdiction initiative. Washington, DC: U.S. Department of the Treasury.

Bureau of Alcohol, Tobacco and Firearms: Fact Sheet. (2010). Washington, DC: U.S. Department of the Treasury. Retrieved from http://www.atf.gov/publications/factsheets/factsheet-facts-and-figures.html.

Callahan, C. M., Rivara, F. P., & Koepsell, T. D. (1994). Money for guns: Evaluation of the Seattle buy-back program. *Public Health Reports, 109*(4), 472–477.

Cerda, M., Messner, S. F., Tracy, M., Vlahov, D., Goldmann, E., Tardiff, K. J., & Galea, S. (2010). Investigating the effect of social changes on age-specific gun-related homicide rates in New York City during the 1990s. *American Journal of Public Health, 100*(6), 1107–1115.

Chilton, R. (2004). Regional variations in lethal and nonlethal assaults. *Homicide Studies, 8*(1), 40–56.

CNN Poll: Race, gender not important in Supreme Court pick. (2009). Retrieved from http://politicalticker.blogs.cnn.com/2009/05/18/cnn-poll-race-gender-not-important-in-supreme-court-pick/.

Coalition to Stop Gun Violence. (2010). Retrieved from http://www.csgv.org/.

Cohen, L. E., & Felson, M. E. (1979). Social change and crime trends: A routine activity approach. *American Sociological Review, 44*, 588–608.

Cohen, D., & Nisbett, R. (1994). Self protection and the culture of honor: Explaining Southern violence. *Personality and Social Psychology Bulletin, 20*, 551–567.

Committee on Law and Justice (2004). *Firearms and violence: A critical review.* Washington, DC: National Academy of Science.

Cook, Philip J. (1987). Robbery violence. *Journal of Criminal Law and Criminology, 70*(2), 357–374.

Cook, P. J., & Ludwig, J. (1995). *Guns in America: Results of a comprehensive national survey on firearms ownership and use.* Washington DC: Police Foundation.

Cook, P. J., & Ludwig, J. (1998). Defensive gun uses: New evidence from a national survey. *Journal of Quantitative Criminology, 14*, 111–131.

Cook, P. J., Molliconi, S., & Cole, T. B. (1995). Regulating gun markets. *Journal of Criminal Law and Criminology, 86*(1), 59–92.

Cook, P. J., Moore, M. H., & Braga, A. A. (2002). Gun control. In J. Q. Wilson & J. Petersilia (Eds.), *Crime: Public policies for crime control.* San Francisco, CA: Institute for Contemporary Studies.

Cork, D. (1999). Examining time-space interaction in city-level homicide data: Crack markets and the diffusion of guns among youth. *Journal of Quantitative Criminology, 15*, 379–406.

Courtwright, D. T. (1996). *Violent land.* Cambridge, MA: Harvard University Press.

Davies, K. (2008). *The murder book: Examining homicide.* Upper Saddle River, NJ: Pearson/Prentice Hall.

District of Columbia v. Dick Anthony Heller, 554 U.S. _56-64 (2008).

Duggan, M. (2001). More guns, more crime. *The Journal of Political Economy, 5,* 1086–1114.

Duggan, M., Hjalmarsson, R., & Jacob, B. A. (2008). The effect of gun shows on gun-related deaths: Evidence from California and Texas (Working Paper 14371). Retrieved from the National Bureau of Economic Research website: http://www.nber.org/papers/w14371.

Ellison, C. G. (1991). Southern culture and firearm ownership. *Social Science Quarterly 72,* 267–283.

Felson, R. B., & Boba, R. (2010). *Crime and everyday life.* Los Angeles, CA: Sage Publications.

Felson, R. B., & Pare, P. (2010). Gun cultures or honor cultures? Explaining regional and race differences in weapon carrying. *Social Forces 88*(3), 1357–1378.

Fox, J. A., Levin, J., & Quinet, K. (2008). *The will to kill: Making sense of senseless murder.* Boston, MA: Pearson.

Garland, T. S. (2010). Guns and victimization. In B. S. Fisher & S. P. Lab (Eds.), *Encyclopedia of victimology and crime prevention* (Vol. 1, pp. 431–433). Thousand Oaks, CA: Sage.

General Licensing Division Application. (2010). Maryland State Police. Retrieved from http://www.mdsp.org/downloads/licensing_application.pdf.

Gimpel, J. G. (1998). Packing heat at the polls: Gun ownership, interest group endorsements, and voting behavior in gubernatorial elections. *Social Science Quarterly, 79*(3), 634–648.

Greenberg, K. S. (1997). *Honor and slavery.* Princeton, NJ: Princeton University Press.

Gun Owners' Action League. (2010). *New residents' overview of Massachusetts gun laws.* (2010). Retrieved from www.goal.org/documents/law_faq_pdfs/newres.pdf.

Harlow, C. W. (2001). *Firearm use by offenders* (NCJ-189369). Washington, DC: U.S. Department of Justice, Bureau of Justice Statistics.

Hart, T. C., & Miethe, T. D. (2009). Self-defensive gun use by crime victims: A conjunctive analysis of its situational contexts. *Journal of Contemporary Criminal Justice, 25*(6), 6–19.

Hawkins, D. F. (1995). *Ethnicity, race and crime: Perspectives across time and place.* Albany, NY: State University of New York Press.

Hemenway, D., Azrael, D., & Miller, M. (2000). Gun use in the United States: Results from two national studies. *Injury Prevention, 6,* 263–267.

Hemenway, D., Prothrow-Stith, D., Bergstein, R. A., & Kennedy, B. (1996). Gun carrying among adolescents. *Law and Contemporary Problems, 59,* 39–53.

Hepburn, L. M., & Hemenway, D. (2004). Firearm availability and homicide: A review of the literature. *Aggression and Violent Behaviour, 9,* 417–440.

Herz, A. D. (1995). Gun crazy: Constitutional false consciousness and dereliction of dialogic responsibility. *Boston University Law Review, 57.*

Hofstadter, R. (1970, October). America as a gun culture. *American Heritage Magazine.*

Jacobs, B. A., & Wright, R. A. (2006). *Street justice: Retaliation in the criminal underworld.* Cambridge, MA: Cambridge University Press.

Johnson, K. (2007, August 21). Most police agencies not making use of ATF gun info. *USA Today, p.* 4A.

Kaplan, D. E. (2007). More stressed, but still safer. *U.S. News & World Report, 142,* 11.

Kates, D. B., & Mauser, G. (2007). Would banning firearms reduce murder and suicide? A review of international and some domestic evidence. *Harvard Journal of Law & Public Policy, 30,* 649–694.

Kellerman, A. L., Rivara, F. P., Rusforth, N. B., Banton, J. G., Reay, B. T., Francisco, J. T., Locchi, A. B., Prosdzinski, B. A., Hackman, B. B., & Somes, G. (1993). Gun ownership as a risk factor for homicide in the home. *New England Journal of Medicine, 267,* 1084–1090.

Kennedy, D. M. (1997). Pulling levers: Chronic offenders, high crime settings, and a theory of prevention. *Valparaiso University Law Review, 31,* 449–484.

Kleck, G. (1991). *Point blank: Guns and violence in America.* New York, NY: Aldine de Gruyter.

Kleck, G. (1997). *Targeting guns: Firearms and their control.* New York, NY: Aldine de Gruyter.

Kleck, G., & DeLone, M. A. (1993). Victim resistance and offender weapon effects in robbery. *Journal of Quantitative Criminology, 9,* 55–81.

Kleck, G., & Gertz, M. (1995). Armed resistance to crime. *Journal of Criminal Law and Criminology, 86*(1), 150–187.

Kleck, G., & McElrath, K. (1991). The effects of weaponry on human violence. *Social Forces, 69*(3), 669–692.

Klein, M. W. (1995). *The American street gang: Its nature, prevalence, and control.* Oxford, England: Oxford University Press.

Klepper, S., & Nagin, D. (1989). The deterrent effect of perceived certainty and severity of punishment revisited. *Criminology, 27,* 712–746.

Kopel, D. (1996). The untold triumph of concealed-carry permits. *Policy Review, 78*(1), 9–11.

Lacey, M. (2010, December 4). Pushing a right to bear arms, the sharp kind. *The New York Times.* Retrieved from http://www.nytimes.com/2010/12/05/us/05knives.html?nl.

Lane, R. (1997). *Violent death in the city: Suicide, accident, and murder in 19th century Philadelphia.* Cambridge, MA: Harvard University Press.

Lewis v. United States, 445 U.S. 55 (1980).

Lizotte, A. J., Bordua, D. J., & White, C. S. (1981). Firearm ownership for sport and protection: Two not so divergent models. *American Sociological Review, 46,* 499–503.

Locker, R. (2009, February 13). Tennessee bills focus on gun owners. *The Commercial Appeal.*

Lott, J. R. (2000). *More guns, less crime: Understanding crime and gun control laws.* Chicago, IL: University of Chicago Press.

Luckenbill, D. (1977). Criminal homicide as a situated transaction. *Social Problems, 25*(2), 176–186.

Ludwig, J. (2005). Better gun enforcement, less crime. *Criminology and Public Policy, 4*(4), 717–708.

Ludwig, J., & Cook, P. J. (2000). Homicide and suicide rates associated with implementation of the Brady Handgun Violence Prevention Act. *Journal of the American Medical Association, 284,* 585–601.

Ludwig, J., & Cook, P. J. (2003). *Evaluating gun policy: Effects on crime and violence.* Washington, DC: Brookings Institution Press.

Luna, E. (2002). The .22 caliber Rorschach test. *Houston Law Review, 39,* 53–131.

Malcolm, J. L. (2003). Lessons of history: Firearms regulation and the reduction of crime. *Texas Review of Law and Politics, 8*(1), 176–178.

Marshall, C. K. (2009). Why can't Martha Stewart have a gun? *Harvard Journal of Law & Public Policy, 32,* 695–735.

McGonigal, M. D. (1993). Urban firearm deaths: A five-year perspective. *Journal of Trauma, 35,* 532–537.

McGarrell, E. F., Chermak, S., Wilson, J. M., & Corsaro, N. (2006). *Justice Quarterly, 23*(2), 214–229.

McGarrell, E. F., Hipple, N. K., Corsaro, N., Bynum, T. S., Perez, H., Zimmerman, C. A., & Garmo, M. (2009). Project Safe Neighborhoods—A national program to reduce gun crime: Final report. Washington, DC: U.S. Department of Justice. Retrieved from http://www.ncjrs.gov/pdffiles1/nij/grants/226686.pdf.

Moorhouse, J. C., & Wanner, B. (2006). Does gun control reduce crime or does crime increase gun control? *Cato Journal, 26*(1), 103–124.

National Research Council (NRC), Committee on Law and Justice. Division of Behavioral and Social Sciences and Education. (2005). Committee to Improve Research Information and Data on Firearms. In C. F. Wellford, J. V. Pepper and C. V. Petrie (Eds.), *Firearms and violence: A critical review.* Washington, DC: The National Academies Press.

O'Connell, V., & Barrett, P. M. (1999, August 16). Cities suing gun firms have a weak spot: They're suppliers, too. *The Wall Street Journal,* p. A1.

O'Shea, T. C. (2007). Getting the deterrence message out: The Project Safe Neighborhoods public-private partnership. *Police Quarterly, 10*(3), 288–307.

Perkins, C. (2003). Weapon use and violent crime (NCJ194820). Washington, DC: U.S. Department of Justice, Bureau of Justice Statistics.

Pierce, G. L., Braga, A. A., Hyatt, R. R., & Koper, C. S. (2004). Characteristics and dynamics of illegal firearms markets: Implications for a supply-side enforcement strategy. *Justice Quarterly, 21*(2), 391–422.

Piquero, A. R. (2005). Reliable information and rational policy decisions: Does gun control fit the bill? *Criminology and Public Policy, 4*(4), 779–797.

Raphael, S., & Ludwig, J. (2003). Prison sentence enhancements: The case of project exile. In J. Ludwig & P. J. Cook (Eds.), *Evaluating gun policy: Effects on crime and violence.* Washington, DC: Brookings Institute Press.

Recycled District of Columbia police guns tied to crimes. (1999, November 12). *The Washington Post,* p. A1.

Riedel, M., & Welsh, W. (2008). *Criminal violence: Patterns, causes and prevention.* New York, NY: Oxford University Press.

Romero, M. P., Wintemute, G. J., & Vernick, J. S. (1998). Characteristics of a gun exchange program, and an assessment of potential benefits. *Injury Prevention, 4*, 206–210.

Rosenfeld, R., Fornango, R., & Baumer, E. (2005). Did Ceasefire, Compstat, and Exile reduce homicide? *Criminology and Public Policy, 4*, 419–450.

Roth, J. (1994). Firearms and violence (NCJ145533). Washington, DC: U.S. Department of Justice, Bureau of Justice Statistics.

Ruth, H., & Reitz, K. R. (2003). *The challenge of crime: Rethinking our response.* Cambridge, MA: Harvard University Press.

Schwartz, E. (2007, July 23). A well-worn path to a gun shop door. *U.S. News & World Report, 143*(3), 29–30.

Sheley, J. F., & Wright, J. D. (1994). *Gun acquisition and possession in selected juvenile samples, research in brief.* Washington, DC: Office of Justice Programs.

Sheley, J. F., & Wright, J. D. (1995). *In the line of fire: Youth, guns and violence in urban America.* New York, NY: Aldine.

Sherman, L. W. (1997). Communities and crime prevention. In L. W. Sherman, D. C. Gottfredson, D. L. MacKenzie, J. E. Eck, P. Reuter, & S. D. Bushway (Eds.), *Preventing crime: What works, what doesn't, what's promising.* Washington, DC: National Institute of Justice, U.S. Department of Justice.

Sherman, L. W., Shaw, J. W., & Rogan, D. P. (1995). The Kansas City Gun Experiment. National Institute of Justice: Research in Brief. Washington, DC: National Institute of Justice, U.S. Department of Justice.

Smith, E. L., & Farole, D. J., Jr. (2009). Profile of intimate partner violence cases in large urban counties (NCJ228193). Washington, DC: U.S. Department of Justice, Bureau of Justice Statistics.

Smith, T. W. (1980). The 75% solution: An analysis of the structure of attitudes on gun control, 1959–1977. *Journal of Criminal Law and Criminology, 71*, 309–311.

Snyder, H. N. (1998). Juvenile arrests 1997 (NCJ173938). Washington, DC: U.S. Department of Justice, Office of Justice Programs, Office of Juvenile Justice and Delinquency Prevention.

Spano, J., Freilich, J. D., & Bollard, J. (2008). Gang membership, gun carrying and employment: Applying routine activities theory to explain violent victimization among inner-city, minority, youth living in extreme poverty. *Justice Quarterly, 25*(2), 381–410.

Spitzer, R. J. (2007). *The politics of gun control.* Washington, DC: Congressional Quarterly Press.

Tark, J., & Kleck, G. (2004). Resisting crime: The effects of victim action on the outcomes of crimes. *Criminology, 42*, 861–909.

Teret, S. P., & Webster, D. W. (1999). Reducing gun deaths in the United States. *British Medical Journal, 318*, 1160–1161.

Texas Penal Code Title 2 (9)(A). Amended September 1, 2007.

Truman, J. L., & Rand, M. R. (2010). *Criminal Victimization, 2009* (NCJ231327). Washington, DC: U.S. Department of Justice, Bureau of Justice Statistics.

Understanding gun control. (1972, June 7). *The Wall Street Journal,* p. 14.

Unnithan, N. P., Pogrebin, M., Stretesky, P. B., & Venor, G. (2008). Gun felons and gun regulation: Offenders' views about reactions to "shall-issue" polices for carrying concealed weapons. *Criminal Justice Policy Review, 19*(2), 196–211.

Vandal, G. (2000). *Rethinking southern violence: Homicides in post-Civil War Louisiana, 1866-1884.* Columbus, OH: Ohio State University Press.

Vizzard, W. (1997). *In the cross fire.* Boulder, CO: Lynne Rienner.

Watkins, A. M., Huebner, B. M., & Decker, S. H. (2008). Patterns of gun acquisition, carrying, and use among juvenile and adult arrestees: Evidence from a high-crime city. *Justice Quarterly, 25*(4), 674–700.

Webster, D. W., & Starnes, M. (2000). Reexamining the association between child access prevention gun laws and unintentional shooting deaths of children. *Pediatrics, 106*(6), 1466–1470.

Webster, D. W., Vernick, J. S., & Bulzacchelli, M. T. (2009). Effects of state-level firearm seller accountability policies on firearm trafficking. *Journal of Urban Health, 86*(4), 525–537

Weisberg, R. (2002). Values, violence and the Second Amendment: American character, constitutionalism, and crime. *Houston Law Review, 39,* 1–51.

Wells, W. (2002). The nature and circumstances of defensive gun use: A content analysis of interpersonal conflict situations involving criminal offenders. *Justice Quarterly, 19,* 127–157.

Welsh, B. C. & Hoshi, A. (2002). Communities and crime prevention. In L. W. Sherman, D. P. Farrington, B. C. Welsh, & D. L. Mackenzie (Eds.), *Evidence-based crime prevention.* New York, NY: Routledge.

Wilkinson, D. L., & Fagan, J. (1996). Role of firearms in violence scripts: The dynamics of gun events among adolescent males. *Law Contemporary Problems, 59*(1), 55–89.

Wilson, J. Q. (1994, Mar. 20). Just take away their guns: Forget gun control. *New York Times,* pp. 46–47.

Wintemute, G. (2000). Guns and gun violence In A. Blumstein & J. Wallman (Eds.), *The crime drop in America.* New York, NY: Cambridge.

Wintemute, G. J., Hemenway, D., Webster, D., Pierce, G., & Braga, A. A. (2010). Gun shows and gun violence: Fatally flawed study yields misleading results. *American Journal of Public Health, 100*(10), 1856–1860.

Wolfgang, Marvin E., & Ferracuti, F. (1967). *The subculture of violence: Towards an integrated theory in criminology.* London, UK: Tavistock Publications.

Wright, J. D. (1988). Second thoughts about gun control. *The Public Interest, 91,* 23–39.

Wright, J. D., & Rossi, P. H. (1985). The armed criminal in America: A survey of incarcerated felons. Washington, DC: National Institute of Justice.

Wright, J. D., & Rossi, P. H. (1986). *Armed and considered dangerous: A survey of felons and their firearms.* Hawthorne, NY: Aldine de Gruyter.

Wright, J. D., Rossi, P. H., & Daly, K. (1983). *Under the gun: Weapons, crime and violence in America.* New York, NY: Aldine.

Wright, J. D., Sheley, J. F., & Smith, M. D. (1992). Kids, guns, and killing fields. *Society, 30*(1), 84–89.

Wyant, B. R., & Taylor, R. (2007). Size of household firearm collections: Implications for subcultures and gender. *Criminology, 45*(3), 519–546.

Young, M. E. (2008, Nov. 24). "Castle law" arms Texas homeowners with right to shoot. *The Dallas Morning News.*

Zawitz, M. W. (1995). Guns used in crime. Washington, DC: Department of Justice, Bureau of Justice Statistics.

Zimring, F. E., & Hawkins, G. (1997). *Crime is not the problem: Lethal violence in America.* New York, NY: Oxford University Press.

CHAPTER 5

Problem-Oriented Policing and Open-Air Drug Markets: Examining the Rockford Pulling Levers Deterrence Strategy

Nicholas Corsaro
Southern Illinois University—Carbondale

Rod K. Brunson
Southern Illinois University—Carbondale

Edmund F. McGarrell
Michigan State University

INTRODUCTION

Since the mid-1980s, a number of criminal justice interventions have been introduced in response to a surge in drug-related offenses (Mazerolle, Soole, & Rombouts, 2006, 2007). There is considerable variation in law enforcement approaches (Weisburd & Eck, 2004), however, and this extends to strategies that target drug markets and related offending. Problem-oriented policing initiatives are directed at specific issues and rely on a host of proactive tactics in an effort to address the underlying causes of crime in varying community contexts (see Goldstein, 1990). This study evaluates a problem-oriented policing strategy used by the Rockford Police Department (RPD) to combat open-air drug markets and related offending in a high-crime neighborhood.

Drug Law Enforcement Strategies

An abundant body of research exists with regard to policing strategies designed to disrupt the flow of illegal drugs in open-air markets. Mazerolle et al. (2007) found that interventions aimed at reducing narcotic activity offer promise in terms of effect. Often-used aggressive policing tactics that rely extensively on crackdowns (e.g., arrests, sweeps, and saturation) in high crime neighborhoods have

Nicholas Corsaro, Rod K. Brunson, Edmund F. McGarrell, Crime & Delinquency, Vol 49, Issue 5, October 14, 2009. Reprinted by permission of SAGE Publications.

produced mixed results, however (Bynum & Worden, 1996; Wood et al., 2004). Prior investigations consistently indicate that, at best, crackdowns have a short-term effect (Best, Strang, Beswick, & Gossip, 2001; Smith, Davis, Hillenbrand, & Goresky, 1992; Smith, 2001). Thus, successful interventions directed at drug offenders in high crime communities require more than identification and arrests.

The literature indicates that the most successful drug market interventions have relied on problem-oriented policing approaches, which involve a variety of tactics designed to tackle problems in specific contexts (e.g., supply-side reductions, improving police-community relations, and nuisance abatement efforts). The use of these strategies has yielded reductions in crime and problem behaviors associated with drug markets in Chicago, Illinois (Coldren & Higgins, 2003), Jersey City, New Jersey (Mazerolle, Ready, Terrill, & Waring, 2000; Weisburd & Green, 1995), Oakland, California (Green, 1995; Mazerolle, Price, & Roehl, 2000; Mazerolle & Ransley, 2006), and San Diego, California (Clarke & Bichler-Robertson, 1998; Eck & Wartell, 1998).

A meta-analysis of drug law enforcement evaluations conducted by Mazerolle et al. (2006) concluded that problem-oriented policing tactics appear to be the most effective approach when dealing with drug crime, incivilities, and overall offenses than were community-wide policing, hot spots policing, and standard (i.e., unfocused or reactive) policing.[1] Similarly, recent research relying on simulation techniques comparing the experimental conditions of random patrol, hot spots policing, and problem-oriented policing found that the latter approach was the optimal strategy for disrupting street-level drug markets, reducing crime, and minimizing harm, regardless of the drug being trafficked (Dray, Mazerolle, Perez, & Ritter, 2008).

Although problem-oriented policing tactics seem to hold promise for minimizing criminal offenses associated with drug markets, few studies have specifically examined the utility of the "pulling levers" problem-oriented approach (see Kennedy, 1997) in an open-air drug market setting. To date, a majority of pulling levers strategies has focused on reducing violence and gang-related crime. The pulling levers intervention appears adaptable in terms of affecting youth, gang, and gun crime in a number of large U.S. cities; thus, it is reasonable to hypothesize that pulling levers can also be used as an approach to reduce nongang-related drug crime.

Pulling Levers: Combining Focused Deterrence and Social Support

Problem-oriented policing strategies have also been suggested as effective tools for preventing violence, in particular when targeted at gang-involved offenders (Decker, 2003). In response to the huge increase in firearms violence in the late 1980s and early 1990s (Blumstein & Rosenfeld, 1998), a large number of criminal justice agencies began experimenting with focused deterrence strategies often referred to as "pulling levers" (Braga, Kennedy, & Tita, 2002; Braga, Kennedy, Waring, & Piehl, 2001; McGarrell, Chermak, Wilson, & Corsaro, 2006; Weisburd & Braga, 2006). The multistage approach consists of diagnosing a specific crime problem, convening an interagency working group of criminal justice personnel, conducting research to identify patterns of chronic offenders and criminal networks, framing a specific response to law violators that uses a variety of sanctions as a coercive approach to stop continuing illegal behavior, providing social services and community resources to targeted offenders, and directly and repeatedly communicating with offenders so that they understand why they are receiving special attention (Braga, Pierce, McDevitt, Bond, & Cronin, 2008; Kennedy, 1997, 2006).

The first pulling levers intervention was implemented in Boston and has since been recognized as an effective strategy for reducing violence, firearm offenses, and youth homicide (Braga et al.,

2001). For example, pulling levers has been replicated, with promising results, in other U.S. cities including Baltimore, Maryland (Braga et al., 2002), Cincinnati, Ohio (Engel, Baker, Tillyer, Eck, & Dunham, 2008), Chicago, Illinois (Papachristos, Meares, & Fagan, 2007), High Point, North Carolina (Coleman, Holton, Olson, Robinson, & Stewart, 1999), Indianapolis, Indiana (McGarrell et al., 2006), Los Angeles, California (Tita, Riley, Ridgeway, Grammich, Abrahamse, & Greenwood, 2003), Lowell, Massachusetts (Braga et al., 2008), Minneapolis, Minnesota (Kennedy & Braga, 1998), and Stockton, California (Braga, 2008; Wakeling, 2003). At the national level, Dalton (2002) described how the pulling levers framework has been applied in a large number of U.S. cities and federal districts through the Strategic Alternatives to Community Safety Initiative and Project Safe Neighborhoods.

Summary and Research Implications

Although the promise of problem-oriented policing strategies has been well-documented as a successful law enforcement approach to combat illegal-drug markets (Mazerolle et al., 2006, 2007), and pulling levers deterrence initiatives have been regarded as promising problem-oriented policing strategies to reduce gang violence (Braga et al., 2008; Decker, 2003), very little research exists examining the capacity of pulling levers to combat open-air drug markets that are not directly driven by violent gang members. The first law enforcement agency to use pulling levers in response to persistent street-level drug markets, beyond those driven by gang members, was the High Point Police Department in North Carolina (Frabutt, Gathings, Hunt, & Loggins, 2006). Information about the High Point campaign gained the attention of RPD administrators. Further, officers from Rockford traveled to High Point to get a better understanding of the specific processes that were necessary for replication.

The purpose of this article is to assess the utility of pulling levers as an effective response to open-air drug markets in a distressed Rockford, Illinois, neighborhood. This study contributes to the drug law enforcement literature and pulling levers research by examining the utility of pulling levers as a specific response to drug sellers in drug hot spots. Although pulling levers has largely been implemented and evaluated on its ability to reduce firearms and violence, its usefulness beyond these contexts is unknown. Our results provide insight into whether the pulling levers campaign holds promise as a viable strategy for combating open-air drug markets.

METHOD AND STUDY SETTING

We employed multiple data collection and analysis methods in this study. Specifically, we used narratives and observational data with criminal justice officials to measure program implementation, RPD crime statistics to measure programmatic impact, and in-depth interviews with residents from Delancey Heights (the target neighborhood) to triangulate both process and impact data.[2]

Activity (i.e., process) data were collected through narratives, interviews, and observations with law enforcement officials, prosecutors, and social service providers in an effort to capture detailed information on program implementation. Specifically, we examined the extent to which the Rockford initiative adhered to the tenets of the pulling levers theoretical framework (see Braga et al., 2001; Kennedy, 1997).

Offense (i.e., impact) data include all crimes reported over a 2-year period, which were aggregated into a monthly format from June 2006 through June 2008. Crime data in Rockford are submitted and conform to the National Incident Based Reporting System maintained by the Federal Bureau of Investigation and offer distinct advantages for both policy analysis and criminal justice research, at least compared with data submitted to the traditional Uniform Crime Report system (Maxfield, 1999). Crime data were operationalized as composite measures of violent and nonviolent offenses that occurred from the first through the last day of each month. Offense data from RPD are more reliable than conventional calls for service data because immediately following their investigations, officers enter detailed information concerning incidents into a computer system mounted in their patrol cars, allowing for improved cross-validation. In addition to employing pre- and post-intervention analyses in Delancey Heights using growth curve models, we also modeled changes in citywide offense trends once the target area was subtracted from the city total for general trend and comparison purposes.

We used qualitative, in-depth interviews with 34 adults in Delancey Heights to complement the narrative, observational, and quantitative data. The interviews lasted approximately 40 minutes to 1 hour. Participation in the study was voluntary and participants were paid $25 and promised strict confidentiality. The in-depth interviews were semistructured and consisted of open-ended questions intended to elicit detailed information about participants' perceptions of and experiences with crime and disorder in Delancey Heights (prior to and following the initiative).[3] The interviews were not audiotaped. Members of the research team, however, meticulously recorded responses by hand. Furthermore, painstaking attention was paid to accurately capture study participants' statements verbatim. We analyzed the data through numerous readings of participants' accounts and were careful that the concepts developed and themes that emerged illustrated the most common (and salient) patterns of residents' descriptions in the target neighborhood. This was accomplished using grounded theory methods involving searches for and highlighting of deviant cases (Strauss, 1987). Finally, we attempted to strengthen the reliability of the data by asking participants about their perceptions and encounters multiple times during the interview.

To place the present pulling levers intervention strategy into context, we provide descriptive information for both Delancey Heights and the city of Rockford. **Table 5-1** displays key demographic characteristics of residents and households in the target community as well as the overall city. Descriptive indicators of neighborhood context include the total population, percent male, percent White, median home income, average educational attainment of inhabitants, and measures of resi-

TABLE 5-1 Demographic Characteristics of Residents: Comparison Between Target Neighborhood and Overall City of Rockford

Census measure	Target neighborhood	Overall city of Rockford
Percent male	47.0%	48.2%
Percent White	46.0%	72.8%
High school graduates (25 years and older)	33.3%	77.8%
Renter occupied units	84.4%	38.9%
Median income	$13,284	$37,667
Population (2000)	2,681 inhabitants	150,115 inhabitants

Source: Corsaro, N., Brunson, R. K., & McGarrell, E. F. Problem-oriented policing and open-air drug markets: Examining the Rockford pulling levers deterrence strategy. *Crime and Delinquency,* forthcoming.

dential stability. These data, taken from the 2000 U.S. Census, were aggregated from block groups in the target neighborhood and the overall city. Delancey Heights accounts for roughly 1.7% of the Rockford population and is generally one of the more distressed neighborhoods within the city.

Variables

Table 5-2 displays the offense data that were aggregated to create measures of violent and nonviolent outcome variables. In terms of the violent crime variable, nine offenses were selected to create an overall index measure. Violent offenses were aggregated from homicides (< 1%), rapes (1.5%), kidnappings (< 1%), robberies (11%), and simple and aggravated assaults (86.6%), which made up the majority of violent crimes. Similarly, nine crimes comprised the nonviolent offenses measure, which was a composite of drug-related incidents, nuisance crimes (including prostitution and vagrancy), and property offenses. Nonviolent offenses included 63.1% property damage, 15.9% drug and drug equipment violations, and 21% of nuisance crimes (including prostitution, curfew violations, vagrancy, and disorderly conduct). Identical selection criteria were employed for both the target neighborhood and citywide offense variables.

The *intervention* variable, seen in **Table 5-3**, captures the pulling levers intervention. In Delancey Heights, treatment was measured as a dichotomous variable (0 = pre-May 2007, 1 = May 2007 and beyond). Specifically, May 2007 was treated as the postintervention date because it was during this month that RPD: (a) arrested a number of violent offenders who were involved in open-air drug trafficking, (b) conducted the pulling levers notification meeting bringing together community leaders and key criminal justice officials to speak with nonviolent drug sellers and (c) worked with community development officers to improve neighborhood conditions by issuing citations for a wide range of code violations. In all, these efforts resulted in 11 months of preintervention and 14 months of postintervention data for the target neighborhood. In the next section, we describe process and impact results of the pulling levers intervention employed by Rockford officials in Delancey Heights.

TABLE 5-2 Description of Violent and Nonviolent Offenses in Rockford

Violent Offenses (offenses against persons)	Nonviolent Offenses (nuisance, drug, and property offenses)
Murder	Stolen property
Nonnegligent manslaughter	Destruction of property
Rape	Vandalism
Kidnapping	Drug/narcotic violations
Abduction	Drug equipment violations
Unlawful restraint	Prostitution
Robbery	Violation of curfew
Aggravated assault	Vagrancy and loitering
Simple assault	Disorderly conduct

Source: Corsaro, N., Brunson, R. K., & McGarrell, E. F. Problem-oriented policing and open-air drug markets: Examining the Rockford pulling levers deterrence strategy. *Crime and Delinquency,* forthcoming.

TABLE 5-3 Descriptive Statistics

Variable	N	M	SD	Minimum	Maximum
Violent offenses	50	299.5	298.5	10	700
Nonviolent offenses	50	482.4	475.2	9	1225
Intervention measure	50	0.28	0.453	0	1
Target neighborhood	50	0.50	0.707	0	1

Source: Corsaro, N., Brunson, R. K., & McGarrell, E. F. Problem-oriented policing and open-air drug markets: Examining the Rockford pulling levers deterrence strategy. *Crime and Delinquency,* forthcoming.

RESULTS

Implementation and Process Assessment

The Rockford pulling levers intervention strategy generally followed the High Point Drug Market initiative (Frabutt et al., 2006) and involved the following three stages: (a) identification, (b) notification, and (c) resource delivery. The identification stage was a data-driven procedural analysis used by RPD to determine the appropriate neighborhood and individuals for the intervention (see Klofas et al., 2006). The notification stage consisted of a two-part process: (1) a targeted investigation that lasted several months and led to the arrest and focused prosecution of seven chronic, violent offenders in Delancey Heights; and (2) a targeted investigation and publicly delivered message of zero-tolerance to five suspected dealers who were given an opportunity to participate in a "last chance" program that afforded them access to a variety of social support services (i.e., a pulling levers notification) because of their limited and nonviolent criminal histories. The resource delivery stage provided these five offenders with positive support mechanisms that were specific to each person's situation—a critical component of the mixed deterrence and social support strategy (Cullen, 1994; Tyler, 1990). In addition, RPD and cooperating agencies worked extensively to improve the quality of life for residents in the target area through order maintenance policing efforts. Thus, the stages of the Rockford strategy were consistent with the pulling levers framework (Kennedy, 1997).[4] A detailed summary of the action plan and the pulling levers process component is displayed in Appendix A.

Impact and Outcome Assessment

The ultimate goal of the Rockford pulling levers strategy implemented in Delancey Heights was to reduce criminal offending, interrupt open-air drug markets, and make the once high crime community more inhabitable. The purpose of the following analyses is to assess the impact of the initiative by examining whether changes in crime patterns occurred after implementation.

As an initial step, percentage differences were examined with regard to the changes in violent and nonviolent offenses for the target neighborhood, the remainder of Rockford, and the overall city both before and after the intervention. Because the number of pre- and postintervention periods is not equivalent, the average percentage change in the number of offenses per month across the city is displayed in **Table 5-4**, which shows that the target neighborhood experienced an average decline of 24.10% in nonviolent and a 14.29% reduction in violent incidents between the pre-

TABLE 5-4 Changes in Nonviolent and Violent Offenses in Rockford Before and After May 2007 Call-In

Location	Number of offenses per month (preintervention)	Number of offenses per month (postintervention)	Percentage
Target neighborhood			
Nonviolent	29	22	−24.10
Violent	21	18	−14.29
Remainder of city			
Nonviolent	944	859	−9.00
Violent	567	554	−2.29
Overall city			
Nonviolent	1013	881	−13.03
Violent	588	573	−2.55

Source: Corsaro, N., Brunson, R. K., & McGarrell, E. F. Problem-oriented policing and open-air drug markets: Examining the Rockford pulling levers deterrence strategy. *Crime and Delinquency,* forthcoming.

and postintervention periods. Comparatively, from a general trend perspective, the remainder of the city also experienced a decline in both nonviolent (–9%) and violent crime (–2.3%). Ultimately, a decline in both violent and nonviolent offenses occurred in the city of Rockford before and after May 2007. It is also apparent that the decline throughout the remainder of the city was not as extensive (in terms of magnitude for either offense type) and that the decline in both violent and nonviolent crime for the entire city was influenced by specific declines in the target neighborhood.

Growth Curve Estimates

The empirical models presented here examine repeated crime data in a monthly format from June 1, 2006 to June 30, 2008, in the target neighborhood and the remainder of Rockford. The use of a mixed model is appropriate for the current data and is well suited to the specific research questions here because the stochastic process in a hierarchical model can be specified using repeated observations nested within a neighborhood or city (Raudenbush & Bryk, 2002). Specifically, simple linear models as well as maximum likelihood count regressions assume mutual dependence in the error estimates. In time-series data, the observations at adjacent points in time are highly intercorrelated, or autocorrelated, and thus, the Hierarchical Generalized Linear Modeling (HGLM) framework is appropriate for this analysis.

HGLM is used to assess within-neighborhood changes in both violent and nonviolent crime from June 2006 to June 2008 by relying on a Poisson sampling model with a correction for overdispersion and the neighborhood population as the exposure variable. In this case, the monthly offense counts were treated as repeated measures nested within the target neighborhood at Level 1. Including the population as the exposure variable means that the dependent variable is interpreted as a crime rate outcome for both violent and nonviolent crime (Raudenbush & Bryk, 2002). In addition, the intervention measure was group-centered to create a unique intercept and slope for the target neighborhood. Group centering a time-varying covariate at Level 1 provides an unbiased estimate of the change effect between the independent variable (X) and violent crime within the neighborhood, which is the focus of this study (see Xie & McDowall, 2008).

The unconditional random effects baseline models for both violent and nonviolent incidents indicated significant variation in crime trends within the target neighborhood as well as the remainder of Rockford ($p < .01$ for both sets of models). **Table 5-5** displays the conditional models where the intervention variable was included as a Level 1 covariate.[5] The intervention measure captures the specific change in the target neighborhood to assess whether there was significant within-neighborhood variation in local offenses after the pulling levers intervention. Because the remainder of the city did not receive the intervention, the measure is always a zero, thus isolating the estimate of the intervention effect to the target neighborhood. Nonviolent crime in Delancey Heights reduced by roughly 22.2% (per 1,000 residents) following the May 2007 pulling levers intervention, and the decline was statistically significant ($p < .05$).[6] Although violent crime also reduced in the target community following the intervention (–8.7%), the decline was not statistically significant ($p = .33$).

We next examined whether the changes in both violent and nonviolent offenses experienced in Delancey Heights were significantly different (i.e., above and beyond) from crime changes in the remainder of the city over the same period. The application of multilevel models is useful in this instance because estimates obtained from Level 2 variables indicate differences across (i.e., between) the units at Level 1. In this case, we used the same intervention variable for both the target neighborhood and the remainder of the city (0 = pre-May 2007 intervention, 1 = May 2007 and beyond) to create a viable comparison. Target designation, a Level 2 measure, distinguished the Delancey Heights neighborhood from the remainder of the city (0 = remainder of the city, 1 = target neighborhood). The slope of the intervention measure at Level 1 was thus modeled as a function of the target designation at Level 2 (i.e., a cross-level interaction effect). The results indicated that nonviolent crimes in the target neighborhood reduced at a marginally significantly greater

TABLE 5-5 Hierarchical Generalized Linear Modeling Fixed Effects Growth Curve

Estimates and standard errors

Variable	Nonviolent offenses		Violent offenses	
	Coefficient	SE	Coefficient	SE
Level 1-only models				
Intercept (β_{00})	.078**	.000	.055**	.003
Intervention (β_{10})	–.250*	.120	–.090	.090
Multilevel models				
Intercept (β_{00})	.078**	.000	.055	.003
Intervention (β_{10})	–.010*	.000	–.000	.000
Target (β_{11})	–.020†	.011	–.000	.000

†$p < .10$. *$p < .05$. **$p < .01$.

Source: Corsaro, N., Brunson, R. K., & McGarrell, E. F. Problem-oriented policing and open-air drug markets: Examining the Rockford pulling levers deterrence strategy. *Crime and Delinquency,* forthcoming.

rate (p = .07) than nonviolent offenses in the remainder of the city following the May 2007 pulling levers intervention. Violent crime in the target area also declined at a greater rate when compared with the remainder of the city, but the difference was not statistically significant (p = .41). Both sets of HGLM models yield similar and consistent results: Nonviolent incidents in the target neighborhood experienced a significant decline after the implementation of pulling levers, whereas violent incidents also declined but not to the level of statistical significance.

To visually display the results seen in the HGLM estimates, nonviolent crime trends were standardized (per 1,000 residents) for the target neighborhood and the remaining city (see **Figure 5-1**). The target area experienced a decline from 10.8 nonviolent offenses per 1,000 residents before to 8.3 nonviolent offenses after pulling levers was implemented in May 2007. Comparatively, the remainder of Rockford experienced a reduction from 6.8 nonviolent offenses to 5.9 nonviolent offenses per 1,000 residents over this same period. Figure 5-1 also indicates that the decreases in the nonviolent offenses within the target area occurred a few months after the intervention and have since remained relatively proximate to nonviolent offense rates seen in the remainder of the city. Thus, an observed lag in the reduction of nonviolent offenses and the observed statistical effect occurred after the early summer months following program implementation. Although this lag was included in the parameter estimates in the growth curve models, it was not specifically isolated using this approach. Although not displayed here, we also used the Autoregressive Integrated Moving Average (ARIMA) identification procedure to identify and isolate the lag effect, which was statistically significant (p < .01).[7] Data obtained from interviews with residents cross-validated the lag-effect finding, which we note in the next section.

Resident Interviews

The majority of study participants report being very pleased with the RPD intervention and tout it as an innovative crime-reduction strategy. For example, several participants noted that they have seen reductions in crime and incivilities in Delancey Heights following the intervention. For instance, Ted remarked, "Now the people who walk down the street aren't outsiders trafficking drugs. Now [when you see people outside] it's residents from this community. Outsiders don't come in and cause problems anymore, at least not as much as they did before." Similarly, James stated, "We used to have 'trash pickup' days every couple of months to make the neighborhood look good. We've

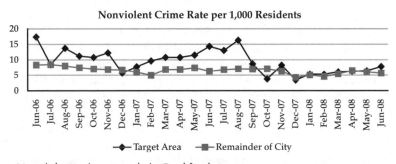

FIGURE 5-1. Nonviolent crime trends in Rockford.

Source: Corsaro, N., Brunson, R. K., & McGarrell, E. F. Problem-oriented policing and open-air drug markets: Examining the Rockford pulling levers deterrence strategy. *Crime and Delinquency,* forthcoming.

had to cancel several of those because we just don't have the amount of trash in this neighborhood as we used to. And that's a good thing." And finally, Mary explained,

> *I wouldn't say it's one hundred percent better, but it's a heck of a lot better. There are a lot less dealers, hookers, and noise around here than there used to be. It's been a long time since we have seen something bad happen, like a shooting. The big difference around here is at night; it's just a lot more peaceful at night now.*

These statements highlight that residents in Delancey Heights have noticed a tangible change with regard to drug dealing, crime, nuisance offenses, litter, and incivilities in the neighborhood.

In terms of specifying when the positive changes occurred, a majority of Delancey Heights residents identified the period when RPD publicly announced its intervention efforts. Furthermore, study participants consistently attributed the observed crime reduction in their neighborhood to increased police presence and shorter response times. This perception was consistent among both heavily involved and disengaged neighborhood residents. For example, William, who attended the pulling levers community notification, noted,

> *It took several months after the call-in before we saw real impact. There were some remaining drug dealers in the neighborhood that refused to leave because this was their turf and they were going to stay. Police were able to eventually drive them out, but it took a few months.*

Similarly, Carla, a resident who was uninvolved in the pulling levers call-in, remarked,

> *Things changed for the better when police got the dealers out of here. Really, when police boarded up [an abandoned building], locked the gates to it, and put up a camera, things got a lot better around then; maybe a little after that. After the dealers couldn't find anywhere else to go, this place has just been a lot better.*

It is also important to note that as time has elapsed since the intervention, a number of participants expressed dissatisfaction with what they considered poor police response times. They were especially troubled because according to them, they enjoyed appreciably quicker response times during the earliest period of the intervention. And in their view, the police department no longer showed the same level of commitment to Delancey Heights. Jason's comment illustrates this point. He reported, "There's a perception among residents in this neighborhood that police [no longer] make us a priority when we call. We'd like to know why this is, especially since problems in this neighborhood used to be a priority." Likewise, Jan said, "Police response takes longer now than it used to. For a long time, police were always here and were so quick to respond to our calls. Now they seem to care less about what goes on here than they used to and that is something they should address." There were other underlying issues and concerns that the interviews seemed to uncover.

Although participants remarked that the most blatant forms of open-air drug dealing had dissipated, they noted that many remaining dealers had simply adapted to enforcement efforts and now sold drugs more covertly (i.e., inside cars and residences rather than on the street). Sheila commented, "We have less dealers than we *used* to, but the ones we still have are also different. They don't sell out on the street anymore but rather in their cars. Now they have to be sneaky about it." In agreement, Kendall noted,

I think the dealers that have been able to avoid getting caught try hard not to bring too much attention to themselves. People who used to sell drugs here sold to outsiders who were coming in, bringing attention to themselves. We don't have those types of dealers anymore, out in the street.

And finally, Kim advised, "I know there are still people here who deal. But it's not 'in and out' anymore. People who are selling drugs now are doing it out of their homes or in their cars. It's not gone, but it's much more out-of-sight."

Although study participants were consistent in the belief that drug crime and related offenses in Delancey Heights had indeed subsided, they desired a continued commitment from RPD to the area.

DISCUSSION

Results from the HGLM growth curve models indicate that Delancey Heights experienced a statistically significant, substantive, and noticeable reduction in property, drug, and nuisance offenses after pulling levers was implemented. This is important given the relationship between these specific types of behaviors and open-air drug markets documented in prior research (Pettiway, 1995; Rengert & Wasilchick, 1989). Comparative statistical analyses reveal that the greater city did not experience a similar effect with regard to changes in crime rates over the same period. Interviews with residents demonstrated that they observed an appreciable transformation in the neighborhood shortly after RPD introduced proactive, strategic, and focused approaches to interrupt the open-air markets that had once flourished in the community. Regardless of their level of involvement with and knowledge of the intervention strategy, the majority of study participants agreed that crime and disorder in Delancey Heights had dropped precipitously as a result of the multiagency crime-control effort.

In sum, our findings are consistent with previous studies, which indicate that strategies relying on both proactive and reactive policing tactics appear to be extremely promising for reducing drug and related crime (Mazerolle et al., 2006, 2007; Weisburd & Green, 1995). It is important that RPD and other public officials sought to strengthen informal social control in Delancey Heights throughout the initiative by involving residents in various stages of the intervention process (Bursik & Grasmick, 1993; Sampson, Raudenbush, & Earls, 1997). Interviews with residents, and in particular with those who were engaged in the pulling levers notification meeting, indicated a heightened sense of awareness and responsibility in terms of cooperating with police to regulate neighborhood behaviors.

In terms of sustainability, once drug, nuisance, and property offense rates declined in the target neighborhood, they remained consistent with those experienced by the remainder of the city. It is not surprising that RPD officials have since implemented additional proactive law enforcement and pulling levers strategies in other high crime, Rockford communities in an effort to replicate the effect seen in Delancey Heights. Resident interviews indicated that many citizens in the target area believed that RPD was not prioritizing Delancey Heights as it did when intervention dosage was highest (i.e., during the implementation of strategies), despite the apparent and sustained effect. In fact, residents feared that RPD had shifted its attention and resources to other problem neighborhoods. As Tyler and Folger (1980) observed, citizens' perceptions of procedural fairness from a criminal justice perspective are directly related to issues such as police response time, regardless of whether quicker responses by law enforcement would actually solve their specific problems. Given that prior research indicates that crime victims want compassion, concern, and sensitivity from law enforcement personnel (see Mawby & Walklate, 1994), it should come as no surprise that residents who greatly appreciate the benefits of enhanced policing strategies (i.e., quicker response times, greater police presence, etc.) struggle with a perceived withdrawal or reduction of those resources once crime rates subside. Further research should be invested in effective "weaning" strategies focused on neighborhood residents' perceptual vantage points as well as on crime rates.

It is interesting that although violent crime in the target area declined following the intervention, it did not reduce at a statistically significant level. A likely explanation is the lack of statistical power given that violent offenses were relatively infrequent in Delancey Heights. As mentioned previously, more than 86% of the violent offenses were classified as assaults. A more detailed analysis should attempt to delineate those physical attacks that were drug market-related, such as retaliatory violence as a means of debt collection (see Anderson, 1999) or assaults that occurred in public, in an effort to better understand this phenomenon. It is unfortunate that our data do not allow for a more in-depth investigation of these events. The fact that only nonviolent offenders were included in the pulling levers program also has implications for the lack of a significant violent crime reduction. It is difficult to assess the generalizability concerning the lack of an observed violent crime reduction that has been seen in other pulling levers strategies because the Delancey Heights neighborhood had such a small number of robberies and homicides, which have been the major focus of pulling levers research to this point (Piquero, 2005). On a related note, the observed gradual or lagged effect on nonviolent crime rates in the Rockford strategy also differs from those seen in prior research. Specifically, some of the initial pulling levers initiatives had an immediate effect, which was seen in Boston, Massachusetts (Piehl, Cooper, Braga, & Kennedy, 2004), Indianapolis, Indiana (Corsaro & McGarrell, 2009), Minneapolis, Minnesota (Kennedy & Braga, 1998), and other sites. Whereas the immediate or "light-switch" effect (see Kennedy, 2006, p. 158) of pulling levers is consistently observed where reducing youth, gang, and gun crime is the target of the strategy, much less is known about how much time should be expected until an effect is observed in an open-air drug market setting. Rather than having an immediate and abrupt effect when dealing with gang offenders, the pulling levers intervention strategy may serve more as a catalyst for change (requiring more lag time before an effect is observed) when directed at open-air drug market offenders. Further research that examines pulling levers in different contexts is vital to our obtaining a better understanding of its utility.

There are a number of limitations to this study that we mention with the hope of informing further research on this topic. First, the pulling levers intervention assessment here is not isolated from the combination of reactive, directed, and proactive/partnership strategies that have been established as successful interventions, which are outlined in Mazerolle et al.'s (2007) systematic review of drug enforcement strategies. In essence, the Rockford intervention could be referred to as "pulling-levers-plus" because there were supplemental strategies associated with the antidrug, law enforcement tactics. The effect of a pulling levers intervention strategy without the nuisance abatement and civil remedy approaches that were also included in the Rockford initiative would be extremely beneficial to this line of inquiry. It is certainly plausible that the correlation between the reduction in nonviolent crime in the target neighborhood and the implementation of the pulling levers strategy could be heavily influenced and confounded by the nuisance abatement programs implemented in Rockford. Future studies that examine pulling levers would benefit from a more singularly focused strategy to address this issue.

Whereas the statistical techniques and in particular the HGLM estimates were appropriate for the data used here, Bushway and McDowall (2006) contend that the use of ARIMA time-series analysis is perhaps the most rigorous criminal justice evaluation approach to assess program impact. The data available equate to 25 observation periods for the target area and the overall city, which is roughly half of the recommended number of observations needed to obtain reliable ARIMA estimates (Box & Jenkins, 1976). Despite the low number of observations, we were able to fit zero-order, permanent transfer function ARIMA models[8] for the nonviolent and violent offenses in the target area that met all of the assumptions of time-series analysis.[9] The time-series results were very consistent with those presented in the Results section above, which indicated a statistically significant reduction in nonviolent offenses ($p < .05$) and a reduction in violent offenses that was statistically insignificant. In addition, the quantitative data used here do not allow us to examine long-term impact change as well as local displacement or diffusion of benefits in contiguous areas (see Green, 1995).

The use of more rigorous, time consuming, and expensive drug offender identification methods would also strengthen research in this area. For example, Beckett, Nyrop, and Pfingst (2006) used needle exchange survey data and extensive ethnographic research methods to uncover discrepancies between official arrest data and the dark figure of crime associated with drug use in open-air drug markets. Future drug market intervention research would benefit greatly from approaches such as those used by Beckett and colleagues, especially if collected throughout the duration of program implementation. In addition, although the use of a baseline comparison of the remainder of Rockford helps reduce the concern that crime in Delancey Heights simply went through a natural reduction (i.e., regression to the mean), a more appropriate methodology would be to use comparisons between multiple neighborhoods that were consistent in terms of size, social structure, and crime rates. Officials in RPD maintained that the target area was unique from all other communities within the city and, thus, a quasi-experimental analysis of within-city neighborhoods would be somewhat unreliable. Future studies should draw from the use of more powerful analytical methodologies including the application of a quasi-experimental or experimental design to assess the effect of the localized intervention (Cook & Campbell, 1979).

SUMMARY

The statistically significant reduction in nonviolent offenses that occurred after pulling levers was implemented in Delancey Heights suggests that the extension of the initiative to drug markets holds promise. On the other hand, the lack of a statistically significant reduction in violent offenses requires further exploration. To this point, most of the research on pulling levers has focused on reducing youth, gun, and gang violence. These prior studies have consistently indicated a reduction in violent offenses driven by changes in gang-related activity. This study builds on prior problem-oriented policing research and suggests that the use of pulling levers, at least in combination with other drug law enforcement strategies, is not limited to affecting youth violence and gang-related offenses but also can be adapted to nuisance, drug, and property crimes. Future studies are needed to assess the capacity of pulling levers both independent of and in addition to other drug law enforcement strategies for eliminating drug markets in crime-ridden communities. The results of the Rockford initiative highlight the utility of such an approach.

Strategy	Description
Identification (February 2007)	Research analysts at RPD mapped index offenses, drug arrests, and drug complaints for the entire city.
Mobilization (March 2007)	Law enforcement officials determined that the Delancey Heights target neighborhood, consisting of two subbeats, would be the ideal locale for the pulling levers intervention.
Intelligence Gathering (March 2007)	A narcotics unit officer at RPD supervised intelligence gathering on individuals who engaged in chronic drug dealing in the target neighborhood.
Incident Review (March 2007)	Narcotics detectives conducted a complete incident review of all known offending in the target area. All reports and contacts with police, including intelligence gathered from cooperating witnesses, were examined. Twelve persistent offenders were identified.
Undercover Investigation (March–April 2007)	Narcotics detectives made controlled buys from the twelve identified drug dealers over the course of eight weeks. Surveillance equipment was used to record the purchases. And, cooperating witnesses were recruited.
DMI Eligibility Meeting (April 2007)	A multi-agency committee reviewed the cases made against the twelve individuals and relied upon the suspects' criminal histories (e.g., the number of violent offenses and the total number of offenses) to identify five dealers who would be eligible for the pulling levers meeting.
Notice to Residents (May 2007)	RPD notified residents at a local community meeting that an undercover investigation had been conducted over the past couple of months and that an immediate response was about to take place.
Sweep of Violent Offenders (May 2007)	Within 48 hours of the initial notification meeting, the seven violent offenders who were ineligible for the pulling levers strategy were subsequently arrested and received $500,000 bonds.
Contact With Eligible Offenders' Families (May 2007)	RPD made phone calls, and relied upon a pastor at a local church to notify offenders of the call-in by contacting their families. The police Chief also wrote a letter to each offender guaranteeing they would not be arrested at the meeting. RPD provided assistance for those out of town to ensure their attendance.

APPENDIX A

Summary of the process indicators of the pulling levers strategy

The Call-In (May 2007)	The offenders, their families, key criminal justice personnel, and community members attended the pulling levers meeting. First, residents spoke of the harm that drug dealing caused in their community. Next, offenders and their families received the deterrent message from multiagency members that continued offending would not be tolerated. Finally, an immediate needs assessment was made by social support services, followed by a more detailed assessment in the following weeks.

| Community Follow Up (May 2007) | RPD and housing inspectors seized five housing complexes where prior drug offending had been prominent. Social service officials assisted in moving residents who did not previously engage in illegal drug distribution into new homes. Maintenance code citations (e.g., lawn, trash, and poor fencing) were written for violations throughout the neighborhood. A street sweeper cleaned the streets to symbolize the change that was occurring. |
| Long-Term Follow Up | RPD continues routine and saturated patrols in the neighborhood. Community source officers and community leaders maintain communication for up-to-date information on neighborhood issues. |

KEY TERMS

Pulling levers
Deterrence
Problem-oriented policing
Open-air drug markets
Law enforcement strategies

NOTES

1. Community-wide policing is focused on drug law enforcement efforts at a broader level than drug hot spots, whereas hot spots policing relied on more traditional methods (i.e., saturation, crackdowns, street sweeps) employed at drug hot spots (see Mazerolle, Soole, & Rombouts, 2006).
2. Pseudonyms are used throughout the article, both for the study neighborhood and for participants.
3. Our interview strategy involved a two-stage approach. First, we interviewed a subsample of participants following a local community policing meeting to capture "engaged citizens'" views. Second, we also interviewed "less than involved" neighborhood residents. Equal numbers of participants were drawn from each setting.
4. It is important to note that David Kennedy, considered the architect of the original pulling levers strategy in Boston, worked with RPD officials prior to program implementation to provide guidance concerning the specific tenets of the pulling levers framework.
5. None of the random effects variance components were statistically significant in the conditional models, and thus, all of the estimates were obtained from fixed-effects models (Raudenbush & Bryk, 2002).
6. The decline of 22.2% was calculated by using exponentiation on the logged coefficient, $(-.250) = -.778$, and subtracting 1.0 to obtain the estimated change between pre- and postintervention.
7. We estimated the following Autoregressive Integrated Moving Average model in the identification stage, which was an appropriate statistical fit to the observed target neighborhood

nonviolent crime data: 1(6), 0, 0; Akaike information criterion = 26.0. This indicated a statistically significant lag in the observed nonviolent offense data without the inclusion of the intervention estimate. Results are available upon request.

8. Both violent and nonviolent offenses fit the Autoregressive Integrated Moving Average (1, 0, 0) models.

9. Specifically, both of the estimated Autoregressive Integrated Moving Average models had mean and variance stationarity and no residuals were statistically significant at key-lags, indicating appropriate model fit.

REFERENCES

Anderson, E. (1999). *Code of the street: Decency, violence, and the moral life of the inner city*. New York, NY: Norton.

Beckett, K., Nyrop, K., & Pfingst, L. (2006). Race, drugs, and policing: Understanding disparities in drug delivery arrests. *Criminology, 44*, 105–137.

Best, D., Strang, J., Beswick, T., & Gossip, M. (2001). Assessment of concentrated, high-profile police operations. *British Journal of Criminology, 41*, 738–745.

Blumstein, A., & Rosenfeld, R. (1998). Explaining recent trends in U.S. homicide rates. *Journal of Criminal Law and Criminology, 88*, 1175–1216.

Box, G. P., & Jenkins, G. M. (1976). *Time series analysis: Forecasting and control*. San Francisco, CA: Holden Day.

Braga, A. A. (2008). Pulling levers focused deterrence strategies and the prevention of gun homicide. *Journal of Criminal Justice, 36*, 332–343.

Braga, A. A., Kennedy, D., & Tita, G. (2002). New approaches to the strategic prevention of gang and group-involved violence. In C. R. Huff (Ed.), *Gangs in America* (3rd ed., pp. 271–286). Thousand Oaks, CA: Sage.

Braga, A. A., Kennedy, D. M., Waring, E. J., & Piehl, A. M. (2001). Problem-oriented policing, deterrence, and youth violence: An evaluation of Boston's Operation Ceasefire. *Journal of Research in Crime and Delinquency, 38*, 195–226.

Braga, A. A., Pierce, G. L., McDevitt, J., Bond, B. J., & Cronin, S. (2008). The strategic prevention of gun violence among gang-involved offenders. *Justice Quarterly, 25*, 132–162.

Bursik, R. J., & Grasmick, H. G. (1993). *Neighborhoods and crime: The dimensions of effective community control*. Lexington, NY: Lexington.

Bushway, S. D., & McDowall, D. (2006). Here we go again—can we learn anything from aggregate-level studies of policy interventions? *Criminology and Public Policy, 5*, 461–470.

Bynum, T., & Worden, R. (1996). *Police drug crackdowns: An evaluation of implementation and effects*. Washington, DC: National Institute of Justice.

Clarke, R. V., & Bichler-Robertson, G. (1998). Place managers, slumlords and crime in low rent apartment buildings. *Security Journal, 11*, 11–19.

Coldren, J. C., & Higgins, D. F. (2003). Evaluating nuisance abatement at gang and drug houses in Chicago. In S. H. Decker (Ed.), *Policing gangs and youth violence* (pp. 131–166). Belmont, CA: Thomson and Wadsworth.

Coleman, V., Holton, W., Olson, K., Robinson, S., & Stewart, J. (1999, October). Using knowledge and teamwork to reduce crime. *National Institute of Justice Journal*, pp. 16–23.

Cook, T. D., & Campbell, D. T. (1979). *Quasi-experimentation: Design and analysis for field settings*. Chicago, IL: Rand McNally.

Corsaro, N., & McGarrell, E. F. (2009). Testing a promising homicide reduction strategy: Re-assessing the impact of the Indianapolis "pulling levers" intervention. *Journal of Experimental Criminology, 5*, 63–82.

Cullen, F. T. (1994). Social support as an ongoing concept for criminology: Presidential address to the Academy of Criminal Justice Sciences. *Justice Quarterly, 11*, 527–559.

Dalton, E. (2002). Targeted crime reduction efforts in ten communities: Lessons for the Project Safe Neighborhoods initiative. *U.S. Attorney's Bulletin, 50*, 16–25.

Decker, S. H. (2003). *Policing gangs and youth violence*. Belmont, CA: Wadsworth.

Dray, A., Mazerolle, L., Perez, P., & Ritter, A. (2008). Policing Australia's "heroin drought": Using an agent-based model to simulate alternative outcomes. *Journal of Experimental Criminology, 4*, 267–287.

Eck, J., & Wartell, J. (1998). *Reducing crime and drug dealing by improving place management: A randomized experiment*. Washington, DC: National Institute of Justice.

Engel, R. S., Baker, S. G., Tillyer, M. S., Eck, J., & Dunham, J. (2008). *Implementation of the Cincinnati Initiative to Reduce Violence (CIRV): Year 1 report*. Cincinnati, OH: University of Cincinnati Policing Institute.

Frabutt, J. M., Gathings, M. J., Hunt, E. D., & Loggins, T. J. (2006). *High Point West End Initiative: Project description, log, and preliminary impact analysis*. Greensboro, NC: University of North Carolina at Greensboro, Center for Youth, Family and Community Partnerships.

Goldstein, H. (1990). *Problem-oriented policing*. New York, NY: McGraw-Hill.

Green, L. (1995). Cleaning up drug hot spots in Oakland, California: The displacement and diffusion effect. *Justice Quarterly, 12*, 737–754.

Kennedy, D. (1997). Pulling levers: Chronic offenders, high-crime settings, and a theory of prevention. *Valparaiso University Law Review, 31*, 449–484.

Kennedy, D. (2006). Old wine in new bottles: Policing and the lessons of pulling levers. In D. Weisburd & A. A. Braga (Eds.), *Police innovation: Contrasting perspectives* (pp. 155–170). New York, NY: Cambridge University Press.

Kennedy, D., & Braga, A. A. (1998). Homicide in Minneapolis: Research for problem solving. *Homicide Studies, 2*, 263–290.

Klofas, J., Hipple, N. K., McDevitt, J., Bynum, T., McGarrell, E. F., & Decker, S. H. (2006). *Crime incident reviews: A Project Safe Neighborhoods strategic intervention*. Washington, DC: U.S. Department of Justice, Office of Justice Programs.

Mawby, R., & Walklate, S. (1994). *Critical victimology: International perspectives*. London, UK: Sage.

Maxfield, M. G. (1999). The National Incident-Based Reporting System: Research and policy applications. *Journal of Quantitative Criminology, 15*, 119–149.

Mazerolle, L., Price, J., & Roehl, J. (2000). Civil remedies and drug control: A randomized field trial in Oakland, California. *Evaluation Review, 24*, 212–241.

Mazerolle, L., & Ransley, J. (2006). *Third party policing*. Cambridge, UK: Cambridge University Press.

Mazerolle, L. G., Ready, J., Terrill, W., & Waring, E. (2000). Problem-oriented policing in public housing: The Jersey City evaluation. *Justice Quarterly, 17*, 129–158.

Mazerolle, L., Soole, D. W., & Rombouts, S. (2006). Street-level drug law enforcement: A meta-analytical review. *Journal of Experimental Criminology, 2*, 409–435.

Mazerolle, L., Soole, D., & Rombouts, S. (2007). Drug law enforcement: A review of the evaluation literature. *Police Quarterly, 10*, 115–153.

McGarrell, E. F., Chermak, S., Wilson, J. M., & Corsaro, N. (2006). Reducing homicide through a "lever-pulling" strategy. *Justice Quarterly, 23*, 214–231.

Papachristos, A., Meares, T., & Fagan, J. (2007). Attention felons: Evaluating Project Safe Neighborhoods in Chicago. *Journal of Empirical Legal Studies, 4*, 223–272.

Pettiway, L. (1995). Copping crack: The travel behavior of crack users. *Justice Quarterly, 12*, 499–524.

Piehl, A., Cooper, S., Braga, A., & Kennedy, D. (2004). Testing for structural breaks in the evaluation programs. *The Review of Econometrics and Statistics, 85*, 550–558.

Piquero, A. R. (2005). Reliable information and rational policy decisions: Does gun research fit the bill? *Criminology and Public Policy, 4*, 479–498.

Raudenbush, S. W., & Bryk, A. (2002). *Hierarchical linear models: Applications and data analysis methods* (2nd ed.). Thousand Oaks, CA: Sage.

Rengert, G., & Wasilchick, J. (1989). *Space, time, and crime: Ethnographic insights into residential burglary*. Washington, DC: National Institute of Justice.

Sampson, R. J., Raudenbush, S., & Earls, F. (1997). Neighborhoods and violent crime: A multilevel study of collective efficacy. *Science, 277*, 918–924.

Smith, B., Davis, R., Hillenbrand, S., & Goresky, S. (1992). *Riding neighborhoods of drug houses in the private sector.* Washington, DC: American Bar Association.

Smith, M. (2001). Police-led crackdowns and cleanups: An evaluation of a crime control initiative in Richmond, VA. *Crime & Delinquency, 47,* 60–83.

Strauss, A. L. (1987). *Qualitative analysis for social scientists.* Cambridge, UK: Cambridge University Press.

Tita, G., Riley, K. J., Ridgeway, G., Grammich, C., Abrahamse, A., & Greenwood, P. (2003). *Reducing gun violence: Results from an intervention in East Los Angeles.* Santa Monica, CA: RAND Corporation.

Tyler, T. R. (1990). *Why people obey the law.* New Haven, CT: Yale University Press.

Tyler, T. R., & Folger, R. (1980). Distributional and procedural aspects of satisfaction with citizen-police encounters. *Basic and Applied Social Psychology, 1,* 281–292.

Wakeling, S. (2003). *Ending gang homicide: Deterrence can work.* Sacramento, CA: California Attorney General's Office.

Weisburd, D., & Braga, A. A. (2006). *Police innovation: Contrasting perspectives.* New York, NY: Cambridge University Press.

Weisburd, D., & Eck, J. E. (2004). What can police do to reduce crime, disorder, and fear? *The ANNALS of the American Academy of Political and Social Science, 593,* 43–65.

Weisburd, D., & Green, L. (1995). Policing hot spots: The Jersey City drug market analysis experiment. *Justice Quarterly, 12,* 711–735.

Wood, E., Spittal, P., Small, W., Kerr, T., Li, K., & Hogg, R., et al. (2004). Displacement of Canada's largest public illicit drug market in response to a police crackdown. *Canadian Medical Association Journal, 170,* 1551–1556.

Xie, M., & McDowall, D. (2008). The effects of residential turnover on household victimization. *Criminology, 46*(3), 539–575.

CHAPTER 6

Preventing Terrorism

Eric S. See
Methodist University

Patricia B. Wagner
Youngstown State University

INTRODUCTION

Prevention of terrorist acts is a major concern for any society. The attacks of September 11, 2001 on the World Trade Center (9/11) forced us as a nation to understand that terrorist attacks can and will take place on American soil. Gone are the days when terrorist events were simply something that Americans read about, or something that occurred at far away military bases and other targets. This awakening to global terrorism has occurred on a number of levels. Our definitions of terrorism have changed, along with our national responses. New laws have been passed, new agencies created, and new facilities built to house captured terrorists. Despite these efforts, several questions remain unanswered, including whether the United States is in a better position to prevent acts of terrorism today than it was a decade ago. Have the legislative and judicial modifications served our nation well and enhanced our safety? Do we really understand terrorism on a more advanced level than we did before? What is the lasting impact of the death of Osama Bin Laden?

No single chapter on terrorism can be all inclusive. This chapter will focus on a basic understanding of terrorism both before and after 9/11. It will examine various definitions and types of terrorism and their impact on society. The United States has created and activated terrorist response teams designed to detect and respond to incidents of nuclear terrorism. It has pursued foreign polices ranging from promoting the spread of democracy in the Middle East to military engagement and regime change. Laws and institutions have changed as well. New laws, such as the Patriot Act, have been passed and updated. The Department of Homeland Security was created to house numerous agencies pursuing a similar goal. In addition, old institutions have been given new life. The role of the secretive Foreign Intelligence Surveillance Act (FISA) Court has been expanded. These changes in American society will be examined to determine if and how terrorism can be prevented, and to analyze whether our nation is safer than before the attacks of 9/11.

What exactly is meant by the words *terrorist* and *terrorism*? The answer depends not only on who is asking the question, but on who provides the answer. A number of different definitions are available. The Federal Bureau of Investigation's (FBI) definition of terrorism is a good starting point:

> *There is no single, universally accepted, definition of terrorism. Terrorism is defined in the* Code of Federal Regulations *as "the unlawful use of force and violence against persons or property to*

intimidate or coerce a government, the civilian population, or any segment thereof, in further-ance of political or social objectives (Code of Federal Regulations, 2010).

The FBI further distinguishes between domestic and international terrorism in the following manner:

Domestic terrorism is the unlawful use, or threatened use, of force or violence by a group or individual based and operating entirely within the United States or Puerto Rico without foreign direction committed against persons or property to intimidate or coerce a government, the civil-ian population, or any segment thereof in furtherance of political or social objectives.

International terrorism involves violent acts or acts dangerous to human life that are a violation of the criminal laws of the United States or any state, or that would be a criminal violation if commit-ted within the jurisdiction of the United States or any state. These acts appear to be intended to intimidate or coerce a civilian population, influence the policy of a government by intimidation or coercion, or affect the conduct of a government by assassination or kidnapping. International ter-rorist acts occur outside the United States or transcend national boundaries in terms of the means by which they are accomplished, the persons they appear intended to coerce or intimidate, or the locale in which their perpetrators operate or seek asylum (FBI, 2009).

While the FBI definition provides a useful introductory view, there are a number of problems with this binary approach. First, there are different types of terrorists beyond domestic and inter-national. While not exhaustive, any typology of terrorists must also include the following: cyber, environmental, super, right wing, left wing, religious, narco, economic, professional and amateur. Terrorism categories overlap, and a particular terrorist or terrorist organization often falls under one or more of these labels simultaneously. There is no widespread agreement among terrorism experts or academics on the definitions of any these terms. In the absence of widespread agreement, and to provide a basis for crime prevention, a brief explanation of the various types of terrorists and terrorism is provided below.

Cyberterrorism. One of the newest forms of terrorism, cyberterrorism refers to the use of technology, computers, and the Internet to launch, direct, or control terrorist attacks. The Internet can be used to recruit new members, and it can be used as a command and control function. This technique allows the leaders of an organization to direct attacks from their home country or state while never meeting the operatives carrying out the attack. The Internet may also be a primary weapon itself. Cyber attacks against banks and other financial institutions, as well as key components of the government such as the Pentagon occur on a daily basis. While many cyber attacks are kept from public view, the economic impact runs into the billions of dol-lars each year.

Superterrorism. In general, superterrorism is a label that has been attached to any organiza-tion that seeks to utilize weapons of mass destruction including nuclear, biological, or chemical weapons. Some authors prefer using the term exclusively for terrorists seeking a nuclear weapon, while others take a more inclusive approach, even including acts of terrorism that include cyber warfare and economic warfare (Schweitzer & Dorsch, 1998).

Religious terrorism (radical Islamic fundamentalism). Perhaps no other type of terrorism generates as much controversy as radical Islamic fundamentalism. While only a small fraction of those following Islam can be classified as fundamentalists, an even smaller fraction can be classified as radical fundamentalists. "It is only possible to equate the use of terrorism with a militant, anti-accommodative version of Islam" (Chalk, 1999). Radical Islamic terrorism can be directed toward the country of origin of the terrorists, or toward America and other countries as well. The goals of radical Islamic fundamentalism seem pretty straight forward. America itself—as well as the entire concept of democracy—is seen as evil and in direct opposition to Islamic beliefs. While only a small subset of the followers of Islam may actually believe this, those that do have a clear mission. America must be destroyed, along with the ideals, values, and belief systems supported by America and Americans. Under this view, the United Sates is seen as an oppressor nation, interested only in expanding and controlling other nations for the purpose of exploiting their resources and imposing their ideas and beliefs upon others. Viewed in this light, attacks on America and Americans are not only permissible, they are necessary and viewed as a defense of Islam. Those who commit these acts are not viewed as terrorists, but rather as champions and martyrs fighting a good and noble fight.

Left-wing (environmental) terrorism. Left-wing terrorist groups most commonly take the form of environmental groups or animals rights groups. For example, the Earth Liberation Front is an environmental group that has been active for over 20 years, and has been identified by the FBI as responsible for a number of arsons (FBI, 2009).

Right-wing (neo-Nazi) terrorism. American right-wing terrorists include neo-Nazi organizations, skin heads, white separatists, and radical antiabortion organizations. Many of these groups have used the Internet both to train and recruit members and to harass those in the community they wish to intimidate or eliminate. Antiabortion groups have established websites complete with the pictures, addresses, phone numbers, and family details of doctors who provide abortions. These sites are then updated when the doctors are hurt or killed.

Narcoterrorism. The term *narcoterrorism* was first used in 1983 by the former President of Peru, Belaunde Terry. In its original form, narcoterrorsim was used to describe attacks on the nation's antidrug efforts and attacks on the police force (Smith, 1991) Today, the narcoterrorism has been expanded to include the use or threat of violence surrounding the drug trade, and it may be applied within or between nations. Terrorist organizations may see their primary revenue generated from the manufacture and sale of illegal drugs, or they may simply use the drug trade as a mechanism to fund other objectives.

Economic terrorism. Economic terrorism encompasses a variety of strategies and techniques. While not the sole intent of the 9/11 terrorists, the economic impact of the attack on Wall Street, the city of New York, and the airline industry was profound. Terrorists have already attacked the tourism industry of Egypt and the wine industry of Chile. Counterfeit currency can also be used to

---

BOX 6-1 Muslims in American Society

With the threat of terrorist attacks coming from certain radical Islamic fundamentalist groups, suspicion has been cast on American Muslims in general. Are they really a threat or just part of the fabric of our diverse society? For more information, see:

Muslim Integration: Challenging Conventional Wisdom in Europe and the United States at http://csis.org/files/media/csis/pubs/070920_muslimintegration.pdf

Mapping Muslim Assimilation: Islam's Growing Social Infrastructure at http://www.religionlink.com/tip_090326.php#civil

erode confidence in a nation's stability. In addition, the introduction of certain animals or bugs into a country's ecosystem could cause serious economic damage (Cetron & Davis, 1994).

State-sponsored (professional) terrorism. This term is generally used to describe traditional, state-sponsored terrorist organizations. This is the type of terrorism most commonly thought of before the attacks of 9/11. "State sponsored" simply means that a nation or government is backing the terrorist organization, supplying them with funds, and directly or indirectly controlling their actions.

Amateur terrorism. Amateur terrorism in large part stems from the rise of technology and the Internet. It includes members that are recruited and trained via the Internet and often poorly equipped to carry out a terrorist operation. Oftentimes, the terrorist scheme is discovered with minimal loss of life or property.

Pandemics. When discussing terrorism, the topics of pandemics and pandemic preparedness often arise. The World Health Organization defines a pandemic as a worldwide epidemic of a disease (WHO, 2009). A pandemic can stem from a variety of causes, and is not limited to any single disease. For instance, an entire country, multiple countries, or the world could face an influenza epidemic at any time. The source of this pandemic could be naturally occurring or the result of a man-made situation.

The focus of a pandemic could be a common virus such as the flu, or it could be a virus that had previously been thought to have been eradicated or at least controlled. Currently, only the United States and the Soviet Union retain samples of the smallpox virus. For years, there has been a worldwide debate concerning the fate of these stockpiles. Should they be destroyed to avoid the risk of improper use, or should samples remain so that scientists can continue to study them? The larger issue is whether the United States is ready to battle a worldwide, or even nationwide pandemic. Regardless of whether a pandemic is naturally occurring or the result of a terrorist attack, our healthcare system may need to be prepared to handle several million people in need of immediate life-or-death treatment.

GOALS OF TERRORISM

Understanding the goals and motives of terrorists is a difficult task. A review of the diverse types of terrorists and terrorism clearly demonstrates that there is no single universal goal that is shared by all. Nevertheless, it is vital to the prevention of terrorism to try to ascertain what it is that terrorists want.

Many of the types of terrorism the world experiences today simply did not exist 20 or 30 years ago. Traditionally, on an international level, terrorism was a state-sponsored activity, carried out by paraprofessionals who directed attacks stemming from one nation towards another. The goals of this type of terrorism were generally directed at policy change. Through the use of fear and violence, the terrorists hoped that their actions would cause a foreign government to change policies and/or procedures. On a domestic level, when the disputes occurred within a single country, the distinction between "terrorist" and "freedom fighter" often depended on the side of the battle one had a vested interest in. The goals of this type of terrorism generally centered on regime change or the recognition of minority rights. Often the terrorist organization simply wanted increased power, representation, or a voice in the direction of the government.

The creation of the Internet and the development of global economies fueled the rise of both international and domestic terrorism worldwide. Continents, countries, and economies became more and more dependent upon one another. The Internet made it increasingly difficult for governments across the world to limit the access of their citizens to the information and cultural influences of other nations. Economic cooperation and joint financial interests became viewed as economic exploitation, and foreign cultural trends became viewed as religious denigration, all fostering new agendas for potential terrorists. Radical groups within and across nations developed a means to quickly and cheaply distribute their message to the masses while maintaining a level of anonymity never before available.

Prior to the 9/11 attacks, the prevailing belief was that the majority of terrorists did not want a high number of casualties. The use of a nuclear weapon, for example, was an option that most traditional state-sponsored terrorist groups never considered (Jenkins, 1985). Instead, what terrorists groups really wanted, and needed to survive, was publicity. "Because publicity for a cause is almost always the reason for terrorism, the media inevitably are drawn into such crises beyond their task of disseminating news" (Agee, Ault, & Emery, 1985). Terry Anderson was the chief correspondent for the Associated Press and a hostage in Lebanon from March of 1985 through December of 1991. He describes a relationship in which terrorist organizations manipulate and use the media. The terrorist act needs to be reported. Without publicity, the act goes unnoticed and can accomplish no goal. Each subsequent reporting or analysis of the attack by any media source is a victory for the terrorists. Often times, factual accounts of the attack, propaganda from the terrorists, and forced "confessions" from hostages are all reported in the same manner and given equal weight. Each of these events benefits the terrorist organization, and once reported, allows that message to become a permanent part of the public record. As noted by Anderson, publicity is a goal and a weapon of the terrorists. It is their lifeblood, and once achieved, it can be used to further their agenda (Anderson, 1993).

The prevailing wisdom before the 9/11 watershed was that generating publicity was more important than maximizing the number of individuals killed in any one attack. While it may have been necessary to kill or injure, killing too many people was viewed as having a negative effect. If an attack amassed a body count that was excessive, sympathy could turn against the terrorist organization. Too much negative publicity could damage the intended goals of policy change and lead to increased pressure to eliminate the terrorist organization itself. In recent years, however, it appears that terrorists have favored a larger body count. Several factors may have contributed to a shift in the goals of terrorist organizations from small to large body counts. One factor is American military might (Carter, Deutch, & Zelikow, 1998). As the last remaining superpower, America has a military unmatched anywhere in the world. The ability of any single nation or rogue terrorist organization to directly conquer the American military on the battlefield is remote. In addition, while not perfect, the American military has the ability to adequately guard hard domestic targets such as nuclear reactors, military bases, airports, and government buildings. While attacks against these targets are certainly possible, responses would be swift and damages limited. This fact has pushed terrorists to consider and plan attacks against softer, nonconventional targets (Carter, Deutch, & Zelikow, 1998; Cetron & Davis, 1994).

The Bush Doctrine, developed by George W. Bush, describes the approach of his administration to the response to terrorism as follows:

First, make no distinction between the terrorists and the nations that harbor them—and hold both to account. Second, take the fight to the enemy overseas before they can attack us again at home. Third, confront threats before they fully materialize. And fourth, advance liberty and hope as an alternative to the enemy's ideology of repression and fear (Bush, 2010).

It is unclear if terrorist groups have actually changed their goals to include higher body counts. As noted previously, experts are divided on the question. It is evident, however, that the elements of the Bush Doctrine are focused on the elimination of terrorist threats before they become terrorist acts. A world view of terrorism however, cannot be formed based upon the events of 9/11 alone.

In the months and years leading to 9/11, many experts tried to predict and understand the changing nature of terrorism. The breakdown of the Soviet Union led to an unknown number of nuclear weapons and nuclear material being unsecured or simply missing. The fear of both superterrorism and cyberterrorism grew, and attempts were made to predict and protect against the next type of attack that might be used. By 1996, security professionals widely believed that the hijacking of airliners was mostly a thing of the past. The value of a hijacked plane was regarded to be small, as more and more countries were refusing to let them land. As a result, this kind of incident was perceived as a terrorist technique that was largely obsolete (Laqueur, 1996).

Fears shifted to nuclear, biological, or chemical attacks. Experts predicted that terrorists would shift to softer, nonmilitary targets. It was also suggested that terrorists would consider a site that allowed for multiple casualities, multiple coordinated attacks, and an event that strained the resources of the government under attack. This would allow the terrorist organization to show their strategic planning ability (Cetron & Davis, 1994). Finally, it was suggested that it would take an attack on the scale of Pearl Harbor to fully get the attention of the United States and its citizens. It was suggested that if such an event were to occur on American soil, it would forever change the face and landscape of America, and divide American history into a pre-event and postevent timeline (Carter, Deutch, & Zelikow, 1998).

Partially in line with the views of the experts, yet in direct opposition to some of their predictions, the attack occurred on September 11, 2001. A large-scale attack was launched using unorthodox methods but conventional weapons. Four airliners were hijacked and used as missiles to attack the World Trade Center and the Pentagon. Three airliners hit their targets, while a fourth crashed in Pennsylvania. The targets were a mixture of both a soft, nonmilitary target that was high in symbolic value (the World Trade Center), and a traditional hard military target (the Pentagon). The fatality and injury rate made it the most deadly terrorist attack in history. It was a new form of superterrorism, yet it was accomplished without the use of nuclear, chemical, or biological weapons. The timeline had been drawn and the landscape had changed in a matter of minutes. American history, and the history of terrorism, will forever be told in the context of pre- and post-9/11.

BOX 6-2 9/11/2001—A Day that Changed History

What have we learned from that tragic day? To find out more, see:

Library of Congress September 11 Web Archive at http://lcweb2.loc.gov/diglib/lcwa/html/sept11/sept11-overview.html

The September 11 Digital Archive at http://911digitalarchive.org/index.php

The 911 Commission Report at http://govinfo.library.unt.edu/911/report/911Report_Exec.pdf

POST-9/11 AMERICA

Since 9/11, terrorism in all its stated forms has never been viewed in the same way. While debate continues as to exactly what terrorism is, there is little doubt that the United States has focused a tremendous amount of time, energy, and resources on the issue. In the context of crime prevention, the United States has taken a variety of measures in several different categories in an attempt to respond to terrorism and terrorists. Three categories will be discussed here: prevention and response, investigation and prosecution, and detention.

The first category is prevention and response. To address this need a new agency, the Department of Homeland Security, was established to investigate, protect from, and respond to terrorist events. In addition, specially trained tactical teams capable of detecting and responding to nuclear, chemical, and biological weapons have been formed and placed on 24-hour standby. The second category deals with the legal aspects of investigating and prosecuting suspected terrorists. Chief among changes in this area are the passage of the Patriot Act and the expansion of the role of the Foreign Intelligence Surveillance Act (FISA) Court. The final category to be considered is detention. The aftermath of 9/11 gave rise to logistical questions regarding where suspected terrorists should be held as they await trial, if they are even to be tried at all.

Prevention and Response

The Department of Homeland Security was officially formed on November 25, 2002 as an umbrella organization to combine numerous related agencies. A partial list of agencies and components that make up the department includes: National Protection and Programs Directorate, Science and Technology Directorate, Directorate for Management, Office of Policy, Office of Health Affairs, Office of Intelligence and Analysis, Office of Operations Coordination, Federal Law Enforcement Training Center, Domestic Nuclear Detection Office, Transportation Security Administration, United States Customs and Border Protection, United States Immigration and Customs Enforcement, Unites States Coast Guard, Federal Emergency Management Agency, and United States Secret Service (DHS, 2011a). As of 2008, the Department of Homeland Security had approximately 225,000 employees, 22 agencies, and 22 discrete missions. The 5 main stated missions of the department are: (1) preventing terrorism and enhancing security, (2) securing and managing the borders, (3) enforcing and administering immigration laws, (4) safeguarding and securing cyberspace, and (5) ensuring resilience to disasters (DHS, 2009). To accomplish these goals,

---

BOX 6-3 Natural Disasters and Lessons Learned

What can we learn about terrorism preparedness from the management of natural disasters? For more information, see:

Federal Emergency Management Administration (FEMA) website at http://www.fema.gov/plan/index.shtm

The Federal Response to Hurricane Katrina: Lessons Learned at http://library.stmarytx.edu/acadlib/edocs/katrinawh.pdf

TABLE 6-1 Terrorist Attacks, Injuries, and Deaths, Worldwide 2005–2009

	2005	2006	2007	2008	2009
Attacks	11,023	14,443	14,435	11,725	10,999
Injuries	24,795	38,314	44,139	34,057	34,057
Deaths	14,482	20,515	22,736	15,727	14,971

Source: Adapted from Cordesman, A. H. (2011, June 29). *U.S. State Department and Counter-Terrorism Center reporting terrorism in the Middle East and Central Asia, August 2010. Patterns of terrorism: Worldwide: 2005–2009.*

the Department of Homeland Security requested a budget for 2011 totaling 56.3 billion dollars. This total represented an increase of 2% over the level of funding provided in 2010 (DHS, 2011a).

The Department of Homeland Security is only one agency among many others, with one budget line among many others working to protect Americans. What exactly is this single agency, with almost a quarter of a million employees and an annual budget exceeding 56 billion dollars, working so hard to prevent? The simplest answer is that they are trying to protect America from terrorism, both foreign and domestic. How likely is it that someone will be killed or injured by a terrorist attack? Looking at the data in **Table 6-1**, it appears to be an unlikely event.

Between 2005 and 2009, the peak year with the highest number of attacks around the world was 2006. In that year, there were 14,443 terrorist attacks. The highest death toll, however, was in 2007 with 22,736 casualties. With over three billion people on earth, the odds of being a victim of terrorism are indeed slim.

With the number so low worldwide, what are the chances of becoming a victim of terrorism in America? Put another way, how likely is it that the United States, or any particular American, will be the victim of either a foreign or domestic terrorist act? Each year since the 1980s, the FBI has compiled a report on acts of terrorism taking place in America. A careful reading of these reports leads to several crucial observations.

As noted in **Table 6-2**, in the 25-year period between 1980 and 2005, there were 245 incidents of domestic and foreign terrorism in the United States, injuring 14,038 people and killing 3,179. In effect, the United States is currently spending over 56 billion dollars in one agency alone to prevent the recurrence of a mere 245 acts. Even these numbers are misleading, as they tend to overstate the chances of being victimized by a terrorist. The attacks of 9/11 were the deadliest terrorist attacks

TABLE 6-2 Terrorism Injuries and Deaths, 1980–2005

Years	# of terrorist incidents	# of injuries	# of deaths
1980–1989	158	82	18
1990–1999	41	1,939	181
2000–2005	46	12,017	2,979
25-year totals	245	14,038	3,179

Source: Federal Bureau of Investigation (FBI). (2007). *Terrorism 2002–2005.*

TABLE 6-3 Impact of 9/11		
Years	**# of injuries**	**# of deaths**
All Attacks 1980–2005	14,038	3,179
Attacks on 9/11	12,000 (estimated)	2,972
Total minus 9/11	2,308	207
Source: Federal Bureau of Investigation (FBI). (2007). Terrorism 2002–2005.		

in history. The numbers of people killed and injured far exceed the typical attack. **Table 6-3** takes a look at how the numbers are affected by the attacks of 9/11.

Making no attempt to diminish the impact of 9/11, it is clear that once the deadliest attack in history is removed from the calculations, America suffered 2,308 terrorist-related injuries, and 207 terrorist-related deaths over 25 years. With a population of more than 300 million, the percentage of Americans who can expect to be victimized by a terrorist is infinitesimally small.

The events of September 11, 2001 were the work of Al Qaeda. This was their second terrorist attack on the World Trade Center. The first attack occurred on February 26, 1993, when a truck loaded with explosives detonated in the parking garage beneath the north tower. A group of Middle Eastern terrorists with ties to Al Qaeda planned and carried out the attack. The attack killed 6 people and injured 1,042. America has suffered from large-scale acts of domestic terrorism as well. On April 19, 1995, the Alfred P. Murrah Federal Building in Oklahoma City was bombed by Timothy McVeigh and his accomplice Terry Nichols, both United States citizens. The truck bomb that exploded at the scene caused over 600 million dollars in damage, killed 168 people, and injured 754. At the time, it was the deadliest terrorist attack in American history.

The loss of life and the number of injuries resulting from the attack in Oklahoma City and the two attacks on the World Trade Center have put Americans on heightened alert. While the losses were staggering to Americans and traumatic to the conscience of the nation, it must be reiterated that all three of these attacks were anomalies, both in the numbers of deaths and injuries. A look at the numbers in **Tables 6-4** and **6-5** illustrates the point.

On the one hand, it may seem imprudent to remove from consideration the biggest three terrorist events in this country. All three events occurred, and the injuries and deaths were very real.

TABLE 6-4 Terrorist Injuries and Deaths, 1980–2005, and by Top Three Events		
Years/Incident	**# of injuries**	**# of deaths**
All attacks 1980–2005	14,038	3,178
1993 attack on World Trade Center	1,042	6
1995 attack Oklahoma City	754	168
2011 attack on World Trade Center	12,000	2,972
Source: Federal Bureau of Investigation (FBI). (2007). Terrorism 2002–2005.		

TABLE 6-5 Terrorist Injuries and Deaths, 1980–2005, Top Three Events Excluded		
Time period	**# of injuries**	**# of deaths**
1980–2005 With the top three events excluded	242	32
Source: Federal Bureau of Investigation (FBI). (2007). Terrorism 2002–2005.		

On the other hand, useful discussions of crime prevention cannot occur until the actual scope of the problem is addressed. Fears aside, the actual odds of any American becoming the victim of a terrorist attack, foreign or domestic, are extremely remote.

Nevertheless, the fear remains. The level of fear reaches a pinnacle when the issue becomes one of nuclear terrorism. Current estimates state that there is enough raw material available to make 250,000 nuclear weapons. There has already been one documented case of a worker in the former Soviet Union stealing small amounts of highly enriched uranium. At the time of his arrest, he had stolen 1.5 kilograms of bomb-grade uranium. Upon being apprehended, he was reported to have said that he hoped to sell the stolen uranium to earn enough money to buy a refrigerator and a washing machine for his family (History Channel, Lutz 2009, Santa Clarita, CA).

While the exact numbers are not known, enough terrorist organizations around the world have been seeking nuclear weapons to make the fear of this type of attack very real. While there is disagreement, experts have predicted that the likelihood of a nuclear weapon or dirty bomb being exploded in an American city over the next 10 years is anywhere from 10% to over 50% (Lugar, 2005). While the numbers of previous injuries and deaths listed in Tables 6-1–6-4 are indeed small, they would pale by comparison to the injuries and deaths caused by the detonation of a nuclear weapon in an American city (Lugar, 2005).

Planning for the nation's response to a nuclear attack following such an event is somewhat limited. Specialized teams have been formed to respond in the wake of a nuclear attack. The primary team is the Chemical, Biological, Incident Response Force (CBIRF). CBIRF members are trained and equipped to enter the hot zone of a nuclear or biological attack and attempt to rescue victims, but the emphasis of the agency is focused primarily upon preventing the attacks from taking place rather than responding to them. A related task force, the Nuclear Emergency Support Team (NEST), is charged with the primary mission of hunting down and securing loose nuclear material and/or weapons. This team can be activated upon receiving a credible tip of an impending nuclear attack on an American city.

NEST provides technical assistance to a lead federal agency to deal with incidents—including terrorist threats—that involve the use of nuclear materials. NEST has been structured to address threats by domestic and foreign terrorists that may have the will and means to employ weapons of mass destruction. NEST would assist in the identification, characterization, rendering safe, and final disposition of any nuclear weapon or radioactive device (DOE, 2009). Under the authority of the Department of Homeland Security, NEST is one of several response teams trained and equipped to track, locate, and disarm nuclear weapons. Members of NEST are stationed across the country and can be activated and deployed anywhere in the country very rapidly.

No matter how the numbers are examined, the odds of becoming the victim of a terrorist attack are slim, both worldwide and in the United States. While response teams have been formed to track down weapons and to enter the affected hot zones, the primary mission of the Department

---

BOX 6-4 A Terrorist Attack of Epidemic Proportions

How quickly could our emergency response and healthcare systems react to an epidemic or pandemic? If a toxic viral agent were integrated into the population, would we be prepared for the consequences? To consider the possibilities, see:

> Dark Winter Bioterrorism Exercise, Andrews Air Force Base at http://www.homelandsecurity.org/
> darkwinter/docs/DARK_WINTER.pdf
> Countering the Twin Threats of Pandemic Flu and Biological Terrorism at
> http://www.americanprogress.org/events/2006/6/b593305ct2628385.html

---

of Homeland Security is to prevent the terrorist attack in the first place. In recognition of this fact, the United States has addressed terrorism prevention since 9/11 through legislation that makes it easier for law enforcement to detect and prosecute terrorist activity before an incident can occur.

Investigation and Prosecution

One of the threshold issues in preventing and defending against any terrorism attack is to identify the attacker. When the incidents of 9/11 took place, it was immediately clear that it was an attack on America, but it was not instantly apparent who the source was and what the proper response should be. Was it an act of war by a foreign power requiring military intervention, or was it to be treated as a garden-variety, albeit large-scale, criminal conspiracy? One of the first reactions to the attacks was the scrambling of military aircraft to protect the airspace over New York City. This was plainly a military response. Yet nearly 10 years later, it is still unclear whether these acts would have been best investigated using traditional law enforcement tactics by a federal agency, such as the FBI or the Central Intelligence Agency (CIA), or by using a straight military approach.

At the request of civilian law enforcement authorities, the U.S. military is permitted to provide certain military support such as natural disaster relief. This support can also include relief in terrorist attack situations. For example, in the Oklahoma City bombing, the military provided medevac aircraft, ambulances, bomb detection dog teams, and various military personnel at the crime scene to assist local authorities (Winthrop, 1997). The Posse Comitatus Act prohibits military personnel from executing the law unless it serves a military purpose, or under some narrowly defined exceptions. Therefore, whether a terrorist attacker is considered to be a military operative rather than a traditional criminal has broad legal implications. The former invites the engagement of military authorities while the latter is handled through civilian law enforcement mechanisms. While the hypothetical debate lingers on, we can examine what has actually occurred. One of the first major responses to the attacks on 9/11 was to strengthen the hand of civilian law enforcement agencies through the Patriot Act.

The Patriot Act

The U.S.A. Patriot Act (Patriot Act) is a vital legal tool for the government to investigate and prosecute terrorists. The Patriot Act was enacted quickly in reaction to the attacks of 9/11. The purpose of the Patriot Act was to prevent future acts of terrorism by expanding the government's authority to collect intelligence involving both foreign and domestic terrorists, to combat money laundering, and to secure our borders. It created new crimes and enhanced penalties for old ones. Congress passed the Patriot Act in a climate of fear and shock on October 24, 2001, a mere 45 days after the worst terrorist attacks in our nation's history. There was virtually no debate on the law at the time of its passage, and it received strong bipartisan support. The Patriot Act swept through Congress by overwhelming margins, passing by 98 to 1 in the Senate and 357 to 66 in the House of Representatives. Some of the lawmakers later admitted that they did not even read the Act before voting to approve it, so great was the sense of urgency at the time (McCullagh, 2005). Further expediting the Act's passage, legislators built in a safeguard against problems that might arise by scheduling much of the Act to expire in 2005, roughly 4 years after its passage.

The Patriot Act amended multiple federal statutes and constituted a voluminous 342 pages. Among the better known federal laws that were revised by the Patriot Act are the Immigration and Nationality Act, the Bank Secrecy Act, the Money Laundering Control Act of 1986, the Electronic Communications Privacy Act of 1986, the Foreign Intelligence Surveillance Act of 1978, and the Victims of Crime Act of 1984, Given the length, complexity, and sweeping scope of the Patriot Act, it was inevitable that it would generate controversy and litigation following its initial adoption. Hundreds of municipal, county, and state governing bodies reacted by passing ordinances or resolutions opposing sections of the Act. Supporters argue that it has been indispensable in the prevention of numerous terrorist plots and successful prosecutions, while opponents claim that it undermines civil liberties by giving law enforcement too much power. Nevertheless, in response to the sunset clause that would have allowed the Act to expire, the Patriot Act was reauthorized in 2006 without major revisions.

There are 10 titles to the Patriot Act. Each title is a separate section of the law devoted to a particular topic of crime prevention. The following is a brief overview of the Act's key areas. Title I of the Patriot Act provides for federal funding to support antiterrorist activities, including money for the FBI Technical Support Center. A nationwide Electronic Task Force was authorized, and the President was given the power to confiscate property from foreign powers or agents who have participated in attacks against the United States. Title I of the Act, as well as Title X, address the issue of racial and religious bigotry and violence, which was documented to have occurred with increased frequency against some minority groups following 9/11. Title I specifically condemns the targeting of Arab and Muslim Americans, and Title X condemns the targeting of Sikh Americans, who report being frequently confused with Muslims. Despite the best intentions of these provisions, controversy over unfair profiling of these groups persists.

Title II of the Patriot Act addresses a myriad of surveillance procedures. It enhances the ability of the government to gather foreign intelligence from suspected terrorists, whether or not the suspects are United States citizens. It authorizes intercepting communications believed to be related to terrorist activities and then provides for the sharing of such information among federal agencies. The means of surveillance permitted was broadened to encompass almost any method practicable. This includes allowing orders for roving surveillance, which permits surveillance to follow a target wherever he or she may travel in the nation, as opposed to more traditional orders for surveillance that limit a wiretap to one telephone line at a specific location. Title II also imposed reporting obligations on information providers such as telecommunications companies and Internet service providers, who now may be required to produce records of suspects' usage without the knowledge of those individuals. With this new power, the government can monitor a terrorism suspect's telephone and computer activity, including the content and times of telephone conversations, and the log-on information for websites they visit.

One of the more controversial sections of Title II provides for so-called "sneak and peak" warrants to be issued, allowing the government to delay giving notice to suspects that physical searches of their private premises have been authorized until after the search has been concluded. Brandon Mayfield, a Muslim American lawyer from Oregon, sued to challenge the constitutionality of this and other provisions after his premises were secretly searched, and he was erroneously linked to a 2004 Madrid train bombing incident. Although the trial court ruled that portions of the Patriot Act were unconstitutional, including the sneak and peek provision, the Ninth Circuit Court of Appeals overturned the ruling (*Mayfield v. United States*, 2009). Another part of Title II that provoked widespread public debate concerned the ability of the government to obtain items that may relate to terrorist activity such as books, papers, documents, and records from sources like schools and public libraries. Critics, including the American Library Association, claim the Act will permit the widespread clandestine gathering of information on people's reading habits where there is no proof that they are engaged in criminal activity (ALA, 2005), while supporters of the Act counter that this rhetoric is mere fear-mongering that serves to undermine prevention efforts (MacDonald, 2003).

Combating money laundering is the primary subject of Title III of the Patriot Act. Money laundering refers to the movement of cash or other valuables that are the fruits or instruments of crime. Title III aims to prevent terrorism by cutting off sources of financial support for individual terrorists and terrorist organizations. It requires stricter and more comprehensive recordkeeping by financial institutions, which may be required to share financial information on suspected terrorists with the government. In addition, Title III expanded the definitions of and increased the penalties for money laundering, smuggling, illegal exportation, bribery, and official corruption. This title also provides procedures for confiscating money and property from those connected with terrorist activities.

Reinforcing border security is the goal of Title IV of the Patriot Act. Title IV allocates increased federal funding for border patrols, customs agents, and immigration and naturalization officials in order to strengthen our national borders. Title IV authorized enhanced identification documentation and background screening to prevent alien terrorists from entering the United States, and further permitted the detention and/or deportation of those already within our borders.

Title IV also provides for enhanced monitoring of foreigners who are in the country on student visas. Moreover, any foreigner with ties to a terrorist organization could be prohibited from entering the United States.

The use of National Security Letters is delineated in Title V of the Patriot Act. A National Security Letter is a formal demand letter for private records about an individual who is under investigation. The types of information that can be obtained with a National Security Letter include credit, financial, telephone, and email records. Court approval is not required prior to the issuance of a National Security Letter. Although such letters can be used to obtain records, ongoing electronic surveillance and physical searches normally would require court approval as discussed below. Among the United States government agencies that may use a National Security Letter to obtain information are the FBI, the Department of Defense, the CIA, and the Department of Homeland Security. A National Security Letter is an extremely flexible and useful tool for investigators because there is no need to demonstrate to a judge that there is probable cause that a crime has been committed, and the letter contains a gag order that prohibits the recipient who is producing the information from disclosing that they received the letter. An exception to the gag rule allows the recipient of a National Security Letter to disclose receipt to their attorney, so that they may request a court to review, modify, or repeal the letter after the fact.

Prior to the Patriot Act, a National Security Letter could only be used if the government could show that the target suspected of terrorism was a foreign power. Title V of the Act relaxed this requirement and permitted National Security Letters to be issued whenever the records sought have relevance to an ongoing investigation. This change allowed the use of National Security Letters even where the subject is a United States citizen who is not being investigated for a crime. Title V of the Act also expanded the number of federal bureaucrats who were eligible to issue National Security Letters, for example, permitting letters to be issued from FBI field agents rather than from headquarters. Not surprisingly, use of these letters is problematic for civil libertarians given the lack of judicial oversight and the secrecy surrounding the process. In 2007, the FBI disclosed the results of an internal probe that documented more than one thousand occasions in which National Security Letters had been used improperly to skirt traditional warrant requirements (Solomon, 2007). The American Civil Liberties Union has successfully challenged the use of National Security Letters in at least two cases (*Doe v. Gonzales*, 2005; *Internet Archive v. Mukasey*, 2008); however, such litigation is relatively rare, and it has not dampened the government's enthusiasm for the use of such letters. Since the Patriot Act became law, the use of National Security Letters has increased dramatically. The Justice Department reported to Congress that in just 1 year (2008), the number of National Security Letter requests increased to 24,744 from 16,804 in the previous year (Department of Justice, 2009).

Title VI of the Patriot Act provides for financial compensation for the victims of terrorism and their families. In the wake of 9/11, this section was intended to improve the way the U.S. Victims of Crime Fund was funded and managed so that public safety officers killed or injured in the tragedy, and their families, would receive aid expeditiously. Under the Act, no means testing would be used to determine who would be compensated, and even citizens who were victimized outside of the United States could qualify. The states could also apply for grants under Title VII to fund state crime victim funds, disaster relief efforts, training, and technical assistance for preventing, responding to, and prosecuting terrorism.

In Title VIII of the Patriot Act, new crimes are defined and added to the list of federal offenses considered to be terrorism. Domestic terrorism was broadened to include offenses that went well beyond obvious examples like instances that involve mass destruction similar to 9/11. Title VIII of the Act created new federal terrorism crimes that include intimidation, kidnapping, assassination, racketeering, money laundering, charity fraud, counterfeiting, computer hacking (cybercrime), and using biological weapons. In addition, Title VIII increased penalties applicable to terrorism crimes already on the books and established stiff penalties for newly defined terrorism crimes. For example, attacking a mass transportation system that is occupied by passengers could result in a sentence of life imprisonment even if there are no injuries. Penalties were enhanced for traditional crimes that a terrorist would be likely to commit, such as conspiracy or arson. Similarly, Title VIII establishes the penalties to be imposed upon people who aid and abet terrorists. This assistance may consist of harboring, training, providing resources, giving expert advice, or providing material assistance to terrorists in any other way.

Title IX of the Patriot Act attempts to ameliorate the problem of poor communication between government entities by creating streamlined procedures for sharing national intelligence between agencies. Finally, Title X of the Patriot Act is the catch-all section for miscellaneous, minor provisions that do not fit neatly into other titles of the Act. Examples of the various unrelated items in this title include provisions for studying the feasibility of employing biometric factors to screen people entering the country, for mandating training and background checks for Hazmat licenses, and for imposing up to 5 years' imprisonment for impersonating a Red Cross member. Title IX also provides for federal funding in the form of foreign law enforcement training grants.

BOX 6-5 Military Law and Civilian Law

The military justice system is a separate, unique legal system from civilian law. What are some of the major differences? How would terrorism suspects be treated under military law? For more information, see:

Constitutional Topic: Military Justice at http://www.usconstitution.net/consttop_milj.html
Library of Congress Military Resources at http://www.loc.gov/rr/frd/Military_Law/

Whether the Patriot Act is a successful tool for preventing terrorism is difficult to measure. Since the Act's passage, no major terrorist attacks have occurred on United States soil. It is impossible to prove, however, that the relative safety from terrorist attacks that our nation has experienced in the last decade is a direct result of the Act. Even so, there can be no doubt that at least some potential terrorist activity has been stymied by the government's use of powers that were conferred by the Patriot Act. No law can be 100% effective in preventing crime, but at least it can serve as a strong weapon in the government's antiterrorism arsenal.

Foreign Intelligence Gathering Under FISA

In order to prevent foreign attacks on the United States, it is essential that the government have the ability to gather intelligence thoroughly and efficiently. The Foreign Intelligence Surveillance Act of 1978 (FISA) was enacted to prescribe the terms under which the government could engage in domestic surveillance in order to monitor foreign intelligence (Department of Justice, 2009). Before the passage of FISA, numerous complaints had been lodged by citizens claiming the government had violated their civil liberties with unbridled warrantless surveillance. In 1975 and 1976, the Church Committee held congressional hearings that documented flagrant government abuses of covert surveillance. FISA was an attempt to remedy this problem by creating a legal mechanism that balances the government's legitimate need to gather intelligence for national security purposes against the expectation of privacy held by citizens.

FISA regulates the gathering of foreign intelligence only within the United States. It does not apply to the gathering of intelligence outside of our national borders. FISA authorizes the government to conduct both physical searches and electronic surveillance in order to collect foreign intelligence. Such "foreign intelligence information" is defined under the law as:

(1) information that relates to, and if concerning a United States person is necessary to, the ability of the United States to protect against—
   (A) actual or potential attack or other grave hostile acts of a foreign power or agent of a foreign power;
   (B) sabotage or international terrorism by a foreign power or an agent of a foreign power; or
   (C) clandestine intelligence activities by an intelligence service or network of a foreign power or by an agent of a foreign power; or
(2) information with respect to a foreign power or foreign territory that relates to, and if concerning a United States person is necessary to—
   (A) the national defense or the security of the United States; or
   (B) the conduct of the foreign affairs of the United States.

FISA was written to prevent random fishing expeditions into the private affairs of United States citizens by requiring that the targets of FISA warrants be foreign powers or agents. Note that the definition above refers to a "foreign power or agent of a foreign power" as the source of the foreign intelligence to be gathered under the Act. In 2004, the definition of "foreign power" was amended to include any noncitizen (or permanent resident alien) who prepares for or engages in international terrorism, even if they are acting alone. The purpose of this so-called "lone wolf" amendment was to allow for FISA warrants where there is no apparent connection between the lone wolf and a terrorist organization or foreign government.

The government need only show probable cause that the target of the surveillance is a foreign power or agent before searches and electronic surveillance can be authorized. In this regard, FISA search or surveillance warrants differ from traditional warrants, which require probable cause that a crime is being or has been committed. FISA warrants do not require probable cause of a crime because their stated purpose is intelligence gathering, not criminal investigation. In 2007, the Protect America Act amended FISA to remove the warrant requirement altogether for monitoring communications that either begin or end in a foreign country, or where the target of surveillance is reasonably believed to be outside of the United States. In situations where court approval is required, the government may request the use of wiretaps, pen registers or trap/trace equipment (the electronic equivalent of a clandestine caller ID device), certain business records, and physical searches of premises.

FISA provided for the establishment of a new court that would have jurisdiction to hear applications for and issue court orders approving warrants for searches and surveillance anywhere in the nation. This specialized FISA Court was created for the express purpose of reviewing requests under FISA to conduct intelligence gathering and to resolve legal issues that arose under the Act. Membership on the United States FISA Court is determined by the Chief Justice of the U.S. Supreme Court. Although FISA originally provided for a 7-member court, the Patriot Act increased the number of judges on the court to 11 to accommodate a larger caseload. Not only did the Patriot Act expand the membership of the FISA Court, it added the requirement that at least 3 of the judges on the court reside within 20 miles of Washington, DC to facilitate urgent requests for court orders. The court meets twice per month, with two of the Washington, DC-based judges available on the other days. One judge must be on call around the clock to preside over emergency hearings that may take place at night or on weekends (Lawton, 1983). The Chief Justice appoints U.S. District Court judges to serve on the FISA Court for 7-year terms. A judge is permitted to serve on the FISA Court for one term only.

The feature that starkly sets the FISA Court apart from other federal courts is its secrecy. Unlike most other federal court proceedings, FISA Court proceedings are closed to the public to protect the government's need for stealth in its investigations. The Court meets behind locked doors in a windowless section of the Justice Department building in Washington, DC. Records of court proceedings are classified and generally unavailable to the public. On the rare occasion that the Court releases records of its proceedings, they are heavily redacted to remove confidential information. Although the Court must make an annual report to Congress, it includes only the barest statistics such as the number of warrant requests sought and approved, without other details that would betray the nature of the requests.

The FISA Court becomes involved in the prevention of terrorism when the government suspects that a certain foreign individual or group, or someone operating as their agent, may be the source of valuable national security information. Requests for so-called "FISA warrants" are processed by the Department of Justice, which screens all applications from the various federal agencies before they can proceed. Once the Justice Department has reviewed and approved an application, a government attorney would then apply to the court for a FISA warrant to obtain records, conduct a physical search, or begin electronic surveillance. Only the government presents evidence, and other affected parties do not participate in any way. If electronic surveillance is approved, common carriers like telecommunications companies and Internet service providers must cooperate with the government while maintaining the confidentiality of the surveillance.

Although an important purpose of the FISA Court is to screen out inappropriate warrant requests, in actuality the FISA Court almost always approves government applications. According to the Department of Justice Annual Reports to Congress, the FISA Court has only denied a total of 11 applications for electronic surveillance and/or physical searches since 1979, the first year reported after FISA's enactment, until the most recent report in 2010. During that same time period, the FISA Court approved 27,855 applications for such warrants. In other words, the Court approves more than 2,000 requests for each one it denies. The Patriot Act also authorizes the government to seek a separate order from the FISA Court for certain business records in terrorism investigations. To date none of these business records requests has ever been denied by the Court (Department of Justice, 2010).

The President of the United States, through the Attorney General, may authorize surveillance in national security investigations without a FISA warrant in some situations. Surveillance within the United States that would otherwise require a warrant can be conducted without one for up to 1 year, as long as there is no substantial likelihood that the surveillance will capture any communication in which a United States person is a party. A United States "person" is defined as a citizen, permanent resident alien, or organization comprised thereof. The President may authorize warrantless domestic surveillance even if it involves United States citizens for up to 15 days when a war is declared by Congress. Finally, the Attorney General may also begin surveillance without prior court approval in an emergency if he or she seeks court approval no later than 24 hours after the surveillance has begun.

FISA also provided for the establishment of the U.S. FISA Court of Review, which serves as an appellate court to review orders of the FISA Court. This appellate court consists of three judges appointed by the Chief Justice of the Supreme Court. They may be chosen from the ranks of U.S. Courts of Appeals judges or U.S. District Court judges, but a judge may not serve on both the FISA Court and the FISA Court of Review. The FISA Court of Review convened for the first time in its history in 2002. Before then, the FISA Court was so consistent in granting government requests that no appeals of its orders were ever filed, making any meeting of the FISA Court of Review unnecessary. In 2002, the FISA Court rejected a warrant application made by the government, leading to an appeal of the rejection to the FISA Court of Review. The Court of Review took jurisdiction over the matter, known as *In re Sealed Case* (*In re Sealed Case*, 2002), and issued a decision overturning the FISA Court's denial of the application. *In re Sealed Case* gave the public a rare opportunity to study case law issued directly from the U.S. FISA Court of Review. In the decision, the Court of Review ruled on the constitutionality of FISA, finding that it is a valid statute. Among other things, they also interpreted the Patriot Act to allow the approval of warrants for the collection of evidence in criminal prosecutions in some circumstances, and acknowledged the President's right to authorize warrantless surveillance of foreign intelligence.

When the FISA Court was established, its authority was limited to surveillance activities in which gathering foreign intelligence was the primary purpose. The FISA Court of Review found that under the Patriot Act, such surveillance could be approved when foreign intelligence is merely a significant purpose, even if not the primary or sole purpose. According to the FISA Court of

Review in *In re Sealed Case*, surveillance for the purposes of prosecuting a criminal case is now permitted under FISA as long as there is also a copurpose of foreign intelligence gathering. In effect, the Patriot Act expanded the scope of powers given to the FISA Court to permit government surveillance in a broader arena.

FISA had originally been written narrowly to prevent the government from manipulating its provisions under the guise of foreign intelligence surveillance when the real purpose was to gather evidence for ordinary criminal prosecutions. There was concern that without a wall of separation between criminal investigations and foreign intelligence gathering, the government would abuse its authority by, for example, initiating a secret wiretap against a criminal suspect without the normal probable cause and discovery protections guaranteed to criminal defendants under the Fourth Amendment (Leahy, 2002). For this reason, when surveillance pursuant to a FISA warrant turned up incidental evidence of criminal activity, it was reviewed and processed independently by a designated official who was not the intelligence officer on the case, prior to being shared with a prosecutor. The unfortunate result of this separation was that there was poor communication between agencies seeking information involving the same targets, hampering prevention. The Patriot Act sought to make FISA a more effective foreign intelligence tool by removing this barrier to cooperation between government entities. The Patriot Act's various amendments to FISA have made the FISA Court a much more attractive vehicle for law enforcement than it was before 9/11, as evidenced by the sharp increase in FISA warrants approved. **Table 6-6** shows the number of FISA warrants issued in the 30 years since the inception of the FISA Court.

Clearly, the FISA Court has become a proactive force in the fight against terrorism. With increased surveillance approved by the Court, terrorist plots can be nullified at the earliest stages. Once terrorists are exposed they can be subject to prosecution in U.S. Courts for any criminal violations.

Detention—Guantanamo Bay

Suspected terrorists arrested in the United States are generally subject to detention in domestic federal facilities just like any other criminals. In the wake of 9/11, however, the United States quickly detained a large number of suspected terrorists operating on foreign soil. What to do with foreign terrorists once they are captured has become a contentious issue. The federal prison located at Guantanamo Bay, Cuba ("Gitmo") was expanded to house the influx of terrorism suspects from Afghanistan and other countries resulting from the so-called "war on terror." The legal status of the prison, as well as the legal rights of these detainees, has been the subject of much controversy.

Reliable facts and figures concerning Gitmo and its occupants are not readily available. The nature of the facility and those housed in it make it very difficult, if not impossible, to accurately describe and quantify the detainees there, what acts of terrorism they might have actually attempted or completed, and how they have been treated at the facility. Best estimates reflect that about 750–800 individuals have been detained at Gitmo since it opened in 2002 (Northam, 2005). Current estimates indicate that about 170–250 individuals remain. President Obama made it a campaign issue to close Gitmo during his presidential campaign in 2008. In 2009, he signed an executive order to close the institution within a year. As of this writing, however, Gitmo remains in operation.

Inmates serving time at Gitmo have been classified as "enemy combatants" (Fetini, 2008). This designation is critical, because it justifies a process to deal with these inmates and their legal cases that is entirely different from the process accorded ordinary criminals. The classification of an individual as an enemy combatant, along with subsequent legislation, allows the government to

TABLE 6-6 Number of Warrants Granted by the FISC by Year

Pre-9/11		Post-9/11	
Year	# of warrants	Year	# of warrants
1979	207	2002	1,228
1980	322	2003	1,724
1981	431	2004	1,754
1982	473	2005	2,072
1983	549	2006	2,176
1984	635	2007	2,370
1985	587	2008	2,083
1986	573	2009	1,376
1987	512		
1988	534		
1989	546		
1990	595		
1991	593		
1992	484		
1993	509		
1994	576		
1995	697		
1996	839		
1997	748		
1998	796		
1999	880		
2000	1,012		
2001	934		

Source: U.S. Department of Justice (2009). FISA annual reports to Congress, 1979–2009.

deny these individuals access to the federal court system. It also allows the government to try them before a military tribunal, or to simply continue to detain them at will, while declining to ever file formal charges.

The current status of inmates at Gitmo is uncertain. To date, five detainees have been convicted by military tribunals, and only one, Ahmed Ghailani, has been convicted at a federal trial in the United States. Several hundred detainees have been released to foreign countries. Critics of the process claim that an estimated 61 that have been released have rejoined terrorist forces in the fight against America, although this number has been challenged (Wilkerson, 2009). President Obama has advocated that more detainees face trial in American courts. Adding to the confusion, however, Congress has passed a law prohibiting the Pentagon from bringing more detainees to this country for trial. In addition, President Obama has reaffirmed one of the more controversial policies of the Bush administration by indicating that at least some of the inmates at Gitmo may continue to be detained without being charged with any crime, or being brought before a military tribunal or a criminal court. The government's position is that because these inmates are classified as enemy combatants, they fall outside the reach of the federal court system.

The impact that Gitmo has on the goal of crime prevention is unclear. Without knowing the full backgrounds of those held at Gitmo, it is impossible to adequately assess the true risk they pose to the security of the United States. Without a precise understanding of how many detainees released from Gitmo have rejoined terrorist forces and why, the basic question of whether Gitmo helps protect America or breeds additional terrorist actions, cannot be considered. It is clear that America needs a facility to house, incarcerate, and punish terrorists. It is also clear that a system to try these suspects, while still protecting the interests of the country, needs to be developed. It is unclear, however, whether Gitmo or military tribunals accomplish either of those necessary goals.

THE POST-OSAMA BIN LADEN ERA OF TERRORISM

On Sunday, May 1, 2011, in an address from the White House, President Obama made the following announcement: "Good evening. Tonight, I can report to the American people and to the world that the United States has conducted an operation that killed Osama Bin Laden, the leader of al Qaeda, and a terrorist who's responsible for the murder of thousands of innocent men, women, and children." That statement by the President ushered in a new age in the fight against terrorism.

At the time of this writing, there are more questions than answers, both about the operation that killed Bin Laden and about the future of the war on terrorism. The official story from the administration has continued to change on a daily basis, and new details are being leaked at a rapid pace. At this point, no academic record exists detailing the actual events. Much of the following information has been gleaned from newspapers, magazines, and online sources. In the coming days, weeks, months, and years, much of what is written here may be contradicted. Nonetheless, it is important to document the early record. While the exact details of what occurred on April 1, 2011 may never be released, the questions raised by the killing of Osama Bin Laden and the effects on the global fight against terrorism, are immense.

Initial debate has focused on whether the assault that resulted in the death of Bin Laden was a capture-or-kill mission, or a straight out kill mission. Reuters news agency reported on April 2, 2011 that the mission was strictly a kill mission, meaning that there was never any intention to capture Bin Laden alive (Hosenball, 2011). Early statements by various administration officials seem to back this up. The narrative soon changed, however, and the mission was described as a kill-or-capture mission (Scherer, 2011). One additional scenario, advanced by a daughter of Bin Laden, is that he was captured alive and killed later by U.S. forces.

These inconsistent scenarios will likely continue to be floated unless and until the United States releases video images of the raid. CBS News reported that the entire 40-minute raid had been captured on helmet cameras worn on by the military strike force (Martin, 2011). While the release of relevant video would not deter all of the conspiracy theorists, it would provide corroboration of the official version of events.

After initial indications that photographs of Bin Laden's body might be released, the administration opted not to release them. It is believed by some in the administration that pictures of that sort could enrage Muslims around the world. As of May 7, 2011, the Associated Press had already filed a Freedom of Information Request for the photographs in question (Winslow, 2011). While releasing the videotapes or the photographs will certainly not convince a worldwide audience, it remains to be seen if the evidence will be released by choice or court order, and what the impact of such a release might be.

The legality of killing Bin Laden under the Constitution and international law has also been the subject of debate. Initial reports claimed that Bin Laden was involved in a gun battle with U.S. Forces. Later reports claim that he was unarmed, but did not surrender. However, if the point was to kill and not capture him all along, then whether he was armed or resisted is immaterial. Attorney General Holder described Bin Laden as an enemy commander in the field and claimed that the mission to capture or kill him was an act of national self-defense (Silverleib, 2011). Adding to the complexity of the debate, Bin Laden was killed in the foreign, sovereign nation of Pakistan, and the United States did not notify Pakistan of the mission until after it was completed. Was Bin Laden a soldier in a war, a mass murderer, or a foreign leader? President Reagan signed executive order 12333 in 1981. Section 2.11 of that order states:

> *Prohibition on Assassination. No person employed by or acting on behalf of the United States Government shall engage in, or conspire to engage in, assassination.*

However, public law 107040, passed by a Joint Resolution of Congress on September 18, 2001 states:

SEC. 2. AUTHORIZATION FOR USE OF UNITED STATES ARMED FORCES.

(a) IN GENERAL.—That the President is authorized to use all necessary and appropriate force against those nations, organizations, or persons he determines planned, authorized, committed, or aided the terrorist attacks that occurred on September 11, 2001, or harbored such organizations or persons, in order to prevent any future acts of international terrorism against the United States by such nations, organizations or persons.

(b) WAR POWERS RESOLUTION REQUIREMENTS.—

(1) SPECIFIC STATUTORY AUTHORIZATION.—Consistent with section 8(a)(1) of the War Powers Resolution, the Congress declares that this section is intended to constitute specific statutory authorization within the meaning of section 5(b) of the War Powers Resolution.

How much the government of Pakistan knew, and whether they are truly a United States ally are questions that will take years to address. The political relationship with Pakistan is complicated and subject to change based upon a number of factors. It seems incredible that Bin Laden could have spent so many years hiding in one place in Pakistan, so close to a military training facility, without the aid of the government of Pakistan. As early as May 4, 2011, a bill was introduced in the House of Representatives to cut off U.S. aid to Pakistan unless it could be established that Pakistan was not involved in hiding Bin Laden (Kasperowicz, 2011). In response to the view that Pakistan was actively involved in protecting and hiding Bin Laden, the President of Pakistan, Asif Ali Zardari, published an editorial in the Washington Post the day after Bin Laden's announced death. In part, he said:

> *Let us be frank. Pakistan has paid an enormous price for its stand against terrorism. More of our soldiers have died than all of NATO's casualties combined. Two thousand police officers, as many as 30,000 innocent civilians and a generation of social progress for our people have been*

lost. And for me, justice against bin Laden was not just political; it was also personal, as the ter-
rorists murdered our greatest leader, the mother of my children. Twice he tried to assassinate my
wife. In 1989 he poured $50 million into a no-confidence vote to topple her first government. She
said that she was bin Laden's worst nightmare—a democratically elected, progressive, moderate,
pluralistic female leader. She was right, and she paid for it with her life.

Some in the U.S. press have suggested that Pakistan lacked vitality in its pursuit of terror-
ism, or worse yet that we were disingenuous and actually protected the terrorists we claimed to
be pursuing. Such baseless speculation may make exciting cable news, but it doesn't reflect fact.
Pakistan had as much reason to despise al-Qaeda as any nation. The war on terrorism is as much
Pakistan's war as it is America's. And though it may have started with bin Laden, the forces of
modernity and moderation remain under serious threat. (Zardari, 2011)

Now that Bin Laden is gone, speculation is rampant as to the future of Al Qaeda. The most
likely successor to Osama Bin Laden is Ayman al-Zawahri. As a long time aid and deputy to Bin
Laden, he seems the most logical selection. It must be stressed that Al Qaeda is not a multinational
corporation with a board of directors, nor is it run like one. Al Qaeda was fueled by a strict devo-
tion to the cult of personality developed by Bin Laden. In the 10 years since 9/11, however, Bin
Laden has been running the organization mostly from behind the scenes. Early indications from
the treasure trove of intelligence that was collected during the raid that killed Bin Laden seems to
demonstrate that he was more in control of the organization than the United States first thought.

This all points to a complex yet fragmented organization left behind after Bin Laden's death.
While Ayman al-Zawahri appears to have the support of Al Qaeda elements in Iraq (AP, 2011),
many in Al Qaeda prefer a different leader at the helm and believe that perhaps no new leader will
be officially named (Santana, 2011). It is possible that a smaller, fragmented, more independent Al
Qaeda may be a greater challenge to U.S. intelligence and military forces.

Reaction in the Muslim world has been a mixture of relief and outrage. The outrage stems
from the killing of a Muslim by the U.S., the perceived invasion of a sovereign nation, the dumping
of Bin Laden's body at sea, and the killing of his son during the raid. As noted by the President of
Pakistan, however, others focus on the thousands of innocent people, including innocent Muslims,
killed by Bin Laden and Al Qaeda. Long-term reaction remains to be seen.

One question that can at least be addressed in the short term is whether there will be attacks in
retaliation to Bin Laden's death. May 13, 2011 marked the first retaliatory attack by Al Qaeda. The
double suicide attack, which occurred outside a training facility in Pakistan, killed at least 80 and
injured dozens more. Various members of Al Qaeda have promised additional attacks, including
attacks on the United States and various U.S. interests.

One benefit of the operation that killed Bin Laden is that intelligence gathered from the raid
may help to prevent future attacks by Al Qaeda. ABC News reported that the United States confiscated a million pages of data to analyze. According to early reports, Al Qaeda had targeted President
Obama and his 88-year-old step-grandmother (Ross, Chuchmach, & Raddatz, 2011). Among the
items recovered from the compound were computers, flash drives, Bin Laden's personal diary, and
pornography. This kind of intelligence directly from the leader of Al Qaeda, combined with the
sheer volume of material, will keep the intelligence community busy for years.

A number of important questions surrounding the raid remain unanswered. The public may
never know why the United States was stymied so long in locating Bin Laden's hiding place, and
whether controversial forms of enhanced interrogation ultimately contributed to the success of
the mission. No doubt some will argue the success of the raid validates the Patriot Act, Gitmo,

and other post 9/11 institutions. Unfortunately, thousands of American soldiers have been killed, and tens of thousands have been injured in the wars in Iraq and Afghanistan. Massive government agencies have been created, and the economy has suffered. Was it worth it and did the ends justify the means? While these questions may take years to answer, the death of Bin Laden has brought them to the forefront again.

CONCLUSION

Adding to the dilemma surrounding terrorism is our inability as a nation to answer a basic question—whether terrorism is a problem for law enforcement, the military, or the political establishment. The prevention of terrorism raises many larger issues that go beyond tinkering with the mechanics of our current law enforcement and legal apparatus. It raises policy issues regarding the proper division of prevention roles between the civilian, military, and political systems.

Should the lead agency be the FBI, the military, or the White House? If terrorism is a law enforcement problem, then changes in the law such as the Patriot Act should aid in the investigation and prosecution of suspected terrorists. If the military is in charge, then it seems to follow that the use of force is the primary weapon to fight terrorism. If this is a political issue, then the spread of democracy has been suggested as the primary tool to change the hearts and minds of would be terrorists. Concerning military and political options however, there are more philosophical and political issues to be resolved, such as whether efforts by the United States to spread democracy would be more likely to preclude or incite terrorism. To date, these issues remain unresolved while the United States has focused its efforts on small, practical solutions that attempt to improve the current crime-fighting bureaucracy.

As described throughout this chapter, the government has embraced many new strategies and mechanisms to prevent terrorism since 9/11. Whether they will succeed in the long run is a current subject of debate. Some of the legal obstacles to effective prevention have been removed through FISA and the Patriot Act; however, not all inefficiencies can be remedied through changes in the law. Many problems involving the collection of intelligence that could possibly prevent future terrorist attacks relate to mundane, recurring issues such as "poor communication, inadequate training, a turf mentality, and cumbersome information management and computer systems that date back to the Dark Ages" (Leahy, 2002). Moreover, no realistic prevention strategy can guarantee a crime-free society, regardless of the category of crime. Terrorism cannot be eradicated completely, but with innovative legal tools, stronger agencies, and better preparation, the United States can at least minimize the threat.

DISCUSSION QUESTIONS

1. In 1995, Timothy McVeigh and his accomplice Terry Nichols were convicted of bombing the Alfred P. Murrah Federal Building in Oklahoma City, Oklahoma, killing 168 people. They were both convicted of murder under traditional state and federal homicide laws, and McVeigh was executed. Do you think subsequent, post-9/11 laws like the Patriot Act would have made any difference in the investigation and prosecution of this crime?
2. Civil libertarians have argued that the Patriot Act and other post-9/11 terrorism prevention policies threaten the privacy and freedom of American citizens. Do you think civil rights are at risk as a result of such changes? Why or why not?

3. The death of Osama Bin Laden is destined to be viewed as a watershed event in the prevention of terrorism. What role will politics play in the aftermath of his killing? How much credit should go to the Bush and Obama administrations for the success of the mission?

4. A major source of terrorist threats against the United States is radical Islamic fundamentalism. Does this justify criminal profiling or disparate treatment of Muslims in particular or Middle Easterners in general in airports or other secured areas?

5. Would more public education regarding terrorist threats be helpful in preventing terrorism, or would it cause undue fear and suspicion in the populace? How much should the public be told?

REFERENCES

Agee, W., Ault, P., & Emery, E. (1985). *Introduction to mass communications*, 8th ed. New York, NY: Harper Row.

Al Qaeda in Iraq pledges support for Al-Zawahiri. (2011, May 9). Associated Press. Retrieved from http://www.foxnews.com/world/2011/05/09/al-qaeda-iraq-pledges-support-al-zawahiri/

American Library Association. (2005). *Resolution on the U.S.A. PATRIOT Act and libraries*. Chicago, IL: ALA Council.

Anderson, T. (1993, June). Terrorism and censorship: The media in chains. *Journal of International Affairs*, 47(1).

Bush, G. W. (2010). *Decision points*. New York, NY: Crown Publishing.

Carter, A., Deutch, J., & Zelikow, P. (1998). Catastrophic terrorism. *Foreign Affairs*, 77(6), 80–94.

Cetron, M. J., & Davis, O. (1994). The future face of terrorism. *Futurist*, 28(6), 10.

Chalk, P. (1999). Evolving dynamic of terrorism in the 1990's. *Australian Journal of International Affairs*, 2, 151–167, 179.

Code of Federal Regulations (2010). 28 C.F.R. Section 0.85.

Cordesman, A. H. (2011, June 29). *U.S. State Department and Counter-Terrorism Center reporting terrorism in the Middle East and Central Asia, August 2010. Patterns of terrorism: Worldwide: 2005–2009.* Retrieved from http://csis.org/files/publication/110629_US_State_Survey_MENA_Cent_Asia_Terrorism_2010.pdf.

Doe v. Gonzales. 546 U.S.1301. (2005).

Federal Bureau of Investigation (FBI). (2007). *Terrorism 2002–2005*. Retrieved from http://www.fbi.gov/stats-services/publications/terrorism-2002-2005/terror02_05.pdf.

Federal Bureau of Investigation (FBI) (2009). *Terrorism 2002–2005*. U.S. Department of Justice, Counter Intelligence Division. Retrieved from http://www.state.gov/s/ct/rls/crt/2009/index.htm.

Fetini, A. (2008). A brief history of Gitmo. *Time*. Retrieved from http://www.time.com/time/nation/article/0,8599,1858364,00.html

Hosenball, M. (2011, May 2). U.S. commandos knew bin Laden likely would die. Retrieved from http://blogs.reuters.com/mark-hosenball/page/3/http://lugar.senate.gov/nunnlugar/pdf/NPSurvey.pdf

In re Sealed Case. 310 F. 3d 717 (2002).

Internet Archive v. Mukasey. No. 07-4943-cv (2008).

Jenkins, B. M. (1985). *The likelihood of nuclear terrorism*. Santa Monica, CA: Rand Corporation. Retrieved from http://www.rc.rand.org/content/dam/rand/pubs/papers/2008/P7119.pdf.

Kasperowicz, P. (2011, May 4). Bill would withhold aid to Pakistan. The Hill.com. Retrieved from http://thehill.com/blogs/floor-action/house/159221-house-bill-would-withhold-aid-to-pakistan-until-bin-laden-cooperation-clarified.

Laqueur, W. (1996). Postmodern terrorism. *Foreign Affairs*, 75(5), 24–36

Lawton, M. C. (1983, Jun 8). Statement before the House Subcommittee on Courts, Civil Liberties, and the Administration of Justice in Washington, DC.

Leahy, P. J. (2002, Spt. 10). Statement before the Committee on the Judiciary of the United States Senate, 107th Congress, Second Session.

Lugar, Richard, G. 2005. *The Lugar Survey on proliferation threats and responses*. Retrieved from http://lugar.senate.gov/nunnlugar/pdf/NPSurvey.pdf.

Lutz, Jill. *Day after disaster*. The History Channel, Santa Clarita, CA (Sept. 28, 2009).

MacDonald, H. (2003, Summer). Straight talk on homeland security. *The Manhattan Institute, City Journal*. Retrieved from http://www.city-journal.org/html/13_3_straight_talk.html retrieved 09/16/11

Martin, D. (2011, May 12). SEAL helmet cams recorded entire bin Laden raid. CBSNews.com. Retrieved from http://www.cbsnews.com/stories/2011/05/12/eveningnews/main20062410.shtml

Mayfield v. United States. No. 07-35865. (2009).

McCullagh, D. (2005, May 9). *Congress plans scrutiny of Patriot Act. News.com*. Retrieved from http://news.cnet.com/Congress-plans-scrutiny-of-Patriot-Act/2100-1028_3-5700986.html?tag=mncol;1n

Northam, J. (2005). Q&A about Guantanamo Bay and the detainees. NPR. Retrieved from http://www.npr.org/templates/story/story.php?storyId=4715916.

Ross, B., Chuchmach, M., & Raddatz, M. (2011). Osama Bin Laden wanted to kill President Obama. ABCNews.com. Retrieved from http://abcnews.go.com/Blotter/osama-bin-laden-wanted-kill-president-obama/story?id=13595181.

Santana, R. (2011, May 10). Al Qaeda may not name Osama Bin Laden successor. HuffingtonPost.com. Retrieved from http://www.huffingtonpost.com/2011/05/11/al-qaeda-osama-bin-laden-successor_n_860176.html.

Scherer, M. (2011, May 2). Official: Bin Laden mission was kill or capture, not just kill. Retrieved from http://swampland.time.com/2011/05/02/official-bin-laden-mission-was-kill-or-capture-not-just-kill/

Schweitzer, G. E., & Dorsch, C. C. (1998). *Super terrorism, assassins, mobsters, and weapons and weapons of mass destruction*. New York, NY: Plenum Trade.

Silverleib, A. (2011, May 4). The killing of bin Laden: Was it legal? CNN.com. Retrieved from http://articles.cnn.com/2011-05-04/world/bin.laden.legal_1_al-qaeda-leader-bin-cia-director-leon-panetta?_s=PM:WORLD

Smith, G. D. (1991). *Commentary No. 13: Terrorism and the rule of law: Dangerous compromise in Colombia*. Ottawa, Canada: Canadian Security Intelligence Service. Retrieved from: http://www.csis-scrs.gc.ca/pblctns/cmmntr/cm13-eng.asp.

Solomon, J. (2007, June 14). FBI finds it frequently overstepped in collecting data. *Washington Post*. Retrieved from http://www.washingtonpost.com/wp-dyn/content/article/2007/06/13/AR2007061302453.html.

U.S. Department of Energy (DOE). (2009). NNSA Fact Sheet: NNSA nuclear/radiological incident response sheet. Retrieved from http://www.nnsa.energy.gov/mediaroom/factsheets/incidentresponse2009.

U.S. Department of Homeland Security (DHS). (2009). *The department's five responsibilities*. Retrieved from http://journal.dhs.gov/2009/06/departments-five-responsibilities.html

U.S. Department of Homeland Security (DHS). (2011a). *Department structure*. Retrieved from http://www.dhs.gov/xabout/structure.

U.S. Department of Homeland Security (DHS). (2011b). *FY 2011 budget in brief*. Retrieved from http://www.dhs.gov/xlibrary/assets/budget_bib_fy2011.pdf.

U.S. Department of Justice (2009). *FISA annual reports to Congress,1979–2009*. Retrieved from http://www.fas.org/irp/agency/doj/fisa/#rept.

Wilkerson, L. (2009). Some truths about Guantanamo Bay. *The Washington Note*. Retrieved from http://www.thewashingtonnote.com/archives/2009/03/some_truths_abo/.

Winslow, D. R. (2011). AP files legal request for Bin Laden photos. *News Photographer*. Retrieved from http://www.nppa.org/news_and_events/news/2011/05/freedom.html.

Winthrop, J. (1997, July). The Oklahoma City bombing: Immediate response authority and other military assistance to civil authority (MACA). *The Army Lawyer*. Retrieved from http://www.loc.gov/rr/frd/Military_Law/pdf/07-1997.pdf.

World Health Organization (WHO) (2009). *Pandemic preparedness report*. Retrieved from http://www.who.int/csr/disease/influenza/pandemic/en/.

Zardari, A. A. (2011, May 2). Pakistan did its part. *Washington Post*. Retrieved from http://www.washingtonpost.com/opinions/pakistan-did-its-part/2011/05/02/AFHxmybF_story.html.

CHAPTER 7

Technology and Crime Prevention

Steven Downing
University of Ontario Institute of Technology

INTRODUCTION

The title of this chapter may seem straightforward, but it actually represents a distinct shift away from the term more commonly used to describe crime related to computers: cyber-crime. This distinction serves as a good starting point for any exploration of technology's relationship with crime, primarily because it is illustrative of a symbolic and cultural evolution of how humans interact with and have come to define the technology they use.

For a "thing" to qualify as technology, it need only meet some basic criteria. The definition of technology is fairly simple. Webster's dictionary defines technology as a "practical application of knowledge...." From this definition we can easily imagine that technology has existed as long as humans have, and probably even longer (Weir et al., 2002). Thus, to address the relationship between technology and crime (and its prevention) it is important to first acknowledge that technology is not novel to contemporary society. While many of the issues discussed in this chapter will echo the themes of lack of preparedness and reactive practices on the part of criminal justice agencies, it would be incorrect to suggest that these agencies have only now had to contend with new technologies for the committing of crime.

To put technological evolution in perspective, we will consider four primary technology "revolutions." Nobel Prize-winning economist Herbert A. Simon recognized three of these as the agricultural revolution, the industrial revolution, and the information revolution (Simon, 1969). This chapter will argue that we are on the verge of a fourth: the postinformation revolution (Smihula, 2010). Essentially each of these stages of evolution has brought with it new promises as well as new challenges.

The agricultural revolution allowed persons to remain in one place for longer, alleviating many of the challenges associated with nomadic lifestyles. In essence agriculture enabled the building of settlements and the institutions and organizational structures associated with modern communal living. One may also consider the nature of social control in pre- and postagricultural and industrial societies. Donald Black (1976) proposes that, for example, the breakdown or diminishing of informal social control has an inverse effect on formal social control. In other words, insofar as informal social control (e.g., controls within the family) diminishes in labor markets that are less home-centered, formal institutions (such as law) will become stronger. Durkheim (1933) offers a similar explanation of social control. He defines deviance as a "break" from norms that are defined by a "collective conscience." He suggests that this conscience exists within organic or mechanical economic, social, and political systems. Both Black and Durkheim would likely agree that a shift from a simple society to a more complex one will result in a shift in social control mechanisms, most typically away from informal controls to more formal ones. They would also agree that the locus of control would shift away from informal societal institutions like the family and into formal ones like the courts and corrections system.

Changes in the nature of social control also accompanied changes in the power of the individual laborer. The industrial revolution introduced the assembly line and mechanization to the production of goods, causing what some theorists such as Marx allege was the removal of power from the working class into the hands of the elite or bourgeois. Nevertheless, industrialization brought with it mass production and concentrations of peoples in larger and larger cities. Along with these phenomena came both benefits and problems. Criminologists like Shaw and McKay (1942) would eventually pay particular attention to some of these issues. Most notably, criminologists have studied the role of urbanization on crime. They also continue to assess the social stratification between rich and poor that industrialization has at least in part helped to create.

The industrial revolution also brought with it changing definitions of social status beyond our contemporary idea of the working class adult. Of particular interest to criminologists and criminal justice agencies are the definitions of youth and subsequently "delinquency" that emerged alongside the industrial revolution. Technology served as a double-edged sword for youth. In early industrial times many youths were still viewed as "miniature adults," and often employed in factories. Later, however, mechanization would make it unnecessary for youths to work in factories, and they began to be viewed more and more as, at best, a protected class of persons, and at worst, an intentionally excluded and marginalized sector of the population (Greenberg, 1985). Regardless of the explanation for this shift, youths also had more "leisure time" on their hands, prompting some criminologists, including those in the Chicago School, to identify this excessive leisure time as a cause of urban delinquency (see, e.g., the works of Park et al.,1925, & Sutherland, 1924).

Today, amidst the communication revolution, youth are again the subject of great inquiry. The communication revolution began long before the invention of the Internet, but the Internet is arguably the most significant and quintessential symbol of the information age. For an overview of the relationship between definitions of childhood and the Internet, see Jewkes (2010). The Internet was used by the public in the late 1980s, but between that time and the date of this writing much has changed. This chapter will largely address the phenomenon emerging within the 2 decades following the 1980s, and will present the framework for what probably represents a fourth technological revolution: the postinformation revolution. This revolution encompasses a shift toward technology that is augmented onto and into normal everyday living. One can already observe the pervasiveness of these types of technologies with respect to cellular phone adoption, use of social networking, GPS, and so on.

These technologies and more have also impacted the criminal justice system, specifically with respect to policing. The relationship between technology and street-level policing issues has historic origins. In Victorian England, police officers did not carry firearms, or indeed any other "offensive" tools. The introduction of the truncheon (baton) and handcuffs were major advancements for policing, allowing officers to apply force as well as incapacitate a suspect while directing his attention elsewhere (Emsley, 1984). The firearm also dramatically changed policing practices and continues to do so today. The formation of SWAT units in the 1960s, for example, was—along with a general shift in policing toward para-militarism—the result of concern over the use of increasingly lethal firearms by suspects encountered by the police (Weber, 1997).

Today, although police still carry truncheons, handcuffs, and firearms, other technologies of criminal justice have changed. This chapter's focus on Internet-related crimes also necessarily encompasses the growing use of the Internet in an effort to prevent crime. Perhaps the most publicized example of this change is the use of the Internet by police to combat child sexual exploitation. The exposure of crime through Internet investigation is warranted since rates of arrests for child sexual exploitation resulting from police Internet operations increased an average of 280% between 2000 and 2006 (Mitchell et al., 2010b). The Internet may be the most visible new policing tool, but it is not the only one. Others include video and audio surveillance, GPS, less lethal offensive and defensive weaponry, and so on.

This general overview of the evolution of technology and its impact on institutions such as the family, economy, and criminal justice system primarily serves to illustrate the reasoning behind this chapter's title and the content contained within it. It will quickly become clear that the term "cyber-crime" fails to encompass the broad and complex relationship between technology, crime, and criminal justice. The popular notion of cyber-crime thus emerges as an artifact of social apprehension about technology. To illustrate how public opinion impacts perceptions of technology, let us consider the results of a 1999 Pew Research Center poll. The findings suggest that upwards of 10% of Americans view modern technologies as "bad for" overall quality of life. While a small percentage, this percentage is not insignificant, especially when one considers the potentially one-sided media depictions of cyber-crime. These concerns also echo reservations about technology as a source of informal social control breakdown. As discussed previously in this chapter, shifts in technology have often been accompanied by this type of breakdown. In this sense apprehensions regarding technology are perhaps well-founded, making it altogether more important that a well-informed strategy for preventing technology-related crime be established.

Despite the importance of and need for such a strategy, there arise two barriers to its creation: (1) the presence of cultural reservations about technology and media depictions that may sensationalize cyber-crime, and (2) the reality that in an academic sense, relatively little is known about various types of cyber-crime, including many of those most reported on by the media, e.g., cyber-bullying, stalking, and harassment (Melander, 2010; Law et al., 2010). These factors result in a fairly skewed social construction of technologically oriented crime that is aptly labeled by even many researchers as "cyber-crime." The frequent underlying tone of this term's use illustrates the moral panic surrounding the public's belief that technology is increasingly being used for nefarious purposes. It also undermines a serious academic and policy effort to address and prevent technological crime.

Nevertheless, cyber-crime does pose some real dangers to individuals, economies, and society as a whole. Many of these actual threats posed by cyber-crime run parallel to threats of traditional crime. These commonalities include, among others, intimate partner and/or acquaintance victimization (Melander, 2010; Sheridan & Grant, 2007), online fraud that mirrors that found offline, and use of technological infrastructures to commit acts of espionage and civil disruption (Yar, 2005b). Extremist groups with offline origins may also increasingly find an outlet for expression and recruitment online (Caiani & Parenti, 2009; Yar, 2005b). Cyber-bullying is also related to and spills over into and from traditional venues of bullying (Mason, 2008). In effect, while there are some novel crimes (Yar, 2005a) emerging from the Internet, there are likely many more that are similar to or derived from traditional offline crimes. In light of actual evidence, the media-generated image of the Internet as a frightening, alien, and lawless domain is most likely exaggerated.

SOCIAL CONTROL AND CYBER-CRIME PREVENTION

Where the media have relied on sensationalism to describe and explain cyber-crime, criminologists have increasingly turned to both traditional and Internet-specific theories of crime and human behavior. Among those theories frequently applied to cyber-crime are routine activities (Holt & Bosslery, 2009; Yar, 2005a), social learning and subcultural theories (Downing, 2009, 2010a). Contrasting these traditional approaches, Brown (2006) suggests that cyber-crime is sufficiently different from traditional crime in that it cannot be effectively studied using traditional crime theories.

While all of these theories (and likely many more) are relevant and useful to the study of cyber-crime, social control perspectives are particularly related to the notion of cyber-crime prevention, and thus, the theme of this chapter. This, in part, is because of the nature of the Internet as a tool for exchanging information, the flow of which is controlled by particular parties. It is the nature of these parties and the extent of their control over information exchange that constitute the basic foundation for both legal and illegal activity on the Internet.

While "social control" as such does not refer to a specific theory—but instead simply to prevention, enforcement, and sanctions (Hinduja, 2004; Lingamneni, 1997)—recognized control theories have begun to see tests in relation to cyber-crime. These theories are distinct from other perspectives in that they assume persons are generally inclined to offend and that control measures (either internal or external) prevent these inclinations from being realized. This theoretical construct creates a framework for understanding how social control relates to Internet deviance and criminality. In essence, individuals as well as groups on the Internet are either constrained or enabled by and through control of their own and other's behaviors, as well as access to and dissemination of information. In the information age, information often equates to power. Some examples of the application of control theory to Internet crime include Bossler and Holt's (2010) test of self-control's relationship to cyber-offending. Although little support is found for this relationship, other control theories have received some support in relation to Internet criminality and deviance, suggesting, for example, that control mechanisms within the context of Internet subcultures may contribute to the nature and extent of deviance and criminality within those groups (Downing, 2010a; Williams, 2007).

These groups (such as software pirates) as well as agents of social control (such as those in the criminal justice system) hold in common that they exist in a shared virtual space whose existence relies on the exchange of information both within and between these groups. Thus the stakes are high for all parties involved. Digital piracy (or file sharing) is a prime example of this relationship, wherein consumers of information fight with producers and distributors of this information for the right to use and duplicate it. The matter is indeed complex: while it stands to reason that publishers are financially harmed by piracy, Katz (2005) suggests that some publishers may choose to be less active in their enforcement of piracy laws in order to maximize exposure of their products and thus increase profit. Gupta et al. (2004) likewise suggest that publishers face a challenging balancing act when weighing the potential for piracy to increase distribution of products against the potential for piracy to decrease revenues if these products are not purchased.

Piracy serves as only one example of the intersection between different groups on the Internet and the dynamics of social control. Victimization is also related to social control, as victimization itself can prevent or deter access to the many constructive uses of the Internet. For example, Hinduja et al. (2008) find that youth who are cyber-bullied are fearful of going online. This represents what is perhaps an unintended consequence of cyber-crime, but nevertheless one that results in the control of individual patterns of behavior (in this case, ceasing to use the Internet).

Most relevant to this chapter is the relationship between social control and cyber-crime prevention. This chapter will approach this relationship by examining formal and informal methods of preventing cyber-crime (Butterfield, 2003), but it is worth briefly acknowledging another vein of research related to technology and social control: surveillance.

Despite media depictions of a surveillance state, the reality is that many police agencies lack the funds, organizational structure, expertise, or even desire to effectively monitor online behavior (Jewkes & Andrews, 2005; Hinduja, 2004). Nevertheless, there is evidence that the balance between privacy and control is shifting toward the state (Koops, 2003). Related to this shifting balance is the concept of anonymity. The reader will find that a large percentage of the research cited in this chapter addresses in at least some part the notion of anonymity, or in other words, the idea that persons acting on the Internet are not identified (Armstrong & Forde, 2005). The anonymity provided by the Internet makes it more difficult to assess the nature of offenders as well as victims. This reality creates a difficulty for preventative strategies that must also remain aware of privacy issues (Armstrong & Forde, 2005). Thus, the main thrust of this chapter will be prevention strategies that do not directly take the form of surveillance—as defined by that body of research—and instead focus on three types of preventative strategies: (1) formal, (2) informal, and (3) a hybrid of formal and informal (or pseudo-formal). It will quickly become evident that no one approach to cyber-crime prevention can be completely effective.

Governments have already begun to recognize the need for a multipronged preventative strategy that takes into account all three of these types of control. In 2001 the Convention on Cybercrime (CC) was signed by a number of nations, including the United States and Canada. This convention in effect promotes and facilitates the use of extra-governmental expertise from Internet service providers (ISPs) and allows policing agencies to request access to information through ISPs (Huey & Rosenberg, 2004). Trim (2003) suggests that governmental and private-sector cooperation is necessary to combine the expertise and "force" necessary to effectively prevent and combat cyber-crime.

Nevertheless, business practices in the private sector also have unintended consequences related to formal prevention and prosecution of cyber-crime. For example, banking policies related to check clearance have a direct impact on the investigation and prosecution of online fraudsters (Fisher, 2008). This reality makes it especially important that the public sector act with the private sector, creating pseudo-formal approaches to combating cyber-crime. This cooperation must also consider the ultimate impact on private Internet users, especially vulnerable populations such as children. Thus, in addition to private-public practices, parental controls and automated control software have been espoused by many in the media as important tools for combating youth victimization and offending online. In this regard, Law et al. (2010) present evidence that content blocking software is a less effective means of controlling youth online behavior than is youth-parent communication. In concert the two approaches may be particularly useful, suggesting again that an informal-formal hybrid may be the best preventative strategy. As the reader, you can assess the review of each cyber-crime type and discussion of the related preventative strategies and assess which domains are most appropriate for effectively preventing these crime types.

How to Read this Chapter

When reading this chapter you should first bear in mind the reality that from a historical perspective, cyber-crime is not completely novel. You should also adopt a critical mindset with respect to media depictions of cyber-crime. With this critical eye, approach cyber-crime through the understanding that effective prevention requires a realistic understanding of crime typologies and victim and offender profiles. This type of understanding can be achieved by surveying the research that has been done already, but also by imagining how future research can be improved. As part of this thinking, you should also critically examine current and proposed strategies since all of these

---

BOX 7-1 Tips for Parents of Children Using the Internet

The Internet is probably not as dangerous as many media reports suggest, but it is a relatively free and open place where the potential for real harm and victimization exists. This chapter outlines some of the myths and realities of these dangers, but its focus is on prevention. Thus, based on a review of the research discussed in this chapter, here are a few tips for parents monitoring child-Internet use.

—Educate yourself beyond what you see and hear in the media. Seek out information about the real dangers of the Internet. Ironically, the Internet is a good place to do this research. Websites such as kidshealth.org have this type of information.

—Perhaps the most important tip for parents is that they communicate openly and frequently with their children. Ask your children what they are doing online.

—Install "nanny software" on your family's or your child's computer. Net Nanny is one particular product, but there are many available.

—As an alternative to nanny software you can use websites and browser plug-ins such as Web of Trust. Based on user feedback, these types of services will rate sites in categories such as obscenity.

—Do not rely on nanny software alone. While it may filter some obscene and potentially dangerous content, most research has shown that its affects are limited.

—It may help to place the family's or child's computer in a shared room. Some research has shown that this type of monitoring is very effective in curbing dangerous Internet surfing.

—Install antivirus software. Some viruses like those called "trojans" can mine personal information from your computer.

—Do not focus solely on "stranger danger." Difficult as it is to think about, peers and even family friends and family members may use the Internet to harm your child.

—Use the Internet with your child. This may include browsing websites of interest to both you and your child, playing games together, or watching videos.

—Encourage your child to use the Internet for "healthy" purposes, realizing that this will probably include communicating with other youths through games, chat, forums, and email.

---

strategies must over overcome the possibility that cyber-crime prevention strategies may not necessarily reduce the chances of victimization (Winterdyk & Thompson, 2008). Finally, as you read the chapter, apply the discussed social control perspectives, examining the benefits and challenges proposed by formal and informal approaches to preventing and controlling cyber-crime. It is likely that a multipronged prevention approach will be necessary.

WEB-BASED VICTIMIZATION

As with most crime, the media play a role in how the public perceives and is educated about computer-related crime, both in terms of victim/offender profiles and how it is investigated. To illustrate, consider the case of Internet sex offenders: The media present an image of the Internet sex offender as a forceful stranger, often likened to a violent rapist. Words such as "predator" are often used to describe these types of offenders (Wolak et al., 2010). In reality, online sexual predators (particularly those preying on youth) are more like a statutory rapist, developing relationships with youth over a long period of time (Wolak et al., 2010). In fact, based on arrests the vast majority of Internet-related sex crimes are categorized as nonforcible (Wolak et al., 2003).

Research has shown that Internet sex offenders are a heterogeneous group, with marked differences between, for example, those who solely consume child pornography and those who target children in offline settings (Bates & Metcalf, 2007; McCarthy, 2010). However, images (both literal and figurative) in media and public awareness campaigns continue to portray Internet predators as traditional predators with computers, a motif of "invasion" often employed to suggest that these offenders use the Internet to come into someone's home. Wolak et al. (2010) argue that the media perpetuate these myths through programs such as "To Catch a Predator." They suggest that such programs depict online sex offenders as "tricky" and "violent." Wolak and his colleagues discuss, in particular, five myths about online sex offenders:

1. Sexual offenses against children have increased alongside adoption rates for the Internet. In reality, they have decreased dramatically since 1990.
2. The Internet represents the largest threat to children. The reality is that parents and family members remain the largest threat.
3. Children should not use the Internet to communicate with others. Instead, Wolak et al. (2010) suggest that the Internet is a valuable tool for children, but should be used safely.
4. The majority of Internet sex offenders are pedophiles. In reality, the majority seek out teens, not children.
5. Internet sex offenders use violence and trickery to lure their victims. The reality, argue Wolak et al., is that victims often know that the offender is an adult and willingly continue their relationship with them.

Not only do these media myths influence parents' assessments of dangers on the Internet, but they may also influence criminal justice policy and procedure, making it doubly important to explore the realities of online sexual offending. As such, this section will examine three types of Internet-related crimes (cyber-stalking, cyber-bullying, and Internet sex crimes) and discuss their larger implications for building a solid knowledge base about Web victimization and investigation.

Cyber-stalking: A Case of Too Little Knowledge

To begin, let us consider cyber-stalking, a much-talked-about issue that has been alleged to be on the rise, especially among youth. In reality, relatively little is known about cyber-stalking, primarily because it is both underreported and because police forces are ill-equipped to effectively categorize, record, and pursue such cases (Parsons-Pollard & Moriarty, 2009).

In addition, there remains a definitional issue pertaining to cyber-stalking. For example, definitions garnered from self-reports of victimization suggest there may be little to distinguish cyber-stalking from traditional stalking (Sheridan & Grant, 2007). Nevertheless, some research has attempted to understand the victim-offender dynamics of cyber-stalking. Particularly, one study of college students has shown that increased exposure to offenders and increased suitability as a target (through, for example, going to websites that house malware) increase the likelihood of being victimized online, while attempts to improve capable guardianship have relatively little effect on victimization (Marcum et al., 2010). In other words, there is evidence that a person's "online routine" has an impact on how likely they are to be victimized on the Web.

The implication of the routine activities explanation for cyber-stalking is that "target harden-ing" measures used online and nanny software may have a limited impact on Internet offenses. This is because a person's behavior online may be largely dictated by his or her interests, associations, and preferences concerning what materials he or she may wish to consume. In other words, nanny software can monitor and prevent the visiting of certain specific sites, but it cannot necessarily thwart the underlying dynamics that form the "routine behavior" of an Internet user. In light of this reality, an understanding of victims and offenders remains a necessary part of preventing cyber-stalking (and other forms of Internet-related crime). In this regard, it is argued that both sociologi-cal and psychological perspectives are important in understanding who is likely to commit and be victimized by cyber-stalking (Patton et al., 2010)

Cyber-Bullying: More Definitional Issues

In the absence of a clear definition of cyber-stalking, we turn to another commonly discussed form of Web victimization: cyber-bullying. Like cyber-stalking, cyber-bullying is purportedly a rapidly increasing social problem, now attracting the attention of celebrity advocacy groups, media reports, and political inquiry, and indeed there is legitimate cause for concern. Cyber-bullying has a marked impact on its victims. Patchin and Hinduja (2006) report that nearly half of bullied respondents in their study felt frustrated and angry after having been bullied, and about a quarter reported feeling sad. Nearly a third reported that cyber-bullying negatively affected them at school, and a quar-ter reported being negatively affected at home. These findings are supported by Raskauskas and Stoltz's (2007) findings that common responses to cyber-bullying include sadness, hopelessness, depression, and fear of attending school. In addition, Raskauskas and Stoltz (2007) find that victims who know their aggressors reflect a general increase in suspicion of others.

Thus, this section will explore cyber-bullying under the informed assumption that it is a real social problem, worthy of inquiry and preventative approaches. Nevertheless, the scope of the problem is somewhat unclear. Empirical research has yielded mixed results in this respect. There is a large body of research that reports similarly low-to-moderate prevalence, while some studies

BOX 7-2 Is Bullying a Crime?

Several high-profile bullying and cyber-bullying cases—including the suicides of a Rutgers student, Tyler Clementi, and a Missouri high school student, Megan Meier—have led the public, school officials, and law makers to reconsider the seriousness of bullying. In New Hampshire, a recent law aims to in part address the question of whether or not bullying is a crime. The 2010 law, called the Pupil Safety and Violence Prevention Act, seeks to improve both prevention of and responses to bullying. To prevent bullying, the act requires that all schools create a prevention policy for bullying. To respond to bullying, the act requires that school employees report all bullying behaviors to a principal, who is then, in some cases, required to report the bullying to the police. In return these parties are granted immunity for liability should any negative consequences arise from the reported bullying. Some New Hampshire residents and legislators are already calling for tougher antibullying laws. The driving force behind the move to toughen bullying laws is the assertion that bullying has real, and sometimes deadly, consequences. The question of whether or not bullying is a crime, however, is difficult to answer. When asked this very question, one New Hampshire district attorney responded, "It depends" (Flynn, 2011).

report startling high rates of cyber-bullying. The contested prevalence of cyber-bullying is best understood against the backdrop of the likelihood that, when viewed as a social problem across the life course, there is strong evidence that cyber-bullying peaks as a problem in middle school (Williams & Guerra, 2007; Worthen, 2007).

Traditional bullying and cyber-bullying are both problems for school-aged youth. One study of traditional and "text" bullying found that 47% of the surveyed youths had been bullied offline and 11% had been text-bullied (Marsh et al., 2010). Although it is clear that cyber-bullying is a problem, its prevalence is difficult to assess since different research efforts have yielded a range of estimates. For example, drawing on data collected as part of the 2000 Youth Internet Safety Survey of 1,501 U.S. youths, Ybarra and Mitchell (2004b) report that 19% of respondents had been involved in online harassment. Of these, 3% were both aggressors and targets, 4% targets only, and 12% aggressors only. Ybarra and Mitchell (2007) draw on more recent YISS data (from 2005) and find that compared to the 2000 data, 19% of respondents had been involved in online harassment. Of these, 3% were aggressors and targets, 4% targets only, and 12% aggressors only; in these 2005 results, 6% reported frequently harassing others, and 17% reported limited perpetration. Yielding similar results, Dehue et al. (2008) report that in their sample, 16% of respondents had engaged in cyber-bullying and 23% had been victims.

Still other recent studies of cyber-bullying also have found supporting evidence that it is only moderately prevalent. Kowalski and Limber (2007) found that of a sample of 1,700 German secondary school students, 11% reported having been bullied in the past 2 months, 7% reported being both the bully and victim, and 4% reported being the bully only. In Wolak et al.'s (2007) study, roughly 9% of respondents reported having been harassed in the last year, and 57% of those reported being bullied by someone met online. Emphasizing the difficulty in defining and addressing cyber-bullying, most of these incidents were not repeat in nature and did not meet school-determined definitions of bullying. Tapping into a different sample (this time university students), Finn (2004) also found that 10–15% of students reported having received email or instant messages that were defined as threatening, insulting, or harassing.

In contrast, a Web survey of 1,154 youth, aged 12–17 (Juvonen & Gross, 2008) found that 72% of respondents reported having been bullied online at least once in the past year, and of those 85% reported also being bullied in school. The most common type of bullying in both cases was reported as name calling and/or insults. Yielding less severe but still high levels of cyber-bullying reports, in a survey of 177 seventh graders, Li (2005) finds that 54% of respondents reported being victims of traditional bullying, and over 25% reported being victims of cyber-bullying. Nearly one-third of respondents reported perpetrating traditional bullying, compared with 15% reporting use of electronic tools to bully. While not a measure of direct victimization, Patchin and Hinduja (2006) also find that of 571 survey respondents, 47% reported witnessing online bullying.

In light of this broad range of findings, it is logical to ask why such variation exists at all. One primary reason is a lack of a consistent definition for cyber-bullying. This problem underscores what will emerge throughout this chapter as an issue for studying and preventing all types of Internet-related crime. Cyber-bullying has been defined in a number of ways, ranging from the succinct "willful and repeated harm inflicted through the medium of electronic text" (Patchin & Hinduja 2006, p. 152) to those definitions that draw on related concepts such as cyber-stalking (Finn, 2004) and online youth gangs (King et al., 2007). Numerous studies have drawn on Patchin and Hinduja's (2006) definitional emphasis of repetition of harassment in cases of cyber-bullying (Smith et al., 2008; Vandebosch & Van Cleemput, 2008). Specifically, Vandebosch and Van Cleemput (2008) suggest that cyber-teasing is distinct from cyber-bullying, noting that the latter requires repetitive harassment over a duration of time. Bryant et al. (2006) also found that "playing tricks" on peers through instant messaging was common among youth in their sample.

With the knowledge that no clear, consistent definition of cyber-bullying prevails, one can reasonably predict that prevention and enforcement strategies will likewise emerge as inconsistent in nature and success. This prediction is largely supported by the current state of formal reaction to cyber-bullying.

To begin with, there may be a problem with the context of prevention efforts. There is evidence that most cyber-bullying occurs outside of school (Agatston et al., 2007). Patchin and Hinduja (2006) suggest that most cyber-bullying occurs in private, out-of-school venues (e.g., email and texting) yet many prevention programs are delivered in school, rather than directly online through awareness ads and programs. This reality is especially problematic in light of a lack of officially defined school strategies for preventing and dealing with cases of cyber-bullying (Mason, 2008). Nevertheless, structural and cultural changes at the school level could have a negative impact on rates and severity of bullying. Williams & Guerra (2007) find that probullying norms and perceived peer support of bullying are positively correlated with all types of bullying. Particularly, negative school climates created by these peer norms also correlate with higher rates of bullying and general acceptance of bullying by classmates. A consequence of this pervasiveness is that bullied children are in some cases unable to escape bullying even when at home. This reality is one reason that cyber-bullying victimization has been linked with increased depression and distrust of others (Raskauskas & Stoltz, 2007).

In essence, there is evidence that programs aimed at reducing cyber-bullying—if they are to be delivered in school—should focus on changing norms and values that encompass antibullying sentiments, rather than attempting to target cyber-bullying as a unique and isolated social problem. While a lack of program evaluations makes it difficult to gauge whether this type of program would be more effective, there is evidence to be found in studies of online cultural structures that relate to bullying. These structures tell us something about the nature of cyber-bullying with respect to the interpersonal dynamics at play within a larger context of macro-level cultural values. For example, Mason (2008) suggests that anonymity reduces or mediates the inhibition to behave in certain ways, bullying included. The Internet also creates a new context for social interaction. Because of these factors, individual identity is replaced with social identity, whereby social norms serve to regulate behavior. Therefore, if the social norms of the Internet present an imperative that values the invisibility of one's self, accountability for individual actions may be compromised.

Since accountability for individual bullying behavior is often diluted because of group participation, it may be beneficial for policy makers and practitioners to engage in situational crime prevention. This type of prevention strategy seeks to reduce opportunities to offend while also decreasing the perceived and actual benefits of the offense (Clarke, 1995). As a part of this approach, effective school programs should attempt to emphasize broad values that stress accountability for individual actions and the actions of peers, whether online or offline. Perhaps more importantly, more tech-savvy approaches should be used to educate youth about the realities of cyber-bullying. This is in part because both schools and parents often lack the knowledge to accurately and convincingly talk to youth about Internet-related issues (King et al., 2007). King et al. (2007) also emphasize that youths use technological superiority to gain a power edge over adults, particularly in the home. These power imbalances may also play out online between youths. Vandebosch and Van Cleemput (2008) point to such imbalances between perpetrators and victims of cyber-bullying, suggesting that frequency and duration of potential bullying should be used in defining whether or not an act actually constitutes cyber-bullying.

The connections among knowledge, power, and culture relate back to the notions of social control discussed in the introduction to this chapter. Such relationships create an imperative whereby prevention policies should acknowledge youth practices in the context of not only school, but also the home and Internet communities. Research and policy can help inform these prevention strategies by understanding how victims and offenders of cyber-bullying operate within the dynamics of this power-control scheme.

Predicting Cyber-Bullying: Lessons for Prevention

Where prevention and reaction strategies to cyber-bullying remain underdeveloped, understanding of cyber-bullying offender and victim profiles fairs slightly better. It may in fact be this understanding that can serve as a more solid foundation for developing consistent definitions of and prevention strategies for cyber-bullying. Several variables arise as important to the prediction of cyber-bullying, namely sex/gender, age, and familiarity between offenders and victims. It is worth noting that all of these factors are among the most commonly correlated with other types of offending.

Perceptions of cyber-bullying among those most affected (i.e., the involved youths themselves) is important for defining and preventing cyber-bullying. Thus, it is of interest that females are more likely to suggest cyber-bullying as a problem than are males (Agatston et al., 2007), yet there is evidence that males and females are equally likely to report harassing someone online (Ybarra & Mitchell (2004). Regarding victim profiles, Li (2005) finds that, although in many traditional crime categories females are less often the victims, 60% of cyber-bullying victims in the studied sample were female, while over half of the bullies were male. Li's (2006) findings reaffirm that the majority of reported bullies were male, but find that females were no more likely to be the victims than males. Also of increasing concern is the role of sexual orientation in the likelihood of being cyber-bullied. In Finn's (2004) cyber-bullying study, sexual orientation emerged as the only significant predicting variable for cyber-bullying victimization.

Slonje and Smith's (2008) study found that gender is not a significant predictor of cyber-bullying or victimization; over one-third of respondents reported that they did not know the gender of the bully. This relates to another of the aforementioned correlates of cyber-bullying: familiarity of victims and offenders. To this end, Juvonen and Gross (2008) find that two-thirds of their respondents knew who their bully was. In contrast, Kowalski and Limber (2007) found that nearly half of the respondents in their study did not know the bully. Another study reports a third of victims did not know their bullies (Raskauskas & Stoltz, 2007).

Also important to predicting and preventing cyber-bullying is an understanding of the motivations for bullying. Raskauskas and Stoltz (2007) found that of their study respondents, 38% reported that they thought cyber-bullies do it for fun, while 25% reported that they do it to get back at someone. Smith et al. (2008) found that cyber-bullying is perpetrated by a few students repeatedly. Interestingly, Smith et al.'s sample had no respondents reporting being bullied by persons from a lower grade level, thus suggesting that age may be of relatively little importance to cyber-bullying victim/offender dynamic. This hypothesis is consistent with the aforementioned idea that peer contexts relate closely to how cyber-bullying unfolds. Lastly, there is little evidence that sexual solicitation is coupled with cyber-bullying, but individuals engaging in this combined behavior are particularly psychologically at risk (Ybarra et al., 2007). A case in point is the recent case at Rutgers University, where a male university student was secretly filmed by his roommate having sex with another male. The roommate then posted the video to the Internet. Shortly after this event, the young man in the video committed suicide. The roommate who secretly taped the event is facing criminal charges. This case illustrates one component of cyber-bullying that is currently underexplored in the research, namely that it may draw on homophobic attitudes (Rochman, 2010). Other motives related to race and sex could also arise as central to the actual quality of cyber-bullying, rather than just to its quantity. Future research and policy intervention need to explore these relationships in an effort to better prevent cyber-bullying cases like the one at Rutgers, but also to help victims cope with and defend against future bullying.

Internet Sex Crimes: Myths, Realities, and Prevention

This section on Web-based victimization began with a discussion of some misconceptions about Internet sex crimes and how these misconceptions relate to preventing such crimes. Returning to this issue we find that many of the same problems inherent to cyber-stalking and cyber-bullying emerge with respect to Internet-related sex crimes, namely that what constitutes this type of crime is debatable, and thus prevention strategies are left with little—or at best, mixed—information about the nature of victims and offenders.

To begin with, the realities of sexual crimes occurring on and stemming from the Internet are somewhat different from those portrayed in the media. In reality, unwanted sexual aggression on the Internet may occur even between dating couples, and is thus not limited to the "stranger" encounter depicted in most accounts of such crimes (Draucker & Martsolf, 2010; Melander, 2010). This reality is often tied in with definition issues. In other words, what constitutes an Internet sex crime? For example, those labeled as "sexual predators" by both the criminal justice system and media are most often statutory rapists engaging in nonforcible sex acts (Wolak et al., 2010; Wolak et al., 2003).

The difficulty in defining force and coercion as they relate to Internet sexual offenses is complicated by the digital nature of imagery and textual communication involved in these offenses. Some argue, for example, that sexually explicit depictions of children should constitute person-victims in the legal sense (Seto, 2010). If possession of sexually explicit depictions of youths qualifies as criminal, then policing agencies are faced with a great increase in workload; a problem exacerbated by the already strained resources (both technologically and in terms of expertise) available to police departments at all levels.

Buzzell's (2007) review of Internet sex crime prosecution offers insight into the relationship between police resources and rates of arrests and prosecution. Both are linked to the presence of special units devoted to investigating these crimes. These units are in turn related to the size and economic well-being of a particular jurisdiction. Many police forces are also still very locally organized, a factor limiting funds and expertise while also facilitating local police cultures resistant to technological change (Jewkes & Andres, 2005).

Thus, police-based prevention of Internet sex crimes is, for the time being, difficult to implement. Other formal interventions over the period of time during which the Internet has been available have ranged widely and often lacked direction from sound research findings (Atkinson & Newton, 2010). Likewise, while public awareness is important, it must also be accurate, especially when portraying "typologies" of offenders. Research findings from studies such as McCarthy's (2010) are useful for distinguishing varieties and severities of offender types and their posed risk to the community. These typologies suggest that, much like the situation with other forms of sex crimes, individuals should be most aware and cautious about their immediate interpersonal sur-

---

BOX 7-3 Virtual Child Pornography?

In *Ashcroft v. Free Speech Coalition* (2002), the U.S. Supreme Court upheld the legality of computer-generated child pornography. In 2003, however, Congress revisited this issue, passing a new law (the PROTECT Act) that outlined what components of computer-generated child pornography were legal and illegal. Specifically, the act makes illegal any portrayal of children engaged in actual sex acts. More controversial (and more difficult to determine) is the Act's prohibition on depictions of children that are considered "obscene." The law uses the "Miller test" for obscenity. This test arose from the 1973 *Miller v. California* case and essentially rules that obscenity must be determined using a three-pronged test, including whether "community standards" or state law define the content as obscene, and whether or not the material lacks artistic, literary, political, or scientific value (Duranske, 2008).

---

roundings. Take for example a recent case involving Kevin Whitty in Florida. Whitty was a family friend of his victims, two young sisters, one 9 and the other 12, who would often spend the night at his house. After being alerted to some inappropriate pictures of their daughters found on a friend's cell phone, the parents alerted the police. When police searched Whitty's home they found—in addition to numerous digital and printed explicit photographs of the two sisters—a number of files containing child pornography downloaded from the Internet. In this case the parents clearly trusted the offender and were not alerted to his behavior until another parent intervened. This case illustrates a need for increased attention to and education about the risks posed by persons close to the victim, and not just the "stranger lurking in the bushes."

Informed education about actual risks of inappropriate Internet behaviors is probably the most economic and realistic way to prevent Internet sexual victimization. For example, with the recent surge in the popularity of social networking sites has arisen a concern over their potential to provide havens for sexual predators. Mitchell et al. (2010a) find, based on arrests, that there is some justification for this concern, although research on the extent and nature of social networking sites' relationship to sexual victimization needs further development. Nevertheless, Mitchell et al. (2010a) propose that educating youth about safe and responsible behavior in general will likely reduce online risk more than measures to monitor and/or restrict use of social networking sites.

Also, in light of the statutory nature of sexual assaults stemming from online interaction, it is important that youth be directly educated about the real dangers of online communication of a sexual nature. Youths should, however, not be directed away from normal, healthy sexual interaction with peers, as this normal, intimate interaction may in fact curb the likelihood of victimization by a person met online (Wolak et al., 2010).

Another option to preventing Internet sex crimes is semiformal in nature, taking the form of nanny software to control or monitor Internet use. Ybarra et al. (2009) examine the extent to which nanny software may reduce unwanted exposure to online sexual content, finding that this software is relatively effective for youths younger than the age of 15 (specifically males) but not terribly effective for older youths.

Definitional dilemmas arise with such research, as "unwanted" in this case applies to pop-ups, spam, etc., but may be correlated with routine Internet browsing behaviors that are intentional. In light of other researchers' suggestions for education of youth about "normal" sexual behavior, both online and offline (Wolak et al., 2010), it becomes particularly important to carefully understand and define common adolescent Internet use. Wolak et al. (2010) offer further findings suggesting that nanny software has a limited effect on child offending online. There is strong evidence that youth education is probably a more appropriate and effective tool for combating online victimization (see also Mitchell et al., 2010a). Through educating children about the Internet, parents can also establish computer-use norms, both in the context of family computer and individual computer use.

In summary, much like the situation with other forms of Internet-related crime discussed in this section (cyber-bullying and cyber-stalking), Internet sex crimes are serious but ill-defined in both policy and research. This definitional dilemma extends into and is complicated by limited enforcement resources. Although arrests and prosecutions for child sex crimes have increased since 2000 (Wolak et al., 2010), it remains unclear whether or not this increase, which is the result of more police "stings," is reflective of a growing number of Internet sex offenders or merely an artifact of increased police attention in the light of high-profile sting operations such as those depicted in NBC's *Dateline* episode "To Catch a Predator" (Wolak et al., 2010). Nevertheless, police agencies remain limited in their resources as well as their ability to keep up with rapidly changing communication technology. Coupled with this limitation are ethical concerns regarding the methods used by police to detect and apprehend Internet sex offenders. Stings are perhaps the most popular method. This method involves police posing as underaged potential victims, talking to potential offenders in chat rooms and through email, and sometimes sending sexually explicit images of children (Burns et al., 2008; Edelmann, 2010). Although research has shown that police officers involved in these stings have developed coping mechanisms to deal with the potential trauma of seeing child pornography, some of which is violent in nature, there remains the ethical question of whether or not use of such materials and strategies is healthy in a larger legal, social, and psychological context (Burns et al., 2008, Edelmann, 2010, Mitchell et al., 2010a).

Ultimately, as with many technology-based crimes, policing is difficult for a number of legal, ethical, but in this case perhaps most importantly, logistical reasons. Mitchell et al. (2010b) note that even their study of policing Internet sex crime between 2000 and 2006 may, because of the rapid adoption of social networking by youth, present outdated information. The nature of technological change coupled with the reality that police agencies are often constrained by budgetary and personnel issues, positions informal and semiformal means of prevention as perhaps the most realistic and impactful. These means range from school-based education to content delivered to at-risk youth in the online venues they frequent. Parental involvement (through the use of software or more conventional means) also emerges as an important factor in preventing cyber-victimization, but researchers caution that too much intervention with "normal" youth behaviors may in fact place youth at greater risk of victimization. Thus, as is usually the case with complex social issues, continued development of research, policy, and prevention efforts is in order.

INTERNET CRIME AND PROPERTY

This section's title is purposely broad. The concept of "property" is an ambiguous one. Philosophers and law makers have long debated its meaning. The Internet and rise of "digital" representations of property have only further complicated the concept. Thus, prevention of property crimes related to the Internet requires—at the very least—a critical examination of the components of property. This section will provide this examination through surveying research on a variety of Internet fraud types as well as digital piracy (or file sharing).

To begin this exploration, one might consider how commerce has shifted away from "paper money" toward the use of "plastic," and increasingly, digital representations of wealth. As Internet commerce increases, so too do the chances for e-fraud victimization. For example, routine activities theory has been used to explain the risk of online fraud, suggesting that regular use of the Internet increases exposure to potential harm, thus increasing the overall likelihood for victimization, regardless of other demographic characteristics (Pratt et al., 2010; Marcum et al., 2010).

This increased exposure to risk has evolved alongside what some suggest is a "culture of fear" orientation toward new technologies. Wall (2008) applies this concept to the development of perceptions about cyber-victimization, suggesting that science fiction depictions and popular cultural notions of technology in a dystopian context help shape what is often an irrational fear of new technologies. In essence, depictions of technology in popular media (such as in the movie, *The Matrix*) often show technology turning on humans or being used against people by a criminal individual or group. Hackers are also a popular topic of media portrayals. In the movie *Scorpion*, for example, John Travolta plays a villain who coerces a hacker into helping him steal large sums of money. Travolta's character's "tech-savvy" approach to crime is also accompanied by violence, reinforcing the notion of dangerousness associated with technology.

While this dystopian perspective is probably just a cultural artifact, it nevertheless represents anxieties about using the Internet for financial transactions. To some extent this anxiety is reflected in Internet usage. While it is easy to assume that modern economies have fully transitioned into this new paperless form, in reality the adoption of and trust in the Internet as a venue for commerce and communication remains stratified. Older individuals are less likely to use the Internet, and older women have been shown to be the least knowledgeable about Internet security risks (Grimes et al., 2010). Essentially, there is evidence that at the very least, age and sex play a role in how (or whether) people perceive and use the Internet. This relationship is a good starting point for understanding Internet-based property crimes and their prevention.

Identity Theft

Part of the dystopian image of the Internet relates to a loss of personhood or identity. Identity theft is interesting in that it represents a crime that draws on an existential notion of personal identity. Thus, the pieces of data (e.g., bank accounts, social security numbers) are now not only digital, but digitally transferable and duplicable. "Black markets" for such data have even emerged, where "data thieves" buy and sell this information at determined or negotiated rates (Holt & Lampke, 2010). The quantification of "value" by black market participants and even the researchers of these markets suggests that identity has indeed been transformed into a commodity to be bought, sold, and where prevention is concerned, secured and protected.

In spite of (or perhaps because of) the many forms of digital identity that exist, criminological research has still not developed a consistent or detailed definition of identity theft, particularly as it relates to the Internet (Meints et al, 2010). A lack of consistent and clear definitions makes it difficult to both analyze identity theft research and create effective preventative strategies. Further complicating the nature of identity theft is the reality that some identity-related crimes involve no direct victim, but rely instead on the creation of entirely fabricated identities used to establish, for example, fake credit card numbers (Meints et al., 2010).

Related to the creation of identity (and part of the reason that identity is such a flexible concept) is that information has been commoditized online, and thus can also be manipulated to misinform.

BOX 7-4 Identity Theft: How Big of a Problem Is It?

The Federal Trade Commission (FTC) takes complaints from the public about a variety of consumer-related issues, including banking, Internet auctions, Internet services, and so on. In 2010, the most complaints received dealt with identity theft. Of all the complaints made to the FTC, 19% (250,854), dealt with identity theft, while issues with debt collection agencies ranking at a somewhat distant 11%. Overall, the FTC estimates that fraud in 2010 cost consumers 1.7 billion dollars. Consumers were fraudulently contacted most frequently through email and websites, emphasizing the connection between fraud (specifically identity theft) and the Internet (FTC, 2011). In light of increasing concern over identity theft, some government agencies are encouraging public awareness and action through informal programs. Several cities across the United States have begun to hold "shred days," where the public is encouraged to visit a location where free document shredding services are provided. Different local government agencies are usually cooperating with private groups such as banks to host these events. This represents a good example of a pseudo-formal preventative strategy (Shred Day Event, 2011).

For example, Daniels (2009) discusses the notion of "cloaked" websites where hidden racist political agendas emerge among other pieces of information that may or may not be factual, emphasizing that information does not necessarily need to be truthful in order to be influential. This case also illustrates the link between identity and crime (in this case hate crime). Thus, while identity is linked with cyber-*victimization* beyond identity theft, *false* identity may be closely related to *commission* of cyber-crime.

Since identity cannot be defined narrowly or consistently, then an understanding of how different people perceive the risk of this type of victimization is just as important as understanding how to prevent identity theft. In addition to the aforementioned relationship between age, sex, and Internet fraud, Reisig et al. (2009) suggest that individuals of lower socioeconomic status as well as more financially impulsive consumers perceive a higher risk when shopping online. As a consequence, they are less likely to spend time online, at least in a consumer capacity. Thus, scholars are faced with a difficult landscape for understanding identity theft and suggesting policies for its prevention. It is readily apparent that not all individuals use the Internet for commerce and of those that do, the perception of and actual risks of victimization are also varied.

In order to overcome some of the complexities involved with understanding identity theft, scholars have begun applying mainstream theoretical tests to identity-related crimes on the Internet. Moon et al. (2010), for example, find support for self-control theory as an explanatory factor in identity theft among a sample of Korean youths. Bossler and Holt (2010) extend self-control theory to online victimization, providing evidence that Internet crime may be somewhat unique in that self-control does reportedly have an impact on the likelihood of being victimized.

This may relate to what other studies (Pratt et al., 2010; Marcum et al., 2010) have discovered regarding the relationship between routine activities of Internet users (e.g., visiting nefarious sites) and the likelihood for their computers to be infected by malware that can lead to fraud or identity theft victimization. Deterrence and labeling theories have also been applied to online copyright infringement, suggesting that the *perception* (though not actual knowledge) of potential negative labels as well as detection and punishment have a negative impact on the likelihood to engage in file sharing (Li & Nergadze, 2009; Downing, 2010a).

Other Forms of Internet Fraud

Phishing is another common form of Internet fraud. Phishing relies on the sending of deceptive messages (Wright et al., 2010) to a large number of recipients among whom only a small percentage may actually be deceived. In other words, phishers cast a wide net of fraudulent emails (usually asking for personally identifying information such as bank account numbers) with the expectation that they will only "catch" a few potential victims. If the net is sufficiently wide, however, they will still catch enough to make the crime profitable.

The Nigerian "advance fee" email frauds are among the most well-known and financially successful phishing scams (Smith, 2009). These frauds rely on cultural perceptions of Africa's financial state as well as conventional components of fraud success including preying on the greed of intended targets and increasing a sense of urgency. In essence, they successfully combine an emotional plea that transforms an illogical proposition into a perceived legitimate business opportunity. This approach draws on traditional confidence game principles such as preying on older persons who are more trusting or are less aware of contemporary technologies that facilitate fraud (Friedman, 1992; Alves & Wilson, 2008). Essentially, confidence games or "swindles" seek out vulnerable victims. Phishing scams allow for a wide net to be cast over many potential types of victims, but the nature and content of these scams still seeks to draw on the same characteristics of a vulnerable victim (e.g., trusting, naïve, or single/widowed).

Online auctions are another fast growing form of e-commerce, and traditional auction frauds have transitioned online. Shill bidding is one such practice. Shill bidding is essentially the artificial inflating of an item's selling value through seller-controlled bidding. Engelberg and Williams (2009) find that shill bidding is not only fairly common on eBay, but is also relatively effective as a means of raising the final purchase price.

Preventing Identity Theft and Internet Fraud

As with most other forms of cyber-crime, formal legal and criminal justice agencies continue to address the issue of Internet fraud and identity theft reactively rather than proactively (Mehra, 2010). In light of the acceleration of identity from physical to digital, one of the most important preventative strategies from a law enforcement perspective may simply be to prevent rather than to react.

In the absence of any consistent formal intervention, we will focus on informal and pseudo-formal measures of preventing these types of victimization. As with the safer use of the Internet by youth discussed in previous sections, there is some evidence that education and training can help prevent fraud victimization online. Davinson and Sillence (2010) tested one such program aimed at educating Internet users about the dangers of phishing scams, finding that the program at least increased the intention of the recipients to use the Internet more securely, although there was no strong evidence that their actual use changed dramatically. Given that many phishing scams rely on false perception and stereotypes about international financial situations and foreign finance laws (Smith, 2009), it is important that Internet users become educated not only to be aware of, but also to *actually* avoid business transactions with unknown parties.

Pseudo-formal prevention of identity theft and fraud relates primarily to service providers (e.g., banks and other financial institutions). It seems logical to assume that any business providing services online has a vested interest in Internet security. Sproule and Archer (2010) find that Internet fraud victimization has a sizable impact (up to a 20% reduction) on the use of the Internet for financial transactions, although problematically, this loss is based on projections rather than actual losses. A similar issue arises when researchers measure the "losses" due to digital piracy. Industry members make projections that assume pirated media would have otherwise been purchased by the user, when in fact this is not always the case. We can only assume that projections of Internet traffic use a similar "opportunity cost" model.

Regardless of these measurement issues, some online businesses may actually benefit from fraudulent or ethically questionable practices. On and offline marketing often relies on the buying and selling of the consumer's personal information (Milne et al., 2009), and auction sites such as eBay may benefit financially from the fraudulently inflated selling prices of items listed through their services (Engelberg & Williams, 2009). Wilbur and Zhu (2009) point to another example where online businesses may permit and even benefit from some forms of fraud. Specifically, they study "click fraud," or the repeated clicking of Internet ads to increase perceived traffic of advertisers to manipulate the profit of advertising sites or the prices to advertise there. Wilber and Zhu demonstrate a financial model that suggests some degree of click fraud may actually benefit the the search engine providers, though excessive click fraud will eventually become harmful to their profits due to decreased use of these search engines.

Ultimately the actions of service providers on the Internet seem, not surprisingly, to be profit motivated. Nevertheless, they remain probably the most powerful and certainly the most "frontline" defense against cyber-fraud. For this reason it is important that preventative strategies involve online businesses, but also that these strategies address potential abuse of information confidentiality, intentionally permitted fraud, and other unethical business practices that could entice businesses to compromise Internet security. This is where prevention strategies come full circle and offer an opportunity for formal systems to become involved at the regulatory level. An intelligent, comprehensive prevention strategy should incorporate enforced regulation, service provider safeguards, and end-user education.

Copyright Violations

Copyright violations include a number of acts defined as illegal. This section will focus specifically on what is commonly referred to as "digital piracy," although increasingly researchers from a sociological tradition are referring to this behavior as "file sharing." Thus, this section will first address the definitional issues surrounding file sharing/piracy and then explore this topic through a focused discussion on the copying and sharing of software (for personal computers and other digital entertainment devices), then draw broader conclusions regarding the prevention of copying, sharing, and selling of digital materials in violation of copyright.

Piracy or File Sharing?

As mentioned before, the distinction between piracy and file sharing is more than a matter of semantics. It suggests something about the nature of the actions being described; what motivates them, and whether they are illegal and immoral. The question of motivation relates both to individual actors and their context within groups of other pirates or file sharers. These contexts also relate to the question of harm (i.e., does this behavior harm specific industries?). The question of illegality seems straightforward, but to those engaged in the behavior of piracy/file sharing, the illegality of their behavior is uncertain. Likewise, the moral issues surrounding this behavior are ambiguous to the pirates/file sharers and other stakeholders.

For example, one critical perspective on piracy proposes that it may represent a socially constructed phenomenon resulting from evolving social, legal, and industry ideas and pressures regarding piracy (Yar, 2005a). The result of this process has been the rise of new global political responses to piracy and intellectual property (Shadlen et al., 2005).

Formal responses from policy makers and industry members have evolved alongside what some have referred to as a "culture of piracy" (Condry, 2004; Kini et al., 2004; Yar, 2005a; North and Oishi, 2006). This perspective suggests that digital piracy/file sharing is widely accepted and practiced. In other words, it is culturally normal. This cultural normalcy may in fact be related to broader political characteristics. For example, Piquero and Piquero (2006) suggest a link between democracy and piracy, citing the political and social climates that help define access to legitimate goods as well as digital access to pirated software.

It is not surprising then, that a lack of established legal and economic institutions in developing countries is linked with higher rates of piracy (Banerjee et al., 2005). Depken and Simmons (2004) suggest that regional economic conditions play an important role alongside social and cultural characteristics in defining rates of piracy. However, in contrast, Andrés' (2006) findings suggest that on a national level, piracy is negatively correlated with economic inequality. Andrés (2006) also suggests that income and education have little explanatory power with regard to rates of piracy. In light of the concern over piracy in countries such as China, this relationship between political economic structure and digital piracy becomes particular interesting. Rates of piracy in China are thought to be high, and this is likely because of a lack of or inability to enforce copyright laws, especially when copyrights are held overseas (Mertha, 2010).

These broad social factors are accompanied by more microlevel group orientations. Downing (2010a) proposes several typologies of digital pirates, suggesting that some are, for example, "socially motivated," seeking friendship, esteem, and recognition within their respective online subcultures. Downing (2010a) and Wang and Zhu (2003) also recognize that some pirates are motivated by profit, but caution that perhaps more are motivated by factors external to cost-benefit analyses. Nevertheless, Chih–Chien (2005) offers evidence that cost-benefit analysis is an important factor in determining whether or not one purchases pirated motion pictures.

Goode and Cruise (2006) and Downing (2010a) also explore the motives of software "crackers" (those who alter pirated software for its end use to be unlocked), finding that the challenge of cracking software inscription and copy-protection measures is their primary motive. Social recognition for these cracks is also illustrative of the social dynamics present in the piracy scene. Thus, in light of these realities, the term "file sharing" emerges as an apt description of the group-oriented nature of this type of copyright violation. Within and emerging from this group orientation is also a legal-moral dilemma. Software "pirates" themselves negotiate the ethics of their behavior, even using informal social control measures to reward and punish behaviors within their communities (Downing, 2010a). These exertions of control range from verbal condemnation or praising to ousting from a particular community through formal means such as banning persons from websites. The distribution of "social capital," or in other words "respect" is also a method by which groups of pirates reward and sanction behaviors within their groups. This phenomenon (or at the least, an understanding of it) may be an important tool for preventing copyright violation.

Preventing File Sharing and Copyright Violation

Regardless of the term applied, there is little doubt that copyright violation is widespread. Industry research shows a rate of PC software piracy in 2008 at 41% (Business Software Alliance [BSA],

2008). This data also suggest that rapid growth of piracy rates in some countries can be attributed to increasing access to the computers as well as the Internet. For economic and social reasons, the Internet facilitates file sharing that is often illegal (Rehn, 2004; Gayer and Shy, 2005).

Due to the technological nature of file sharing, certain "automatic" or "organic" artifacts of social computing may serve to prevent piracy. For example, Wolfe et al. (2008) found that fear of computer viruses influences engagement in digital piracy. Higgins (2005) also found that subject-generated deterrents (deterrents identified as effective by study respondents) lend credibility to the notion that there is at least some form of risk or sanction that will deter piracy.

Specifically regarding the tenets of deterrence (severity, certainty, and celerity), Peace et al. (2003) found that all three factors are important to deterring software piracy (in workplace environments), whereas Higgins (2005) found that certainty of detection is a greater deterrent to piracy than is the severity of a proposed sanction. Further, Chiang and Assane (2008) provide evidence that males are less likely to be deterred by economic risk factors when pirating through file-sharing networks.

Evidence in support of deterrence theory, however, is not universal (Al-Rafee & Cronan, 2006). Some industry responses would also seem to suggest that this is the case. Gillespie (2006) points to a shift in corporate strategies for dealing with copyright enforcement that prefer preventing piracy through code and other built-in barriers rather than relying on the threat of law enforcement (i.e., formal deterrence).

As an alternative to deterrence through built-in (target hardening) and legal barriers to piracy, Al-Rafee and Cronan (2006) suggest that changing attitudes about file sharing may yield more positive results. They draw on the social dynamics of file sharing to suggest that deterrent strategies aimed at individuals are unlikely to have a great impact on what is a largely group-oriented behavior. Downing (2010a) reinforces this position. Many digital pirates seem to download and share software not because they wish to "cheat" producers out of money, but because they enjoy the social aspects of sharing these files as well as the freedom to control the software in the absence of digital rights management. Similarly to some computer hackers, some digital pirates also engage in piracy and/or "cracking" software mainly because it offers a challenge and test of their skills. Software

---

BOX 7-5 Want to Stop Piracy? Try Making it Free

Whether a legitimate justification or not, many pirates cite the high prices of music, movies, or software as their motivation for downloading and copying these materials (Downing, 2010a). The responses to piracy usually involve attempting to block these attempts in some way, either through legislation or the creation of built-in mechanisms. Some media producers, however, are turning to a different model. Radiohead was one of the first widely publicized examples of a copyright owner offering their product to consumers for free, but also encouraging them to purchase the album if they enjoyed it. This strategy has been followed by a "pay what you want" trend that spans a gamut of media types from music to computer software. The Bandcamp website uses a similar model where consumers name their own price for the music (Bandcamp, 2011). Independent computer game developers often employ this same strategy. The idea behind this approach is that it will encourage fan loyalty and reduce consumer hostility toward what they may perceive as rich, greedy, corporate producers. It also allows consumers the opportunity to reward work they perceive as particularly well made. As of yet it is too early to tell how well this model will work, but it provides an interesting alternative to stricter, more formal approaches to piracy.

crackers essentially break codes in software that are intended to prevent copying or running the software on an unauthorized device. Because of the sheer size of the piracy community and the presence of these crackers, it is extremely difficult if not impossible for software producers and publishers to prevent piracy through "target hardening" or coding against copying and unintended use.

Thus, a comprehensive prevention strategy aimed at curbing rates of piracy should consult not only industry members and criminal justice policy makers, but also end users. These users may provide a surprising willingness to engage in initiatives that reward media developers while also acknowledging the social and individual preferences and rights of those who consume this media.

EMERGING ISSUES: CRIME, DEVIANCE, AND VIRTUAL WORLDS

The socio-legal complexity of copyright violation serves as a good transition into understanding emerging issues related to crime, deviance, and computers. Returning to the notion of technological revolutions, the reader may recall this chapter's earlier discussion of the postinformation revolution. This section will present what it is argued are components of this revolution, namely that "reality" and online communication are becoming increasingly enmeshed, creating a state of "virtual reality." It is within these virtual contexts that criminology has a unique opportunity to explore deviance and criminality on the frontier of technologically enabled communities and cultures. Alongside this exploration emerges the sobering reality that—though they certainly offer many promising possibilities—virtual realities are not utopias.

Gaming, Crime, and Deviance

There are essentially two avenues of research regarding the connection among gaming, crime, and deviance. The most common avenue of research in criminology explores the relationship between playing games and propensity for violence or an increase in aggression in general. The other avenue of research that is more common in the general sociological and communications fields approaches games as contexts for human interaction that includes a wide gamut of behaviors going beyond violence. This body of research is critical of gaming studies that focus solely on real-world aggression, citing that even though gaming has grown to become an important social leisure activity, criminological studies continue to focus narrowly on the connection between video games and negative behaviors (Bryce & Rutter, 2003).

Gaming and Violence

The proposed connection between gaming and antisocial behavior is not a new notion. For example, a 1987 study found that video-game playing youths exhibited more problem behaviors than "gambling" youths (Huff & Collinson, 1987). Irwin and Gross (1995) also find that youth are more aggressive, though primarily during actual play sessions. Studies continue to propose a connection between problem behavior and game playing, but now focus primarily on aggression and violence (Anderson & Bushman, 2001; Anderson & Murphy, 2003; Kronenberger & Mathews, 2005). However, the literature does offer some competing evidence with regard to the connection between aggression and gaming. Cooper and Mackie (1986) found that violent video gaming has little effect on male play with friends. Another study found that violent video games have less of a negative impact on behaviors than violent television (Sherry, 2001). A comprehensive review of

29 video game-aggression studies suggests that young adults and adults are minimally affected by exposure to violent video games (Bensley & Eenwyk, 2001).

Thus, the reader is encouraged to draw his or her own conclusions on the video game-violence debate—although the reader should consider the methodologies employed in the cited studies (many of which are laboratory experiments), and whether or not these methodologies translate well into real-world situations where there is strong evidence that complex social and individual variables contribute to the committing of violent and aggressive acts. Likewise, such issues should raise a cautionary flag regarding premature or overzealous intervention on the part of lawmakers and practitioners. Most studies that support a link between gaming and violence have suggested policy implications related to changing the content of games or restricting access to them. These approaches, however, should be considered with great care, as they may easily shift from preventative strategies to forms of restricting freedom of expression.

Beyond the Violence Connection

As previously mentioned, a second avenue of research in gaming and social interaction considers a wider range of behaviors. As the previous sections have shown, a great deal of the cyber-victimization literature, for example, focuses on either violent or sexual crimes related to the Internet (Beech, Elliot, & Birgden, 2008; Wolak, Finkelhor, & Mitchell, 2008; Wolak, Mitchell, & Finkelhor, 2007; Walsh & Wolak, 2005; Mitchell, Wolak, & Finkelhor, 2007; Burke, Sowerbutts, & Blundell, 2002; Craven, Brown, & Gilchrist, 2007). The research on crime and deviance within game worlds considers these types of crimes including "cyber-rapes" (Michals, 1997; Gorrindo & Groves, 2010). While cyber-rape is not currently defined as a crime on the same level as physical rape, it nevertheless involves emotional trauma brought on by exposure to text, spoken words, and images that seek to degrade the victim.

Nevertheless, in reality, as this chapter has shown, victimization online is not limited to sexual or violent assaults. To this end, the sociological literature has begun to address virtual worlds with a focus on interactions from the perspective of communications scholarship, which emphasizes the changing nature of sharing friendships on the Internet (Colwell & Kato, 2003). Criminological research in this area has been limited, but emerging studies suggest that the nature of deviance in online gaming contexts is similarly complex to these behaviors offline. Specifically, offline individual and culturally held beliefs and values may transition into game worlds (Downing, 2009, 2010b, Gorrindo & Groves, 2010).

BOX 7-6 Virtual Murder?

How serious is "virtual crime?" In 2008, a Japanese woman was arrested and charged after she hacked into a man's online game account and deleted his character. She was married to this man in the game and committed the "virtual murder" after a particularly messy game-divorce. She was subsequently arrested and faced potential charges related to illegally accessing and manipulating data. These charges can result in up to a 5-year prison sentence or $5,000 fine (Geere, 2008). This case reflects the changing landscape of criminal justice as it relates to computer technology and social life. As the line between the virtual and the real becomes more blurred, these cases may become more common.

It is important to also recognize that cyber-victimization occurs within the context of settings characterized by relatively free speech (Graca & Stader, 2007). In the case of online gaming, this speech is also connected with actions ranging from the mundane to simulated violence and theft (Downing, 2009). Therefore, cyber-victimization serves as a catalyst for reframing definitions of both online and offline crime, criminal, and victim (Wykes, 2007).

This line of research is currently too underdeveloped to offer firm recommendations related to preventing "virtual harm" but it does suggest that more attention should be paid to human interaction in the context of gaming, and not solely on the relationship between exposure to violence in games and real world behaviors. Future policies will likely have to address increasing cases of in-game harm impacting individuals offline. There is already a precedent for this relationship with respect to cyber-bullying (Mitchell at al., 2007).

SUMMARY

The gaming and crime connection offers a mere glimpse into the future of Internet-related crime and its surrounding issues. Preventing these crimes in the future will be even more challenging than it is today. Some futurists predict that within just a few decades humans will "transcend" their biological selves (Kurzweil, 2005). Even if this prediction is only partially fulfilled, it suggests that the difference between technological and nontechnological interaction will become less and less distinct. As has been mentioned in this chapter, we can already observe these trends with respect to augmentations of current technology into everyday life—cell phones, GPS, social networking, and so on. Interactive games are now experimenting with augmentation using GPS that allows, for example, individuals to play games by physically traveling to real-world locations and interacting with other people. Coupled with increasing realism and immersion through simulated and real 3D, this augmentation promises to fundamentally alter human interaction, further blurring the line between real and virtual.

While these changes probably sound like science fiction, they underscore an important trend with respect to crime prevention: that *prevention* of technology-related crime absolutely requires *prediction*. Current research on Internet-related crime not only offers glimpses into current problems and their potential prevention, but more importantly, offers the information with which policy makers can develop prevention strategies for emerging and future technology-based crimes.

Thus, if there is one important lesson to be drawn from this chapter, it should be that prevention of Internet crime should be proactive rather than reactive. This proves difficult in the absence of adequate budgets. Each section of this chapter has shown that police and other agencies are almost always understaffed and underfunded to combat Internet-related crimes. This reality is agitated by the lack of common legal and even socially agreed-upon definitions of many of the crimes in question. The line between crime, deviance, and "normal" behavior online is indeed a blurry one.

The presence of these challenges should not, however, discourage attempts at prevention. The wealth of empirical research on these issues that has been conducted and continues to amass is encouraging. Prevention strategies should first and foremost consult this body of research. This chapter has shown that informed prevention methods work best. Interestingly, the lack of financial and human capacity to prevent Internet-related crime is not as great of an obstacle when one consults the literature. This is because the literature generally supports the contention that informal prevention methods work best. Thus, education, parental involvement, and cooperation among individuals, private companies, and public agencies is probably the best way to create a climate in which Internet crime is least likely to become an unwieldy problem.

In addition to this informal push, the Internet should not be regarded solely as a place where negative behavior thrives. Instead, these informal prevention strategies can be combined with pro-social uses of technology. For example, Mawby (2004) suggests that the Internet can facilitate victim healing, sharing, and consultation with experts. There is no reason that prevention methods such as education and open communication among involved parties cannot also thrive on the Internet, or whatever form of technologically enabled social contexts prevail in the future.

KEY TERMS

Cyber-bullying
Phishing
Click fraud
Auction fraud
Nanny software
Social control
Piracy
File sharing
Cyber-stalking
Information revolution
Situational crime control
Routine activities theory
Virtual victimization

DISCUSSION QUESTIONS

1. In your opinion, what technological innovation has most influenced society? What innovation has most influenced crime?
2. What are some examples of movies or books that depict technology as being harmful? How do these depictions influence fears about cyber-crime?
3. Why do studies find such varying rates of cyber-bullying? What are some ways to reduce these discrepancies?
4. Is it ethical for the police to pose as children during sting operations against potential Internet child-sex offenders?
5. Estimates of losses due to digital piracy are often based on the assumption that every copied or downloaded piece of digital media would have otherwise been purchased by the pirate. What might be a better way to estimate these losses?
6. Can software creators ever fully protect their software against copying and cracking? If not, what are some other ways they can reduce piracy?
7. Are "virtual crime and victimization" real crime and victimization? How will changing technologies alter the nature of this type of victimization?

REFERENCES

Agatston, P., Kowalski, R., & Limber, S. (2007). Students' perspectives on cyber bullying. *Journal of Adolescent Health, 41*, S59–S60.

Al-Rafee, S., & Cronan, T. (2006). Digital piracy: Factors that influence attitude toward behavior. *Journal of Business Ethic, 63*(3), 237–259.

Alves, L., & Wilson, S. (2008). The effects of loneliness on telemarketing fraud vulnerability among older adults. *Journal of Elder Abuse and Neglect, 20*(1), 65–85.

Anderson, C., & Bushman, B. (2001). Effects of violent video games on aggressive cognition, aggressive affect, physiological arousal, and prosocial behavior: A meta-analytic review of the scientific literature. *Psychological Science, 12*(5), 353–359.

Anderson, C., & Murphy, C. (2003). Violent video games and aggressive behavior in young women. *Aggressive Behavior, 29*(5), 423–429.

Andrés, A. R. (2006). Software piracy and income inequality. *Applied Economics Letters, 13*(2), 101–105.

Armstrong, H. L., & Forde, P. J. (2003). Internet anonymity practices in computer crime. *Information Management & Computer Security, 11*(5), 209–215.

Atkinson, C., & Newton, D. (2010). Online behaviours of adolescents: Victims, perpetrators and web 2.0. *Journal of Sexual Aggression, 16*(1), 107–120.

Bandcamp. (2011). Retrieved from http://bandcamp.com/

Banerjee, D., Khalid, A., & Sturm, J. (2005). Socio-economic development and software piracy: An empirical assessment. *Applied Economics, 37*(18), 2091–2097.

Bates, A., & Metcalf, C. (2007). A psychometric comparison of Internet and non-Internet sex offenders from a community treatment sample. *Journal of Sexual Aggression, 13*(1), 11–20.

Beech, A., Elliot, I., & Birgden, A. (2008) The Internet and child sexual offending: A criminological review. *Aggression and Violent Behavior: A Review Journal, 13*(3), 216–228.

Bensley, L., & Van Eenwyk, J. (2001). Video games and real-life aggression: review of the literature. *Journal of Adolescent Health 29*(4), 244–257.

Black, D. (1976). *The behavior of law.* New York, NY: Academic Press.

Bossler, A., & Holt, T. (2010). The effect of self-control on victimization in the cyberworld. *Journal of Criminal Justice, 38*(3), 227–236.

Brown, S. (2006). The criminology of hybrids: Rethinking crime and law in technosocial networks. *Theoretical Criminology, 10*(2), 223–244.

Bryant, J., Sanders-Jackson, A., & Smallwood, A. (2006). IMing, text messaging and adolescent social networks. *Journal of Computer-Mediated Communication, 11*(2),http://jcmc.indiana.edu/vol11/issue2/bryant.html.

Bryce, J., & Rutter, J. (2003). Gender dynamics and the social and spatial organization of computer gaming. *Leisure Studies, 22*, 1-15.

Burke, A., Sowerbutts, S., & Blundell, B. (2002). Child pornography and the Internet: Policing and treatment issues. *Psychiatry, Psychology and Law, 9*(1), 79–84.

Burns, C., Morley, J., Bradshaw, R., & Domene, J. (2008). The emotional impact on and coping strategies employed by police teams investigating Internet child exploitation. *Traumatology, 14*(2), 20–31.

Business Software Alliance (2008). *Software piracy fact sheet.* Retrieved from http://www.bsa.org.

Butterfield, L. (2003). The New Zealand model for prevention of cyberviolence. *Journal of School Violence, 2*(1), 95–104. Retrieved from www.csa.com.

Buzzell, T. (2007). The effects of organizational and community context on local prosecution of computer child pornography cases. *Criminal Justice Studies: A Critical Journal of Crime, Law and Society, 20*(4), 391–405.

Caiani, M., & Parenti, L. (2009). The dark side of the web: Italian right-wing extremist groups and the Internet. *South European Society & Politics, 14*(3), 273–294.

Chiang, E. P., & Assane, D. (2008). Music piracy among students on the university campus: Do males and females react differently? *Journal of Socio-Economics, 37*(4), 1371–1380.

Chih-Chien, W. (2005). Factors that influence the piracy of DVD/VCD motion pictures. *Journal of American Academy of Business, Cambridge, 6*(1), 231–237.

Clarke, R. (1995). Situational crime prevention. *Crime and Justice*, 19, 91–150.

Colwell, J., & Kato, M. (2003) Investigation of the relationship between social isolation, self-esteem, aggression and computer game play in Japanese adolescents. *Asian Journal of Social Psychology*, 6(2), 149–158.

Condry, I. (2004). Cultures of music piracy: An ethnographic comparison of the US and Japan. *International Journal of Cultural Studies*, 7(3), 343–363.

Cooper, J., & Mackie, D. (1986). Video games and aggression in children. *Journal of Applied Social Psychology*, 16, 726–744.

Craven, S., Brown, S., & Gilchrist, E. (2007). Current responses to sexual grooming: Implication for prevention. *Howard Journal of Criminal Justice*, 46(1), 60–71.

Daniels, J. (2009). Cloaked websites: Propaganda, cyber-racism and epistemology in the digital era. *New Media & Society*, 11(5), 659–683.

Davinson, N., & Sillence, E. (2010). It won't happen to me: Promoting secure behaviour among Internet users. *Computers in Human Behavior*, 26(6), 1739–1747.

Dehue, F., Bolman, C., & Vollink, T. (2008). Cyberbullying: Youngsters' experiences and parental perception. *Cyber Psychology & Behavior*, 11(2), 217–233.

Depken, C. A., & Simmons, L. C. (2004). Social construct and the propensity for software piracy. *Applied Economics Letters*, 11(2), 97–100.

Douglas, R. (2009, November 17). Floral City man charged with video voyeurism, having hundreds of child porn pictures. *Citrus Daily*. Retrieved from http://citrusdaily.com/local-news/ floral-city-man-charged-video-voyeurism-hundreds-chld-porn-pictues/2009/11/17/16760.html

Downing, S. K. (2009). Attitudinal and behavioral pathways of deviance in online gaming. *Deviant Behavior*, 30(3), 293–320.

Downing, S. (2010a). Social control in a subculture of piracy. *Criminal Justice and Popular Culture*, 17(1), 77–123.

Downing, S. K. (2010b). Virtual victimization and validation through social construction. *Eludamos: Journal for Computer Game Culture*, 4(2), 287–301.

Draucker, C., & Martsolf, D. (2010). The role of electronic communication technology in adolescent dating violence. *Journal of Child and Adolescent Psychiatric Nursing*, 23(3), 133–142.

Duranske, B. (2008, May 23). New supreme court opinion discusses virtual child pornography law; Linden Lab's 2007 ban clarified. *Virtually Blind*. Retrieved from http://virtuallyblind.com/2008/05/23/ageplay-ban-clarified/

Durkheim, E. (1933). *The division of labor in society*. New York, NY: MacMillan Publishing Co.

Edelmann, R. (2010). Exposure to child abuse images as part of one's work: Possible psychological implications. *Journal of Forensic Psychiatry & Psychology*, 21(4), 481–489.

Emsley, C. (1984). Arms and the Victorian policeman. *History Today*, 34(11), 37–42.

Engelberg, J., & Williams, J. (2009). eBay's proxy bidding: A license to shill. *Journal of Economic Behavior & Organization*, 72(1), 509–526.

Federal Trade Commission (FTC). (2011). *FTC list of top consumer complaints in 2010*. Retrieved from http:// www.ftc.gov/opa/2011/03/topcomplaints.shtm.

Finn, J. (2004) A survey of online harassment at a university campus. *Journal of Interpersonal Violence*, 29(4), 468–483.

Fisher, J. (2008). The UK's faster payment project: Avoiding a bonanza for cybercrime fraudsters. *Journal of Financial Crime*, 15(2), 155–164.

Flynn, J. (2011, Feb. 17). Hampton district attorney Mark G. Mastroianni calls for mandatory reporting of bullying cases. *The Republican*. Retrieved from http://www.masslive.com/news/index.ssf/2011/02/ hampden_district_attorney_mark.html

Friedman, M. (1992). Confidence swindles of older consumers. *Journal of Consumer Affairs*, 26(1), 20–46.

Gayer, A., & Shy, O. (2005). Copyright enforcement in the digital era. *CESifo Economic Studies*, 51(2/3), 477–489.

Geere, Duncan. (2008, October 24). Japanese woman jailed for killing virtual husband. *Tech Digest*. Retrieved from http://www.techdigest.tv/2008/10/japanese_woman.html

Gillespie, T. (2006). Designed to "effectively frustrate": Copyright, technology and the agency of users. *New Media & Society*, 8(4), 651–669.

Goode, S., & Cruise, S. (2006). What motivates software crackers? *Journal of Business Ethics, 65*(2), 173–201.

Gorrindo, T., & Groves, J. (2010). Crime and hate in virtual worlds: A new playground for the id? *Harvard Review Psychiatry, 18*(2), 113–118.

Graca, T., & Stader, D. (2007) Student speech and the Internet: A legal analysis. *NASSP Bulletin, 91*(2), 121–128.

Greenberg, D. F. (1985). Age, crime, and social explanation. *American Journal of Sociology, 89*, 1–21.

Grimes, G. A., Hough, M. G., Mazur, E., & Signorella, M. L. (2010). Older adults' knowledge of Internet hazards. *Educational Gerontology, 36*(3), 173–192.

Higgins, G. E. (2005). Can low self-control help with the understanding of the software piracy problem? *Deviant Behavior, 26*(1), 1–24.

Hinduja, S. (2004). Perceptions of local and state law enforcement concerning the role of computer crime investigative teams. *Policing: An International Journal of Police Strategies & Management, 27*(3), 341–357.

Hinduja, S., & Patchin, J. W. (2008). Cyberbullying: An exploratory analysis of factors related to offending and victimization. *Deviant Behavior, 29*(2), 129–156.

Holt, T. J., & Bossler, A. M. (2009). Examining the applicability of lifestyle-routine activities theory for cybercrime victimization. *Deviant Behavior, 30*(1), 1–25.

Holt, T. J., & Lampke, E. (2010). Exploring stolen data markets online: Products and market forces. *Criminal Justice Studies: A Critical Journal of Crime, Law and Society, 23*(1), 33–50.

Huey, L., & Rosenberg, R. (2004). Watching the Web: Thoughts on expanding police surveillance opportunities under the cyber-crime convention. *Canadian Journal of Criminology and Criminal Justice, 46*(5), 597–606.

Huff, G., & Collinson, F. (1987). Young offenders, gambling and video game playing. *British Journal of Criminology, 27*, 401–410.

Irwin, R., & Gross, A. (1995). Cognitive tempo, violent video games, and aggressive behavior in young boys. *Journal of Family Violence, 10*, 337–350.

Jewkes, Y. (2010). Much ado about nothing? Representations and realities of online soliciting of children. *Journal of Sexual Aggression, 16*(1), 5–18.

Jewkes, Y., & Andrews, C. (2005). Policing the filth: The problems of investigating online child pornography in England and Wales. *Policing & Society, 15*(1), 42–62.

Juvonen, J., & Gross, E. (2008). Extending the school grounds?—Bullying experiences in cyberspace. *Journal of School Health, 78*(9), 496–505.

Katz, A. (2005). A network effects perspective on software piracy. *University of Toronto Law Journal, 55*(2), 155–216.

King, J., Walpole, C., & Lamon, K. (2007). Surf and turf wars online—Growing implications of Internet gang violence. *Journal of Adolescent Health, 41*, S66–S68.

Kini, R., Ramakrishna, H., & Vijay Ayaraman, B. (2004). Shaping of moral intensity regarding software piracy: A comparison between Thailand and U.S. students. *Journal of Business Ethics, 49*(1), 91–104.

Koops, B. (2003). The shifting "balance" between criminal investigation and privacy. *Information, Communication & Society, 6*(3), 380–403.

Kowalski, R., & Limber, S. (2007). Electronic bullying among middle school students. *Journal of Adolescent Health, 41*, S22–S30.

Kronenberger, W., Mathews, V., & Dunn, D. (2005). Media violence exposure in aggressive and control adolescents: Differences in self- and parent-reported exposure to violence on television and in video games. *Aggressive Behavior, 31*, 201–216.

Kurzweil, R. (2005). *When humans transcend biology the singularity is near.* New York, NY: Penguin Group.

Law, D., Shapka, J., & Olson, B. (2010). To control or not to control? Parenting behaviours and adolescent online aggression. *Computers in Human Behavior, 26*(6), 1651–1656.

Li, Q. (2005). New bottle but old wine: A research of cyberbullying in schools. *Computers in Human Behavior, 23*, 1777–1791.

Li, Q. (2006). Cyberbullying in schools: A research of gender differences. *School Psychology International, 27*(2), 157–170.

Li, X., & Nergadze, N. (2009). Deterrence effect of four legal and extralegal factors on online copyright infringement. *Journal of Computer-Mediated Communication, 14*(2), 307–327.

Lingamneni, J. R. (1997). Computer crime. *Caribbean Journal of Criminology & Social Psychology, 2*(1), 85–95.

Marcum, C., Higgins, G., & Ricketts, M. (2010). Potential factors of online victimization of youth: An examination of adolescent online behaviors utilizing routine activity theory. *Deviant Behavior, 31*(5), 381–410.

Marsh, L., McGee, R., Nada-Raja, S., & Williams, S. (2010). Brief report: Text bullying and traditional bullying among New Zealand secondary school students. *Journal of Adolescence, 33*(1), 237–240.

Mason, K. L. (2008). Cyberbullying: A preliminary assessment for school personnel. *Psychology in the Schools, 45*(4), 323–348.

Mawby, R. (2004) Surfing the crime net: Victim support and victim assistance programmes. *Crime Prevention and Community Safety: An International Journal, 6*(1), 65–69.

McCarthy, J. (2010). Internet sexual activity: A comparison between contact and non-contact child pornography offenders. *Journal of Sexual Aggression, 16*(2), 181–195.

Mehra, S. K. (2010). Law and cybercrime in the United States today. *The American Journal of Comparative Law, 58,* 659–685.

Meints, M., Leenes, R., van der Meulen, N. Koops, B., & Jaquet-Chiffelle, D. (2009). A typology of identity-related crime. *Information, Communication & Society, 12*(1), 1–24.

Melander, L. A. (2010). College students' perceptions of intimate partner cyber harassment. *Cyberpsychology, Behavior, and Social Networking, 13*(3), 263–268.

Mertha, A. (2010). Intellectual property rights in China: Politcs of piracy, trade and protection. Routledge Contemporary China Series. *Public Affairs, 83*(3), 579.

Michals, D. (1997, March/April). Cyber-rape: How virtual is it? *Ms. Magazine.* Retrieved from http://www.terry.uga.edu/~dawndba/4500CyberRape.html

Milne, G. R., Rohm, A., & Bahl, S. (2009). If it's legal, is it acceptable? Consumer reactions to online covert marketing. *Journal of Advertising. Special Issue: Advertising Regulation and Self-Regulation, 38*(4), 107–122.

Mitchell, K., Finkelhor, D., Jones, L., & Wolak, J. (2010a). Use of social networking sites in online sex crimes against minors: An examination of national incidence and means of utilization. *Journal of Adolescent Health, 47*(2), 183–190.

Mitchell, K., Finkelhor, D., Jones, L., & Wolak, J. (2010b). Growth and change in undercover online child exploitation investigations, 2000–2006. *Policing & Society, 20*(4), 416–431.

Mitchell, K., Wolak, J., & Finkelhor, D. (2007). Trends in youth reports of sexual solicitations, harassment and unwanted exposure to pornography on the Internet. *Journal of Adolescent Health, 40*(2), 116–126.

Mitchell, K., Ybarra, M., & Finkelhor, D. (2007) The relative importance of online victimization in understanding depression, delinquency, and substance abuse. *Child Maltreatment, 12*(4), 314–324.

Moon, B., McCluskey, J. D., & McCluskey, C. P. (2010). A general theory of crime and computer crime: An empirical test. *Journal of Criminal Justice, 38*(4), 767–772.

North, A. C., & Oishi, A. (2006). Music CD purchase decisions. *Journal of Applied Social Psychology, 36*(12), 3043–3084.

Park, Robert E., Burgess E., McKenzie, R. (1925). *The city.* Chicago, IL: University of Chicago Press.

Parsons-Pollard, N., & Moriarty, L. (2009). Cyberstalking: Utilizing what we do know. *Victims & Offenders, 4*(4), 435–441.

Patchin, J., & Hinduja, S. (2006). Bullies move beyond the schoolyard: A preliminary look at cyberbullying. *Youth Violence and Juvenile Justice, 4*(2), 148–169.

Patton, C., Nobles, M., & Fox, K. (2010). Look who's stalking: Obsessive pursuit and attachment theory. *Journal of Criminal Justice, 38*(3), 282–290.

Peace, A. G., Galletta, D. F., & Thong, J. (2003). Software piracy in the workplace: A model and empirical test. *Journal of Management Information Systems, 20*(1), 153–177.

Piquero, N., & Piquero, A. (2006). Democracy and intellectual property: Examining trajectories of software piracy. *Annals of the American Academy of Political and Social Science, 605,* 104–127.

Pratt, T., Holtfreter, K., & Resig, M. (2010). Routine online activity and Internet fraud targeting: extending the generality of routine activity theory. *Journal of Research in Crime and Delinquency, 47*(3), 267–296.

Raskauskas J., & Stoltz, A. (2007). Involvement in traditional and electronic bullying among adolescents. *Developmental Psychology, 43*(3), 564–575.

Rehn, A. (2004). The politics of contraband: The honor economies of the Warez scene. *Journal of Socio-Economics*, *13*(3), 359.

Reisig, M. D., Pratt, T. C., & Holtfreter, K. (2009). Perceived risk of Internet theft victimization: Examining the effects of social vulnerability and financial impulsivity. *Criminal Justice and Behavior*, *36*(4), 369–384.

Rochman, B. Cyberbullying? Homophibia? Tyler Clementi's death highlights online lawlessness. (2010, October 1). *Time Magazine*. Retrieved from http://healthland.time.com/2010/10/01/cyberbullying-homophobia-tyler-clementis-death-highlights-online-lawlessness/.

Seto, M. (2010). Child pornography use and Internet solicitation in the diagnosis of pedophilia. *Archives of Sexual Behavior*, *39*(3), 591–593.

Shadlen, K. C., Schrank, A., & Kurtz, M. J. (2005). The political economy of intellectual property protection: The case of software. *International Studies Quarterly*, *49*(1), 45–71.

Shaw, C., & McKay, H. (1942). *Juvenile delinquency in urban areas*. Chicago, IL: University of Chicago Press.

Sheridan, L. P., & Grant, T. (2007). Is cyberstalking different? *Psychology, Crime & Law*, *13*(6), 627–640.

Sherry, J. (2001). The effects of violent video games on aggression: A meta-analysis. *Human Communication Research*, *27*, 409–431.

Shred day event helps public fight identity theft. (2011, March 4). *NJ Today*. Retrieved from http://njtoday.net/2011/03/04/shred-day-event-helps-public-fight-identity-theft/.

Simon, H. A. (1969). The impact of the computer on management. Proceedings of the 15th International Management Congress. CIOS, 25–30.

Slonje, R., & Smith, P. (2008). Cyberbullying: Another main type of bullying? *Personality and Social Sciences*, *49*, 147–154.

Smihula, D. (2010). Waves of technological innovations and the end of the information revolution. *Journal of Economics and International Finance*, *2*(4), 58–67.

Smith, A. (2009). Nigerian scam e-mails and the charms of capital. *Cultural Studies*, *23*(1), 27–47.

Smith, P., Mahdavi, J., Carvalho, M., Fisher, S., Russell, S., & Tippett, N. (2008). Cyberbullying: Its nature and impact in secondary school pupils. *Child Psychology and Psychiatry*, *49*(4), 376–385.

Sproule, S., & Archer, N. (2010). Measuring identity theft and identity fraud. *International Journal of Business Governance and Ethics*, *5*(1/2), 51–63.

Sutherland, E. (1924) *Principles of criminology*. Chicago, IL: University of Chicago Press.

The Pew Research Center for the People & the Press (1999). *Technology triumphs, morality falters: Scientific inventions and social trends*. Retrieved from http://people-press.org.

Trim, P. R. J. (2003). Public and private sector cooperation in counteracting cyberterrorism. *International Journal of Intelligence and Counterintelligence*, *16*(4), 594–608.

Vandebosch, H., & Van Cleemput, K. (2008). Defining cyberbullying: A qualitative research into the perceptions of youngsters. *Cyber Psychology & Behavior*, *11*(4): 499–503.

Wall, D. S. (2008). Cybercrime and the culture of fear. *Information, Communication & Society*, *11*(6), 861–884.

Walsh, W., & Wolak, J. (2005). Nonforcible Internet-related sex crimes with adolescent victims: Prosecution issues and outcomes. *Child Maltreatment*, *10*(3), 260–271.

Wang, S., & Zhu, J. (2003). Mapping film piracy in China. *Theory, Culture & Society*, *20*(4), 97–125.

Weber, D. C. (1997). Warrior cops: The ominous growth of para-militarism in American police departments (briefing paper 50). Retrieved from http://www.cato.org/pubs/briefs/bp50.pdf.

Weir, A. S., Chappell, J., & Kacelnik, A. (2002). Shaping of hooks in New Caledonian crows. *Science*, *297*(5583), 981.

Wilbur, K. C., & Zhu, Y. (2009). Click fraud. *Marketing Science*, *28*(2), 293–308.

Williams, K., & Guerra, N. (2007). Prevalence and predictors of Internet bullying. *Journal of Adolescent Health*, *41*(6), S14–S21.

Williams, M. (2007). Policing and cybersociety: The maturation of regulation within an online community. *Policing & Society*, *17*(1), 59–82.

Winterdyk, J., & Thompson, N. (2008). Student and non-student perceptions and awareness of identity theft. *Canadian Journal of Criminology and Criminal Justice/Revue Canadienne De Criminologie Et De Justice Penale*, *50*(2), 153–186.

Wolak, J., Finkelhor, D., Mitchell, K., & Ybarra, M. (2010). Online "predators" and their victims: Myths, realities, and implications for prevention and treatment. *Psychology of Violence, 1*(S), 13–35.

Wolak, J., Mitchell, K., & Finkelhor, D. (2003). *Internet sex crimes against minors: The response of law enforcement* (NCMEC 10-03-022). Alexandria, VA: National Center for Missing & Exploited Children.

Wolak, J., Mitchell, K., & Finkelhor, D. (2007) Unwanted and wanted exposure to online pornography in a national sample of youth Internet users. *Pediatrics, 119*(2), 247–257.

Wolfe, S. E., Higgins, G. E., & Marcum, C. D. (2008). Deterrence and digital piracy. *Social Science Computer Review, 26*(3), 317–333.

Worthen, M. (2007). Education policy implications from the expert panel on electronic media and youth violence. *Journal of Adolescent Health, 41*, S61–S63

Wright, R., Chakraborty, S., Basoglu, A., & Marett, K. (2010). Where did they go right? Understanding the deception in phishing communications. *Group Decision and Negotiation, 19*(4), 391–416.

Wykes, M. (2007). Constructing crime: Culture, stalking, celebrity and cyber. *Crime, Media, Culture, 3*(2), 158–174.

Yar, M. (2005a). The Global "epidemic" of movie "piracy": Crime-wave or social construction? *Media, Culture & Society, 27*(5), 677–696.

Yar, M. (2005b). The novelty of "cybercrime": An assessment in light of routine activity theory. *European Journal of Criminology, 2*(4), 407–427.

Ybarra, M., & Mitchell, K. (2004). Youth engaging in online harassment: Associations with caregiver-child relationships, Internet use, and personal characteristics. *Journal of Adolescence, 27*, 319–336.

Ybarra, M., Espelage, D., & Mitchell, K. (2007). The co-occurrence of Internet harassment and unwanted sexual solicitation victimization and perpetration. *Journal of Adolescent Health, 42*, 31–41.

Ybarra, M., & Mitchell, K. (2007). Prevalence and frequency of Internet harassment instigation: Implications for adolescent health. *Journal of Adolescent Health, 41*, 189–195.

Ybarra, M., Finkelhor, D., Mitchell, K., & Wolak, J. (2009). Associations between blocking, monitoring, and filtering software on the home computer and youth-reported unwanted exposure to sexual material online. *Child Abuse & Neglect, 33*(12), 867–869.

CHAPTER 8

Spatial Analysis of Property Crimes, Foreclosure, and Other Socioeconomic Variables: An Examination of Garfield Heights, Ohio

Harry J. Wilson
Ohio Northern University

Kevin Cieplowski
Ohio Northern University

Seungmug Lee
Western Illinois University

INTRODUCTION

Much debate exists regarding the relationship between foreclosures and crime, especially since the onset of the recession in late 2007 (Finklea, 2009). The implications for neighborhoods and entire cities are particularly important as foreclosures and crime affect real estate investment, lending, and homeownership rates. They also influence the overall image of communities and their ability to attract and retain residents, businesses, and industries.

Most agree that the main threat is that foreclosed properties, if left unsold and vacant, will facilitate neighborhood decay, and problems common to blighted areas will increase, including crime (Immergluck & Smith, 2006). The ability of neighborhoods to quickly sell foreclosed properties seems important since it ensures that homes remain occupied and land values remain steady. The loss of residents also undermines the ability of neighborhoods to police themselves and engage in other activities that ensure the safety, appeal, and overall worth of their communities (Goodstein & Lee, 2010).

Identifying the extent of the foreclosure problem is especially challenging, primarily because of the myriad of socioeconomic factors involved (Immergluck & Smith, 2006). Lower-income neighborhoods and those already struggling to address other social problems may be most at risk of slipping into blight and may experience the greatest difficulty recovering. Upper-income areas may have more safeguards in place that would help ensure the cohesiveness and safety of their neighborhoods.

Analysis of the impact of foreclosures at the community and neighborhood levels provides a more comprehensive picture of the implications regarding the recent foreclosure crisis and promises to help concerned parties target their resources more efficiently. This paper presents a method for identifying areas that are most at risk of slipping into blight, areas where recent foreclosure and crime rates are elevated or rising, and where residents may not be equipped to adjust to these emerging problems. This paper presents an efficient method for initiating such research, utilizing readily available public data and common statistical and spatial techniques. Those conducting research can easily acquire foreclosure and crime data from local municipalities and neighborhood information from the U.S. Census Bureau. Pearson correlations and factor analysis reveal the relationship between these variables, and when mapped utilizing Geographic Information Systems (GIS), can identify patterns within communities where crime and foreclosure rates are most problematic.

Garfield Heights, Ohio, provides an excellent landscape to analyze the relationship between foreclosures and crime and for identifying neighborhoods that are most affected. The community is a suburb of Cleveland located in the southeast section of the metropolitan area within Cuyahoga County (**Figures 8-1 & 8-2**). Foreclosure and property crime rates in Garfield Heights have increased in recent years and have affected every section of the community. Garfield Heights, however, is not a uniform landscape. The typical race, age, and family structure of residents in neighborhoods in southern sections are very different from those to the north, as are their incomes and land values. Residential foreclosure and property crime rates also vary across the community. Examining the relationship between these variables at the block group level reveals not only the neighborhoods most affected by foreclosures and crime, but also identifies demographic groups who are more at risk than others within this community.

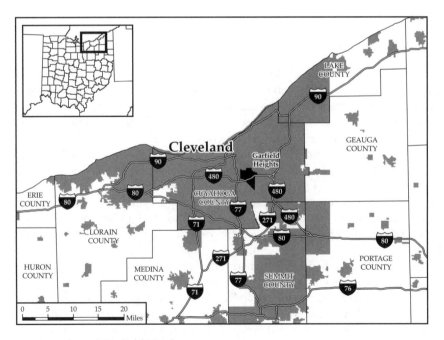

FIGURE 8-1. Location of Garfield Heights.

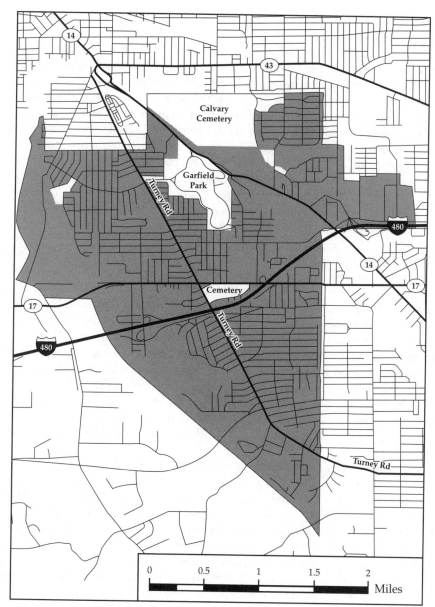

FIGURE 8-2. Garfield Heights.

BACKGROUND

Very few scholars have examined the relationship between residential foreclosures and crime, a reality that has not gone unnoticed (Finklea, 2009). Given recent economic events and the importance of the national foreclosure problem, this may seem surprising, especially with the "anecdotal evidence" cited in many newspaper articles linking a positive relationship between the two.

However, the few articles that do exist contain information worth mentioning and certainly provide a foundation on which to build.

Immergluck and Smith (2006) offer one of the more important recent scholarly articles on the subject, in which they analyze foreclosures and crime in Chicago neighborhoods in 2000 and 2001. They conclude that higher foreclosure levels contribute to increased rates of violent crime in Chicago, but that no significant correlation existed between foreclosures and property crime. This, they postulated, may be due to underreporting of crime in lower income areas. The authors also write that increased foreclosure rates in certain neighborhoods do not immediately lead to a rise in crime rates. Rather, a predictable chain of events transpires over what could be a considerable length of time. Areas with high rates of foreclosures could easily degrade as vacant properties increase. If unoccupied homes remain vacant or unsold for extended periods, their neighborhoods may become blighted and crime rates would increase. This is especially true in lower-income areas where "various forms of economic duress" exist as serious obstacles to community improvement. In middle- and upper-income neighborhoods, where property tends to sell quicker, this phenomenon is not as prevalent.

Michael Bess (2008) provides a similar community-level study for Charlotte-Mecklenburg, North Carolina, and presents similar results. A positive correlation exists between violent crime and foreclosures, but not between property crime and foreclosures. Analysis of 5 years of data between 2003 and 2007 further suggests that higher foreclosure rates correspond to older neighborhoods, and that newer subdivisions "might simply be at an early stage of the foreclosure process and may not yet have experienced the subsequent impact on crime and disorder" (p. 4).

Goodstein and Lee (2010) use a national county-level dataset of foreclosures between 2002 and 2007 and conclude that a positive correlation exists between foreclosures and property crime, and particularly burglary. This result, they write, is primarily because of the loss of homeowners who typically provide informal policing in their respective neighborhoods. With their removal, property crime eventually increases. "A one percentage point increase in foreclosure rates is estimated to increase burglary rates by 10.1 percent" (p. 1), with accrued costs of burglary between $4.6 and $17.4 billion.

Scholars do generally agree that the dramatic increase in foreclosure rates, especially in concentrated areas within communities such as the Cleveland metropolitan area, if left unchecked will only increase the odds of those neighborhoods slipping into blight (Baxter & Laurie, 2000; Schuetz, Been & Ellen, 2008; Immergluck & Smith, 2006; Li & Morrow-Jones, 2010; Harding, Rosenblatt, & Yao, 2009). If this is allowed to happen, property crime rates are sure to increase. This phenomenon, some scholars (Tuthill, 2008) note, is consistent with the "broken windows" theory developed by Wilson and Kelling (1982) that essentially states that physical and social signs of disorder increase the amount of apathy and fear in neighborhood residents, which in turn decreases the willingness of residents to participate in community improvement programs.

While the broken windows theory and other similar processes are important to understand because they address the various factors that feed into neighborhood deterioration and blight, it should be mentioned that certain criminal activity does capitalize on recent increases in foreclosures. In Cleveland (Mentel, 2008), for example, organized crime groups have capitalized on readily available public foreclosure information from the Cuyahoga sheriff's office and also from HUD. After obtaining these lists, these groups quickly identified and entered recently foreclosed and vacated properties from which they snatched copper pipes, wires, and other items that they sold at scrap yards.

GARFIELD HEIGHTS OVERVIEW

In terms of size, Garfield Heights is approximately 3–5 miles wide and encompasses about 7.3 square miles (Figure 8-2). Interstate 480 and two state routes go through the municipality. Most sections of Cleveland, including its airport, are approximately 15 minutes away from Garfield Heights. Businesses and industrial complexes line the Cuyahoga River near the western portion of the community, and parks and cemeteries occupy much of the northern sections. The Garfield Heights police department has a force of about 90 patrol and auxiliary officers (Garfield Heights Chamber of Commerce). Marymount Hospital serves as the city's largest employer, providing some 1,200 jobs, followed by a district office of Ohio Department of Transportation (~500 jobs), the City of Garfield Heights (~370 jobs), and the Garfield Heights City Schools (~350 jobs). The community's chamber of commerce has over 250 member businesses. CNN/Money referenced Garfield Heights in 2007 and its neighbor Maple Heights as two of the nation's affordable communities (CNN/Money). The Chamber of Commerce website touts that "the city is currently experiencing a construction boom as CityView Center; a $80,000,000 shopping complex at the Transportation Boulevard exit comes to completion," and construction of another shopping complex is in the planning stage (Garfield Heights Chamber of Commerce).

Table 8-1 provides demographic information from the U.S. Census in 2000 pertaining to Garfield Heights, Cleveland, and Cuyahoga County. Garfield Heights had just over 30,000 persons. The proportion of the community's white population exceeds that of Cleveland and the county while the percentages of African Americans and other minorities are lower. Some four of five persons are high school graduates, and 12% have bachelor's degrees from college. Garfield Heights had nearly 13,000 housing units in 2000, and the homeownership rate was just under 80%, far above that for Cleveland and Cuyahoga County. The median value of owner-occupied houses

TABLE 8-1 Garfield Heights Descriptive Data, Census 2000			
	Cleveland	**Garfield Heights**	**Cuyahoga County**
Population	478,403	**30,734**	1,393,978
White persons, percent	41.50%	**80.70%**	68.70%
Black persons, percent	51.00%	**16.80%**	28.20%
Persons reporting two or more races	2.20%	**1.00%**	1.50%
High school graduates, persons age 25+	69.00%	**80.20%**	81.60%
Bachelor's degree or higher, persons age 25+	11.40%	**12.00%**	25.10%
Housing units	215,856	**12,998**	616,903
Homeownership rate	48.50%	**79.90%**	63.20%
Median value owner-occupied houses	$72,100	**$87,900**	$113,800
Median household income	$25,928	**$39,278**	$39,168
Persons below poverty, percent	26.30%	**8.50%**	10.30%

was $87,900. Median income for the community mirrored that of the county at just over $39,000, and the poverty rate of 8.5% was lower than both that of Cleveland and the county.

Despite its small size, the community does exhibit socioeconomic differences among neighborhoods. Most of the neighborhoods south of Interstate 480 are composed predominantly of white homeowners with the highest incomes and land values. Residents in this quarter are predominantly married, older than age 50, and live without children. Other areas are ethnically more diverse, have more rental properties, more vacant households, and have lower incomes and land values.

MATERIALS AND METHODS

The materials and data used in this study were procured from a variety of sources and pertain to crime, foreclosures, and demographics. Garfield Heights (Ohio) Police Department (GHPD) provided the property crime data through dispatch reports and property logs dating between May 2004 and April 2009. The crime information includes burglary, breaking and entering, criminal damaging, criminal trespass, alarm drop, premise violations, robbery, suspicious activity, and theft. The dispatch reports contain information recorded in the initial calls for service, taken before official police investigations began. The information provided to dispatch from these initial reports is the basis for categorizing the offenses. The dispatch report contains the date, time, and location of the reported offense, the report number assigned by the GHPD, the call type (offense originally attributed to the report), and a narrative section for additional information.

The property log corresponds with the dispatch report and lists categorical descriptions of all property reported stolen, received, and seized by the GHPD. The property log also includes the date of the offense, an offense code, and other identifying information about the property stolen. GHPD used the same report numbers from both the dispatch report and the property log.

Spatial analysis in GIS required the street addresses of each property crime. A specific, valid address was provided in nearly all reports (1,314 of 1,340 cases). Reports without identifying information, such as a valid address, were removed. To facilitate spatial analysis, crime data was address-matched within GIS. This process resulted in a dot or point displayed on the map of Garfield Heights for each crime event. For example, an address of 25 S. Main St. would result in a point being placed one quarter along the line representing the one hundred block of South Main Street. Address matching of places points generally close to where they should be, but seldom in their exact and real-world locations. To account for this level of error, points were then individually moved to their correct locations using parcel data from the Cuyahoga County Auditor and Recorder as a reference.

The Cuyahoga County Auditor and Recorder provided the residential foreclosure data for Garfield Heights. The Northeast Ohio Community and Neighborhood Data for Organizing (NEO CANDO) system, a multiagency organization operated and maintained by Case Western Reserve University, facilitated data querying, gathering, and downloading. The foreclosure data were current as of April 2009 and amounted to 1,328 foreclosures in Garfield Heights. Foreclosures were address-matched in GIS and manually adjusted in the same manner described previously for crime data.

The demographic data utilized in the analysis originated from the 2000 decennial census from the U.S. Census Bureau. The specific census level of analysis utilized in this study was the census block group. The Census Bureau also provided the block group boundaries as a GIS feature class used in this study.

After address matching and manually adjusting individual addresses for property crimes and residential foreclosures, density maps were developed to indicate the location of hotspots of these events. For analyzing and comparing property crime, maps were created pertaining to each of the 5 years between May 2004 and April 2009, and also one map for the entire period. Only one map shows foreclosures, for April 2009.

While the authors recognize the conventionality of creating maps revealing the locations of individual crime and foreclosure events, we consider this type of illustration bordering on unethical as these types of maps could be used to facilitate criminal activity (Curtis, Mills & Leitner, 2006). We suggest that density or hotspot maps offer a compromise for scholars and analysts who may be concerned with this issue.

The socioeconomic variables chosen for analysis are among those commonly used in similar studies (Kurbin & Squires, 2004; Morenoff et al., 2001). Fourteen were chosen as potentially being related to property crime and foreclosures. These included percent white population, percent black population, percent multiple races, percent households with one male, percent households with one female, percent married head of household with children, percent married head of household with no children, percent male head of household with children, percent female head of household with children, percent vacant housing units, percent owner-occupied housing units, percent renter-occupied housing units, median family income, and median land values. The values were determined for each of the 33 census block groups in Garfield Heights.

Two statistical methods proved useful in analyzing the correlations among these variables at the community level and within block groups. Calculating the Pearson correlation revealed the strength of correlation for each variable for the entire community. Factor analysis identified certain groups of highly correlated variables within sections of Garfield Heights and, when mapped, showed their spatial orientation within the community. Factor analysis is especially useful when attempting to determine which variables are more important than others in terms of their explanatory power for the entire population. For this research, factor analysis isolated four groups or components within the block groups in Garfield Heights. Each component has certain highly correlated variables, and each is unique with respect to its variable strengths and spatial orientation. Factor analysis utilized Varimax rotation and Principal Components extraction with Eigenvalues over one.

RESULTS

Table 8-2 provides an overview of property crime in Garfield Heights during the 5-year period between May 2004 and April 2009. There were 1,314 crimes, most of which were burglaries (638, 48.6%), breaking and entering (480, 36.5%), or theft (117, 8.9%). Lower numbers of other property crimes (79, 6.0%) were recorded and consisted primarily of premise violations and alarm drops.

Only 337 of the 1,314 dispatch reports mentioned items stolen, primarily associated with crimes classified as theft (75%). Far fewer burglaries and breaking-and-entering incidents mentioned what was taken. Most of the items reported stolen were related to construction activities (103, 30.6%) and included copper plumbing and wiring, tools, building materials, and equipment. Lower numbers of electronics, personal items, home items, bicycles, vehicle parts, firearms, and other items were reported taken.

Figure 8-3 shows the location of property crime hotspots throughout Garfield Heights for the 5-year period. It illustrates that despite some fluctuation, every residential section of town was

TABLE 8-2 Property Crime in Garfield Heights

Crime	#	%	Items stolen	%
Burglary	638	48.6%	122	36.2%
B&E	480	36.5%	127	37.7%
Theft	117	8.9%	88	26.1%
Other	79	6.0%		
Total	1,314		337	

affected by property crime. The northeast corner experienced the highest overall rates. Increases in property crimes also occurred in the western portion of the city, especially in the final year of study.

As of April 2009 Garfield Heights had 1,328 foreclosed residential properties. Of these, most properties were owned for a very brief time, typically less than 5 years (see **Figure 8-4**). That is, properties purchased in the last 5 years had a much greater chance of being in foreclosure status. Of the 390 properties purchased between January and April 2009, 205 (52.6%) were already fore-closed. Of the 1,009 properties purchased in 2007, 339 (33.6%) were in foreclosure.

Figure 8-5 provides the location of hotspots of foreclosed residential properties in Garfield Heights as of April 2009. At first glance the dispersion of foreclosures emphasizes the severity of

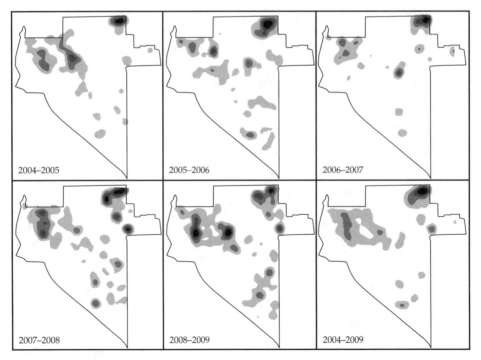

FIGURE 8-3.   Property crime hotspots. (From: Garfield Heights Police Department.)

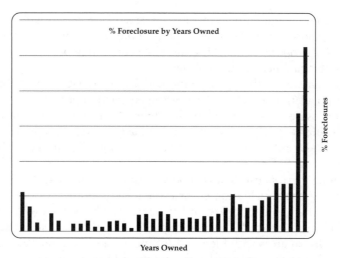

FIGURE 8-4. Foreclosures in Garfield Heights as of April 2009 and years owned. (From: Cuyahoga County, Cuyahoga County Auditor and Recorder)

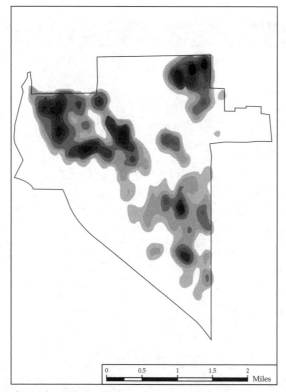

FIGURE 8-5. Foreclosed residential properties. (From: Cuyahoga County, Cuyahoga County Auditor and Recorder.)

this problem to the entire community in that every residential section is affected. Higher concentrations do exist in the northeast and northwest parts of the city in the same areas that were experiencing elevated rates of property crime. This suggests a correlation between the two but cannot be confirmed based on this rudimentary level of analysis.

Pearson correlation affords the opportunity to test the strength of the relationship between variables in a given population. In this study, Pearson correlation provides the correlations among property crime, foreclosure rates, and each of the other 12 census variables for all block groups in Garfield Heights (**Table 8-3**). The values closest to 1 have the strongest positive correlation while the values closest to –1 have the strongest negative correlation. Significant levels are shown at the 0.05 and 0.01 levels.

When interpreting these statistics, it is important to remember that they indicate correlations and not the extent that one variable causes, or even affects, another. In other words, we cannot assume that, given the high value for percent female head of household with children and crime, the first causes or affects the other. We can say, however, that there is a strong positive correlation between the two so that in areas with high rates of the former there tend to be high rates of the latter. That being said, we can infer correlation with regard to certain areas within the community where these variables are higher (or lower).

TABLE 8-3 Pearson Correlations

	Percent property crime	Percent residential foreclosures
Percent white	−0.74**	−0.62**
Percent black	0.73**	0.63**
Percent multiple races	0.64**	0.09
Percent households with 1 male	0.13	−0.36*
Percent households with 1 female	−0.48**	−0.69**
Percent married head of household with children	−0.43**	−0.04
Percent married head of household with no children	−0.52**	−0.09
Percent male head of household with children	0.22	0.3
Percent female head of household with children	0.85**	0.44*
Percent vacant housing units	0.53**	0.07
Percent owner-occupied housing units	−0.44*	0.11
Percent renter-occupied housing units	0.44*	−0.11
Median family income	−0.67**	−0.22
Median land values	−0.62**	−0.63**
Percent Crime	1	0.62**
Percent foreclosures	0.62**	1

** Correlation significant at the 0.01 level.
* Correlation significant at the 0.05 level.

Property crime in Garfield Heights is correlated with nearly every variable, and most with significant levels at the 0.01 level. In fact, only households with one male and male head of household with children are not correlated with property crime. Areas with high property crime rates are most associated with, in ascending order, female head of household with children, blacks, multiple races, foreclosures, vacant housing units, and renters. Areas with low property crime rates are correlated with low percentages of whites, median family income, median land values, married head of household with and without children, household with one female, and owner-occupied households. The differences between these two groups should be obvious, and strongly suggests that Garfield Heights is stratified spatially along socioeconomic lines and that property crime rates are very different in these areas.

Unlike property crime, residential foreclosures are not significantly correlated with as many of these variables. Areas with more foreclosures have higher rates of blacks in their populations, property crime, and female head of household with children. Conversely, areas with lower rates of households with one person (male or female) and lower median land values have significantly fewer residential foreclosures, as do the areas with more whites.

It should also be apparent that there are areas where both property crime and residential foreclosures are a serious problem, given their strong correlation value. However, for these areas, it is impossible to see their relationship with other variables when utilizing Pearson correlation.

Factor analysis provides a more detailed look at the correlation existing among the selected variables for each block group in Garfield Heights, and allows us to identify groups (or components) of highly correlated variables. These can be mapped to reveal spatial trends associated with any significant correlations.

Analysis reveals that four factors are necessary to adequately describe the data population. **Table 8-4** provides the total variance explained of the first five components and shows that the four with the highest Eigenvalues account for just under 84% of all components. The fifth component has an Eigenvalue of 0.715, far enough below the threshold of one to be included as an individual component.

The rotated component matrix is provided in **Table 8-5** and reveals the correlations among the variables in this study. The positive or negative values closest to 1 indicate the strongest relationship with each component. For example, the first component (explaining about 47% of all components) has the strongest correlation with, in ascending order, percent blacks, residential foreclosures, property crime, and female head of household with children. This can be translated as meaning that areas with high rates of one of these variables should have high rates of the others. Also, areas associated with the first component have strong negative correlations with median land values and percent whites, meaning these areas have lower values for these variables. The second component (explaining about 21%) is strongly related to households with one male, renter occupancy, and also have far fewer owner-occupants and married head of household with no children. Areas associated with component three (explaining about 10%) have higher rates of multiple races, vacant housing units, female head of household with children, and to a lesser degree property crime. The fourth component (explaining about 6%) is strongly correlated with male and married head of household with children.

The first component contains the strongest relationship between property crime and foreclosures. This confirms the analysis of the Pearson correlations and also reveals the strength of relationship between these two variables and others. The fact that the explanation value is high (about 47%) indicates not only the importance of this component across Garfield Heights, but also the

TABLE 8-4 Total Variance Explained for Components

Component	Initial Eigenvalues			Extraction sums of squared loadings			Rotation sums of squared loadings		
	Total	% of variance	Cumulative %	Total	% of variance	Cumulative %	Total	% of variance	Cumulative %
1	7.476	46.723	46.723	7.476	46.723	46.723	4.350	27.186	27.186
2	3.412	21.324	68.046	3.412	21.324	68.046	4.038	25.236	52.423
3	1.533	9.584	77.631	1.533	9.584	77.631	3.508	21.926	74.348
4	1.006	6.284	83.915	1.006	6.284	83.915	1.531	9.567	83.915
5	.715	4.470	88.385						

TABLE 8-5 Rotated Component Matrix for Variables

	Component			
	1	2	3	4
Percent white	−.842	−.059	−.373	.303
Percent black	.855	.052	.346	−.303
Percent multiple races	.119	.334	.810	.024
Percent households with 1 male	−.100	.904	.113	−.031
Percent households with 1 female	−.444	.549	−.514	−.191
Percent married head of household with children	−.400	−.404	−.322	.666
Percent married head of household with no children	−.272	−.791	−.281	−.335
Percent male head of household with children	.143	.199	.209	.757
Percent female head of household with children	.605	.298	.691	−.053
Percent vacant housing units	.095	.475	.711	.118
Percent owner-occupied housing units	−.134	−.843	−.446	.034
Percent renter-occupied housing units	.134	.843	.446	−.034
Median family income	−.388	−.199	−.587	.002
Median land values	−.851	−.257	.039	−.234
Percent crime	.684	.137	.591	.080
Percent foreclosures	.825	−.335	.115	.318

relevance of the correlation between its strongest variables, including residential foreclosures and property crime. The other three components combined can only explain about 37% of the entire community.

Mapping the factor scores provides an effective method for visualizing the spatial impact of each component from factor analysis. When brought into a GIS environment and symbolized according to factor scores (**Figure 8-6**), the spatial orientation of the first component is revealed as existing primarily in nine block groups in the northern section of Garfield Heights. Seven of these are near the intersection of Interstate Highway 480 and State Route 14, while three are just west of Turney Avenue. These are areas with higher rates of residential foreclosures, property crime, blacks, and female head of household with children.

The map also shows that two block groups have negative values for component 1, symbolized with hatching, as existing in the southwest part of the city in areas with higher rates of owner-occupants, ages 50 and older, who are married and are not living with children. The rates of property crime and residential foreclosures are lower in these areas than in any other part of Garfield Heights.

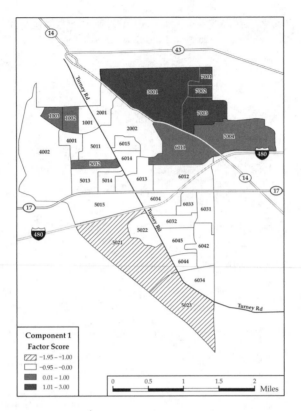

FIGURE 8-6. Component 1 mapped.

CONCLUSIONS

This study demonstrates the worth of analyzing social problems while utilizing a variety of different methods and incorporating readily available data. The results provide a more comprehensive perspective of the issues involved and, when integrated into a GIS, afford the opportunity to observe patterns over a given landscape. In this manner a more objective and factual analysis is developed, and if warranted a more detailed analysis can be conducted.

Within Garfield Heights, a relatively small municipal suburb of Cleveland, Ohio, analysis reveals the areas most affected by the recent foreclosure crisis. Mapping the occurrences of crimes and foreclosures reveals hotspots in specific areas in Garfield Heights and suggests a strong relationship between the two. Pearson correlation confirms this, indicates a significant positive correlation between property crime and foreclosures, and hints at strong relationships between these two and other socioeconomic variables associated with lower-income neighborhoods. Factor analysis identifies the strength of the correlations between these variables and shows that the highest rates of property crimes and foreclosures exist in areas where the rates of black population and female head of household with children are higher, and where those of land values and white population are lower. Mapping the factor scores reveals the spatial orientation of these areas within Garfield Heights as being in the northern sections of the community.

The authors stress again that the current methods do not attempt to isolate the causes of these problems, or the specific effect of these on neighborhoods or their residents. Other methods are better suited to address these issues, such as those that incorporate qualitative data or others that observe these phenomena over time. The worth of this type of analysis resides in its ability to easily identify areas that are most affected by property crime and residential foreclosures, and to efficiently interpret socioeconomic factors in these areas. Programs designed to help mitigate the adverse effects of these issues can then be more efficiently implemented in these neighborhoods.

Increasing numbers of law enforcement agencies are using geographic information systems to help them do their jobs. Utilizing GIS to analyze spatial patterns, whether related to criminal activity, demographics, or economic trends, is becoming more common as agencies realize the benefits of investing in GIS. Tracking and analyzing crime has never been easier and is leading to a more comprehensive understanding of the relationship among illegal activities, neighborhoods, and communities. Further, we can more easily examine how economic factors such as foreclosure rates are related to certain criminal activities.

The ultimate benefit of a more comprehensive spatial analysis is that it improves our ability to prevent crime. Understanding, for example, that increased residential foreclosure rates will eventually lead to neighborhood blight and increased crime allows us to look for areas where foreclosures are common and target those areas for revitalization. Further, as our understanding increases regarding the factors leading to foreclosure, we are increasingly able to identify those neighborhoods where foreclosures are not yet problematic, but may be if preventative measures are not taken. The rewards, it would seem, extend beyond just the neighborhoods where crime and foreclosure rates are currently greatest. Entire communities stand to benefit from these types of comprehensive spatial analyses.

ACKNOWLEDGMENTS

The authors are grateful to the Garfield Heights Police Department for their patience and courtesy, and for providing us with 5 years of dispatch reports and property logs. We also thank the Cuyahoga County Cuyahoga County Auditor and Recorder and the Northeast Ohio Community and Neighborhood Data for Organizing (NEO CANDO) system administered through Case Western Reserve University for residential foreclosure data and parcel information.

REFERENCES

Baxter, V., & Laurie, M. (2000). Residential mortgage foreclosure and neighborhood change. *Housing and Policy Debate 11*(3), 675–699.

Bess, M. (2008). Assessing the impact of home foreclosures in Charlotte neighborhoods. *Geography and Public Safety 1*(3), 2–5.

CNN/Money. (2007). Best places to live: Where homes are affordable. Retrieved from http://money.cnn.com/galleries/2007/moneymag/0707/gallery.BPTL_most_affordable.moneymag/23.html.

Curtis, A. J., Mills, J. W., & Leitner, M. (2006). Spatial confidentiality and GIS: Re-engineering mortality locations from published maps about Hurricane Katrina. *International Journal of Health Geographics 5*(44) 4–12.

Finklea, K. M. (2009). Economic downturns and crime. *Congressional Research Service Report for Congress.* Washington, DC: Prepared for members and committees of Congress.

Garfield Heights Chamber of Commerce. (2011). Retrieved from http://www.garfieldchamber.com/.

Goodstein, R. M., & Lee, Y. Y. (2010, May). Do foreclosures increase crime? *Federal Deposit Insurance Corporation Center for Financial Research Working Paper*.

Harding, J. P., Rosenblatt, E., & Yao, V. W. (2009). The contagion effect of foreclosed properties. *Journal of Urban Economics 66*, 164–178.

Immergluck, D., & Smith, G. (2006). The impact of single family mortgage foreclosures on neighborhood crime. *Housing Studies 21*(6), 851–866.

Kurbin, C., & Squires, G. (2004, April). The impact of capital on crime: Does access to home mortgage money reduce crime rates? Paper presented at the Annual Meeting of the Urban Affairs Association, Washington DC.

Li, Y., & Morrow-Jones, H. A. (2010). The impact of residential foreclosure on neighborhood change and succession. *Journal of Planning Education and Research 30*, 22–39.

Mentel, Z. (2008). Mortgage crisis is affecting local property crime. *Community Policing Dispatch 1*(9). Retrieved from http://www.cops.usdoj.gov/html/dispatch/index.asp.

Morenoff, J. D., Sampson, R. J., & Raudenbush, S. W. (2001). Neighboring inequality, collective efficacy, and the spatial dynamics of urban violence. *Criminology 39*, 517–559.

Schuetz, J., Been, V., & Ellen, I. G. (2008). Neighboring effect of concentrated foreclosures. *Journal of Housing Economics 17*(4), 306–319.

Tuthill, L. (2008). Breaking new windows—examining the subprime mortgage crisis using the broken windows theory. *Geography and Public Safety 1*(3), 9–10.

Wilson, J. Q., & Kelling, G. (1982, March). Broken windows: The police and neighborhood safety. *The Atlantic*, 29–38.

CHAPTER 9

Employing Surveillance in Situational Crime Prevention

David A. Mackey
Plymouth State University

INTRODUCTION

It is quite easy to say that technology has affected every facet of social life. The impact of technology on both crime prevention and law enforcement's ability to apprehend those who violate the law has also been profound, as numerous examples attest. Technology and gadgets that made their public debut in movies, such as the scanning devices in the Arnold Schwarzenegger films *Total Recall* (1990) and *True Lies* (1994), have been installed in numerous airports and other sensitive locations in the United States, including federal buildings (Mackey, 2007). Applications such as Google Earth® have been used by municipal officials to identify backyard swimming pools installed without the proper permits or required fees ("Google Earth Used," 2010). Global positioning satellite (GPS) tracking, employed in popular services that provide turn-by-turn driving directions and timely dispatch of assistance in the event of emergencies, now comes standard in some new vehicle models; it can also be used to monitor the locations of individuals under supervision by the criminal justice system, of a company's fleet vehicles, and even of one's children or spouse (Guardian Angel Technology, 2008; Marx & Steeves, 2011).

This chapter examines the nature and extent of contemporary surveillance strategies and their application to crime prevention. These strategies often have the stated purpose of safeguarding individuals from harm, but the use of such strategies may also seek to verify an individual's identity and categorize individuals, thus allowing any number of social control agents to supervise or surveil their actions. Surveillance strategies and techniques vary in the degree to which members of the public consent to their use. In some cases, individuals consent to participate in the strategy in order to gain a particular benefit, such as a discount on a product or service (Marx & Steeves, 2011). For example, a customer can obtain a vehicle insurance discount by permitting the installation of a GPS tracking device that would assist police in locating the vehicle if it is stolen. Some products and applications also record driving patterns and seat-belt usage, with the resulting data being used to determine insurance rates and damage awards. Some strategies may be a condition of employment, such as drug testing or Web monitoring, while others may be place-specific, such as the use of closed-circuit television (CCTV) in a business or public area. There are also surveillance techniques, in both proactive and reactive applications, that provide data mining opportunities for homeland security and general crime prevention by creating a searchable database of information.

Such data can be used to proactively identify individuals of interest or to aid in after-the-fact investigations (described more fully in subsequent sections of this chapter). In addition, surveillance products have been marketed to businesses as a means of limiting liability exposure specifically in relationship to crimes committed against their employees and customers and even to parents hoping to protect children from external threats and the consequences of the youth's own decision making (Marx & Steeves, 2011). With the widespread use of technology to monitor people, members of society may see a diminishment in their expectation of privacy and autonomy, benefits they may have assumed and recognized as reasonable. Surveillance through technology, once thought of as solely a governmental action, has penetrated the workplace and even the home. It is thus important to examine the balance between maximizing the common good of preventing crime versus maintaining personal autonomy given the increasing use of surveillance strategies.

Scholarship on evidence-based evaluation of various crime prevention proposals has appeared regularly and is a primary focus in this book. In contrast, however, there is a relative scarcity of high-quality evaluation research (such as true experimental designs) in many areas of surveillance, and evidence-based policy and evaluation depend upon such research. Much that has been written in the area of contemporary surveillance, with some exceptions, is more anecdotal in nature, focusing on the social, ethical, and legal implications of specific surveillance policies and techniques. Contemporary surveillance strategies utilize tenets of rational choice theory and situational crime prevention. Contemporary surveillance is designed to increase the probability of detecting criminal events as well as criminal perpetrators.

CRIME PREVENTION THEORIES AND SURVEILLANCE

The primary stated purpose for surveillance efforts typically centers on their crime prevention functions. From a crime prevention standpoint, surveillance efforts can be employed in both proactive and reactive applications. Proactive efforts seek to prevent a criminal act from occurring or to reduce the harm that may occur as a result of the act. Proactive surveillance strategies can take many different forms. Data mining is a common surveillance strategy in which databases are searched, most easily by computer, to identify patterns that depart from the norm. On several occasions drug dealers have been identified by abnormalities in their electric bills. For example, indoor marijuana cultivation requires substantially more electricity than the average household would consume. In reactive surveillance efforts, officials attempt to identify perpetrators and prepare a criminal case for adjudication. Reactive types of investigation may involve reviewing CCTV video and conducting forensic examinations of a suspect's financial records, telecommunications records, or travel history in an effort to build the prosecution's case against the individual. In an example of a proactive surveillance strategy, the Transportation Security Administration (TSA) uses its Secure Flight Program to screen air travelers for individuals on its "no-fly" list. Secure Flight requires passengers to provide their full name, date of birth, gender, and redress number, if applicable (TSA, 2008), at the time of booking. The redress number is a mechanism that allows officials to track complaints filed with the Department of Homeland Security's Traveler Redress Inquiry Program (DHS TRIP).

The manifest functions of surveillance technology are fairly straightforward. Surveillance strategies seek to increase physical safety by deterring antisocial behavior. Some types of technology seek to verify the trustworthiness of individuals in terms of their actual identity as well as their background and threat potential. Data collection and analysis procedures also seek to increase the efficiency of business transactions and services provided to customers. Data surveillance and tracking efforts may be seen as less physically intrusive than various alternatives. According to some authors (Staples, 2000; Torpey, 2007), these more technical efforts are essentially a more egalitarian approach to surveillance and entail a greater level of objectivity in surveillance. This seeming neutrality arises from the idea that all individuals receive equal treatment—as potential suspects.

The manifest dysfunctions of surveillance and data collection strategies include diminished expectations for privacy, the possibility of restrictions on employment for those individuals whose data profile might raise concerns, and security breaches of databases, which often result in significant financial ramifications as well as the possible erosion of confidence in the sponsoring organization. Individuals also face possible restrictions in movement and travel, negative impacts on life course trajectory, digital segregation, a false sense of physical security because of the reliance on technology, an ongoing quest for more data, and a decline in personal trust (Marx & Muschert, 2007). According to Marx and Muschert, "We seek privacy and anonymity, but we also know that secrecy can hide dastardly deeds and that visibility can bring accountability. But too much visibility may inhibit experimentation, creativity, and risk taking. And although we value disclosure, we also believe in redemption and new beginnings after individuals have been sanctioned for misdeeds or overcome limitations" (Marx & Muschert, 2007, p. 385).

Surveillance efforts draw from the principles of situational crime prevention, which often relies on a rational choice approach to deterring offenders. Clark (1992) declares that situational crime prevention seeks to reduce the opportunity for criminal behavior and to increase the chances of detecting the offense through systematic changes in the environment. Surveillance strategies draw upon many of the 12 techniques of situational crime prevention (Clark, 1992, p. 13), which include, among others, surveillance by employees, formal surveillance, reducing inducements, rule setting, and deflecting offenders.

AUTONOMY AND SURVEILLANCE

One of the unintended consequences of crime prevention efforts is the threat to individual privacy and autonomy presented by the normalization of everyday surveillance. A free society always faces a dilemma regarding the appropriate balance between the powers of the government to protect the public and the right of the individual to be free from government intrusion. Society must ask itself how individual rights can be maximized so that individuals may enjoy a private life while at the same time ensuring that other individuals enjoy similar freedom. In many ways, the discussion of individual rights versus the common good may be misleading if we simply characterize the tension between the two as a balancing act. For instance, Dinh states that "freedom does not refer simply to the absence of governmental restraint; it also refers, at a more fundamental level, to the absence of fear" (Dinh, 2004, p. 106). Dinh also contends that "security and freedom are not rivals in the universe of possible goods; rather, they are interrelated, mutually reinforcing goods. Security is the very precondition of freedom" (p. 106). Implied in this view is the idea that individuals are not completely unfettered in their pursuit of liberty but in fact have an obligation to society to help promote mutual security. In contemporary society, the security–privacy dilemma is also confounded by the involvement of nongovernmental entities, such as schools and businesses, in surveillance activities, and further complicating the situation is the recent introduction of private surveillance tools such as home drug test kits (TestMyTeen LLC, 2009).

Intrusions on individual autonomy, whether recognized in the objective sense as true intrusions or only perceived as such by an individual, may be rationalized for personal and community safety, validation of personal trustworthiness, and efficient business practices. The terrorist attacks on September 11, 2001, have accelerated a pattern for the use of technology-based surveillance. In many ways, this trajectory was already in motion prior to the 9/11 attacks due in part to the downsizing of the military–industrial complex and the growth of the safety and security complex (Staples, 2000). As the market for military hardware contracted, the business focus shifted to security-related research and products. The most striking area of surveillance business growth may arguably be products and services marketed to parents for the protection and monitoring of their children (Marx & Steeves, 2011) and their own aging parents. These products and services can include home drug test kits, remote monitoring of driving patterns, GPS tracking devices to monitor location, confidential home visits by a drug dog (Sniff Dogs, 2011), electronic cards to monitor children's lunch habits at school, as well as fall detection monitoring for elderly parents. Youths may not fully appreciate the nature of parental surveillance since they may also possess their own gadgets with surveillance capabilities, readily available online from retailers such as www.spygear.net.

The preponderance of both official and private surveillance constitutes postmodern social control, which has four salient features (Staples, 2000, pp. 4–6). First, surveillance tends to be systematic, methodical, and automatic, thus generating a permanent record of evidence. This feature is most evident in the compilation of databases that can be searched and that may provide fairly detailed insight into someone's life. The second feature is a shift to the body in an effort to influence behavior; Staples states "it is the individual's body that will 'tell us what we need to know'" (p. 5). For instance, the body can provide a record of drug use, alcohol use, and exposure to environmental toxins as well as clues to one's travel. The third feature is the shift in location of social control from formal institutional settings to more everyday settings. The fourth feature is a shift to a more democratic application of surveillance, one that affects a broader category of people rather than targeting persons based on suspicions about an individual or about a whole category of persons. In effect, various systems of surveillance, whether based in the home, the workplace, or the community, are designed to bring a broader range of individuals under surveillance and, to some degree, to presume guilt with respect to motives and behavior.

Building on these ideas, Torpey (2007) identifies two types of contemporary surveillance: thin and thick. Torpey notes that "thin surveillance monitors our movements, our business transactions, and our interactions with government, but generally without constraining our mobility per se. Thick surveillance, on the other hand, involves confinement to delineated and often fortified spaces, in which observation is enhanced by a limitation of the range of mobility of those observed" (2007, p. 116). Thin surveillance usually impacts people who are better off economically, while thick surveillance disproportionately impacts the poor, minorities, and individuals under supervision by the criminal justice system. Many of the practices that fall under the heading of thin surveillance are also based on the concept of benevolent intentions. Individuals experience benefits by participating in the surveillance system; they may receive financial discounts for products and services or at least avoid the awkwardness that might accompany attempting to opt out of surveillance monitoring (Marx, 2006). Persons attempting to opt out might raise suspicions and prompt a business or other entity to ask what such individuals may be trying to hide and why they would not want to participate in a process that can verify trustworthiness.

ILLUSTRATIVE HYPOTHESES FOR SURVEILLANCE

A number of illustrative hypotheses guide the following surveillance discussion. For example, Marx and Muschert (2007) contend that "the more generous a system of exchange (information in return for something the individual wants), the more likely it is to be tolerated" (p. 384). In addition, one may also state that the greater the psychological impact of an event, the more extensive will be the surveillance strategies consensually imposed in its wake. Some anecdotal support for the latter hypothesis is found with the reactions to the anthrax mailings in October 2001 and new airport rules following an attempt to blow up an airliner with a "shoe bomb," a report on the explosive capabilities of small quantities of liquids in carry-on luggage, and the deployment of hundreds of additional full body x-ray scanners in U.S. airports after a plot to bring down a commercial airliner with an "underwear bomb" (Resnick, 2010). For instance, as Rosen (2004, p. 217) notes,

> *Immediately after 9/11, more than six in ten Americans agreed that the average person would have to give up civil liberties to fight terrorism. By June 2002, however, the number had fallen to 46 percent. Along the same lines, recall the shift in public opinion about national identification cards. A poll conducted the week after the 9/11 attacks found that 70 percent of the respondents supported the idea of a national ID card that would have to be shown to officials on demand. Six months later, however, another poll found that only 26 percent of Americans backed the proposal, while 41 percent opposed it.*

In terms of prevention, widespread application of data surveillance strategies can both identify potential offenders during the planning stages of an incident as well as enhance the data collection potential of retroactive investigations in a postevent environment. Rosen (2004) identifies four models for protecting liberty and security in relation to surveillance strategies: the transparency model, the control-use model, the judicial-oversight model, and the political-oversight model (p. 194). Of particular significance is the control-use model, which would permit the executive branch to employ surveillance strategies very broadly but limit the use of any information so obtained when prosecuting lower level crimes. Such information could still be used when prosecuting more serious offenses, such as those involving homeland security. Rosen (2004) states that "mass dataveillance could be permitted as a tool of risk prediction, as opposed to criminal investigation, only when there are limitations imposed on how the government can use evidence of ordinary crimes unrelated to terrorism" (p. 202). In this view, the government would be able to collect and analyze information for the purpose of protecting national security but would be unable to use the data for traditional law enforcement purposes. This type of authorization creates an environment in which surveillance takes place but is not revealed to the public as a result of more typical criminal investigations.

Since 9/11, a number of incidents have highlighted threats to public safety in the United States. While airports, international borders, ports, mass transit, tourist destinations, and high profile installations, such as power generating stations, remain highly visible areas of concern for homeland security, softer targets with potential for mass casualties, dramatic economic impact, and psychological toll have relatively little security, and these locations are more easily accessible because of the nature of the U.S. social and economic system. For example, schools provide a high profile target with the potential for mass casualties and an extreme psychological impact on the American public. To illustrate, Giduck (2005) details the history of terrorist-related activities Chechens committed against Russia. Hospitals were targeted in terrorist attacks on June 14, 1995 and January 9, 1996. In another violent event, Chechen terrorists took about 800 hostages at a Nord-Ost theater production on October 23, 2002. In this incident, 129 hostages were killed, as were all 42 of the terrorists (Giduck, 2005, p. 83). The Russian military used gas to render the terrorists unconscious and then shot many of them in the head while retaking the theater. In one of the most horrific attacks, everyone in Beslan Middle School No. 1 was taken hostage in September 2004. In the aftermath of the three-day siege, 330 people were killed and 700 wounded; 172 children were among the dead.

Giduck (2005) recommended a number of measures that could be used to defend U.S. schools against a Beslan-style attack. Some of these measures are arming teachers, deploying three-person special operations teams in each school, and using counter-intelligence operations, such as identifying individuals who seek information about school architectural plans and building layouts. One may view the presence of three-member response teams in schools as extreme; such a measure may have the effect of making data surveillance and information gathering techniques seem like a much more reasonable alternative. Rosen's (2004) control-use model of data surveillance would authorize fairly widespread data collection efforts emphasizing the protection of youths from large-scale threats to public safety.

TECHNOLOGY AND SURVEILLANCE APPLICATIONS IN CRIME PREVENTION

Stanley and Steinhardt (2003) contend that three interconnected issues have accelerated the use of video surveillance for crime prevention efforts. These issues are (1) improved digital technology, (2) capability for centralized surveillance, and (3) unquestioned assumptions that video surveillance provides security (2003, pp. 2–3).

Closed-Circuit Television (CCTV)

Changes in CCTV technology have increased surveillance capability, while the cost of such technology has decreased, making it more accessible for a wider range of potential clients.

While London has traditionally been seen as the surveillance capital of the Western world, the technology has spread both in terms of its use and its acceptance. Welsh and Farrington (2009) note that the United Kingdom has spent the equivalent of 375 million dollars for CCTV over a 10-year period. Welsh and Farrington have conducted the most extensive review of the effectiveness of CCTV studies to date, and research findings on the effectiveness of CCTV in preventing crime have shown mixed results. CCTV technology is also far from uniform in both quality and application. There is much variation in the technical capabilities of the cameras (e.g., movement, zoom, quality of image, interactivity, sound) and the percentage of the targeted area. There are also monitoring issues (i.e, whether surveillance is by police or private security or is simply recorded for later examination) as well as measurement issues, such as the time period under study, quality of the control group, measures of displacement, and maintenance of CCTV equipment. Multiple treatment effects (see Chapter 1) can also be a major issue when CCTV is combined with other security measures such as improved lighting, a strengthening of the role of place managers, and implementation of "hotspot" policing tactics. It becomes difficult to sort out the effects of CCTV alone when it is being used in combination with other surveillance tactics.

In a meta-analysis of 41 high-quality studies on the effectiveness of CCTV, Welsh and Farrington (2009) reported that CCTV had a statistically significant impact on crime, but more than half of the studies (23 of 41) in the meta-analysis did not report a statistically significant change in the amount of crime during the study period, and few of the studies considered the economic benefits of implementing CCTV by comparing the costs of the program to actual savings. From their discussion of the evaluation literature on CCTV use, numerous points emerge. First, many of the quality studies on the effectiveness of CCTV to date used data obtained in the United Kingdom, and these studies were more likely to indicate positive results than were studies conducted in U.S. settings. Second, based on the studies in Welsh and Farrington's meta-analysis, effective CCTV programs are more likely to be associated with parking facilities in the United Kingdom. Their findings indicated that CCTV programs in city centers or public transportation settings tended not to produce statistically significant reductions in crime. They note that 10 of the 22 CCTV studies targeting city centers were associated with a statistically significant drop in crime during the study period in contrast to 5 studies that showed an increase in crime because more crimes were made known to the police by either citizen reports or police observations, with the remainder showing no difference (2009, p. 65). They note on average a 7% reduction in crime with the presence of CCTV in city centers, a figure that did not reach statistical significance. Welsh and Farrington also examined four studies measuring the effectiveness of CCTV in addressing crime reduction in public transportation. Three of the studies targeted the underground rail system in London and one targeted the underground rail system in Montreal. Two studies showed a decrease in crime (one noting a 61% decrease), one showed an increase in crime, and one showed no effect (p. 70). Regarding six studies of CCTV-equipped parking garages in the United Kingdom, Welsh and Farrington note that crime in parking garages covered by CCTV showed a 50% decrease compared to control groups.

According to Saville (2004), there are social impacts associated with improved lighting and CCTV in center city areas and that these impacts may be associated with other factors related to crime. Saville notes that the heavier pedestrian traffic in parks and city centers provides greater natural capabilities for surveillance, a positive condition in both Crime Prevention Through Environmental Design and routine activity theory. Likewise, Burns-Howell and Pascoe (2004) note that the use of CCTV in the United Kingdom accelerated not so much as a result of positive evaluation results but mainly because the national government provided funds for the purchase of CCTV systems.

Total Information Awareness (TIA) and Its Legacy

Much of what the average person does each day leaves some sort of electronic trail. These electronic trails may include credit card purchases, grocery purchases tracked with the store's preferred customer card, and electronic communications. A person's electronic trail can provide interested parties with yet another useful source of data that does not require a camera to capture. Total Information Awareness (TIA) was a program developed by the Defense Advanced Research Projects Agency (DARPA), and it was designed to provide interconnectedness across several large databases . Commenting on the TIA program, Parenti (2004) notes that, "from the digital trails of credit cards, electronic tolls, banking transactions, health records, and library use it sought to create one 'virtual, grand database' that could be data-mined for interesting and incriminating patterns" (p. 119). Stanley and Steinhardt (2003) note that one motivation driving the growth in data surveillance is the commodification of information; information about consumers and potential customers has tremendous value to companies that seek to market products more efficiently to their target audience. Marketing is only one of the reasons that the collection of information is widespread; the government also has an interest in collecting and analyzing information. Some theorists consider TIA to be a modern analogue or electronic version of the Panopticon. Students who have taken a corrections course may recognize the Panopticon as Jeremy Bentham's circular prison design that permitted the continuous monitoring of prisoners (see Foucault, 1977). Rather than arranging the inmate cells in a line, which would limit direct observation into each cell, the Panopticon design placed cells on the outer circumference of a circle that had a guard tower in the center. Bentham's design also utilized a system of shades and lighting that would give guards a full view into each cell but not the other way around. The presumption behind the Panopticon design was that individuals would alter their behavior (Strub, 1989). Inmates would never know when they were under surveillance and would thus be motivated to constantly control their own behavior to avoid negative consequences. The modern electronic Panopticon would operate using a similar motivating force. Individuals exercising rational choice would be deterred from antisocial and deviant behavior due to the threat of continuous electronic surveillance. Their behaviors would not escape the watchful eyes of the keepers.

After 9/11, there was a call for increased government surveillance capabilities. In this climate U.S. Attorney General John Ashcroft proposed Project Tips. It was an interesting but controversial program that called for enlisting the help of utility company workers and numerous private employees, such as delivery people and contractors, in enhancing the government-sponsored data collection effort. These workers would be asked to report to the appropriate governmental agency any suspicious activity they observed while performing their normal job duties. In effect, the program would involve average citizens in surveillance activities. Due to public opposition, neither Project Tips nor Total Information Awareness was implemented. Stanley and Steinhardt (2007) contend that similar data mining efforts, which targeted global financial transactions and telecommunications, actually were implemented, some at the state level and others in the private sector. President George W. Bush authorized the National Security Agency to monitor without prior judicial review the electronic communications of targets of interest outside the United States, even in situations when the second party to the communication was in the United States (*In Re: National Security Agency Telecommunications Records Litigation*, 2009). In similar circumstances throughout American history, a warrant would have been required in order to conduct such surveillance on U.S. citizens. In this case, however, the administration had secured the cooperation of telecommunications companies, which agreed to tap into domestic and international telephone and electronic transmissions. In litigation, the government asserted state secret privilege, noting that further discovery in open court would threaten national security interests. The decision also noted that participating telecommunications companies would be granted narrow civil immunity through federal legislation for their participation in the surveillance program from September 11, 2001 to January 7, 2007.

Passenger Screening

After 9/11, transportation security and passenger screening were identified as areas in need of dramatic improvement. Miller (2005) noted that the FBI maintained 257.5 million records for people who were passengers on commercial flights from June 2001 to September 2001. The passenger record information included names, credit card information, travel itineraries, addresses, telephone numbers, and meal requests. The U.S. government launched CAPPS II (Computer Assisted Passenger Prescreening System), which facilitated inquiries into passengers' bank accounts, credit reports, and travel history. The CAPPS database was designed to be administered and managed by the TSA. Transportation Secretary Norman Mineta stated that the system would enable the government to verify a person's identity more efficiently (Miller, 2003). The TSA's passenger screening procedures as of 2010, which include the Secure Flight program, utilize multiple layers of screening. Specific passenger screening begins at the time of ticket purchase, when ticket information is compared against databases of persons of interest, such as the no-fly list. In theory, large-scale electronic communication surveillance efforts would have a significant effect on transportation security (Stanley & Steinhardt, 2003).

Drug Dogs

Some surveillance approaches use a nonelectronic approach to crime detection. In *Illinois v. Caballes* (2005), the Supreme Court of the United States held that the use of a narcotics-detection dog to detect the presence of drugs during a lawful traffic stop does not violate the Fourth Amendment so long as the drug dog sweep is conducted during the time it takes to normally process the traffic stop. Based on the facts in *Illinois v. Caballes*, Caballes was stopped by the police for driving 71 mph in a 65-mph zone. While the original trooper was writing a warning to Caballes for a motor vehicle violation, a second state trooper arrived on the scene of the traffic stop with a drug dog. The animal alerted to the presence of illegal drugs in the trunk; the alert was then used as probable cause to search the trunk. The Court ruled that the drug dog search occurred during the time ordinarily required to process the traffic stop and specifically that the driver was not unlawfully or unreasonably detained in order to execute the drug dog search. The majority opinion in *Illinois v. Caballes* (2005) noted that individuals do not have an expectation of privacy for the possession of contraband.

Interestingly, in a dissenting opinion in *Illinois v. Caballes* (2005), Justice Ruth Bader Ginsburg cautioned that every traffic stop may become an occasion to employ a drug dog. The majority opinion did not impose any type of restriction that would require the police to associate a particular driver or automobile with illegal drug possession. Also, Ginsburg's dissent noted that the Court did not adopt a standard similar to that attached to a Terry Stop, in which a subsequent search (e.g., a drug dog search) must be related in scope to the circumstances that led to the initial inquiry (e.g., a traffic stop).

Global Positioning System (GPS)

As mentioned previously, there have been many advances in global positioning technology and numerous new applications of it. Lost or endangered hikers have been rescued thanks to GPS-enabled cell phones. GPS-implanted products such as the LoJack system aid in the recovery of stolen vehicles; LoJack also offers a product line called ReuniteIT, which offers similar technology for smaller electronic items, such as MP3 players, laptop computers, or even bicycles (LoJack, 2009).

If GPS technology can be used to reunite a person with his or her vehicle, it could be used to reunite parents with their children or at least let parents know that their daughter, instead of going to the library as she told them, was at a boyfriend's house instead. Kennedy (2007) describes a product called "Peace of Mind"—sneakers with embedded GPS technology. The GPS feature is activated by the wearer using a button in the sneaker or by the parent using a password to the remote monitoring service. The sneakers' designer stated that the tracking device should be used only in emergencies (Associated Press, 2007), although the company later introduced a similar shoe with a social networking feature so friends could track the wearer's location (Isaac Daniel Technology, 2010). Similar technology exists for cell phones (Kim, 2006). One service, marketed by GTXC and called Loopt, constantly monitors consenting users in a user's group list (Kim 2006). Sneakers with this feature could be marketed to parents concerned about their children as well as to spouses concerned about their significant other. GTXC has also developed a "smart shoe'" with embedded GPS capability. Burris (2007) states that this product "enables parents to set up safe (green zone) and unsafe (red zone) areas. If a child leaves a green zone and heads to a red zone, parents will receive a text and/or Internet message immediately. Ditto, if the shoes cease moving for an extended period—such as if they've been removed" (p. B6).

GPS tracking can be used in divorce cases as well. While adultery generally is not viewed as a criminal matter, at least one state has such a law. New Hampshire criminal code RSA 645:3 states that "a person is guilty of a class B misdemeanor if, being a married person, he engages in sexual intercourse with another not his spouse or, being unmarried, engages in sexual intercourse with another known by him to be married" (Title LXII Criminal Code, 1992). Bartlett (2009) describes the benefit of using GPS tracking to either confirm or dispel fears of an unfaithful spouse. Brickhouse Security (2011) offers a whole product line tailored to detecting infidelity, including technology to recover deleted text messages.

Radio Frequency Identification (RFID)

Most people have had some experience with or exposure to the use of RFID tags. For instance, the E-Z Pass streamlines highway toll collection with a system in which electronic readers in toll booths detect RFID signals from vehicles equipped with transponders, and the authority then deducts tolls from drivers' dedicated electronic accounts. RFID chips are also present in many products and service applications, including pet identification, identification badges for schools and workplaces, casino chips, inventory tracking, and instant payment systems (e.g., ExxonMobil's Speedpass®). RFID products such as E-Z Pass transponders have been used in criminal investigations, and RFID reader placement has been employed to track individuals and products.

There are two types of RFID tags: active and passive. Active tags have an internal power source. Examples of this type include E-Z Pass transponders. Passive tags need to be powered by an external source for the transmitter to function. These RFID transmitters may have an effective range varying from a few feet to several hundred yards (Anderson & Labay, 2006). Anderson and Labay note that widespread adoption of RFID is already a reality; Wal-Mart and the Department of Defense and their respective suppliers are large entities that use such technology to provide better inventory control, loss prevention, and convenience to the consumer by helping to ensure inventory availability and avoiding price increases due to shoplifting and employee theft.

Albrecht and McIntyre (2005) note that the difference between a universal product code (UPC) and an RFID chip is that, with UPCs, each product *type* has the same UPC but, with RFID chips, each individual *item* has a unique identifying chip with a 16-digit identifier. That unique number links the individual chip to a database that records each time the RFID chip was sighted by a reader. A beneficial feature of RFID is that it is not limited by the electronic reader's line of sight. The information supplied by the RFID chip as the product is carried throughout a retail environment provides data on shopping patterns. Marketing specialists can then use these data in making product placement decisions and even in crafting direct marketing appeals to the consumer in the store.

Lewan (2008) describes how the RFID chips have become ubiquitous in both physical and social environments. The tiny chips can be embedded in an endless range of products. Paired with electronic "sniffers," or devices that read the RFID chips, they can provide a wealth of information about an individual. Even U.S. passports have RFID chips, and Albrecht and McIntyre (2005) contend that individuals could similarly be under surveillance via chips in their shoes, automobile tires, or wallets. RFID chips could be detected by readers strategically placed at highway access ramps, along highways, in doorways, beneath carpets, or above ceiling tiles.

The possible uses of the chips seem limitless. Lewan (2007) notes that Verichip Corporation and its parent, Applied Digital Solutions, sold about 2,000 chips for implantation into persons. Lewan (2007) describes the agreement a surveillance equipment company reached to "chip" two of its employees in an effort to safeguard access to a restricted area of its facility. In discussing permissible instances of human RFID chipping, Lewan characterizes them as a slippery slope on which there might be specific categories of people targeted for chipping. There are situations in which people might consider human chipping appropriate. A patient with Alzheimer's disease might be such a situation, but the looming question is then how many groups would eventually fall into the category of "appropriate for chipping."

Elderly persons living alone might be candidates for the "caring plant," described by Albrecht and McIntyre (2005). This electronic plant can monitor in-home movement and activity, such as the opening and closing of a medicine cabinet or refrigerator. The use of electronic monitoring has numerous applications for criminal justice and special offender populations. One might advocate chipping sex offenders so that strategically placed readers could detect their presence near parks, schools, or other places of interest. Chip readers in offenders' homes could provide a variety of information, such as the presence of alcohol or a missed curfew. Albrecht and McIntyre (2005) note that using RFID could be viewed as an updated version of "Operation Identification," begun in the early 1980s, when ID numbers were inscribed into items so that, if stolen, they could be returned to their rightful owner. However, as Albrecht and McIntyre (2005) point out, RFID can also provide thieves, equipped with readers, with the opportunity to scan targets (people or vehicles) to determine their value prior to committing an overt theft or robbery.

Vehicle Black Boxes

Burris (2007) notes that in addition to GPS-equipped watches, shoes, and phones, "black boxes" to monitor teens' driving habits are becoming more popular for both fleet vehicle owners and parents. Vehicle black boxes record driving information such as steering, braking, engine RPMs, seat-belt usage, and speed (Morris, 2004; "What's a Black Box", 2004; Wickham, 2005). Once the box is activated, it records about 5 seconds worth of data ("What's a Black Box", 2004). The information can be accessed by law enforcement agencies or insurance companies to aid in the investigation of accidents. The device can register speeds at impact and braking. In New Hampshire, Morris (2004) notes, state police would have to obtain a warrant before downloading information, but insurance companies would not have the same limitations. It is currently against federal law to disable the black box since it is a component of the airbag system. Morris (2004) notes that GM began equipping some of its vehicles with black boxes in 1994, and all GM models now contain them. Morris (2004) notes that customer notification about the recording device is contained in the owner's manual, in a less than prominent fashion—a situation referred to as a "burial notification."

An insurance company has offered drivers a discount if they participate in the voluntary data collection program. Fordahl (2004) states that "Progressive says it will use the data only for potential discounts and not to penalize customers whose devices reveal risky driving habits" (p. A22). One issue this situation raised was the possibility that other insurance companies might offer similar programs to "safe" drivers. Williamson (2005) notes that some services include installation of a camera to capture activity within the passenger compartment of the vehicle or send driving data directly to a parent's computer. This technology is identical to that used for monitoring business fleet vehicles (Marx & Steeves, 2011).

Genetic and Health-Related Databases

As noted above, Staples (2000) contends that postmodern surveillance targets the body. Genetic and health-related databases can provide insights into aspects of an individual's lifestyle, such as alcohol and drug use. In one instance, a Pennsylvania man named Emerich disclosed to the medical doctor treating him for an irregular heartbeat that he drank about a six-pack of beer each day (Raffaele, 2004). This patient had had a DUI conviction 23 years earlier. His doctor notified the state's Department of Motor Vehicles about the patient's drinking behavior, which could affect his ability to safely operate a vehicle. Upon this notification, the state court suspended the patient's driver's license pending the installation of an ignition-monitoring device to test for alcohol even though the man stated that he didn't drink and drive but chose to drink only at home.

As noted previously, there are also a number of drug testing products developed and marketed for private home use, especially by parents concerned about drug use by their children (Marx & Steeves, 2011).

REAL ID and Biometrics

Health care, transportation security, and immigration reform efforts have prompted a renewed interest in identification technology. Stanley and Steinhardt (2007) contend that the federal REAL ID Act of 2005 seeks to nationalize the states' systems for licensing drivers. Each state's license database would be interconnected, and each license would be machine readable as part of an overall effort to standardize license validity. An interconnected system of this sort might prevent individuals from concealing their true identities when moving across state lines. The case of "Edward Davies" is an example of why such a system might be useful. When Edward Davies, known in his local community as Uncle Buddha, died from liver failure, the medical examiner learned that this man who babysat children in his home was actually Edward F. Bessette, Jr. He had fled from another state 18 years earlier and was wanted for five counts of sexual assault of a child under the age of 15. More precise methods of identification might have resulted in the capture of this person wanted for crimes committed against children and also prevented his further contact with such a vulnerable population.

Biometric systems are increasingly being used to ascertain one's identity. The US-VISIT system for people entering the United States or using a rental locker at various types of high-profile locations, utilizes biometrics (Bergstein, 2004). Federal officials view biometrics as a mechanism with which to address problems in verifying airline passenger identification. The REAL ID legislation passed in 2005 requires states to certify that the potential licensee is in the country legally. Privacy advocates decry the plan to link data among states so that a state can determine whether the applicant already has a license issued by another state or has lost his or her privileges in another state. Some states note that one unintended consequence of interstate access would be the vulnerability of data; many more people would have access to confidential databases. REAL ID has been viewed by some as a national identification card issued at the state level. Some states, including New Hampshire, already comply with many of the act's requirements, such as ensuring machine readability of licenses and adding physical security features to them to prevent counterfeiting. One section of the REAL ID Act that some find troubling is that "states must provide electronic access to all other states to information contained in the motor vehicle database of the state" (Wickham, 2005, p. A1).

DNA and Cold Case Files

Physical traces left by people in public places are viewed differently from traces left in the home. Thompson (2007) describes a case in which law enforcement officers collected DNA evidence as part of an ongoing criminal investigation of cold cases. When a man who was a suspect in a cold case spat on the sidewalk, police collected a DNA sample from his spittle and compared it to physical evidence from a 30-year-old unsolved rape and murder case. The spittle (and the DNA it contained) is legally considered abandoned by the individual and would therefore make it unnecessary for police to obtain a warrant to compel the person to produce a DNA sample. In this view, abandoned DNA, from spittle, gum, or even flatware used at a restaurant, is much like trash, which is a key determinant in how it can be treated by the police and third parties. The Supreme Court of the United States ruled in *California v. Greenwood* (1988) that people do not have an expectation of privacy in regard to their trash. In a sense, a person knowingly relinquishes control over the discarded items or objects with the understanding that someone else will come along and take them. In this case, the Court ruled that the police would not need a warrant to collect discarded property or trash, although New Hampshire has ruled that the police would need a warrant to seize and then search someone's trash (*State of New Hampshire v. Goss*, 2003).

Backscatter X-rays

Backscatter technology uses x-rays to produce a very detailed image of the selected target. This type of x-ray is not strong enough to penetrate the skin of the person being scanned, unlike a tra-

---

BOX 9-1 Contemporary Issues in Surveillance

Gary T. Marx, Professor Emeritus of Sociology at Massachusetts Institute of Technology has written extensively on the topic of surveillance, privacy, and social control. His article with Valerie Steeves, titled "From the Beginning: Children as Subjects and Agents of Surveillance," provides a detailed and thought provoking analysis of surveillance technologies marketed to parents intended to keep their children safe. These products include covert cameras, RFID-enabled clothing, GPS trackers, computer and cell phone monitoring, and home drug test kits.

CRITICAL THINKING QUESTIONS

1. Marx and Steeves observe a technology fallacy of meeting rather than creating consumer needs for products and services. While true dangers exist, to what extent are threats children face exaggerated by the media? Are children today safer than in the past?
2. Do you think the use of technology to monitor children would create more distrust and resentment between the child and the parent, or would parents be irresponsible for not taking advantage of available technology designed to keep children safe?
3. Does this wave of technology have the potential to do more harm than good in the pursuit of raising children with an internalized set of beliefs about what behavior is right and wrong?

ditional medical x-ray (Stoughton, 2002). The purpose of this scanning technology is to provide an efficient and effective means of screening persons for potentially dangerous items concealed under clothing (and thus not visible to the casual observer) without doing a physical pat-down search (Mackey, 2007). Backscatter x-ray technology does not have the same limitations as a metal detector. Metal detectors cannot detect nonmetallic objects such as drugs and plastic explosives or weapons. According to Murphy and Wilds (2001, p. 334), backscatter technology is capable of "pinpointing not only weapons, drugs, and contraband, but also the traveler's breasts, buttocks, and genitalia. In fact, the resolution is so clear that the operator can literally count the hairs on a man's chest or measure the depth of a woman's navel." One product utilizing this technology is Rapiscan Systems' Secure 1000 Personnel Scanner. Further details of the backscatter x-ray machines are provided in Chapter 10.

SUMMARY

The Fourth Amendment states that citizens are to be protected against unreasonable searches and seizures. Therefore, reasonable searches are legally justified, regardless of how intrusive the search may seem. Although the government is considered a prime threat to individual liberty, businesses and individuals with less than noble intentions present threats to individual autonomy as well. The appropriate uses of surveillance have been discussed and analyzed in a variety of settings, including the academic literature, corporate boardrooms, legislative sessions, and court cases. The manifest and latent functions of technology serve a variety of surveillance functions emphasizing positive goals for society, but they usually produce some unintended consequences. For instance, Anderson and Labay (2006) note that "an example of one potential use would be the court-ordered 'chipping' of known child molesters and the installation of readers near areas known to be frequented by potential victims. The detection of a chip by one of these readers, indicating the person chipped had been in the area, would constitute a violation of parole" (p. 268). Would the proposal above create a false sense of security among parents, leading them to believe that, if a predator is in the vicinity, alarm bells would immediately sound? To what extent would children be protected against perpetrators they know well or to whom they are related?

Society should evaluate policy recommendations using evidence-based approaches to measure the effectiveness of various surveillance strategies. In addition to the relative effectiveness of an approach, research should consider social, legal, ethical, and monetary considerations. Withholding or selectively disclosing information about oneself is critical to how people define themselves. Marx (1998) emphasizes respect for the dignity of the person subjected to surveillance, an emphasis on the avoidance of harm, validity of the processes used, trust in the management of the process and data, fair notice of its use, and permission when crossing personal boundaries. Do individuals have full awareness of the implications of various security measures at the time of consent to their use?

Situational crime prevention provides a useful framework for crafting technological solutions to specific problems. When developing situational crime prevention measures, government and law enforcement officials can craft technological solutions that will reduce the benefits of particular crimes as well as increase the probability of detection. Etzioni's (1999) communitarian perspective provides a useful framework for discussing and evaluating the current application of technology. It seeks to provide a standard to determine the correct and just balance for proposed policies based upon their reasonableness. If something is technologically possible, should we do it? According to Etzioni, "a good society seeks a carefully crafted balance between individual rights and social responsibility, between liberty and the common good" (p. 5). To pass the test of reasonableness, the proposal must address not only the level of intrusion the individual will experience but also the substantial public interest or common good that will result from the action. Furthermore, society must rule out less intrusive measures to achieve the same purpose. The spectrum between expected privacy and intrusive searching is broad, and the debate is at times loud and fierce. However, the public demand for increased personal security may be incompatible with the seemingly equal public demand for complete personal privacy. This dichotomy, when viewed against the backdrop of rapidly advancing technology that facilitates the surreptitious collection of data on our every activity, from the important to the most mundane, will undoubtedly spur continued controversy and legal argument.

KEY TERMS

Closed circuit television
Data mining
Secure Flight
Panopticon
Radio frequency identification
Backscatter x-ray

DISCUSSION QUESTIONS

1. What are some examples that illustrate an exchange in which people freely give up personal information in exchange for some anticipated benefit?
2. How would you counter the claim that, if you have nothing to hide, you have nothing to fear from surveillance?
3. While preventing crime is a noble and worthwhile objective, what are some of the benefits of being able to selectively release information about oneself?
4. Should parents use covert techniques to monitor their children's behavior?
5. Should states be compelled to require drivers' licenses to have biometric information?

REFERENCES

Albrecht, K., & McIntyre, L. (2005). *Spychips: How major corporations and government plan to track your every move with RFID*. Nashville, TN: Nelson Current.

Anderson, A. M., & Labay, V. (2006). Ethical considerations and proposed guidelines for the use of radio frequency identification: Especially concerning its use for promoting public safety and national security. *Science and Engineering Ethics, 12*, 265–272.

Associated Press. (2007, February 9). GPS sneakers help locate wearer: Quantum Satellite Technology line requires $19.95 monthly subscription. Retrieved from http://www.msnbc.msn.com/id/17063608.

Bartlett, G. (2009, January 25). GPS tracking unfaithful spouses. *GPS Tracking News*. Retrieved from http://www.rmtracking.com/blog/2009/01/25/gps-tracking-unfaithful-spouses/.

Bergstein, B. (2004, August 23). Biometrics arrives at the touch of a button. *The New Hampshire Union Leader*, p. C2.

Brickhouse Security. (2011). How to catch a cheater, catch a cheating spouse: Suspect your partner is cheating? Here's the proof. Retrieved from http://www.brickhousesecurity.com/catch-a-cheater.html.

Burns-Howell, T., & Pascoe, T. (2004). Crime prevention evaluation: A realistic framework based on experience and reality. *Criminology & Public Policy, 3*(3), 527–534.

Burris, J. (2007, November 1). Tracking kids with cellphones and gum shoes. *The New Hampshire Union Leader,* p. B6.

California v. Greenwood. 486 U.S. 35. (1988). Retrieved from http://laws.findlaw.com/us/486/35.html.

Clark, R. V. (1992). Introduction. In R. V. Clark (Ed.), *Situational crime prevention: Successful case studies* (pp. 3–36). Albany, NY: Harrow and Heston.

Dinh, V. D. (2004). Freedom and security after September 11. In M. K. B. Darmer, R. M. Baird, & S. E. Rosenbaum (Eds.), *Civil liberties vs. national security in a post-9/11 world* (pp. 105–113). Amherst, NY: Prometheus Books.

Etzioni, A. (1999). *The limits of privacy.* New York, NY: Basic Books, Perseus Books Group.

Fordahl, M. (2004, October 10). Insurer offers discounts for black-box drivers. *The New Hampshire Sunday News,* p. A22.

Foucault, M. (1977). *Discipline and punish: The birth of the prison.* (Alan Sheridan, Trans.). New York, NY: Vintage.

Giduck, J. (2005). *Terror at Beslan: A Russian tragedy with lessons for America's schools.* Golden, CO: Archangel Group.

Google Earth used to find unpermitted pools in N.Y. town. (2010, August 2). *The New Hampshire Union Leader,* p. D10.

Guardian Angel Technology. (2008). Guardian Angel Technology: Helping parents know where and when through technology. Retrieved from http://www.guardianangeltech.com/.

Illinois v. Caballes. 543 U.S. 403 (2005). Retrieved from http://laws.findlaw.com/us/000/03-923.html.

In Re: National Security Agency Telecommunications Records Litigation. (2009). Retrieved from http://www.eff.org/files/filenode/att/orderhepting6309_0.pdf.

Isaac Daniel Group, Inc. (2010). "Social networking with your feet": Isaac Daniel Group announces newest, cutting edge GPS shoe, "Blue GPS": New GPS shoes allow sharing location with friends. Retrieved from http://www.isaacdanielgroup.com/blue-gps-shoes-press-release.php.

Kennedy, K. (2007, February 11). GPS sneakers locate wearer with press of a button. *The New Hampshire Sunday News,* p. D4.

Kim, R. (2006, December 19). New services allow you to track your friends. *The New Hampshire Sunday News,* p. D7.

Lewan, T. (2007, July 22). Microchips in humans: High-tech helper or big brother? *The New Hampshire Sunday News,* p. A5.

Lewan, T. (2008, January 27). Microchips: Boon for retailers, bane for privacy. *The New Hampshire Sunday News,* p. A8.

LoJack. (2009). LOJACK security systems for stolen vehicle recovery, GPS anti-theft and persons at risk. Retrieved from http://www.lojack.com/.

Mackey, D. A. (2007). The "X-rated X-ray": Reconciling liberty, privacy, and community safety. Special issue: Criminal justice and homeland security. *Criminal Justice Studies: A Critical Journal of Crime, Law, and Society, 20*(2), 149–159.

Marx, G. T. (1998). An ethics for the new surveillance. *The Information Society, 14*(3). Retrieved from http://web.mit.edu/gtmarx/www/ncolin5.html.

Marx, G. (2006). Soft surveillance: The growth of mandatory volunteerism in collecting personal information. In T. Monahan (Ed.), *Surveillance and security.* Devon, UK: Willan Publishing. Retrieved from http://web.mit.edu/gtmarx/www/softsurveillance.html.

Marx, G. T., & Muschert, G. W. (2007). Personal information, borders, and the new surveillance studies. *Annual Review of Law and Social Science, 3,* 375–395.

Marx, G. T., & Steeves, V. (2011). From the beginning: Children as subjects and agents of surveillance. *Surveillance & Society, 7*(3/4), 192–230. Retrieved from http://web.mit.edu/gtmarx/www/childrenandsurveillance.html.

Miller, L. (2003, February 28). Air passengers' backgrounds to be checked. *The New Hampshire Union Leader,* pp. A1–A2.

Miller, L. (2005, January 15). FBI keeping records on air travelers who flew just before 9/11. *The New Hampshire Union Leader,* p. A3.

Morris, J. (2004, October 10). Is big brother under your car's dash? *The New Hampshire Sunday News,* pp. A1, A22.

Murphy, M. C., & Wilds, M. R. (2001). X-rated x-ray invades privacy rights. *Criminal Justice Policy Review, 12*(4), 333–343.

Parenti, C. (2004). Fear as institution: 9/11 and surveillance triumphant. In M. K. B. Darmer, R. M. Baird, & S. E. Rosenbaum (Eds.), *Civil liberties vs. national security in a post-9/11 world* (pp. 115–131). Amherst, NY: Prometheus Books.

Raffaele, M. (2004, August 18). Court OKs suspension of license of beer drinker reported by doctor. *The New Hampshire Union Leader,* p. D10.

Resnick, S. (2010). TSA deploys more full-body scanners despite EPIC protests. Retrieved from Security Zone: The Medill National Security Journalism Initiative, http://medillnsj.org/05/2010/medill-reporting/us-security-civil-liberties-reporting/tsa-deploys-more-full-body-scanners-despite-epic-protests.

Rosen, Jeffrey. (2004). *The naked crowd: Reclaiming security and freedom in an anxious age.* New York, NY: Random House.

Saville, G. (2004). Editorial introduction: Surveillance and crime prevention. *Criminology and Public Policy, 3*(3), 493–496.

Sniff Dogs. (2011). Sniff Dogs—discreet narcotics detecting dogs for drug detection work. Retrieved from http://www.sniffdogs.com/.

Stanley, J., & Steinhardt, B. (2003). *Bigger monster, weaker chains: The growth of an American surveillance society.* New York, NY: American Civil Liberties Union.

Stanley, J., & Steinhardt, B. (2007). *Even bigger, even weaker: The emerging surveillance society; Where are we now?* New York, NY: American Civil Liberties Union.

Staples, W. G. (2000). *Everyday surveillance: Vigilance and visibility in postmodern life.* New York, NY: Rowan & Littlefield.

State of New Hampshire v. Goss. No. 2002-445. (2003). Retrieved from http://www.courts.state.nh.us/supreme/opinions/2003/goss120.htm.

Stoughton, S. (2002, January 7). Err-to air combat. *The Boston Globe,* pp. C1, C4.

Strub, H. (1989). The theory of panoptical control: Bentham's Panopticon and Orwell's *Nineteen Eighty-Four. The Journal of the Behavioral Sciences, 25,* 40–59.

TestMyTeen LLC. (2009). "No, my parents test me." Retrieved from http://www.testmyteen.com/default.aspx.

Thompson, C. (2007, March 18). Questions raised as police get creative in collecting DNA. *The New Hampshire Sunday News,* p. B7.

Title LXII Criminal Code, N.H. Stat., RSA chap. 645: Public Indecency, §645:3 Adultery (1992). Retrieved from http://www.gencourt.state.nh.us/rsa/html/NHTOC/NHTOC-LXII-645.htm.

Torpey, J. (2007). Through thick and thin: Surveillance after 9/11. *Contemporary Sociology, 36*(2), 116–119.

Transportation Security Administration (TSA). (2008). Secure Flight Program: Secure flight passenger data definitions. Retrieved from Office of Transportation Threat Assessment and Credentialing (TTAC), Transportation Security Administration, U.S. Department of Homeland Security, http://www.tsa.gov/assets/pdf/secure_flight_passenger_data_definitions.pdf.

Welsh, B. C., & Farrington, D. P. (2009). *Making public places safer: Surveillance and crime prevention.* New York, NY: Oxford University Press.

What's a black box, and what does it do? (2004, October 10). *The New Hampshire Sunday News,* p. A22.

Wickham, S. K. (2005, September 18). NH not sold on "national ID card." *The New Hampshire Sunday News,* pp. A1, A15.

Williamson, E. (2005, March 28). With the car keys, a monitoring device. *The New Hampshire Union Leader,* p. C10.

CHAPTER 10

The "X-Rated X-Ray": Reconciling Fairness, Privacy, and Security

David A. Mackey

Plymouth State University

Commercial airline flights have been targeted in the events of September 11, later by Richard Reid in December, 2001, and more recently in the terrorist plot foiled by British investigators involving an estimated ten transatlantic flights. Since September 11, 2001, the screening of airline travelers has been redefined in light of its threat to homeland security. Global events have fueled the momentum of policies designed to strengthen homeland security. Some policies, which have the intended goal of protecting individuals and the larger community from harm, may produce unintended negative consequences. A question remains as to what expectation of privacy society is willing to accept as reasonable for travelers on commercial airlines. In particular, X-ray screening using backscatter technology is one technique which has been used to screen airline travelers for weapons and contraband in a number of major U.S. airports. The legal, social, and ethical considerations of airport screening are discussed in the context of homeland security.

A number of works (Agre and Rotenberg, 1998; Lyon, 2003; Mizell, 1998; Stanley and Steinhardt, 2003; Staples, 2000; Sykes, 1999; Whitaker, 1999) have chronicled a decline in the realization of individual privacy caused by intrusions from the government and other organizations. Among the technologies and policies being debated are national identification cards using smart-technology (Etzioni, 1999; Hempel, 2001; O'Harrow, 2002; O'Harrow & Krim, 2001), video surveillance (Electronic Privacy Information Center [Epic], 2005; Lyon, 2003; Stanley and Steinhardt, 2003), data mining frameworks (American Civil Liberties Union [ACLU], 2004; Stanley and Steinhardt, 2003), and scanning equipment (Hawn, 1999; Murphy and Wilds, 2001; Stoughton, 2002). Many of these efforts, as well as the general trend of increasing levels of security in our society, pre-date the attacks of September 11, 2001.

Commercial airline flights have been targeted by Khalid Sheikh Mohammed during 1995, on September 11th, later by Richard Reid in December 2001, and more recently in the terrorist plot foiled by British investigators involving an estimated ten transatlantic flights. These events have fueled the momentum of additional policies and procedures designed to strengthen homeland security, yet some of which use technologies that may have a number of unintended negative consequences. For about 40 years, airlines have been the target of terrorist plots including hijackings

The X-Rated X-Ray: Reconciling Fairness, Privacy and Security, David A. Mackey, Criminal Justice Studies, Vol. 20, Issue 2, June 1, 2007. Reprinted by permission of Taylor & Francis Ltd.

and bombings (Crank and Gregor, 2005; Fagin, 2006), but recent events have made airline security a central concern of homeland security.

The 9/11 Commission was created to investigate the events leading up to the terrorist attacks, the nation's response to the attacks, as well as to produce recommendations to prevent future attacks. It must be noted that 19 of 19 hijackers on September 11successfully passed security checkpoints although eight were flagged for additional screening by the CAPPS program (9/11 Commission, 2004). Additional screening requirements at that time, only called for screening of checked bags which would then be loaded only after the passenger had boarded the plane. Among the recommendations was the creation of the Transportation Security Administration (TSA) and federal responsibility for passenger screening. Other recommendations by the 9/11 Commission called for screening of passengers for explosives not just luggage, as well as improving screener performance (2004, p. 562).

Crank and Gregor (2005) note that reoccurring problems plagued airline security prior to the attacks on September 11; the problems concerning passenger screening include: low wages to screeners, inadequate training, and rapid turnover (p. 119). In addition to replacing private security at airports, the TSA has upgraded screening equipment at the nation's largest airports, all walk through metal detectors (WTMD) are now enhanced status (TSA, 2006), which has contributed to a staggering amount of confiscations of prohibited items (see Sweet, 2006, p. 368). Years after the attacks on September 11 and following recommendations from the 9/11 Commission, airline security is very visible but still maintains significant shortcomings (Crank and Gregor, 2005, p. 243) often with reactionary measures such as questioning passengers as to whether they packed their own luggage, prohibiting potential cutting instruments, removing shoes, and prohibitions on gels and liquids in carry-on luggage (Chertoff, 2006). Although several of the 9/11 terrorists were selected for additional screening, the response was to confirm that they had boarded the flight prior to their checked luggage being loaded on board the aircraft (9/11 Commission, 2004). The sensitivity of metal detectors could not detect knives with blades less than four inches in length while written policy did not prohibit the items from carry-on luggage or passenger possession (p. 122). Among the current issues are: the adequacy of no-fly lists, the adequacy of passenger screening, luggage/cargo screening, and the utility of the air marshal program.

While x-rays using backscatter technology have been used for some time to screen employees and visitors as they enter sensitive government facilities (Hawn, 1999), more recently, backscatter x-rays have been used to screen airline travelers in a number of major U.S. airports (Cannon, 1999; EPIC, 2005; Murphy and Wilds, 2001; Stoughton, 2002) as well as other mass transit locations (Webster, 2005). This type of technology would be viewed as a significant upgrade of technological capabilities over traditional metal detectors. As a society, we should avoid evaluating backscatter scanning technology based on a single criterion, even if that criterion is to maximize community safety against a real or perceived threat. The effectiveness of the screening technology and procedures for implementation are a key concern. Legality also should not be the only criterion used to determine whether or not a search using backscatter technology should be allowed. Ethical and social issues associated with the use of this technology should also be considered. Ethical concerns address issues of passenger consent, awareness of the procedure, equality of application, and proportionality of the intrusion of the search compared to the desired government objective. In addition to ethical dimensions, Etzioni's (1999) communitarian perspective provides one model to evaluate the fit between the stated goal of protecting commercial airlines from terrorist attacks and individual privacy.

TECHNOLOGY

X-rays using backscatter technology use low power energy beams to produce a very detailed image of the target. The energy does not penetrate the object or person being scanned as it does with a traditional x-ray (EPIC, 2005; Stoughton, 2002) although clothes are rendered transparent. The purpose of this scanning technology is to provide an efficient and effective means to screen persons for potentially dangerous items concealed under clothing, not visible to the casual observer, without requiring a physical pat-down search. Objects on the outside of the body, yet concealed with clothes, are visible to the operator. Backscatter technology does not suffer from the same limitations as the conventional metal detector, which cannot detect non-metallic objects including bombs, drugs, or non-metallic weapons although backscatter scans cannot detect items smuggled internally (EPIC, 2005). Backscatter scans expose persons to the rays of energy whereas other similar technology uses passive imaging (Mackey, 1997) which relies on energy naturally emitted from the person as well as the composition of the object on the person.

According to Murphy and Wilds (2001, p. 334) backscatter technology is capable of pinpointing not only weapons, drugs, and contraband, but also the traveler's breasts, buttocks, and genitalia. In fact, the resolution is so clear that the operator can literally count the hairs on a man's chest or measure the depth of a woman's navel.

Stoughton (2002) presents graphic evidence of the results of backscatter scans by providing a detailed image of a male with concealed weapons but also "love handles" around his abdomen. One product utilizing this technology is Rapiscan Systems' Secure 1000 Personnel Scanner; the company also produces a model capable of scanning a tractor-trailer, which seems highly suitable for homeland security needs.

LEGAL CRITERIA FOR EVALUATION

One question which emerges from the discussion of backscatter scanning technology is whether its use constitutes an unreasonable search in violation of the Fourth Amendment. It is proposed that backscatter scanning in the context of enhanced airport security does not rise to the level of a Fourth Amendment violation for two reasons. First, as a matter of policy, the scan could be made a condition of purchasing a ticket, converting it into a voluntary search to which a person knowingly and voluntarily submits to as a condition of travel on a commercial aircraft. Secondly, the Fourth Amendment does not create an absolute right to privacy, but one which is qualified to protect individuals against unreasonable searches rather than against all intrusive searches (Etzioni, 1999). The individual may be subject to an intrusive search, such as a body cavity search (*United States v. Montoya De Hernandez*, 1985), which is a lawful and constitutional search so long as the Courts rule it is reasonable considering the context in which it arises. Aronson (2001) notes that judges rather than the community will determine the reasonableness of potential intrusions by the government. Since the Courts will make this determination for backscatter X-rays using logic from previous cases, it is important to identify patterns in previous rulings.

Advances in technology have had a significant impact on law enforcement practices designed to uncover that which was previously hidden. The U.S. Supreme Court continues to recognize the sanctity of the home while recognizing less privacy for the individual in public places and in particular engaging in regulated activities. For instance, in *Kyllo v. United States* (2001), the U.S. Supreme

Court ruled that a warrantless search of a home using a thermal imaging device was unreasonable. The Court ruled that such devices would reveal intimate details of lawful activities occurring inside the home in addition to potentially illegal activity. More importantly, the Court marked a firm and bright line for police at the entrance to a home. Fourth amendment cases involving the home have traditionally been held to higher scrutiny than those involving more public places. The U.S. Supreme Court has taken a more permissive view when looking at searches conducted outside the home.

The U.S. Supreme Court has ruled that warrantless searches conducted without specific suspicion on a particular individual can be reasonable, such as consent searches (*Florida v. Bostick*, 1991), sobriety checkpoints (*Michigan Dept. of State Police v. Sitz*, 1990), border searches (*United States v. Montoya De Hernandez*, 1985), drug dog searches (*Illinois v. Caballes*, 2005; *United States v. Place*, 1983), and drug testing (*Vernonia School District 47J v. Acton*, 1995). Searches of this nature are relevant to the present discussion since the same logic could be applied to backscatter scanning at airports.

In *Florida v. Bostick* (1991), the U.S. Supreme Court reversed a Florida court's ruling that every police encounter with a citizen while on a bus is a seizure. Bostick claimed that a seizure took place and he was not free to leave. He reasoned that he was on a bus about to depart for an interstate trip and if he left the bus he would have been stranded without his luggage away from his departure city and his destination city. The U.S. Supreme Court ruled that Bostick was not seized, was free to terminate the encounter, and voluntarily consented to a search of his luggage. The key concern for the Court was whether the police adequately communicated the right to refuse the search to the suspect so that a reasonable person would know the encounter was voluntary. For instance, in *United States v. Guapi* (1998), a federal circuit court ruled that the police did not effectively communicate the right to refuse the search to the suspect and also created a situation where the average person would not feel free to terminate the encounter.

The police have used other techniques to counter significant threats to society. For instance, in *United States v. Place* (1983) the U.S. Supreme Court noted that the use of a drug dog is not considered a search. In *United States v. Holloman* (1997), a drug dog alerted to the presence of drugs inside a vehicle stopped by police for a minor motor vehicle infraction. The search and seizure was considered reasonable since the driver was not detained longer than was necessary to process the initial traffic stop. The ruling in *United States v. Holloman* has been supported in the U.S. Supreme Court case *Illinois v. Caballes* (2005). The vehicle driven by Caballas was stopped by police for traveling 71 mph on Interstate 80. While the police officer was processing the warning for speeding, another police officer responded to the stop with a drug dog subsequently detecting the presence of marijuana and producing probable cause for the search of the vehicle. The Court ruled that the search was constitutional since the search was conducted during the time necessary to process a lawful traffic stop and the dog detected a substance that the individual had no right to possess.

In *Delaware v. Prouse* (1979), the U.S. Supreme Court ruled that roving police patrols which stop vehicles without individualized suspicion are unreasonable. A police officer stopped a vehicle during a lull in calls and, upon approaching the vehicle, smelled marijuana and saw marijuana in plain view in the vehicle. There was no probable cause or articulable suspicion for an alleged traffic violation as a basis for the stop. The officer wanted to check the driver's license and vehicle registration. The roving patrol is substantially different from the drunk driving roadblock where vehicle stops are more objective. In *Michigan Dept. of State Police v. Sitz* (1990), the U.S. Supreme Court ruled that the use of a sobriety checkpoint was reasonable. The preliminary stop of a vehicle may last about 30 seconds. The duration and level of intrusion of the stop were viewed as reasonable by the Court given the costs of drunken drivers to society. Data may also be produced on alcohol enforcement checkpoints to determine their effectiveness while also documenting the procedures for vehicle stops.

With similar reasoning applied to the use of drug-sniffing dogs to combat the significant social problem of drugs, the U.S. Supreme Court ruled that the government has a substantial interest in keeping the roads safe; but spot checks conducted without probable cause or articulable suspicion are not sufficiently productive to justify their use for safety. In addition, the Court also reasoned that people would be more frightened during a roving patrol stop than in a roadblock-style search. Prohibiting roving patrols was done in an effort to control what Justice White called the unconstrained exercise of discretion by police. It was stated that 'consent to regulatory restrictions is presumptively concurrent with participation in the regulated enterprise' (*Delaware v. Prouse*, 1979). While the concept of regulated enterprise originally referred to driving an automobile, it may also be applied to commercial airline passengers.

While roadblock stops lasting 30 seconds designed to detect and deter drunk drivers may be seen as only a minor intrusion, some searches may be considered very intrusive yet reasonable by the Court. In *United States v. Montoya De Hernandez* (1985) a woman was suspected of being a balloon swallower who was attempting to smuggle drugs into the USA. She was held 16 hours prior to a judicial warrant to conduct a rectal exam and an involuntary X-ray. The court reasoned that the search initially based on reasonable suspicion was reasonable. The Court based their decision on the sanctity of international borders, the method chosen to smuggle, and De Hernandez's refusal to voluntarily submit to an X-ray. It was noted in the dissenting opinion that only about 15–20% of all body cavity searches conducted by customs revealed drugs.

As these cases indicate, the U.S. Supreme Court tends to view searches in public, or within regulated activities such as driving or border crossings, differently from searches involving the home. The constitutional test of searches is based on reasonableness. The Court recognizes that the state may require a search which is considered intrusive in an effort to achieve a compelling state interest. The degree of intrusiveness would be weighed in light of the government's interests. Would an X-ray scan taking about 30 seconds of an airline traveler which reveals bare breasts and buttocks be considered reasonable? From the cases identified above, different approaches could be used to insure 'reasonableness.' First, backscatter scanning can be performed in a timely, efficient manner with minimal physical intrusion similar to a roadblock stop in the Sitz case. Secondly, backscatter scanning can rely on voluntary informed consent. Passengers would have the right to refuse the search and to seek alternative methods of travel. Third, TSA officials, again using the Sitz case, would need to be collected to demonstrate the effectiveness of backscatter X-ray scanning in detecting potential weapons. Fourth, the procedures used must be implemented in an objective manner with consideration to avoid discriminatory application.

ETHICAL CRITERIA FOR EVALUATION

Marx (1998) provides 29 criteria which can be used to assist in determining the ethical use of technology. Many of the criteria are relevant to the present discussion of backscatter scans. A preliminary application of the criteria to the use of backscatter scans in airports, with some modification to the actual scanning procedures, weighs in favor of using the technology. Among the key criteria identified by Marx are the absence of physical or psychological harm, awareness of the procedures, consent to the procedures, the golden rule, proportionality of the intrusion given the objectives, consequences of inaction, adequate data stewardship, and who benefits from the intervention. Using this framework, if individuals do not consent to the backscatter X-ray they would be denied access to the secure areas of the airport. Travelers have alternatives to travel by air if they choose not to consent to a search. The golden rule is particularly interesting. Are people willing to have other people scanned for weapons, explosives, or other prohibited items using a fairly revealing technology but not willing to undergo the same procedure themselves? Also, given the significance of passenger screening to homeland security interests, it is difficult to justify any exceptions to scanning all passengers, airport staff, and crews.

Several of Marx's (1998) criteria cluster around awareness and consent of the process by the individuals being affected. Marx notes that ethical concerns are raised when the procedures are applied to people without their knowledge and consent. Equality could also be an issue if profiling is used to select only a small percentage of people for scanning. Also, the potential for unequal application of the technology is of concern with regard to private, corporate, and charter flights. Individuals with the economic means could avoid the scanning process associated with commercial flights; private and charter flights pose a threat to homeland security. Also, while passengers and their luggage may be subject to X-ray scanning, cargo from known shippers aboard passenger airlines may not be adequately screened (Sweet, 2006). Marx also warns of the creation of unwanted precedents. For instance, backscatter scanning for all passengers could be seen as reasonable given the risks to society, but this same argument could be used to introduce scanning for sporting events, such as professional football, major league baseball, NASCAR events or even college football games with large attendance. Likewise, would the nexus of technology and case law allow the application of scanning in gun-crime hotspots which is a similar issue raised by Justice Ginsburg in a dissenting opinion in *Illinois v. Caballes* (1995)? Backscatter technology is already used by 30 federal agencies in a variety of settings (EPIC, 2005).

THEORETICAL CRITERIA FOR EVALUATION

Privacy and autonomy are key values for members of U.S. society. The majority of individuals would question laws which overtly favor the state's interest in homeland security over the individual's right to privacy and autonomy, like the social control exercised in Singapore which includes limitations on magazines, compulsory police/military service, and proscribed hair length for men (Austin, 1987). The nature of individual rights which limit governmental action is the cornerstone of the Bill of Rights. The expectations which arise from the Bill of Rights include, but obviously are not limited to, protections against unreasonable searches and seizures, protections against self-incrimination, and the right to counsel.

The communitarian perspective provides another framework for discussing and evaluating the current technology and the context of its use. Etzioni's communitarian model (1999) provides a standard to determine the correct and just balance to be struck when policies are designed to protect both the public good, in this case homeland security, and the individual's privacy. According to Etzioni (1999, p. 5), 'a good society seeks a carefully crafted balance between individual rights and social responsibility, between liberty and the common good.' From this perspective, the balance between the individual and the community is based on reasonableness of the proposed policy. To pass the test of reasonableness the proposal must consider not only the level of intrusion the individual will experience, but also the substantial public interest or common good that will result.

Etzioni's communitarian model criteria call for the well balanced, communitarian society (1) to take steps to limit privacy only if it faces a *well-documented and macroscopic threat* to the common good, not merely a hypothetical danger (p. 12, italics in original); (2) to act initially to counter a tangible and macroscopic danger by other means rather than *first resorting to measures that might restrict privacy* (p. 12, italics in original); (3) to make privacy-curbing measures that must be introduced as *minimally intrusive* as possible (p. 13, italics in original); (4) to *treat the undesirable side effects* of needed privacy diminishing measures openly rather than ignore them (p. 12, italics in original) and, when given a choice between two or more policies which equally protect the community's interest, to adopt the measure which best limits potential intrusions upon the individual. These criteria will be applied to the current uses of backscatter scans discussed below.

THE CONTEXT OF SCANNING TECHNOLOGY

Murphy and Wilds (2001, p. 339) contend that the utilization of X-ray search devices allows unreasonable, subjective searches of an innocent traveler when little or no evidence of criminality is present. The backscatter device effectively reduces the traveler's body to the same legal status as a piece of luggage on a conveyor belt. Murphy and Wilds contend that backscatter scanning is an unreasonable intrusion into a person's privacy.

The Fourth Amendment states that we are protected against unreasonable searches and seizures. Therefore, reasonable searches are legally justified regardless of how intrusive the search may seem. Contemporary society faces the reality of terrorists using commercial airlines as weapons of mass destruction to cause both mass casualties as well as a severe negative impact on the economy. The reality of the threat calls for responses which effectively screen passengers and luggage on airplanes and requires intrusions into the privacy of passengers. And, according to Etzioni's communitarian model, less intrusive alternatives to widespread implementation of scanning technology at airports for passengers, luggage, and personnel risks compromising the public good.

With a real, documented macroscopic threat to both travelers and the non-flying public posed by unsafe airline travel, the communitarian perspective would focus on making these intrusions as minimally intrusive as possible by treating the undesirable side effects of the intrusion. One concern is the level of detail of the image produced by the scanning technology (EPIC, 2005). Approaches could be devised to address this issue satisfactorily for the vast majority of travelers. For instance, passive imaging technology described elsewhere (Mackey, 1997) utilized technology which did not reveal an image to the operator unless an anomaly indicating the presence of an object was detected by the scan (see also Huguenin, 1994). Without an anomaly present, no detailed image need be revealed to the operator. With knowledge and awareness of the scanning procedures, travelers can avoid carrying any item on their body which may be detected as an anomaly and cause a detailed image output. Another option, described by EPIC (2005), provides for a digital fig leaf imposed on the displayed image. While the recommended security guidelines call for a physical design of security areas which prevents the public from viewing the X-ray screen (TSA, 2006), EPIC has also questioned the long-term storage and retrieval of the images produced by the scans.

As a society, we must determine the reasonable expectation of privacy for individuals in particular contexts. In the aftermath of September 11 when terrorists hijacked four commercial airliners and used them as weapons of mass destruction, do airline travelers have a reasonable expectation of privacy? What level of privacy is society willing to recognize as reasonable for passengers who voluntarily elect to fly on commercial aircrafts? Scanning for all passengers may eliminate the fairness issues associated with profiling practices. As a society, we should be aware of Marx's warning of the creation of unintended precedents. To what extent can entertainment venues, seen as a soft target for homeland security, require either a pat-down, metal detector, or even a backscatter X-ray as a requirement for entrance? Because a person has purchased a ticket to an event, does it guarantee her or him entrance to the event?

DISCUSSION

The right to be left alone, to be an autonomous individual, and to control access to information about oneself is central to a free society. Without a doubt, technology has fueled the intrusion into individual privacy by government and profit-minded organizations and current technology permits these intrusions to be far more intrusive and coordinated, potentially without the individual's knowledge and consent, than in the past. But, as recognized by Etzioni (1999), individual privacy does not trump all other considerations such as public safety and the rights of other individuals to life, liberty, and property. Homeland security, and by implication the public good associated with other's rights, is threatened by unrestricted personal autonomy and right to privacy. Legality should not be the only criterion used to determine whether or not a search should be allowed. Ethical issues associated with the use of the technology should also be considered. Ethical concerns address issues of consent, awareness, equality, and proportionality. The communitarian perspective provides one model to evaluate the fit between the goals of the community and individual privacy.

Aviation security experienced significant changes during the late 1960s and early 1970s when Fagin (2006) notes eight airplanes were hijacked to Cuba within a month in 1969 prompting the installation of metal detector screening for passengers. Airline bombings and hijackings continued in the 1970s, according to Fagin, but were mostly international incidents. According to the 9/11 Commission, onboard explosives were viewed as the most significant threat to domestic aviation. On September 11, the existing metal detectors were designed to detect items with a metal content equivalent to a .22 caliber handgun (9/11 Commission, 2004, p. 4). Contemporary concerns have been expressed regarding the effectiveness of airport screening procedures for passengers and cargo (Sweet, 2006). Department of Homeland Security (2006) notes there are currently 56,000 screeners deployed in all 429 commercial airports in the USA. Background qualifications and training of screening personnel have still been determined inadequate. Effective screening should be a component of improved airline security which addresses airport security, passenger identification and screening (potentially with biometric identification to screen and validate passengers as recommended by the 9/11 Commission, but certainly with the most comprehensive and coordinated no-fly list), airport proximity security, and in-flight security (Fagin, 2006, p. 157). The use of backscatter technology without substantial improvements to other airport screening efforts may be viewed as unreasonable. For instance, two terrorists on 9/11 triggered alarms at the metal detector station, but follow-up hand wand detection, as indicated by videotape records, failed to identify what triggered the alarm (9/11 Commission, 2004). In addition, steps should be taken to safeguard documents to validate someone's identity such as the USVISIT system and Secureflight. 'For terrorists, travel documents are as important as weapons. Terrorists must travel clandestinely to meet, train, plan, case targets, and gain access to attack' (9/11 Commission, 2004, p. 548) We must recognize the dangers of public safety policies which not only erode personal privacy, liberty, and autonomy, but are also ineffective in their goals of protecting the public from harm.

KEY TERMS

Global events
Individual privacy
Legal criteria
Ethical criteria
Scanning technology

REFERENCES

Agre, P. E., & Rotenberg, M. (Eds.). (1998). *Technology and privacy: The new landscape.* Cambridge, MA: MIT Press.

American Civil Liberties Union (ACLU). (2004). *Matrix: Myths and realities.* Retrieved March 12, 2005, from http://www.aclu.org/Privacy/Privacy.cfm?ID=14894&c=130.

Aronson, B. (2001). *New technologies and the fourth amendment: The trouble with defining a "reasonable expectation of privacy."* Findlaw's Legal Commentary. Retrieved January 15, 2002, from http://writ.news.findlaw.com/aronson/20010309.html.

Austin, W. T. (1987). Crime and custom in an orderly society: The Singapore prototype. *Criminology, 25*(2), 279–294.

Cannon, S. (1999). X-ray vision. *Latin Trade, 7*(10), 34.

Chertoff, M. (2006, August 10). Remarks by Homeland Security Secretary Michael Chertoff. Press Office, U.S. Department of Homeland Security. Retrieved from http://www.tsa.gov/press/speeches/dhs_press_conference_08102006.shtm.

Crank, J. P., & Gregor, P. E. (2005). *Counter terrorism after 9/11: Justice, security, and ethics reconsidered.* Dayton, OH: Anderson.

Delaware v. Prouse, 440 U.S. 648 (1979). Retrieved from http://laws.findlaw.com/us/440/648.html.

Department of Homeland Security. (2006). *Travel and transportation.*

Electronic Privacy Information Center (EPIC). (2005, June). *Spotlight on surveillance: Transportation agency's plan to x-ray travelers should be stripped of funding.* Retrieved from http://www.epic.org/privacy/surveillance/spotlight/0605/.

Etzioni, A. (1999). *The limits of privacy.* New York, NY: Basic Books, Perseus Books Group.

Fagin, J. A. (2006). *When terrorism strikes home: Defending the United States.* Boston, MA: Pearson Education.

Florida v. Bostick, 501 U.S. 429 (1991). Retrieved from http://laws.findlaw.com/us/501/429.html.

Hawn, C. (1999, November 29). Yes, we have no illegals. *Forbes, 164*(13), 144.

Hempel, C. (2001, December 31). Whether for business or "National ID," smart cards are moving into limelight. *The Union Leader,* p. C2.

Huguenin, G. R. (1994). *Testimony to the Crime and Criminal Justice Subcommittee of the House Judiciary Committee.* South Deerfield, MA: Millitech Corporation.

Illinois v. Caballes, 543 U.S. __ No. 03-923 (2005). Retrieved from http://laws.findlaw.com/us/000/03-923.html.

Kyllo v. United States, 533 U.S. 27 (2001). Retrieved fromhttp://laws.findlaw.com/us/533/27.html.

Lyon, D. (2003). *Surveillance after September 11.* Cambridge, MA: Polity Press.

Mackey, D. (1997). The ethics of new surveillance. *Criminal Justice Policy Review, 8*(2-3), 295–307.

Marx, G. T. (1998). An ethics for the new surveillance. *The Information Society, 14*(3). Retrieved from http://web.mit.edu/gtmarx/www/ncolin5.html.

Michigan Dept. of State Police v. Sitz, 496 U.S. 444 (1990). Retrieved from http://laws.findlaw.com/us/496/444.html.

Mizell, L. R., Jr. (1998). *Invasion of privacy.* New York, NY: The Berkley Publishing Group.

Murphy, M. C., & Wilds, M. R. (2001). X-rated x-ray invades privacy rights. *Criminal Justice Policy Review, 12*(4), 333–343.

9/11 Commission. (2004). *The 9/11 Report: The national commission on terrorist attacks upon the United States.* New York, NY: St Martin's Press.

O'Harrow, R., Jr. (2002, January 14). Driver's license as a national ID is pushed. *The Union Leader,* p. A12.

O'Harrow, R., Jr., & Krim, J. (2001, December 17). National ID card gaining support. *Washington Post Online.* Retrieved from http://www.highbeam.com/doc/1P2-497048.html.

Stanley, J., & Steinhardt, B. (2003). *Bigger monster, weaker chains: The growth of an American surveillance society.* New York, NY: American Civil Liberties Union.

Staples, W. G. (2000). *Everyday surveillance: Vigilance and visibility in post modern life.* New York, NY: Rowman and Littlefield.

Stoughton, S. (2002, January 7). Err-to air combat. *The Boston Globe,* pp. C1, C4.

Sweet, K. M. (2006). *Transportation and cargo security: Threats and solutions.* Upper Saddle River, NJ: Pearson Education.

Sykes, C. J. (1999). *The end of privacy.* New York, NY: St. Martin's Press.

Transportation Security Administration (TSA). (2006). *Recommended security guidelines for airport planning, design and construction.* Washington, DC: U.S. Department of Justice. Retrieved from http://www.tsa.gov/assets/pdf/airport_security_design_guidelines.pdf.

United States v. Guapi, 144 F.3d 1393 (1998). Retrieved from http://laws.findlaw.com/11th/976289opn.html.

United States v. Holloman, No. 96-2714 (1997). Retrieved from http://laws.findlaw.com/11th/962714opa.html.

United States v. Montoya De Hernandez, 473 U.S. 531 (1985). Retrieved from http://laws.findlaw.com/us/473/531.html.

United States v. Place, 462 U.S. 696 (1983). Retrieved from http://laws.findlaw.com/us/462/696.html.

Vernonia School District 47J v. Acton, 515 U.S. 646 (1995). Retrieved from http://laws.findlaw.com/us/515/646.html.

Webster, B. (2005, July 8). Body scan machines to be used on Tube passengers. *Times Online.* Retrieved from http://www.yasni.com/ext.php?url=http%3A%2F%2Ftechnology.timesonline.co.uk%2Ftol%2Fnews%2Ftech_and_web%2Fpersonal_tech%2Farticle541746.ece&name=On+You+Tube&cat=filter&showads=1.

Whitaker, R. (1999). *The end of privacy.* New York: The New Press.

CHAPTER 11

Sentencing Philosophies and Intermediate Sanctions

Katherine Polzer

Texas Christian University

INTRODUCTION

Over the last 30 years, the United States has gone on an imprisonment binge. When Martinson (1974) decided "nothing works," the United States completely overhauled sentencing philosophies and structure, turned away from rehabilitation, and focused on punitive sanctions and harsher punishments. In the last decade, the United States has been experiencing an overhaul in many areas in terms of sanctioning, such as the effect of sanctions on reentry and diversionary programs.

The prison system is exceedingly overcrowded, and criminal justice practitioners and academics are searching for ways to reduce the number of inmates being sent to prison, help ex-prisoners be successful once released, and identify evidence-based graduated sanctions that are successful. Punishment and sentencing are not only significant issues in criminology and criminal justice, but also hold great importance for the general public. How offenders are sentenced, punished, and released directly affects local communities and society as a whole. This chapter focuses on the various sentencing philosophies and intermediate sanctions currently being used, risk and resiliency factors for adults, and evidence-based graduated sanctions. The rationale across this chapter is to explore the broad scope of punishment and sentencing by focusing on sentencing models, procedures, and effectiveness. The main issues discussed can have significant policy implications for the future of criminal justice and the affected communities.

GOALS OF MODERN SENTENCING

Since the late 1970s, our sentencing philosophies have drastically changed. As aforementioned, after Martinson and corresponding lawmakers decided "nothing works," the United States saw a dramatic shift in sentencing. Prior to this shift, punishment had a rehabilitation component, which was the basis for indeterminate sentencing. Indeterminate sentences are based on the philosophy that treatment must be based on the needs of offender. Since the sentence has a maximum and minimum time frame, inmates can get early time off for good behavior, and if released early, be under continued supervision for a specified amount of time. But the maximums and minimums on sentences can also be very beneficial for inmates who are clearly not ready to be released or if the parole board has serious doubts about their release.

Indeterminate sentences are advantageous for many reasons. First of all, they allow for the full implementation of the rehabilitation ideal. Also, they tailor the sentence to the individual offender's circumstances and behavior. If an offender goes before a parole board and the parole board does not think the offender is ready to be released, they do not have to allow release. Finally, it helps maintain an orderly environment in the correctional institution. If an offender knows they will get time reduced from their sentence for good behavior, it will likely be a serious deterrent to disruptive behavior. Indeterminate sentences can also have some disadvantages. They can easily ignore the underlying causes of crime and can be more often used as a form of inmate control, which can hinder the rehabilitation process. Along with this, if rehabilitation is not internalized by many inmates and treatment is merely a token gesture, then inmates can "play the system" by appearing to do just enough to obtain early release.

Currently, though, we are operating under determinate sentencing, which is arguably the main reason our prison system is so overcrowded. Along with the determinate sentencing came the idea of "just deserts" in punishment philosophy. Von Hirsch (1976) believed in adopting just deserts sentencing, which focuses on making the punishment equal to the crime committed. He believed that indeterminate sentencing and parole should be replaced with guidelines for specific penalties for specific crimes (Petersilia, 2003). The just deserts theory is retrospective rather than prospective (Carlsmith, Darley, & Robinson, 2002) by design. In other words, the correctional institutions carrying out the punishing need not be concerned with future outcomes, only with providing appropriate punishment for the given harm perpetrated (p. 285). Rehabilitation is clearly no longer a factor in the just deserts approach. Proponents of just deserts feel justified because their philosophy is based on retributive justice, but not vengeance (Lokanan, 2009, p. 295).

In the 1980s, the United States took a "get tough on crime" approach, and that mentality has continued. Also, the "War on Drugs" effort has been a major contributor to our burgeoning prison population because of the harsh mandatory minimum sentences placed on drug offenses. Also, we adopted a new sentencing philosophy at the time: incapacitation. The primary goal of incapacitation is to simply lock up offenders, mainly repeat offenders, for as long as possible. As Walker (2011) puts it, incapacitation further assumes that if we keep them locked up twice as long, we are preventing twice as many crimes.

In the United States corrections system, we have two different types of incapacitation: selective and general. Selective incapacitation serves to get the career criminals off the street for good by giving them exceptionally long prison sentences. General incapacitation refers to the idea of locking up large numbers of people, regardless of criminal history. Currently, the United States emphasizes the use of general incapacitation, and has ignored the selective approach, which has led to the overcrowded prison system. A brief discussion of determinate sentencing will give a better idea of where it all went wrong.

Determinate sentencing seemed great in theory but has cost the United States billions of dollars and created a rapidly increasing ex-offender population, one with no skills or education and extremely high rates of recidivism. **Figure 11-1** shows the dramatic increases in the prison population since determinate sentencing laws were enacted, as well as outlining the increase in the community corrections population. Determinate sentences—sometimes referred to as structured, fixed, or mandatory sentences—were initially prompted by discontent over the disparity and uncertainty of indeterminate sentences. Also, lawmakers and the public thought many offenders were getting off too easy. Determinate sentences require offenders to serve a specified number of years, and judges determine this by using sentencing guidelines. Sentencing guidelines have been criticized as being too harsh and rigid, failing to take into account juvenile convictions, resulting in longer

Sourcebook of criminal justice statistics Online
http://www.albany.edu/sourcebook/pdf/t612009.pdf

Table 6.1.2009

Adults on probation, in jail or prison, and on parole

United States, 1980-2009

	Total estimated correctional population[a]	Probation	Jail	Prison	Parole
1980	1,840,400	1,118,097	182,288[b]	319,598	220,438
1981	2,006,600	1,225,934	195,085[b]	360,029	225,539
1982	2,192,600	1,357,264	207,853	402,914	224,604
1983	2,475,100	1,582,947	221,815	423,898	246,440
1984	2,689,200	1,740,948	233,018	448,264	266,992
1985	3,011,500	1,968,712	254,986	487,593	300,203
1986	3,239,400	2,114,621	272,735	526,436	325,638
1987	3,459,600	2,247,158	294,092	562,814	355,505
1988	3,714,100	2,356,483	341,893	607,766	407,977
1989	4,055,600	2,522,125	393,303	683,367	456,803
1990	4,350,300	2,670,234	405,320	743,382	531,407
1991	4,535,600	2,728,472	424,129[c]	792,535	590,442
1992	4,762,600	2,811,611	441,781[c]	850,566	658,601
1993	4,944,000	2,903,061	455,500[c]	909,381	676,100
1994	5,141,300	2,981,022	479,800	990,147	690,371
1995	5,342,900	3,077,861	507,044	1,078,542	679,421
1996	5,490,700	3,164,996	518,492	1,127,528	679,733
1997	5,734,900	3,296,513[d]	567,079	1,176,564	694,787
1998	6,134,200	3,670,441[d]	592,462	1,224,469	696,385
1999	6,340,800	3,779,922[d]	605,943	1,287,172	714,457
2000	6,445,100	3,826,209	621,149	1,316,333	723,898
2001	6,581,700	3,931,731	631,240	1,330,007	732,333
2002	6,758,800	4,024,067	665,475	1,367,547	750,934
2003	6,924,500	4,120,012	691,301	1,390,279	769,925
2004	6,995,000	4,143,792	713,990	1,421,345	771,852
2005	7,045,100	4,166,757	740,770	1,448,344	780,616
2006	7,176,000	4,215,361	759,717	1,492,973	799,875
2007[e]	7,267,500	4,234,471	773,341	1,517,867	821,177
2008[e]	7,274,600	4,244,046	777,852	1,522,834	824,834
2009	7,225,800	4,203,967	760,400[f]	1,524,513	819,308
Average annual percent change 2000 to 2008	1.5%	1.3%	3.0%	1.8%	1.6%

Note: Counts for probation, prison, and parole populations are for December 31 of each year; jail population counts are for June 30 of each year. Counts of adults held in jail facilities for 1993 and 1994 were estimated and rounded to the nearest 100. Data for jail and prison are for inmates under custody and include those held in private facilities and may include a small number of juveniles in the six States that have combined jail-prison systems. Totals for 1998-2004 exclude probationers held in jail or prison. Beginning in 2005, totals exclude probationers and parolees held in jail or prison. These data have been revised by the Source based on the most recently reported counts and may differ from previous editions of SOURCEBOOK. For information on methodology and explanatory notes, see Appendix 15.

[a]Some offenders have multiple correctional statuses. Beginning in 2005, the data were adjusted to account for multiple statuses. For this reason and because the totals are rounded to the nearest 100, detail will not sum to total.
[b]Estimated.
[c]Includes an unknown number of persons supervised outside jail facilities.
[d]Coverage of probation agencies was expanded. For counts based on the same reporting agencies, use 3,266,837 in 1997 (to compare with 1996); 3,417,613 in 1998 (to compare with 1997); and 3,772,773 in 1999 (to compare with 1998).
[e]Includes population counts estimated by the Source because some States were unable to provide data.
[f]In 2009, counts were revised to include adult only jail counts and therefore may not be comparable to earlier data.

Source: U.S. Department of Justice, Bureau of Justice Statistics, *Correctional Populations in the United States, 1994*, NCJ-160091, Table 1.1; *1995*, NCJ-163916, Table 1.1; *2009*, Bulletin NCJ 231681, Table 1 (Washington, DC: U.S. Department of Justice); U.S. Department of Justice, Bureau of Justice Statistics, *Probation and Parole in 1999*, Press Release NCJ 183508 (Washington, DC: U.S. Department of Justice, July 2000), p. 3, Table 1; U.S. Department of Justice, Bureau of Justice Statistics, *Probation and Parole in the United States, 2002*, Bulletin NCJ 201135, p. 1; *2004*, Bulletin NCJ 210676, p. 1; *2008*, Bulletin NCJ 228230, p. 3 (Washington, DC: U.S. Department of Justice); and data provided by the U.S. Department of Justice, Bureau of Justice Statistics. Table adapted by SOURCEBOOK staff.

FIGURE 11-1. Sourcebook of criminal justice statistics online.

Source: Maquire, Katleen. ed. Sourcebook of Criminal Justice Statistics, Table 6.1.2009. Adults on probation, in jail or prison, and on parole, United States, 1980–2009. Retrieved from http://www.albany.edu/sourcebook/pdf/t612009.pdf.

prison terms, and being biased against African Americans. These sentences bar any judicial discretion, can often exclude parole/probation, and sometimes do not take into account any good time behavior credits acquired. One of the major flaws with determinate sentences is the automatic release of prisoners. This is extremely problematic because they do not have to prove they are fit to be in society, do not have to come before the parole board, show any remorse, or improve themselves in any way. Sometimes, a parole board will impose additional postincarceration stipulations or supervision. This most often occurs with inmates convicted of sexual crimes.

Three-Strikes Law

The three-strikes law, an extremely harsh but popular determinate sentence in some states, provides for a significantly longer prison term for any offender convicted of three felonies. It varies by state but most often the statute imposes a 25 years–to-life sentence for a third serious or violent felony.

In some states such as California, the three felonies do not even have to all be violent crimes, causing many offenders to be locked up for a possible life sentence for nonviolent felony offenses, such as writing bad checks. Another problem with three-strikes in California is that there is no consideration given if a large amount of time has passed between a first and second strike and can include convictions that occurred while the offender was still a juvenile. The first woman prosecuted under three-strikes was arrested for a $20 cocaine purchase, which occurred 14 years after her second strike (Walker, 2011, p. 167). Also, California has different stipulations for a second strike and a third strike. A second strike in California equates to doubling the sentence for an offender previously convicted of a felony that was designated a "strikeable" offense, and the third strike stipulation requires life in prison with no parole eligibility before 25 years has been served (p. 167). Some states, such as Washington, utilize a two-strike philosophy. These enacted statutes require a life sentence for two specific violent felonies, but California's is still the toughest and most expansive.

The idea behind three-strikes is to keep habitual offenders locked up for much longer periods of time, which lawmakers believe will help reduce recidivism rates. Despite enacting this law, recidivism rates have not declined, while the U.S. prison population continues to grow. During the significant reduction in violent crimes in the 1990s, states that did not use three-strikes experienced greater reductions than those states that did (Greenwood et al., 1998). With this enormous growth, we are seeing more and more individuals convicted of nonviolent offenses, such as drug possession, being locked up for lengthy sentences due to many states' three-strikes legislation. Greenwood et al. (1994) found that under California's three-strikes law, 192 offenders were sentenced for marijuana possession for second and third strikes, compared to 40 murderers, 25 rapists, and 24 kidnappers. Despite being the nation's toughest determinate sentencing law, it is clear that it is not providing the results originally intended.

CAPITAL PUNISHMENT

Arguably the most controversial and severe sentencing model or philosophy in the United States is the use of capital punishment. The United States is the only Westernized country that continues to use capital punishment. States have the right to decide on its use, with 34 states having it as a punishment option. In 1972, the United States Supreme Court ruled in *Furman v. Georgia* that capital punishment violated the Eighth Amendment prohibition on cruel and unusual punishment due to the potentially arbitrary way it was imposed, and the practice was halted across the country.

Four years later, *Gregg v. Georgia* (1976) reinstated capital punishment and attempted to fix the bias problems in its use; the Court stated that jurors must consider aggravating circumstances (e.g., defendant tortured the victim; defendant had a prior record) and mitigating circumstances (e.g., defendant was abused as a child; defendant had no criminal record) during the sentencing portion of the trial. In the *Gregg* case, they also added that a capital trial must occur in two phases: the first phase to determine guilt or innocence, and the second phase to determine punishment, be it life in prison or death. In other notable Supreme Court cases relating to capital punishment, *Roper v. Simmons* (2005) ruled that an individual must be at least 18 years old at the time of the crime to be sentenced to death, and *Atkins v. Virginia* (2002) banned states from executing mentally ill offenders.

It is extremely important to look at how the death penalty is administered because it represents a microcosm of underlying problems in the criminal justice system as a whole, such as racial and class biases. Obviously, the death penalty is the ultimate punishment in the United States that can only be handed down for a capital murder conviction. The result is that only a miniscule percentage of offenders receive this sentence. Although the Supreme Court reinstated the death penalty with the *Gregg* decision, and executions resumed in 1977, it was not until the 1980s that it became a more commonly used sentencing option. Lethal injection is the primary method used in executing capital offenders.

Currently, the popularity of capital punishment has declined because of numerous men on death row being found innocent. The only point supporters and those in opposition to capital punishment agree on is that they are both against convicting, sentencing, and executing innocent people. According to the Death Penalty Information Center, between 1973 and 1999, there was an average of 3.1 exonerations per year, but between 2000 and 2007, there was an average of 5 exonerations a year.

The biggest argument against the death penalty is the use of discretion and racial bias, with 4 out of 10 inmates on death row being African Americans, while that group accounts for only approximately 12% of the U.S. population (Costanzo, 2007). A recent study on race and murder in California found that those who killed whites were three times more likely to receive the death penalty than offenders who killed blacks, and over four times more likely than those who killed Latinos (Pierce & Radelet, 2005).

Next, considering the severity and irreversible nature of capital punishment, it does not seem to carry the deterrent effect some have theorized it should have, see **Figure 11-2**. The Death Penalty Information Center used 2009 FBI Uniform Crime Reports to show that while the South accounted for 80% of all executions in the United States, they also had the highest murder rate; the Northeast, which had the lowest murder rates in the country, accounts for less than 1% of all executions. A *Los Angeles Times* article from 2005 found that taxpayers in California spent over $250 million on each execution the state had conducted, and the death penalty system in that state cost the citizens $114 each year more than the cost of a life in prison without possibility of parole. Those against capital punishment find it morally wrong to kill people just to show that killing is wrong and think that it is just a vehicle for misplaced vengeance (Amnesty International, 2011).

On the other side, at least four major arguments are commonly made in favor of the death penalty: (1) public support, (2) deterrence, (3) retribution, (4) cost-effectiveness (Riedel & Welsh, 2011, p. 318). First, public support for the death penalty has always remained relatively high. Since 2005, support for capital punishment has not dropped below 64%, and a Gallup Poll examining capital punishment trends between 2001 and 2010 also shows that support (Newport, 2010) (see **Figure 11-3**). Next, the underlying assumption for supporters is that the threat of execution will prevent someone from committing murder—the deterrence theory. The problem with this argument is that

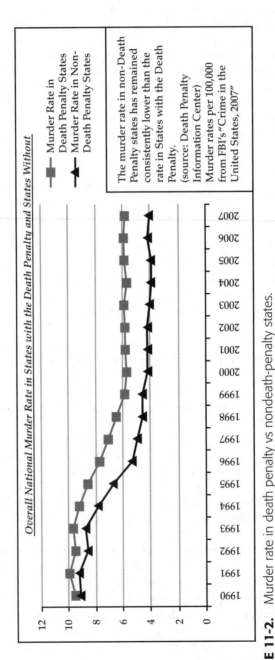

FIGURE 11-2. Murder rate in death penalty vs nondeath-penalty states.

Source: Amnesty International. (2011). Overall national murder rate in states with the death penalty and states without. Retrieved from http://www.amnestyusa.org/our-work/issues/death-penalty/us-death-penalty-facts/the-death-penalty-and-deterrence.

Are you in favor of the death penalty for a person convicted of murder?

2001–2010 trends from Gallup poll crime survey, conducted each October

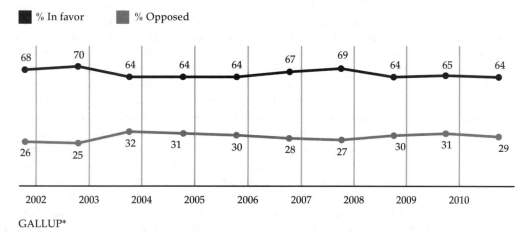

GALLUP*

FIGURE 11-3. Gallup poll on death penalty opinions.
Source: Newport, F. (2010, November 8). In U.S., 64% support death penalty in cases of murder: Half say death penalty not imposed often enough. Gallup. Retrieved from http://www.gallup.com/poll/144284/support-death-penalty-cases-murder.aspx.

it assumes criminals are rational when they commit crime. If this were the case, we would not need the different levels of homicide we have on the books, such as second degree murder, involuntary or voluntary manslaughter, or crimes of passion. Last, another general assumption is that executing someone is cheaper than locking them up for life. With the bifurcated (two-part) trial, careful jury selection, and mandatory process, a capital murder trial is significantly more expensive than keeping someone in prison for life.

INTERMEDIATE SANCTIONS

Intermediate sanctions is a punishment option that falls between probation and prison. The front end, by design, is less punitive and focuses on rehabilitation and restitution as the primary goals. A variety of punishments are available under intermediate sanctions. A defendant who receives an intermediate sanction sentence avoids the harsher prison term, but is faced with a tougher sentence than a defendant placed on traditional probation. In prison, rehabilitation program funding has been cut to almost zero, while a traditional probation sentence can be seen as too lenient. A desirable aspect of intermediate sanctions is that it does meet the proportionality requirement of our just deserts sentencing philosophy (Morris & Tonry, 1990).

Throughout the history of our punishment and sentencing philosophies, rehabilitation theory has received significant support from both social service providers and various aspects of the justice system. However, each peak of support seems to have been followed by a trough of backlash, prison overcrowding, budgetary crises, and then renewed support again (Banks & Gottfredson, 2003). As previously mentioned, the concept of rehabilitation lost its luster in the 1970s, and within the next several years the criminal justice system saw sweeping changes to policies and a shift back to strict deterrence and incapacitation (Banks & Gottfredson, 2003).

Sociologist Jeffrey Ulmer (2001) looked at intermediate sanctions and found that the sentences were more structured and involved more treatment and surveillance than the typical probation sentences. Furthermore, Ulmer concluded that intermediate sanctions have become increasingly popular because they maintain our "get tough on crime" approach while still helping solve the massive prison overcrowding problem we are currently facing. Intermediate sanctions come in many forms. Electronic monitoring, which can include house arrest, intensive program supervision, drug courts, DWI courts, supervised work programs, and substance abuse treatment are some of the most used forms of intermediate sanctions, and we see them used in those offenders who are on parole as well.

Not only do intermediate sanctions have the extremely important cost-saving advantage as opposed to a prison sentence, they can help reduce the stigmatization that accompanies being in prison. The offender can maintain ties in the community while still paying his or her debt to society and getting the needed rehabilitation at the same time. For example, offenders sent to drug court are able to deal with the underlying issues associated with substance abuse, get treatment for the addiction, and gain skills and knowledge on how to stay clean. Drug courts map out individualized plans for each offender, which can be very strict and comprehensive, and involve numerous weekly meetings, random drug tests, and counseling sessions to name a few requirements. Electronic monitoring is a very efficient way to keep track of people in real time and appears very advantageous for people convicted of sexual offenses. Electronic monitoring will also be discussed in more depth in the Chapter 13. All the intermediate sanctions require the offender to complete all the assigned stipulations, and if they do not a prison or jail sentence usually follows.

Since the majority of our overcrowded prisons are filled with nonviolent offenders, usually convicted of lower level drug offenses, it makes sense to offer this opportunity for these types of offenders. Also, intermediate sanctions are more often applied to repeat violators than to one-time violators (Harris, Petersen, & Rapoza, 2001). Offenders convicted of violent crime are generally not eligible for an intermediate sanction sentence.

Intermediate sanctions are based on labeling, social control, and differential association theories. John Braithwaite's (1989) concept of shaming is classified into two types: reintegrative and stigmatized. Reintegrative shaming is a powerful groundwork for the use of intermediate sanctions because it allows the community to assist in the punishment but also reaccept the reformed offender back into their community. According to Makkai & Braithwaite (1994), the key factors in reintegrative shaming include:

1. Disapproval while sustaining a relationship of respect
2. Ceremonies to certify deviance terminated by ceremonies to decertify deviance
3. Disapproval of the evil of the deed without labeling the person as evil
4. Not allowing deviance to become a master status trait

In terms of intermediate sanctions, reintegrative shaming is based on the idea that we need to reduce the use of prison sentences and instead rely on community service-based sentences. It takes into account the public and criminal justice system's need to punish criminals but helps reduce the stigma of convictions and maintains open lines of communication within the community. Prison sentences can often do more harm than good, leading to increased criminality, psychological and emotional issues, and social stigmatization associated with incarceration. In contrast, intermediate sanctions help restore social bonds, which can make the offender less likely to engage in criminal activity, and helps reduce the revolving door effect in the criminal justice system.

How far is too far in terms of shaming? Miethe, Lu, & Reese (2000) examined reintegrative shaming and recidivism risks in drug courts with some surprising results. Miethe et al. found that the drug court program was more stigmatizing than the conventional courts and that it did not focus enough on reintegration in its approach to punishment. This stigmatizing effect was seen in hostile attitudes toward the drug court participants who had noncompliance issues, which degraded them in a public setting, and the program gave only a token of recognition to the defendants' efforts to successfully complete the program (p. 536).

Although intermediate sanctions are still a relatively new type of punishment, they seem promising in many respects. Diverting first-time, low-level, nonviolent offenders out of prison increases their chances of maintaining ties with the community and receiving treatment they otherwise would not be getting. Also, the reduction in prisoners in an already overcrowded, deteriorating system makes intermediate sanction sentences much more cost effective, and therefore very appealing.

Drug Courts

The most used type of intermediate sanction, drug courts, has become very successful and is serving as a model for other types of problem-solving courts. The Office of National Drug Control Policy (2004) refers to drug courts as alternatives to incarceration that coerce drug offenders into abstaining from drug use by escalating sanctions, requiring mandatory drug testing and treatment, and by providing strong aftercare programs. Even a brief glance at the literature on drug courts reveals that the primary goal of these programs is to divert offenders from prison into treatment due to prison overcrowding. State prisons are not the only correctional facilities facing massive drug overcrowding issues; federal court drug cases nearly tripled in number between 1984 and 1999 from 11,854 to 29,306 (Scalia, 2001). The Office of National Drug Control Policy estimates that expansion of drug court programs could reduce the nation's prison population by 250,000 inmates within 5 years (Hughes, 2004). The advancement and improvement of drug courts can continue to help reduce prison populations while helping drug offenders actually deal with their substance abuse problems and the underlying issues contributing to their addictions, in addition to helping the community understand the importance of drug addiction and its relation to crime.

The drug court movement began in the 1980s as the criminal justice system was trying to combat an alleged epidemic of drug use and to help relieve the massive prison overcrowding facing the United States (Goldkamp, 2001). After many years of just incarcerating drug offenders with no success, probation officers, judges, and researchers began to examine addiction differently, and the need to cure drug addiction became a top priority (Gottfredson, Najaka, & Kearley, 2003). With the cost of operating, constructing, and maintaining prisons and jails on the rise, drug courts seemed like a viable option. Between 1980 and 1996, that cost rose from $7 billion to $38 billion (Belenko, 1998).

Miami, Florida (Dade County) pioneered the first drug courts due to their overwhelming increase in drug-related offenses throughout the 1980s (Goldkamp, 2001). The outdated punishment of mandatory minimums, intensive probation, and court-imposed special conditions did not address the main problems facing these offenders, namely, their drug addictions (Banks & Gottfredson, 2003). The traditional system of treating drug addiction within the criminal justice system obviously was not working well. On the other hand, drug courts give judges something constructive and hopefully rehabilitative to do with drug-addicted offenders other than putting them in jail or prison or returning them to the streets with little or no supervision (Anderson, 1998).

Drug treatment courts deal with the issue of rehabilitation, but there are still offenders who continue to use while in the program, drop out, or resume drug use once the program is completed

(Banks & Gottfredson, 2003). However, policy makers and researchers have expressed confidence in the power of sanctions to force treatment (Maxwell, 2000).

According to Belenko (1998), the public and policymakers find drug courts attractive for many reasons. First, drug court programs offer more intensive community supervision than standard probation. Second, the drug court process tends to treat drug cases more seriously and rigorously than other types of programs. Offenders are held to a higher degree of accountability for violations of their probation while in drug court (Gottfredson & Exum, 2002), which will be discussed further in the graduated sanctions discussion. Next, drug courts increase cooperation among community treatment providers, which concurrently reduces the duplication of services and taxpayer expense because of the collaboration. In other words, they are being punished and rehabilitated at the same time, a component sorely lacking in prison. Last, drug courts free criminal courts from hearing drug cases, allowing them to deal with more serious issues, such as violent felony charges. The positive effects of the drug court movement may turn out to be one of the major criminal justice policy reforms implemented in the latter part of the 20th century (Goldkamp, 2001). Wolfe and Guydish (2002) found drug court retention rates of 65–85%, a reduction in drug use while in drug court, and lower rearrest rates that dropped 2–20% for participants in drug court.

Day Reporting

Another type of intermediate sanction that has seen success is day reporting. Day reporting requires offenders to come to an assigned facility every day or on a designated regular basis for a specified length of time to participate in activities such as counseling, job training, social skills training, or various other types of treatment programs (Clarke, 1994). This rehabilitative aspect in day reporting is commonplace throughout other intermediate sanctions. Marciniak (1999) examined the 1994 North Carolina Structured Sentencing Act, which led to an increased use of intermediate sanctions and looked at day reporting specifically. She found that retention rates for the program were low but also found that certain offender characteristics affected the likelihood of termination from the day reporting center. Gender, race, and age did not appear to affect termination rates, while being employed and having more years of education did seem to be significant predictors of success (Marciniak, 1999). Despite this particular program in North Carolina having higher termination rates than other day reporting centers, we now know what types of offenders are more likely to cause problems and which are more likely to succeed.

Electronic Monitoring

Electronic monitoring is often used in conjunction with other programs or sentences, such as intensive community supervision, tracking of offenders awaiting trial, and as part of house arrest/home confinement. Electronic monitoring is another popular intermediate sanction because while it keeps the offender out of the overcrowded prisons and jails, it still has the retribution component without the financial and social costs of actually being in prison, including: (1) satisfying the demand for punishment, (2) providing a deterrent effect, and (3) providing for community protection (Abadinsky, 2003).

Shock Programs—Shock Probation/Incarceration/Boot Camps

Shock programs are part of a relatively new approach intended to frighten offenders by instilling uncertainty about whether they will be released and, if so, when (Masters et al., 2011). The shock concept has been effective in the need for social control, because the offenders sentenced to shock incarceration would have been placed on standard probation if shock incarceration did not exist (Petersen & Palumbo, 1997). Shock programs that will be discussed include a probation/incarceration combination and a probation sentence that can involve boot camp participation.

Shock probation/incarceration is an intermediate sanction that combines a probation sentence with short-term incarceration. Shock probation originally started in Ohio, and many other states adopted the idea. In Texas in 1977, shock probation was introduced as a rehabilitation method in which an offender is given a sample of prison and then placed on probation for the remainder of the sentence (Abadinsky, 2003). The time spent in prison is generally between 30 and 120 days and is mostly given to younger adult offenders or juveniles. The research is mixed on whether or not shock probation reduces recidivism and has long-lasting effects on the offender.

Another type of shock program is a boot camp program, sometimes also referred to as shock incarceration. Typically reserved for juvenile offenders, boot camps use the military model of basic training: rigid style, rigid rules, and behavior modification to command the attention and respect of these offenders (Masters et al., 2011). Public sentiment indicates that boot camps are popular because they are still providing the punishment aspect the community desires while keeping young people out of the correctional system. Similarly to shock probation, boot camps appear to be no more effective than traditional probation sentences or programs in reducing recidivism (MacKenzie, Gover, Armstrong, and Mitchell, 2001; MacKenzie & Parent, 1991; Dickey, 1994; Meade & Steiner, 2010). Tyler, Darville, and Stalnaker (2001) suggest providing a better aftercare component in boot camp programs to help reduce recidivism. Also, boot camps have come under enormous scrutiny due to the recent deaths of juveniles while at boot camp facilities. Martin Lee Anderson, 14 years old, died on January 6, 2006 while at a boot camp in Florida. Video surveillance showed guards kicking and beating him. This brought national attention to boot camps and caused Florida to close down all boot camps for juvenile offenders after their investigation was concluded (CBS News, 2010).

REINTEGRATIVE SANCTIONS

Intermediate and reintegrative sanctions are, by design, less punitive and more diversionary on the front end, while focusing on rehabilitation as the primary goal. Many argue that even first-time offenders should be punished more severely, but the fact is that most first-time offenders will not reoffend, and their crimes are generally less serious and nonviolent. Upon committing the first offense, the system should ensure that first-time offenders get the full rehabilitative measures needed to remain out of the system in the future. Also, a prison sentence can do more harm than good in many cases, leading to the stigma of being in prison and the additional invisible consequences that come along with it, such as losing voting rights after a felony conviction and restriction on access to public welfare and housing subsidies. Some researchers have suggested that the laws and policies once enacted to protect society might actually contribute to higher rates of crime and exacerbate the criminal problems they were intended to address (Petersilia, 2003). The criminals who habitually reoffend will continue to filter through the system and then can be given more punitive sanctions. Reintegrative sanctions include stigma, restorative justice, and various types of problem-solving courts, such as mental health courts, DWI courts, and domestic violence courts.

Restorative justice is a sentencing philosophy that promotes reparation over retribution (Lubitz & Ross, 2001) and helps divert offenders away from the formal criminal justice process commonly used with juvenile offenders. The concept behind restorative justice is to ensure the community's safety while still seeking a joint resolution between the offender and the victim. According to the National Institute of Justice, restorative justice recognizes that a crime has been committed but uses a more subjective understanding of the harm done and the unique circumstances of the offender (Lubitz & Ross, 2001). This approach individualizes each punishment and makes it fit the specific crime committed and avoids using a "one-size-fits-all" sentencing approach. By using the restorative justice framework and tailoring each punishment to fit the individual, distrust in the criminal justice system and disproportionality among sentences can be reduced.

Stigmatization is conceptually similar to restorative justice. Derived from the labeling perspective and the other type of shaming, stigmatization relies on labeling the offender as a criminal; in essence, letting society know this person did something wrong. Shaming that takes the form of stigmatization, in contrast to reintegrative shaming, emphasizes the labeling of the offender as deviant and pays little attention to delabeling in order to signify forgiveness and reintegration (Miethe et al., 2000, p. 528). This can cause the offender to internalize their new, negative label and create conditions in which the offender becomes an outsider, and then cannot recover from this position.

How the individual responds to the stigma is the most important question. Is he or she going to internalize the new label that has been placed on him or her, or is the individual going to respond positively, attempt to make amends, and get back on the straight and narrow? Also, does social class, other demographic characteristics, or simply the effects of being labeled contribute to recidivism one way or the other? It is reasonable to conclude that how one responds to stigmatization is strongly associated with social class and relative powerlessness (Beirne & Messerschmidt, 2010)?

Chiricos, Barrick, Bales, and Bontrager (2007) found that one of two things can happen with stigmatization: the more socially advantaged offenders have more to lose from a criminal label while recidivists are less disadvantaged by a former label. Hirshfield (2008) found that disadvantaged youth in inner-city Chicago experienced no stigmatizing consequences from contact with the criminal justice system. This could be due to the fact that people in those neighborhoods with arrests records, convictions, currently serving time, or under some other form of criminal justice control are more commonplace than in other communities. These findings are quite alarming, especially if juveniles no longer feel the negative effects of the stigma of being a criminal. Without those effects, they will not feel the need to change their behavior or assume they are doing something wrong because "everyone" in their community is doing it.

Risk and Resiliency Factors for Adults

With the enormous number of men and women under some form of criminal justice control, it is important to examine what factors put offenders at risk for recidivism and what factors help them stay out of trouble. According to the Bureau of Justice Statistics, at the end of 2008, the United States had approximately 5.1 million adults under some form of community supervision, with 84% of those on a probation sentence. In the 1970s, there was another shift in the probation arena, with a new focus on agency resources and structure, followed by a shift in the 1980s in which caseloads became dominated by risk classifications. In terms of returning prisoners, research shows that finding employment and housing are the main success factors for offenders once released (Petersilia, 2003). This will be examined more thoroughly in Chapter 13.

Regarding those on probation/intermediate sanctions sentences, there is a need for a strong risk classification instrument. The risk/needs concept developed in Wisconsin has been adopted by most jurisdictions and the National Institute of Corrections (Abadinsky, 2003). The goal behind the risk/needs assessment is to predict the successes or failures of probationers and parolees. For the purposes of this discussion we will be focusing on probationers.

With a growing number of offenders being placed on community corrections, it is important for these organizations to find evidence-based practices to assist in guiding their decision making, effective offender supervision strategies, and risk assessments. Evidence-based principles that have been developed through stringent scientific research include three basic considerations: (1) risk principle, (2) need principle, and (3) treatment principle. These three primary considerations coincide with secondary issues such as responsivity factors, well-trained staff members, appropriate monitoring strategies, and consistent quality assurance (Latessa, 2006). The size of a probation officer's caseload has always been a main concern in how effective these community correction sentences can be in terms of reducing recidivism.

Intensive supervision programs (ISPs) were originally developed to look at caseload sizes and were once thought to be an optimal approach for supervising high-risk offenders because the offenders would get extra attention, the community would be safer, and supervisors would be more available to assist high-risk offenders in completing their sentences (Banks et al., 1977). This approach eventually also became a very effective way to supervise prisoners in the community and thus reduce the pressures from prison overcrowding and budgetary shortfalls. The early ISPs coincided with the shift in sentencing in the late 1970s and early 1980s that focused on deterrence and incapacitation, virtually omitting the rehabilitation ideal. These early ISP caseloads have extremely high failure rates because additional monitoring led officers to detect violations at higher rates, including technical violations of supervision (e.g., being late or missing a meeting with your probation officer) (Petersilia, Turner, & Deschenes, 1992). Then the American Probation and Parole Association (APPA) developed an ISP model that integrated more rehabilitation and treatment components into the traditional risk-control strategies. By including these treatment-oriented components, this more balanced approach led to higher success rates and lasting changes in the offender, but there were no significant differences in recidivism rates among those offenders under regular supervision versus ISP (Fulton, Latessa, Stichman, & Travis, 1997).

Despite not seeing the reduction in recidivism rates, ISPs have helped create new models to be implemented within community supervision. Some of these include specialized caseloads based on offender needs, such as sex compulsions, mental illness, domestic abuse, and substance abuse; and specialized surveillance and field models. In 2008, Klein, Wilson, Crowe, and DeMichele found that the special domestic violence probation supervision program in Rhode Island showed significantly lower recidivism rates as opposed to those for domestic batterers who were placed under traditional probation supervision. The new norm includes having a maximum caseload burden for dealing with sexual offenders that allocates the greatest amount of resources, treatment, time, and surveillance for each offender. This concept has gained notable popularity due to empirical research showing that offenders on a community corrections sentence are more likely to have their sentence revoked if they have a mental illness than offenders who do not suffer from a mental illness (Dauphinot, 1996). Even more recently a new shift has emerged, not just focused on caseload sizes but also on improving community supervision efforts and increasing rapport between officers and offenders.

There have been several other evidence-based principles shown to work effectively in community supervision. Motivational interviewing techniques used by counselors helping those undergoing drug or alcohol treatment have also found success in community corrections. These motivational techniques improve the quality of interactions between officer and offender (Taxman, Shepherson, & Byrne, 2004; Walters, Clark, Gingerich, & Meltzer, 2007), while a confrontational style of counseling seems to limit effectiveness (Miller & Rollnick, 2002; Hubble, Duncan, & Miller, 1999). If proper training is implemented, motivational interviewing can be an important evidence-based principle associated with successful completion of supervision. A properly trained staff that understands how to conduct and successfully use these practices is crucial to their success. The research on rapport and successful outcomes shows that this evidence-based practice works when all the pieces are successfully merged (Mair & May, 1997; Springer, Applegate, Smith, & Sitren, 2009; Ireland & Berg, 2008; Taxman, 2008).

For this approach to work, it is imperative to first assign an offender to the correct caseload. As aforementioned, specialized caseloads have become increasingly common, most significantly with sexual offenders, but also for those with substance abuse problems. Next, special conditions may be placed on the offender. For example, a sexual offender may not be allowed to go within a specified range of playgrounds or schools, or drug offenders may be required to undergo regular drug testing. Then, the offender must be followed up consistently to ensure all conditions are being met.

Graduated Sanctions

With more and more offenders being placed on some type of community correction, making sure that these programs are properly designed and implemented is of utmost importance. With the correct design and implementation, it is more likely that offenders will comply, succeed, and stay out of the criminal justice system once they complete their sentences. Graduated sanctions are structured, incremental responses to noncompliant behavior of probationers while they are under supervision (Taxman, Soule & Gelb, 1999, p. 183). The concept of graduated sanctions gives probation officers more discretion and allows them to act quickly with noncompliant probationers. The probation officer can increase restrictions on the probationer, such as increased reporting, or go as far as putting them in jail for a few days. Graduated sanctions can be extremely effective because they provide swift and certain punishment for offenders, and therefore increased accountability. This deterrent effect can prevent future noncompliance.

It is important to note that graduated sanctions are not intermediate sanctions, but can be used simultaneously with them. For example, drug courts are an effective intermediate sanction that has pioneered the use of graduated sanctions as a response to those who commit noncompliant acts while in drug court (Taxman et al., 1999). The typical noncompliant acts in drug court are testing positive for drugs or failing to attend scheduled meetings. To deal with those offenders, a graduated sanction is placed upon them as opposed to immediately revoking their probation and sending them to jail or prison. Once an offender is given a graduated sanction, his or her increased level of supervision goes up, and he or she could also be given stricter requirements in order to fulfill the sentence, such as increasing drugs tests in drug court. By using incremental sanctions or increased supervision, offenders who have substance abuse problems can potentially get the help they need and would not get it if they were incarcerated. Harrell and Roman (2001) found evidence of the impact of graduated sanctions on reducing drug use. The offenders who participated in their study were significantly less likely to use drugs prior to sentencing and during the following year; in addition they were significantly less likely to be rearrested and had fewer arrests (Harrell & Roman, 2001).

Graduated sanctions appear to be the most successful in drug courts, but that is simply because they are the largest type of problem-solving court in the United States, and drug offenders account for a significant portion of those arrested each year. As mentioned previously, the use of graduated sanctions in drug courts is based on deterrence theory, which specifies that behavior is a product of the perceived costs and benefits associated with the behavior (Lindquist, Krebs, & Lattimore, 2006, pp. 119–120). The reasoning behind graduated sanctions—in drug courts in this case—is that the costs will outweigh the potential benefits of any wrongdoing, since offenders know that sanctions will be handed down. Marlowe and Kirby (1999) have identified several characteristics of effective sanctions:

1. The expectations must be clear and the sanction predictable.
2. The appropriate behavior must be achievable and the sanction controllable.
3. The infraction must be detected.
4. Every infraction must be met with a sanction.
5. The sanction should be delivered immediately after the infraction.
6. The sanction must be of sufficient intensity, although ultimately a maximum upper limit will be reached in a graduated sanction program.

Roman and Harrell (2001) found another significant benefit to using this type of punishment for drug offenders versus using a standard prison sentence—saving money. Their cost-benefit analysis found a two-dollar savings for every dollar spent by using the graduated sanction program implemented in Washington, DC. Ultimately, graduated sanctions have the ability to deter and prevent future crimes without increasing the prison population. Another key benefit of graduated sanctions is that drug courts, being more treatment oriented than traditional courts, will try to tailor the sanction to each individual as opposed to a "one-size-fits-all" approach, while also identifying many more types of behaviors that could potentially result in a sanction (Lindquist et al., 2006). Maxwell (2000) examined the effects of the use of threats of sanctions in court-ordered drug treatment programs. She found that both legal status and legal pressure had significant independent effects on retention, but one was not conditional on the other (p. 559); meaning that the greater perceived threat increased offenders' retention rates.

SUMMARY

Issues in sentencing philosophies and ideas can take many forms but all retain priority in the criminal justice system in order to attempt to prevent crime, and deter and rehabilitate those who do come in contact with the system. How we choose to punish, rehabilitate, and socialize offenders can have broad implications for the functioning of the justice system and for public safety. Sentencing philosophies can be felt throughout communities, can influence public policy and sentiment, and affect the familial structure and obligations of offenders and their families. Even with decades of research conducted, we still see policy debates on the most effective and efficient ways to sentence and ultimately punish those who break the law. This chapter provides a glimpse into the various types of punishment and sentencing, while providing ample evidence for examining alternatives to prison and punishment.

KEY TERMS

Sentencing philosophies
Determinate sentencing
Indeterminate sentencing

Intermediate sanctions
Probation
Drug courts
Rehabilitation
Prison overcrowding
Restorative justice
Graduated sanctions
Reintegrative shaming
Stigmatization
Three-strikes law
Capital punishment
Shock probation
Boot camps

DISCUSSION QUESTIONS

1. What is the current sentencing philosophy the United States is using and why did we switch?
2. What is the difference between determinate sentencing and indeterminate sentencing?
3. What is the difference between intermediate sanctions and a traditional probation sentence?
4. What are the main aspects of restorative justice and how does it attempt to punish and rehabilitate the offender at the same time?
5. What is the difference between reintegrative shaming and stigmatization?
6. What is the main purpose behind using graduated sanctions?
7. Why were drug courts invented?

REFERENCES

Abadinsky, H. (2003). *Probation and parole: Theory and practice* (8th ed.). Upper Saddle River, NJ: Prentice Hall Publishing.

Amnesty International. (2011). Overall national murder rate in states with the death penalty and states without. Retrieved from http://www.amnestyusa.org/our-work/issues/death-penalty/us-death-penalty-facts/the-death-penalty-and-deterrence.

Anderson, D. (1998). *Sensible justice: Alternatives to prison*. New York, NY: The New Press.

Atkins v. Virginia. 536 U.S. 304 (2002).

Banks, D., & Gottfredson, D. (2003). The effect of drug treatment and supervision on time to rearrest among drug court participants. *Journal of Drug Issues, 33*(2), 385–413.

Banks, J., Porter, A., Rardin, R., Sider, R., & Unger, V. (1977). Evaluation of intensive special probation projects: Phase 1 report (Grant No. NI-99-0045). Washington, DC: U.S. Department of Justice.

Beirne, P., & Messerschmidt, J. (2010). *Criminology: A sociological approach* (5th ed.). New York, NY: Oxford University Press.

Belenko, S. (1998). Fighting crime by substance abuse. *Issues in Science and Technology, 15*(1), 53–61.

Braithwaite, J. (1989). *Crime, shame, and reintegration*. Cambridge, UK: Cambridge University Press.

Bureau of Justice Statistics, Office of Justice Programs. Retrieved from http://bjs.ojp.usdoj.gov/index.cfm?ty=tp&tid=15 on April 1, 2011.

Carlsmith, K., Darley, J., & Robinson, P. (2002). Why do we punish? Deterrence and just deserts as motives for punishment. *Journal of Personality and Social Psychology, 83*(2), 284–299.

CBS News (2010, April 16). Florida juvenile boot camp death: No charges. Retrieved from http://www.cbsnews.com/stories/2010/04/16/national/main6402852.shtml.

Chiricos, T., Barrick, K., Bales, W., & Bontrager, S. (2007). The labeling of convicted felons and its consequence for recidivism. *Criminology, 45*(3), 547–581.

Clarke, S. (1994). 1994 supplement to law of sentencing, probation, and parole in North Carolina: The structured sentencing act of related legislation, 1993–94. Chapel Hill, NC: Institute of Government, The University of North Carolina at Chapel Hill.

Costanzo, M. (1997). *Just revenge: Costs and consequences of the death penalty.* New York, NY: Saint Martin's Press.

Dauphinot, L. (1996). The efficacy of community correctional supervision for offenders with severe mental illness. (Unpublished doctoral dissertation). Department of Psychology, University of Texas at Austin.

Death Penalty Information Center. (2011). http://www.deathpenaltyinfo.org/documents/FactSheet.pdf.

Dickey, W. (1994). Evaluating boot camp prisons. In *Campaign for an effective crime policy.* Washington, DC: U.S. Government Printing Office.

Fulton, B., Latessa, E., Stichman, A., & Travis, L. (1997). The state of ISP: Research and policy implications. *Federal Probation, 61*(4), 65–75.

Furman v. Georgia. 408 U.S. 238, 309–10 (1972).

Goldkamp, J. (2001). Do drug courts work? Getting inside the drug court black box. *Journal of Drug Issues, 31*(1), 27–72.

Gottfredson, D., & Exum, L. (2002). The Baltimore city drug treatment court: One year results from a randomized study. *Journal of Research in Crime and Delinquency, 39*(3), 337–356.

Gottfredson, D., Najaka, S., & Kearley, B. (2003). Effectiveness of drug treatment courts: Evidence from a randomized trial. *Criminology & Public Policy, 2*(12), 171–196.

Greenwood, P., Everingham, S., Chen, E., Abrahamse, A., Merritt, F., & Chiesa, J. (1998). Three strikes revisited: An early assessment of implementation and effects (NCJ 194106). Washington, DC: U.S. Department of Justice, Office of Justice Programs, National Institute of Justice.

Greenwood, P., Rydell, C., Abrahamse, A., Caulkins, J., Chiesa, J., Model, K., & Klein, S. (1994). Three strikes and you're out—Estimated benefits and costs of California's new mandatory sentencing law. Santa Monica, CA: RAND Corporation. Retrieved from http://www.rand.org/publications/MR/MR509/.

Gregg v. Georgia. 428 U.S. 153 (1976).

Harrell, A., & Roman, J. (2001). Reducing drug use and crime among offenders: The impact of graduated sanctions. *Journal of Drug Issues, 31*(1), 207–232.

Harris, P., Petersen, R., & Rapoza, S. (2001). Between probation and revocation: A study of intermediate sanctions decision-making. *Journal of Criminal Justice, 29*, 307–318.

Hirschfield, P. (2008). The declining significance of delinquent labels in disadvantaged urban communities. *Sociological Forum, 23*(3), 575–601.

Hubble, M., Duncan, B., & Miller, S. (1999). The heart and soul of change: What works in therapy. Washington, DC: American Psychological Association.

Hughes, L. (2004). Where miracles happen: The promise of drug court programs. *Human Rights: Journal of the Section of Individual Rights and Responsibility, 31*(1), 5.

Ireland, C., & Berg, B. (2008). Women in parole: Respect and rapport. *International Journal of Offender Therapy and Comparative Criminology, 52*(4), 474–491.

Klein, A., Wilson, D., Crowe, A., & DeMichele, M. (2008). Evaluation of the Rhode Island probation specialized domestic violence supervision unit (Grant No. 2002-WG-BX-2011). Washington, DC: National Institute of Justice.

Latessa, E. (2006). From theory to practice: What works in reducing recidivism? Washington, DC: National Institute of Corrections.

Lindquist, C., Krebs, C., & Lattimore, P. (2006). Sanctions and rewards in drug court programs: Implementation, perceived efficacy, and decision making. *Journal of Drug Issues, 36*(1), 119–146.

Lokanan, M. (2009). An open model for restorative justice: Is there room for punishment? *Contemporary Justice Review, 12*(3), 289–307.

Lubitz, R., & Ross, T. (2001). Sentencing guidelines: Reflections on the future. Washington, DC: National Institute of Justice.

MacKenzie, D., Gover, A., Armstrong, G., & Mitchell, O. (2001). A national study comparing the environments of boot camps with traditional facilities for juvenile offenders. Washington, DC: National Institute of Justice.

MacKenzie, D., & Parent, D. (1991). Shock incarceration and prison overcrowding in Louisiana. *Journal of Criminal Justice, 19*, 225–237.

Mair, G., & May, C. (1997). Offenders on probation. *Home Office Research Study*, 167.

Makkai, T., & Braithwaite, J. (1994). Reintegrative shaming and compliance with regulatory standards. *Criminology, 32*, 361–383.

Marciniak, L. M. (1999). The use of day reporting as an intermediate sanction: A study of offender targeting and program termination. *The Prison Journal, 79*(2), 205–225.

Marlowe, D., & Kirby, K. (1999). Effective use of sanctions in drugs courts: Lessons from behavioral research. *National Drug Court Institute Review, II*, 1–15.

Martinson, R. (1974). What works—questions and answers about prison reform. *The Public Interest, 35*, 22–54.

Masters, R., Way, L., Gerstenfeld, P., Muscat, B., Hooper, M., Dussich, J., Pincu, L., & Skrapec, C. *CJ: Realities and Challenges*. New York, NY: McGraw-Hill Publishing.

Maxwell, S. R. (2000). Sanction threats in court-ordered programs: Examining their effects on offenders mandated into drug treatment. *Crime & Delinquency, 46*(4), 542–563.

Meade, B., & Steiner, B. The total effects of boot camps that house juveniles: A systematic review of the evidence. *Journal of Criminal Justice, 38*, 841–853.

Miethe, T., Lu, H., & Reese, E. (2000). Reintegrative shaming and recidivism risks in drug court: Explanations for some unexpected findings. *Crime & Delinquency, 46*(4), 522–541.

Miller, W., & Rollnick, S. (2002). *Motivational interviewing: Preparing people for change* (2nd ed.). New York, NY: Guildford Press.

Morris, N., & Tonry, M. (1990). *Between prison and probation: Intermediate punishments in a rational sentencing system*. New York, NY: Oxford University Press.

Newport, F. (2020, November 8). In U.S., 64% support death penalty in cases of murder: Half say death penalty not imposed often enough. Gallup. Retrieved from http://www.gallup.com/poll/144284/support-death-penalty-cases-murder.aspx.

Office of National Drug Control Strategy. (2004). *Healing America's drug users: Getting treatment resources where they are needed*. Washington, DC: Author.

Petersen, R., & Palumbo, D. (1997). The social construction of intermediate punishments. *The Prison Journal, 77*(1), 77–91.

Petersilia, J. (2003). *When prisoners come home*. New York, NY: Oxford University Press.

Petersilia, J., Turner, S., & Deschenes, E. (1992). Costs and effects of intensive supervision for drug offenders. *Federal Probation, 56*(4), 12–17.

Pierce, G. & Radelet, M. (2005). The impact of legally inappropriate factors on death sentencing for California homicides, 1990–1999. *Santa Clara Law Review, 46*(1), 1–47.

Riedel, M., & Welsh, W. (2011). *Criminal violence: Patterns, causes, and prevention* (3rd ed.). New York, NY: Oxford University Press.

Roman, J., & Harrell, A. (2001). Assessing the costs and benefits accruing to the public from a graduated sanctions program for drug-using defendants. *Law and Policy, 23*(2), 237–268.

Roper v. Simmons. 543 U.S. 551 (2005).

Scalia, J. (2001). *Federal drug offenders, 1999 with trends 1984–99*. Bureau of Justice Statistics Special Report. Washington, DC: U.S. Department of Justice, Office of Justice Programs.

Springer, N., Applegate, B., Smith, H., & Sitren, A. (2009). Exploring the determinants of probationers' perceptions of their supervising officers. *Journal of Offender Rehabilitation, 48*, 210–227.

Taxman, F. (2008). To be or not to be: Community supervision déjà vu. *Journal of Offender Rehabilitation, 47*(3), 209–219.

Taxman, F., Shepherson, E., & Byrne, J. (2004). *Tools of the trade: A guide to incorporating science into practice*. Washington, DC: National Institute of Corrections Publications.

Taxman, F., Soule, D., & Gelb, A. (1999). Graduated sanctions: Stepping into accountable systems and offenders. *The Prison Journal*, *79*(2), 182–204.

Tempest, Rone. (2005, March 6). Death row often means a long life. *The Los Angeles Times*, p. B1.

Tyler, J., Darville, R., & Stalnaker, K. (2001). Juvenile boot camps: A descriptive analysis of program diversity and effectiveness. *The Social Science Journal*, *38*(3), 445–460.

Ulmer, J. (2001). Intermediate sanctions: A comparative analysis of the probability and severity of recidivism. *Sociological Inquiry*, *71*(2), 164–193.

Von Hirsch, A. (1976). *Doing justice: The choice of punishments*. New York, NY: Hill and Wang Publishing.

Walker, S. (2011). *Sense and nonsense about crime, drugs and communities* (7th ed). Belmont, CA: Wadsworth Cengage Learning.

Walters, S., Clark, M., Gingerich, R., & Meltzer, M. (2007). Motivating offenders to change: A guide to probation and parole. Washington, DC: National Institute of Corrections.

Wolfe, E., & Guydish, J. (2002). A drug court outcome evaluation comparing arrests in a two year follow-up period. *Journal of Drug Issues*, *32*(4), 1155–1173.

CHAPTER 12

Promising Programs for Delinquency Prevention and the Rehabilitation of Juvenile Offenders

Danielle McDonald
Northern Kentucky University

Michael Bush
Northern Kentucky University

INTRODUCTION

When one thinks of crime prevention and juveniles, the first thoughts that come to mind are programs that attempt to prevent all youth from engaging in criminal or delinquent behavior. In the 1980s, for example, the "Just Say No" campaign targeted all elementary school children and asked them to "just say no" to drugs. In the 1990s, a popular television public service announcement used an egg frying in a pan to illustrate the effect of drugs on one's brain. However, the most common types of juvenile prevention programs target at-risk youth and are referred to as secondary crime prevention, or target juveniles already involved in the juvenile justice system, also known as tertiary prevention.

Secondary crime prevention is defined as an activity that "engages in early identification of potential offenders and seeks to intervene in their lives in such a way that they never commit criminal violation" (Brantingham & Faust, 1976, p. 290). Both primary and secondary crime prevention are concerned with initial prevention of criminal violation although secondary crime prevention focuses on preventing delinquency in people, areas, or situations that are at higher risk for delinquent behavior to occur. Without question, the large majority of crime prevention strategies are, by definition, secondary crime prevention activities. Thus, it is important for researchers and policymakers to identify those factors that either increase or decrease the propensity for juvenile offending. A variety of criminal justice and noncriminal justice agencies engage in secondary crime prevention, including police, courts, probation and parole services, general social services, educational institutions, planners, private citizens, businesses, and religious institutions (Brantingham & Faust, 1976). A criticism of secondary crime prevention is that these efforts are thought to focus on symptoms of crime and delinquent behavior rather than root causes.

Tertiary crime prevention "deals with actual offenders and involves intervention in their lives in such a fashion that they will not commit further offenses" (Brantingham & Faust, 1976, p. 290). Tertiary crime prevention efforts occur in the correctional component of the criminal justice system. These efforts assume that, through effective treatment, offenders are able to return to society as productive, responsible, and socially acceptable citizens. Similarly to secondary crime prevention efforts, there are a number of both criminal justice and noncriminal justice agencies that engage in tertiary crime prevention. A criticism of tertiary crime prevention efforts is that they tend to be more ideologically satisfying than practically effective.

This chapter will examine what characteristics or risk factors make juveniles more vulnerable to involvement in deviant and/or delinquent behavior, while also exploring why some children who are exposed to these risk factors don't participate in these negative behaviors. Next, the types of crimes that juveniles engage in will be discussed by looking at who is arrested and for what types of crimes, as well as what types of cases are adjudicated. The original intention of the juvenile court also will be compared to the current juvenile justice system and its constant struggle to balance punishment with treatment. The chapter will conclude with a discussion of promising programs for delinquency prevention and the rehabilitation of juvenile offenders.

JUVENILES AT HIGH RISK FOR OFFENDING AND JUVENILE OFFENDERS

Traditionally the focus in juvenile justice has been on the identification of risk or protective factors. Research suggests that delinquency, mental health disorders, and substance use increase with exposure to a greater number of risks. Thus, researchers and policymakers have attempted to identify certain individual and environmental risk and protective factors, arguing that more effective prevention strategies can be developed if key elements that increase or decrease propensities for juvenile offending are identified (Herrenkohl et al., 2000).

Risk factors are those characteristics, or attributes, that are thought to increase the likelihood of offending for juveniles (Arthur et al., 2002; Herrenkohl et al., 2000; Martin, 2005; Welsh & Farrington, 2007). Protective factors take those features that pose a particular risk to youth and turn them into positive features or protective factors. Thus, protective factors are those factors that reduce the likelihood of offending for juveniles perceived to have a higher propensity for offending behavior (Arthur et al., 2002; Benard, 1991; Mullis, Cornille, Mullis, & Huber, 2004).

Risk factors and protective factors are often categorized into five domains: individual, family, school, peer, and community (Herrenkohl et al., 2000; Howell, 2003). **Table 12-1** lists these domains along with persistent individual and environmental elements that increase the likelihood for offending. The interrelated nature of these risk and protective factor domains must be kept in mind. Therefore, if a child is exposed to major risks in the family system, then those factors identified as protective factors will likely come from one or more of the remaining domains: individual, school, peer, or community. Likewise, when a child's major risk factors stem from the community, then protective factors might come from the individual, family, or school domains. The following sections discuss the five risk and protective factor domains.

Individual

Individual risk factors "include biological and psychological characteristics identifiable in children at very young ages that may increase their vulnerability to negative social and environmental influences over the course of development" (Herrenkohl et al., 2000, p. 177). Research studies, for example, have indicated that gender alone is considered a biological risk factor since males are more likely to engage in crime or delinquency. Other examples of risk factors in the individual domain

TABLE 12-1 Risk Factor Domains and Persistent Individual and Environmental Elements

Individual	1. Early or persistent antisocial behavior
	2. Rebelliousness and aggressiveness
	3. Early commencement of problem behaviors
	4. Use of alcohol or other drugs
Family	1. Family history of problem behaviors
	2. Family management toward problems
	3. Chronic family conflict
	4. Parental approval of problem behavior
	5. Parental involvement in criminal or delinquent behavior
School	1. Academic failure
	2. Poor commitment to school
	3. Truancy
	4. Dropping out
	5. Moving frequently to new schools
Peer	1. Peer rejection
	2. Peer influence
	3. Gang involvement
Community	1. Availability of alcohol or other drugs
	2. Availability of firearms
	3. Laws and social norms favoring crime and delinquency
	4. Media portrayals of neighborhood characteristics
	5. Community disorganization
	6. Economic deprivation

Source: Adapted from Martin, G. (2005) and Howell, J. C. (2003).

include early or persistent antisocial behavior, rebelliousness, aggressiveness, early commencement of problem behaviors, and use of alcohol or other drugs. Youths who are able to succeed in spite of the adverse circumstances they must endure are referred to as "resilient" (Benard, 1991).

Benard (1991) described the resilient youth as being socially competent, possessing problem-solving skills, autonomous, and having a sense of purpose and future. Social competence is defined as one's ability to interact within various social settings and includes a range of personality traits such as responsiveness, flexibility, empathy, communication skills, a sense of humor, and other prosocial skills. Problem-solving skills refer to an individual's ability to develop solutions to both cognitive and social situations. Youths who are autonomous have a sense of their own identity and attempt to exert some control over their environment. Autonomous youths are able to "psychologically distance" themselves from a situation or environment that may cause another to succumb to negative influence. Having a sense of purpose and future includes educational aspirations, goal orientations, achievement motivation, persistence, and hopefulness, to name a few. This factor is perhaps the most powerful protective factor for juveniles since it promotes long-term perspective and perseverance. As a result, the youth who has a sense of purpose is more successful at establishing positive relationships with others (Benard, 1991).

Although researchers ascribe a variety of characteristics to resilient youth, the previously mentioned attributes of social competence, problem-solving skills, autonomy, and a sense of purpose and future are consistent themes in the literature. Some research indicates that individuals already experiencing problems with crime, delinquency, alcohol, drug abuse, and/or mental illness are often lacking these qualities. Developmental theory argues that the early years in life are most influential for later development; thus, early prevention efforts tend to focus on improvement of cognitive skills, social and emotional development, and school resources (Welsh & Farrington, 2007).

Family

The family domain refers to the notion that the manner in which children are socialized within the family structure is strongly related to positive and negative developmental outcomes (Herrenkohl et al., 2000). Risk factors within the family domain include family history of problem behaviors, chronic family conflict, poor family management of conflict, parental approval of problem behavior, and parental involvement in criminal or delinquent behavior. Numerous studies exist that suggest children will largely mimic the behavior of their parents, including such behaviors that are perceived as favorable to crime and delinquency, antisocial interaction with peers, and behaviors prone to violence. Additionally, parents' inability to set clear rules for their children, failure to appropriately or effectively monitor their children's behavior, or use of inconsistent discipline can increase the risk for offending (Herrenkohl et al., 2000). However, some children are able to succeed despite the conditions that surround them.

The quality of the family environment is determined by the amount of care and support the children receive, what is expected of the children within the family structure, and the level of participation that is encouraged for children within the family environment (Benard, 1991). Children with a secure attachment to at least one person—typically the mother or father, but not necessarily—who will provide them with stable care and from whom they will receive adequate and appropriate attention are more likely to develop the foundation needed for human bonding and social development. Families that establish high expectations at an early age assist their children with developing certain characteristics that will reduce the likelihood that they will offend. Beyond expectations, children need to see that they are meaningful participants within their social spheres. When children are given responsibilities—such as assigned chores, or taking care of their siblings, or working part-time—they feel like worthy and capable members of society. Thus, children are considered more resilient when they have received adequate and appropriate attention at an early age that resulted in a secure attachment to an authority figure; families that established high expectations for them; and families that provided meaningful opportunities for them to participate.

School

The school domain refers to a youth's level of academic achievement and educational experiences and how they are related to the likelihood of offending (Herrenkohl et al., 2000). Academic failure, poor commitment to school, truancy, dropping out, and moving frequently to new schools are common risk factors associated with the school domain. In addition, children and adolescents attend school at a time when they are more susceptible to developing aggressive behavior and the use of violent means (Hawkins et al., 1998).

Public schools in the United States hold unique positions in their communities since they are expected to provide children with the requisite knowledge and skills to become productive and useful citizens in a very competitive world (Marans & Schaefer, 1998). Families, communities, and schools have traditionally been the three social institutions responsible for the development of youth into productive and successful members of society (Stetson, Stetson, & Kelly, 1998). In recent years, schools have had to compensate for the deterioration of these other institutions (Elliott, Hamburg & Williams, 1998; Elliott, Williams, & Hamburg, 1998; Stetson et al., 1998). Furthermore, schools have become progressively more responsible for an economically and ethnically diverse population, including students of teenage parents, overstressed parents, and parents who lack parenting skills (Stephens, 1998). As a result, public schools have increasingly been expected to assume a larger role in areas of public health, public safety, moral instruction, and addressing social and psychological problems related to youth development (Elliott, Williams et al., 1998).

Protective factors within the school domain are the same as those for the family domain: caring and support, high expectations, and youth participation and involvement. Having a strong commitment to school and maintaining positive relationships with teachers serve as strong protective factors for juveniles, as well as having high academic expectations. Youth participation and involvement is also a strong protective factor in the school environment. The current mantra calls for the creation of safe schools. A safe school is defined as "a warm and welcoming environment, free of intimidation and fear of violence" and should foster a sense of acceptance and care for children (Stephens, 1998, p. 253).

Therefore, prevention and intervention strategies in schools are modeled after traditional school health programs, which also contain numerous psycho-educational approaches acquired from various disciplines such as education, social work, and psychology (Marans & Schaefer, 1998). These strategies generally include a specific curriculum, workshops, or series of group sessions that deal with students' knowledge, assumptions, beliefs, behavior changes, and development of life skills. Of particular interest are issues related to alcohol and drug use, anger management, conflict resolution, dropping out, social competence, self-esteem, sexual abuse, racism, interpersonal mediation, and bullying.

Peers

The peer domain refers to the pressures that juveniles face from other youths within the socialization process. Risk factors in this domain refer to such influences as peer rejection, peer influence, and gang involvement. Early research studies in the United States focused on low peer status or peer rejection (see Asher & Coie, 1990). Peer rejection refers to children who are considered widely disliked by their peers or who are identified as individuals to avoid playing or working with (Perry, Hodges, & Egan, 2001). These children often are targeted for further harassment; however, not all rejected youth are further victimized. Some rejected children do not experience negative actions from others; they are just not part of the group. Other individuals are more sensitive and less comfortable in group settings and may be excluded because of their awkwardness or may choose to isolate themselves. Thus, not all rejected youths are victimized, which means that two separate groups of rejected youths are possible, the victimized-rejected and the nonvictimized-rejected (see Schuster, 2001).

Perhaps the strongest predictor of juvenile offending is involvement with antisocial or delinquent peers, particularly gang involvement. Reflecting various stages of adolescent development, violence and aggression within social interactions provides functional, material, and symbolic meaning—or social status, a sense of belonging, and a social hierarchy—for juveniles (Fagan & Wilkinson, 1998). Part of the developmental process for adolescents is discovering power within social settings and among social groups (Thompson & Cohen, 2005). Some adolescents create an aggressive or violent "aura" that is used as a shield for protection against possible negative social experiences (Fagan & Wilkinson, 1998). This can eventually create an atmosphere where beliefs and norms pertaining to violence and aggression are absorbed into students' cognitive frameworks, impacting their interpretations of and responses to future adolescent encounters or criminal opportunities.

Similarly to the individual domain, possessing attributes of the resilient youth serves as the best protective factor against peer-influenced delinquency. In other words, a juvenile is likely to overcome peer-related risk factors that increase the likelihood of offending if he or she is capable of interacting confidently in social situations, possesses the ability to solve various problems either cognitively or socially, has a sense of his or her own identity, and is working toward future goals pertaining to success.

Community

Community risk factors refer to such elements as the availability of alcohol or other drugs in a community as well as the availability of firearms. Additional risk factors include laws and social norms favoring crime and delinquency, media portrayals of neighborhood characteristics, community disorganization, and economic deprivation (Herrenkohl et al., 2000). Exposure to these types of risk factors can increase the risk for later delinquency and violence. Understanding the various community factors that increase juveniles' risk for delinquent behavior at various stages of development is necessary for developing effective prevention and intervention strategies. Furthermore, a better understanding of the effects that multiple risk factors have within and across domains will assist in determining protective factors for those domains as well.

As with family and school institutions, the community must emphasize and support the positive development of youth through building traits of resiliency within individuals and by collectively fostering an environment that provides caring and support (e.g., health care, child care, housing, education, job training, employment, and recreation), high expectations, and opportunities for community involvement (Benard, 1991).

Juvenile Offenders

In 2008, law enforcement agencies arrested approximately 2.11 million persons younger than 18 (Puzzanchera, 2009). The total number of arrests for the four crimes that make up the Violent Crime Index (i.e., murder and nonnegligent manslaughter, forcible rape, robbery, and aggravated assault) was 96,000; 17% of those arrested for one of these categories were female and 27% were younger than 15. Aggravated assault contained the highest number of offenses with 56,000; 24% of those offenders were female and 31% were younger than 15. Although juveniles accounted for 16% of all violent crime arrests in 2008, juvenile arrests for violent crime in 2008 were lower than any year in the 1990s; juvenile arrests for forcible rape were lower than any year since 1980; and juvenile arrests for aggravated assault were lower than any year since 1988. On the other hand, juvenile arrests for robbery have increased more than 46% since 2004, and robbery was the only one of the four offense categories included in the Violent Crime Index that increased in 2007–2008 with an increase of 2%.

Juvenile offenders accounted for 26% of all property crime arrests in 2008. A total of 439,600 arrests were made for offenses included in the Property Crime Index (i.e., burglary, larceny/theft, motor-vehicle theft, and arson); 36% of juvenile offenders arrested for property crime offenses were female and 29% were younger than 15. The larceny/theft offense category contained the highest number of juvenile arrests with 324,100; 44% of these offenders were female and 29% were younger than 15. In 2006 and 2007, the Property Crime Index increased for the first time since 1993–1994. This growth is largely attributed to the 8% increase in the number of juvenile arrests for larceny/theft that occurred in each of those years. It is also important to note that the number of juvenile arrests for motor-vehicle theft and arson were at their lowest points in history, although the number of arrests for burglary increased 3% from 2007 to 2008. Three categories of Part II, or nonindex, crimes that contained the highest number of juvenile arrests were "Other Assaults" with 231,700 arrests (34% female and 37% younger than 15); "Vandalism" with 107,300 juvenile arrests (13% female and 40% younger than 15); and "Drug Abuse Violations" with 180,100 juvenile arrests (15% female offenders and 15% younger than 15).

In 2007, juvenile courts handled an estimated 1.7 million delinquency cases (Knoll & Sickmund, 2010). Despite showing some generally increasing trends, the number of delinquency cases handled in the United States has remained relatively stable in the period 2000–2007. Person offense cases were relatively stable from 1985 to 1993, rose sharply, and then leveled off, and property offense cases increased 26% from 1985 to 1992, and then steadily declined through 2007, resulting in the one general offense category that displayed an overall decline from 1985 to 2007. Drug law violation cases were relatively stable from 1985 to 1993, rose sharply, and then leveled off through 2005 while public order offense cases have increased steadily over time since 1985.

The juvenile court handled 1,400 homicide cases in 2007, but the majority of person offense cases (i.e., cases that involve an offense against a person) involved assault. Simple assault cases (274,900) and aggravated assault cases (49,600) accounted for 79% of all person offense cases handled in 2007. Over half (56%) of person offense cases handled in 2007 involved white youth, 41% involved black youth, 1% involved American Indian youth (including Alaskan Native), and 1% involved Asian youth (including Native Hawaiian and other Pacific Islander). Of the 409,200 person offense cases handled in 2007, 58% (238,400) were handled formally—meaning a petition was filed requesting either an adjudicatory or transfer hearing. Of these cases that were petitioned, 60% (143,600) resulted in the youth being adjudicated delinquent in the juvenile justice system, 38% (90,700) resulted in the youth being adjudicated not delinquent, and 2% (4,100) were judicially transferred to adult criminal court. It is important to note that although the overall number of person offense cases has remained relatively stable from 1985 to 2007, the female proportion of person offense cases has increased from 21% to 30%.

One area worth continued attention is the persistently disproportionate number of minorities that come into contact with the juvenile justice system. The racial composition of the U.S. juvenile population ages 10–17 in 2008 was 78% white (includes Hispanics), 16% black, 5% Asian/Pacific Islander, and 1% American Indian/Native Alaskan (Knoll & Sickmund, 2010; Puzzanchera, 2009). Of all juvenile arrests for violent crimes in 2008, 47% involved white youths, 52% involved black youths, 1% involved Asian youths, and 1% involved American Indian youths. The black proportion of juvenile arrests in 2008 was 58% for murder; 37% for forcible rape; 67% for robbery; and 42% for aggravated assault. More notably, black youths were arrested at five times the rate of white youths for offenses included in the Violent Crime Index, six times the rate for American Indian youths, and thirteen times the rate for Asian youths.

The disproportionate representation was also evident for property crime arrests. White youths accounted for 65% of property crime cases, 33% were black youths, 2% Asian youths, and 1% American Indian youths. Furthermore, black youths were arrested at more than double the rate that white youths and American Indian youths were and nearly six times the rate that Asian youths were arrested. White youths accounted for a larger proportion of drug offense cases (72%) than for any other offense category, and person offenses had the greatest proportion of offense cases involving black youths with 41%. Asian and American Indian youths accounted for a very small proportion of cases across all categories. Essentially, black youths were overrepresented in juvenile arrests. Regarding the number of delinquency cases handled in juvenile court in 2007, 64% involved white youths, 33% involved black youths, 1% Asian youths, and 1% American Indian youths.

Age is another factor that needs additional consideration. Youths younger than 15 accounted for more than 27% of all juvenile arrests for Violent Crime Index offenses and 29% of all property crime index offenses in 2008 (Puzzanchera, 2009). A year earlier, in 2007, juveniles younger than 16 at the time of court referral accounted for 54% of all delinquency cases handled. This age group accounted for 61% of person offense cases, 56% of property offense cases, 39% of drug law violation cases, and 50% of public order offense cases (Knoll & Sickmund, 2010). Person offense cases had the largest proportion (24%) of very young juveniles (younger than 14 at the time of referral), followed by property offense cases (20%). There were smaller proportions of cases involving juveniles younger than age 14 among public order offense cases (15%) and drug offense cases (8%). It is important to note that the definition for juvenile varies slightly across jurisdictions. For instance, 37 states and the District of Columbia define a juvenile as anyone younger than the age of 18; 3 states define juveniles as those younger than age 16; and 18 states define juveniles as persons younger than age 17 (Lab et al., 2011).

The delinquency caseload for female offenders has steadily risen from 19% in 1985 to 30% in 2008; 17% of juvenile Violent Crimes Index crime arrests, 36% of juvenile Property Crime Index arrests, and 44% of juvenile larceny/theft arrests (Knoll & Sickmund, 2010; Puzzanchera, 2009). From 1985 to 2007, the number of delinquency cases increased more for females than males for each of the four general offense categories (i.e., person offenses, property offenses, drug law violations, and public order offenses). There was a significant increase in person offense cases for both males and females from 1985 to 2007; however, the increase was greater for females. From 1999 to 2008, the number of female juvenile arrests decreased less than the number of juvenile male arrests for most offense categories; most notably for burglary, which decreased 3% for females and 16% for males (Puzzanchera, 2009). For some offense categories, female juvenile arrests increased while male juvenile arrests decreased. For example, the number of arrests for simple assault increased 12% for females and decreased 6% for males, and DUI arrests increased 7% for females and decreased 34% for males. Also from 1999 to 2008, the number of juveniles arrested for robbery increased 38% for females and 24% for males and motor-vehicle theft arrests decreased 52% for females and 50% for males. Although the overall numbers of female juvenile arrests have increased, they remain a relatively small proportion of the total delinquency caseload.

CREATION OF THE JUVENILE JUSTICE SYSTEM

Historically, the juvenile justice component of the criminal justice system has operated from a rehabilitative *parens patriae* philosophy, which allows the state to assume parental responsibility of juvenile offenders. Until the early 1800s, there was no special consideration for dealing with youthful offenders. Interestingly, changes in youth status and the beginnings of the juvenile justice system can be traced to social policies aimed at dealing with poverty (Bartollas & Miller, 2008; Lab et al., 2011). Many groups in society focused their attention on poor children since it was believed that they were most in need of attention and the most receptive to assistance. Various institutions were created for housing children, such as houses of refuge, reformatories, and cottages. The first house of refuge was established in New York City in 1825 and was quickly replicated in Boston in 1826 and again in Philadelphia in 1828. Other cities would soon follow. These institutions provided assistance to those in need while emphasizing education, skills training, hard work, religious training, and parental discipline.

The houses of refuge gave way to reformatories in the mid-1800s. The reformatories shared the same basic goals of the houses of refuge, yet differed in two significant ways: the reformatories handled only youths who needed assistance and not adults; and they typically were structured as small cottages in order to resemble a family setting where the authority figures were considered surrogate parents who would provide the love and attention needed by children. Three major changes that influenced juvenile institutions near the end of the 19th century were "the increasing size of institutional populations, a decrease in funding from state legislatures, and the admission of more dangerous offenders" (Bartollas & Miller, 2008, p. 11).

The development of the juvenile court adopted the same logic as these early institutions, assuming that youthful offenders needed assistance rather than punishment to become law-abiding, productive members of society. The first juvenile court was established in Cook County (Chicago), Illinois in 1899 and was founded on the philosophy of *parens patriae* (Lab et al., 2011; Small, 1997). *Parens patriae* encourages the nurturing, protection, and training of youths, who are amenable to such treatment, to assist them in overcoming their mistakes through a system of reform. The new juvenile court had jurisdiction over youths aged 15 and younger, regardless of the charges against the juvenile, and the court was intended to operate in a very informal manner in order to avoid any resemblance to the adult court system. In essence, the juvenile court was to approach youthful offenders in a paternalistic manner and to provide assistance in a similar way that a family would provide support.

This was not only a shift in philosophy for dealing with juvenile offenders, but also acknowledgement that juveniles were developmentally different from adult offenders. For instance, rather than assume that juveniles chose to engage in crime as a result of careful thought and deliberation as it is assumed for adults, the system now believed that youths were incapable of forming intent and chose to engage in crime either because of forces beyond their control or because they did not understand the consequences of their behavior. The *parens patriae* philosophy remained as the dominant view for the juvenile justice system until the 1960s, when a series of court decisions would dramatically alter the juvenile justice landscape. Since then, the *parens patriae* philosophy has gradually diminished.

BOX 12-1 The History of Juvenile Justice

Read *The History of Juvenile Justice—Part I* found at http://www.americanbar.org/content/dam/aba/migrated/publiced/features/DYJpart1.authcheckdam.pdf.

Do you think there should be a juvenile justice system, or should all offenders go through the adult system? Explain your answer.

JUVENILE JUSTICE AND THE IMPACT OF THE "GET-TOUGH" APPROACH

During the 1990s, issues of violence were considered more significant than living costs, unemployment, poverty, homelessness, and health care (Elliott, Hamburg, et al., 1998). For this reason, policies and programs for the prevention and control of violence at state and national levels included such initiatives as the use of judicial waivers for young offenders; gun control policies; the development of boot camps and shock incarceration programs; and community policing. School safety has also become a national concern in recent years, evidenced by the adoption of measures to increase incarceration and punishment for school crimes (Van Patten & Siegrist, 2000). Survey results for 78 elementary, middle, and high school teachers revealed that 95% felt violence in society had increased and 84% felt violence or civil disobedience had increased in their respective schools (Stetson, Stetson, & Kelly, 1998). Furthermore, 71% of respondents had experienced an increase in violence, despite having some type of conflict management or conflict resolution program in place.

The real or perceived threat of violence has altered the landscape for juvenile justice. As a result, society continues to support these punitive-based policies, despite the general agreement among experts that punitive methods alone do not work (Garnes & Menlove, 2003; Rigby, 2002).

Juvenile Transfer

Some juvenile offenders are processed, or dealt with, in the adult criminal court system rather than the juvenile court system (Whitehead & Lab, 2009; Lab et al., 2011). Juvenile transfer is defined as "a process whereby someone who is legally a juvenile is determined to be beyond the help of the juvenile justice system" (Lab et al., 2011, p. 181). All states allow for juveniles to be prosecuted in adult criminal court under some circumstances, and various methods exist depending on jurisdiction (Griffin, 2008; Knoll & Sickmund, 2010). Three common methods for transferring juveniles to adult criminal court are judicial waiver, prosecutorial waiver, and statutory exclusion (see also **Table 12-2**).

Judicial waiver is the most commonly used method for transferring juveniles to adult criminal court. There are three broad types of judicial waiver: discretionary waiver, presumptive waiver, and mandatory waiver (Adams & Addie, 2010). Currently, 46 states have discretionary waiver provisions, which allow juvenile court judges the discretion to waive juvenile jurisdiction over some cases. Presumptive waiver provisions exist in 15 states, which designate certain cases that are presumed appropriate for waiver to criminal court. Finally, other states (15) have mandatory waiver provisions where cases that meet certain age, offense, or prior record criteria are automatically waived to criminal court. A judicial waiver requires that a hearing take place—usually referred to as a waiver hearing, fitness hearing, or certification hearing. The hearing is conducted in front of a judge who subsequently decides whether the case is more suitable for either the adult or juvenile court system. During the hearing, the prosecutor must show probable cause that the juvenile committed the offense he or she is charged with and must also argue that the juvenile is beyond the help of the juvenile justice system. A decision is made about whether to transfer the youthful offender based on such factors as the age and maturity of the child; the child's relationship with his or her parents, school, and community; whether the child is perceived as dangerous; and whether court officials believe the child can benefit from the juvenile justice system and related agencies. Factors that typically lead to a juvenile being transferred to adult court include the seriousness of the offense, the juvenile's prior record, the age of the offender, previous dispositions from the juvenile court system, and the low likelihood that the offender could still benefit from the juvenile justice system.

TABLE 12-2 Types of Juvenile Transfer, or Waiver, to Adult Court	
Judicial waiver	Requires a waiver hearing in front of a judge who determines the suitability of removing the case to the adult court.
Prosecutorial waiver	The decision to try a juvenile in the adult court is made by the prosecutor, who has sole discretion in the matter.
Statutory exclusion or legislative waiver	The legislature has dictated, through a statute, that certain youths must be tried in the adult court—the juvenile court is excluded from hearing the case.
Demand waiver	Youths demand a transfer to adult court, possibly to ensure greater due process protections.
Once an adult, always an adult	Once a youth has been adjudicated in adult court, the youth is permanently under the adult court's jurisdiction.
Blended sentencing	Refers to youths who have received a prosecutorial waiver to adult court and who reside under the concurrent jurisdiction of the juvenile and adult court.
Reverse waiver	A case is returned to juvenile court after initially being transferred to adult court through judicial waiver, prosecutorial waiver, or statutory exclusion; a case thought better suited for juvenile court.

Judicial waivers peaked in 1994 with 13,100 cases and since then declined to 35% in 2007 with 8,500 cases (Adams & Addie, 2010; Knoll & Sickmund, 2010). Less than 1% of delinquency cases in 2007 where the juvenile was adjudicated delinquent resulted in judicial waiver (Adams & Addie, 2010). The decrease in the number of judicial waivers is undoubtedly driven by the decline in juvenile violent crime; however, part of the decline is also due to the increased use of nonjudicial transfer laws (Adams & Addie, 2010). Therefore, some cases that were filed directly in criminal court in more recent years might have been subjected to judicial waiver proceedings and been transferred anyway.

Another method for transferring juveniles to adult court is through prosecutorial waiver. Prosecutorial waiver occurs in states with concurrent jurisdiction statutes, which refers to those states that contain statutes that grant both juvenile court and adult court jurisdiction to prosecutors for certain types of cases. This process is similar to a judicial waiver, yet differs in that the prosecutor has sole authority to decide whether to file charges in juvenile court or adult court. State statutes assist prosecutors in identifying which offenses and what circumstances can be used to make a determination in their decision making. Generally speaking, the age of offender, type of offense, and prior record are taken into consideration. The use of prosecutorial waivers has increased in recent years amid growing concerns regarding the frequency and nature of juvenile crime, combined with the public's desire for safety and security.

Juvenile offenders are also commonly transferred to adult court through statutory exclusion or legislative waiver. Statutory exclusion refers to the process of creating and implementing laws that determine automatic transfer to adult court for offenders committing certain types of offenses and thus, are legally excluded from juvenile court processing. Statutory exclusion is generally reserved for cases involving violent crimes or chronic offenders, and there is typically a minimum age requirement determined by state legislatures. It is important to note that states vary in the age at which juveniles are eligible for transfer to adult court. Most states require juveniles to be at least 16 years old to be eligible for waiver to adult court. Other states allow minors as young as 13 to be transferred to adult court, and a few states allow children of any age to be tried as adults for certain crimes, such as homicide, and the minimum age of eligibility for some states is between 6 and 10 years old. The current trend is for states to lower the minimum age of eligibility for transfer, which is partially due to the public's misperception that juvenile crime is on the rise as well as the public's desire for punitive responses to crime.

Additional provisions for transferring juveniles to adult court exist in various jurisdictions. Some jurisdictions allow juvenile offenders to exercise a demand waiver to adult court (Lab et al., 2011). A demand waiver is a process within which a juvenile offender demands a transfer to adult court, likely in an attempt to ensure greater due process protections. It is also important to note that 34 states have created provisions for juvenile offenders that require offenders who have been transferred to adult court once to be automatically transferred to adult court for certain subsequent violations (Griffin, 2008; Lab et al., 2011; Whitehead & Lab, 2009). Commonly referred to as "once an adult, always an adult" provisions, most states require a conviction for the original offense before enforcing the provisions while other states apply "once an adult, always an adult" provisions for a broad range of offenses—usually those considered more serious. Nearly all states have legislative guidelines for enforcing these provisions. Oregon is currently the only state that allows the juvenile courts to decide whether or not to enforce the "once an adult, always an adult" provisions.

Blended sentencing is an additional option of the courts, where juveniles are concurrently under the jurisdiction of the juvenile court and the adult court (Bartollas & Miller, 2008). This procedural option is reserved for juvenile offenders who have been transferred to adult court though a prosecutorial waiver. Juvenile offenders receive sentences from both the juvenile and adult courts, but are first given the opportunity to fulfill the conditions of the juvenile disposition. If the juvenile successfully fulfills the conditions of his or her juvenile disposition, then the adult disposition is suspended. In contrast, if the juvenile does not successfully fulfill the conditions of his or her juvenile disposition, then the juvenile is required to fulfill the conditions of the adult disposition. In some cases, the juvenile may be expected to fulfill the conditions of the juvenile disposition until reaching the age of majority and then be expected to fulfill the conditions of the adult disposition.

Finally, reverse waiver provisions are used in 25 states for determining the best method for processing juvenile offenders (Griffin, 2008). A reverse waiver occurs when a case is returned to juvenile court after initially being transferred to adult court because of judicial waiver, prosecutorial waiver, or statutory exclusion (Bartollas & Miller, 2008; Whitehead & Lab, 2009). A reverse waiver is typically allowed for juvenile offenders who are over the maximum age of jurisdiction and whose cases are better suited for juvenile court (Griffin, 2008).

Aside from cases where state law mandates that a juvenile offender be transferred to adult criminal court, various processes exist where individuals must decide on whether to transfer an offender to adult court or have them remain in juvenile court. The decision to process a juvenile in the adult court system rather than juvenile court is significant for several reasons (Lab et al., 2011; Whitehead & Lab, 2009). Processing a juvenile in adult court potentially subjects the youth to adult penalties. For example, a juvenile transferred to adult court may receive a lengthy prison sentence in an adult institution rather than a relatively shorter period of incarceration inside a juvenile training school. Additionally, a conviction in adult court results in the creation of an adult criminal record for the juvenile, which may have an effect on future opportunities for success. A juvenile record typically remains confidential and is often perceived less negatively than an adult record.

There are several concerns regarding the process of juvenile transfer to adult court. One concern is about the factors that are taken into consideration for transferring individuals to adult court (Whitehead & Lab, 2009). Although the likelihood of judicial waiver has decreased, person offense cases were more likely to be waived in 2007 than cases within the other general offense categories (Hockenberry, 2010). Property offense cases were more commonly waived to adult court until the mid-1990s, and then person offense cases began to outnumber property offense cases (Knoll & Sickmuund, 2010). In 2007, person offense cases (4,100) totaled nearly half of the 8,500 cases that were waived that year. This was followed by property offense cases (2,300), drug law violations (1,100) and public order offenses (900). In addition, cases involving males were four times as likely to be judicially waived than cases involving females as well as cases involving juveniles 16 or older. Also in 2007, person offense cases involving American Indian youths were more likely to be waived to adult criminal court than person offense cases involving white, black, or Asian youths.

Additional concerns include whether transferred individuals receive harsher sentences than those that are not transferred and concerns about the effectiveness of transfer. The general conclusion is that transferring individuals to adult court has little to no general deterrent effect in preventing serious juvenile crime. On the other hand, there are several advantages to being transferred to adult court, such as the increased constitutional protections or due process procedures that adult court provides. In addition, jury members may be more sympathetic to a child defendant, or the child may receive a lighter punishment because of full courtroom dockets or crowded facilities. Disadvantages of being transferred to adult court include being subjected to adult penalties, being subjected to a narrow range of punishment and treatment options, and the potential for a permanent criminal record if convicted.

Scared Straight or Child Abuse

Another example of a politically popular program that has been shown to be ineffective is the Scared Straight Program. Scared Straight originated in a New Jersey prison in the 1970s as a way to deter children from a life of crime (Petrosino, Turpin-Petrosino, & Buehler, 2003). The program brought at-risk children or children involved in the juvenile justice system into an adult male prison, where they were subjected to adult male inmates who told them highly exaggerated stories of prison life and the violence that occurs within prison. The idea behind the program was to scare the children so badly that they literally would not want to participate in delinquency for fear of being brutalized in prison. In 1979, a television documentary was made about the New Jersey program, which popularized the program, and it subsequently spread rapidly to 30 other

---

BOX 12-2 Juvenile Offender Case Analysis

Go to the FRONTLINE website found at http://www.pbs.org/wgbh/pages/frontline/shows/juvenile/four/.

Read through the four case descriptions about four juvenile offenders. Two of the juvenile offenders were transferred to adult court while the other two remained in the juvenile court system. Do you agree with the decisions to try Shawn and Marquese in juvenile court? Why or why not? Do you agree with the decisions to try Jose and Manny in adult court? Why or why not?

states as well as into other countries. In 1982, the New Jersey program was evaluated, and it was determined that the program did not have any effect on those who participated in comparison to a control group that did not participate. However, the program continued to grow in popularity because it fit with the "get tough on crime" approach that was popular in the 1980s, it was cheap to operate, and it gave inmates a way to contribute to society (Petrosino, Turpin-Petrosino, & Buehler, 2003).

Today, this program is still in operation in many states despite the fact that other program evaluations also have shown the program to be ineffective. A few program evaluations have actually found that children who participated in the program were more likely to engage in delinquency than children who did not participate. A study by Finckenauer (1982), for example, found that 6 months after participating in a Scared Straight program, 41% of the children committed a new offense in comparison to 11% of children in the control group who did not participate in the program. However, the popularity of these programs continues, and there is a new television show on A&E called Scared Straight that documents in weekly episodes the experiences of children who participate in these programs. In fact, this new television show is unintentionally responsible for bringing to light the abuses that children in these programs have been experiencing. In an episode shot in a Maryland institution, an 8-year-old boy who had participated in the program was so traumatized by the experience that a family member contacted the child abuse hotline upon his return. This case is being investigated by child and youth services and prompted the program to be suspended. Other states, such as California, also have suspended their programs after the Department of Justice, through a letter to the editor of the *Baltimore Sun*, threatened to reduce federal funding for states that utilize these programs and do not comply with the Juvenile Justice and Delinquency Prevention Act (Dishneau, 2011).

The Juvenile Justice System and Punishment Today

In 2007, 56% of delinquency cases where the juvenile was adjudicated delinquent resulted in formal probation as the disposition for the youthful offender, and 25% of delinquency cases resulted in residential placement, or detention, as the disposition (Hockenberry, 2010; Knoll & Sickmund, 2010). A smaller number of cases (19%) resulted in some other type of disposition agreed upon within the respective juvenile courts where those dispositions were received.

Juvenile courts handled approximately 1.7 million delinquency cases in 2007 (Livsey, 2010). One-third of those delinquency cases resulted in probation as the most serious disposition. Probation can be either court-ordered or voluntary. Court-ordered probation occurs after a juvenile has been adjudicated delinquent. Youths who are not adjudicated delinquent by the court may voluntarily agree to court-imposed probation conditions, with the understanding that their case will be terminated if they successfully abide by those conditions. In 2007, 58% of cases receiving probation as the most severe disposition were placed on court-ordered probation after being adjudicated delinquent. The remaining delinquency cases resulted in probation because of a voluntary or informal arrangement between the juvenile and the court.

In 2007, the majority of delinquency cases placed on probation involved white males. For instance, 68% of cases ordered to probation involved white juveniles, 29% involved black juveniles, and 3% involved juveniles of other races or ethnicities (Livsey, 2010). Furthermore, most delinquency cases resulting in probation involved males (74%), although the proportion of female cases has increased from 18% in 1985 to 26% in 2007. In addition, juveniles aged 14–16 accounted for about 64% of the probation caseload in 2007. Property offense cases made up the greatest proportion of the overall probation caseload; however, their overall proportion has declined over time. The most likely to be ordered to probation were youths age 15 or younger, females, and whites.

The number of juveniles placed in residential placement, or detention, in publicly or privately operated facilities has steadily declined since 2000 (Sickmund, 2010). In 2007, rates for placement in residential facilities (the number of juveniles in placement for every 100,000 juveniles in the general population) varied significantly from state to state, with a low of 69 in Vermont to a high of 513 in South Dakota. Delaware and Wyoming also had rates greater than 400. Eleven states had residential placement rates below 200: Connecticut, Hawaii, Maine, Maryland, Massachusetts, Mississippi, New Hampshire, New Jersey, New Mexico, North Carolina, and Tennessee. Interestingly, nearly half (46%) of all juvenile offenders in residential placement were held by the six states with the largest placement populations: California (329), Texas (287), Florida (315), Pennsylvania (344), Ohio (41), and New York (239). In 2008, fewer than 81,000 juvenile offenders were in residential placement, which was the lowest number since 1993, when slightly less than 79,000 juveniles were housed.

Juveniles may be placed in secure detention at various times during case proceedings, although it is primarily used for temporarily holding youths who are awaiting adjudication, disposition, or placement elsewhere (Knoll & Sickmund, 2010). All states require that a hearing take place within a few days where a judge reviews the initial detention decision and decides whether to continue detention for the youth or some alternative disposition. Detention is used as a sanction in most states, as either an initial disposition or as punishment for a violation of probation conditions. The likelihood of detention varies by general offense category. In 2007, person offense cases were the most likely to involve detention (28%). Actually, based on demographics, the most likely to receive a disposition of residential placement in 2007 for person offense cases were youths age 16 or older, males, and American Indian youths. Person offenses were followed by public order offense cases (23%), while drug offense cases (20%) and property offense cases (17%) were less likely to result in detention.

JUVENILE TREATMENT PROGRAMS

Even with the shift in philosophy to the current "get-tough" approach to crime and criminality, there remains some debate as to whether juvenile justice systems should focus on punishment or treatment with juvenile offenders. The Office of Juvenile Justice Delinquency Prevention has identified several programs that are either exemplary, effective, or promising that address the root causes of juvenile delinquency and attempt to rehabilitate and reintegrate juveniles back into their communities in the spirit of the original intention of the juvenile court.

OJJDP's Model Programs Guide

The Office of Juvenile Justice and Delinquency Prevention (OJJDP) created a Model Programs Guide to assist practitioners, communities, researchers, and administrators in implementing evidence-based juvenile justice programs in their communities ("OJJDP Model Programs Guide," n.d.). The Model Programs Guide is available at their website and offers a comprehensive searchable database of model juvenile programs across every phase of prevention including primary, secondary, and tertiary prevention programs. The database allows one to find programs based on risk and/or protective factors, program type, model program guide rating, demographics, special population, and phase of prevention ("OJJDP Model Programs Guide," n.d.).

The Model Programs Guide is based on a review of juvenile program evaluations, where program effectiveness was ranked using a rating scale created by the OJJDP ("OJJDP Model Programs Guide," n.d.). The ratings scale was designed to assist those searching the database to provide a better understanding of the quality of research currently available that supports the program he or she is examining. The rating scale is based on four criteria. First, the conceptual framework or theoretical basis for the program must be sound and based on prior research. Second, program fidelity is examined, or how well the program was implemented according to the original plan. Third, the scientific methods used in the program evaluation are analyzed. Finally, the empirical evidence is examined to find out if the research findings actually supported an increase in protective factors and/or decrease in risk factors. A program's rating on these four criteria determines whether the program is classified as exemplary, effective, or promising ("OJJDP Model Programs Guide," n.d.).

An exemplary rating is the highest ranking a program can receive. Exemplary status is determined by the program being implemented effectively and based on a conceptual framework that has been well-researched ("OJJDP Model Programs Guide," n.d.). An exemplary program uses an experimental evaluation design with random assignment to a control and experimental group, as well as tests prior to and after participation in the program. Exemplary programs demonstrate strong empirical evidence that a program is increasing protective factors and/or decreasing risk factors. The second highest ranking is effective. A program is found to be effective if it did a good job of implementing the program as intended and is based on a sound conceptual model. The effective program evaluation design involves a quasi-experimental design, where random assignment was not used to assign research participants to a control or experimental group. Effective programs demonstrate adequate empirical evidence that their programs increase protective factors and/or decrease risk factors. Finally, programs are found to be promising if they minimally implemented the program as planned and are based on a reasonable conceptual framework. Promising programs have a weak research design that typically only includes a pre- and posttest for a single group without a comparison group. The empirical evidence for promising programs tends to show potential, but the findings are often inconsistent ("OJJDP Model Programs Guide," n.d.).

The OJJDP also has a link on their Model Programs Guide website to their best practices database for reducing disproportionate minority contact for minority youth who are at risk and/or involved in the juvenile justice system ("OJJDP Model Programs Guide," n.d.). This database assists one in selecting a program, based on his or her specific needs, to be implemented to reduce disproportionate minority contact. The programs highlighted in the database are not ranked in the same way as the programs found in the Model Programs Guide because not enough research has been conducted on these programs and their impact on disproportionate minority contact. However, some of the programs listed as model programs also have illustrated

---

BOX 12-3 OJJDP Model Programs Guide

Go to the OJJDP website for the Model Programs Guide found at http://www.ojjdp.gov/mpg/programTypesDefinitions.aspx.

Read through the different types of programs that are offered. Select two programs that you believe would be effective with juveniles and explain why. Be sure to include who the program targets, how the program operates, and program evaluation findings.

a reduction in disproportionate minority contact. These programs will be noted during the discussion that follows. Although these programs were not originally intended to reduce dispro-portionate minority contact, their empirical findings illustrate that they do ("OJJDP DMC—Reduction Best Practices Database," n.d.).

Secondary Prevention Programs for Juveniles

Community Oriented Policing

Community oriented policing (C.O.P.) occurs when the police and the community come together to identify and solve community problems (U.S. Departement of Justice, n.d.). The community (community groups, businesses, nonprofits, media, and/or government agencies) and the police strengthen their relationship through this collaboration. This style of policing became popular in 1994, after 8.8 billion dollars in grant funding was made available from the Violent Crime Control and Law Enforcement Act to create C.O.P. programs and hire and train new C.O.P. officers (U.S. Department of Justice, n.d.).

There are three main components in C.O.P.: community partnership, organizational trans-formation, and problem solving (U.S. Department of Justice, n.d.). The community partnership is the collaboration between the community and the police, where they work together as one to solve the problem at hand. The organizational transformation occurs as new staff are hired and trained and current personnel accept the philosophy of C.O.P. and incorporate it into their work. Problem solving occurs when the community and police identify and prioritize the problems within the community, research what is known about the problem, develop strategies to address the problem, and later evaluate the effectiveness of the strategy (U.S. Department of Justice, n.d.).

C.O.P. helps to address secondary prevention by creating a venue for the community and po-lice to come together and assess what the risk factors are in the community and create a plan for how to decrease them as well as increase protective factors (U.S. Department of Justice, n.d.). Two programs from the Model Programs Guide that illustrate C.O.P. strategies and target at-risk youth are the Richmond Comprehensive Homicide Initiative and Weed and Seed.

The Richmond Comprehensive Homicide Initiative focuses on preventing homicides and has been rated as an effective model program ("OJJDP Model Programs Guide," n.d.). This program was created in 1995 after a spike in violent crime in Richmond, California (White et al., 2003). Richmond is an urban area near San Francisco that saw an increase in violent crime, particularly homicides, during the early 1990s. This program was created as a response to this violence in col-laboration with the U.S. Department of Justice. The first task was to better understand homicide trends and risk factors by comparing homicide rates in Richmond from 1985 to 1989 to rates from 1990 to 1994. It was discovered that during the early 1990s, there were more people dying out-doors, more people being killed by guns, more offenders committing the crime of homicide with prior records, and more people joining gangs (White et al., 2003). The next step involved the police and community using this knowledge and working together to identify risk factors for juveniles who were likely to commit violent crime and to specify plans to target these at-risk youth. The program they created is multifaceted and targets at-risk youth from a variety of angles. Domestic violence, for example, is addressed through collaborations with the women's crisis center to pro-mote programs aimed at ending domestic violence. Gang- and drug-related violence also is tar-geted through partnerships with the Drug Enforcement Administration and the Federal Bureau of

Investigation (FBI), whose assistance helps track down violent gang members. Programs also were developed to improve investigations; for example, hiring evidence specialists, improving technology, and intervening in the lives of at-risk youth with programs such as job skills training and Drug Abuse Resistance (DARE) mentoring (White et al., 2003).

In 2003, White et al. evaluated the Richmond Homicide Initiative by comparing homicide data in Richmond from 1985 to1989, a stable period for homicides, to 1990–1994, a time period where there was a dramatic increase in homicides, to 1995–1998, when the program had been implemented. Interviews with homicide and gang detectives also were examined and time series analysis was used to analyze and compare the three time periods. The empirical evidence suggests that the program decreased risk factors for at-risk youth by decreasing violence in both their communities and their homes. Domestic murders, for example, decreased by 55%, and female victimization within the home decreased by two-thirds, while drive-by shootings decreased by 64%, and gun-related homicides returned to the more stable rate of the late 1980s. Drug-related homicides also decreased by 60% (White et al., 2003).

The Weed and Seed program began in the early 1990s ". . . as a community-based, comprehensive, multi agency approach to law enforcement, crime prevention and community revitalization in high-crime neighborhoods" (Trudeau, Barrick, Williams, & Roehl, 2010, p. 2). This program is rated in the Model Programs Guide as promising, and its goals include reducing violent crime and drug trafficking while improving the quality of life in the community through neighborhood revitalization programs ("OJJDP Model Programs Guide," n.d.). Neighborhoods with high crime rates can apply for a 1 million dollar grant over 5 years from the Community Capacity Development Office to implement Weed and Seed programming in their own communities. Currently, there are 256 Weed and Seed sites in 46 states in the United States (Trudeau et al., 2010). These programs are composed of three components: weed, seed, and community policing. The first component, weed, involves law enforcement officials from all levels working together to remove violent and/or drug offenders from the targeted neighborhood. The second component, seed, involves social services being recommended and made available to those who need them and the community working together to improve the physical appearance of the community. The third component, community policing, involves the community and the police working together to identify problems and create solutions.

Trudeau et al. (2010) conducted a program evaluation of over 200 Weed and Seed sites across the United States. Data were collected through crime data reports from the agencies and Web-based surveys that had been distributed to residents in the targeted communities, as well as to agency representatives. Thirteen sites also were randomly selected to gather more in-depth information. The information gathered included surveys completed by residents of the targeted communities and a comparison group from a neighboring community, program documents, and interviews with key stakeholders. The results of the program evaluation showed a decrease in crime in the targeted neighborhoods. In comparison to surrounding communities, the targeted areas saw a greater decrease in robberies, burglaries, and aggravated assaults. A few of the targeted communities had decreases in crime rates prior to the program being implemented in their communities. However, these drops in crime continued after the program was implemented, and the community's decrease in crime was greater than that in surrounding communities where the program had not been implemented. Key stakeholders also revealed, during interviews, that relations between the community and police had improved, along with community involvement and the availability of social services to the community (Trudeau et al., 2010).

Gang Prevention

Juveniles who are involved in gangs tend to be more violent than their peers and commit more serious crimes (Howell & Decker, 1999). Gang membership has been found to have a greater influence on a juvenile's violent behavior than association with other types of delinquent nongang juveniles (Howell, 1997). Surveys conducted with urban youths from gang-prone areas have shown that 14–30% of these youths will join a gang (Howell, 1997). Therefore, secondary prevention programs targeting at-risk youth for gang membership are extremely important. By intervening early in the lives of at-risk youth, violent crime in gang-prone neighborhoods can be reduced dramatically. This can be accomplished by identifying the risk and protective factors for this at-risk youth population and providing the necessary programming to reduce youth gang membership. Two programs from the Model Programs Guide that illustrate gang prevention strategies and target at-risk youth are Boys and Girls Club Gang Prevention Through Targeted Outreach and Movimiento Ascendencia.

In 1991, the Boys and Girls Club created a gang prevention program, Gang Prevention Through Targeted Outreach, with the support of the Office of Juvenile Justice and Delinquency Prevention (Boys and Girls Club of America, n.d.). This program has been rated as promising by the Model Programs Guide ("OJJDP Model Programs Guide," n.d.). There are four components to the program, including: community mobilization, recruitment, mainstream programming, and case management (Boys and Girls Clubs of America, n.d.). The first component, community mobilization, occurs when the club works with community agencies to better understand the extent of the youth gang problem and mobilizes community leaders to assist in developing solutions. The second component, recruitment, occurs through either direct outreach, where the club solicits at-risk youths, or referrals from the school, community, and/or juvenile justice system. The third component, mainstreaming and programming, occurs when the recruited youths are placed in typical Boys and Girls Clubs programming with other youths who attend the club based on their needs and interests. Each recruited youth is assigned a staff person who mentors the youth. The fourth component, case management, involves the youth being assigned a case manager for a period of 1 year who meets monthly with the child to monitor problems and successes provides access to necessary programming (Boys and Girls Clubs of America, n.d.).

In 2002, Arbreton and McClanahan evaluated 21 Gang Prevention Through Targeted Outreach programs with a total of 932 youth. Each of the 21 Boys and Girls Clubs had implemented the program within 1 to 3 years prior to the program evaluation. Data were collected through a review of the case management records and a pretest/posttest survey. The survey was distributed 12 months prior to participating in the program and 12 months after participating in the program to the youths who participated and to a control group who did not. The authors concluded that the programs were effectively targeting at-risk youth who had significant social service needs, and the clubs were doing a good job of keeping the recruited youths involved. Seventy-three percent of youths, for example, were still attending the club 12 months later, and 50% reported attending multiple times a week. Those youths who attended the club more regularly were less likely to start wearing gang colors, have contact with the juvenile court, and smoke marijuana. These youths also reported an increase in positive peer and family interactions (Abreton & McClanahan, 2002).

Movimiento Asendencia was created in 1991 by the Colorado Youth Services Bureau. This program has been rated as promising by the Model Programs Guide ("OJJDP Model Programs Guide," n.d.). Movimiento Ascendencia targets Mexican-American girls between the ages of 10 and 17 who are at risk for gang involvement and substance abuse ("Movimiento Ascendencia," n.d.).

There are three main components to the program, including: (1) mediation or conflict resolution, (2) social support or self-esteem, and (3) cultural awareness. The first component, mediation or conflict resolution, includes providing a safe environment for the girls and case managers to advocate and support the girls through social services. The second component, social support or self-esteem, occurs through a variety of programs such as mentoring, tutoring, organized social events, and life skills programs. The third component, cultural awareness, occurs through day trips and by attending cultural fairs.

Williams, Curry, and Cohen (2002) conducted a program evaluation of Movimiento Ascendencia. The control group consisted of girls referred by the school or juvenile system, while program participants were randomly selected to participate. Pretest surveys and records showed the two groups to be demographically similar. The girls were interviewed about seven types of delinquent behavior, such as running away from home, damaging property, theft of an item less than $50 and over $50 and asked to reflect on their own delinquent behavior. The study concluded that participating in the program decreased delinquent behavior significantly (Williams, Curry, & Cohen, 2002).

Job Training

If a juvenile is a high school dropout, he or she will have a difficult time obtaining legitimate work, which creates a risk factor for delinquent behavior. Juveniles who had dropped out of high school, for example, were unemployed at a rate of 36% in comparison to 21% of those who were unemployed, had completed high school, and did not go on to college (Snyder & Sickmund, 2006). In order to reduce this risk factor, government job training programs target at-risk juveniles who have either dropped out of high school, or are from poor communities and/or impoverished families (Sherman et al., 1997). The intention of job training is to intervene early in the lives of at-risk youth to help them become a part of their communities as successfully employed juveniles and eventually adults (Sherman et al., 1997). Job training programs also have been shown to reduce disproportionate minority contact ("OJJDP DMC—Reduction Best Practices Database," n.d.).

There are three types of job training programs aimed at youth: summer work, short-term training and long-term training (Sherman et al., 1997). Summer work lasts during the summer months and provides minimum wage job opportunities to disadvantaged children. Short-term training targets out-of-school youth and provides job training and educational programs for 6 months along with assistance in finding a job at the end of the training. Long-term training lasts approximately 1 year and includes a residential program that provides educational, vocational, and life skills training with job placement assistance upon completion. Long-term training programs target seriously dis-

---

BOX 12-4 Disproportionate Minority Contact Best Practices Database

Go to the OJJDP website for Disproportionate Minority Contact Best Practices Database found at http://www2.dsgonline.com/dmc/dmc_default.aspx.

How does disproportionate minority contact occur in the juvenile justice system? Examine the three DMC strategies (direct services, training and technical assistance, system change). Which of these strategies or combination of strategies do you believe would be the most effective in reducing disproportionate minority contact for juveniles?

advantaged populations and have been found to be the most effective type of job training program (Sherman et al., 1997). A program found in the Model Programs Guide that illustrates long-term job training for at-risk youth is Job Corps ("OJJDP Model Programs Guide," n.d.).

Job Corps is a career development program that provides vocational and educational training to disadvantaged youths 16–24 years of age in a residential setting (Job Corps, n.d.). Job Corps is rated as effective in the Model Programs Guide ("OJJDP Model Programs Guide," n.d.). Originally started in 1964, Job Corps is funded today by the Workforce Investment Act of 1998 and is the largest government vocational and educational training program in the United States (Job Corps, n.d.). In order to be eligible for Job Corps, one must be between 16–24 years of age, register with selective service if male, be a legal U.S. citizen or alien, meet the criteria for low income, and have one or more of the following characteristics: dropped out of school; need intense vocational and educational training and/or career counseling; be homeless, a runaway, or foster child; or be a parent. The applicant also must be drug free. Those who have a criminal background or are under court supervision are not automatically disqualified; however, those under supervision must obtain a waiver from the court stating that face-to-face supervision will not be necessary and be able to show a history of good behavior during their time under supervision. If an individual meets the criteria, eligibility is determined through a face-to-face interview (Job Corps, n.d.).

Once an individual has been admitted to the Job Corps program, he or she will start the first of the three phases of this program. The first phase, career preparation period, typically lasts about 60 days. This phase is a period of transition as the program participant becomes acquainted with the program environment and expectations. The second phase, career development period, involves educational and vocational training, as well as programming on communication and problem-solving skills. During this phase, the participant also begins to search for jobs and prepares to eventually live on his or her own. The third phase, career transition period, is where the participant will obtain his or her first job and make arrangements, with the assistance of Job Corps, to live on his or her own (Job Corps, n.d.).

Schochet, Brughardt, and Glazerman (2000) conducted a program evaluation to determine the effectiveness of Job Corps. The authors evaluated Job Corps programs nationwide through pretest and posttest surveys administered 12 months before and 30 months after program participation. Over 11,000 youths participated in the study from start to finish. The experimental group consisted of participants who were eligible for Job Corps and randomly assigned to participate. The control group consisted of those who were eligible for Job Corps but were not given the option to participate. The authors concluded that program participants were more likely to receive a GED or other vocational certificate, completed more hours in vocational training, and had increased their weekly earnings by 11%. Job Corps participants also decreased their arrest rates by 22%. The most significant findings were found for those who were 16–17 years of age. This age group increased their weekly earnings by 20% and high school diploma/GED rates by 80%. This age group also decreased their arrest rates by 14% and incarceration due to a conviction by 26% (Schochert, Brughardt, & Glazerman, 2000).

Community-Based Mentoring

A mentor provides interaction with a positive adult role model through regular meetings between the two (Sherman et al., 1997). Mentors are assigned to mentees based on common interests matched during the application process. Meetings between the two provide a forum for the mentee to develop and practice coping mechanisms such as problem-solving and social skills. Meetings can take place in a variety of community settings or in the home. Mentoring provides the most interaction between an adult and child of all community-based programming. These interactions provide the two an opportunity to develop a strong bond, which can help to counteract negative peer influences such as substance use and gang involvement (Sherman et al., 1997). Mentoring programs also have been shown to reduce disproportionate minority contact ("OJJDP DMC—Reduction Best Practices Database," n.d.). Big Brothers Big Sisters of America is an example of a community-based mentoring program that is found in the Model Programs Guide ("OJJDP Model Programs Guide," n.d.).

In 1904, Big Brothers was created by a New York City court clerk who began pairing boys involved in the court system with positive adult role models (Big Brothers Big Sisters, n.d.). Shortly thereafter, a similar program was created for girls called Catholic Big Sisters. Both of these programs were successfully implemented nationwide and by 1977 they had paired up to become Big Brothers Big Sisters of America (BBBS). Currently, Big Brothers Big Sisters of America operates in over 500 local agencies, pairing more than 75,000 littles (mentees) with bigs (mentors) (Big Brothers Big Sisters, n.d.). Big Brothers Big Sisters community-based mentoring has been rated as exemplary by the Model Programs Guide ("OJJDP Model Programs Guide," n.d.).

BBBS offers community-based mentoring to children ages 5–18 who are from a single-parent background (Tierney, Grossman, & Rosch, 2000). Children who have both parents living at home are not eligible for services. BBBS also offers specialized community-based mentoring for children from different racial/ethnic backgrounds, children with parents in the military, and children who have parents who are incarcerated (Big Brothers Big Sisters, n.d.). Children who are eligible must complete a written application, a home assessment, and an interview that is conducted with both the parent and child (Tierney, Grossman, & Rosch, 2000). Mentors are carefully screened through background checks and must complete a written application as well as an interview. Mentors also must commit to meeting with their assigned little between two and four times a month for approximately 4 hours each meeting for a minimum of 1 year. Once a big and little are paired, the agency will continue to monitor the relationship and offer training (Tierney, Grossman, & Rosch, 2000).

In 2000, Tierney, Grossman, and Rosch conducted a nationwide program evaluation to determine the program effectiveness of Big Brothers Big Sisters of America. The authors compared a total of 959 youth 10–16 years of age who were either randomly assigned to the waiting list or to the Big Brothers Big Sisters program. Interviews were conducted with all participants prior to being assigned to the control or experimental groups and again 18 months after being assigned to one of the two groups. The results were positive and illustrate the impact of community-based mentoring on reducing delinquency risk factors and improving resiliency factors. Study participants who were involved in BBBS were 46% less likely to start using drugs, 27% less likely to start using alcohol, and nearly one-third less likely to hit another person. Those involved in BBBS improved their school attendance and missed half as many days of school as those in the control group. Improvements also were noted in family and peer relationships, including littles reporting that they had a higher level of trust with their parents than those who did not participate in BBBS (Tierney, Grossman, & Rosch, 2000).

Tertiary Programs for Juveniles

Restorative Justice

The traditional criminal justice system is based on a retributive approach, where the offender is punished for his or her actions, and the victim has little to no involvement in the process (*Restorative*

Justice Online, n.d.). Restorative justice offers a different approach to the criminal justice system that provides both the offender and the victim the opportunity to participate in the process by having the chance to explain their actions or how they were harmed by another's actions. This provides the offender the opportunity to understand that their behavior is not only wrong, but has real consequences for real people, and it gives the victim an opportunity to have his or her voice heard. Ultimately, the offender receives a punishment, but also has the opportunity to apologize to and, along with the victim, determine a way to repair the harm done. Restorative justice programs also have been shown to help reduce disproportionate minority contact ("OJJDP DMC—Reduction Best Practices Database," n.d.).

There are three main components to restorative justice ("Restorative Justice Online," n.d.). First, both the offender and the victim must voluntarily participate. Second, the offender must be willing to acknowledge his or her part in the delinquent act and accept responsibility. Third, there must be a face-to-face encounter between the victim or person(s) representing the victim and an offender, where both parties are able to voice their concerns and how the harm might be repaired ("Restorative Justice Online," n.d.).

Restorative justice can be implemented in multiple ways, but all of the program varieties include the three main components. The most commonly used program format is Victim–Offender Mediation where the victim and offender are provided a safe arena to meet face to face to discuss the harms caused by the offender's actions and how to repair it ("Restorative Justice Online," n.d.). The majority of victim–offender mediation programs are funded by the state or local government with the most common offenses referred being vandalism, minor assault, theft, and burglary. The offender is typically diverted out of the juvenile justice system prior to admitting a formal statement of guilt (Umbreit & Greenwood, 2000). The Minneapolis Center for Victim–Offender Mediation, the Albuquerque Victim–Offender Mediation Program, and the Oakland Victim–Offender Reconciliation Program have all been rated as promising restorative justice programs by the Model Programs Guide ("OJJDP Model Programs Guide," n.d.).

Umbreit and Coates (1993) conducted a program evaluation of victim–offender mediation programs in the states of New Mexico, California, Texas, and Minnesota. A total of 1,153 victims and offenders were interviewed. Those who participated in the mediation process were interviewed prior to and after the mediation session, and their results were compared to those who were eligible, but did not participate in victim–offender mediation. The authors concluded that the majority of those who participated in the victim–offender mediation felt the process was fair and they were satisfied with the outcome. Victims who participated in the mediation sessions reported reducing their fear and anxiety significantly more than those who did not participate, while offenders who participated were more likely to complete their restitution payments (Umbreit & Coates, 1993).

Problem-Solving Courts

Problem-solving courts, such as juvenile gun or drug courts, are based on the idea of therapeutic jurisprudence or "… the study of the role of law as a therapeutic agent" (Wexler, 1999, p. 1). Therapeutic jurisprudence is based on the idea that the experience an individual has as he or she proceeds through the court system can have positive and negative effects on his or her emotional and psychological well-being and therefore behavior (Wexler, 1999). This theory requires the court to become aware of these unintended consequences and to maximize the positive and minimize the negative impacts of the court system.

Problem-solving courts tackle a wide variety of social and delinquency problems ranging from guns to drugs. However, all of these problem-solving courts are based on the same six principles (Center for Court Innovation, n.d.). First, all those working within the court must be trained to better understand the specific population, victims, and community that they are targeting. This training and knowledge will allow judges and attorneys to make more informed decisions. Second, the community needs to become engaged in the process by helping to identify the problem and assisting in developing possible solutions. Community engagement also will help to improve relations and trust between the court system and the community. Third, collaboration must occur between the court, schools, and social services to improve communication. Fourth, the court must provide individualized services to each client by assessing what services each person needs upon intake and helping them to connect to these services. Fifth, each court client must be held accountable for his or her actions. Therefore, if someone does not comply with the rules of the program, there must be clear consequences for their behavior. Finally, each program must assess its effectiveness in order to improve its outcomes (Center for Court Innovation, n.d.).

One example of a problem-solving court is juvenile drug court, which has been rated as promising in the Model Programs Guide ("OJJDP Model Programs Guide," n.d.). Juvenile drug courts are diversion programs that target those who have committed nonviolent delinquent or status offenses and who are abusing substances (National Drug Court Institute, 2003). These juveniles are diverted from the traditional juvenile court to a juvenile drug court, where the judge and the rest of the staff have been trained to work with this specific population. The judge and his or her team (school officials, probation officers, social services, and treatment representatives) determine the best way to help the juvenile participant to remain substance and delinquency free. The drug court participant remains in the community with his or her family, but under the supervision of the juvenile drug court judge who oversees the juvenile's progress on a weekly basis. If the juvenile graduates from the drug court program, the charges are dropped against the participant, however, if he or she is not successful in drug court then the participant will be sent back to the juvenile court system where charges will be filed.

Juvenile drug courts can be implemented slightly differently, but there are five main goals that have been identified by the National Drug Court Institute (2003) that all juvenile drug courts should strive to achieve. First, the juvenile drug court should provide structure through its daily schedule of school, treatment, and the oversight of weekly visits with the judge. Second, the court should decrease substance use by helping the juvenile to improve daily functioning and problem-solving skills to eliminate the need to use substances. Third, the court should seek to improve the overall life opportunities for the juvenile by strengthening community relations, educational opportunities, and self-esteem. Fourth, the court should seek to strengthen the child's family and enable them to provide guidance and support for their child, while the fifth goal is to ensure accountability both with the juvenile participant and the social service providers (National Drug Court Institute, 2003).

Hickert, Becker, and Prospero (2010) conducted a program evaluation of six juvenile drug court programs across the state of Utah. They compared those who had participated in the juvenile drug court program (n = 622) to those who had committed similar alcohol and other drug-related offenses, but were sentenced to probation (n = 596). Across the six programs, 70.4% of the drug court participants had completed the program successfully, and those in the juvenile drug court were rearrested significantly less than those on probation. Thirty months after being assigned to probation or drug court, juvenile drug court participants were rearrested at a rate of 34% in comparison to those assigned to probation, who were rearrested at a rate of 48%. The authors also

BOX 12-5 Addicted to Courts

Read the Justice Policy Institute's report "Addicted to Courts: How a Growing Dependence on Drug Courts Impacts People and Communities" found at http://www.justicepolicy.org/uploads/justicepolicy/documents/addicted_to_courts_final.pdf.

Do the issues discussed in this report, which focuses on adult drug courts, pertain to juvenile drug courts as well?

found juvenile drug court programs to be the most successful in reducing delinquent behavior with those who had committed the most delinquent offenses prior to participation. However, those who had committed between one and three delinquent acts prior to participating in the juvenile drug court had only a slight decline in delinquent behavior afterwards, and those who had not committed any delinquent acts prior had a slight increase in delinquent behavior after participating in the program (Hickert, Becker, & Prospero, 2010).

Juvenile gun courts are a second example of problem-solving courts that have been found to be promising by the Model Programs Guide ("OJJDP Model Programs Guide," n.d.). Juvenile gun courts target first-time nonviolent gun offenders who did not cause any physical harm (Sheppard & Kelly, 2002). The goal of this program is to hold the youth accountable for his or her crime, but also to simultaneously provide early intervention through community-based programming with the hopes of decreasing future gun crime and delinquent offenses. Juvenile gun courts can operate differently from one site to the next, for example, some programs are supplemental for the juvenile as he or she moves through the juvenile system and other programs operate in place of the regular juvenile justice system. However, all juvenile gun court programs have four common elements. First, the juvenile gun court program provides early intervention for the juvenile offender, where the first gun court session should occur as close to the arrest as possible to increase accountability. Second, the participant is exposed to short, intense programming that is tailored to fit the individual's needs. Third, community members and professionals present on topics such as harm caused by gun violence to the community, making good choices, and problem solving without using guns or weapons. Fourth, court officials, law enforcement and community members all must collaborate and help to create solutions to the problems faced by participants and the community (Sheppard & Kelly, 2002).

An example of a juvenile gun court program is the Jefferson County Juvenile Gun Court in Birmingham, Alabama. This program has been rated as promising by the Model Programs Guide ("OJJDP Model Programs Guide," n.d.) and targets juveniles 17 years old and younger who have committed first-time nonviolent gun offenses (Sheppard & Kelly, 2002). Juveniles who are admitted to the program enter a 28-day boot camp program within 10 days of being referred to the program. The parents attend a parent education program while the juveniles are in boot camp. These parent education classes discuss mental health issues and the consequences of gun violence, and provide opportunities for parents to connect to social services. Once the juvenile participant has completed the boot camp program, he or she is placed on house arrest under probation supervision and must attend substance abuse classes, pass urine screens, attend parent education classes with parents, and complete community service.

The intensity of supervision decreases as the participant moves through the program, and the participant is released from the program upon successful completion of probation. Two years after program completion, the juvenile can petition to have his or her record sealed if he or she has not been convicted of any misdemeanor or felony offenses. If the participant has remained crime free by age 24, he or she can petition to have his or her juvenile record destroyed permanently (Sheppard & Kelly, 2002).

Sheppard and Kelly (2002) conducted a program evaluation of the Jefferson County Juvenile Gun Court program by examining case processing and recidivism rates of juvenile gun court participants; those not in the juvenile gun court, but who had a brief stay in detention followed by probation; and those who had committed a gun offense, but were on probation only in the neighboring community. The authors found that juvenile gun court participants spent less time on probation (10 months) compared to those who went to detention, but did not participate in gun court (12 months) and those who were assigned to probation only (16 months). Recidivism rates for those involved in the juvenile gun court also were significantly lower than those who did not participate in the juvenile gun court program (Sheppard & Kelly, 2002).

Intensive Supervision Probation

Traditional probation is the most common sanction used in the juvenile justice system ("Juveniles on Probation," n.d.). The juvenile court uses traditional probation as a way to divert low-risk non-violent and/or status offenders out of the juvenile court system and as an alternative to incarceration for juveniles who have committed more serious offenses. Traditional probation allows the juvenile to be supervised, but also at the same time remain in his or her community to attend school, work, and to participate in programming, if needed ("Juveniles on Probation," n.d.). However, traditional probation has been criticized because juvenile probation officers manage heavy caseloads, which does not allow them to supervise their juvenile probationers as closely as needed. Intensive supervision probation programs were created to fill this gap (Sherman et al., 1997).

The goal of Intensive Supervision Probation (ISP) is to reduce the cost of a high-risk juvenile's sanction by supervising him or her in the community with more intense probation services (Sherman et al., 1997). ISP officers are assigned small caseloads in order to be able to supervise closely their juvenile probationers and typically meet with the juvenile in person multiple times a week. The conditions of ISP are determined by the court and the probation officer and are typically stricter than traditional probation. ISP can include terms such as a curfew, drug/alcohol tests, school attendance checks, house arrest, electronic monitoring, and/or programming. ISP officers also are simultaneously responsible for assessing the juvenile to determine if he or she should be connected to additional community and/or health services. As long as a juvenile continues to meet the terms of his or her ISP, he or she will be released from the juvenile system upon completion of the sentence. However, if a juvenile violates the terms of his or her ISP, then he or she will be sent back to the juvenile court system (Sherman et al., 1997). The Repeat Offender Prevention Program is an example of an ISP that has been rated as promising by the Model Programs Guide ("OJJDP Model Programs Guide," n.d.).

The Repeat Offender Prevention Program (ROPP) of San Diego County, California targets juvenile offenders who are at high risk of becoming serious chronic repeat offenders (Howard, Misch, Burke, & Pennell, 2002). ROPP targets first-time offenders who are younger than 15.5 years of age and have any three of the following four risk factors: school problems (truancy, low grades, school suspension), family problems (victim of neglect or abuse, domestic violence in home, family with criminal background), substance abuse problems, or at high risk for predelinquent behavior (status offender, property crimes, gang association). After a youth is referred to the program by a probation officer, a team of social service providers collaborate to determine the youth's needs and what programs are appropriate, such as mental health services, vocational/educational programming, individual/group counseling, and/or transportation. Throughout the program the probation officer monitors the youth closely with the guidance of the team of social service providers. Once the youth nears completion of the program, he or she begins to transition into family and social services provided within the community (Howard et al., 2002).

Howard et al. (2002) conducted a program evaluation of the San Diego County Repeat Offender Prevention Program by randomly assigning 196 youths to intensive supervision probation and 171 youths to traditional probation. Every 6 months after program intake, assessments were conducted and probation records were examined for a period of 2 years. Both the comparison and experimental groups were similar upon intake. In both groups, the participants were on average 14 years of age and most were ethnic minorities; all of the youths had family and school issues and associated with delinquent peers. Those who participated in ROPP had a higher grade point average and passed more classes than those who were assigned to traditional probation. ROPP participants also failed fewer drug tests, and were more likely to complete the payment of their restitution/fines and community service than youth assigned to traditional probation. Upon exiting the program, ROPP participants also were found to be less at risk for education, substance use, and delinquent behavior problems and were associating less often with delinquent peers than those on traditional probation (Howard et al., 2002).

Aftercare

Approximately 100,000 juveniles are detained and placed outside of the home each year ("Juveniles in Corrections," n.d.). Nearly all of these juveniles will return to their communities, and 50% of serious juvenile offenders if left untreated will recidivate and return to the juvenile justice system (Gies, 2003). Aftercare programs attempt to interrupt this cycle through an intensive intervention of supervision and social services that occurs while incarcerated and continues upon the juvenile's release back into the community. Juvenile offenders are assessed upon intake into the detention center to determine what specific services (educational, vocational, mental health, substance abuse, counseling) the individual needs to be successful upon release, and the juvenile participates in these services under the supervision of the detention center. Prior to the youth's release back into the community, a parole officer meets with the juvenile offender and begins to enroll the youth in community programs and social services in anticipation of his or her release. Once back in the community, the juvenile offender remains under the supervision of the parole office while participating in programming tailored to the individual's needs. If the juvenile parolee is successful on parole, then he or she will have completed his or her sanction at the end of the parole term. If a juvenile parolee is not successful on parole, then his or her case will be sent back to the juvenile court for further assessment (Gies, 2003). The Family Integrated Transitions program is an example of a juvenile aftercare program that has been rated as effective by the Model Programs Guide ("OJJDP Model Programs Guide," n.d.).

The Family Integrated Transition (FIT) program targets juveniles who are younger than 17.5 years old, have substance abuse problems along with mental health problems (suicide attempt, diagnosed with serious mental illness or prescribed psychotropic medication), and are incarcerated and set to be released for 4 months or more on parole supervision (Aos, 2004). The goals of the program are to reduce recidivism; connect the youth's family with social services in the community; help the youth to abstain from substances; and improve mental health and prosocial behaviors. The program begins 2 months before the juvenile offender is released from detention and continues for 4 to 6 months after the juvenile is released to the community and on parole supervision. Participants are referred by the parole office to a team of therapists who work closely with the youth to create individualized programming. The therapists work with the youth directly to help him or her develop the necessary coping skills needed to be successful at home, in the community, at school, and on parole. The parents or guardians of the juvenile also work closely with the therapist to improve their relationships with the community, school, and parole office in order to serve as better advocates for the child (Aos, 2004).

Aos (2004) conducted a program evaluation of FIT by examining the recidivism rates of 104 youths who participated in the FIT program and 169 youths who were eligible for the program, but did not live in a county that had a program. Those who participated in the FIT program were significantly less likely to have been convicted of a felony than those who did not participate in the program. Eighteen months postrelease, for example, 41% of non-FIT participants had been convicted of a felony offense in comparison to 27% of FIT participants. Although FIT participants were less likely to be convicted of a misdemeanor and felony or a violent felony, the differences between the two groups was not found to be significant (Aos, 2004).

SUMMARY

By investing in secondary and tertiary prevention programs, we are investing in our future. Secondary prevention programs help to reduce the number of children who become involved in the juvenile justice system by targeting at-risk youth and providing them with the support they need to mitigate the risk factors in their lives. Tertiary prevention programs help to reduce the number of juveniles who commit another delinquent act after being released from the juvenile justice system by providing the child with the necessary tools needed to reduce their risk factors and increase their protective factors. Tertiary programs delve into the root causes of the delinquent behavior, thus allowing the juvenile to successfully reintegrate back into his or her community upon release from the juvenile system. Both secondary and tertiary prevention programs help to reduce the number of children involved in the juvenile justice system and will help to create safer communities with children who are productive members and eventually successful adults.

KEY TERMS

Risk factors
Protective factors
Parens patriae
House of refuge
Cottage
Juvenile transfer
Judicial waiver
Prosecutorial waiver
Statutory exclusion/Legislative waiver
Demand waiver
Once an adult, always an adult

Blended sentencing
Reverse waiver
Court-ordered probation
Residential placement
Detention
Office of Juvenile Justice & Delinquency Prevention (OJJDP)
Model Programs Guide
Mentor
Restorative justice
Problem-solving courts

DISCUSSION QUESTIONS

1. Think about the environment where you were raised. Were there any characteristics or attributes of that environment (i.e., individual, family, school, peer, and community) that you would consider risk or protective factors? Which of these do you think were most influential for your own behavior?
2. Discuss the advantages and disadvantages of the *parens patriae* philosophy.
3. Discuss the various methods for transferring juveniles to adult court. What do you think the minimum age should be for transferring juveniles to adult court? Explain your answer.
4. Should secondary and tertiary prevention programs be developed specifically to reduce disproportionate minority contact with the juvenile justice system? If yes, explain why and what these programs would look like. If no, explain why not.
5. How would you convince your state or local lawmaker to fund secondary and tertiary prevention programs for juveniles? Be sure to consider items such as recidivism rates, the costs of incarceration, and program evaluation findings.
6. Should all juvenile offenders who are incarcerated complete an aftercare program? If yes, explain why. If no, explain why not.

REFERENCES

Adams, B., & Addie, S. (2010). Delinquency cases waived to criminal court, 2007. Office of Juvenile Justice and Delinquency Prevention. Retrieved from http://www.ojjdp.gov.

Aos, S. (2004). *Washington State's family integrated transitions program for juvenile offenders: Outcome evaluation and benefit-cost analysis.* Olympia, WA: Washington State Institute for Public Policy.

Arbreton, A. J. A., & McClanahan, W. S. (2002). *Targeted outreach: Boys and Girls Clubs of America's approach to gang prevention and intervention.* New York, NY: Public/Private Ventures.

Arthur, M. W., Hawkins, J. D., Pollard, J., Catalano, R. F., & Baglioni, Jr., A. J. (2002). Measuring risk and protective factors for substance use, delinquency, and other adolescent problem behaviors: The communities that care youth survey. *Evaluation Review, 26*(6), 575–601.

Asher, S. R., & Coie, J. D. (1990). *Peer rejection in childhood.* New York, NY: Cambridge University Press.

Bartollas, C., & Miller, S. J. (2008). *Juvenile justice in America* (6th ed.).Upper Saddle River, NJ: Prentice Hall.

Benard, B. (1991, August). *Fostering resiliency in kids: Protective factors in the family, school, and community.* Portland, OR: Northwest Regional Educational Laboratories.

Big Brothers Big Sisters of America (BBBS). (n.d.). *100 years of history.* Retrieved from http://www.bbbs.org.

Boys and Girls Clubs of America. (n.d.). *Gang prevention through targeted outreach*. Retrieved from http://www.bgcnj.org.

Brantingham, P. J., & Faust, F. L. (1976). A conceptual model of crime prevention. *Crime & Delinquency, 22*(3), 284–296.

Center for Court Innovation. (n.d.). *Problem-solving justice*. Retrieved from http://www.courtinnovation.org/index.cfm?fuseaction=page.viewPage&pageID=505&document.

Dishneau, D. (2011, February 4). Md., Calif. Suspend "scared straight" programs. *Associated Press*. Retrieved from http://abcnews.go.com/Entertainment/wireStory?id=12845875&page=1.

Elliott, D. S., Hamburg, B. A., & Williams, K. R. (1998). Violence in American schools: An overview. In D. S. Elliot, B. A. Hamburg, & K. R. Williams (Eds.), *Violence in American schools* (pp. 3–28). Cambridge, UK: Cambridge University Press.

Elliott, D. S., Williams, K. R., & Hamburg, B. (1998). An integrated approach to violence prevention. In D. S. Elliot, B. A. Hamburg, & K. R. Williams (Eds.), *Violence in American schools* (pp. 379–386). Cambridge, UK: Cambridge University Press.

Fagan, J., & Wilkinson, D. L. (1998). Social contexts and functions of adolescent violence. In D. S. Elliot, B. A. Hamburg, & K. R. Williams (Eds.), *Violence in American schools* (pp. 55–93). Cambridge, UK: Cambridge University Press.

Finckenauer, J. O. (1982). *Scared straight and the panacea phenomenon*. Englewood Cliffs, NJ: Prentice Hall.

Garnes, L., & Menlove, R. (2003). *School-wide discipline practices: A look at the effectiveness of common practices*. Paper presented at American Council on Rural Special Education 23rd Annual Conference. Salt Lake City, Utah.

Gies, S. V. (2003). Aftercare services (NCJ 201800). Washington, DC: U.S. Department of Justice, Office of Justice Programs, Office of Juvenile Justice and Delinquency Prevention.

Griffin, P. (2008). National overviews. *State Juvenile Justice Profiles*. Pittsburgh, PA: National Center for Juvenile Justice. Retrieved from http://www.ncjj.org/Research_Resources/State_Profiles.aspx.

Hawkins, J. D., Farrington, D. P., & Catalano, R. F. (1998). Reducing violence through the schools. In D. S. Elliot, B. A. Hamburg, & K. R. Williams (Eds.), *Violence in American schools* (pp. 188–216). Cambridge, UK: Cambridge University Press.

Herrenkohl, T. I., Maguin, E., Hill, K. G., Hawkins, J. D., Abbot, R. D., & Catalano, R. F. (2000). Developmental risk factors for youth violence. *Journal of Adolescent Health, 26*(3), 176–186.

Hickert, A. O., Becker, E. E., & Prospero, M. (2010). *Evaluation of Utah juvenile drug courts*. Utah Criminal Justice Center, University of Utah. Retrieved from http://ucjc.law.utah.edu/wp-content/uploads/110.pdf.

Hockenberry, S. (2010). Person offense cases in juvenile court, 2007. Office of Juvenile Justice and Delinquency Prevention. Retrieved from http://www.ojjdp.gov.

Howard, L., Misch, G., Burke, C., & Pennell, S. (2002). *San Diego County Probation Department's Repeat Offender Prevention Program final evaluation report*. Retrieved from http://sandiegohealth.org/crime/publicationid_753_1432.pdf.

Howell, J. C. (1997). Youth gangs (FS-9722OJJDP). Washington, DC: U.S. Department of Justice, Office of Justice Programs, Office of Juvenile Justice and Delinquency Prevention.

Howell, J. C. (2003). *Preventing & reducing juvenile delinquency: A comprehensive framework*. Thousand Oaks, CA: Sage Publications, Inc.

Howell, J. C., & Decker, S. H. (1999). The youth gangs, drugs, and violence connection (NCJ 171152). Washington, DC: U.S. Department of Justice, Office of Justice Programs, Office of Juvenile Justice and Delinquency Prevention.

Job Corps. (n.d.). About Job Corps. Retrieved from http://www.jobcorps.gov.

Juveniles in corrections. Office of Juvenile Justice and Delinquency Prevention. Retrieved from https://www.ncjrs.gov/html/ojjdp/202885/contents.html.

Juveniles on probation. Office of Juvenile Justice and Delinquency Prevention. Retrieved from http://www.ojjdp.gov/ojstatbb/probation/index.html.

Knoll, C., & Sickmund, M. (2010). Delinquency cases in juvenile court, 2007. Office of Juvenile Justice and Delinquency Prevention. Retrieved from http://www.ojjdp.gov.

Lab, S. P., Williams, M. R., Holcomb, J. E., Burek, M. W., King, W. R., & Buerger, M. E. (2011). *Criminal justice: The essentials* (2nd ed.). New York, NY: Oxford University Press.

Livsey, S. (2010). Juvenile delinquency probation caseload, 2007. Office of Juvenile Justice and Delinquency Prevention. Retrieved from http://www.ojjdp.gov.

Marans, S., & Schaefer, M. (1998). Community policing, schools, and mental health: The challenge of collaboration. In D. S. Elliot, B. A. Hamburg, & K. R. Williams (Eds.), *Violence in American schools* (pp. 312–347). Cambridge, UK: Cambridge University Press.

Martin, G. (2005). *Juvenile justice: Process and systems*. Thousand Oaks, CA: Sage Publications, Inc.

Movimiento Ascendencia. Office Juvenile Justice and Delinquency Prevention. Retrieved from http://www.nationalgangcenter.gov/SPT/Programs/94.

Mullis, R. L., Cornille, T. A., & Mullis, A. K., & Huber, J. (2004). Female juvenile offending: A review of characteristics and contexts. *Journal of Child and Family Studies, 13*(2), 205–218.

National Drug Court Institute. (2003). Juvenile drug courts: Strategies in practice (NCJ 197866). Washington, DC: U.S. Department of Justice, Office of Justice Programs, Bureau of Justice Assistance.

OJJDP DMC—Reduction Best Practices Database. Office Juvenile Justice Delinquency Prevention. Retrieved from http://www.2dsgonline.com/dmc/dmc_default.aspx.

OJJDP Model Programs Guide. (n.d.). Office Juvenile Justice Delinquency Prevention. Retrieved from http://www.ojjdp.gov/mpg/.

OJJDP Statistical Briefing Book. Office of Juvenile Justice and Delinquency Prevention. Retrieved from http://ojjdp.gov/ojstatbb/.

Perry, D. G, Hodges, E. V. E., & Egan, S. K. (2001). Determinants of chronic victimization by peers: A review and a new model of family influence. In J. Juvonen & S. Graham (Eds.), *Peer harassment in school: The plight of the vulnerable and victimized* (pp. 73–104). New York, NY: The Guilford Press.

Petrosino, A., Turpin-Petrosino, C., & Finckenauer, J. O. (2000). Well-meaning programs can have harmful effects! Lessons from experiments of programs such as Scared Straight. *Crime and Delinquency, 46*, 354–379. doi:10.1177/0011128700046003006

Puzzanchera, C. (2009). Juvenile arrests 2008. Office of Juvenile Justice and Delinquency Prevention. Retrieved from http://www.ojjdp.gov.

Restorative justice online. Prison Fellowship International. Retrieved from http://www.restorativejustice.org/.

Rigby, K. (2002). *New perspectives on bullying*. London, UK: Jessica Kingsley Publishers.

Schochet, P., Brughardy, J., & Glazerman, S. (2000). *National Job Corps study: The impacts of Job Corps on participants' employment and related outcomes*. Washington, DC: U.S. Department of Labor, Employment and Training Administration.

Schuster, B. (2001). Rejection and victimization by peers: Social perception and social behavior mechanisms. In J. Juvonen & S. Graham (Eds.), *Peer harassment in school: The plight of the vulnerable and victimized* (pp. 290–309). New York, NY: The Guilford Press.

Sheppard, D., & Kelly, P. (2002). Juvenile gun courts: Promoting accountability and providing treatment (NCJ 187078). Washington, DC: U.S. Department of Justice, Office of Justice Programs, Office of Juvenile Justice and Delinquency Prevention.

Sherman, L. W., Gottfredson, D., MacKenzie, D., Eck, J., Reuter, P., & Bushway, S. (1997). *Crime prevention: What works, what doesn't, what's promising*. Retrieved from https://www.ncjrs.gov/works/.

Sickmund, M. (2010). Juveniles in residential placement 1997–2008. Office of Juvenile Justice and Delinquency Prevention. Retrieved from http://www.ojjdp.gov.

Small, M. A. (1997). Introduction to this issue. *Behavioral Sciences and the Law, 15*, 119–124.

Snyder, H. N., & Sickmund, M. (2006). *Juvenile offenders and victims: 2006 national report*. Washington, DC: U.S. Department of Justice, Office of Justice Programs, Office of Juvenile Justice and Delinquency Prevention.

Stephens, R. (1998). Safe school planning. In D. S. Elliot, B. A. Hamburg, & K. R. Williams (Eds.), *Violence in American schools* (pp. 253–289). Cambridge, UK: Cambridge University Press.

Stetson, R., Stetson, E., & Kelly, J. (1998, April 13–15). *Building a civil society: Are schools responsible?* Paper presented at AERA Annual Meeting, San Diego, CA.

Thompson, M., & Cohen, L. (2005). When the bullied must adjust. *Education Digest, 70*(6), 16–19.

Tierney, J. P., Grossman, J. B., & Resch, N. (2000). *Making a difference: An impact study of Big Brothers Big Sisters.* New York, NY: Public/Private Ventures.

Trudeau, J, Barrick, K., Williams, J., & Roehl, J. (2010). *Independent evaluation of the national weed and seed strategy.* Retrieved from http://www.weedandseed.info/docs/reports/WnS_Final_Evaluation_Report.pdf.

Umbreit, M. S., & Coates, R. B. (1993) Cross-site analysis of victim–offender mediation in four states. *Crime & Delinquency, 39*(4), 565–585.

Umbreit, M. S., & Greenwood, J. (2000). National survey of victim–offender mediation programs in the United States (NCJ 176350). Washington, DC: U.S. Department of Justice, Office of Justice Programs, Office for Victims of Crime.

U. S. Department of Justice. (n.d.). Community policing defined. Retrieved from http://www.cops.usdoj.gov/default.asp?item=36

Van Patten, J. J., & Siegrist, J. (2000). *Developing a common faith and ethic for school safety.* Paper presented at Annual Meeting of the American Educational Research Association, New Orleans, LA.

Welsh, B.C., & Farrington, D. P. (2007). Save the children from a life of crime. *Criminology and Public Policy, 6*(4), 871–880.

Wexler, D. (1999). Therapeutic jurisprudence and the culture of critique. *Journal of Contemporary Legal Issues, 10,* 263–293.

White, M. D., Fyfe, J. F., Campbell, S. P., & Goldkamp, J. S. (2003). The police role in preventing homicide: Considering the impact of problem-oriented policing on the prevalence of murder. *Journal of Research on Crime & Delinquency, 40,* 194–225. doi: 10.1177/0022427803251126.

Whitehead, J. T., & Lab, S. P. (2009). *Juvenile justice: An introduction* (6th ed.). Albany, NY: Matthew Bender & Company, Inc.

Williams, K., Curry, G. D., & Cohen, M. (2002). Gang prevention programs for female adolescents: An evaluation. In W. L. Reed & S. H. Decker (Eds.), *Responding to Gangs: Evaluation and research* (pp. 225–263). Washington, DC: U.S. Department of Justice, National Institute of Justice.

CHAPTER 13

Adult Offender Recidivism Reduction Programs

Kristine Levan
Plymouth State University

INTRODUCTION

There are currently more than seven million adults under some form of correctional supervision. This number comprises over five million parolees and probationers, and two million individuals who are confined in either prisons or jails (Glaze, 2010). Approximately 95% of inmates will eventually return to the community (Hughes, Wilson, & Beck, 2001, as cited in Petersilia, 2003), and of all of the admissions made to prison each year, approximately 33% are those who failed or violated their parole (Blumstein & Beck, 2005; Steen & Opsal, 2007, as cited in Bahr, Harris, Fisher, & Armstrong, 2010).

It is apparent that society ultimately will need to contend with these offenders upon their release from prison. More than 630,000 prisoners return to the community annually, a number that is approximately four times as high as just a few decades ago (Hughes & Wilson, 2002, Travis & Lawrence, 2002, Harrison & Karberg, 2004, as cited in Solomon, Johnson, Travis, & McBride, 2004). As such, it seems logical that the appropriate programs are intact for released offenders to successfully reintegrate back into society without continuing to commit offenses. Programs exist both inside correctional facilities and in the community in an attempt to prevent offenders from recidivating and ultimately returning to prison. However, since modern prisoners serve longer sentences than in the past, they are exposed to the negative aspects of prison for a longer period of time, and a lack of financial support for various programs and services means that fewer inmates are able to participate in them than before (Solomon et al, 2004).

Most inmates leaving prison return to the communities they resided in prior to their incarceration. Many of these communities are fraught with issues such as high crime rates, poverty, and unemployment (Lynch & Sabol, 2001, La Vigne, Kachnowski et al., 2003, La Vigne, Mamalian, Travis, & Visher, 2003, La Vigne, Thomson et al., 2003, Visher, La Vigne, & Travis, 2004, as cited in Solomon et al., 2004). This means that many are returning to communities where conditions exist that encourage criminal activity. Individuals who are released to communities that exhibit high levels of poverty and unemployment are significantly more likely to recidivate (Harer, 1994; Austin & Hardyman, 2004). Ex-offenders who are at the greatest risk of recidivism are those who have committed financially related crimes such as burglary, robbery, and motor vehicle theft, or those who have been arrested for substance abuse (Langan & Levin, 2000, as cited in Petersilia, 2003).

Whereas the process of a return to a life of crime is called recidivism, the process by which offenders cease to commit crime is often called desistance (Maruna, 2001). Many of the notions of desistance by way of correctional programming are based on the ideas of social bond theory, which states that conventional ties to institutions such as family, education, and employment help prevent criminality (Gottfredson & Hirschi, 1990). Programs offered in prison or after release often center on rebuilding the bonds between the offender and these institutions in an effort to prevent offenders from continuing to commit crimes.

PRISON-BASED RECIDIVISM REDUCTION PROGRAMS

Many of the issues surrounding prison-based recidivism reduction programs center on a lack of finances coupled with a lack of public interest in funding these programs. The principle of least eligibility is one that guides the types of programs and services offered to inmates. This principle states that prisoners should only receive services similar to those offered for free to the nonoffending general community (Feest, 1999; Petersilia, 2003). As more and more prisoners are released on mandatory parole rather than discretionary parole, many have less incentive to participate in any type of recidivism reduction program (Haney, 2002).

As prison overcrowding continues to be an issue, the country builds more correctional facilities in an attempt to accommodate the influx of inmates. Funding the construction of new correctional facilities, as well as staffing and maintaining these facilities, means that there is less funding for recidivism reduction programs (Petersilia, 2003). Programs such as those focusing on rehabilitation, treatment, education, and vocational training are becoming more and more scarce.

Rehabilitation Programs

Rehabilitation is a term that is used differently in various contexts. For purposes of discussion herein, rehabilitation means anything that is designed to change how prisoners respond to their environment, as well as alter their lifestyles and motivations (Alleman, 2002; Ross, 2008). Ultimately, the goal of rehabilitation is to provide ex-offenders with the skills and abilities necessary for them to be returned to their communities and not reoffend. Prison-based rehabilitation programs take on a variety of forms and cover a wide range of behaviors for which changes are sought. Some examples of rehabilitation programs are treatment programs, therapeutic programs, educational programs, vocational training programs, work-release programs, and family-based intervention programs.

Throughout much of the 1960s and 1970s, correctional ideologies focused on rehabilitation as a major purpose of punishment in an attempt to reduce recidivism of offenders. In 1974, this philosophy was called into question when a researcher indicated that "the rehabilitative efforts that have been reported so far have had no appreciable effect on rehabilitation" (Martinson, 1974, p. 25). As a result of this assessment, many began to question whether rehabilitation programs were worth the time, effort, and financial resources that were being poured into them.

The rehabilitation ideal can be contrasted with other purposes of punishment, including deterrence, retribution, and just deserts. After Martinson's claims, many began to revert to the ideologies that these other purposes of punishment entail. Van den Haag, in particular, states that rehabilitation has already failed with first-time offenders, and does not seem to be working for repeat offenders. He cites a return to the ideas of punishment for offenders (1982). Some believe that rehabilitation has never been an idea that is supported by correctional administrators. As stated by Newman (2002), "... rehabilitation became simply a catch-word of correctional administrators who sought to soften the cruel conditions of imprisonment used to justify asking for more funding" (p. 244).

Treatment Programs

Of all the services available to inmates, substance abuse treatment is the most common. According to a national survey, 74% of prisons and 61% of jails offer some form of substance abuse treatment (Taxman, Perdoni, & Harrison, 2007). The use of the word *treatment* should, however, be considered with caution, as many prisons classify various programs as drug treatment, including therapeutic communities, group therapies, 12-step programs, and methadone maintenance (MacKenzie, 2006). Studies indicate that those who participate in substance abuse treatment are less likely to recidivate once they are released (Sherman, Farrington, Welsh, & MacKenzie, 2002, as cited in Bahr et al., 2010). The effectiveness of the programs varies, though, in terms of what type of program is being offered. Therapeutic communities and group counseling are the most effective at reducing recidivism (Mitchell, MacKenzie, & Wilson, 2005, as cited in MacKenzie, 2006)

The number of individuals incarcerated for substance abuse-related crimes has continued to increase, in part as a result of the War on Drugs and subsequent increases in penalties associated with these types of crimes. Mandatory minimum sentences and three-strikes laws mean that there are more substance abusers behind bars than in previous years (Harrison, 2001). On the federal level, those imprisoned for drugs account for more than 74,000 prisoners, and at the state level they represent more than 250,000 inmates (West & Sabol, 2010). This means that drug offenders comprise approximately 20% of state inmates and around 56% of federal inmates. These numbers do not represent the full spectrum of drug abuse and addiction among the incarcerated population since only the most serious offense for which the offender is incarcerated is reported.

If an offender was using drugs or was in possession of an illicit substance while committing a more serious offense, the drug offense would not be reflected in these numbers. Chronic substance abusers who use drugs such as crack, cocaine, and heroin commit a disproportionate amount of crime (Ball, Rosen, Flueck, & Nurco, 1981; Pettiway, 1987, Inciardi & Pottieger, 1998, and Lipton & Johnson, 1998, as cited in Harrison, 2001). Nor do these numbers include more than 30% of state inmates and nearly 20% of federal inmates who admitted to being under the influence of alcohol at the time of their offense (Rand, Sabol, Sinclair, & Snyder, 2010). Only about 10% of substance abusers and 8% of alcohol abusers claim to have ever received any type of treatment prior to their current sentence (Mumola, 1999).

The criminal justice system is an ideal setting to assist with drug treatment because there are so many individuals with substance abuse issues gathered in one place (Harrison, 2001). Because of the high costs of housing these offenders in the custody of the criminal justice system and the high costs to society in their likely continued involvement in crime upon their release, delivering quality substance abuse treatment should be of the utmost concern (Martin & Inciardi, 1993(a), and Martin & Inciardi, 1993(b), as cited in Harrison, 2001). However, there are several issues with trying to deliver treatment services behind bars. "Treatment" may be accomplished simply by attending group meetings, with little or no participation or desire to change from the offender (Harrison, 2001). The waiting lists for in-prison treatment programs are lengthy (Harrison, 2001), and as such, only a fraction of the inmates who need treatment will actually be able to receive it (Petersilia, 2003). When inmates are able to receive treatment, the programs are often not lengthy enough, nor intensive enough, to have an appreciable effect on their dependency issues (Harrison, 2001).

The Federal Bureau of Prisons tackles the drug problem with what they call a layered approach. This three-pronged approach mandates that any inmates with a history of substance abuse complete a drug treatment program while incarcerated. Additionally, they may volunteer to attend drug abuse counseling, which may be self-help, individual, or group based. Finally, residential drug treatment units would be available in order to provide intense therapy for substance abusers (Murray, 1992, as cited in Leukefeld & Tims, 2009).

Although the drug abuse and addiction situation seems bleak, substance abuse treatment programs show promise. There has been a vast amount of research conducted on the efficacy of treatment programs. Drug treatment programs, especially those that are conducted in group or therapeutic community settings, lead to decreased levels of recidivism among participants (Wexler, Falkin, & Lipton, 1990, Wexler, Williams, Early, & Trotman, 1996, Pearson & Lipton, 1999, Prendergast, Podus, Chang, & Urada, 2002, Mitchell & MacKenzie, 2003, and Mitchell et al., 2005, as cited in Turner, Myers, Sexton, & Smith, 2007; Messina, Burdon, Hagopian, & Prendergast, 2006). Because many inmates who have substance abuse issues also suffer from psychiatric illnesses or disorders, this information underscores the need to have more collaborative efforts between substance abuse treatment programs and some form of psychological treatment (Messina et al., 2006).

Therapeutic and Psychological Programs

Psychotherapy is often used in an attempt to modify the attitudes and behaviors of inmates. Although both individual and group therapy settings are found in correctional facilities, group therapies have become increasingly common in recent decades. A recent national survey found that approximately 20% of inmates participate in group therapy (Morgan, Winterowd, & Ferrell, 2006). This is in part due to prison overcrowding and the costs associated with individual-level therapy (Corsini, 1964, Yong, 1971, as cited in Morgan et al., 2006; Lipton, 1988). Aside from the practical aspects of group therapy, these types of settings also allow inmates to increase their social and communication skills (Yalom, 1995, as cited in Morgan et al., 2006), skill sets which are often lacking among the inmate population.

There are some limitations to group therapies. Many of the individuals who facilitate group therapy sessions have not received a doctorate degree and, in many instances, are not supervised by an individual who has received a doctorate degree (Morgan et al., 2006), leading some to believe that underqualified staff may be placed in charge of these therapeutic efforts. Confidentiality is also an issue. Not only is there concern that some inmates in group therapy sessions may not keep the discussions private, but there is also concern that, because therapists may need to report concerns over potential suicides, violent activities, riots, or escape attempts, that the inmates participating in these sessions may not be entirely forthcoming (Morgan et al., 2006).

Cognitive behavioral therapy is one type of therapy that may be used to change an inmate's behavior. This form of therapy is used to try to change how the inmate thinks and perceives his or her life situation (Dobson & Khatri, 2000, as cited in MacKenzie, 2006), and is based on the notion that in order to change unwanted behavior, people must alter their cognitions (Dobson & Craig, 1996, as cited in MacKenzie, 2006). It focuses on disentangling problematic thinking that may lead to criminal behavior and helps to build problem-solving skills and rational thought processes (Quinn,

2003). A major advantage cited for this type of therapy is that it can be used on various types of of-fenses, ranging from domestic abuse to substance abuse (MacKenzie, 2006), making it applicable to many types of offenders. Cognitive behavioral therapy has been shown to be effective at reducing criminogenic behavior among participants (Walters, 1999; Polaschek, Wilson, Townsend, & Daly, 2005; MacKenzie, 2006)

Participation in a therapeutic community while incarcerated has been shown to be effective in reducing recidivism upon release. This type of treatment is the most effective when it is combined with some form of postincarceration effort (Butzin, Martin, & Inciardi, 2002; Inciardi, Surratt, Martin, & Hooper, 2002). This is likely because once an offender is released from prison, he or she may need to continue to address the issues that led to his or her criminogenic tendencies.

Education Programs

Offenders generally have been found to have received less formal education than their law-abiding counterparts. More than 40% of all individuals who are incarcerated have less than a high school education, and less than 13% of all inmates have obtained some college education, as compared with nearly 50% of the general population (Harlow, 2003). Disparities become even more apparent when considering the differences by gender and race. Males and minorities in state prisons are less likely to have completed high school or obtained a GED than those who are female and/or white (Harlow, 2003).When inmates were asked what the most important factor was for dropping out of school, the most frequently cited reasons were behavioral or academic problems or lost interest in school (34.9%), family or personal problems (16.4%), beginning work or enlisting in the military (13%), and being convicted of a crime (11.1%) (Harlow, 2003).

These results indicate that there is something qualitatively different between those who are incarcerated and those who are not. Those who are incarcerated are more likely to grow up and reside in disadvantaged communities and have greater levels of exposure to criminogenic activities. As such, they are less likely to place great value on formal education and are more likely to have academic difficulties, making it more difficult to achieve academic success.

The mainstays of prison-based education programs are three-fold. As inmates become more ed-ucated and more knowledgeable, their job prospects postprison are believed to increase. Education also is believed to allow inmates to become more responsible and to hold them accountable for their own individual learning (McCollum, 1994). Ultimately, these two factors contribute to the fact that those who participate in educational programs are less likely to recidivate than those who do not (Chappell, 2004; Messemer & Valentine, 2004). Those who benefit the most from in-prison education programs and recidivate the least seem to be those who start out with the lowest levels of education or who are illiterate (Fabelo, 2002).

Basic education is more frequently available to inmates than postsecondary education (Lahm, 2000). Eighty nine percent of prisons and nearly 60% of jails offer some form of remedial educa-tion program (Taxman et al., 2007). The range of educational programs provided by an institution often depends on the security level; maximum security and super-max prisons are usually limited to either General Equivalency Diploma (GED) program, or Adult Basic Education programs, which provide skills up to an eighth-grade level (Ross, 2008). In terms of basic literacy programs, many states and the federal government require that inmates demonstrate basic literacy prior to their release into the community (Thomas, 1995, and Bosworth, 2002, as cited in Guerrero, 2011). This requirement is often ignored however, due to a combination of overcrowding issues and a lack of available programs to guarantee that literacy is obtained (Applegate, 2001, as cited in Quinn, 2003).

A GED is used to demonstrate that an individual has the knowledge and skills necessary to earn a high school diploma. Because many inmates lack a basic high school education, these programs are frequently found in correctional facilities. Studies also indicate a high level of correlation between inmates who earn their GED while incarcerated and the ability to desist from crime upon their release from prison (Walsh, 1985, Langenbach, North, Aagaard, & Chown, 1990, Schumaker, Anderson, & Anderson, 1990, and Jeffords & McNitt, 1993, as cited in MacKenzie, 2006; Aos, Phipps, Barnoski, & Lieb, 2001 and Nuttall, Hollmen, & Staley, 2003, as cited in Guerrero, 2011).

College level course instructors are often either graduate students or college professors that are either volunteering their services or earning internship credit for their participation in the program. The benefits of obtaining either an associate's or a bachelor's degree while incarcerated are vast. Most notably, earning a degree has consistently been linked with lowered recidivism rates upon release to the community (Schumaker et al, 1990; Batiuk, Moke, & Rountree, 1997, Stevens & Ward, 1997, Wilson, Gallagher, & MacKenzie, 2000, Ross & Richards, 2002, Ross, 2008, and Thomas & Thomas, 2008, as cited in Guerrero, 2011). Additionally, those who participate in educational programs while incarcerated are significantly more likely to find employment postrelease (Ubah, 2004, as cited in Guerrero, 2011).

Since 2004, the Inviting Convicts to College Program has been active. Coordinated by the University of Wisconsin-Oshkosh, this program allows undergraduate and graduate students to teach college level courses in convict criminology to inmates at two state prisons (Rose, Reed, & Richards, 2005; Richards, Rose, & Reed, 2006; Ross, 2008). In addition to learning convict criminology, these inmate–students are given guidance and information about applying to college, such as financial aid and college application information (Ross, 2008; Offender to College Program, 2011). The courses are run like traditional college courses, expecting the inmate–students to attend class, write papers, and complete exams. Upon completion of the course, inmate–students are issued a certificate of completion, which may be helpful in gaining admittance to a university upon their release from prison (Ross, 2008). Research results indicate that the program has been successful in achieving its goals, including reducing recidivism rates among participants, and participants' enrolling in universities upon their release from prison (Ross, 2008; Rose, Reschenberg, & Richards, 2010).

There has been a significant decline in the number of prisons that offer college level courses (Tewksbury, Erickson, & Taylor, 2000). Some believe that outside instructors may be seen by prison administrators as a threat to daily routine and security. Educated inmates may also be seen as a threat since they may communicate issues such as poorly run facilities or inappropriate prison conditions to the media or other outsiders (Ross, 2008). In fact, this decline is primarily a result of the Violent Crime Control and Law Enforcement Act of 1994. This act makes anyone who was found guilty of a felony ineligible for Pell Grants. Although the public showed little interest in funding college level education for inmates, the total amount that was rewarded to inmates under Pell Grants was less than 1% (Molitor, 1994; Petersilia, 2003).

The Drug Free Student Act of 1998 further restricts many inmates and ex-offenders from participation in college level courses. This act disallows any individual who has been convicted of a drug-related offense from receiving student loans or participating in work-study programs (Ross, 2008). Given the significant number of offenders who are convicted of an offense involving illegal substances, this means that many are denied the opportunity to receive funding for college education throughout the remainder of their lives.

One of the issues in studying the effects of education on recidivism is the issue of self-selection. Because these programs are voluntary, it may be that those who participate in the programs are more motivated to change their behavior (Gottfredson & Hirschi, 1990; Ubah, 2002). It may therefore not be the education programs, but the attitudes and motivations of the inmates themselves, that are more likely to lead to change. The individual's view of the value of education may be ultimately what prevents them from engaging in criminal activity (Loeber, Stouthamer-Loeber, Van Kammen, & Farrington, 1991).

When considering male and female prison education programs, it is crucial to understand the differences in learning styles between genders. Males often are more independent learners and enjoy competition, while females are more likely to thrive in a cooperative environment that is more teamwork oriented (Hayes & Richardson, 1995, as cited in Quinn, 2003).

Many argue that the idea behind prison education programs defeats some of the very purposes of correctional facilities. Inmates are sent to prison to be punished and fulfill purposes such as retribution, just deserts, and deterrence. Allowing them to participate in educational programs, especially those that are college level, may violate the principle of least eligibility. Many law-abiding citizens cannot afford higher education, so many believe it is unfair to provide these services to inmates at the expense of taxpayers. In order to justify prison education to the public, the reductions in recidivism must be noted and addressed since the benefit to society of releasing inmates who are more educated would ultimately be a lower crime rate and increased feelings of safety from crime.

Vocational Training Programs

When examining the differences between offenders and nonoffenders, there are stark differences in their typical employment histories. Those who are involved in crime are consistently less likely to maintain stable and legitimate work than their law-abiding counterparts. They are also significantly less likely to have marketable job skills (Andrews & Bonta, 2003). Correctional facilities may offer some form of vocational training in order to increase the likelihood of securing legitimate employment upon release.

Vocational training is meant to be training in a specific job area, such as mechanics, maintenance, or technology. Increasing specialized skills can greatly increase an offender's likelihood of obtaining legitimate employment, and therefore greatly reduce their risk of recidivism upon returning to their community (Schumaker et al, 1990). It has also been shown that those who participate in vocational training are less likely to have disciplinary issues while they are incarcerated (Ward, 2009). As with all programs designed to rehabilitate or reintegrate inmates back into their community, vocational programs suffer from self-selection issues, as those who are more likely to volunteer for these programs may be more motivated to desist from crime (Saylor & Gaes, 1987, as cited in Ward, 2009).

Implementing effective vocational training is difficult. Many inmates may be released before they complete the full cycle of their training (Marquart et al., 1994). Additionally, the overcrowding issue plays a role in a lack of training and in-prison employment opportunities for inmates (Ross, 2008; Hassine, 2010). Moreover, all prisons generally offer what they deem to be vocational training, but some of this training equates to prison maintenance duties (Conley, 1980). Most inmates who are participating in what is deemed vocational training are actually completing duties such as washing laundry, cleaning the correctional facility, groundskeeping, maintenance, or kitchen duty and are supervised by correctional officers, who do little more than simply supervise their work

(Conley, 1980; Ross, 2008). These types of employment positions do little to prepare inmates for employment in the community after their release, and therefore are likely ineffective at preventing recidivism (Maguire, Flanagan, & Thornberry, 1988; Saylor & Gaes, 1992; MacKenzie, 2006).

Ross and Richards (2002) explain that on a typical day, about 20% of inmates are working in a prison industry, such as a factory. Five percent of inmates are participating in each of the following activities: mopping floors, working in the kitchen, maintenance, or groundskeeping. Approximately 10% are engaged in one of the following: GED classes, spending time in the correctional infirmary or their cell due to a medical issue, or being confined in solitary confinement. Only about 2.5% of the inmates are in drug treatment classes. The remaining inmates (over 30%) are confined to their housing units with idle time on their hands.

Women's vocational training programs have historically illustrated marked gender stereotyping. For instance, female prisons are more likely to offer training in fields such as sales, administrative work, and the service industry (Lahm, 2000). These are the fields that are also the most underpaid in society, perhaps putting female offenders at a further disadvantage when released from prison. Females leaving prison are often in a position where not only do they have to be able to support themselves, but also dependent children (Fleisher, Rison, & Helman, 1997).

Work-Release Programs

Work-release programs can consist of a variety of different types of programs. Some prisoner work-release programs allow offenders to live in the community, while others temporarily allow them to return to their communities while still serving their prison sentences.

Rearrest rates for those participating in work-release programs have been shown to be lower than for those who do not participate in these programs (Turner & Petersilia, 1996, and Uggen, 2000, as cited in Petersilia, 2003). Offenders who participate in a work-release program may have the opportunity to transition the position into employment postrelease. At a minimum, these programs allow offenders to increase both their job skills and their readiness to return to the work force after they have served their sentences (Petersilia, 2003).

Family-Based Intervention Programs

There is no doubt that imprisonment has a negative impact on both the prisoner and the family members that he or she has left behind. A lack of family support is often a detriment to inmates while they are incarcerated. More than half of all inmates are parents of at least one minor child (Travis, McBride, & Solomon, 2005). A lack of both financial and social support is reported for family members who are left behind after a parent has been incarcerated (Hagan & Dinovitzer, 1999). Marital relationships are often strained and may even end in divorce as a result of spousal incarceration. The effects of incarceration on both the inmate and the family members left behind may be tempered with family visitation, as well as parent-education classes that benefit the family upon the prisoner's release.

There are stark gender differences with respect to parent–child relationships for prisoners. More than 60% of mothers sentenced in a state prison and more than 80% of mothers sentenced in a federal prison had custody of at least one minor child at the time of their incarceration, in contrast with approximately 50% of fathers (Parke & Clarke-Stewart, 2002).

Maintaining social bonds to spouses, children, and other family members can not only reduce in-prison rule violations, but also assist in reducing recidivism (Toch, 1992; Hairston, 1998; Casey-

Acedevo & Bakken, 2001; Petersilia, 2003; Tewksbury & DeMichele, 2005; Haney, 2006; Listwan et al., 2006; Bales & Mears, 2008). Prison administrators often use family visitation as a way to ensure that some inmates abide by the rules of the correctional institution (Carlson & Garrett, 2008). Inmates who engage in frequent or major rule infractions, such as engaging in prison violence or possessing contraband, may have these visitation privileges temporarily revoked.

The effects of having a parent incarcerated can be devastating to the child. Some of the consequences to the child may include anxiety and fear (Wright & Seymour, 2000; Bilchik, Seymour, & Kreisher, 2001), failure in school (Bouchet, 2008), difficulty paying attention (Snyder, Carlo, & Mullins, 2001), difficulties in social settings (Eddy & Reid, 2002), stigmatization by the community (Lowenstein, 1986; Travis, Solomon, & Waul, 2001), and juvenile delinquency (Johnston, 1995; Travis, 2009). Ultimately, children of incarcerated parents may continue the cycle of crime and become criminals themselves as adults, leading to intergenerational incarceration (Raeder, 1993; Johnston, 1995; Bilchik et al., 2001; Jarvis, Graham, Hamilton, & Tyler, 2004; Travis, 2009). The negative behavioral effects of having an incarcerated parent can be tempered by having more frequent visits and more positive experiences with that parent while they are institutionalized (Petersilia, 2003).

There are many barriers for visitation and contact between parents and children, as well as between spouses or significant others. A lack of visits may be due to the distance from the home to the correctional institution, coupled with a lack of transportation to the correctional facility (Sabbath & Cowles, 1992; Covington, 2002, as cited in Petersilia, 2003). This is particularly an issue for female inmates. Many states only have one correctional facility for females, which often means families must travel over 100 miles to visit their incarcerated loved one (Casey & Wiatrowski, 1996; Incarcerated parents and their children, 2000). Visiting hours are often during the day, when the caregiver may be most likely to be at work (Petersilia, 2003). If the relationship between the child's custodian and the incarcerated parent is strained, the custodian may be unwilling to take the child to visit their parent (Covington, 2002, as cited in Petersilia, 2003). The only visitors who are legally allowed to accompany a minor child are those who are either the child's legal guardians or immediate family members of the inmate (Travis, 2009). Although phone calls may seem the easiest method of contact between those who are incarcerated and their families, there are limits to the number of calls that can be placed, as well as the lengths of phone calls (Travis, 2009). The costs of these phone calls may be astronomical. The inmates generally have to make collect calls to their loved ones, costing $1–3 per minute, as compared to the 10 cents per minute that is typically charged for similar phone calls in the free community (Petersilia, 2003; Travis, 2009).

Even for those who are able to overcome these barriers, other difficulties with visitation and contact remain. Many family members report a dislike for visiting prisons and jails (Sturges, 2002; Arditti, 2003; Arditti, 2005). Those visiting their incarcerated loved ones report feeling degraded and stigmatized by the process involved (Hairston, 1998, as cited in Sturges, 2002; Arditti, 2005), and some even state that the strict rules and regulations of visitation make them feel that they have been imprisoned themselves (Comfort, 2003). Over time, visits and other forms of contact begin to decrease in frequency (Brodsky, 1975; Lynch & Sabol, 2001; Arditti, 2005).

One recommendation has been to increase the "child friendliness" of visiting areas (Bilchik et al., 2001; Sturges, 2002; Bales & Mears, 2008). Because many families are forced to stay in the waiting area for long periods of time, including a small play area for children may help alleviate some of the boredom and potentially unruly or disruptive behavior from younger visitors (Sturges, 2002). Other facilities have begun to utilize technology as an answer to the difficulties involved in familial visitation. Video visitation is increasing in frequency across the country (Arditti, 2005).

A recent study conducted in Ireland allowed researchers to examine the effects of inmates who were granted brief furloughs from prison to visit with their families; this study was conducted as a result of Ireland's policy that allows inmates to temporarily leave prison for vocational or family reasons. The results indicate lower recidivism rates for these offenders upon their return to the community (Baumer, O'Donnell, & Hughes, 2009). Maintaining contacts with the community may be essential to provide a buffer, even while individuals are still incarcerated, and allow them to more successfully reintegrate back into the community.

Another solution to maintaining positive parent–child relationships may be to increase parental education with parenting classes (Gonzalez, Romero, & Cerbana, 2007). Participants in parenting classes while incarcerated have indicated that they feel stronger and healthier bonds with their children, and an increased knowledge of issues such as child development and appropriate management of their children (Showers, 1993, and Thompson & Harm, 2000, as cited in Gonzalez et al., 2007). It is believed that these education programs will subsequently lead to a parent being motivated to not continue to commit crime since they have stronger bonds with their children (Gonzalez et al., 2007). Unfortunately, many facilities are simply not well-funded enough to offer parent-education programs, although they are desperately needed to improve and repair parent–child relationships (Austin & Hardyman, 2004).

COMMUNITY-BASED RECIDIVISM REDUCTION PROGRAMS

Offenders may be supervised in the community, either on probation or on parole. At the end of 2009, the United States had 4,203,967 probationers under supervision, compared with 819,308 parolees (Glaze, Bonczar, & Zhang, 2010). Although these terms are sometimes used synonymously, they are very different concepts. Probation is usually given as an alternative to incarceration and means that offenders are supervised in the community by a probation officer. Individuals who serve probation generally have not served a prison or jail sentence, and therefore are likely to be less serious and less frequent offenders. In part due to the burgeoning prison population, more and more offenders are given probation. Sixty percent of those convicted of a crime are sentenced to a community-based sanction in lieu of serving a prison sentence (May, Wood, Mooney, & Minor, 2005, as cited in Williams, May, & Wood, 2008). Intermediate sanctions such as probation are shown to be at least as effective at reducing recidivism among offenders as prison sentences (May et al., 2005, as cited in Williams et al. 2008).

In contrast, parole is a conditional release that is handed down after an offender has been incarcerated and involves community supervision by a parole officer. Parole decisions are made by a parole board. There are currently two methods of parole release: discretionary and mandatory. Discretionary parole means that the power of the decision to grant parole is vested solely in the hands of the parole board, which can consider issues such as whether the offender has been rehabilitated when making a decision. In contrast, mandatory parole occurs when an inmate has accumulated enough "good time" to comprise the end of their sentence. Good time is earned on a monthly basis and is given to inmates who have had no rule infractions for the previous month. Important to note with mandatory parole is that the decision to parole is taken out of the hands of the parole board; the board simply stipulates the terms and conditions of the individual's parole (Quinn, 2003). Because mandatory parole allows no discretion for decision making by the parole board on an offender's readiness to be released, some argue that it is ineffective at preventing offenders from committing crimes once they are returned to the community (Seiter & Kadula, 2003).

There are differences in the method of exit between probationers and parolees. Individuals on probation are less likely to recidivate than those who have served a prison sentence and are out on parole (Spohn, 2007). Fifty-one percent of parolees successfully completed their parole in 2009, compared with 65% of probationers. Incarceration as a result of either a new crime or a violation of supervision accounted for 34% of parolees, and only 16% of probationers (Glaze et al., 2010). (For a complete breakdown of exits from parole and probation, see **Table 13-1**.) The question remains whether parolees are simply more likely to continue a life of crime postrelease when compared with probationers, or if parolees are more likely to be caught and incarcerated because they are being supervised and scrutinized more closely by authorities.

Many of those released from prison will continue to be under some form of community supervision (Latessa & Smith, 2007). Those offenders who reoffend are likely to recidivate soon upon their release. Rearrests are most likely to occur soon after release from prison, decreasing over time (Visher, Lattimore, & Linster, 1991; Kurlychek, Bushway, & Brame, 2006). Therefore, it has been recommended that the most intensive supervision and services be given to inmates immediately upon their release from prison and continue from 6 months to 1 year after their release (Rauma & Berk, 1987, and Finn, 1998, as cited in Petersilia, 2003; Visher & Travis, 2003; Harrison & Schehr, 2004).

Recidivism rates of released prisoners tend to be relatively high. In 1994, researchers examined those released from prison in 15 different states, and found that within 3 years two-thirds of offenders recidivated (Hughes, Wilson, & Beck, 2001; Langan & Levin, 2002; Listwan, Cullen, & Latessa, 2006). The length of a prisoner's sentence seems to be positively correlated with their likelihood of recidivating, meaning that those who have served the longest sentences will have the most difficulty in reintegrating back into society. This seems intuitive when considering the prison experience. Prison exposes individuals to high levels of violence, distrust, and criminogenic behavior while removing them from the free community. As a result, they likely suffer from deteriorated bonds with family, friends, and community, as well as lack of both educational and employment opportunities.

TABLE 13-1 Exits from Parole and Probation, 2009 (Percentages)

Reason for exit	Parolees	Probationers
Completion	51	65
Incarceration	34	16
with new sentence	9	—
with revocation	24	—
other/unknown	1	—
Absconder	9	3
Other unsatisfactory	2	10
Transferred to other state	1	—
Death	1	1
Discharged to custody, detainer or warrant	—	1
Other	3	4

Source: Glaze, Bonczar, & Zhang (2010)

In comparison with prison-based interventions, there has been significantly less research conducted on effective community-based programming to reduce recidivism (Turner et al., 2007). Effective programs are those that allow offenders to complete rehabilitation in an environment that mimics their own natural environment, incorporate cognitive and behavioral approaches, target those who are the highest risk, use a rewards system for prosocial behavior, and account for the individualized learning styles of offenders (Lipsey, 1992; Gendreau, 1996; Cullen & Gendreau, 2000; Allen, MacKenzie, & Hickman, 2001; Andrews & Bonta, 2003; Wilson, Bouffard, & MacKenzie, 2005; Listwan, Cullen, & Latessa, 2006). Moreover, it has been suggested that by matching an offender's needs with the appropriate reintegration services, recidivism may be reduced by up to 50% (Andrews et al., 1990, as cited in Zhang, Roberts, & Callanan, 2006).

Those who receive the most intensive treatment should be those who are at the greatest risk for recidivism (Gendreau, 1996; Andrews et al., 1990, as cited in Lowenkamp & Latessa, 2005; Bonta, 2002; Andrews & Bonta, 2003; Listwan et al., 2006). For instance, those who are chronic offenders, do not have stable employment, or who have little or no attachment with family or noncriminogenic friends, may be considered high risk. It may also be necessary to target individual needs, such as changing antisocial attitudes and addressing deficiencies in areas such as self-control, impulse control, and self-management (Gendreau, 1996; Van Voorhis, 1997; Andrews & Bonta, 2003; Listwan et al., 2006; Listwan, Van Voorhis, & Richey, 2007). Finally, it is of utmost importance that the intervention be appropriate for the offender. This aspect focuses on the individual characteristics of the offender when considering the type of treatment, rehabilitation, or program that best suits the individual (Andrews & Bonta, 1998; Listwan et al., 2006).

Halfway Houses

Halfway houses, also known as residential treatment centers, are intended to provide a transitional facility for offenders who have been released from prison. These centers are intended for those who may not be ready to completely return to the community. In recent years, these facilities have also become residential facilities as an alternative for going to prison or jail (Latessa & Smith, 2007). These facilities are designed to help in transitioning the offender back into the community by assisting them with finding employment, and providing counseling or treatment, as well as providing their basic needs such as food and shelter.

However, these facilities are often criticized for doing little to prevent recidivism. Some issues that plague halfway houses include poor quality of staff, not providing enough individualized treatment, not properly assessing inmates' risk, and being little more than simply a place for ex-offenders to sleep and eat (Latessa, 1998, as cited in Latessa & Smith, 2007). In terms of whether they are effective at reducing recidivism, the results are mixed (Homant, 1984; Twill et al., 1998, as cited in Quinn, 2003). Although it seems counterintuitive, it may be that halfway houses benefit high-risk offenders by reducing recidivism, but among middle- and low-risk groups may actually increase the likelihood of crime commission (Andrews et al., 1990, as cited in Lowenkamp & Latessa, 2005).

Day Reporting Centers

Day reporting centers are facilities for newly released inmates from jail or prison, and are generally reserved for those who do not have employment upon their release (Quinn, 2003). Unlike halfway houses, residents reside at their own residence. They are required to physically report to the day reporting center each day and are often required to contact the center via telephone several times throughout the day. Failure to report constitutes a technical violation of the conditions of their parole and may result in a return to prison or jail. Other stipulations for participants may include random drug testing and providing a list of their planned activities to the center (Gowdy, 1993, as cited in Latessa & Smith, 2007). The major goals of day reporting centers include preventing recidivism by maintaining supervision over the participants and making it easier for probation and parole services to be available to the participants (Neito, 1998, and Marciniak, 1999, as cited in Quinn, 2003).

The majority of day reporting centers are operated by nonprofit, private organizations rather than the government (Parent, 1990, and Parent et al., 1995, as cited in Latessa & Smith, 2007). They provide services to anywhere between 10 and 150 individuals, although the capacity for many centers is around 50 participants (Parent, 1990, as cited in Latessa & Smith, 2007). The centers offer a range of programs to assist participants, including job skills, literacy, education, job placement, counseling, and drug treatment and education (Quinn, 2003; Latessa & Smith, 2007).

The results on whether or not day reporting centers are successful at reducing recidivism among participants are mixed (Craddock & Graham, 2001, as cited in Ostermann, 2009). One study that examined participants in Massachusetts indicates that approximately two-thirds of participants successfully completed the program, with only 2% being reincarcerated for a new crime (Curtin, 1990). Other evaluations have indicated similar rates of success among participants (Craddock, 2000; McBride & VanderWaal, 1997, as cited in Quinn, 2003). Others indicate that recidivism may actually be higher among participants than nonparticipants (Latessa, Travis, Holsinger, & Hartman, 1998).

The difficulty in studying the success rates of day reporting centers seems to be in the wide range of services offered and the various types of participants involved. Some centers are more successful at offering work-release programs, or can offer greater levels of supervision, more intense programming, and higher quality services, which have all been linked to lower rates of recidivism among participants (Parent, 1990, as cited in Latessa & Smith, 2007; Marciniak, 2000, as cited in Quinn, 2003). The other issue is how evaluations determine success. Although some measure recidivism of participants, others simply measure whether participants complete the programs at the day reporting centers (Marciniak, 1999, as cited in Ostermann, 2009).

Substance Abuse Treatment

Substance abuse treatment in the community is especially important for those who have been released from prison. It has been argued that because of the issues surrounding program availability as a result of overcrowding in prison, community-level treatment is a necessity for those with substance abuse issues (Gregrich, 1992, as cited in Leukefeld & Tims, 2009; Hiller, Knight, & Simpson, 2006; MacKenzie, 2006; Messina et al., 2006). Parolees and probationers often have substance abuse treatment as a stipulation of their parole or probation (Harrison, 2001; MacKenzie, 2006). Many of the issues with overcrowding and waiting lists for substance abuse treatment continue for offenders, even while they are in the community. Some community-based programs are hesitant to accept offenders as clients (MacKenzie, 2006).

Substance abuse treatment in the community may take a few different forms. Residential treatment programs are often more intensive since participants do not leave the facility and receive all treatment services in-house. Outpatient services are also utilized. These often constitute having ex-offenders report to treatment once a week, or however frequently is determined necessary. In comparing the types of programs, it is often found that those who have more intensive therapy, such as residential treatment, are more likely to recidivate than those who report to a treatment facility on a periodic basis. Although this may be unanticipated, it should be remembered that those undergoing more intensive treatment are also subject to more intense supervision, which means that violations are more likely to be detected than those who participate in outpatient programs (Knight, Simpson, & Hiller, 1999, as cited in Hiller et al., 2006).

One of the pitfalls in any drug treatment program is the broad definition given to the word *treatment*. As is the case with in-prison programs, many 12-step programs and Narcotics Anonymous programs are classified as substance abuse treatment (MacKenzie, 2006). Many programs offer little in the way of medical or psychological treatment, and may consist of little more than various members gathering together to discuss their substance-related issues.

Substance abuse is often symptomatic of other issues, such as a lack of employment, lack of education, or broken family ties (Harrison, 2001). As such, it seems that substance abuse may be a foundational issue that must be addressed in order to also provide assistance in other avenues of the offenders' lives.

Drug Courts

As it has become more apparent that traditional criminal justice interventions are not effective with substance abusers, drug courts have emerged as an alternative sanction (Latessa & Smith, 2007). Drug courts are a way of combining standard probation with drug abuse treatment programs. Those who are supervised under the jurisdiction of the drug court are more closely monitored, have more opportunities for substance abuse treatment, and are more frequently tested for substance abuse than those who are involved in standard parole or probation supervision (Harrison, 2001; Mateyoke-Scrivner, Webster, Stanton, & Leukefeld, 2004). As of December 31, 2009, there were 2,459 drug courts, 354 of which were hybrid DWI/drug courts that contend with both illicit substance users and those convicted of a DWI offense (NDCI, 2009).

One purpose of drug courts is to process and manage drug offenders in an expeditious manner so that they can begin substance abuse treatment as soon as possible. Drug courts are also designed so that judges can take a more active role in offenders' progress. They constantly monitor the offenders and meet with both probation officers and treatment providers to monitor their progress. (Belenko, 1998, as cited in Bouffard & Richardson, 2007; Latessa & Smith, 2007). The ultimate goal of drug courts is to rehabilitate and treat offenders so that they can successfully reintegrate into the community.

Drug courts have been shown to be effective at reducing recidivism and substance use of illicit drug users (Belenko, 1998, Belenko, 1999, Belenko, 2001, and Gottfredson, Najaka, & Kearly, 2003, as cited in Bouffard & Richardson, 2007). In one study, over a 4-year period of time in California, 17% of drug court graduates were rearrested. In contrast, similar substance abusers who did not undergo processing through drug courts were rearrested in 41% of the cases (Carey, Finigan, Crumpton, & Waller, 2006; NDCI, 2009).

There have been mixed results for DWI offenders, but treatment programs have generally been less effective at reducing recidivism among DWI offenders. This may be because DWI offenders are more likely to be in denial and less likely to hold themselves accountable for their offense because alcohol is a licit substance (Bouffard & Richardson, 2007). DWI courts are relatively new, so in comparison with the number of drug courts, there are fewer cases to analyze (Crancer, 2003, as cited in Bouffard & Richardson, 2007).

Electronic Monitoring

Although the terms are often used interchangeably, home confinement, house arrest, and electronic monitoring refer to very different correctional practices. Home confinement requires an offender to stay in their residence, with the exceptions of therapy, counseling, employment, or other preapproved activities. In contrast, house arrest is more stringent. The offender is required to remain in their home at all times, except for medical emergencies. In comparison with home confinement, house arrest is used much less frequently and is generally reserved for more severe offenses (Quinn, 2003).

Electronic monitoring may be combined with home confinement or house arrest, and there are two types of monitoring currently available. In random monitoring, a bracelet is worn on the offender's ankle, and a transmitter is placed on the telephone. Either a representative from the company or a computer-based program randomly calls the offender to ensure that they are in their residence. In continuous monitoring, the offender is monitored by a parole or probation officer, or by a representative of the monitoring company, to ensure that they remain in their home. About one out of every three offenders who are sentenced to house arrest or home confinement are also placed on electronic monitoring (Latessa & Smith, 2007).

Electronic monitoring has been used for a variety of offenses, including theft, embezzlement, and domestic violence, but it is most commonly prescribed for sex offenders (Gable & Gable, 2005; Button, DeMichele, & Payne, 2009; Killias, Gillie'ron, Kissling, & Villettaz, 2010). For offenders who are mandated to avoid specific locations, such as those who engage in domestic violence or substance abuse, electronic monitoring may be combined with global positioning systems (GPS) (Taxman, 2002; Nussbaumer, 2008, as cited in Killias et al., 2010).

Many question the punitiveness of these sanctions, stating that offenders who are sentenced to time in their home are not being punished severely enough for their crimes, especially those convicted of serious offenses. Many offenders indicate that they would rather serve time behind bars than be subjected to home confinement or electronic monitoring, in part because of the high levels of supervision associated with these sanctions (Payne & Gainey, 1999; Quinn, 2003). Even those who do prefer home confinement and electronic monitoring indicate that there are many negatives to these forms of punishment, such as the financial costs, a deprivation of autonomy, a loss of access to goods and services and multiple negative effects on their family members (Payne & Gainey, 2009).

More importantly, studies that analyze the recidivism rates for electronic monitoring generally indicate that they are ineffective. High-risk offenders show some promise under these programs, but low recidivism rates usually result when electronic monitoring is combined with cognitive behavioral therapy (Bonta, Wallace-Capretta & Rooney, 2000). Others posit that they have little effect on recidivism (Renzema & Mayo-Wilson, 2005). Some researchers indicate that home confinement may actually increase the likelihood of recidivism, especially among low-risk offenders (Bonta et al., 2000; Gendreau, Goggin, Cullen, & Andrews, 2000). As with other studies involving recidivism and intermediate sanctions, it should be remembered that those on electronic monitoring are more likely to be more intensely supervised than those on standard alternative sanctions (Hucklesby, 2009).

Employment

Postincarceration employment can greatly reduce the likelihood an individual will recidivate (Sampson & Laub, 1993; Lipsey, 1995; Uggen, 2000; Solomon et al., 2004; Listwan et al., 2006), and obtaining employment is usually a condition of an individual's parole. When combining employment with a commitment to work and maintaining a feeling of job stability, the likelihood of criminality greatly decreases (Sampson & Laub, 1995). Parolees who are able to secure an employment position that allows them to work at least 40 hours per week are less likely to be involved in crime and more likely to successfully reintegrate back into their communities (Laub & Sampson, 2003; Bahr et al., 2010).

All forms of employment are not equally likely to prevent individuals from recidivating. Individuals who hold positions that enable them to earn reasonable wages are less likely to engage in crime (Finn, 1998, Bernstein & Houston, 2000, and Western & Petit, 2000, as cited in Solomon et al, 2004; Uggen, 1999; Harrison & Schehr, 2004). As stated by Shover (1996), and as cited in Maruna (2001), those who are the most likely to *not* engage in crime after their release from prison are those who are employed in a position that enables them to "return a decent income, enable the individual to exercise intelligence and creativity, and allow for some autonomy in structuring the day's activities" (p. 127).

Those released from prison often face an uphill battle when securing legitimate employment opportunities and report difficulty in securing employment upon their return to the community (Henderson, 2001). Additionally, although states vary in their provisions for releases, the average amount of "gate money" given to ex-offenders is $69, and some states only provide a bus or a plane ticket for their return to the community (Harrison & Schehr, 2004). Many offenders lack the stable employment history to obtain a position. Some have parole stipulations that limit the types of employment that a convicted offender may hold. For example, anyone convicted of a financial crime is often prevented from holding employment that involves handling money. Some states restrict felons from working in specific fields, such as child care, law enforcement, or human resources (Rothstein, 1999, and Mukamal, 2000, as cited in Harrison & Schehr, 2004). Other types of offenders may be prohibited from maintaining employment where they are not home before dark.

It is often difficult to find an employer who is willing to hire a convicted felon (Holzer, Raphael, & Stoll, 2003; Graffam, Shinkfield, & Hardcastle, 2008), especially if they have been convicted of a crime that is either violent or financial in nature. Many employers perceive ex-offenders as potentially less trustworthy, less productive, and with a less intensive work ethic than nonoffenders (Freeman, 2008, as cited in Tarlow, 2011). Research does suggest, however, that employers may be more willing to hire ex-offenders if a third party, such as a community service program or counseling program, is involved and oversees the employment process (Wirthlin Worldwide, 2000, as cited in Petersilia, 2003).

One program that helps ex-offenders secure a job postincarceration in an attempt to reduce recidivism is the Texas RIO (Re-integration of Offenders) program. The Texas RIO project has 62 offices with over 100 staff members and is a collaborative effort of two state-based agencies: The Texas Workforce Commission and the Texas Department of Criminal Justice (Finn, 1998, as cited in Petersilia, 2003; Tarlow, 2011).

Since 1985, the RIO project has placed over 75% of more than 200,000 ex-offenders, and maintains a pool of 12,000 employers who have hired ex-offenders (Petersilia, 2003). Additionally, RIO provides vouchers for necessities, such as food, medical care, and clothing, likely lessening the burden on ex-offenders (Harrison & Schehr, 2004). The Texas Workforce has predicted that as many as 66% of those who have been placed in a position of employment through this program will not recidivate (Fulp, 2001). The program has proven to be successful, as only 23% of high-risk offenders participating in RIO were returned to prison, compared with 38% of non-RIO participants (Buck, 2000). It has been estimated that in 1990 alone, more than five million dollars was saved by RIO participants not returning to prison as a result of their successfully finding employment and subsequently desisting from crime (Petersilia, 2003).

Families

A lack of familial bonds, including both marriage and having dependent children, are shown to increase an individual's likelihood of recidivating (Bahr et al., 2010; Huebner & Berg, 2010). After their release from a correctional institution, families can offer various forms of support, such as emotional encouragement and financial assistance (Petersilia, 2003; Scott, Dewey, & Leverentz, 2006; Leverentz, 2006; Leverentz, 2011). Those who feel their families are supportive report being more optimistic for their future opportunities and may be less likely to engage in crime (Nelson, Deess, & Allen, 1999, as cited in Petersilia, 2003)

Family-based programs seek to rebuild the structure of a family that has been damaged as a result of parental incarceration. These programs have been shown to be successful at reducing recidivism (Patterson, Chamberlain, & Reid, 1982; Gordon, Arbuthnot, Gustafsori, & McGreen, 1988; Henggeler & Borduin, 1990; Listwan et al., 2006).

Peers

Bonds with peers also may play a role in successful reintegration of ex-offenders. One of the most important factors is whether the peers are engaging in criminogenic behavior. Returning to previous patterns of behavior, such as engaging in one-night stands and searching for a means to make easy money, are associated with repeated criminogenic behaviors upon release from prison (Seal et al., 2007; Leverentz, 2011).

Offenders who spend time participating in activities with their noncriminogenic friends are less likely to recidivate. Some may isolate themselves from former friends and try to establish new connections with law-abiding peers (Laub & Sampson, 2003; Seal et al., 2007; Leverentz, 2011). Additionally, those who maintain relationships with fewer friends are more likely to indicate feelings of loneliness, which may in fact lead them to return to their criminogenic behaviors (Bahr et al., 2010).

CONCLUSION

Overall, it has been suggested that the correctional system needs to put more emphasis on community-based programs (Turner et al., 2007). Providing appropriate programming and resources is essential to ensuring that ex-offenders who are released are successfully reintegrated into their communities and continue to desist from crime. For those serving an alternative sanction, such as probation, ensuring that the appropriate treatment or program is given to the offender may prevent them from continuing to commit crimes and eventually being given a prison sentence.

One of the repercussions of the "get tough on crime" approach that has dominated criminal justice in the United States in the past three decades has been a significant increase in the prison and jail population. An unintended consequence of this increase is an inability to provide the appropriate treatment and programs to prevent ex-offenders from continuing to commit crimes once they are released back into the community. Although many argue that offenders who cannot desist from crime should simply be reincarcerated, the impact on the larger community of having crime continue should be considered when taking programs and services to prevent recidivism into account.

KEY TERMS

Recidivism
Desistance
Principle of least eligibility
Rehabilitation
Cognitive behavioral therapy
Vocational training
Work-release programs
Probation
Parole
Mandatory parole
Discretionary parole
Halfway houses
Day reporting centers
Drug courts
Home confinement
House arrest
Electronic monitoring

DISCUSSION QUESTIONS

1. Why do you think the principle of least eligibility is generally the guiding principle used to determine which programs and services will be available to inmates? Do you think other considerations should be made?
2. What are the positive and negative aspects of group therapy? How could we overcome some of these limitations to make group therapy more effective?
3. Why do you think cognitive behavioral therapy has been shown to be so effective at reducing recidivism?
4. Why has the number of inmates needing substance abuse treatment increased? How can we deal with this increasing population and provide them adequate treatment?
5. How does education prevent recidivism? Make an argument that educating prisoners also benefits society.
6. Why is the type of work classified as vocational important? What types of in-prison jobs do inmates benefit the most from?
7. What are the barriers to family visitation of inmates?
8. Explain both the potential positives and negatives of a child visiting their parent while he or she is incarcerated.
9. Why are parolees more likely to recidivate than probationers?
10. What are some of the difficulties in studying whether postimprisonment community supervision initiatives (such as day reporting centers and halfway houses) are effective?

11. Why do you think drug courts are shown to be more effective at reducing recidivism among substance abusers than traditional sanctions?

12. What types of postimprisonment employment are more likely to help offenders desist from crime and why?

13. If you were an employer do you think you would be willing to hire an ex-offender? Why or why not? Would the type of offense committed make a difference to you? What other factors might you consider?

REFERENCES

Alleman, T. (2002). Correctional philosophies: Varying ideologies of punishment In R. Gido & T. Alleman (Eds.), *Turnstile justice: Issues in American corrections.* Upper Saddle River, NJ: Prentice Hall.

Allen, L. C., MacKenzie, D. L., & Hickman, L. (2001). The effectiveness of cognitive behavioral treatment for adult offenders: A methodological quality-based review. *International Journal of Offender Therapy and Comparative Criminology, 45*(4), 498–514.

Andrews, D. A., & Bonta, J. (2003). *The psychology of criminal conduct.* Cincinnati, OH: Anderson.

Andrews, D. A., Zinger, I., Hoge, R. D., Bonta, J., Gendreau, P., & Cullen, F. T. (1990). Does correctional treatment work? A clinically relevant and psychologically informed meta-analysis. *Criminology, 28*(3), 369–404.

Aos, S., Phipps, P., Barnoski, R., & Lieb, R. (2001). *The comparative cost and benefits of programs to reduce crime, version 4.0.* Olympia, WA: Washington State Institute for Public Policy.

Applegate, B. K. (2001). Penal austerity: Perceived utility, desert, and public attitudes toward prison amenities. *American Journal of Criminal Justice, 25*(2), 253–268.

Arditti, J. A. (2003). Locked doors and glass walls: Family visiting at a local jail. *Journal of Loss and Trauma, 8,* 115–138.

Arditti, J. A. (2005). Families and incarceration: An ecological approach. *Families in Society: The Journal of Contemporary Social Services, 86*(2), 251–260.

Austin, J., & Hardyman, P. L. (2004). The risks and needs of the returning prisoner population. *Review of Policy Research, 21*(1), 13–29.

Bahr, S. J., Harris, L., Fisher, J. K., & Armstrong, A. H. (2010). Successful reentry: What differentiates successful and unsuccessful parolees? *International Journal of Offender Therapy and Comparative Criminology, 54*(5), 667–692.

Bales, W. D., & Mears, D. P. (2008). Inmate social ties and the transition to society: Does visitation reduce recidivism? *Journal of Research in Crime and Delinquency, 45*(3), 287–321.

Ball, J. C., Rosen, L., Flueck, J. A., & Nurco, D. N. (1981). The criminality of heroin addicts when addicted and when off opiates. In J. A. Inciardi (Ed.), *The drug crime connection.* Beverly Hills, CA: Sage Publications.

Batiuk, M. E., Moke, P., & Rountree, P. W. (1997). Crime and rehabilitation: Correctional education as an education of change—a research note. *Justice Quarterly, 14*(1), 167–180.

Baumer, E. P., O'Donnell, I., & Hughes, N. (2009). The porous prison: A note on the rehabilitative potential of visits home. *The Prison Journal, 89*(1), 119–126.

Belenko, S. (1998). Research on drug courts: A critical review. *National Drug Court Institute Review, I*(1), 1–42.

Belenko, S. (1999). Research on drug courts: A critical review. *National Drug Court Institute Review: 1999 update, II*(2), 1–58.

Belenko, S. (2001). Research on drug courts: A critical review. *National Drug Court Institute Review: 2001 update.* New York, NY: The National Center on Addiction and Substance Abuse at Columbia University.

Bernstein, J., & Houston, E. (2000). *Crime and work: What we can learn from the low-wage labor market.* Washington, DC: Economic Policy Institute.

Bilchik, S., Seymour, C., & Kreisher, K. (2001). Parents in prison. *Corrections Today, 63,* 108–114.

Blumstein, A., & Beck, A. J. (2005). Reentry as a transient state between liberty and recommitment. In J. Travis & C. Visher (Eds.), *Prison reentry and crime in America* (pp. 50–79). New York, NY: Cambridge University Press.

Bonta, J. (2002). Offender risk assessment: Guidelines for use. *Criminal Justice and Behavior, 29*(4), 355–379.

Bonta, J., Wallace-Capretta, S., & Rooney, J. (2000). A quasi-experimental evaluation of an intensive rehabilitation supervision program. *Criminal Justice and Behavior, 27*(3), 312–329.

Bosworth, M. (2002). *The U.S. federal prison system.* London, UK: Sage Publications.

Bouchet, S. (2008). *Children and families with incarcerated parents: Exploring development in the field and opportunities for growth.* Baltimore, MD: Annie A. Casey Foundation.

Bouffard, J. A., & Richardson, K. A. (2007). The effectiveness of drug court programming for special kinds of offenders: Methamphetamine and DWI offenders versus other drug involved offenders. *Criminal Justice Policy Review, 18*(3), 274–293.

Brodsky, S. (1975). *Families and friends of men in prison.* Lexington, MA: Lexington Books.

Buck, M. (2000). *Getting back to work: Employment programs for ex-offenders.* Field Report Series. Public/Provate Ventures. Retrieved from http://eric.ed.gov/PDFS/ED449365.pdf.

Button, D. M., DeMichele, M., & Payne, B. K. (2009). Using electronic monitoring to supervise sex offenders: Legislative patterns and implications for community corrections officers. *Criminal Justice Policy Review, 20*(4), 414–436.

Butzin, C. A., Martin, S. S., & Inciardi, J. A. (2002). Evaluating component effects of a prison based treatment continuum. *Journal of Substance Treatment, 22,* 63–69.

Carey, S. M., Finigan, M., Crumpton, D., & Waller, M. (2006). California drug courts: Outcomes, costs and promising practices: An overview of phase II in a statewide study. *Journal of Psychoactive Drugs, SARC Supplement 3,* 345–346.

Carlson, P. M., & Garrett, J. S. (2008). *Prison and jail administration: Practice and theory.* Sudbury, MA: Jones and Bartlett Publishers.

Casey, K. A., & Wiatrowski, M. D. (1996). Women offenders and "Three strikes and you're out." In D. Schichor & D. K. Sechrest (Eds.), *Three strikes and you're out: Vengeance as public policy* (pp. 222–243). Thousand Oaks, CA: Sage.

Casey-Acevedo, K., & Bakken, T. (2001). The effects of visitation on women in prison. *International Journal of Comparative and Applied Criminal Justice, 25,* 48–69.

Chappell, C. A. (2004). Post-secondary correctional education and recidivism: A meta-analysis of research conducted 1990–1999. *The Journal of Correctional Education, 55*(2), 148–169.

Comfort, M. (2003). In the tube at San Quentin: The "secondary prisonization" of women visiting inmates. *Journal of Contemporary Ethnography, 32*(1), 77–107.

Conley, J. A. (1980). Prisons, production and profit: Reconsidering the importance of prison industries. *Journal of Social History, 14*(2), 257–275.

Corsini, R. J. (1964). Group psychotherapy in correctional rehabilitation. *British Journal of Criminology, 4,* 272–274.

Covington, S. (2002). A woman's journey home: Challenges for female offenders and their children. Paper presented at The Urban Institute's From Prison to Home Conference, Washington, DC.

Craddock, A. (2000). *Exploratory analysis of client outcomes, costs, and benefits of day reporting centers—Final report.* Rockville, MD: National Institute of Justice.

Craddock, A., & Graham, L. (2001). Recidivism as a function of day reporting center participation. *Journal of Offender Rehabilitation, 34*(1), 81–97.

Crancer, A. (2003). *An analysis of Idaho's Kootenai Count DUI Court: An alcohol treatment program for persons arrested for their second DUI offense or BAC of 0.20% or higher.* National Highway Traffic Safety Administration. Retrieved from www.isc.idaho.gov/dcourt/dc128fin.pdf.

Cullen, F. T., & Gendreau, P. (2000). Assessing correctional rehabilitation: Policy, practice and prospects In J. Homey (Ed.), *Criminal justice 2000: Vol. 3—Policies, processes and decisions of the criminal justice system* (pp. 109–175). Washington, DC: U.S. Department of Justice, National Institute of Justice.

Curtin, E. (1990). Day reporting centers, In A. Travisino (Ed.), *Intermediate punishment: Community-based sanctions* (pp. 72–73). Laurel, MD: American Correctional Association.

Dobson, K. S., & Craig, K. D. (1996). *Advances in cognitive behavioral therapy.* Newbury Park, CA: Sage Publications.

Dobson, K. S., & Khatri, N. (2000). Cognitive therapy: Looking backward, looking forward. *Journal of Clinical Psychology, 56*, 907–923.

Eddy, J. M., & Reid, J. B. (2002). The antisocial behavior of the adolescent children of incarcerated parents: A developmental perspective. Paper prepared for The Urban Institute's From Prison to Home Conference, Washington, DC.

Fabelo, T. (2002). The impact of prison education on community reintegration of inmates: The Texas case. *Journal of Correctional Education, 53*(3), 106–110.

Feest, J. (1999). Imprisonment and prisoners work: Normalization or less eligibility? *Punishment and Society, 1*(1), 99–107.

Finn, P. (1998). *Texas' Project Rio (Re-integration of Offenders).* Washington, DC: National Institute of Justice.

Fleisher, M. S., Rison, R., & Helman, D. W. (1997). Female inmates: A growing constituency in the Federal Bureau of Prisons. *Corrections Management Quarterly 1*(4), 28–35.

Freeman, R. (2008). Incarceration, criminal background checks, and employment in a low(er) crime society. *Criminology and Public Policy, 7*(3), 405–412.

Fulp, E. (2001). Project Rio (Reintegration of Offenders). *In State of Corrections.* Proceedings, Annual Conference 2000. Lanham, MD: American Correctional Association.

Gable, R. K., & Gable, R. S. (2005). Electronic monitoring: Positive intervention strategies. *Federal Probation, 69*(1), 21–25.

Gendreau, P. (1996). The principles of effective intervention with offenders In A. Harland (Ed.) *Choosing correctional options that work* (pp. 117–130). Thousand Oaks, CA: Sage Publications.

Gendreau, P., Goggin, C., McCullen, F., & Andrews, D. (2000). The effects of community sanctions and incarceration on recidivism. *FORUM, 12*(2), 10–13.

Glaze, L. E. (2010). Correctional populations in the United States, 2009 (NCJ 231681). U.S. Department of Justice, Bureau of Justice Statistics.

Glaze, L. E., Bonczar, T. B., & Zhang, F. (2010). Probation and parole in the United States, 2009 (NCJ 231674). U.S. Department of Justice, Bureau of Justice Statistics.

Gonzalez, P., Romero, T., Cerbana, C. B. (2007). Parent education program for incarcerated mothers in Colorado. *The Journal of Correctional Education, 58*(4), 357–373.

Gordon, D. A., Arbuthnot, J., Gustafson, K., & McGreen, P. (1988). Home-based behavioral-systems family therapy with disadvantaged juvenile delinquents. *American Journal of Family Therapy, 16*, 243–255.

Gottfredson, D. C., Najaka, S. S., & Kearly, B. (2003). Effectiveness of drug treatment courts: Evidence from a randomized trial. *Criminology and Public Policy, 2*, 401–426.

Gottfredson, M., & Hirschi, T. (1990). *A general theory of crime.* Stanford, CA: Stanford University Press.

Gowdy, V. (1993). *Intermediate sanctions.* Washington, DC: U.S. Department of Justice.

Graffam, J., Shinkfield, A. J., & Hardcastle, L. (2008). The perceived employability of ex-prisoners and offenders. *International Journal of Offender Therapy and Comparative Criminology, 52*, 673–685.

Gregrich, R. J. (1992). Management of the drug abusing offender. In C. G. Leukefeld & F. M. Tims (Eds.), *Drug abuse treatment in prisons and jails* (pp. 211–231). Washington, DC: U.S. Government Printing Office.

Guerrero, G. (2011). Prison-based educational and vocational training programs, In L. Gideon & H. Sung, (Eds.), *Rethinking corrections: Rehabilitation, reentry and reintegration* (pp. 219–252). Thousand Oaks, CA: Sage Publications.

Hagan, J., & Dinovitzer, R. (1999). Collateral consequences of imprisonment for children, communities and prisoners. *Crime and Justice, 26*, 121–143.

Hairston, C. F. (1998). The forgotten parent: Understanding the forces that influence incarcerated fathers' relationships with their children. *Child Welfare, 77*, 617–638.

Haney, C. (2002). The psychological impact of incarceration: Implications for post-prison adjustment. Paper prepared for the Urban Institute's re-entry roundtable, Washington, DC.

Haney, C. (2006). *Reforming punishment: Psychological limits to the pains of imprisonment.* Washington, DC: American Psychological Association.

Harer, M. D. (1994). *Recidivism among federal prison releases in 1987: A preliminary report.* Washington, DC: Federal Bureau of Prisons.

Harlow, C. W. (2007). Education and correctional populations (NCJ 195670). U.S. Department of Justice, Bureau of Justice Statistics.

Harrison, B., & Schehr, R. (2004). Offenders and post-release jobs: Variables influencing success and failure. *Journal of Offender Rehabilitation, 39*(3), 35–68.

Harrison, L. D. (2001). The revolving prison door for drug-involved offenders: Challenges and opportunities. *Crime and Delinquency, 47*(3), 462–484.

Harrison, P., & Karberg, J. (2004). Prison and jail inmates at mid-year 2003 (NCJ 203947). U.S. Department of Justice. Bureau of Justice Statistics.

Hassine, V. (2010). *Life without parole: Living in prison today.* New York, NY: Oxford University Press.

Hayes, K., & Richardson, J. T. E. (1995). Gender, subject and context as determinants of approaches to studying in higher education. *Studies in Higher Education, 20*(2), 215–221.

Henderson, M. (2001). Employment and crime: What is the problem and what can be done about it from the inmate's perspective. *Corrections Management Quarterly, 5,* 36–42.

Henggeler, S. W., & Borduin, C. M. (1990). *Family therapy and beyond: A multisystemic approach to treating the behavior problems of children and adolescents.* Pacific Grove, CA: Brooks/Cole.

Hiller, M. L., Knight, K., & Simpson, D. D. (2006). Recidivism following mandated residential substance abuse treatment for felony probationers. *The Prison Journal, 86*(2), 230–241.

Holzer, H., Raphael, S., & Stoll, M. (2003). Employment barriers facing ex-offenders. Paper prepared for the reentry roundtable: The employment dimensions of prisoner reentry: Understanding the nexus between prisoner reentry and work, New York, NY.

Homant, R. (1984). Employment of ex-offenders: The role of prisonization and self esteem. *Journal of Offender Counseling, Services and Rehabilitation, 8,* 5–23.

Hucklesby, A. (2009). Vehicles of desistance? The impact of electronically monitored curfew orders. *Criminology and Criminal Justice, 8,* 51–71.

Huebner, B., & Berg, M. (2010). Examining the sources of variation in risk for recidivism. *Justice Quarterly, 28*(1), 146–173.

Hughes, T., & Wilson, D. J. (2002). Inmates returning to the community after serving time in prison. Bureau of Justice Statistics, Washington, DC. Retrieved from http://bjs.ojp.usdoj.gov/index.cfm?ty=pbdetail&id=1138.

Hughes, T., Wilson, D., & Beck, A. (2001). Trends in state parole, 1990–2000 (NCJ 184735). U.S. Department of Justice. Bureau of Justice Statistics.

Incarcerated parents and their children. (2000). U.S. Department of Justice, Bureau of Justice Statistics.

Inciardi, J. A., & Pottieger, A. E. (1998). Drug use and street crime in Miami: An almost twenty-year retrospective. *Substance Use and Misuse, 33*(9), 1839–1870.

Inciardi, J. A., Surratt, H. L., Martin, S. S., & Hooper, R. M. (2002). The importance of aftercare in a corrections-based treatment continuum. In C. G. Leukefeld, F. M. Tims, & D. Farabee (Eds.), *Clinical and policy responses to drug offenders* (pp. 204–216). New York, NY: Springer.

Jarvis, J., Graham, S., & Tyler, D. (2004). The role of parenting classes for young fathers in prison: A case study. *The Journal of Community and Criminal Justice, 5*(1), 21–33.

Jeffords, C. R., & McNitt, S. (1993). *The relationship between GED attainment and recidivism.* Austin, TX: Texas Youth Commission Department of Research and Planning.

Johnston, D. (1995). Effects of parental incarceration. In K. Gabel & D. Johnston (Eds.), *Children of incarcerated parents* (pp. 59–88). New York, NY: Lexington Books.

Killias, M., Gillie'ron, G., Kissling, I., & Villettaz, P. (2010). Community service versus electronic monitoring—What works better? Results of a randomized trial. *British Journal of Criminology, 50,* 1155–1170.

Knight, K., Simpson, D. D., & Hiller, M. L. (1999). Three-year reincarceration outcomes for in-prison therapeutic community treatment in Texas. *The Prison Journal, 79*(3), 337–351.

Kurlychek, M., Bushway, S., & Brame, R. (2006). Scarlet letters and recidivism: Does an old criminal record predict future offending? *Criminology and Public Policy, 5,* 483–504.

Lahm, K. F. (2000). Equal or equitable: An exploration of educational and vocational program availability for male and female offenders. *Federal Probation, 64*(2), 39–46.

Langan, P. A., & Levin, D. J. (2002). Recidivism of prisoners released in 1994 (NCJ 193427). U.S. Department of Justice, Bureau of Justice Statistics.

Langenbach, M., North, M. Y., Aargaard, L., & Chown, W. (1990). Televised instruction in Oklahoma prisons: A study of recidivism and disciplinary actions. *Journal of Correctional Education, 41,* 87–94.

Latessa, E. (1998). *Public protection through offender risk reduction: Putting research into practice.* Washington, DC: National Institute of Corrections.

Latessa, E. J., & Smith, P. (2007). *Corrections in the community.* Cincinnati, OH: Anderson Publishing.

Latessa, E., Travis, L., Holsinger, A., & Hartman, J. (1998). *Evaluation of Ohio's pilot day reporting program final report.* Cincinnati, OH: Division of Criminal Justice, University of Cincinnati.

Laub, J. H., & Sampson, R. J. (2003). *Shared beginnings, divergent lives: Delinquent boys to age 70.* Cambridge, MA: Harvard University Press.

La Vigne, N., Kachnowski, V., Travis, J., Naser, R., & Visher, C. (2003). *A portrait of prisoner reentry in Maryland.* Washington, DC: The Urban Institute.

La Vigne, N., Mamalian, C., Travis, J., & Visher, C. (2003). *A portrait of prisoner reentry in Illinois.* Washington, DC: The Urban Institute.

La Vigne, N., Thomson, G., Visher, C., Kachnowski, V., & Travis, J. (2003). *A portrait of prisoner reentry in Ohio.* Washington, DC: The Urban Institute.

Leukefeld, C. G., & Tims, F. R. (2009). Drug abuse treatment in prison and jails. In R. Tewksbury & D. Dabney (Eds.), *Prisons and jails: A reader* (pp. 263–274). New York, NY: McGraw Hill.

Leverentz, A. (2006). I put her through a particular hell: The role of family and friends in onset and desistence. Paper presented at The American Society of Criminology meeting, Los Angeles, CA.

Leverentz, A. (2011). Barriers to reintegration. In L. Gideon & H. Sung, (Eds.), *Rethinking corrections: Rehabilitation, reentry and reintegration* (pp. 359–382). Thousand Oaks, CA: Sage Publications.

Lipsey, M. (1992). Juvenile delinquency treatment: A meta-analysis inquiry into the variability of effects. In T. D. Cook, H. Cooper, D. S. Cordray, H. Hartman, L. V. Hedges, R. J. Light, … F. Mosteller (Eds.), *Meta-analysis for explanation: A casebook.* New York, NY: Russell Sage Foundation.

Lipsey, M. W. (1995). What do we learn from 400 research studies on the effectiveness of treatment with juvenile delinquency? In J. McQuire (Ed.), *What works: Reducing reoffending* (pp. 63–78). West Sussex, UK: Wiley Publishing.

Lipton, D.S. (1988). Treatment for drug abusing offenders during correctional supervision: A nationwide overview. *Journal of Offender Rehabilitation, 26*(3/4), 1–45.

Lipton, D. S., & Johnson, B. D. (1998). Smack, crack and score: Two decades of NIDA-funded drugs and crime research at NRDI 1974–1994. *Substance Use and Misuse, 33*(9), 1779–1816.

Listwan, S. J., Cullen, F. T., & Latessa, E. J. (2006). How to prevent prisoners reentry programs from failing: Insights from evidence-based corrections. *Federal Probation, 70*(3), 19–25.

Listwan, S. J., Van Voorhis, P., & Ritchy, P. N. (2007). Personality, criminal behavior and risk assessment: Implications for theory and practice. *Criminal Justice and Behavior, 34*(1), 60–75.

Loeber, R., Stouthamer-Loeber, M., Van Kammen, W., & Farrington, D. (1991). Initiation, escalation and desistence in juvenile offending and their correlates. *Journal of Criminal Law and Criminology, 82,* 36–82.

Lowenkamp, C. T., & Latessa, E. J. (2005). Increasing the effectiveness of correctional programming through the risk principle: Identifying offenders for residential placement. *Criminology & Public Policy, 4*(2), 501–528.

Lowenstein, A. (1986). Temporary single parenthood: The case of prisoners' families. *Family Relations, 35,* 79–85.

Lynch, J., & Sabol, W. (2001). *Prisoner reentry in perspective.* Washington, DC: The Urban Institute.

MacKenzie, D. L. (2006). *What works in corrections: Reducing the criminal activities of offenders and delinquents.* New York, NY: Cambridge University Press.

Maguire, K. E., Flanagan, T. J., & Thornberry, T. P. (1988). Prison labor and recidivism. *Journal of Quantitative Criminology, 4,* 3–18.

Marciniak, L. M. (1999). The use of day reporting as an intermediate sanction: A study of offender targeting and program termination. *The Prison Journal, 79*(2), 205–225.

Marciniak, L. M. (2000). Addition of day reporting to intensive supervision probation: A comparison of recidivism rates. *Federal Probation, 64*(1), 34–39.

Marquart, J. W., Cuvelier, S. J., Burton, V. S., Adams, K., Gerber, J., Longmire, D., . . . Fritsch, E. (1994). A limited capacity to treat: Examining the effects of prison population control strategies on prison education programs. *Crime and Delinquency, 40*(4), 516–531.

Martin, S. S., & Inciardi, J. A. (1993a). Case management approaches for criminal justice clients. In J. A. Inciadri (Ed.), *Drug treatment and criminal justice* (pp. 81–96). Newbury Park, CA: Sage Publications.

Martin, S. S., & Inciardi, J. A. (1993b). A case management treatment program for drug involved prison releases. *The Prison Journal, 73*(3/4), 319–333.

Martinson, R. (1974). "What works?" Questions and answers about prison reform. *Public Interest, 35,* 22–54.

Maruna, S. (2001). *Making good: How ex-convicts reform and rebuild their lives.* Washington, DC: American Psychological Association.

Mateyoke-Scrivner, A., Webster, J. M., Stanton, M., & Leukefeld, C. L. (2004). Treatment retention predictors of drug court participants in a rural state. *The American Journal of Drug and Alcohol Abuse, 3*(3), 605–625.

May, D. C., Wood, P. B., Mooney, J. L., & Minor, K. I. (2005). Predicting offender generated exchange rates: Implications for a theory of sentence severity. *Crime and Delinquency, 51,* 373–399.

McBride, D., & VanderWaal, C. (1997). Day reporting centers as an alternative for drug using offenders. *Journal of Drug Issues, 27*(2), 379–397.

McCollum, S. (1994). Mandatory literacy: Evaluating the Bureau of Prisons' long-standing commitment. *Federal Prisons Journal, 3*(2), 33–36.

Messemer, J. E., & Valentine, T. (2004). The learning gains of male inmates participating in a basic skills program. *Adult Basic Education, 14*(2), 67–89.

Messina, N., Burdon, W., Hagopian, G., & Prendergast, M. (2006). Predictors of prison-based treatment outcomes: A comparison of men and women participants. *The American Journal of Drug and Alcohol Abuse, 32,* 7–28.

Mitchell, O., & MacKenzie, D. L. (2003). Crime prevention via prison-based drug treatment: A systematic review and assessment of the research. In H. Kury & J. Obergfell-Fuchs (Eds.), *Crime prevention: New approaches.* Weberstrabe, Germany: Weisser Ring.

Mitchell, O., MacKenzie, D. L., & Wilson, D. B. (2005). The effectiveness of incarceration based drug treatment: An empirical synthesis of the research. In D. P. Farrington & B. C. Welsh (Eds.), In *Preventing crime: What works for children, offenders, victims and places.* Belmont, CA: Wadsworth Publishing.

Molitor, G. T. (1994). Should prison inmates receive education benefits. *On the Horizon, 2*(4), 9–10.

Morgan, R. D., Winterowd, C. L., & Ferrell, S. W. (2006). A national survey of group psychotherapy services in correctional facilities. In R. Tewksbury (Ed.), *Behind bars: Readings on prison culture* (pp. 348–357). Upper Saddle River, NJ: Pearson Education.

Mukamal, D. (2000). Confronting the employment barriers of criminal records: Effective legal and practical strategies. *Clearinghouse Review, January-February,* 597.

Mumola, C. J. (1999). Substance abuse and treatment, state and federal prisoners, 1997 (NCJ 172871). U.S. Department of Justice, Bureau of Justice Statistics.

Murray, D. W. (1992). Drug abuse treatment programs in the Federal Bureau of Prisons: Initiatives for the 90's. In C. G. Leukefeld & F. M. Tims (Eds.), *Drug abuse treatment in prisons and jails* (pp. 62–83). Washington, DC: U.S. Government Printing Office.

National Drug Court Institute (NDCI). (2009). National Association of Drug Court professions. Retrieved from http://www.ndci.org/research.

Nelson, M., Deess, P., & Allen, C. (1999). *The first month out: Post-incarceration experiences in New York City.* New York, NY: Vera Institute of Justice.

Newman, D. J. (2002). Prisons don't work. In T. Gray (Ed.), *Exploring corrections: A book of reading* (pp. 243–249). Boston, MA: Allyn and Bacon.

Nieto, M. (1998). *Probation for adult and juvenile offenders: Options for improved accountability.* Sacramento, CA: California Research Bureau.

Nussbaumer, D. (2008), Massnahmen gegen nicht fassbare Gewalt. (Unpublished doctoral dissertation). University of Zurich.

Nuttall, J., Hollmen, L., & Staley, E. M. (2003). The effect of earning a GED on recidivism rate. *Journal of Correctional Education, 54*, 90–94.

Offender to College Program. (2011). University of Wisconsin-Oshkosh. Retrieved from http://www.uwosh.edu/public_affairs/criminal-justice/inviting-convicts-to-college-4/OSCIOffenderstoCollege.pdf.

Ostermann, M. (2009). An analysis of New Jersey's day reporting center and halfway back programs: Embracing the rehabilitative ideal through evidence based practices. *Journal of Offender Rehabilitation, 48*, 139–153.

Parent, D. (1990). *Day reporting centers for criminal offenders—A descriptive analysis of existing programs.* Washington, DC: National Institute of Justice.

Parent, D., Byrne, J., Tsarfaty, V., Valade, L., & Esselman, J. (1995). *Day reporting centers: Volume 1.* Washington, DC: National Institute of Justice.

Parke, R., & Clarke-Stewart, K. A. (2003). Effects of parental incarceration on children. In J. Travis & M. Waul (Eds.), *Prisoners once removed: The impact of incarceration and reentry on children, families and communities.* Washington, DC: The Urban Institute Press.

Patterson, G. G., Chamberlain, P., & Reid, J. B. (1982). A comparative evaluation of a parent-training program. *Behavior Therapy, 13*, 638–650.

Payne, B. K., & Gainey, R. R. (1999). How monitoring punishes. *Journal of Offender Monitoring, 12*(1), 23–25.

Payne, B. K., & Gainey, R. R. (2009). A qualitative assessment of the pains experienced on electronic monitoring. *Prisons and jails: A reader* (pp. 533–544). Boston, MA: McGraw Hill.

Pearson, F. S., & Lipton, D. S. (1999). A meta-analytic review of the effectiveness of corrections-based treatment for drug abuse. *Prison Journal, 79*, 384–410.

Petersilia, J. (2003). *When prisoners come home: Parole and prisoner reentry.* New York, NY: Oxford University Press.

Pettiway, L. E. (1987). Participation in crime partnerships by female drug users: The effect of domestic arrangements, drug use, and criminal involvement. *Criminology, 251*, 741–766.

Polaschek, D. L. L., Wilson, N. J., Townsend, M. R., & Daly, L. R. (2005). Cognitive-behavioral rehabilitation for high-risk offenders: An outcome evaluation of the violence prevention unit. *Journal of Interpersonal Violence, 20*(12), 1611–1627.

Prendergast, M. L., Podus, D., Chang, E., & Urada, D. (2002). The effectiveness of drug abuse treatment: A meta-analysis of comparison group studies. *Drug and Alcohol Dependence, 67*, 53–73.

Quinn, J. F. (2003). *Corrections: A concise introduction.* Long Grove, IL: Waveland Press.

Raeder, M. S. (1993). Gender and sentencing: Single moms, battered women, and other sex- based anomalies in the gender free world of the federal sentencing guidelines. *Pepperdine Law Review, 20*, 905–990.

Rand, M. R., Sabol, W. J., Sinclair, M., & Snyder, H. (2010). Alcohol and crime: Data from 2002 to 2008. U.S. Department of Justice. Bureau of Justice Statistics. Retrieved from http://bjs.ojp.usdoj.gov/index.cfm?ty=pbdetail&iid=2313.

Rauma, D., & Berk, R. (1987). Remuneration and recidivism: The long-term impact of unemployment compensation on ex-offenders. *Journal of Quantitative Criminology*, 3–27.

Renzema, M., & Mayo-Wilson, E. (2005). Can electronic monitoring reduce crime for moderate to high risk offenders? *Journal of Experimental Criminology, 1*, 215–237.

Richards, S. C., Rose, C. D., & Reed, S. O. (2006). Inviting convicts to college: Prison and university partnership, In *The State of Corrections: 2005 Proceedings ACA Annual Conferences* (pp. 171–180). Lanham, MD: American Corrections Association.

Rose, C. D., Reed, S. O., & Richards, S. C. (2005). Inviting convicts to college: A free college preparatory program for prisoners. *Offender Programs Report, 8*(6), 81, 91–93.

Rose, C. D., Reschenberg, K, & Richards, S. C. (2010). The inviting convicts to college program. *Journal of Offender Rehabilitation, 49*(4), 293–308.

Ross, J. I. (2008). *Special problems in corrections.* Upper Saddle River, NJ: Pearson Education.

Ross, J. I., & Richards, S. C. (2002). *Behind bars: Surviving prison.* Indianapolis, IN: Alpha Books.

Rothstein, M. (1999). *Employment Law.* St. Paul, MN: West Group.

Sabbath, M. J., & Cowles, E. L. (1992). Problems associated with long term incarceration. *Forum on Corrections Research, 4*(2), 9–11.

Sampson, R. J., & Laub, J. H. (1993). *Crime in the making: Pathways and turning points through life.* Cambridge, MA: Harvard University Press.

Sampson, R. J., & Laub, J. H. (1995). Understanding variability in lives through time contributions of life-course criminology. *Studies in Crime and Crime Prevention, 4,* 143–158.

Saylor, W. G., & Gaes, G. G. (1987). Post release employment project: The effects of work skills acquisition in prison on post-release employment. Presented at The American Society of Criminology Meeting, Montreal, Canada.

Saylor, W. G., & Gaes, G. G. (1992). *PREP study links UNICOR work experience with successful post-release outcome.* Washington, DC: U.S. Federal Bureau of Prisons.

Schumaker, R., Anderson, D., & Anderson, S. (1990). Vocational and academic indicators of parole success. *Journal of Correctional Education, 41,* 8–13.

Scott, G., Dewey, J., & Leverentz, A. (2006). *Community reintegration trajectories: A qualitative comparative study of gang-affiliated and non-gang-affiliated ex-offenders.* Chicago, IL: Illinois Criminal Justice Information Authority.

Seal, D. W., Eldrige, G. D., Kacanek, D., Binson, D., & Macgowan, R. J. (2007). A longitudinal, qualitative analysis of the context of substance use and sexual behavior among 18-to-29-year-old men after their release from prison. *Social Science & Medicine, 65*(11), 2394–2406.

Seiter, R. P., & Kadula, K. P. (2003). Prisoner reentry: What works, what does not, and what is promising. *Crime and Delinquency, 49*(3), 360–388.

Sherman, L. W., Farrington, D. P., Welsh, B. C., & MacKenzie, D. L. (2002). *Evidence-based crime prevention.* London, UK: Routledge.

Shover, N. (1996). Great pretenders: *Pursuits and careers of persistent thieves.* Boulder, CO: Westview Press.

Showers, J. (1993). Assessing and remedying knowledge among women inmates. *Journal of Offender Rehabilitation, 20*(1/2), 35–46.

Snyder, Z. K., Carlo, T. A., & Mullins, M. M. (2001). Parenting from prison: An examination of a children's visitation program at a women's correctional facility. *Marriage and Family Review, 32*(3/4), 33–61.

Solomon, A. L., Johnson, K. D., Travis, J., & McBride, E. C. (2004). From prison to work: The employment dimensions of prisoner reentry. Paper prepared for the Urban Institute's re-entry roundtable, Washington, DC.

Spohn, C. (2007). The deterrent effect of imprisonment and offenders' stake in conformity. *Criminal Justice Policy Review, 18*(1), 31–50.

Steen, S., & Opsal, T. (2007). Punishment on the installment plan: Individual-level predictors of parole revocation in four states. *The Prison Journal, 87,* 344–366.

Stevens, D. J., & Ward, C. S. (1997). College education and recidivism: Educating criminals in meritorious. *Journal of Correctional Education, 48*(3), 106–111.

Sturges, J. E. (2002). Visitation at county jails: Potential policy implications. *Criminal Justice Policy Review, 13,* 32–45.

Tarlow, M. S. (2011). Employment barriers to reintgration, In L. Gideon & H. Sung, (Eds.), *Rethinking corrections: Rehabilitation, reentry and reintegration* (pp. 329–358). Thousand Oaks, CA: Sage Publications.

Taxman, F. S. (2002). Supervision—Exploring the dimensions of effectiveness. *Federal Probation, 66*(2), 14–27.

Taxman, F. S., Perdoni, M. L., & Harrison, L. D. (2007). Drug treatment services for adult offenders: The state of the state. *Journal of Substance Abuse Treatment, 32*(3), 239–254.

Tewksbury, R., & DeMichele, M. (2005). Going to prison: A prison visitation program. *The Prison Journal, 85,* 292–310.

Tewksbury, R., Erickson, D. J., & Taylor, J. M. (2000). Opportunities lost: The consequences of eliminating Pell Grant eligibility for correctional education students. *Journal of Offender Rehabilitation, 31*(1/2), 43–56.

Thomas, J. (1995). The ironies of prison education. In H. S. Davidson (Ed.), *Schooling in a "total institution": Critical perspectives of prison education* (pp. 573–574). Westport, CT: Bergin & Garvey.

Thomas, R. G., & Thomas, R. M. (2008). *Effective teaching in correctional settings: Prisons, jails, juvenile centers, and alternative schools.* Springfield, IL: Charles C. Thomas.

Thompson, P. T., & Harm, N. J. (2000). Parenting from prison: Helping children and mothers. *Issues in Comprehensive Pediatric Nursing, 23,* 61–81.

Toch, H. (1992). *Mosaic of despair: Human breakdowns in prison*. Washington, DC: American Psychological Association.

Travis, J. (2009). Families and children. In R. Tewksbury & D. Dabney (Eds.), *Prisons and jails: A reader* (pp. 335–350). Boston, MA: McGraw Hill.

Travis, J., & Lawrence, S. (2002). *Beyond the prison gates*. Washington, DC: The Urban Institute.

Travis, J., McBride, E. C., & Solomon, A. L. (2005). *Families left behind: The hidden costs of incarceration and reentry*. Washington, DC: The Urban Institute.

Travis, J., Solomon, A., & Waul, M. (2001). *From prison to home: The dimensions and consequences of prisoner reentry*. Washington, DC: The Urban Institute.

Turner, S., Myers, R., Sexton, L., & Smith, S. (2007). What crime rates tell us about where to focus programs and services for prisoners. *Criminology and Public Policy, 6*(3), 623–631.

Turner, S., & Petersilia, J. (1996). Work release in Washington: Effects on recidivism and corrections costs. *The Prison Journal, 76*(1), 138–150.

Twill, S. E., Nackerud, L., Risler, E. A., Bernat, J. A., & Taylor, D. (1998). Changes in measured loneliness, control and social support among parolees in a halfway house. *Journal of Offender Rehabilitation, 27*(3/4), 77–92.

Ubah, C. (2002). A critical examination of offender rehabilitation-correctional education: Lessons for the 21st century. *Journal of Correctional Education, 53*(1), 13–16.

Uggen, C. (1999). Ex-offenders and the conformist alternative: A job quality model of work and crime. *Social Problems, 46*, 127–151.

Uggen, C. (2000). Work as a turning point in the life course of criminals: A duration model of age, employment and recidivism. *American Sociological Review, 65*, 529–546.

van den Haag, E. (1982). Could successful rehabilitation reduce the crime rate? The *Journal of Criminal Law and Criminology, 73*(3), 1022–1035.

Visher, C. A., Lattimore, P. K., & Linster, R. L. (1991). Predicting the recidivism of serious youthful offenders using survival models. *Criminology, 28*(3), 329–366.

Visher, C., LaVigne, N., Travis, J. (2004). *Returning home: Understanding the challenges of prisoner reentry. Maryland pilot study: Findings from Baltimore*. Washington, DC: The Urban Institute.

Visher, C., & Travis, T. (2003). Transitions from prison to community: Understanding individual pathways. *Annual Review of Sociology, 29*, 89–113.

Walsh, A. (1985). An evaluation of the effects of adult basic education on rearrest rates among probationers. *Journal of Offender Counseling, Services, and Rehabilitation, 9*, 69–76.

Walters, G. D. (1999). Short-term outcome of inmates participating in the lifestyle change program. *Criminal Justice and Behavior, 26*(3), 322–337.

Ward, S. A. (2009). Career and technical education in United States prisons: What have we learned? *The Journal of Correctional Education, 60*(3), 191–200.

West, H. C., & Sabol, W. J. (2010). Prisoners in 2009 (NCJ 231675). U.S. Department of Justice, Bureau of Justice Statistics.

Western, B., & Petit, B. (2000). Incarceration and racial inequality in men's employment. *Industrial and Labor Relations Review, 54*, 3–16.

Wexler, H. K., Falkin, G. P., & Lipton, D. S. (1990). Outcome evaluation of a prison therapeutic community for substance abuse treatment. *Criminal Justice and Behavior, 17*, 71–92.

Wexler, H. K., Williams, R., Early, K., & Trotman, C. (1996). Prison treatment for substance abusers: Stay'N out revisited. In K. E. Early (Ed.), *Drug treatment behind bars: Prison-based strategies for change*. Westport, CT: Praeger.

Williams, A., May, D. C., & Wood, P. B., (2008). The lesser of two evils? A qualitative study of offenders' preferences for prison compared to alternatives. *Probation and Parole: Current Issues, 46*, 71–90.

Wilson, D. B., Bouffard, L. A., & MacKenzie, D. L. (2005). A qualitative review of structured, group-oriented, cognitive-behavioral programs for offenders. *Criminal Justice and Behavior, 32*, 172–204.

Wilson, D. B., Gallagher, C. A., & MacKenzie, D. L. (2000). A meta-analysis of corrections based education, vocation and work programs for adult offenders. *Journal of Research in Crime and Delinquency, 37*, 347–368.

Wirthlin Worldwide. (2000). *Member survey: Taking the next step. Welfare to work partnership*. Vol. 1. McLean, VA. Retrieved from www.welfaretowork.org.

Wright, L. E., & Seymour, C. B. (2000). *Working with children and families separated by incarceration: A handbook for child welfare agencies*. Washington, DC: CWLA Press.

Yalom, I. D. (1995). *The theory and practice of group psychotherapy* (4th ed.). New York, NY: Basic Books.

Yong, J. N. (1971). Advantages of group therapy in relation to individual therapy for juvenile delinquents. *Corrective Psychiatry and Journal of Social Therapy, 19*, 34–39.

Zhang, S. X., Roberts, R. E. L., & Callanan, V. J. (2006). Preventing parolees from returning to prison through community-based reintegration. *Crime and Delinquency, 52*(4), 551–571.

CHAPTER 14

Prevention of Sex Offenses and Sex Offenders

Kristine Levan
Plymouth State University

INTRODUCTION

In 2004, the body of 22-year-old Dru Sjodin was found near Crookston, Minnesota in a ravine, after 5 months of searching. An autopsy of her body revealed that she had been beaten, raped, and stabbed to death after being abducted as she walked to her car after shopping. The public outcry over this horrific crime intensified once the public learned that the suspect, Alfonso Rodriguez, Jr., was a convicted rapist who had finished his prison sentence and was residing in the community. Rodriguez had served the entire length of his prison sentence of 23 years and was released from prison with essentially no supervision. Six months after his release from prison, he abducted, raped, and murdered Sjodin.

The Rodriguez case illustrates one of the most heinous acts of sexual offending, a kidnapping followed by a sexual offense and then a murder. Other types of particularly egregious acts include those against children and those by serial rapists. These high-profile horrific events lead to questions about the best way to prevent these types of crimes from occurring in the first place. If more stringent laws were in place, would sex offenders still be able to commit their crimes?

OVERVIEW OF SEX OFFENDERS

Until the 1960s, the only sexual acts defined as criminal were rape and sodomy. Rape was narrowly defined as forced heterosexual penetration and sodomy as consensual homosexual penetration. These overly constricted definitions left many individuals who were sexually victimized without much choice for legal recourse against their attackers. Over the years, the laws have been redefined and restructured so that more inclusive definitions of sex offenses are applied.

The term *sex offender* is generally used to describe any individual who has been convicted of a sex offense. *Sexual assault* is a broad term that includes unwanted sexual conduct, attempted rape, and completed rape. Sex offenses range from a single instance of public indecency to more severe acts such as repeated violent sex crimes against children. *Rape* is defined as an act of forced, non-consensual sexual intercourse. *Acquaintance rape*, which comprises approximately 70% of all sex crimes, is a rape that occurs between intimate partners, family members, or friends (Fisher, Cullen

& Turner, 2000, Johnson & Sigler, 2000, as cited in Dabney, 2004).[1] Someone who engages in consensual sexual conduct with a minor has committed *statutory rape* (Dabney, 2004). A *pedophile* is an individual who engages in sexual activity with a child.

The perceived frequency of sexual offenses also creates concern. Many fear the *serial rapist*—the individual who rapes random victims over a period of time. *Habitual rapists* often rape the same individual over and over again. Some common forms of habitual rapes include date rape and spousal rape.

Date rape begins with the perpetrator and victim engaging in legitimate and consensual behavior. Over the course of time, the offender will engage in forceful or coercive behavior against the victim (Holmes & Holmes, 2009). Date rape may be accomplished with or without the use of drugs or alcohol. In recent years, Rohypnol has been coined as "the date rape drug," since it can have potentially severe effects on the individual consuming it. Loss of inhibitions, loss of memory, and "blacking out" completely, have all been associated with Rohypnol (Terry, 2006). Other types of drugs and alcohol are also commonly linked to incidents of date rape. Date rape is a particularly problematic crime since the victims are often embarrassed or feel partially responsible for the crime, especially if they were consuming alcohol or drugs at the time they were victimized.

Spousal rape is relatively new in terms of legal recognition; it was not recognized as criminal until the 1970s. States differ in their definition of what constitutes spousal rape, with some including only legally married couples. Other states also include couples who cohabitate or couples who are legally separated or divorced. Sexual assault may be accompanied by other forms of physical abuse (Pagelow, 1988; Pence & Paymar, 1993; Bergen, 1998, as cited in Holmes & Holmes, 2009). Reporting issues are very similar to those associated with date rape, with a relatively low incidence of reporting (Moriarty & Earle, 2000, as cited in Holmes & Holmes, 2009). However, many victims of spousal rape also may fear continued abuse at the hands of their spouses, the fear that the criminal justice system will not take their claim seriously, feelings of loyalty to their spouses or family (Russell, 1990), or the belief that they have not been raped (Bergen, 1996).

Sexual offenses are also sometimes classified by the number of perpetrators. Acts involving single perpetrators constitute the vast majority of offenses, with over 90% of rapes and sexual assaults involving a single perpetrator. In contrast, gang rapes, which involve three or more perpetrators, make up only about 1% of all sexual assaults and rapes. The remaining cases involve two perpetrators acting in conjunction with each other to complete a rape or sexual assault.

Offenses perpetrated by three or more offenders have the unique characteristic of the perpetrators engaging in "group think" activities, a phenomenon not seen in offenses involving only two perpetrators (O'Sullivan, 1991). Despite the infrequent occurrence of gang rapes, this type of sexual assault has been brought to the forefront in recent years. Situations in which men are competing against one another for status or prestige may be commonplace for these crimes. For example, prisoners, soldiers, fraternity members, and athletes are at an increased risk of committing gang-perpetrated rapes (O'Sullivan, 1991). These individuals may feel compelled to compete with one another for power or status, and want to exert dominance over each other. They may feel this task can be accomplished by sexually degrading someone in an attempt to prove their own masculinity in a competitive environment.

The university campus environment is one in which a great number of sexual assaults and rapes occur (Johnson & Sigler, 1996, as cited in Holmes & Holmes, 2009). It has been estimated that approximately one in four college females will be sexually assaulted or have a sexual assault attempt made against them while they are enrolled in college (Brenner, McMahon, Warren, & Douglas, 1999; Fisher, Cullen, & Turner, 2000, as cited in Holmes & Holmes, 2009). As many as 90% of college-aged males admit to acting in a sexually aggressive manner in social settings (Thompson & Cracco, 2008). The frequency with which sexual assaults occur on campus may be explained by the nexus of several contributing factors. Not only are college students the likely age at which most victims are sexually assaulted, but they are also exposed to various people on a daily basis, many of whom they have some form of a relationship with, in an environment that encourages social gatherings.

Time and location are both particularly relevant when exploring sex offenses. Sexual assaults are more likely to occur in urban locations than rural ones. Sexual assaults are also more likely to occur during the night-to-early-morning hours, between 6:00 PM and 6:00 AM (Riedel & Welsh, 2008). This means that these types of crimes are more likely to occur in areas and during time frames in which many people are interacting with each other and are more likely to be involved in social settings rather than educational or work-related settings.

In comparison with other forms of violent crimes, sexual assaults and rapes are significantly less likely to involve a weapon. For instance, in comparison with robbery, where 47% of offenses did *not* include a weapon, a weapon was *not* used in 85% of sexual assault and rape cases. The weapon most frequently used in a sexual assault or rape is a knife, comprising about 8% of the total cases (BJS, 2009b). This lack of reliance on a weapon to complete a sexual offense is likely correlated with the complexity of the victim–offender relationship. Since most victims already know their attackers, it seems less likely that a weapon would be necessary to complete the criminal act.

Similarly, most victims of sexual assault and rape are highly unlikely to seek medical treatment for injuries. Reporting to police is highly correlated with seeking medical treatment. For rape victims, 59% of those who reported their victimization to the police sought treatment, compared with only 17% of unreported rapes. For sexual assault victims, 37% of those who reported to the police also sought medical treatment, compared with 18% of those who did *not* report their victimization to the police (BJS, 2002).

Most citizens obtain a majority of their information about crime from the local news and other media outlets. Although the most severe and heinous form of sexual crimes do occur, they do not occur nearly as frequently as much of the public believes, primarily as a result of the media exposure of these types of incidents. The old adage of "if it bleeds, it leads" sums up the relationship between the media and crime. The result of the frequent media portrayals of the most gruesome, yet least frequent types of offenses serves to generate fear in the public by presenting skewed information about crime (Kappeler & Potter, 2005; Dowler, 2006; Zilney & Zilney, 2009).

A sexual attack against a child is one that simultaneously ignites both hatred and fear among the public. Seeing innocent individuals with little to no ability to protect or fend for themselves is enough to garner the drive en mass for changes in policies. The reaction from the public of the news of a crime against a child is often to place blame on the criminal justice system for doing too little to prevent such atrocities (Lieb, Quinsey, & Berliner, 1998; Terry, 2006; Zilney & Zilney, 2009). However, it seems intuitive that it is the complete picture of sexual offenses that should be examined, rather than focusing on a handful of sensationalized cases.

MEASUREMENT AND RATES OF SEXUAL OFFENSES

Although both males and females can be sexually assaulted, females are disproportionately the targets of sexual offenses. There are so few reported male victims for sex offenses that they cannot be compared to female victims. In terms of sexual assaults, only about 2% of all completed sexual assaults that are reported to the police are against males (Chilton & Jarvis, 1999). About 95% of all completed adult rapes are committed against females, and about 90% of sexual assaults are committed against females. Both victims and offenders of sexual assault are predominantly white. Age also plays a prominent factor in determining the likelihood of being victimized. The highest rates occur among those between the ages of 16 and 24.

The official measurement tools for sex offenses are the Uniform Crime Report (UCR)/ National Incident Based Reporting System (NIBRS), and the National Crime Victimization Survey (NCVS). However, the NCVS has historically been seen as a more reliable measurement tool for sexual offenses than the UCR or NIBRS since these measures are based solely on crimes reported to the police. In 2009, approximately 55% of all rapes and sexual assaults were reported to the police (BJS, 2009a). This rate shows an increase from previous years, which indicates that on average, 36% of rapes and 26% of sexual assaults were reported to law enforcement (BJS, 2002).

Feelings of shame, guilt, embarrassment, or fear often overwhelm the victims of sexual offenses, making it one of the most unreported violent crimes (Bachman & Taylor, 1994; Baumer, Felson, & Messner, 2003). The likelihood of reporting the crime to the police is highly correlated with the victim–offender relationship. Approximately 90% of victims who do not report their crime to the police indicate that they had a prior relationship with their attacker (Bohmer & Parrot, 1993). This issue of nonreporting is exacerbated for male victims, who in addition to the previously mentioned reasons, also cite the stigmatization of being labeled as a male victim of a sexual offense as a reason to not report their victimization to the police (Scarce, 1997).

In order to increase the likelihood of reporting a crime to the police, rape shield laws have been passed in most states. Victims of sexual assault have historically reported feeling a process of double victimization—once by the offender during the criminal transaction and again by the criminal justice system itself (Belknap, 2007). For instance, victims may be reluctant to report the crime because they do not want to endure cross-examination by prosecutors. Rape shield laws vary on a state-by-state basis, but in general they provide additional protections for the victim of a sexual offense, such as limiting the amount of information on her or his sexual past that can be called into question during a trial or prohibiting the victim's name from being publicized. The effectiveness of rape shield laws is uncertain since the credibility of the victim continues to often be called into question (Kruttschnitt, 1994, as cited by Riedel & Welsh, 2008). Many of the issues related to the reliability of the victims' claims may be based on the continued belief in several rape myths, which will be discussed later in this chapter.

As with other types of criminal offending, sexual assault can also be measured by researchers, who often focus either on the victim or on the offender. Researchers can narrow the focus on the topic at hand by choosing an issue such as motivation of offenders, effects of victimization, or actions taken by the victims after the offense. Researchers can provide invaluable information by capturing data beyond what is offered by the official measurement tools.

RISK MANAGEMENT OF SEX OFFENDERS

Regardless of whether a sexual offender serves a standard prison sentence, receives treatment, undergoes chemical castration, or becomes civilly committed, a risk assessment tool is typically completed before he or she is considered for release back into the community. Various assessment tools are available, including the Minnesota Sex Offender Screening Tool, Sexual Violence Risk-20, and the Risk for Sexual Violence Protocol. It is critical to note that these risk management tools apply to adult males, and that they are not applicable to either juvenile or female offenders (Zilney & Zilney, 2009).

Predicting risk proves to be a difficult task, and these tests have been faulted for overpredicting recidivism among sexual offenders, especially among those who are the most serious offenders (Quinsey, Lalumiere, Rice, & Harris, 1995; von Hirsch & Ashworth, 1996; Craig, Browne, Stringer, & Beech, 2005; Terry, 2006; Zilney & Zilney, 2009). Ultimately, there is no one measure of which test best assesses the likelihood of recidivism, but as these methods continue to be developed and refined, the belief is that their predictive capabilities will improve (Gideon & Sung, 2001).

THE ISSUE OF RECIDIVISM

The actual recidivism rate of sex offenders continues to be a hotly debated topic. Because our criminal justice policies are ultimately driven by information on rates of reoffending, accurate recidivism information is crucial to any discussion on how to handle sexual offenders. Despite the importance placed on obtaining accurate recidivism rates, there does not seem to be a consensus on how likely a sex offender is to commit a subsequent sexual offense.

As with most crimes, the definition of recidivism is somewhat unclear. If someone commits a technical infraction of his or her parole conditions, this may be counted as recidivating. Someone may also be considered a sexual recidivist if they commit a new crime, regardless of whether or not it is a crime of a sexual nature. Furthermore, some researchers measure recidivism by new arrests, while others ask the offenders to self-report any new sexual crimes that they may have committed. The length of time to recidivate also varies by study, with some studies having a follow up as short as 3 months and others as long as 25 years (Harrison & Beck, 2005, as cited in Riedel & Welsh, 2008; Zilney & Zilney, 2009; Bynum, Carter, Matson, & Onley, 2011).

Most researchers compare the recidivism rates of sex offenders versus those of nonsex offenders. These findings suggest recidivism rates ranging between 5.6% and 24% (Kruttschnitt, Uggen, & Shelton, 2000, as cited in Bynum et al., 2011; Zgoba & Simon, 2005; Meloy, 2006; Webster, Gartner, & Doob, 2006; Terry, 2006; Zilney & Zilney, 2009). Almost uniformly, these findings indicate higher recidivism rates for nonsex offenders than for sex offenders.

When analyzing sex offenders, some studies compare various types of sex offenders and their recidivism rates, the most common being adult victims versus juvenile victims. Snyder (2000) contends that child molesters are significantly less likely to reoffend than adult rapists, with recidivism rates of 3% and 40%, respectively (as cited by Zilney & Zilney, 2009). In contrast, other studies have indicated that child molesters have a significantly higher recidivism rate of 52% versus the 39% reported for those who commit sex offenses against adults (Prentky, Lee, Knight, & Cerce, 1997, as cited in Bynum et al., 2011; Lussier, LeBlanc, & Proulx, 2005, as cited in Zilney & Zilney, 2009).

Of course other factors may be influencing these recidivism rates. If sex offenders are found to have higher rates of recidivism, perhaps it is an artifact of the increased levels of supervision they endure and, subsequently, their greater propensity to be detected by authorities. Furthermore, if sex offenders have more scrutiny placed on them and more restrictions placed on their parole supervision, they may have more opportunities to fail and be rearrested.

Despite the low numbers indicated in many studies, it appears the public is convinced that sex offenders have above-average recidivism rates when compared to other types of offenders. In 2007, researchers questioned the public on their beliefs about the reoffense rate of sex offenders. Respondents indicated that they believe these offenders to have the highest rates of recidivism among all criminal offenders, with a recidivism rate of about 75% (Levenson, Brannon, Fortney, & Baker, 2007, as cited in Zilney & Zilney, 2009).

THEORETICAL EXPLANATIONS OF SEX OFFENDING

Once it was believed that all rapists and sexual offenders were motivated by sexual desire. Therefore, many policies revolved around attempting to curb their sexual urges. However, the last several decades of research have revealed that violent sex offenders are often motivated by a need to exert power over their victims. Understanding the motivations behind commission of the crime is paramount to prevention of the crime.

Psychological Explanations

Psychological explanations of sexual offending attempt to use past behavioral patterns to predict future behavioral patterns (Vito & Holmes, 1995, as cited in Holmes & Holmes, 2009). Trends among sex offenders indicate that events occur over time that "trigger" their criminogenic tendencies (Schultz, 2005). It has been noted that nearly all sex offenders display loneliness and intimacy problems (Marshall, 1989). Negative childhood experiences, such as growing up in an abusive household, may be seen as a pattern among those who commit sex crimes (Greenfeld, 1997, as cited in Riedel & Welsh, 2008; Dabney, 2004). These negative experiences may lead some individuals to become less likely to form healthy attachments to others, which may then lead to an increased likelihood of committing sex offenses (Ward, Hudson, & Marshall, 1996, as cited in Zilney & Zilney, 2009). For example, the *family dysfunction model* focuses on the mother's role in the family unit. Some sex offenders grow up in a family with a mother who is physically or emotionally unavailable, prompting the father to seek comfort and love with his children (MacLeod & Sarago, 1987, as cited in Terry, 2006). This may prompt a cycle of violence that becomes self-perpetuating as the child grows into an adult.

Childhood sexual or physical abuse is not found among all sex offenders, however. Moreover, not all sex offenders are caught. Therefore, there remains an unknown in the equation to correlate abnormal childhood experiences with the likelihood to offend as an adult (Zilney & Zilney, 2009). What is known about a sexual offender's psyche is that he or she often turns to drugs and alcohol in an effort to deal with depression and anxiety. While these factors contribute to lowering the inhibitions of the offender (and in some cases, the victim), they can certainly not be considered a causal mechanism for sexual offending (Riedel & Welsh, 2008).

Some researchers fault psychological explanations of rapists. Many studies have been conducted that falsify the claim that most sexual offenders have a mental illness (Bart & O'Brien, 1985, as cited in Riedel & Welsh, 2008; Scully, 1994). The act of medicalizing an issue sets forth not only the belief that there is a cure for the sex offender's sickness, but also relieves the individual of responsibility and accountability for his or her actions. Because medical research has been unable to find a consistent pattern among sex offenders, these researchers conclude that sex offenders must be seen as being accountable for their crimes (Scully & Marolla, 1985, as cited by Riedel & Welsh, 2008).

Social Learning Theory

Can individuals "learn" to commit rape and other sexual offenses? Social learning theory would suggest that the answer to this question is "yes." If an individual experiences more favorable than unfavorable responses to sexual offending, he or she may be more likely to commit this type of offense. Continued exposure, either directly (through personal experiences) or indirectly (through the media) may play a role in an individual's involvement in sexual crimes.

Social learning of sexual offending can occur in multiple contexts. For example, if an individual experiences the "cycle of violence" in which he or she has been sexually victimized by a parent, other family member, or acquaintance throughout childhood, he or she may be more likely to adopt these behaviors as his or her own upon emergence into adulthood. The cycle of violence approach would posit that sexual misconduct may be perpetrated against the potential offender's children, other family members, or community members.

Learning theory may also be used to explain the presence of many "rape myths" that exist. For example, the "no-means-yes" myth claims that individuals who say no to a sexual advance may actually be too intimidated or demure to acknowledge their willingness to participate in a sexual encounter (Mayerson & Taylor, 1987, as cited in Holmes & Holmes, 2009; Koss & Harvey, 1991, as cited in Riedel & Welsh, 2008). Others indicate that the answer of "no" to a sexual advance may not occur until the male has reached the peak of sexual frustration (Glavin, 1986, as cited in Riedel & Welsh, 2008). Additionally, women who dress provocatively or who are flirtatious may be seen as being overly sexually aggressive (Workman & Freeburg, 1999, as cited in Riedel & Welsh, 2008; Holmes & Holmes, 2009). Others believe that individuals who make reports or claims of rape are individuals who simply regretted their original decision to engage in sexual activity with the assailant. These myths, which perpetuate the beliefs that most sexual conduct is consensual, are often learned from peers, family members, or media depictions of sexual activity.

Similarly, individuals may learn that sexual offenses are acceptable through various media avenues. Movies, television shows, music, and video games all may convey prodeviant sexual attitudes that endorse violent sexual acts. Once the potential offender learns that these prodeviant attitudes are acceptable, these attitudes may translate into unacceptable sexual behavior, such as sexual assault and rape (Holmes & Holmes, 2009). Media explanations may become particularly relevant when considering the offending histories of those individuals who were not victims of sexual abuse as a child.

Learning theory can also be used to explain unique subcultures that may exist where sex offenders operate as "colleagues." If, as learning theory would suggest, the peers that you associate with have the greatest influence over your behavior (Sutherland, 1950), then it seems intuitive that individuals who offend may be likely to keep company with other individuals who offend. Best and Luckenbill (1994) have coined the term *colleagues* to describe these peer-related groups who commit similar offenses (as cited in Dabney, 2004). Continued exposure to an underground media that condones abnormal sexual behavior coupled with a subculture of individuals who endorse sexually violent or deviant behavior as acceptable, may also lend some credibility to a learning theory perspective (Dabney, 2004). One extreme example of subculture groups that promote deviant sexual behavior are those groups that condone pedophiliac lifestyles, such as the North American Man/Boy Love Association (NAMBLA) (DeYoung, 1989; Holmes & Holmes, 2009).

Feminist Theories

Feminist theories state that sexual offenses occur as a result of cultural-level rather than individual-level explanations (Terry, 2006). Sociologically, sex offenses may be partially explained by the male-dominated culture of American society. As boys, males are socialized to be authoritative, powerful, and assertive, while girls are taught to be passive and demure. Males and females are often socialized into traditional gender-specific roles, roles that illustrate to females that they should allow themselves to be controlled by males (Brownmiller, 1975; Baron & Strauss, 1989; Scully, 1994; Jackson, 1995; Dabney, 2004; Riedel & Welsh, 2008; Zilney & Zilney, 2009). As adults, this division in gender roles is reiterated by situations such as a traditional division of labor for household chores and discrepancies in employment and pay between males and females. Men who are sexually aggressive as adults have often been taught throughout their lives that they should not place any value on issues such as intimacy and empathy (Lisak & Ivan, 1995, as cited in Terry, 2006).

This continued oppression, no matter how well hidden, remains pervasive and contributes to feelings of male superiority and female inferiority. Women may feel powerless to stop sexual offenses from being committed against them. Once victimized, they may continue to feel powerless at the hands of the criminal justice system, one that is dominated by white males (Belknap, 2007). Feminist theories that center on gender inequality note that those civilizations in which women are oppressed and thought to be the sexual servants and inferiors of males are likely to also see high rates of sexual victimization.

The Rape–Pornography Link

An idea that is closely related to feminist theories about sex offending is the specific belief that exposure to pornography may increase the likelihood that an individual will become a perpetrator of sexual crimes (Russell, 1998, as cited in Holmes & Holmes, 2009). Images of women being repeatedly degraded and dominated may allow some potential assailants to feel that violent sexual behavior is acceptable. A study conducted by Baron and Strauss (1989) concluded that states with the largest circulation of common adult magazines, such as *Hustler* and *Playboy*, also experience the highest rates of rape (as cited in Dabney, 2004).

Some researchers believe that it is not necessarily all forms of pornographic material that elicit sexual violence from viewers. Rather, it may be the viewing of particular types of pornography that leads to an increased likelihood of sexual offending. *Violent* sexual images may play a much larger role in condoning sexual violence than images that display nonviolent sexual activity (Goode, 1984, as cited in Holmes & Holmes, 2009). It may also be that there is not necessarily a causal relationship between pornography and sexual offending. Other issues from the individual's background may aggravate the effects of pornography, such as a history of being sexually abused or an abusive family environment (Harris & Staunton, 2000, as cited in Holmes & Holmes, 2009). Exposure to pornographic images may simply reinforce violent sexual ideas that already exist within the individual (Holmes & Holmes, 2009).

PREVENTION OF SEXUAL OFFENSES

Many forms of sexual offense have been decreasing in the last several years. For example, even though the United States has the highest rate of rape in the world, with about 28.6 rapes per 100,000 people ("Rape at the National Level," 2008), rapes and other sexual offenses have been on the decline since the mid-1990s. Many people attribute this decrease in offenses to the increased attention given to sex offenses and sex offenders. Efforts such as an increase in the length of time a sex offender may serve in prison, as well as sex offender prevention and treatment programs may be credited for this decrease.

The Containment Model

Because of the situational nature of most sexual offenses, it is a difficult crime to prevent. Most of the prevention mechanisms offered by the criminal justice system focus on convicted sex offenders in an attempt to prevent them from recidivating. Prevention of repeat sexual offenses has proven to be a difficult task. The classification of a sex offense encompasses a wide variety of crimes. In order to prevent a sex offender from recidivating, it is important to consider the actual offense in order to individualize a management strategy. The containment model is often seen as the most effective strategy for managing sex offenders. This model is best described as an interagency approach that understands that sexual offenses generally involve a great deal of deception, secrecy, and manipulation (Thomas, 2000, as cited in Terry, 2006).

The containment model is a three-pronged approach that includes treatment, supervision, and polygraph examinations to assist in monitoring progress in treatment and adherence to supervision (English, Pullen, & Jones, 1996, as cited in Terry, 2006). Several goals can be accomplished with this model. Not only can communities feel safer in the presence of sex offenders, the offender can also receive the treatment necessary to assist in rehabilitation. Collaboration among agencies is the most important aspect of this approach. Not only is collaboration necessary for individual-level cases, but also for policy-level issues (Terry, 2006). The polygraph examinations serve as a safety net to address problem of offenders who are not abiding by the terms of treatment and monitoring, as required by the terms of their probation and parole. Polygraph examinations may also be used by therapists and counselors to determine whether the offenders are truthful in their therapy or counseling sessions (Wilcox, 2000).

The ultimate purpose of the containment model is to closely monitor the sex offender and use internal and external controls on him or her. The offender is held accountable for any infractions (English et al., 1996, as cited in Terry, 2006). Although the containment model works well in some jurisdictions, it is not ideal for larger cities due to the sheer number of agencies involved in the communication effort, as well as the large number of sex offenders who are being supervised (Terry, 2006).

Conditions of Parole and Probation

Many sex offenders may be given probation instead of serving time in a correctional facility. Those who are sentenced to institutional confinement are often released on parole once they have completed their sentences. It is estimated that at any given time, 60% of offenders are under some form of community supervision ("Strategically Monitoring Sex Offenders," 2008). Because they are considered special-needs offenders, they often require more intensive supervision by their parole and probation officers than other types of offenders. They are often required to complete a treatment program and may be required to wear an electronic monitor in order to track their whereabouts. They also may be required to submit to HIV and AIDS testing and have the results of these tests disclosed to their victims, as well as be financially responsible for any treatment or counseling that their victims complete as a result of their sexual victimization.

In order to ensure the sex offender abides by the stipulations of his or her probation or parole, the supervising officer must be diligent and thorough. Because of the taxing nature of supervising only sex offenders, it is often recommended that their parole officers seek counseling or therapeutic support (Terry, 2006). Additionally, because sex offenders are such a unique population, careful selection and training of probation and parole officers is crucial. They must be able to understand the nature of sexual offenses, as well as the unique and specific needs of sex offenders.

Although sex offenders usually heed the requirements of their probation and parole (Terry, 2006), the restrictions for sex offenders on parole or probation are among the strictest for all criminal offenses, in part because of the severity of the crimes committed. One restriction that is unique to sex offenses is the residency restriction. Those convicted of a sex offense are restricted from living in close proximity to a school, park, or daycare center, usually with a 500–2,000 foot restriction, depending on the jurisdiction's guidelines. Other common restrictions may apply to using the Internet (see the discussion on "Cracking Down on Internet Crime" in this chapter), owning pornographic material, and owning items of particular interest to children, such as video games or toys.

The radius restriction requirements on a sex offender's residency have created cause for concern in recent years. A residency restriction only places limitations on where the sex offender lives, and has no bearing on where he or she can travel outside of the home (Zilney & Zilney, 2009). Thus, it is possible for a registered sex offender to freely move about and visit locations that he or she is restricted from living near, such as schools and playgrounds. These restrictions have been faulted for interfering with an offender's ability to successfully reintegrate back into the community. The communities that offenders are eligible to reside in are often dilapidated and far removed from the larger community. Additionally, they are often locations the offenders may not want their family members, especially their children, exposed to. This may prevent them from being able to construct or reconstruct a bond with their loved ones, a facet of reintegration that is often key to successful rehabilitation (Zilney & Zilney, 2009).

Large cities such as Miami and Los Angeles have seen a surge in the number of registered sex offenders, along with a lack of available housing that meets the requirements of their probation or parole restrictions. In large urban areas, this creates issues because there may be very few areas that are not within the designated distance from schools, churches, parks, or playgrounds. As such, sex offenders residing in some cities may find themselves forced into a state of homelessness. For example, in Miami, as many as 100 sex offenders have taken up residence at the Julia Tuttle Causeway sex offender colony. This is in part due to Miami's restriction on housing, which states that sex offenders must remain 2,500 feet from where children congregate. Although colonies such as these give sex offenders a place to stay, they have been criticized for being comparable to shanty towns. As of March 2010, the Julia Tuttle Causeway was being evacuated, and sex offenders were being sent to designated trailer parks and hotels to take up residence (Brown, 2010).

Registration Laws and Community Notification

The United States is not alone in its stance on sex offenders. Many countries, including Australia, Canada, Ireland, and the United Kingdom all require sex offenders to register with local law enforcement upon their return to the community (Zilney & Zilney, 2009). The United States is, however, unique in its stance on notification laws. A comparison with the Canadian system illustrates this difference. Individual provinces determine how much information is disseminated to the public, and the public does not have access to the sex offender registry (Murphy, Fedoroff, & Martineau, 2009; Zilney & Zilney, 2009).

In the United States convicted sex offenders are required by law to register in their city or town as a sex offender. These registries are designed to inform the local public that a sex offender is residing in the area and to allow the government to track his or her place of residence. Failure to register can result in severe penalties that may include revocation of an offender's parole. The information included in the registry is available to the general public, often via the Internet. The registries will often list the type of offense committed, as well as the age and gender of the victim.

However, jurisdictions vary in how they report the age of the victim. Some only list the age at the time of the offense, while others update the victim's age annually (Zilney & Zilney, 2009).

The Jacob Wetterling Act was passed in 1994 to require each state to have some form of registration system for individuals convicted of a sexual offense against a child. Individuals convicted of a sex offense must register with local law enforcement once they are released from prison. For 10 years, offenders must update their addresses annually, and those convicted of a violent sexual offense must update their information on a quarterly basis. They also must update their address when and if they move. The Jacob Wetterling Act served as a basis for subsequent registration laws that were passed, such as Megan's Law.

Megan's Law was passed in 1996. This federal statute allows local law enforcement agencies to keep the public informed when a registered sex offender is living or working within their community. The law is named after 7-year-old Megan Kanka, who was sexually victimized and killed by a convicted child molester after he moved in across the street from the Kanka family. It is up to the discretion of the individual state as to whether they want to notify the community of all sex offenders' statuses, or only those at a particular risk level (Levenson, D'Amora, & Hern, 2007, as cited in Zilney & Zilney, 2009). Some states include additional restrictions on sex offenders. West Virginia, Delaware, and Alabama require that an individual's driver's license indicates that he or she has been convicted of a sex offense (Zilney & Zilney, 2009). Other states may require that the offender provide law enforcement agencies with a DNA sample. If the offender changes his residence, it is his or her responsibility to register with the law enforcement agencies in the new community.

Other notification practices have been initiated in recent years as a response to the availability of the sex offender registry database. For example, some districts post "sex offender free" signs that state that the location is prohibited to sex offenders. These signs are meant to deter sex offenders from entering the area and to promote feelings of safety for residents and visitors of these communities. Other states such as Ohio have pushed for colored license plates for convicted sex offenders (Zilney & Zilney, 2009). This measure in particular is directed at warning children and other potential victims against those who have committed offenses.

Signed into law by President George W. Bush in 2006, the Adam Walsh Act requires states to take the three-tiered approach to classifying sex offenders. Sexual offenders are divided into three different tiers, each with a different corresponding level of seriousness and different requirements for registration and notification (McPherson, 2007).

Level III offenders are considered the most serious, are often labeled as sexual predators or violent sexual offenders, and the public at large is notified of their residence in the community. They are required to remain in the sex offender registry throughout their lifetimes (McPherson, 2007). Because they are the most serious offenders and pose the greatest risk to the community, they are usually required to check in with local law enforcement for verification purposes on a quarterly basis (McPherson, 2007). They are also required to notify the public of their presence and publicly provide their address (Zilney & Zilney, 2009). Some examples of Level III offenders include those whose victims were less than 12 years of age, or who engaged in nonparental kidnapping, acts in which the offender drugged the victim, sexual assault against a stranger, or who have no employment or community ties (Terry, 2006; McPherson, 2007). Additionally, those who previously committed a Level II offense and then subsequently committed another offense may be labeled as a Level III offender.

For Level II offenders, schools and other community organizations in which children and women are involved are notified, but generally not the public at large (Zilney & Zilney, 2009). Often, states will consider the individual offender and offense when determining the level of community notification necessary for these offenders. For example, if there are "high-risk" groups in the offenders' neighborhoods, such as church or community groups that should be made aware, they may receive notification (Terry, 2006). They are considered to pose a risk to the community, though not as serious of a risk as those classified under Level III. They are required to check in for residency verification on a semiannual basis and must remain on the sex offender registry for 25 years (McPherson, 2007). Some offenses included under this tier include distribution or production of child pornography, sexual acts with minors between the ages of 12 and 15, sex trafficking of minors, or offenses involving multiple victims (Terry, 2006; McPherson, 2007). As with a Level III offense, if the offender was previously sanctioned for a Level I offense and committed a subsequent offense, he or she may be classified as a Level II offender.

Finally, for the least serious group of offenders, those classified as Level I, only law enforcement, victims, and witnesses are notified of the sex offender's whereabouts (Terry, 2006; Zilney & Zilney, 2009), and their residency is verified on an annual basis. They are only required to remain a registered sex offender for up to 15 years (Terry, 2006; McPherson, 2007). These offenders may have committed offenses such as possession of child pornography, public indecency, voyeurism, or sexual contact without permission (Terry, 2006; McPherson, 2007). These offenders are seen as the least risky for the community, and are often believed to be the least likely to recidivate.

Individual states vary greatly in their requirements for registration and notification of sex offenders. Some states require all sex offenders, even those convicted prior to 1996 when Megan's Law was officially passed, to register, while others only place this requirement on those convicted after 1996. States also have various definitions as to what types of sex offenses merit registration. Many states, though not all, require juveniles who have been convicted of sex offenses to meet the same requirements as adults who committed similar offenses (Terry, 2006).

Another geographical variation is the system of community supervision for life (CSL). A handful of states now require that some sex offenders remain supervised in the community for the rest of their lives. Under this requirement, sex offenders classified as CSL would have to remain in the same state, although they are able to petition to leave after a 15-year period. CSL offenders would need to meet with a supervising officer throughout the remainder of their lives and, if their status is revoked, could be returned to prison (Terry, 2006).

The constitutionality of registration and notification laws has been called into question. Offenders who have been subjected to these laws who were convicted prior to 1996 have charged that they are being sentenced ex post facto, or punished under an existing sanction that was not in existence at the time of their crime. Some have also claimed that registration and notification laws violate the concepts of double jeopardy (being tried twice for the same crime), and protection from cruel and unusual punishment, as guaranteed by the Eighth Amendment.

In a ruling on the ex post facto issue, the courts have ruled that registration and notification laws are not in violation. In *Doe v. Poritz* (1995), the New Jersey Supreme Court ruled that registration and community notification have the sole purpose of community protection. For this reason, it was stated that ex post facto was not an issue and did not constitute cruel and unusual punishment. In this same case, the court provided specific guidelines to the states to ensure that they are not infringing on individual offenders' rights, with a specific emphasis on offenders who are categorized as Level II and III, since they are the ones whom the public is the most likely to receive notification of. More recently, in *Smith v. Doe* (2003), the court again found that these laws do not constitute punishment since they are centered on the safety of the community members rather than for purposes of continued punishment of the individual offender.

Registration and notification laws have the obvious benefit of making citizens more aware of a sex offender's location, allowing them to use caution in both their own and their children's daily activities. Under the tier system, community members are differentially notified as to whether a sex offender is living in their community. As is the law's intention, those who are considered more dangerous are more likely to be publicized to community members (Zevitz, 2003), while those who are less likely to recidivate or pose a lesser risk to community members are less likely to have attention drawn to them (Craun, 2010). The laws also provide more assistance to law enforcement in finding and apprehending sex offenders in order to arrest them for new offenses (Lewis, 1988, as cited in Zilney & Zilney, 2009). Some studies also indicate that these measures are effective in preventing offenders from reoffending (Barnoski, 2005, and Duwe & Donnay, 2008, as cited in Zilney & Zilney, 2009).

Despite the obvious benefits for the criminal justice system, mandatory registration laws have received much criticism. First, some studies have questioned the effectiveness of these laws, claiming that they have little or no effect on recidivism rates for sexual offenses[2] (Lewis, 1988; Adkins, Huff, & Stageberg, 2000; Walker et al., 2006; Riedel & Welsh, 2008; Vasquez, Madden, & Walker, 2008; Zilney & Zilney, 2009; Zgoba, Veysey, Dalessandro, 2010). Some states do not acknowledge differences among the variations of what may constitute a sex offense in their online or public registries (Schultz, 2005). For example, many states require young teenagers who engage in consensual sex, or individuals convicted of indecent exposure, to register as sex offenders ("America's Unjust Sex Laws," 2009). There is obviously a marked difference between individuals who commit these types of offenses and those who engage in violent, predatory sex crimes. Many argue that having a uniform process for all sex offenders creates an unfair system in which even low-level offenders are required to register and consequently become labeled with the stigma of "sex offender."

As a consequence of the "one-size-fits-all" approach to sex offender registration laws, there may be more individuals registered than can be adequately monitored. There are currently more than 674,000 registered sex offenders in the United States, many of whom have been convicted of nonviolent sexual offenses. The result of the burgeoning population of registrants means that those on whom law enforcement should be focusing may be losing the attention that they should have to those convicted of lesser offenses.

Some of the unintended consequences of registration and notification laws include harassment of the offender by neighbors and other community members, loss of employment, and even eviction from their residence. There are also concerns with vigilantism, either by the victims, their family members, or the community in general. There are several documented cases of sex offenders receiving harassing phone calls, as well as having their homes vandalized or burned by outraged community members. If a registered sex offender fails to change his or her address with the registry, such vigilante justice may fall into the laps of the current homeowners, as has occurred in the past (Farley, 2008).

These factors combined may lead to a reduced likelihood of the offender being able to successfully reintegrate back into the community. A further unintended consequence may be that individuals who register may fear this harassment and, as a result, leave the community and fail to register, causing the criminal justice system to lose track of them altogether (Zilney & Zilney, 2009). This raises some serious questions about the number of sex offenders who are unaccounted for. In 2007, of the 603,000 sex offenders who were supposed to be registered, over 100,000 were unaccounted for (National Center for Missing and Exploited Children, 2007). In comparing the systems in the United States and Canada, we note that convicted sex offenders in Canada are more likely to comply with registration laws than those living in the United States, which may be attributed to Canadian law not requiring dissemination of information to the community (Murphy et al., 2009).

Finally, some researchers argue that registration laws illustrate a general lack of understanding of the nature of sexual assault and other sexual offenses. Although some sex offenders target strangers, the vast majority commit crimes against family, friends, or acquaintances (Koss, 1992). Moreover, despite the public's fear and belief that most sexual offenders are repeat offenders, many studies indicate they exhibit lower recidivism rates than any other type of offender, with the exception of those convicted of homicide (Hanson & Mourton-Bourgon, 2005). Thus, although mandatory registration laws may make sense from a crime prevention standpoint for a few offenders, because the majority of offenders are nonrecidivists, or who are committing crimes against individuals they already know, these laws may be missing the mark on their original intention of community protection.

Increased Sentences for Sex Offenders

In 2005, 9-year-old Jessica Lunsford was abducted from her home in Florida. Three weeks later, John Couey, a registered sex offender, admitted to sexually assaulting and murdering her. Couey had not attended his required counseling sessions and had moved without notifying the authorities, as he was required to. The Jessica Lunsford Act was passed later that year, which requires a mandatory minimum sentence for anyone who sexually assaults a child younger than the age of 12. After release from prison, the offender is also required to remain on electronic monitoring for the remainder of his or her life. Similar measures have been adopted in over 30 states nationwide (Zilney & Zilney, 2009).

Sex offenders comprise approximately 12% of current state-level prison populations. Approximately 4% of these offenders have been convicted of rape and about 8% have been convicted of other forms of sexual assault (Harrison & Beck, 2005, as cited in Riedel & Welsh, 2008; Sabol, West, & Cooper, 2009). Prescribed sentences for sex offenders have remained somewhat stable over the years. For example, in 2004, the maximum sentence length imposed for a rapist was 154 months (almost 13 years), and for other types of sex offenders the maximum time imposed was 90 months (7.5 years). The only other crime that saw harsher sentences imposed was murder, which had a maximum sentence of 241 months (just over 20 years) (*Sourcebook of Criminal Justice Statistics*, 2004). However, the actual amount of time served has increased. A convicted rapist will serve an average of 5 years, while an individual convicted of other sexual offenses will typically serve about 8.5 years. These increases represent 1 to 1.5 years more than the average sentence served from just a decade ago for similar offenses (Greenfeld, 1997, as cited in Riedel & Welsh, 2008).

Part of the reason for the increase in time served is due to the "truth in sentencing" movement. Passage of truth in sentencing laws began in 1984, and in 1994 truth in sentencing legislation required all states to mandate that offenders serve at least 85% of their sentence before they are eligible for parole. If states meet this requirement, they receive additional funds from the truth in sentencing project. Most states currently qualify for these funds. By way of example, the rapist serving the maximum sentence discussed previously would need to serve almost 131 months (almost 11 years) to qualify for having served 85% of his or her sentence.

Another mandatory minimum sentence that impacts sex offenders is a highly controversial piece of legislation known as the "three-strikes law." Many states have adopted three-strikes legislation, with varying requirements on what constitutes a "strike" and lengths for the sentences imposed after the third "strike." All three-strikes states indicate that after the third offense, the penalty becomes extremely severe. In some states, felonies that qualify as a strike must be violent, while in other states, they only need to be a felony (which includes nonviolent felonies). With respect to sanctions, some states mandate that the third felony lead to an automatic 25-year sentence, while others mandate life in prison without the possibility of parole.

Regardless of which state is under consideration, sex offenders are obviously impacted by three-strikes legislation. Although many states were already considering legislation similar to three-strikes, California spearheaded much of the public support for this law. The 1993 murder of Polly Klaas garnered significant public interest in the topic. Again, an innocent youth was the victim in this case. Polly Klaas was abducted during a slumber party by Richard Allen Davis, a previously convicted child rapist. Her raped and murdered body was later discovered. The public outcry against having repeat violent offenders free to reoffend, combined with a gubernatorial election that could use three-strikes as a platform for policy making, practically guaranteed the passage of this highly controversial law (Moore, 1999).

Supporters of three-strikes laws advocate these policies on the basis that they serve both specific and general deterrence. Specifically, a potential three-time offender may reconsider committing their third offense for fear of being caught and receiving the most severe penalty, with no possibility of leniency at the hands of a mandatory sentence. General deterrence may be accomplished by members of the public not committing felonious crimes for fear of being punished severely under three-strikes legislation. Advocates of three-strikes penalties also express a need to achieve retribution by punishing repeat offenders with the most severe sanction available.

Despite the potential benefits of three-strikes legislation, there are many potential costs in this type of mandatory minimum sentence. Many argue that three-strikes legislation is unconstitutional since it imposes penalties that may be seen as cruel and unusual punishment. This is often cited for instances of more minor crimes, such as those receiving the maximum available sentence for stealing a slice of pizza or a pair of blue jeans (Zeigler & del Carmen, 1997). Although three-strikes legislation was originally designed for the most severe repeat offenders, such as Richard Allen Davis, other types of less severe sexual offenders may be impacted by these laws. Moreover, if a previously convicted sex offender is on parole and commits a third felony, he or she may be faced with a life sentence, depending on the specifics of the three-strikes law in his or her state. In the end, this may prohibit some sex offenders from ever becoming completely rehabilitated since they may never be returned to their communities.

Cracking Down on Internet Crime

The invention of the Internet has introduced relatively new groups of sexual offenses that are not only largely underreported, but also difficult to detect. Sexual predators now have several new avenues in which they can be introduced to their victims. The Internet also provides anonymity, especially for predators who possess emotional or psychological dysfunctions (Holmes & Holmes, 2009; Zilney & Zilney, 2009).

In some cases, technology allows predators to physically lure in their victims, such as by enticing children into their homes with video games (Schultz, 2005). However, behind the protection of the Internet, sexual offenders also use tools such as chat rooms, social networking websites, discussion boards, online games, and personal advertisements. Using these sources, potential offenders may misrepresent personal information about themselves to gain access to and earn the trust of their potential victims. For example, they may lie about their gender or age to make the potential victim feel safe in disclosing personal information to them (Grienti, 1997, as cited in Holmes &

Holmes, 2009). The Internet provides sex offenders with a potential forum to interact with other sex offenders and potentially maintain ties with a deviant sexual underworld (Holmes & Holmes, 2009). This social network of sexual offenders hearkens back to the idea of learning theory and subcultures since offenders are able to have their deviant and criminal sexual attitudes and beliefs reinforced by others.

The Internet can also be used to access and distribute pornographic material. The online pornography industry has become massive in recent years, producing $2.8 billion annually and comprising approximately 12% of all available websites (Ropelato, 2006; Edelman, 2009). The darkest side of this is that both the production and dissemination of pornographic images of children is much easier and less expensive than in years past ("Child Pornography," 2010).

Much of the effort in preventing Internet sex crimes is focused on protecting potential juvenile victims. Some websites take precautions to prevent minors from accessing information that is inappropriate by requiring them to enter a credit card number for validation purposes. Major social networking sites, such as MySpace and Facebook, require a birth date for members and allow minors to have their information listed as private and unavailable to strangers. Some have also placed bans on individuals who have committed a sexual offense, and may even delete their accounts if they discover registered sex offenders are using their website ("My Space Deletes," 2008, as cited in Zilney & Zilney, 2009).

As part of their probation or parole guidelines, most states ban sex offenders from using the Internet altogether. The exceptions to this are use for employment seeking or other employment-related purposes. Some local and federal law enforcement agencies also have task forces that focus on capturing sexual predators who lurk online. In 2002, the Child Obscenity and Pornography Prevention Act made it illegal to possess sexually explicit digital images of children.

Internet technology continues to advance on a daily basis. Some crimes that exist today were not possible even a decade ago. Because of this, it is critical for the criminal justice system to stay apprised of current technologies and the potential dangers that each form of technology may have. Despite law enforcement efforts, some criticize the criminal justice system for lacking in its available resources to prevent sexual predators from carrying out their crimes online (Holmes & Holmes, 2009).

Treatment and Rehabilitation Programs

A variety of both in-prison and postprison rehabilitation programs are available for sex offenders. Those that are the most effective in preventing recidivism are those that use a combination of social learning programs and risk assessment, and take into account the needs of the offender (Dowden & Andrews, 2000). The level of risk of recidivating must be considered in assigning treatment programs, as well as examining the individual needs of the offender, such as chemical dependency, antisocial attitudes, and antisocial peer relationships.

Multiple assessment measures may be considered in determining an offender's risk level and their amenability to treatment. Common personality tests, such as the Minnesota Multiphasic Personality Inventory (MMPI) are often used, but more specific tools may also be considered, ones that focus on sex offenders in particular. For example, the Abel Assessment for Sexual Interest is specifically used to determine whether there is a sexual interest in underage children (Abel, Huffman, Warberg, & Holland, 1998). The Multiphasic Sex Inventory-II is meant to measure deviant sexual behaviors, thoughts, and interests. Based on self-reported data, this test requests information from the offender on his or her sexual history, as well as information on current sexual interests (Nicholas & Molinder, 1984).

Psychological treatment for sex offenders has shown promise in reducing rates of reoffending (Polizzi, MacKenzie, & Hickman, 1999; Hanson et al., 2002 as cited in Terry, 2006; Riedel & Welsh, 2008). However, the most effective treatment programs seem to be those that use cognitive behavioral therapy (CBT). Two factors have been cited as key to effective treatment of offenders. The first is ensuring that offenders are accurately assessed to assign them to the correct treatment program (Andrews et al., 1990; O'Connell, Leberg, & Donaldson, 1990; Terry, 2006). The second is making sure that staff members who have the appropriate training are selected to work with the client (Sampson, 1992; Hogue, 1995; Terry, 2006).

Cognitive behavioral therapy is based on the belief that sex offenders have control over their thoughts and actions and can therefore be taught how to alter their behavior. Offenders are taught to understand the environments in which their offenses are likely to occur and to recognize their individual warning signs to prevent a relapse into sexual offending (Burdon & Gallagher, 2002, as cited in MacKenzie, 2006; Riedel & Welsh, 2008). The focus of cognitively based treatment centers on building prosocial behaviors as replacements for antisocial or deviant behaviors, specifically those behaviors that may be linked to the offender's deviant or violent sexual behaviors.

Therapeutic communities may also assist in preventing future sex offenses. Therapeutic communities are residential treatment facilities and are sometimes used in place of a prison sentence. Although they are most commonly used for drug and alcohol offenders, in recent years they have been used for other types of offenders, including sex offenders. Therapeutic community interventions often take the form of group therapy and often include strategies such as anger management, stress management, developing communication skills, and learning to feel empathy for others. Because of the level of intensity of these programs, they often have a high dropout rate among residents; however, those who successfully complete the programs are shown to have much lower recidivism rates.

The effectiveness of treatment programs continues to be controversial when applied to sex offenders. There is evidence that sex offender treatment programs can reduce the likelihood of committing future sexual offenses. Recent studies indicate that cognitive behavioral therapy programs are more effective at reducing recidivism rates (McGrath, Cumming, Livingston, & Hoke, 2003; Scalora, & Garbin, 2003; Zilney & Zilney, 2009).

Studies of the effectiveness of treatment programs show that certain offender characteristics may help explain an inability to be rehabilitated. For example, deviant sexual behaviors and antisocial personality disorder are two conditions that may be predictors of continued sexual offending, even after treatment (Hanson & Morton-Bourgon, 2005; Langton, Barbaree & Peacock, 2006). Other factors, such as the gender and age of the victim, the victim–offender relationship, and the extremity in the use of violence also seem to be predictive of recidivism. In general, though, studies indicate that offenders who complete a treatment program are more likely to successfully reintegrate back into the community without committing a new sexual offense (Gallagher et al., 1999; Losel & Schmucker, 2005).

There are many obstacles to successful treatment of sex offenders. First and foremost, the financial resources must be available, and concerns over retribution often prevent the public and policymakers from being willing to invest tax dollars into rehabilitation programs. This is even truer for sex offenders than for other types of criminal offenders (Vaughn & Sapp, 1989, as cited in Holmes & Holmes, 2009). Policymakers, in an effort to avoid the label of being "soft on crime," will generally not advocate for pricey rehabilitation program (Holmes & Holmes, 2009, p. 284), especially when there is widespread belief that sex offenders are at an increased likelihood to recidivate.

Similar issues exist for those who seek treatment while incarcerated. In prison, sex offenders are subjected to isolation and potential victimization by other inmates (Dumond, 1992; Human Rights Watch, 2001). Because of this, they are often removed from the general population and placed in protective custody. This then creates logistical issues for prison administrators and staff since they must contend with keeping a protected population separate from the general inmate population, while ensuring that they are given the appropriate treatment for their offenses (Cotton & Groth, 1982).

Chemical Castration

Chemical castration has been used in nine states in an attempt to prevent serious sex offenders, such as rapists and child molesters, from recidivating. The extent of the use of chemical castration varies by state, ranging from a few experimental cases to being a mandatory condition of parole. Both California and Florida mandate that after two convictions of child molestation, an offender may be required to submit to chemical castration as a condition of his or her parole (Scott & Holmberg, 2003).

In chemical castration, medication is given to the offender in an attempt to reduce sexual activity and lower libido. Depo-Provera is the most commonly used drug for the procedure. The procedure does not render the offender sterile, unlike surgical castration, and is generally reversible by discontinuing the medication, usually within 7–10 days of termination of the medication (Stohr, Walsh, & Hemmens, 2009).

Critics of the practice of chemical castration may cite violations of the Eighth Amendment's protection from cruel and unusual punishment. In the case of *State v. Brown*, the South Carolina Supreme Court ruled that the procedure did indeed violate the Eighth Amendment. Furthermore, issues relating to informed consent may be particularly pertinent, since it requires that the individual be competent enough to consent to such treatment, that the consent is informed, and that such consent is given without coercion (Schwartz, 1994). Offenders can make the argument that such consent is not voluntary, since some states require that the individual undergo chemical castration as a condition of their parole. Furthermore, as stated in *People v. Gauntlett*, there is concern over whether chemical castration is accepted by the medical profession as both reliable and safe.

The effectiveness of chemical castration has also been called into question. Chemical castration lowers testosterone levels, which also reduces an individual's sex drive. However, it is widely noted that sexual assault is a crime that is typically motivated by anger and a need to dominate and generally not by sexual desire. By engaging in practices such as chemical castration, the system may be releasing individuals into the community who have not fully addressed the motivations behind their offenses. This is particularly at issue when considering that the states that allow for chemical castration do not mandate that either a psychiatric or medical examination be conducted prior to the injections.

Individuals who do not take responsibility for their actions, or who are motivated by anger or power, will likely not benefit from chemical castration and may commit other forms of violence against their potential victims. Studies have shown varying results on whether sexual activity is still feasible after castration (Wille & Beier, 1989, and Stone, Winslade, & Klugman, 2000, as cited in Zilney & Zilney, 2009). Furthermore, chemical castration is reversible by taking additional medications or injections that provide testosterone, or ceasing medication for a short period of time (Zilney & Zilney, 2009).

Civil Commitment Laws

Civil commitment laws allow states to confine convicted sex offenders to a mental hospital or mental care facility, often indefinitely, after completing their prison sentence. There are currently 20 states in the United States that allow for civil commitment, with a total population of over 4,500 sex offenders currently committed (Zilney & Zilney, 2009).[3] Those sentenced to civil commitment are those offenders that are believed to have a higher risk of recidivism and a greater level of threat due to a personality disorder or a mental abnormality (Janus, 2003, and Levenson, 2004, as cited in Zilney & Zilney, 2009). Thus, a special category of sex offender, known as a Sexually Violent Predator (SVP), has been created. An SVP is an individual who is noted to be more likely to recidivate than to not recidivate (Terry, 2006; Zilney & Zilney, 2009). Although definitions of SVP vary from state to state, generally speaking the SVP offender must be charged with a sexually violent offense and have a personality or mental disorder that makes it likely that they will continue to commit sexual offenses (Terry, 2006).

In order for an individual to be civilly committed, the state must file a petition to have the offender involuntarily committed. A mental health professional completes an evaluation on the dangers the individual may pose to members of the community. There is no standardized professional criteria used in making the determination, but this method of confinement is reserved for those who are deemed to be sexually violent predators.

In order to be released, the offender must petition the court for his or her release. Both the court and the psychologist must agree that the offender is ready for release back into the community, a condition that hinges on being able to prove that the individual's mental abnormality is no longer an issue. In reality, sex offenders who are civilly committed are confined throughout the remainder of their lifetimes, with very few successfully petitioning for their release back into the community (Janus, 2000; Zilney & Zilney, 2009).

Because the courts have recognized that the civil commitment of sexually violent predators is a civil, rather than a criminal, issue, the process of civil confinement has not been viewed as unconstitutional. In *Kansas v. Hendricks*, the U.S. Supreme Court ruled that, as long as the individual is not housed with the general prison population, civil commitment is constitutionally permitted with sex offenders. Because the commitment is seen as treatment rather than punishment, it has been found to be constitutionally sound. Commitment is allowed as long as the individual poses a threat to themselves or to the community (Zilney & Zilney, 2009). In cases of commitment of a sexually violent predator, there also must be continual communication with the court on the status of the patient, as well as the expectation that rehabilitation will continue with an eventual release to the community as an end goal.

Civil commitment tends to be relatively costly. In comparison with a standard prison sentence, civil commitment can cost between four and eight times more than housing an offender in prison. For example, in California, the average annual cost to house an inmate in jail or prison is approximately $43,000. To civilly commit an individual in the state of Pennsylvania costs about $166,000 per year (Zilney & Zilney, 2009). Concerns over already scarce mental health resources may point to other potentially dangerous offenders who, because of the increase in the number of civil commitment of sex offenders, can no longer be housed. The result may be increases in other forms of violent crime by those that the mental health system could not handle appropriately due to the increased attention given to sex offenders (Janus, 2000, as cited in Zilney & Zilney, 2009).

Capital Punishment

Many states that still have the death penalty on their books have listed as one of the aggravating circumstances murders committed during the commission of another felony, or a select group of felonies. For example, murders that occur during a transaction that also includes a robbery, kidnapping, or sexual assault would qualify many potential murderers to receive capital punishment. But, what about a sexual assault committed as a singular crime?

In 2008, the U.S. Supreme Court ruled in *Kennedy v. Louisiana* that the death penalty as a punishment for sexual assault, even when that sexual assault is committed against a child, is considered unconstitutional on the grounds that it violates the cruel and unusual punishment clause of the Eighth Amendment. The opinion of the court stated it had issues with disproportionality, citing that death and rape are not equivalent crimes (Zilney & Zilney, 2009). The goal of "just deserts" would indicate that offenders are given punishments that are only as severe as the crime that they have committed, an idea that is not compatible with capital punishment as a potential consequence for any type of nonlethal sexual offense. The just deserts viewpoint would reserve capital punishment for sex offenses only when the victim of the sex offense is also murdered.

Furthermore, this court ruling posits that by executing sex offenders, the criminal justice system may be doing more harm than good. Giving the same potential punishment for both murder and a sex crime may indeed have adverse effects. A rational thinking offender may choose to murder his victim if he or she knows that they could potentially receive the punishment for both crimes. By eliminating the victim, the offender is also in fact eliminating a witness, and with no additional potential penalty for doing so.

The 1972 case of *Furman v. Georgia* brought many flaws in capital punishment to the attention of both the public and policymakers, including issues of it being applied to crimes other than murder. As part of our "get tough on crime" approach, some policymakers and members of the general public seem to want to reinstate the death penalty for crimes other than premeditated and intentional murder. Various reasons may be given for this, including the beliefs that general deterrence and retribution are being served. Some of the most heinous cases of sexual assault, such as those committed during the course of a murder, would already be eligible for capital punishment under many states' existing guidelines. It remains to be seen whether the death penalty will be reinstated as a punishment for sex offenders or any other offenders, in addition to those who commit murder.

Taking a Routine Activities Approach to Prevention of Sexual Offenses

If criminal justice policies, such as increased sentence length, sex offender registration and notification laws, and other mechanisms fail to prevent the occurrence of sex crimes, other measures may be more effective. One such measure may be to consider the routine activities approach. As posited by the original theorists, in order for a crime to occur, three conditions must exist. There must be a suitable target, a motivated offender, and an absence of capable guardians (Cohen & Felson, 1979).

Many of our current criminal justice prevention programs focus on the motivated offender aspect. However, measures can be taken to make targets less suitable. For example, providing potential victims with the ability to defend themselves or making them more aware of their surroundings may prevent a motivated offender from viewing them as a potential victim (Barone, Wolgemuth, & Linder, 2007, as cited in Riedel & Welsh, 2008). Potential victims who use avoidance strategies, such as using physical force or screaming for help, may be more likely to avoid becoming a victim than those who use more subtle forms of prevention, such as pleading with their attacker (Bart & O'Brien, 1985, as cited in Riedel & Welsh, 2008). Increasing capable guardians may also be beneficial to prevention. Simply not traveling alone at night may be enough to deter potential offenders. Increased lighting in parking lots and on streets is another approach that may make sexual crimes less likely to occur (Riedel & Welsh, 2008). For instance, increasing the lighting in parking lots of shopping centers and universities may make targets less suitable because the number of capable guardians (those who can clearly see the potential crime scene) could increase.

These measures may be effective at potentially deterring sexual assaults that occur in public or semipublic areas. However, as previously discussed, most sexual offenses occur in a residence or other private area. Because of this, it may also be beneficial to consider how to change the mentality of the potential offender prior to their commission of a sexual offense in order to prevent situational sexual offenses from occurring.

The Role of Education

Some forms of sexual offense are indeed preventable. In considering the theories discussed in this chapter, it seems that various explanations of why an individual commits these crimes may be plausible. Many of the theories focus on the offender's lack of empathy in viewing the victim as a victim, or a need to exert power over someone else in order to increase their own feelings of power.

As such, it may be that an increase in education for the society at large may be necessary. This education might focus on prevention by disentangling the previously discussed rape myths, or allowing for victim impact panels to explain the effects of sexual victimization. A major obstacle to these types of programs may be the extreme resistance expressed by males, including those most "at risk" for committing sexual offenses (Rich, Utley, Janke, & Moldoveanu, 2010). However, in taking a social learning perspective, frequent exposure to nondeviant sexual behavior and attitudes may also be beneficial in preventing acceptance of deviant sexual attitudes and ascribing to common rape myths among those who are the most likely to perpetrate sexual crimes or who have been exposed to deviant behavior as normative throughout their lives.

SUMMARY

Sex offenders continue to be a cause for concern, both for community members and for the criminal justice system as a whole. The criminal justice system has greatly overhauled not only the definition of what constitutes a sex offense, but also the treatment of and responses to these types of offenders. The theoretical underpinnings behind the potential causal mechanisms of sex offenses continue to create debate and policy discussions, but these are important in understanding the best way in which society can prevent sex offenses from occurring.

In recent years, there has been a significant increase in the sentences served for sex offenses, and there has also been an attempt to create more innovative solutions to deter individuals from committing offenses. Public concern over the presence of sexually violent predators in the community has fueled such initiatives as community notification and registration laws. Concern over future acts against the community also has resulted in measures such as civil commitment and chemical castration. A more rehabilitative approach centers on treatment and therapy. It remains to be seen which type of sex offender management is the most effective in prevention of future acts.

KEY TERMS

Sex offender
Sexual assault
Rape
Acquaintance rape
Statutory rape
Pedophile
Serial rapist
Habitual rapist
Gang rape
Rape shield laws
The containment model
The Adam Walsh Act
The Jacob Wetterling Act
Megan's Law
Therapeutic community
Chemical castration
Civil commitment

DISCUSSION QUESTIONS

1. What are the different types of offenses that are included in the category of sex offenses? What are some of the problems with categorizing this broad range of offenders as one classification?
2. A majority of sex offenses are committed among acquaintances. Should the prevention of acquaintance sex offenses take a different approach than those committed by strangers? Why or why not?
3. Explain why the NCVS might be a better reporting tool for sex crimes than the UCR or NIBRS. What problems might still exist in relying on the NCVS?
4. Compare and contrast the various theories that may be applied to explaining sex offenses. Which one(s) do you think most adequately explain them and why?
5. What are some "rape myths"? Why do you think these myths continue to exist, and what role might they play in both the occurrence of the offense and the sentencing of the offender?
6. What is meant by the containment model? Do you think this model is different for sex offenders than for other types of offenders? Why or why not?
7. What kinds of issues might arise as a result of the radius restrictions placed on sex offenders?
8. Do you think that treatment is an effective replacement for imprisonment for sex offenders? Why or why not?

9. Do you think treatment may work better for some types of sex offenders than others? Which ones do you think are more suited for treatment, rehabilitation, and eventual release back into the community?

10. Why do you think cognitive-based therapies are particularly beneficial for sex offenders?

11. Do you believe measures such as chemical castration and civil commitment laws are constitutionally sound? Why or why not?

12. What types of efforts do you think the criminal justice system may need to enforce in order to successfully combat issues associated with Internet-perpetrated sex offenses?

13. What might some arguments be for and against using capital punishment as a sentence against sexual offenders?

14. What types of settings do you believe would be most important and effective in education on sexual offenses and why?

NOTES

1. This number is a marked difference from victims of other forms of violent crime, in which only about 50% of victims knew their attacker (Rennison, 1999).

2. Some of these studies do, however, show a decline in the number of nonsexual offenses committed with community notification and registration laws.

3. States with civil commitment laws include Arizona, California, Florida, Illinois, Iowa, Kansas, Massachusetts, Minnesota, Missouri, Nebraska, New Hampshire, New Jersey, New York, North Dakota, Pennsylvania, South Carolina, Texas, Virginia, Washington, and Wisconsin.

REFERENCES

Abel, G. G., Huffman, J. Warberg, B., & Holland, C. L. (1998). Visual reaction time and plethysmography as measures of sexual interest in child molesters. *Sexual Abuse: A Journal of Research and Treatment, 10,* 81–95.

Adkins, G., Huff, D., & Stageberg, P. (2000). *The Iowa sex offender registry and recidivism.* Des Moines, IA: Iowa Department of Human Rights, Division of Criminal and Juvenile Justice Planning and Statistical Analysis Center.

America's unjust sex laws. (2009). *The Economist, 392*(8643), 9.

Andrews, D. A, Zinger, I., Hoge, R. D., Bonta, J., Gendreau, P., & Cullen, F. T. (1990). Does correctional treatment work? A clinically relevant and psychologically informed meta-analysis. *Criminology, 28,* 369–397.

Bachman, R., & Taylor, B. M. (1994). The measurement of family violence and rape by the redesigned National Crime Victimization Survey. *Justice Quarterly, 11,* 499–512.

Barnoski, R. (2005). *Sex offender sentencing in Washington state: Has community notification reduced recidivism?* Olympia, WA: Washington State Institute for Public Policy.

Baron, L., & Strauss, M. A. (1989). *Four theories of rape in American society.* New Haven, CT: Yale University Press.

Barone, R. P., Wolgemuth, J. R., & Linder, C. (2007). Preventing sexual assault through engaging college men. *Journal of College Student Development, 48*(9), 585–594.

Bart, P. B., & O'Brien, P. H. (1985). *Stopping rape: Successful survival strategies.* New York, NY: Pergamon.

Baumer, E. Felson, R., & Messner, S. (2003). Changes in police notification for rape (1973–2000). *Criminology, 41*(3), 841–872.

Belknap, J. (2007). *The invisible woman: Gender, crime and justice.* Belmont, CA: Thompson Wadsworth.

Bergen, R. K. (1996). *Wife rape: Understanding the response of survivors and service providers*. Thousand Oaks, CA: Sage.

Bergen, R. (1998). Wife rape. *Violence Against Women, 5*(9), 989–1085.

Best, J., & Luckenbill, D. F. (1994). *Organized deviance*. Englewood Cliffs, NJ: Prentice Hall.

Bohmer, C., & Parrot, A. (1993). *Sexual assault on campus*. New York, NY: Lexington Books.

Brenner, N. D., McMahon, P. M., Warren, C. W., & Douglas, K. A. (1999). Forced sexual intercourse and associated health-risk behaviors among female college students in the United States. *Journal of Consulting and Clinical Psychology, 67*, 252–259.

Brown, J. (2010, March 6). "There will be another Julia Tuttle," sex offender says. *The Miami Herald*.

Brownmiller, S. (1975). *Against our will: Men, women and rape*. New York, NY: Bantam.

Burdon, W. M., & Gallagher, C. A. (2002). Coercion and sex offenders: Controlling sex offender behavior through incapacitation and treatment. *Criminal Justice and Behavior, 29*, 87–109.

Bureau of Justice Statistics (BJS). (2002). *Rape and sexual assault: Reporting to police and medical attention, 1992–2000*. Retrieved from http://bjs.ojp.usdoj.gov/content/pub/pdf/rsarp00.pdf.

Bureau of Justice Statistics (BJS). (2009a). *Violent and property crime rates declined in 2009, continuing the trend observed in the last ten years*. Retrieved from http://bjs.ojp.usdoj.gov/content/pub/press/cv09pr.cfm.

Bureau of Justice Statistics (BJS). (2009b). *Weapon use by offense type*. Retrieved from http://bjs.ojp.usdoj.gov/index.cfm?ty=tp&tid=43.

Bynum, T., Carter, M., Matson, S., & Onley, C. (2011). Recidivism of sex offenders. In J. Latessa & A. M. Holsinger (Eds.), *Correctional contexts: Contemporary and classical readings*. New York, NY: Oxford University Press.

Child pornography. (2010). *Child exploitation and obscenity*. U.S. Department of Justice. Retrieved from http://www.justice.gov/criminal/ceos/childporn.html.

Chilton, R., & Jarvis, J. (1999). Victims and offenders in two crime statistics programs: A comparison of the National Incident Based Reporting System (NIBRS) and the National Crime Victimization Survey (NCVS). *Journal of Quantitative Criminology, 15*(2), 193–205.

Cohen, L. E., & Felson, M. E. (1979). Social change and crime trends: A routine activity approach. *American Sociological Review, 44*, 588–608.

Cotton, D., & Groth, A. (1982). Inmate rape: Prevention and intervention. *Journal of Prison and Jail Health, 59*(2), 47–75.

Craig, L. A., Browne, K., Stringer, I., & Beech, A. (2005). Sexual recidivism: A review of the static, dynamic and actuarial predictors. *Journal of Sexual Aggression, 11*(1), 65–84.

Craun, S. (2010). Evaluating awareness of registered sex offenders in the neighborhood. *Crime and Delinquency, 56*(3), 414–435.

Dabney, D. (2004). *Crime types: A text/reader*. Belmont, CA: Wadsworth.

DeYoung, M. (1989). The world according to NAMBLA: Accounting for deviance. *Journal of Sociology and Social Welfare, 16*(1), 111–126.

Doe v. Poritz, 283 N.J. S.C. 372, 661 (1995).

Dowden, C., & Andrews, D. A. (2000). Effective correctional treatment and violent reoffending: A meta-analysis. *Canadian Journal of Criminology, 42*(4), 449–468.

Dowler, K. (2006). Sex, lies and videotape: The presentation of sex crime in local television news. *Journal of Criminal Justice, 34*, 383–392.

Dumond, R. W. (1992). The sexual assault of male inmates in incarcerated settings. *International Journal of Sociology of Law, 20*(2), 135–157.

Duwe, G., & Donnay, W. (2008). The impact of Megan's Law on sex offender recidivism: The Minnesota experience. *Criminology, 46*(2), 411–446.

Edelman, B. (2009). Red light states: Who buys online adult entertainment? *Journal of Economic Perspectives, 23*(1), 209–220.

English, K., Pullen, S., & Jones, L. (1996). *Managing adult sex offenders: A containment approach*. Lexington, KY: American Probation and Parole Association.

Farley, L. (2008). The Adam Walsh Act: The scarlet letter of the twenty-first century. *Washburn Law Journal, 47*, 471–503.

Fisher, B., Cullen, F., & Turner, M. (2000). *The sexual victimization of college women*. Washington, DC: Bureau of Justice Statistics.

Furman v. Georgia, 408 U.S. 238 (1972).

Gallagher, C. A., Wilson, D. B., Hirschfield, P., Coggeshall, M., & MacKenzie, D. L. (1999). A quantitative view of the effects of sex offender treatment on sexual reoffending. *Corrections Management Quarterly, 3*, 19–29.

Gideon, L. and Sung, H. (2011). *Rethinking Corrections: Rehabilitation, Reentry and Reintegration*. Thousand Oaks. CA: Sage.

Glavin, A. P. (1986, March). *Acquaintance rape: The silent epidemic*. Cambridge, MA: Institute of Technology, Campus Police Department.

Goode, E. (1984). *Deviant behavior*. Englewood Cliffs, NJ: Prentice-Hall.

Greenfeld, L .A. (1997). *Sex offenses and offenders: An analysis of data on rape and sexual assault*. Washington, DC: Bureau of Justice Statistics.

Grienti, V. (1997). Pedophiles on the Internet. *Gazette, 59*(10), 14–15.

Hanson, R. K., Gordon, A., Harris, A. J. R., Marques, J. K., Murphy, W., Quinsey, V. L., & Seto, M. C. (2002). First report of the collaborative outcome data project on the effectiveness of psychological treatment for sex offenders. *Sexual Abuse: A Journal of Research and Treatment, 14*(2), 169–194.

Hanson, R., & Morton-Bourgon, K. (2005). The characteristics of persistent sexual offenders: A meta-analysis of recidivism studies. *Journal of Consulting and Clinical Psychology, 73*(6), 1154–1163.

Harris, V., & Staunton, C. (2000). *The antecedents of young male offenders*. London, UK: Whurr.

Harrison, P. M., & Beck, A. J. (2005). *Prisoners in 2004* (NCJ 210677). U.S. Department of Justice, Bureau of Justice Statistics.

Hogue, T. E. (1995). Training multi-disciplinary teams to work with sex offenders: Effect on staff attitudes. *Psychology, Crime and Law, 1*, 227–235.

Holmes, S. T., & Holmes, R. M. (2009). *Sex crimes: Patterns and behaviors*. Los Angeles, CA: Sage Publications.

Human Rights Watch. (2001). No escape: Male rape in U.S. prisons. Retrieved from http://www.hrw.org/reports/2001/prison/report.html.

Jackson, S. (1995). The social context of rape: Sexual scripts and motivation. In P. Searles & R. J. Berger (Eds.), *Rape and society: Readings on the problem of sexual assault*. Boulder, CO: Westview Press.

Janus, E. S. (2000). Sexual predator commitment laws: Lessons for law and the behavioral sciences. *Behavioral Sciences and the Law, 18*, 5–21.

Janus, E. S. (2003). Legislative responses to sexual violence: An overview. *Annals of the New York Academy of Sciences, 989*, 247–264.

Johnson, I., & Sigler, T. (1996). Forced sexual intercourse on campus: Crime or offensive behavior. *Journal of Contemporary Criminal Justice, 12*(1), 53–68.

Johnson, I., & Sigler, T. (2000). Forced sexual intercourse among intimates. *Journal of Family Violence, 15*(1), 95–108.

Kansas v. Hendricks, 521 U.S. 346 (1997).

Kappeler, V. E., & Potter, G. W. (2005). *The mythology of crime and criminal justice*. Long Grove, IL: Waveland.

Kennedy v. Louisiana, 554 U.S. 407 (2008).

Koss, M. (1992). The underdetection of rape: Methodological choices influence incidence estimates. *Journal of Social Issues, 48*, 61–75.

Koss, M. P., & Harvey, M. H. (1991). *The rape victim: Clinical and community interventions*. Newbury Park, CA: Sage.

Kruttschnitt, C. (1994). Gender and interpersonal violence. In A. J. Reiss & J. Roth (Eds.), *Understanding and preventing violence: Social influences* (Vol. 3). Washington, DC: National Academy Press.

Kruttschnitt, C., Uggen, C., & Shelton, K. (2000). Predictors of desistance among sex offenders: The interaction of formal and informal social controls. *Justice Quarterly, 17*, 62–87.

Langton, C., Barbaree, H., & Peacock, E. (2006). Sex offenders' response to treatment and its association with recidivism as a function of psychopathy. *Sex Abuse, 18*(1), 99–120.

Levenson, J. (2004). Sexual predator civil commitment: A comparison of selected and released offenders. *International Journal of Offender Therapy and Comparative Criminology, 48*(6), 638–648.

Levenson, J. S., Brannon, Y. N., Fortney, T., & Baker, J. (2007). Public perceptions about sex offenders and community protection policies. *Analysis of Social Issues and Public Policy, 7*(1), 1–25.

Levenson, J. S., D'Amora, D. A., & Hern, A. L. (2007). Megan's Law and its impact on community re-entry for sex offenders. *Behavioral Sciences and the Law, 25*(25), 587–602.

Lewis, R. (1988). *Effectiveness of statutory requirements for the registration of sex offenders: A report to the California state legislature.* Sacramento, CA: California Department of Justice.

Lieb, R., Quinsey, V., & Berliner, L. (1998). Sexual predators and social policy. *Crime and Justice, 23,* 2–49.

Lisak, D., & Ivan, C. (1995). Deficits in intimacy and empathy in sexually aggressive men. *Journal of Interpersonal Violence, 10,* 296–308.

Losel, F., & Schmucker, M. (2005). The effectiveness of treatment for sexual offenders: A comprehensive meta-analysis. *Journal of Experimental Criminology 1,* 117–146.

Lussier, P., LeBlanc, M., Proulx, J. (2005). The generality of criminal behavior: A confirmatory factor analysis of the criminal activity of sex offenders in adulthood. *Journal of Criminal Justice, 33*(2), 177–189.

MacLeod, M., & Saraga, E. (1987). Family secrets: Child sexual abuse. *Feminist Review, 7.*

MacKenzie, D. L. (2006). *What works in corrections: Reducing the criminal activities of offenders and delinquents.* New York, NY: Cambridge.

Marshall, W. L. (1989). Intimacy, loneliness and sexual offenders. *Behavior Research and Therapy, 27,* 491–503.

Mayerson, S., & Taylor, D. (1987). The effects of rape with pornography on women's attitudes and the mediating role of sex role stereotyping. *Sex Roles, 17,* 321–338.

McGrath, R. J., Cumming, Livingston, J. A., & Hoke, S. E. (2003). Outcome of a treatment program for adult sex offenders: From prison to community. *Journal of Interpersonal Violence, 18*(1), 3–17.

McPherson, L. (2007). Practitioner's guide to the Adam Walsh Act. National Center for the Prosecution of Child Abuse. Retrieved from www.ojp.usdoj.gov/smart/pdfs/practitioner_guide_awa.pdf.

Meloy, M. L. (2006). The sex offender next door: An analysis of recidivism, risk factors and deterrence of sex offenders on probation. *Criminal Justice Policy Review, 16,* 211–236.

Moore, M. J. (Director) (1999). *The legacy: Murder and media, politics and prisons* [Motion picture]. New York, NY: Public Broadcasting System.

Moriarty, L., & Earle, M. (2000). An analysis of services for victims of marital rape: A case study. *Journal of Offender Rehabilitation, 29*(3/4), 23–44.

Murphy, L., Fedoroff, J. P., & Martineau, M. (2009). Canada's sex offender registries: Background, implementation and social policy considerations. *The Canadian Journal of Human Sexuality, 18*(1/2), 61–72.

MySpace deletes 146 profiles of NE sex offenders. (2008, August 15). *KPTM Fox 42 News.* Retrieved from http://www.kptm.com/global/story.asp?S=8848236.

National Center for Missing and Exploited Children. (2007). National Center for Missing and Exploited Children Creates a new unit to help find 100,000 missing sex offenders and calls for states to do their part. Retrieved from http://www.missingkids.com/missingkids/servlet/PageServlet?LanguageCountry=en_US&PageId=3081.

Nicholas, H. R., & Molinder, I. (1984). *The multiphasic sex inventory manual.* Fircrest, WA: Nicholas & Molinder.

O'Connell, M. A., Leberg, E., & Donaldson, C. R. (1990). *Working with sex offenders: Guidelines for therapist selection.* Newbury Park, CA: Sage.

O'Sullivan, C. (1991). Acquaintance gang rape on campus. In A. Parrot & L. Bechhofer (Eds.), *Acquaintance rape: The hidden crime.* New York, NY: John Wiley & Sons.

Pagelow, M. (1988). Marital rape. In V. B. VanHasselt, R. L. Morrison, A. S. Bellack, & M. Hersen (Eds.), *Handbook of family violence* (pp. 207–232). New York, NY: Plenum Press.

Pence, E., & Paymar, M. (1993). *Education groups for men who batter: The Duluth model.* New York, NY: Springer.

People v. Gauntlett, 352 N.W.2d 310, 313–14 (Mich. App. 1984)

Polizzi, D. M., MacKenzie, D. L., & Hickman, L. J. (1999). What works in adult sex offender treatment? A review of prison and non-prison-based treatment programs. *International Journal of Offender Therapy and Comparative Criminology, 43,* 357–374.

Prentky, R. A., Lee, A. F., Knight, R., & Cerce, D. (1997). Recidivism rates among child molesters and rapists: A methodological analysis. *Law and Human Behavior, 21*(6), 635–659.

Quinsey, V. L., Lalumiere, M. T., Rice, M. E., & Harris, G. T. (1995). Predicting sexual offences. In J. C. Campbell (Ed.), *Assessing dangerousness: Violence by sexual offenders, batterers, and child abusers.* Thousand Oaks, CA: Sage.

Rape at the national level, number of police-recorded offenses. United Nations Office on Drugs and Crime. Retrieved from http://www.unodc.org/documents/data-and-analysis/Crime-statistics/Sexual_violence_sv_against_children_and_rape.xls

Rennison, C. (1999). *Criminal victimization, 1998: Changes 1997–1998 with trends 1993–1998.* Washington, DC: Bureau of Justice Statistics, U.S. Department of Justice.

Rich, M. D., Utley, E. A., Janke, K., & Moldoveanu, M. (2010). "I'd rather be doing something else": Male resistance to rape prevention programs. *The Journal of Men's Studies, 18*(3), 268–288.

Riedel, M., & Welsh, W. (2008). *Criminal violence: Patterns, causes and consequences.* New York, NY: Oxford.

Ropelato, J. (2006). Internet pornography statistics. Retrieved from http://internet-filter-review.toptenreviews.com/internet-pornography-statistics.html.

Russell, D. (1998). *Dangerous relationships: Pornography, misogyny, and rape.* Thousand Oaks, CA: Sage.

Russell, D. E. (1990). *Rape in marriage.* Indianapolis, IN: Indiana University Press.

Sabol, W. J., West, H. C., & Cooper, M. (2009). Prisoners in 2008 (NCJ 228417). Bureau of Justice Statistics. U.S. Department of Justice.

Sampson, A. (1992). Treatment programs: From theory to practice. In Prison Reform Trust (Ed.), *Beyond Containment: The penal response to sex offending.* London, UK: Prison Reform Trust.

Scalora, M. J., & Garbin, C. (2003). A multivariate analysis of sex offender recidivism. *International Journal of Offender Therapy and Comparative Criminology, 47*(3), 309–323.

Scarce, M. (1997). *Male on male rape: The hidden toll of stigma and shame.* New York, NY: Insight Books.

Schultz, P. D. (2005). *Not monsters: Analyzing the stories of child molesters.* Lanham, MD: Rowman & Littlefield.

Schwartz, H. I. (1994). Informed consent and competency. In R. Rosner (Ed.), *Principles and practice of forensic psychiatry* (pp. 103–110). New York, NY: Chapman and Hall.

Scott, C. L., & Holmberg, T. (2003). Castration of sex offenders: Prisoners' rights versus public safety. *The Journal of the American Academy of Psychiatry and the Law, 31,* 502–509.

Scully, D. (1994). *Understanding sexual violence: A study of convicted rapists.* New York, NY: Routledge.

Scully, D., & Marolla, D. (1985, February). Riding the bull at Gilley's: Rapists describe the rewards of rape. *Social Problems, 32*(3): 251–263.

Smith v. Doe, 123 S.C. 1140 (2003).

Snyder, H. (2000). *Sexual assault of young children as reported to law enforcement: Victim, incident, and offender characteristics.* Washington, DC: Bureau of Justice Statistics, U.S. Department of Justice.

Sourcebook of criminal justice statistics online (2004). Bureau of Justice Statistics. Retrieved from http://www.albany.edu/sourcebook/pdf/t5482004.pdf.

State v. Brown, 326 S.E.2d 410, 412 (S.C. 1985)

Stohr, M., Walsh, A., & Hemmens, C. (2009). *Corrections: A text/reader.* Thousand Oaks, CA: Sage.

Stone, H. T., Winslade, W. J., & Klugman, C. M. (2000). Sex offenders, sentencing laws and pharmaceutical treatment: A prescription for failure. *Behavioral Sciences and the Law, 19,* 83–110.

Strategically monitoring sex offenders: Assessing community corrections' resources to enhance law enforcement capabilities. (2008). The Bureau of Justice Assistance. Retrieved from http://www.ojp.usdoj.gov/BJA/pdf/IACPSexOffenderCommCorr.pdf.

Sutherland, E. (1950). The diffusion of sexual psychopath laws. *American Journal of Sociology, 56*(2), 142–148.

Terry, K. T. (2006). *Sexual offenses and offenders: Theory, practice and policy.* Belmont, CA: Wadsworth.

Thomas, T. (2000). *Sex crime: Sex offending and society.* Cullompton, Devon, UK: Willan.

Thompson, E. H., & Cracco, E. J. (2008). Sexual aggression in bars: What college men can normalize. *Journal of Men's Studies, 16*(1), 82–96.

Vasquez, B. E. Maddan, S., & Walker, J. T. (2008). The influence of sex offender registration and notification laws in the United States: A time-series analysis. *Crime and Delinquency, 54,* 175–192.

Vaughn, M., & Sapp, A. (1989). Less than utopian: Sex offender treatment in a milieu of power struggles, status positioning, and inmate populations in state correctional institutions. *Prison Journal, 69*(2), 73–89.

Vito, G. F., & Holmes, R. M. (1994). *Criminology: Theory, research and policy.* Belmont, CA: Wadsworth.

Von Hirsch, A., & Ashworth, A. (1996). Protective sentencing under section 2(2)(b): The criteria for dangerousness. *Criminal Law Review*, 175.

Walker, J. T., Maddan, S., Vasquez, B. E., Van Houten, A. C., & Ervin-McLarty, G. (2006). *Influence of sex offender registration and notification laws in the United States* (NCJ 214626). Little Rock, AR: Arkansas Crime Information Center.

Ward, T., Hudson, S. M., & Marshall, W. L. (1996). Attachment style in sex offenders: A preliminary study. *Journal of Sex Research, 33*(1), 17–26.

Webster, C. M., Gartner, R., & Doob, A. N. (2006). Results by design: The artefactual construction of high recidivism rates for sex offenders. *Canadian Journal of Criminology and Criminal Justice, 48*(1), 79–93.

Wilcox, D. T. (2000). Application of the clinical polygraph examination to the assessment, treatment and monitoring of sex offenders. *Journal of Sexual Aggression, 5*(2), 134–152.

Wille, R., & Beier, K. M. (1989). Castration in Germany. *Sexual Abuse: A Journal of Research and Treatment, 2*(2), 103–133.

Workman, J., & Freeburg, E. (1999). An examination of date rape, victim dress and perceiver variables within the context of attribution theory. *Sex Roles, 41*(3/4), 261–277.

Zeigler, F. A., & del Carmen, R. V. (1997). Cruel and unusual punishment and other Constitutional issues arising from Three Strikes You're Out legislation. In D. L. Sehrcrest (Ed.), *Three Strikes You're Out: Vengeance as public policy.* Beverly Hills, CA: Sage Publishing,

Zevitz, R. G. (2003). Sex offender community notification and its impact on neighborhood life. *Crime Prevention and Community Safety: An International Journal, 5*, 41–61.

Zgoba, K. J., & Simon, L. (2005). Recidivism rates of sexual offenders up to 7 years later. *Criminal Justice Review, 30*(2), 155–173.

Zgoba, K., Veysey, B. M., & Dalessandro, M. (2010). An analysis of the effectiveness of community notification and registration: Do the best intentions predict the best practices? *Justice Quarterly, 27*(5), 667–691.

Zilney, L. J., & Zilney, L. A. (2009). *Perverts and predators: The making of sex offending laws.* Lanham, MD: Rowman and Littlefield.

CHAPTER 15

Preventing White-Collar Crime

George W. Burruss
Southern Illinois University—Carbondale

Jessica L. Deaton
Southern Illinois University—Carbondale

INTRODUCTION

During his 1939 American Sociological Society presidential address, Edwin Sutherland was the first to call for the study of white-collar crime. There had certainly been interest in the harmful behavior of society's elites before Sutherland; however, he argued that sociologists, legal scholars, and other academics had neglected to formally study the problem (Geis, 2007). Sutherland cataloged the many injurious acts carried out by doctors, judges, corporate heads, politicians, and robber barons, noting that they often escaped prosecution and punishment. Sutherland was not just interested in criminal violations, but also regulatory infractions and civil injuries. Sutherland stressed that white-collar crimes had far greater financial costs than street crimes, yet crimes by blue-collar workers and the poor were the subject of most criminological studies and theories at that time. Thus, choosing to focus on this problem and coining a new word during his presidential address was regarded as a scholarly critique of existing theory, an appeal for empirical research, and a call for social action.

Despite Sutherland's call to action for the study of white-collar crime almost 70 years ago, no consensus has emerged about how to define white-collar crime. Sutherland defined "white-collar crime," as: "A crime committed by a person of respectable and high social status in the course of his occupation" (Sutherland, 1949). Since then, criminologists and legal scholars have vigorously debated about which behaviors constitute white-collar crime. Sutherland's definition stresses the status of the offender—a person of respectability and high social status. This definition applied to wrongful acts today would include corporate offenders, such as those in the Enron scandal of 2000, but would leave out low-level managers who embezzle from a company or a used-car salesman who knowingly sells a vehicle using false claims. Sutherland's definition was broad in the offenses it covered, but narrow on the offenders by including only persons of high social status. Thus, other scholars have sought to develop different definitions of white-collar crime that focus on either the offense or the offender.

More recent attempts to refine white-collar crime's definition tend to fall into two broad categories—offender based and offense based. Offender-based definitions focus on the status or respectability of the offender. The status might refer to the socioeconomic standing of the offender (e.g., upper class or high standing) or the professional nature of the offender's occupation (e.g., doctor, lawyer, accountant). Offender-based definitions narrow the scope of who should be studied, but often leave out many offenses that do not typically fall under the study of street crime. A fraud committed by someone of low social status and no education, for example, would fall outside the scope of an offender-based definition.

Offense-based definitions, on the other hand, focus on the offense. Typically, these definitions include crimes committed through fraud or an abuse of trust, regardless of the status of the offender. Thus, a fraud committed by a low-social status person would be suitable for study. The benefit of this kind of definition is that it broadens the scope of study. Some scholars argue, however, that such a definition is too broad, taking the focus away from high-status offenders, which was Sutherland's point in calling attention to white-collar crime in the first place. For example, a used-car salesperson who misrepresents the history of an auto in a sale does far less economic harm than a CEO of a corporation whose fraudulent claims wipe out the value of a corporation's stock price.

Besides these two definitions, Freidrichs (2009, p. 7) has offered five categories of illegal or injurious acts that fall under the white-collar crime concept: (1) corporate crime; (2) occupational crime; (3) governmental crime; (4) state–corporate crime, crimes of globalization, and high finance crime; (5) enterprise crime, entrepreneurial crime, technocrime and avocational crime. Each category allows scholars to pick an area that is about white-collar crime generally, but is specific enough to be sure that the activities contained within are conceptually distinct from the others. For example, officers and agents of corporations can only commit corporate crimes. This would exclude crimes by legitimate small businesses owners, which would fall under the category of occupational crime. As you can see, the definitional problems associated with the study of white-collar crime are many. Further discussion is beyond the scope of this chapter.

THE 2008 U.S. ECONOMIC CRISIS

The U.S. economic crisis of 2008 shows the devastating impact that harmful corporate behavior can have on the entire economy. According to the U.S. Financial Crisis Inquiry Commission's report (2011, pp. 390–401) the recent crisis caused a deep recession that adversely affected essential parts of the economy: lowering housing values; raising home mortgage foreclosures; reducing available consumer and small business credit; laying off millions of employees; depleting tax revenues from local, state, and federal coffers; diminishing the value of stocks and bonds; and reducing consumer confidence. The commission's report indicates that while most of the activities were not illegal, they were risky, unethical, and avoidable. This recent economic catastrophe highlights the continued need for the study of white-collar crime; it also reveals how little we still know about the phenomenon.

The causes of the crisis were many, but a root cause was risky corporate ventures. Most were not criminal acts; however, there were certainly clear acts of misrepresentation in many mortgage loans. According to the Financial Crisis Inquiry Commission (2011), the causes of the economic meltdown were avoidable, due in part to

> . . . an explosion in risky subprime lending and securitization, an unsustainable rise in housing prices, widespread reports of egregious and predatory lending practices, dramatic increases in household mortgage debt, and exponential growth in financial firms' trading activities, unregulated derivatives, and short-term "repo" lending markets, among many other red flags. Yet there was pervasive permissiveness; little meaningful action was taken to quell the threats in a timely manner. (p. xvii)

The Commission further stated that market players weakened the regulatory constraints (but see the report's dissenting statements for a counter view). Financial regulators who did have oversight over lending and financial instruments failed to intervene in cases where there were clear signs of market destabilization. The Commission concluded that financial markets' accountability and ethics broke down. For example, lenders who witnessed increasing defaults and knew the high risk associated with subprime mortgages continued to lend to virtually anyone who applied for a loan, bringing in large fees for themselves. In sum, the regulatory climate in the United States during the first decade of the 21st century was lax: corporate actors could engage in increasingly risky behavior without any fear of punishment.

The catastrophic collapse of U.S. financial markets in 2008 reminds us that risky corporate acts, though not always criminal, can have a devastating impact on the public's economic well-being. Sutherland's concern about elites avoiding detection, prosecution, and study thus continues to be relevant. The activities that led up to the economic crisis were committed by powerful corporate and finance leaders as well as mid-level bureaucrats and low-level mortgage brokers; yet, very few have been prosecuted for wrongdoing. Despite the importance of white-collar and corporate crime as a social problem, the phenomenon remains poorly understood. The reasons stem partially from a lack of data from which to test theories of causation or to even make simple descriptions of the prevalence of such behaviors.

DATA PROBLEM

Despite the harm caused by corporate crime relative to street crime, few data sources exist to study the phenomenon. Critical criminologists attribute this lack of data to the fact the criminal justice system is run by the same people who are likely to commit white-collar offenses. Street offenders, on the other hand, have little control over official sources of data. The data that do exist for the study of corporate crime come from three sources: official data, victimization surveys, and corporations. Two sources of official data exist: criminal and regulatory. The most-cited official crime data source in the United States comes from the FBI's Uniform Crime Reports (UCRs). Serious crimes, as reported by the FBI, are Part 1 offenses. White-collar crime is not among them. Instead, white-collar crimes are listed as Part 2 crimes, which include the broad categories of fraud, forgery/counterfeiting, embezzlement, and all other offenses. The data report the count of arrests along with the offenders' ages, races, and sexes. While some researchers have used the UCR data to test theory (Schoepfer & Piquero, 2006), these data are too general to provide any real measure of the prevalence of many white-collar offenses, especially corporate crime (Barnett, 2000).

Another potential official source of criminal data is the National Incident Based Reporting System (NIBRS). The NIBRS systems expands the available crime data, including white-collar crimes, by further delineating the categories of the UCR as false pretenses, swindles, confidence games, credit card/ATM fraud, impersonation, welfare fraud, and wire fraud (Barnett, 2000). Thus, NIBRS is an improvement over the UCR; however, both sources represent imperfect counts of the behavior, which is true for many street-level offenses as well. Both measure of white-collar crime represent an offense-based definition of white-collar crime because offenders' respectability or social status is not recorded.

A third data source of official corporate and white-collar offending comes from regulatory agencies. Because of the diversity in the kinds of goods and services that corporations produce, many regulatory agencies have oversight over specific markets. For example, the U.S. Food and Drug Administration (FDA) regulates the medicines produced by pharmaceutical companies. Besides regulation of medicine, other state and federal regulatory agencies also oversee pharmaceutical corporations, such as state and federal revenue departments, employment security, and the U.S. Occupational Safety and Health Administration (OSHA). Much of the potential harm done by corporations falls under regulatory actions and administrative law; thus, these data are important to understand corporate wrongdoing. Like criminal records, however, these data have the same limitations—these are infractions known to the authorities and thus represent only a fraction of potential harm done by corporations. In addition, the purview of the different regulatory agencies varies as legislation limits or expands regulations over businesses. Thus, unlike criminal law that remains fairly stable, administrative and regulatory law can change significantly over time.

The second major source of information that informs our understanding of white-collar crime is victimization surveys. The National Crime Victimization Survey (NCVS), which has measured criminal victimizations since the 1970s, was instituted to uncover those crimes that did not get reported to the police (and therefore were not part of the UCR). The NCVS does not acquire much information about white-collar crimes. The NCVS asks household respondents about larcenies that were committed through fraud, and in some years asks about Internet victimizations. The NCVS data are therefore not helpful in measuring white-collar crime.

In 2000, the National White-Collar Crime Center (NWCCC), a nonprofit law enforcement member supported agency, surveyed a random sample of U.S. adult residents about their experience with white-collar crime. The survey was given again in 2005 and 2010. According to the 2010 survey, 24% of households and 17% of individuals reported a victimization that included mortgage fraud, credit card fraud, identity theft, unnecessary home or auto repairs, price misrepresentation, stock fraud, business fraud, or Internet scams (Huff, Desilets, & Kane, 2010). Of those victimizations reported, only about 55% were reported to an external public or private agency, and only about 12% were reported to a law enforcement agency. While the NWCCC survey tells us much about white-collar victimization experiences as well as reporting behavior, most of the crimes reported are not by corporations. This survey does help measure some kinds of white-collar victimizations. Corporate offending, however, is still mostly unmeasured.

In addition to uncovering white-collar victimizations, the NWCCC survey asked respondents about their attitudes toward white-collar crime (Huff, Desilets, & Kane, 2010). The survey showed that respondents viewed white-collar crime as being slightly more serious than street crimes. Also, crimes committed by organizations were viewed as more harmful than those by individuals, and crimes committed by persons of high status were more troubling than those committed by low-status persons. When asked about the recent economic crisis of 2008, a majority (70%) of respondents agreed that white-collar crime was a major contributor.

One final source of data that would be important for the study of corporate crime is corporations themselves. While it is unlikely that corporations or their executives would self-report their own misdeeds, corporations have data that can help examine the structural pressures that can lead to corporate wrongdoing. In their 1979 landmark study, Clinard and Yeager (2006) studied official corporate wrongdoing (criminal, civil, and administrative). They found that the size of the organization and underperforming firms were categories that were more likely to have been sanctioned. Clinard and Yeager purchased most of the corporate data on Fortune 500 companies for a significant amount of money and, not surprisingly, a replication of their findings has yet to be done. Corporations, however, routinely use their own data to detect fraud committed within or against their own interests. Corporations collect much information about their own structure and operations. Using the same data mining techniques that corporations use to protect themselves, researchers could explore the structural correlates of white-collar crime. Such a release of data, however, seems unlikely.

Given the issues associated with existing data, how can researchers and government agencies create data sources to explain, predict, and understand white-collar crime? Because many white-collar crimes fall outside of local law enforcement agencies' jurisdictions, most consumer and financial crimes are reported to state and federal authorities. In most states, for instance, the attorneys general have jurisdiction over consumer fraud; in a few states, the governor or secretary of state has such jurisdiction. Thus, depending on one's definition of white-collar crime, the incidents reported

---

BOX 15-1 The Enron Scandal

The Enron scandal that became public in 2001 makes a good case study for the kind of corporate offending that has become commonplace in the financial sector of the U.S. economy. Some of the schemes employed at Enron were also responsible for the recent economic crisis. Two kinds of business actions taken by Enron executives, notably Jeff Skilling and Andy Fastow, were main reasons why Enron collapsed into bankruptcy and ultimately dissolution: mark-to-market accounting and special-purpose entities. Neither of these practices were illegal, but they were used in illegal schemes; Enron executives sought to make Enron look more profitable than it actually was, thereby driving up its stock price and subsequently their own wealth.

Mark-to-market accounting is a legitimate accounting practice that Jeff Skilling proposed Enron use to reward its adventurous practices and to spur growth. Prior to Skilling's appointment as president of the company, Enron was simply a natural gas-trading firm headquartered in Houston, Texas. Skilling proposed that Enron consider the profit from future earnings at the time of settling a contract. Thus, if Enron had a contract to sell natural gas over 5 years, all the profit from the life of the contract would be added to Enron's books at the beginning of the contractual period. While Enron would certainly earn money over the 5 years of the contract, adding the future earnings to the current budget would make Enron look more profitable in the short run. The use of mark-to-market accounting was not illegal, but it did drive the need to make Enron look like it was growing every quarter in order to justify its growing stock price. This pressure for growth then led to the use of special-purpose entities to buy debt from Enron's books, creating the illusion that it was more profitable than was actually the case.

Andy Fastow, Enron's chief financial officer, introduced special-purpose entities (hereafter SPE), also a legitimate practice, into Enron's trade. In short, a special-purpose entity is a paper company—or limited partnership—that exists to purchase something, typically some kind of resource. In the case of Enron, Fastow would set up special-purpose entities, often naming them after Star Wars characters, like JEDI or Chewco, and use them to buy assets from Enron, such as a factory. Thus the debt Enron had for owning the factory would be removed from its books, increasing Enron's value. The money for the SPE would be borrowed from a bank with the collateral for the loan unofficially guaranteed by Enron stock. Enron would eventually buy back the factory from the SPE since it needed the factory for its operations. As the need for profit increased, the shuffling of debt off of Enron's books became more frequent. Eventually, the fraud was revealed and Enron's stock price and reputation plummeted. Many of the Enron executives responsible for the scandal had sold their own stock as they realized their schemes were about to be made public.

Andy Fastow pleaded guilty to wire and securities fraud and was sentenced to 6 years in prison. Jeff Skilling was sentenced to 24 years in prison for conspiracy, insider trading, and securities fraud.

to these agencies represent white-collar crimes known to the authorities. Like the UCR, these data sources will certainly undercount white-collar crime; however, they are likely to be more accurate than the fraud and embezzlement cases currently counted in the UCR. These data, however, are not uniform. Each state has different means of collecting and recording the data. Before they could be combined into one data source, there would need to be a coding protocol in place.

Also, states are unlikely to relinquish the data to build a common data source. The UCR was mandated by the U.S. Congress. Without a similar national mandate, it is unlikely that states' attorneys general will release their consumer and financial crime data to a third party given that attorney general is an elected office. Many would fear that the data would be used to show ineffective or preferential enforcement. Thus, few studies have used state-level data for research purposes. Until there is a movement to create a clearing house of agency and corporate data, our knowledge about white-collar and corporate crime will remain limited.

Most research that has been conducted on white-collar offending comes from case studies, especially organizational studies after a serious case of fraud, violence, or economic crisis has occurred. For example, Vaughan (1990, 1996) explored the causes of the 1986 Space Shuttle Challenger explosion. In the NASA case study, Vaughan documented many organizational factors that contributed to the tragedy, which she called an organizational–technical system accident. She argued that regulatory ineffectiveness arose from the interdependence between NASA and its regulators; many decisions made on the day of the fatal launch should have led to scuttling the mission, but organizational pressures to launch on time overrode such concerns. Vaughan's case study was grounded in research and theory, but often white-collar crime case studies are more journalistic in their approach but nonetheless important for understating the causes of some white-collar crimes.

For example, two books on the collapse of Enron, the energy trading company, documented the lives of the individuals responsible, the cutthroat organizational culture , and the industry structural factors that contributed to the company's collapse (McLean & Elkind, 2004; Eichenwald, 2005). In *The Smartest Guys in the Room*, McLean and Elkind interviewed many Enron executives and employees and examined official documents to produce an exhaustive and compelling explanation for why Enron rose to prominence and then collapsed. While the books lack an academic focus, they provide invaluable facts and insight about an important white-collar criminal case. In the case of Enron, many of the corporate officers were tried and found guilty or pleaded guilty.

THEORY PROBLEM

The lack of reliable data and a clear definition of the problem not only prevent a general understanding about the prevalence of white-collar crime, but also prevent a thorough testing of criminological theories to explain the causes. Most of the criminological theories applied to explain street offenses have also been posited to explain white-collar crime. For example, Sutherland's own differential association theory has been used to explain juvenile delinquency: juveniles who associate with delinquents will be more likely to commit delinquent acts as they learn the definitions, or justifications, for doing so. This hypothesis has been supported empirically (both as differential association theory and its later reformulation in social learning theory). Sutherland thought that white-collar offending would work in the same way. To test this hypothesis, Sutherland interviewed salesmen and white-collar professionals, finding that they often learned the value of being dishonest to make more sales (Sutherland, 1949). While individual accounts can be important sources of information, they fail to adequately support the hypothesis. Other prominent criminological theories such as the general theory of crime, strain theory, or routine activities theory also suffer from a lack of empirical support given the data limitations mentioned above.

A CHOICE MODEL OF WHITE-COLLAR OFFENDING

A recent theoretical development is Shover and Hochstetler's (2006) choice model of white-collar crime. This model offers an explanation for the variation in white-collar crime rates without explaining the root causes of individual behavior (e.g., low self-control, criminal peers, or low IQ). Theories such as Gottfredson and Hirschi's (1990) general theory of crime or Aker's social learning theory (1973) reveal individual-level factors that explain criminal behavior. The choice model, on the other hand, appears to be a macro-level theory that explains changes in overall crime rates. This theory offers some possible value in exploring the potential for preventing white-collar crime.

Shover and Grabosky (2010) offer a choice model of white-collar offending that focuses on the level of criminal opportunities and size of offender pool to explain the rate of white-collar crime. The offender pool includes those individuals and organizations that are tempted or predisposed to commit white-collar crime. Organizations or individuals who are predisposed have some characteristic that allows them to recognize an opportunity when presented. Criminal opportunities are, "arrangements or situations that offer potential or criminal reward with little apparent risk of detection or penalty" (Shover & Grabosky, 2010, p. 432). The level of these two concepts varies in degree based on three additional concepts.

First, the *supply of lure* increases the offender pool and criminal opportunity. Lure is something appealing that attracts those tempted or predisposed to violate the law in order to gain an advantage in the market (Shover & Grabosky, 2010). In a white-collar crime context, lure can be a policy or practice that can be exploited or avoided. An example of lure is the financial practices that allowed the bundling of risky and safe mortgages into bonds that were part of the cause of the 2008 economic crisis (Shover & Grabosky, 2010, p. 431). According to the model, as lure increases, the volume of those tempted or predisposed will increase.

Second, the prevailing beliefs about the *credibility of external oversight* can reduce the size of the offender pool and criminal opportunity, such that when businesses believe that external parties are not likely to intervene in fraudulent activities, temptation increases. Oversight can come from professional associations, whistle-blowers, civil actions, or government agencies (Shover & Hochstetler, 2006). The form of oversight can include criminal, civil, regulatory, or professional sanctions. Shover and Hochstetler (2006, p. 94) offer some insight into how perceptions of oversight might be measured. For example, they chart the rate of referrals and actual prosecutions for federal white-collar crimes over a 17-year period, noting the variation. It is likely that members of the business and financial communities are also aware of the variation and make note of when prosecutions are rare.

Third, the deployment of extensive and effective *internal oversight* and self-restraint reduce the size of the offender pool and criminal opportunity. According to Shover and Hochstetler (2006, p. 76), "Self-restraint is . . . the willingness of the individuals and groups to be constrained in their consideration of options not by fear or legal penalties but instead by potential self-reproach borne of a guilty conscience or concern for the opinions of others." This might indicate moral or ethical sensibilities. Research has shown that moral considerations have an important impact on decision making, even when the threat of sanctions is low (Paternoster & Simpson, 1996).

The choice model also offers insight into the variation in rates of white-collar crime. When self-restraint, regulation, and law enforcement are lax, the pool of temptations increases and the supply of criminal opportunities rises. But like all scholarship in white-collar crime, the quantitative data needed to test this theory are unavailable. For example, in order to understand the level of oversight, a researcher would need to have data on the changes in regulatory behavior in a single industry as well as valid and reliable measures of offending. As stated previously, such data are hard to come by. On the other hand, qualitative research has provided some insight into the utility of the choice perspective. For example, Nguyen and Pontell (2010) interviewed 23 individuals employed in the subprime mortgage industry. From their interviews they found that a lax regulatory environment encouraged fraud within the industry. Nguyen and Pontell argue for better industry standards and practices, increased accountability for originating loans that fail, and increased formal oversight over the industry.

SENTENCING

One area of white-collar offending that we do have data for is sentencing. Because these data are available, we can look at the punishments that federal and state judges give to white-collar offenders. We can examine not only the severity of punishment, but the variation in punishment over time. In addition, changes in the law are also easily observed, so that how the government chooses to respond to white-collar crime—either leniently or harshly—can be measured.

Traditionally, white-collar offenders have been treated less harshly than individuals who have committed other types of crimes. Before 2002, the average prison length for white-collar offenders was less than 2 years according to the sentencing guidelines. However, white-collar offenders received fines the majority of the time and very rarely saw imprisonment (Kahan & Posner, 1999). In 2001, the total economic loss from burglary, larceny, and motor vehicle theft was $17.2 billion. This amount is only one-third of the amount lost just by the Enron scandal alone (Dutcher, 2005). There are many reasons for this disparity in sentencing. The public does not typically fear white-collar offenders. Violent crimes or theft via trespassing evoke more fear because the victims can physically observe the results of the offense; white-collar crimes, however, often occur away from the victims' presence. Also white-collar crime is very hard to detect and punish compared to ordinary crime. Since 2002, the U.S. government has been pushing for harsher punishments for white-collar offenders by sentencing them to much longer prison terms than in the past (Dutcher, 2005).

A new emphasis on preventing corporate crime by establishing corporate regulations and increasing criminal liability for offenders, has been a result of large corporate fraud scandals that hit the U.S. economy since the beginning of the 21st century. Traditional post hoc punishment has slowly been pushed aside while emphasis on prevention, regulation, and rehabilitation has become the primary focus of white-collar policies. The use of deferred prosecution agreements has increased in order to prevent recidivism. These agreements are contracts between the government and corporate official saying that the government (prosecutor) will not prosecute if the corporate official (defendant) agrees to their requirements. These agreements are not only a tool to aid in investigation and punishment, but are also used for rehabilitation in order to prevent recidivism by exposing the corporate official to criminal sanctions (Meeks, 2006).

White-collar criminals are now facing more severe punishments than in previous years. The structure of the federal sentencing guidelines has increased the length of the prison sentences, usually doubling the term. The guidelines take into consideration the economic loss, the positional power of the defendant, prior criminal conduct, number of victims, and the extent of planning that went into the crime. Federal judges were originally required to impose a sentence that was within the range of the guidelines. There is still some flexibility on the sentences received because of the Supreme Court decision in *United States v. Booker* (Dutcher, 2005). This case ruled that only evidence admitted by the defendant or evidence that was proved beyond a reasonable doubt could be used when calculating the sentence (*United States v. Booker*, 2005). This case struck down the statute that made the sentencing guidelines mandatory and ultimately made them advisory.

Because there is no longer federal parole, white-collar offenders are often faced with serving the actual time they were sentenced to. Usually white-collar offenders are first-time offenders with no prior criminal conduct. Often, these new harsher sentences have been longer than what some people would see for committing a violent crime, especially for a first-time offence. For example, the executives from WorldCom and Enron, Bernard Ebbers and Jeffrey Skilling, were both sentenced to 25 years and 24 years respectively as a result of the sentencing guidelines. Even though judges have been given more flexibility in sentencing, the guidelines continue to be used in the majority of cases (Podgor, 2007). The harsher punishments can be justified by various perspectives such as deterrence, incapacitation, and retribution (Dutcher, 2005).

To control white collar-crime, criminal penalties might deter. Criminal penalties should not only deter the individual who is committing the crime, but also the community by setting the legal limitations. This sends a message to the community that this kind of behavior is considered inappropriate and will be punished accordingly; it is often called general deterrence. In order for deterrence to be effective, the punishment must be severe but appropriate to the crime. A punishment that is too light will send the message that the crime is worth the risk, resulting in deterrence not being effective. Even though the federal guidelines have provided longer prison terms for white-collar crimes, the fines are still not proportional to the crime. In sentencing, the economic loss in the crime and the economic gain for the offender must be accounted for in order for deterrence to be effective. Take the example of Michael Milken: He manipulated the financial market by engaging in racketeering and securities fraud, resulting in a loss of over a billion dollars from investors. He only paid back 600 million dollars, however, and served less than 2 years of his 10-year prison sentence. After being released from prison, his economic gain from the scandal was 700 million dollars because he was not required to pay back the entire amount lost in the crime. This was a widely public scandal with no effective deterrence. Most corporate criminals would gladly spend this amount of time in prison because of the enormous economic gain they receive when they get out (Dutcher, 2005). Deterrence can be a valuable tool in preventing future crime but the physical punishments and fines must be more costly than the economic gains.

Incapacitation is used to prevent individuals from committing further crime. Incapacitating forms of punishments can result in the offender being prohibited from holding an office in a public company because of the regulations set by the Sarbanes-Oxley Act (Dutcher, 2005). Incarceration is also a form of punishment to go along with the fines. By issuing fines only, the offender can see the punishment as being comparable merely to a tax on the sum of money he or she has collected, and thus fines only will not prove an effective form of deterrence. In regards to the retribution approach, the punishment must be proportional to the crime. According to retributivists, a fine is not proportional to the effect of a white-collar crime, so other forms of punishment must be carried out. They also believe that corporate offenders must be punished in the same manner as one would punish a street criminal. Incarceration can also be justified by the fact that the liberty of the corporate offender is being removed; this will have a significant effect on whether the offender will violate another law (Silberfarb, 2003).

Retribution is justified because the offender deserves to be punished; punishment is morally fitting. Retribution does not always mean a harsh punishment, but that the punishment should be proportional to the crime (Recine, 2002). With this being said, a retributivist claims that harsh punishments are appropriate for crimes that cause enormous damage. In relation to white-collar crime, offenders who break the law and cause a massive financial burden to countless victims should receive harsh punishments. In the HealthSouth scandal, for example, employees falsely reported the company's earnings in order to meet the expectations of the stockholders. This action cost the stockholders 400 million dollars. Only 1 of the 10 corporate executives, Emery Harris, served time in prison; his time served was only 5 months, while the other executives were given probation, home detention, and fines. In relation to the millions this scandal brought in losses to its shareholders, many claim that the punishment for the executives was too light. Many others claim that "too light" is an understatement (Dutcher, 2005).

In the last several years, the U.S. Department of Justice (DOJ) has increased their investigations and has launched a crackdown on white-collar crime. The DOJ has the ability to punish and deter by using criminal action through indictments and prosecutions of corporate entities (Meeks, 2006).

RECENT CHANGES IN WHITE-COLLAR CRIME LAW

Sarbanes-Oxley Act of 2002

In 2002, President George W. Bush signed the Sarbanes-Oxley Act to establish new standards for all U.S. public accounting firms. This law was designed to heighten the confidence of the capital markets in reaction to recent corporate scandals like Enron, Tyco International, Adelphia, Peregrine Systems, and WorldCom that cost investors billions of dollars. The act contains 11 titles that established specific requirements for financial reporting.

Title I established the Public Company Accounting Oversights Board, which consists of five members who perform duties like regulating and inspecting all public accounting firms. It also establishes standards and rules for auditing and enforces compliance with the standards for auditing. The auditing standards include any of the following requirements: any public accounting entity that has involvement in the auditing report must register with the Board; audited papers must have a 7-year retention period; a second person must review and approve the audit reports and conduct evaluations that check to see if the records are accurately representing the transactions and dispositions of assets. The Board is also allowed to enforce disciplinary sanctions for any intentional or repeated negligence.

Title II establishes new requirements and prohibitions to maintain auditor independence. Auditors are prohibited from engaging in any nonaudit services unless the audit committee has approved an activity that is not prohibited by the Act. Requirements of auditor approval and reporting were established along with restricting firms from providing consulting services to limit conflicts of interest. Auditor rotation was also established to limit any one auditor from being the leader for more than five consecutive terms. Auditors must report accounting policies used in the audit, written material between the auditor and management, and alternative treatments and ramifications, to the auditing committee. A 1-year probation term can be enforced on an auditor's services if their management had been previously employed by that auditor.

Title III requires members of the audit committee to be independent, but they must be a member of the board of directors. This title also establishes corporate responsibility for each senior executive member to oversee the accuracy and completeness of all financial reports and requires the Securities and Exchange Commission (SEC) to instruct the CEO and CFO of any public firm to certify financial reports. They must agree that the reports do not contain any false information; the financial statements accurately represent the financial conditions; and any significant changes to the internal controls, along with a review of their effectiveness, must be reported. If an accounting restatement must be made due to the noncompliance of an issuer, the CEO and CFO must forfeit all bonuses and compensation for 1 year after the original statement. Also, to benefit the victims of any securities violations, civil penalties are contributed to a fund.

Title IV establishes in-depth reporting requirements for all financial transactions to assure accuracy and disclosure. All financial reports filed with the SEC must reflect all corrected adjustments and disclosures, and all off-balance sheet transactions must be stated in the financial status. Changes in securities ownership or securities swap agreements must be disclosed within 2 days instead of the former 10 days. Information regarding whether senior financial officers have adopted a code of ethics and if there is a financial expert in the auditing committee must be disclosed. Disclosures by issuers have to undergo regular and systematic reviews by the SEC.

Title V establishes a code of conduct for security analysts to restore investor confidence in reporting. Investment bankers are not allowed to preapprove research reports, and research analysts cannot be supervised by an individual who is involved in investments services. This section also requires conflict of interest disclosures by a research analyst who participate in a public appearance and by brokers in research reports, to include: if the analyst has held securities in the company that is the subject of the appearance; if any compensation was received by the analysts or broker from the company in the appearance; if the company making the appearing has been a client of the broker; and finally, if the analyst received compensation regarding a report.

Title VI establishes authority for the SEC to censure and bar specific professionals who have engaged in improper and unethical behavior from the practice, and also prohibits individuals who have engaged in a securities violation from participating in the penny stock exchange. The SEC's disciplinary authority is expanded, which allows it to limit services and operations of brokers and dealers.

Title VII requires the SEC to set up various studies to ascertain the factors leading to accounting firms' consolidating and security violations, as well as the role of credit rating agencies in any violations, and to also report the findings of these studies. The enforcement actions taken by the SEC regarding reporting violations and restatements must be included in the studies and findings. A limitation on pursuing a right of action for a securities violation is limited to 2 years after discovery or 5 years after the violation.

Title VIII is the Corporate and Criminal Fraud Accountability Act. This title imposes the specific criminal penalties that will be enforced for altering or manipulating, falsifying, or destroying any financial records to interfere with investigations by the federal government. This title also provides whistleblower protection. This protection makes it illegal for anyone to enforce criminal penalties against whistleblowers. Any person who knowingly aids in defrauding a shareholder is subject to a fine or imprisonment of up to 25 years.

Title IX consists of the White-Collar Crime Penalty Enhancement Act (WCCPA). This Act implements stronger penalties and increases punishments for mail and wire fraud from a maximum of 5 years to 20 years. Violations against the Employee Retirement Income Security Act of 1974 increase to a fine of up to $500,000 and 10 years in prison. It also adds failure to certify financial reports as a criminal offense. This increases the maximum imprisonment time to 10 years for knowing the report does not comply with the Act or 20 years for knowingly certifying a statement that does not comply with the Act. Title X only consists of one section, which states that company tax returns should be signed by the Chief Executive Officer.

The last title, Title XI, is also known as the Corporate Fraud Accountability Act. This section combines the criminal offenses of record tampering and corporate fraud and assigns specific penalties to them. A maximum 20 year sentence is established for tampering with a record or impeding an official proceeding. This act also prohibits an individual who has engaged in a violation of manipulative governing, deceptive devices, and false transactions, from serving as an officer or director of a public corporation. The penalty for violating the Securities Exchange Act of 1934 increased to a fine of up to $25 million and imprisonment of up to 20 years. This section also allows the SEC to temporarily freeze transactions and payments that are under possible investigation.

The Sarbanes-Oxley Act and the White-Collar Crime Penalty Enhancement Act (WCCPA) have proven to be insufficient when dealing with the current practice of business crime and has made the punishment less of a fear instead of a more of a deterrent (Perino, 2002). Judges have been inconsistent when imposing the stricter punishments set forth by the WCCPA and have also increased the departures from the Federal Sentencing Guideline; this is not only destroying the deterrent effect but is also creating sentencing disparities between jurisdictions by not having consistent sentences given, and allowing judges to exhibit their own discretion in the process (Comey, Jr., 2009). Instead of following the base guidelines and imposing the average sentences for these crimes, the WCCPA has broadened the range of sentencing disparity by simply increasing the maximum sentence. By stabilizing the sentencing and pursuing more proportionate sentences, the deterrence effect would increase along with fairness (Comey, Jr., 2009).

Consumer Financial Protection Bureau

Because of irresponsible lending by large banks, President Obama proposed the establishment of a new financial regulatory agency in 2009. Instead of focusing on the lenders and the financial agencies, this new agency will focus directly on the consumers and their protection. This agency serves as protection against deceptive financial agencies by enforcing and supervising the laws that pertain to lenders of consumer products and services. The Dodd-Frank Wall Street Reform and Consumer Protection Act was passed by Congress and signed by President Obama in 2010. This act, in turn, created the Consumer Financial Protection Bureau (CFPB). This bureau centralizes all consumer financial protection into one place, while focusing on the American consumers who are looking for financial services. The bureau is accountable for making sure that the consumer has all the information he or she needs when deciding on a product or service. The bureau has the responsibility of ensuring that there is understandable information about credit cards, loans, and checking accounts, while at the same time minimizing the policies in the fine print that would constitute traps for the consumer. Under the Dodd-Frank Wall Street Reform Act, the CFPB will

- Require mortgage lenders to determine that a borrower has the ability to repay a loan by verifying income and making sure borrowers can afford loans even after teaser rates expire and payments rise.
- Prohibit repayment penalties, which can make it expensive to refinance, for high-cost loans and adjustable-rate mortgages.

- Put an end to practices like paying bonuses to mortgage brokers and loan officers who steer borrowers into higher-cost loans than they otherwise qualify for.
- Require clearer and simpler disclosures about international money transfers.

The CFPB is increasing oversight by having a strong, diverse team of leaders to ensure that there is a clear purpose for the bureau. Policy efforts to make this a data-driven agency have produced a plan to have updates on spending and other budget related information available to outside groups. Multiple meetings have been conducted to gather ideas and concerns from various groups ranging from consumers to banks and executive officers. A sharp decline in penalty fees was noted due to the many sources of collected information. The bureau is in the process of making the financial market a better place for all American consumers.

KEY TERMS

White-collar crime
Offense-based definitions
Offender-based definitions
State-corporate crime
National Incident Based Reporting System (NIBRS)
Supply of lure
External oversight
Sarbanes-Oxley Act
Dodd-Frank Wall Street Reform and Consumer Protection Act
Consumer Financial Protection Bureau (CFPB)

DISCUSSION QUESTIONS

1. What are some of the difficulties for law enforcement agencies in preventing white-collar crime?
2. What are some key differences between offense-based definitions and offender-based definitions of white-collar crime?
3. To what degree does the complexity of regulations concerning white-collar crime and organizational crime contribute to its cause?
4. What are some concerns associated with sources of data for white-collar crime?
5. Describe specific elements of the Sarbanes-Oxley Act related to preventing white-collar crime.

REFERENCES

Akers, R. L. (1973). *Deviant behavior: A social learning approach*. Belmont, CA: Wadsworth Publishing.
Barnett, C. (2000). *Measurement of white-collar crime using Uniform Crime Reporting (UCR) data*. Clarksburg, WV: U.S. Department of Justice, Federal Bureau of Investigation.
Clinard, M. B., & Yeager P. C. (2006). *Corporate crime*. New Brunswick, NJ: Transaction Publishers.

Comey Jr., J. B. (2009). Go directly to jail: White collar sentencing after the Sarbanes-Oxley Act. *Harvard Law Review, 122*, 1728–1749.

Dutcher, J. S. (2005). From the boardroom to the cellblock: The justifications for harsher punishment of white-collar and corporate crime. *Arizona State Law Journal, 37*(4), 1295–1320.

Eichenwald, K. (2005). *Conspiracy of Fools*. New York, NY: Broadway Books.

Financial Crisis Inquiry Commission. (2011). *The financial crisis inquiry report: Final report of the National Commission on the Causes of the Financial and Economic Crisis in the United States*. Washington, DC: Author.

Freidrichs, D. (2009). *Trusted criminals: White collar crime in contemporary society*. Belmont, CA: Wadsworth Publishing.

Geis, G. (2007). *White-collar and corporate crime*. Upper Saddle River, NJ: Pearson Prentice Hall.

Gottfredson, M. R., & Hirschi, T. (1990). *A general theory of crime*. Stanford, CA: Stanford University Press.

Huff, R., Desilets, C., & Kane, J. (2010). The 2010 National Public Survey on White Collar Crime. Fairmont, WV: National White Collar Crime Center.

Kahan, D. M., & Posner, E. A. (1999). Shaming white-collar criminals: A proposal for reform of the federal sentencing guidelines. *Journal of Law and Economics, 42*(S1), 292–365.

McLean B., & Elkind, P. (2003). *The smartest guys in the room: The amazing rise and scandalous fall of Enron*. New York, NY: Penguin Group.

Meeks, W. (2006). Corporate and white-collar crime enforcement: Should regulation and rehabilitation spell an end to corporate criminal liability? *Columbia Journal of Law and Social Problems, 40*(77), 77–124.

Nguyen T. H., & Pontell H. N. (2010). Mortgage origination fraud and the global economic crisis: A criminological analysis. *Criminology & Public Policy, 9*(30), 591–612.

Paternoster R., & Simpson, S. S. (1996). Sanction threats and appeals to morality: Testing a rational choice model of corporate crime. *Law & Society Review, 30*(3), 549–584.

Perino, M. A. (2002). Enron's legislative aftermath: Some reflection on the deterrence aspects of the Sarbanes-Oxley Act of 2002. *St. John's Law Review, 76*(4), 672–674.

Podgor, E. S. (2007). The challenge of white collar sentencing. *The Journal of Criminal Law & Criminology, 97*(3), 731–759.

Recine, J. S. (2002). Examination of the white collar crime penalty enhancements in the Sarbanes-Oxley Act. *American Criminal Law Review, 39*(4), 1535–1570.

Schoepfer, A., & Piquero, N. L. (2006). Exploring white-collar crime and the American dream: A partial test of institutional anomie theory. *Journal of Criminal Justice 34*(3), 227–235.

Shover, N., & Grabosky, P. (2010). White-collar crime and the Great Recession. *Criminology and Public Policy, 9*(3), 429–433.

Shover, N., & Hochstetler, A. (2006). *Choosing white-collar crime*. New York, NY: Cambridge University Press.

Silberfarb, M. D. (2003). Justifying punishment for white-collar crime: A utilitarian and retributive analysis of the Sarbanes-Oxley Act. *Public Interest Law Journal, 13*, 95–115.

Sutherland, E. H. (1949). *White collar crime*. New York: Dryden Press.

United States v. Booker, 220 U.S. 543 (2005).

Vaughan, D. (1990). Autonomy, interdependence, and social control: NASA and the Space Shuttle Challenger. *Administrative Science Quarterly, 35*, 225–257.

Vaughan, D. (1996). *The Challenger launch decision: Risky technology, culture, and deviance at NASA*. Chicago, IL: The University of Chicago Press.

CHAPTER 16

Preventing Crimes Against Special Populations

Kimberly A. DeTardo-Bora
Marshall University

Dhruba J. Bora
Marshall University

INTRODUCTION

An elderly couple lost a significant amount of their life savings after a pair of men claiming to be financial advisors swindled them into signing over more than 100,000 dollars in certificates of deposit. The couple was treated to fancy dinners at a local country club where they were assured a 12% return on their investment. This couple was hardly alone in the financial fraud committed by these men on unsuspecting senior citizens.

A 17-year-old and two 10-year-old boys attacked a homeless man, leaving him bruised and bloody. The crime would have gone unreported had not a video clip showing the crime appeared on the Internet several days later. When the assailants were finally identified and apprehended, they showed no signs of remorse for the gruesome attack and indicated that victimizing the homeless was a pastime among their group of friends.

While walking home from a nearby public park, a 43-year-old women suffering from mental illness was raped by a young man wielding a knife. When she reported the crime to the local authorities, the crime was initially dismissed. Further evidence indicated that she had indeed been sexually assaulted, and the officers involved were suspended pending an internal investigation. Upon apprehension of the offender, it turned out that he had once worked as a custodian at the mental health facility where the victim went for treatment.

These are but a few accounts of the types of crimes that demonstrate the inherent vulnerability in our elderly, homeless, and mentally ill. While these special populations are prone to victimization at varying rates (e.g., the elderly less likely than the mentally ill), policymakers and criminal justice administrators must treat them just as seriously as crimes against the general population. Toward that end, there are several important pieces of legislation that function as general deterrence measures (i.e., crime prevention) to protect these special groups. With the elderly, efforts to protect them have been noted via the Family Violence Prevention and Treatment Act of 1984, The Reauthorization of the Older Americans Act of 1993, and the Telemarketing Fraud Bill in 1996. To support collaborative efforts between the criminal justice system and mental health institutions, the Mentally Ill Offender Treatment and Crime Reduction Act of 2004 provided funds so that law enforcement could receive additional training in order to better recognize and understand mental illness, and therefore respond in more appropriate ways to this population's needs. The act also included provisions for establishing mental health courts. In regard to the homeless, the legislative efforts have not been as direct. For example, the Matthew Shepard and James Byrd, Jr. Hate Crimes Prevention Act of 2009 was established to increase penalties against those who criminally offend due to a person's actual or perceived gender, sexual orientation, or disability. Therefore, this act covers the homeless within its broad umbrella. Despite all these efforts, it is clear that legislation alone, while necessary, cannot diminish the crimes committed against the elderly, homeless, and mentally ill in our society.

Undoubtedly, these special populations warrant our attention in the criminal justice system and in the health professions. To better serve these groups, it is of utmost importance for members of the criminal justice community as well as the community at large to explore the epidemiology and etiology of victimization, so that in turn, crime prevention strategies can be developed and implemented. It is in this chapter that each special population is described, the research related to factors of victimization is discussed, and methods of crime prevention for each population are presented. While victimization of these special populations is the primary focus of the following discussion, these groups, just like any other group in our society, can also contribute to crime; and thus, the prevention strategies discussed here will tangentially address them as offenders where relevant.

CRIME PREVENTION AND THE ELDERLY

It is predicted that by 2020 there will be 65 million elderly Americans who will make up 20% of the total U.S. population. In 2009, the Census Bureau reported that elderly individuals comprised 12.9% of our population, which equals 1 in every 8 individuals. The term "elderly" can be defined in a few ways. In this chapter, an elderly person is defined as an individual who is 65 years of age or older, as stated by the Social Security Administration and the U.S. Census Bureau. The majority of these Americans are often referred to as "Baby Boomers," or those who were born between 1941 and 1960.

The elderly include both men and women whose required care ranges from no care or additional assistance to some who may be under the care of family or an in-home care provider, adult daycare, or who take residence at a retirement community or assisted living facility. It is important to consider that the process of aging is often unpredictable, and senior citizens may be impacted by the aging process in different ways. Some may be plagued with a severe disability or may have cognitive, mental, and emotional deficits, while others may have few to no aliments that hinder their daily activities.

When it comes to understanding the elderly, many researchers and senior citizen advocates claim that the elderly are virtually an ignored population (Davis & Medina-Ariza, 2001). In the field of criminal justice and criminology, this is due mostly to the fact that when examining rates of victimization, research indicates that younger individuals are at an increased risk of victimization versus an individual 65 or older (Bachman, Dillaway, & Lachs, 1998; Bachman & Meloy, 2008). Thus, some see little to no need to study and examine the elderly, as the focus has been and continues to be to examine the rates of crime and victimization of those in younger age categories. Nonetheless, research shows that the elderly are susceptible to being victims of a variety of crimes and possess a relatively high fear of crime (Dietz & Wright, 2005). Researchers have examined some of the most

---

BOX 16-1 The Role of the AARP

The website for the American Association of Retired Persons (AARP) contains information to assist the elderly in identifying risks associated with not only street crime, but financial fraud, email scams, and cyber-crime. For more information, visit www.aarp.org.

---

common crimes against the elderly, which include telemarketing and email scams, elder abuse, and some of the less common but still alarming crimes such as robbery, and even homicide.

According to the National Crime Prevention Council, senior citizens are the primary targets for telemarketing and email scams. This is of such great concern that it has been proclaimed as a leading concern by the American Association of Retired Persons (AARP). Con artists will purpose-fully reach out to older Americans and have perfected ways in which to solicit credit card numbers, Social Security numbers, and insurance information from them. Senior citizens may be victims of healthcare and investment fraud, reverse mortgage scams, funeral and cemetery fraud, and invest-ment scams, just to name a few.

The FBI's website has compiled numerous fraudulent schemes that telemarketers will use. Enticing phrases such as, "Act now or the offer won't be good" or, "You have won a free gift and you must send money now to receive it," are very common. Some will prey on senior citizens by appealing to their good nature and trustworthiness by disguising themselves as a local charity.

While senior citizens can be financially victimized by phone and email, they are often subject to numerous forms of elder abuse. Elder abuse, sometimes referred to as elder mistreatment, is de-fined as any intentional or negligent act by a known or unknown caregiver who causes harm or puts an elderly person at risk of harm (National Center on Elder Abuse, 2010). This includes physical abuse, emotional abuse, sexual abuse, neglect, and financial exploitation. Every year, the number of victims of elder abuse ranges from 500,000 to 2 million (Payne, 2005), the most common type of elderly abuse being neglect (National Center on Elder Abuse, 1997). Moreover, elderly women are more likely to be victims than men, and adult male children of the elderly are more likely to be the perpetrators of abuse.

The recent well-publicized case of actor Mickey Rooney highlights this ever-increasing prob-lem. Rooney, at age 90, testified in front of Congress on March 2, 2011 to being a victim of elder abuse. The actor claimed that his stepson had financially drained him over numerous years while depriving him of food and medicine. As a result of Rooney's efforts, the U.S. Senate's Committee on Aging was compelled to request $20 million in federal funds to create the Office of Elder Justice. This office, housed under the U.S. Department of Justice, would assist local law enforcement in protecting elders from financial, emotional, and physical abuse (Fleck & Schmidt, 2011).

Gainey and Payne (2006) highlight multiple factors that predispose a person to commit el-der abuse, including offenders who have drug or mental health problems, are dependent on their elder(s), have experienced a history of family violence, caregiver burden, and stress. The authors further researched levels of stress associated with the care of the elderly with Alzheimer's or de-mentia compared to the elderly without any mental impairment. They concluded that regardless of whether the elder person had Alzheimer's or not, there were no differences in a caregiver's stress level. However, this is not to discount the fact that caring for individuals afflicted with Alzheimer's can be challenging.

For the elderly housed in assisted-care facilities, the perpetrators of elder abuse are often nurses' aides as opposed to nurses or doctors (Bachman & Meloy, 2008). Specifically, many nurses' aides have the most direct contact with the elderly resident. Perpetrators of elder abuse are characterized as young, with less education, and with less experience working with geriatric populations. In addition, they report higher levels of job dissatisfaction.

For some elderly women, there is an increased risk of being sexually assaulted by a male perpetrator. In a study of 284 male and female elderly victims, Burgess (2006) found that a majority of elderly women reported being victims of sexual abuse (61.4%). Most of the cases involved a person not known to the victim (26.1%) or a relative or family member (23.2%). There were fewer cases of abuse perpetrated by a staff member or unrelated care provider (10.9%). Similar to other studies, the vulnerability of the elderly is facilitated by their frailty, mental status and memory deficits, and their dependence on others to care for them.

With a growing senior citizen population, there are an increasing number of financial crimes committed against our senior citizens (Malks, Buckmaster, & Cunningham, 2003). Surprisingly, 60–90% of those who financially exploit the elderly are family members or those who provide in-home care, and the majority of victims are usually between the ages of 70 and 89. The following is a case history to illustrate this type of abuse:

> The 86-year-old Mr. H., whose name has been changed to protect his identity, came to live with his daughter in Santa Clara County after his wife died in Hawaii. Before long, his daughter amended his trust to name herself as co-trustee, prevailed upon him to deed a $300,000 beach-front cottage in Hawaii to her, had two vehicles transferred to her name, and made out checks totaling $85,000 to herself and her family members. (Malks et al., 2003, p. 66)

This case reinforces the notion that senior citizens can be exploited by sons, daughters, or other caregivers who have access to their bank accounts and any other financial assets. It cannot be forgotten that the scenario provided at the beginning of this chapter is also one that demonstrates how the elderly can be victimized in fraudulent and financially exploitative ways by those posing to be legitimate financial advisors.

In terms of property crimes, research shows that both men and women aged 65 and older are equally vulnerable to becoming victims of robbery, where clearly the motive is financial gain (Bachman et al., 1998). While robberies are more likely to be committed by those unknown to the elderly victim, assault victimizations against the elderly are often perpetrated by family members or acquaintances. Elderly victims of robbery more often than not require medical assistance, which is also more true for female elderly victims. Another important finding is that for elderly males, a weapon is more likely to be used when compared to all other age groups but they were not as likely to sustain any injuries. Conversely, for female elderly victims, there is a higher incidence of assaults committed by intimates and members of the family, whereas for elderly males, the perpetrator is more likely to be a stranger.

To reiterate, elderly homicide rates are much lower than those of their younger counterparts. However, taking a closer look at the National Crime Victimization Survey (NCVS) and Supplementary Homicide Reports data, Bachman and Meloy (2008) found that in comparison to younger individuals, in homicide cases, the elderly are more likely to be injured by way of a knife stabbing or blunt object, more likely to be victimized by a stranger, and more likely to be a victim in a situation where another felony is being committed.

Primary and Secondary Prevention Efforts

Given the contextual characteristics and correlates of elderly crime victimization as previously discussed, there are a number of primary and secondary prevention methods that can be implemented in order to reduce future victimizations of the elderly (see Bachman & Meloy, 2008). Similar to any individual of any age group, there are precautions and preventative measures with which senior citizens can alter the physical and social environment to buffer themselves from criminals who are not known to them. These primary prevention techniques include, but are not limited to environmental manipulation, security or police patrols, and neighborhood watch programs.

One strategy to address the concerns of the elderly is to establish a senior citizen policing unit or senior citizen police advocate. Such initiatives have taken hold in Milwaukee, Wisconsin and East Providence, Rhode Island (Gilfillan, 1994), for example. The goal is to provide the elderly community with a trained police officer who not only responds to crimes against the elderly but works with the community's elderly population to educate them about fraud, increase home surveillance, and increase security. For example, in order to prevent fraud, the elderly are empowered as consumers to feel adequate in asking questions directly to the caller or salesperson. They are advised to never offer bank account numbers, credit card numbers, Social Security numbers, or any other personal information over the phone. Another way in which elderly fraud can be prevented is through Public Service Announcements from the National Crime Prevention Council for seniors, which explain how to distinguish legitimate phone calls from fraudulent telemarketing scams.

Because senior citizens can be victimized by their own family members or caregivers, they must be provided with additional tools and resources to protect themselves. To combat financial exploitation, one particular initiative created by the Department of Aging and Adult Services (DAAS) and supported by the U.S. Department of Justice, Office of Crime, known as FAST (Financial Abuse Specialist Team), has taken hold in some communities (Malks, Buckmaster, & Cunningham, 2003). In Santa Clara County, California, a FAST program was established in 1999 as the number of financial abuse cases was approaching an alarming 30%. The FAST team included multiple agencies such as DAAS, Adult Protective Services and Public Administrator/Guardian Conservator, the District Attorney's Office, and the County Counsel. A 24-hour hotline was created for reporting financial abuse using an outreach media campaign to provide the community with examples of elder abuse and proper reporting procedures. The goal of FAST is to provide a rapid response to ensure that any asset will be frozen and that any necessary litigation will be carried out swiftly and with little cost to the elderly victim.

Although rates of victimization are typically lower for senior citizens, there have been numerous efforts to assist elderly crime victims to prevent future offending and to reduce fear of crime (Bachman & Meloy, 2008). The U.S. Census reported that in 1993, the population of elderly was the highest (i.e., 19%) in Florida, Pennsylvania, Iowa, Rhode Island, and West Virginia. In these states and many others, it is not unusual for the local sheriff's department, local law enforcement, prosecuting attorneys, victim advocates, and social workers to integrate resources and create programs to assist and inform the elderly. For example, the Triad Program was created in the late 1980s among members of the International Association of Chiefs of Police (IACP), National Sheriffs' AARP (Cross, 1995). A framework was established so that "triads" could be formed in virtually any community where local law enforcement, sheriffs, and the elderly of the community could work together (Bachman & Meloy, 2008). With a triad in place, law enforcement and senior citizens can further establish advisory councils, called SALT (Seniors and Lawmen

Together). Such a support network aims to provide strategies for crime prevention and to create methods for victim assistance.

As reported by Acierno et al. (2010), there is an undeniable link between most forms of elder mistreatment and the lack of social support that exists for senior citizens in our communities. To thwart elder abuse, efforts such as connection with community resources, improved housing designs for older adults that maximize communal interaction, funding for familial and "community programs that bring together the elderly and their neighbors or family members, or—perhaps most important—affordable transportation" are necessary and may aid in other preventative efforts (Acierno et al., 2010, p. 295).

With respect to secondary prevention, research has clearly provided ways in which to identify risk factors and characteristics of potential offenders. One of the most important is to alleviate or reduce stress for family members who are coping with the care of a loved one and to reduce staff burnout at assisted living and retirement communities. Also, primary healthcare providers and in-home care providers need to know the signs of elder sexual abuse (Burgess, 2006). The elder person may exhibit psychological indicators such as distress, cognitive difficulties, withdrawal, or fear. Physical indicators also may be apparent, including evidence of forcible restraints being used to render the victim defenseless. Evidence of sexually transmitted disease may be apparent as well.

Additional recommendations can be inferred from the research. For instance, interventions need to be directed toward the victim and not focus solely on the stress of the caregiver or offender (Gainey & Payne, 2006). Here, a restorative justice model could be used in elder abuse cases. In this model, the community, victim, and offender engage in a cooperative process to repair the harm caused by crime. In situations where the elder person has an in-home caregiver or resides in a care facility, another commonsense approach is to conduct background checks among those who work with the elderly (Burgess, 2006).

CRIME PREVENTION AND THE HOMELESS

To some, the homeless are perceived as dirty wanderers, crazy drunkards, panhandlers, or vagrants who tarnish our society. To others, the homeless are victims of harsh economic conditions and deserving of charitable services, which many agencies in our society strive to provide. Because the indigent remain one of the most powerless groups in our society and dependent on the streets or those who provide shelter care, they are also extremely vulnerable to victimization. Regardless of the economic climate in our country, homelessness does not discriminate. Men, women, teenagers, children, or individuals of any race or ethnicity are susceptible to living a penniless life in both rural and urban areas.

Unlike counts of other subpopulations, exact figures about the number of homeless individuals in our country are more difficult to come by. This issue of innumerability has even plagued our U.S. Census Bureau, preventing them from acquiring a true estimate. One estimate provided by the National Alliance's 2007 study stated that there are approximately 750,000 people homeless on any given night. Much higher estimates are cited by the U.S. Department of Housing and Urban Development with estimates of approximately 2 million homeless. In addition, the National Center on Family Homelessness (2009) estimates that over 1.5 million children are homeless.

There are numerous ways in which the homeless can be defined. One point of contention is whether homelessness equates to the "shelter homeless" or the "street homeless" or both. The definition as stipulated by the McKinney-Vento Homeless Assistance Act (1987) encompasses both. This act states that a homeless person is:

(1) *an individual who lacks a fixed, regular, and adequate nighttime residence and; (2) an individual who has a primary nighttime residence that is—*
   (A) *a supervised publicly or privately operated shelter designed to provide temporary living accommodations (including welfare hotels, congregate shelters, and transitional housing for the mentally ill);*
   (B) *an institution that provides a temporary residence for individuals intended to be institutionalized; or*
   (C) *a public or private place not designed for, or ordinarily used as, a regular sleeping accommodation for human beings.*

In order to develop ways to prevent crimes against the homeless from occurring, it is important to examine the myriad factors that contribute to this condition. However, the risk factors that must be considered are sourced in larger social forces such as our economy, which often translates to the issue of homelessness being unequivocally linked to poverty. Data from 2009 indicated that the poverty rate is 14.3%, which translates to 44 million Americans or 1 in 7 individuals (DeNavas-Walt, Proctor, & Smith, 2010). Aside from these larger social issues that are interlocked with crime, many scholars have taken a closer look at the ways in which the homeless as a population are at risk of sexual and physical assault, robbery, and hate crimes.

In addition to the impact that the changing global and national economy has had on Americans, there are other risk factors that lead to homelessness. One major factor is the deinstitutionalization of the mentally ill, which will be discussed in more detail toward the end of the chapter. Furthermore, substance abuse, a history of childhood violence and disruption, gang activity, and unstable employment are other risk factors associated with homelessness (Dietz & Wright, 2005; Evans & Forsyth, 2004). Considering these reasons that relate to homelessness, there are then added factors to consider regarding their victimization. Victimization of the homeless in general is associated with the lack of a protective structure or dwelling, living in proximity to crime-prone areas, mental illness, previous victimizations, as well as high risk behaviors such as soliciting sex and substance abuse (Dietz & Wright, 2005; Kushel, Evans, Perry, Robertson, & Moss, 2003).

For youth, yet another background factor, running away from home, appears to be a precursor to their homeless state and life on the streets (Tyler & Johnson, 2004; Walsh & Donaldson, 2010). According to the National Safe Place annual report in 2009, 2.8 million youths ran away from home. Of those who entered the program, about 50% reported that they were asked to leave and told not to return home by their parents or guardians. These are youths who are referred to as "throwaways." In addition, most of the youths served were ages 15–17, white (43%) or African American (36%), and almost equally female (53%) and male (47%).

It has been established in the field of criminal justice and criminology that those with a history of victimization are often likely to be perpetrators of crime. This dyadic relationship was examined among 40 homeless youths in a study that employed semistructured interviews (Tyler & Johnson, 2004). The authors found that homeless youth offend for purposes of financial gain, for purposes of demonstrating invincibility, and for paybacks. Alternatively, homeless youths reported that they perceived they were victimized by others for reasons of financial gain, paybacks, and exploitation (most commonly sexual exploitation).

In a qualitative study of 42 homeless men and women, Evans and Forsyth (2004) found that men and women shared similarities and some differences in their victimization. They were equally victims of theft, yet men experienced robbery and assaults at a higher rate than women, who were more likely to be victims of sexual assault. For homeless women, the rate of being sexually assaulted is 3.5 times higher than women in the general population (Jasinski, Wesely, Mustaine, & Wright, 2005). In a study of 1,508 homeless men and women, sleeping outdoors increased the chances of victimization as did mental illness, such as schizophrenia or depression (Wenzel, Koegel, & Gelberg, 2000). For women, drug dependence was another major factor related to victimization and for men, it was alcohol dependence.

Among a larger sample of 974 homeless women in Los Angles County, California, Wenzel, Leake, and Gelberg (2001) found that living on the street for prolonged periods of time led to an increase in major violence. Major violence included incidents where a woman was beaten, kicked, bitten, choked, burned, or threatened with a weapon. Moreover, homeless women who experienced major violence during childhood were more prone to being violently victimized. Not surprisingly, engaging in panhandling activities and trading sex were predictors of major violence, also. These findings are also true for younger homeless women in that they have experienced major violence in the form of sexual victimization at higher rates than their male counterparts (Tyler, Whitbeck, Hoyt, & Cauce, 2004).

In contrast, there are additional issues pertinent to those who are 50 years of age and older and homeless (Dietz & Wright, 2005). Apparently, the differences between homeless men and women become less distinct with age. That is, older homeless men and women are equally likely to be victims of theft and physical assault. However, older homeless women are perceived to be an easy and defenseless target; therefore, there is an increased likelihood that they will be the victims of sexual assault.

With respect to hate crimes, a startling report was issued from the National Coalition for the Homeless (NCH) in August 2010. According to the NCH, from 1999–2010, approximately 1,074 acts of hate crime and bias/violence were committed against the homeless. Examples of these crimes are provided in the following box. Moreover, 291 homeless individuals died due to the injuries that they sustained from these attacks. The perpetrators of violent attacks against the homeless are often young (under 30 years of age) and male (98%). Many homeless are attacked due to their racial or ethnic background, religious beliefs, or sexual orientation. Victims of hate crimes are typically males who are in their 40s. Like other populations discussed in this chapter, what compounds this problem is the lack of reporting crimes that occur against the homeless.

Primary and Secondary Prevention Efforts

Preventing crimes against the homeless may be one of the most challenging issues for members of the criminal justice system in the 21st century. A major impediment is that the homeless are a marginalized and stigmatized population, typically blamed for their own situation. Moreover, they are easy crime targets since they live day to day without any means of protecting themselves. Protection and safety then fall on homeless shelters, social workers, medical personnel, the police, and victim advocates. With this said, the prevention strategies to combat crimes against the homeless are plentiful, yet the resources to implement them are lacking. The few crime prevention initiatives and programs presented here are ones that take into account gender-specific programming, depression and other mental illnesses, substance abuse, and previous childhood victimization.

BOX 16-2 Hate Crimes and the Homeless

- **Teen Bragged About Killing Homeless Man**

  COLORADO SPRINGS, COLORADO—February 5, 2009. David Doyle, fifty-five, was sleeping on a pedestrian bridge when Taylor Lane Gwaltney, nineteen, biked past him; Gwaltney later returning to kill Doyle, hitting him up to sixteen times with a skateboard. Gwaltney, then, bragged to over a dozen other teens that he had "killed a bum." Doyle was a local dirt bike racer in the 70's and 80's and worked in Colorado Springs for years before recently becoming homeless. Many community members and friends gathered together in honor of Doyle after his death. Gwaltney was convicted of first-degree murder and received a mandatory life sentence without parole.

- **Student Kills Homeless Man Based on Prejudice**

  HOUSTON, TEXAS—February 7, 2009. A thirty-two year-old university student has been charged in the early morning killing of a forty-seven year-old homeless man named Joe Tall. Jeremy Lee Pierce remains jailed after being formally charged with the shooting murder. Joe Tall was found lying on a Metro bus bench with at least one bullet hole in his head on the University of Houston campus. He was discovered by a student riding his bike to work when he noticed blood dripping from the victim. The school has offered any video recordings from their 500 on-campus security cameras for use in the Houston Police Department investigation. The murder of Tall is being referred to by investigators as a "thrill kill." Pierce was known by other students as an aggressive individual and is quoted as saying that the homeless are a "blight to society."

- **Two Homeless Men Attacked and One Murdered**

  SAN FRANCISCO, CALIFORNIA—February 15, 2009. Police believe four men were involved in an extremely aggressive assault on two homeless men. One homeless man was able to escape the assailants with minimal injuries but Peter Azadian, fifty-seven, who had been living under a door frame in the area, later died at a hospital. His death was caused by blunt force impacts.

- **Homeless Women Murdered in Brutal Beatings**

  GALVESTON, TEXAS—February 20, 2009. An inmate has been charged in connection with the murder of two homeless women. The women were fifty-six and fifty-one years old and their bodies were found fifteen days apart, on February 5th and on February 20th, near vacant houses. According to police, homeless people have been using the houses as refuge from the elements. David Ray Williams, twenty-two years-old, allegedly murdered two women by beating them around their neck, face, and head. The bodies of the women were discovered by children playing in the building and by an electric meter worker, respectively. Police believe that the women were sexually assaulted based on the haggard condition of their clothing. Patrols were increased in the area in the hopes of finding potential leads but the case broke when DNA evidence linking Williams to the murder was discovered.

Source: Hate crimes against the homeless. National Coalition for the Homeless, 2010, p. 20.

One prevention program that provides prevention and outreach to homeless youth is known as National Safe Place (NSP) (Walsh & Donaldson, 2010). With 138 Safe Place programs in 38 states, and approximately 17,000 national sites, homeless youth on the street can identify the diamond-shaped yellow and black logo and seek help. Trained volunteers assist youths by connecting them to resources such as counseling or shelters. Additional services provided by the NSP include a

"Txt 4 Help" initiative that links over 200 emergency youth shelters. Programs such as these take youths off the streets and can get them the help they need; hopefully, before they are victimized or revictimized.

For homeless women it is imperative that interventions are ready to address their vulnerability to sexual and physical assault and at the same time address the coexisting problems such as drug and alcohol abuse that further deepen their likelihood of being victimized (Wenzel et al., 2001). Many advocate for safe and regulated housing or shelter care that may reduce the rate of sexual assault among younger and older women (Dietz & Wright, 2005; Evans & Forsyth, 2004; Kushel et al., 2003). Moreover, screenings administered in these shelters or in a healthcare setting can be implemented so that a determination can be made about the extent to which a woman has experienced childhood and adult violence.

This approach falls in line with the recommendation that violence prevention needs to be gender specific. As noted by Wenzel et al. (2000), the antecedents for homeless men and women are similar in some respects but different in others. Therefore, comprehensive assistance plans need to be created and tailored to men and women. This extends naturally to substance abuse and mental illness treatment, training and education opportunities, and safe and permanent residences.

A more progressive approach to providing the homeless with an avenue of safety is presented in a study by Eyrich-Garg (2010). With the known lack of access to a permanent mailing address, landline, or mobile phone, a sample of nonsheltered homeless men and women were provided with mobile phones in an effort to address physical and mental health needs. At least 14 of the 100 homeless men and women reported that having a mobile phone was important for safety reasons and could be used as a vehicle to report attacks. Similar use of cell phones has been carried out with domestic violence shelters. Ultimately, the provision of cell phones for the homeless allows them to be reconnected. And, as mentioned earlier in the discussion about the elderly, the purpose of providing a mobile phone would be to increase social support.

As first responders, the police are often needed to assist the homeless. In-service and specialized trainings are needed for law enforcement about how to respond to the noncriminal homeless with the resources they need, and at the same time, respond effectively to the concerns of the public when the homeless have violated the law. Regarding the latter, the Los Angeles police department has had to address this issue as it has one of the most well-known and largest concentrated encampments of homeless individuals in the country, a place known as skid row (Berk & MacDonald, 2010). Due to the number of public nuisance crimes committed by the homeless, including public intoxication, loitering, panhandling, prostitution, public urination, vandalism, etc., the LA police targeted the homeless encampments with a strategy known as the Safer Cities Initiative (SCI).

BOX 16-3 National Safe Place

Until our streets are safe ... Until families can understand each other ... Until drugs and violence disappear ... Until no young person needs to run away or feel afraid ... There must be Safe Place.

—From the website of National Safe Place

National Safe Place is an outreach program targeting runaway youths by providing safe locations where they can go, rather than living a homeless, unsafe existence on the streets. Furthermore, their mission includes a proactive approach aiming to educate youth about the dangers of running away before it occurs. For more information, see www.nationalsafeplace.org.

SCI began in 2005 as a pilot project called Main Street Pilot Project and after some success in its implementation was launched on a wider scale in 2006 (Berk & MacDonald, 2010). For the most part, the initiative involved increasing the number of police officers in downtown LA as well as increasing the number of undercover vice squads and special undercover officers who could combat open drug markets, prostitution, and local robberies. According to Berk and MacDonald, using a targeted approach was successful in reducing crimes without displacing the problem to other parts of the city. Despite the success of SCI, the authors caution that this type of initiative essentially does not address the root of the problem, which is homelessness:

> *In our view, the wisdom of such police action depends on what services are made available to the homeless. . . . Getting the homeless off the streets and into shelters is probably a sensible stop-gap approach. In practice, however, there will often be too few shelter beds. Then, the appropriate public policy will require difficult trade-offs. There is also the matter of costs. (Berk & MacDonald, 2010, p. 835)*

While aggressive policing strategies may remove the homeless from the streets and into shelters, it is possible that primary prevention efforts such as these may not be the most effective. That is, criminalizing homelessness may in fact send the wrong message and enable citizens with bias and violence-motivated desires to justify their actions as they take on a sort of vigilante role in crime fighting, perceiving the homeless as the "enemy." For example, according to a report on hate crime by the National Coalition for the Homeless (2010):

> *Many cities in Florida have enacted severe anti-camping, panhandling, antifeeding, and other criminalization of homelessness laws . . . In fact, four of the ten meanest cities identified in Homes Not Handcuffs were cities in Florida. Florida is also the state with the highest number of bias-motivated crimes against homeless individuals. One possible explanation for this is the message that criminalizing homelessness sends to the general public: 'Homeless people do not matter and are not worthy of living in our city.' This message is blatant in the attitudes many cities have toward homeless people and can be used as an internal justification for attacking someone who is homeless. (p. 17)*

Evans and Forsyth (2004) make similar arguments and echo that the problem of homelessness will not be ameliorated simply by warehousing them in jail. Instead, policies and programs need not only to address social problems but to ensure that the homeless maintain normative ties to the social structure.

As mentioned, hate crimes and the prevention of these offenses necessitate further discussion. However, a detailed discussion is beyond the scope of this chapter, so readers are encouraged to pursue additional sources beyond what is provided in the reference list (see Levin & McDevitt, 2002, for example).

Hate crimes or bias-motivated crimes as defined currently in the United States, are criminal acts committed against a person or property based on an offender's bias toward another person or group due to their real or perceived status on the basis of race, religion, sexual orientation, ethnicity/national origin, and disability. The first piece of hate crime legislation was enacted by the U.S. Congress in 1968, calling for federal officers to investigate and prosecute crimes motivated by race, color, religion, or national origin. Recognizing the seriousness and nature of these crimes, Congress also passed the Hate Crime Statistics Act (HCSA) in 1990, mandating that the U.S. Attorney General establish guidelines for collecting and compiling hate crime data on an annual basis. In turn, the FBI was designated to gather such information via the Uniform Crime Reporting (UCR) program. With the passing of the Violent Crime Control and Law Enforcement Act of 1994, Congress further amended that the HCSA include hate crime victims who have a disability. However, as stated earlier in this chapter, the definition does not include marginalized groups such as the homeless.

In 2009, the FBI's report revealed that there were 8,336 victims of hate crimes, and of these, 4,793 were crimes against persons, while the remaining were crimes against property. The majority of personal crimes involved intimidation (45%) or simple assault (35.3%), whereas for property crimes the majority involved destruction/vandalism (83.7%). When official statistics are referenced, it is important to note that these figures most likely underestimate the actual number of hate crimes since many go unreported to police (Steinberg, Brooks, & Remtulla, 2003).

The largest number of hate crimes are committed due to a person's race (48.8%; 4,057 victims), followed by religion (18.9%; 1,575 victims), sexual orientation (17.8%; 1,482 victims), ethnicity/national origin (13.3%; 1,109 victims), and disability (1.2%; 99 victims) (U.S. Department of Justice—Federal Bureau of Investigation, 2009). Unlike nonbias crimes, victims of hate crime are more likely to sustain greater physical injury as a result of an attack. Also, the attacks are often far more assaultive and brutal in nature. In addition, victims of hate crimes are more likely to experience greater psychological harm (i.e., posttraumatic stress, etc.) compared to those who are victims of nonbias crimes. Most hate crimes take place in or near residences or homes and are disproportionately committed by teens and youth in their 20s (Steinberg et al., 2003).

When examining the data further, homosexual males are the most targeted population when it comes to hate crimes based on sexual orientation (Willis, 2004), and African Americans are more likely to be targeted on the basis of race (Steinberg et al., 2003). Even though these groups are frequently at risk, it cannot be ignored that transgendered individuals, Asians, Hispanics, and immigrants are similarly victims of bias-motivated crimes. Hate crime victims who have a disability face similar risks as do the elderly. In essence, they are at an increased risk of sexual, physical, and emotional abuse. It may be that the victim's condition is targeted and not necessarily their "person" (McMahan et al., 2004). Last, of the crimes that are committed on the basis of religion, the events of September 11, 2001 have produced a surge of anti-Muslim intolerance that continues to plague our country even after a decade.

In the field of criminal justice and criminology, one single causal explanation is typically difficult to pinpoint, but for bias-motivated crimes, the underlying factor is simple: hate. Research has only begun to fully comprehend how hate manifests into anger, intimidation, aggression, and sometimes violence. What researchers have often turned up is that hate crimes are bred by negative attitudes and stereotypes, ethnocentrism, and generalizations about others. Built-up anger and resentment may reach a point too, where violence is seen as a legitimate outlet for the hate felt toward another person or group. Even with the knowledge of these factors, the solution to combating hate crimes is not simple. Bias-motivated crimes are far more complex since they involve deep-rooted normative behaviors and attitudes that are socially and culturally transmitted.

In terms of hate crime prevention, over the past several decades law enforcement and prosecutors have teamed up to create a better systems response via training, protocol development, and innovative programs. These efforts signal the willingness and determination to quell hate crimes and to rid society of the barriers and attitudes that nourish hate. The International Association of Chiefs of Police (IACP), the Department of Justice, the American Prosecutors' Research Institute, and the Bureau of Justice Assistance are but a few agencies invested in producing the necessary mechanisms to improve law enforcement and prosecutorial practices. For instance, the Department

---

BOX 16-4 Hate and Violence

For more information on hate crimes, visit the website of Dr. Jack Levin at www.jacklevinonviolence.com. Levin is the Irving and Betty Brudnick Professor of Sociology and Criminology as well as co-director of the Brudnick Center on Violence and Conflict at Northeastern University.

---

of Justice distributed a national training curriculum for police officers that includes topics such as the history of hate crimes, identifying hate crimes, legal issues, investigation techniques and evidence protection, and improving community relations (Wessler, 2000).

Monitoring the activities of hate groups and handing over valuable information to law enforcement and the media is an important element in stopping hate crimes before they occur. The Southern Law Poverty Center (SLPC), a nonprofit civil rights organization founded in 1971, tracks the activities (i.e., publications, meetings, rallies, speeches, criminal acts) of hate groups and produces educational materials to teach tolerance, among other services. Furthermore, they produce an updated "hate map" that charts the types and numbers of hate groups around the country. To date, the SLPC has reported over 1000 active hate groups in the United States.

Moreover, the National Crime Prevention Council (NCPC) (2011) offers several hate crime prevention strategies. They range from tolerance and diversity education to raising cultural awareness and counseling hate group offenders. For purposes of education, activities and lesson plans are provided on the website for school-aged children and teens. The council reports that children ages 4–9 are best suited for curriculum-based education on diversity before deep-rooted stereotypes take hold. Such a curriculum reinforces prosocial messages about race, gender, culture, and religious differences. Children perform critical thinking exercises and role playing exercises to build a greater understanding of tolerance in an effort to ultimately reduce bigotry. Another effort is to build effective communication and trust among law enforcement and immigrant communities so that cultural awareness can be attained. Because of a lack of trust and fear of police, many crimes or suspicious activities go unreported. By holding community meetings, police, translators, and interpreters can work together to strengthen communication, and at the same time reduce any barriers. Last, the NCPC offers guidance on implementing a counseling program for hate crime offenders or potential offenders. These programs challenge deeply entrenched belief systems that have evolved into hatred and help to broaden the offender or potential offender's views about race, culture, and religion.

Another possible solution is to engage conflicting persons or groups in a restorative justice dialogue (Coates, Umbriet, & Vos, 2006). This novel approach to breaking down hate is one of open dialogue. Restorative justice is a concept that involves establishing offender accountability and restitution or reparation to the victim or community through a process of mediation. A restorative justice dialogue is one where the community, victim, and offender gather in family group conferencing or peacemaking circles for face-to-face discourse. Prior to the exchange of dialogue, preparatory meetings take place. Cases that are more serious may involve several preparatory meetings as well as several dialogue sessions. The process typically begins with the victim having an opportunity to express the details of how he or she was harmed, etc. Then, the offender has an opportunity to explain the situation or circumstances that led to the offense. Once each side has an opportunity to express their point of view, then hopefully hatred can be overcome with understanding and respect so that future negative behaviors will be prevented.

Clearly hate crimes mark some of the most insidious behaviors that law enforcement, community leaders, and the general public have to combat. Overall, researchers conclude that negative attitudes beget hatred, where hatred begets violence, and so on. To deescalate violence and restore communities to a more peaceful and tranquil environment, an ongoing and cooperative endeavor must continue to plant the seeds for tolerance and understanding.

CRIME PREVENTION AND THE MENTALLY ILL

Persons with a mental disability or illness are a misunderstood population. This misunderstanding largely stems from media representations, a lack of knowledge about mental illness, and preconceived notions of this special population that often result in labeling their behavior as "mad and bad." Since negative stereotypes often prevail, it is easy to assume that those with a mental illness are not only incapable of reasoning but are violent and dangerous to society (Choe, Templin, & Abram, 2008). These misconceptions are even more problematic if members of law enforcement possess them, especially when responding to a call that involves a person struggling with a diminished capacity for coping with and resolving issues (Ruiz & Miller, 2004).

Mental illness can be defined in simple terms as "medical conditions that disrupt a person's thinking, feeling, mood, ability to relate to others and daily functioning" (National Alliance on Mental Illness, 2011). More specifically, a mental illness is a diagnosable psychiatric condition (for which a psychiatrist will use the *Diagnostic and Statistical Manual-IV* or DSM-IV), which impairs an individual's normal cognitive, emotional, or behavioral functioning, and is caused by physiological or psychosocial factors. Other terms like *mental disease*, *mental disorder*, or *mental disability* also are used in reference to those who are afflicted with such impairments. For those specializing in the field of mental health, there are deeper nuances associated with the use of these terms. Nonetheless, a person plagued with a mental illness may experience profound negative consequences such as disorganized thought patterns, impulsivity, difficulty with problem solving, and the inability to accurately perceive risks (Teplin, McClelland, Abram, & Weiner, 2005).

According to the DSM-IV, these disorders may include but are not limited to mood disorders, dissociative disorders, anxiety disorders, and psychotic disorders such as schizophrenia. Given the numerous disorders diagnosed by psychiatrists, only a few are described here.

Mood disorders like bipolar disorder are marked by periods of drift between elevated feelings of euphoria to periods of major depression. During the more euphoric periods, a person suffering from bipolar disorder (manic depression) is susceptible to making very rash personal and business decisions as they adopt a sense of inferiority. For those afflicted with a dissociative disorder (sometimes referred to as multiple personality disorder), the person suffers from distinct identities that take control of the person depending on the situation, without the person being consciously aware that this is happening. Sadly, the disorder is brought on by severe trauma or psychological stress during childhood. In many cases the child was a victim of extreme sexual or physical abuse. On the other hand, anxiety disorders, such as posttraumatic stress disorder (PTSD), are caused by a traumatic event that produced intense fear and helplessness. Those afflicted with PTSD have reoccurring thoughts or flashbacks of the traumatic incident, exhibit increased anxiety, and are oftentimes easily startled. Last, schizophrenia is known to begin during young adolescence and early adulthood. The person suffers from delusions, hallucinations, disorganized behaviors, and disorganized speech patterns.

Given the nationwide initiative to deinstitutionalize mental healthcare facilities in the 1950s and 1960s, treatment for the mentally ill shifted from mental health institutions to community outpatient care centers, increased use of psychotropic medications, and other more cost-effective community-based alternatives (Ruiz & Miller, 2004). Thus, a number of mentally disordered individuals were released from mental hospitals that closed their doors, leaving the mentally ill to rely on the care of family, friends, and community outpatient facilities (Silver, 2002). For those who do not have sufficient community resources or access to outpatient care, homelessness may be the end result, complicating the matter even more.

The National Alliance on Mental Illness (NAMI) (2011) estimates that 57.7 million adults will have symptoms of a diagnosable mental illness in a given year. Roughly, this means that 1 in 4 American adults experience a mental health disorder. Of the different types of mental illness, anxiety disorders—which include PTSD—phobias, and obsessive compulsive disorders affect most American adults (about 18.7% or 40 million individuals), followed by major depressive disorder (6.7% or 14.8 million individuals).

To date, a great deal of research has exclusively focused on the mentally ill as perpetrators rather than victims of crime (Choe et al., 2008). However, the research clearly demonstrates that the mentally ill who perpetuate violence range from 2.3% to 13%, whereas violent victimization of the mentally ill ranges from 8.2% to 55% (Choe et al., 2008; Teplin et al., 2005). Research conducted by Teplin and colleagues is worth mentioning in more detail since it utilized the National Crime Victimization Survey (NCVS) and distributed it to 936 selected patients at random. The majority of respondents were from outpatient or residential mental health facilities in Chicago. Results were then compared to over 32,000 respondents from the annual NCVS, which is conducted by the Bureau of Census in conjunction with the Bureau of Justice Statistics (BJS). Annual rates of violent crime victimization are 11 times higher for those individuals who have a severe mental illness compared to the general population and they are 4 times more likely to be victims of property crimes (Teplin et al., 2005). In comparison to victims as a whole, those who have a serious mental illness are more likely to be violently victimized at or near their home and by a person known to them. What is more troubling is that the victimization is less likely to be reported to the police, and the mentally disabled person is more likely to be victimized again.

Clearly, these findings lead one to wonder why the mentally ill are so vulnerable to victimization. With the impairments to a person's internal processes and perceptions, the mentally ill are easy targets. They are weaker in a sense as they have a diminished ability to protect themselves or use self-defense tactics. Also, it is speculated that they are less likely to report their victimization to police and that some may actually fear the police due to their mental illness (Silver, Arseneault, Langley, Caspi, & Moffitt, 2005).

BOX 16-5 Miranda

Students of criminal justice will no doubt be familiar with the name Ernesto Miranda, from whose case the Miranda Warnings originate (*Miranda v. Arizona*, 1966). What most may not know is that his victim was an 18-year-old mentally disabled woman. With the notoriety that the Miranda decision brought to the rights of suspects in terms of self-incrimination, the susceptibility of the victim due to mental impairment often has been overlooked.

Among the mentally ill who receive outpatient and inpatient care, susceptibilities to physical assault, sexual assault, and robbery are most common (Choe et al., 2008). The mentally ill who are homeless report being victims of physical or sexual abuse, robbery, theft, and being threatened with a weapon. In comparison to those who do not have a mental illness, individuals who have an anxiety disorder are more likely to be victims of sexual assaults, and those who have schizophrenia are more likely to be threatened with physical assault or actually physically assaulted (Silver et al., 2005).

When a mentally ill person is victimized, it may exacerbate other mental health conditions (Perron, Alexander-Eitzman, Gillespie, & Pollio, 2008; Teplin et al., 2005). For instance, when a person is a victim of theft, or is threatened with a weapon, it brings on depression. The mentally ill who are robbed by force or physically and sexually assaulted are more likely to experience lower levels of perceived safety. Aside from bringing on a sense of fear, victimization also has been found to be most frequently associated with alcohol/drug abuse, homelessness, and symptoms of severe mental illness (Choe et al., 2008; Cordner, 2006; Maniglio, 2009; Teplin et al., 2005) in addition to factors like conflicted social relationships.

It is estimated that about 25% of all homeless people have a mental illness (National Resource and Training Center on Homelessness and Mental Illness, 2003). This relationship also exists among homeless youth and in some ways has been shown to be much more prevalent in that group. Rates of psychiatric disorders range from 66% to 89% among the homeless youth population (Cauce, 2000). For many of these homeless youths, in tandem with their mental illness, they possess a substance abuse problem. In a study of homeless and mentally ill youths in Denver, Colorado, the majority reported marijuana as the drug of choice, followed by alcohol, nicotine, and methamphetamine (Merscham, Van Leeuwen, & McGuire, 2009). A significant relationship also was found for bipolar youth and their preference for polysubstances (i.e., abuse of three or more substances over a 12-month period). Youths with PTSD preferred to use heroin.

Recently, research studies have also pinpointed those who have a "severe mental illness" (SMI) as having an increased likelihood of victimization (Maniglio, 2009; Teplin et al., 2005). This term encompasses those who have a schizophrenia, schizoaffective disorder, manic depressive disorder, severe forms of panic disorder, and obsessive-compulsive disorder. In over a half a dozen different studies, those who have a diagnosable psychotic disorder such as schizophrenia were more likely to be victimized violently than those without a mental disorder in the general population (Maniglio, 2009). Further, victimization of those with SMI was often related to drug and/or alcohol abuse, homelessness, severe clinical symptoms, and criminal behavior.

Silver (2002) also found that the mentally ill are more likely to be violently victimized when they are involved in highly conflicted social relationships with family, friends, and other caretakers than nonmentally disordered individuals. The impact is even greater when the victim consumes illegal drugs. In essence, a mentally disordered individual who uses illegal drugs has more tumultuous and strained relationships with their family, friends, or caregivers. The additional strain produces negative emotions on the part of these individuals and results in increased social control against the mentally disabled that often is more violent in nature.

Primary and Secondary Prevention Efforts

When it comes to persons with mental illness, reducing criminal opportunity is a daunting task. Crime prevention methods must be created with a clear understanding of the factors that lead to the victimization of the mentally ill and must be built on comprehensive measures that work, while avoiding the ones that simply penalize those who are sick. The conservative and quick-fix approach has been to incarcerate the mentally ill. Roughly half of the inmates in state prison report having a mental illness, which is about five times higher than in the non-incarcerated adult population (Human Rights Watch, 2006). Among female prisoners, the rates of mental illness are even higher than those for their male counterparts. The bottom line is that for either men or women, prisons and jails are ill-equipped to provide adequate treatment.

As mentioned throughout this chapter, all-encompassing crime prevention strategies and techniques need to be created, and with the mentally ill, there is no exception. First, social program investments by our government need to continue to improve the existing mental health treatment establishments that exist in the United States. Outpatient and inpatient care remain at the forefront in protecting our mentally ill by providing them and their families the care and support they need (Wallace, 2007). It is imperative that these programs continue to receive the funding and support necessary to improve patient treatment practices, hire qualified staff, and develop better community outreach. Second, mental health facilities need to establish skills-based prevention programs, especially for persons with SMI (Teplin et al., 2005). Based on the research, high-risk groups need to be educated about the ways that they can improve or manage their own safety. And, special attention must be paid to those who have a drug/alcohol problem, for instance. In those cases where the person is homeless, shelter staff can assist the mentally ill with monitoring their activities and referring them to additional resources, if necessary. Last, improving law enforcement practices by means of developing collaborative mechanisms between the mental health system and the criminal justice system, reducing negative stereotypes about the mentally ill, and training are essential (Teplin et al., 2005). For the latter, most of these law enforcement efforts are under the umbrella of community policing.

Because law enforcement personnel are the first responders in most situations, the safety of the community and the needs of the mentally ill must be carefully balanced (Cordner, 2006). With a limited response time, police officers must use their discretion to make a decision about the best way to respond to the mentally ill. Police may be called to deal with background factors such as drug and alcohol abuse that have aggravated the person's condition. The police officer then must be fully equipped and trained to respond informatively and tactfully. If appropriate training and attitudes are lacking, the tendency is to criminalize the mentally ill. For law enforcement "this reasonability thrusts them into the role of primary gatekeepers who determine whether the mental health or the criminal justice system can best meet the needs of the individual with acute psychiatric problems" in which case, training is essential (Lamb, Weinberger, & DeCuir, 2002, p. 1266).

Known as Crisis Intervention Team (CIT) Training, this program was developed in 1988 by the Memphis, Tennessee Police Department to provide police officers with better tools and resources to assist the mentally ill, which had repeatedly proved to be challenging (Ketteler & Dodge, 2009). Today there are as many as 24 CIT programs in major cities across the United States. While

---

BOX 16-6 Office of Community Oriented Policing Services

The Office of Community Oriented Policing Services (COPS), under the U.S. Department of Justice, published a guide in 2006 for law enforcement personnel called "People with Mental Illness." This resource examines the various types of situations that police may encounter when dealing with the mentally ill, not just as offenders, but as victims of crime. This manual can be downloaded from the website at www.cops.usdoj.gov.

the program may vary from jurisdiction to jurisdiction, it involves 45 hours of training that includes recognizing mental illness symptoms, crisis intervention, mental health resources, and role-playing activities. Moreover, police officers learn how to use tactics that will deescalate a situation as opposed to imposing force, which has been shown to exacerbate the symptoms of a mentally ill person. Overall, the CIT program has been shown to be effective in reducing stigma and stereotypes, decreasing the use of deadly force and restraints, as well as producing lower arrest rates.

Another method is to use a mobile crisis team or specialized unit of police that involves the cooperation of mental health professionals to reduce criminalization and at the same time to resolve the concerns that were initially brought to the police officer's attention (Lamb et al., 2002). The success of this approach is marked by diverting the mentally ill to the appropriate healthcare resources as opposed to jail. However, some speculate that these units may result in an increased number of arrests compared to those that do not use a team approach.

To conclude, television and news media tend to portray those with mental illnesses as deranged and violent offenders. Yet, it must be noted that incidents that represent this stereotype make up a very small fraction of all violent attacks in the United States (Cordner, 2006). In other words, the mentally ill are not all violent and criminal. At the same time, police officers are quite fearful of persons with a mental illness because they believe that most are unpredictable and dangerous. Yet, those with a mental illness also may fear the police. "Neither has an understanding of the other, and this can set the stage for a physical confrontation" (Ruiz & Miller, 2004, p. 360).

SUMMARY

After reading this chapter, one can deduce that preventing crimes against special populations is a complex undertaking. Furthermore, crime prevention strategies for the mentally ill, homeless, and the elderly are largely unstudied and underdeveloped. While primary preventative measures can be taken such as changing the physical environment or altering an exterior's design with increased surveillance, lighting, alarms, locks, etc., in many instances, these subpopulations are frequently dependent on others to provide a safe space. In some cases, such as with the unsheltered homeless, preventative measures are null and void. There are no windows to close or doors to lock. However, it can be argued that preventative measures can be taken by the shelters and healthcare facilities that are responsible for caring for these groups.

What may prove to be the best preventative approach is the use of secondary measures; that is, identifying risk factors and predicting the ways in which individuals are vulnerable to victimization may be the best line of defense in protecting these groups. Based on the current efforts to prevent crime against these special populations, nothing is more certain than the need to have the substantive knowledge about what plagues a person who is aging, homeless, or mentally disabled. In addition, while many criminal justice majors turn to the noble cause of law enforcement, it is equally important that majors seek employment in other professions, such as advocacy and social service, which are just as important.

Many of the programs and strategies described in this chapter are "victim-centered." Specifically, they are aimed at shielding the vulnerable person from dangerous criminals and from family members who do not genuinely care for them. To combat elder abuse, a coordinated community response among law enforcement, prosecutors, social services, victim's advocates, and medical personnel is required (Davis & Medina-Ariza, 2001). For the homeless, preventative strategies need to be two-fold: they need to be invested in addressing the factors that lead to homelessness, plus the factors that lead to their victimization while living on the streets or in shelters. For the mentally ill, the take-home message to crime prevention is simple. Criminal justice and mental health care professionals must continue collaborative efforts in their communities. With law enforcement, existing efforts must be bolstered by better training so that officers will be more equipped to make decisions about the mentally ill who are at risk to themselves or others, and with the mental health community, providing adequate inpatient and outpatient services (Lamb et al., 2002).

Legislatively speaking, tertiary efforts by way of increasing sanctions for those who assault or offend against a special population or increasing incapacitation for those who are likely to reoffend is another approach that has been taken. However, it seems that our society still takes a "blaming the victim approach," which inhibits our ability to combat crimes perpetrated against a particular group. With this mindset, the costs to victims and society are likely to continue.

With technology expanding exponentially, it is likely that more researchers, legislators, and victim advocates will continue to think outside the box and develop crime prevention methods that will ultimately reduce victimizations. While there are still many challenges, considerable progress has been made in protecting these special groups, especially by numerous grassroots organizations and victim advocacy agencies. However, these advocate groups cannot go about this alone; crime prevention requires a total commitment by the individual, the criminal justice system, and the community.

KEY TERMS

Elder abuse
Telemarketing Fraud Bill
Crisis intervention team
Community Oriented Policing
Homelessness
National Safe Place
Safer Cities Initiative
Hate Crime Statistics Act
Southern Poverty Law Center
National Crime Prevention Council
Restorative justice
Mental illness

DISCUSSION QUESTIONS

1. What factors are associated with elder abuse? Why are the elderly targeted?
2. Why are the homeless blamed for their homeless state and in essence for their own victimization?
3. How is the issue of crimes against the mentally ill affected by the issue of homelessness?
4. Who must be involved in developing effective and comprehensive crime prevention strategies? Why?
5. Why is crime prevention for special populations so challenging?

REFERENCES

Acierno, R., Hernandez, M. A., Amstadter, A. B., Resnick, H. S., Steve, K., Muzzy, W., & Kilpatrick, D. G. (2010, February). Prevalence and correlates of emotional, physical, sexual, and financial abuse and potential neglect in the United States: The National Elder Mistreatment Study. *American Journal of Public Health, 100*(2), 292–297.

Bachman, R., Dillaway, H., & Lachs, M. S. (1998). Violence against the elderly: A comparative analysis of robbery and assault across age and gender groups. *Research on Aging, 20*(2), 183–198. doi:10.1177/0164027598202002

Bachman, R., & Meloy, M. L. (2008). Implications for primary and secondary prevention. *Journal of Contemporary Criminal Justice, 24*(2), 186–197. doi:10.1177/1043986208315478

Berk, R., & MacDonald, J. (2010). Policing the homeless: An evaluation of efforts to reduce homeless-related crime. *Criminology & Public Policy, 9*(4), 813–840.

Burgess, A. W. (2006, December). *Elderly victims of sexual abuse and their offenders.* Washington, DC: National Institute of Justice, Office of Justice Programs (Award No. 2003-WG-BX-1007).

Cauce, A. M. (2000). The characteristics and mental health of homeless adolescents: Age and gender differences. *Journal of Emotional & Behavioral Disorders, 8,* 1063–4266.

Choe, J. Y., Teplin, L. A., & Abram, K. M. (2008). Perpetration of violence, violent victimization, and severe mental illness: Balancing public health concerns. *Psychiatric Services, 59*(2), 153–164.

Coates, R. B., Umbreit, M. S., & Vos, B. (2006). Responding to hate crimes through restorative dialogue. *Contemporary Justice Review, 9*(1), 7–21.

Cordner, G. (2006). *People with mental illness.* U. S. Department of Justice Office of Community Oriented Policing Services. Retrieved from http://www.cops.usdoj.gov/files/RIC/Publications/e04062003.pdf.

Cross, W. M. (1995, January). Crimes against the elderly: Is the criminal justice system doing all we can? (SLP-3). Florida Criminal Justice Executive Institute's Senior Leadership Program Research. Retrieved from http://www.fdle.state.fl.us/Content/getdoc/508f8695-2877-4b83-bf11-01222c0248ee/FCJEI-Home.aspx.

Davis, R. C., & Medina-Ariza, J. (2001) *Results from an elder abuse prevention experiment in New York City.* U.S. Department of Justice, National Institute of Justice. Retrieved from http://www.ncjrs.gov/pdffiles1/nij/188675.pdf.

DeNavas-Walt, C., Proctor, B. D., & Smith, J. C. (2010, September). *U.S. Census Bureau current population reports, Income, poverty, and health insurance coverage in the United States: 2009.* Washington, DC: U.S. Government Printing Office.

Dietz, T. L., & Wright, J. D. (2005). Age and gender differences and predictors of victimization of the older homeless. *Journal of Elder Abuse & Neglect, 17*(1), 37–60. doi:10.1300/J084v17n01_03

Evans, R. D., & Forsyth, C. J. (2004). Risk factors, endurance of victimization and survival strategies: The impact of the structural location of men and women on the experiences within homeless milieus. *Sociological Spectrum, 24*(4), 79–505.

Eyrich-Garg, K. (2010). Mobile phone technology: A new paradigm for the prevention, treatment, and research of the non-sheltered "street" homeless? *Journal of Urban Health: Bulletin of the New York Academy of Medicine, 87*(3), 365–380. doi:10.1007/s11524-010-9456-2

Fleck, C., & Schmidt, T. (2011, March 2). Mickey Rooney claims elder abuse. *AARP Bulletin.* Retrieved from http://www.aarp.org.

Gainey, R. R., & Payne, B. K. (2006). Caregiver burden, elder abuse and Alzheimer's disease: Testing the relationship. *Journal of Health & Human Services Administration, 29*(1/2), 245–259.

Gilfillan, C. J. (1994). Senior citizens police advocates. *FBI Law Enforcement Bulletin, 63*(14), 14–16. Washington, DC: Federal Bureau of Investigation. Retrieved from http://www.fbi.gov/stats-services/publications/law-enforcement-bulletin/leb.

Human Rights Watch. (2006, September). *U.S.: Number of mentally ill in prisons quadrupled.* Retrieved from http://www.hrw.org/en/news/2006/09/05/us-number-mentally-ill-prisons-quadrupled.

Jasinski, J. L., Wesely, J. K., Mustaine, E., & Wright, J. D. (2005). *The experience of violence in the lives of homeless women: A research report* (final report to the National Institute of Justice). Orlando, FL: Institute of Social and Behavioral Sciences.

Ketteler, L., & Dodge, M. (2009). Improving police interactions with the mentally ill: Crisis Intervention Team (CIT) training. In R. L. Gido & L. Dalley (Eds.), *Women's mental health issues across the criminal justice system* (pp. 84–97). Upper Saddle River, NJ: Pearson Education.

Kushel, M. B., Evans, J. L., Perry, S., Robertson, M. J., & Moss, A. R. (2003). No door to lock: Victimization among homeless and marginally housed persons. *Archives of Internal Medicine, 163*(20), 2492–2499.

Lamb, H. R., Weinberger, L. E., & DeCuir, W. J., Jr. (2002). The police and mental health. *Psychiatric Services, 53*(10), 1266–1271.

Levin, J., & McDevitt, J. (2002). *Hate crimes revisited: America's war on those who are different.* Cambridge, MA.: Westview.

Malks, B., Buckmaster, J., & Cunningham, L. (2003). Combating elder financial abuse—A multi-disciplinary approach to a growing problem. *Journal of Elder Abuse & Neglect, 15*(3/4), 55–70. doi:10.13000/J084v15n03_04

Maniglio, R. (2009). Severe mental illness and criminal victimization: A systematic review. *Acta Psychiatrica Scandinavica, 119*, 180–191.

McMahon, B. T., West, S. L., Lewis, A. N., Armstrong, A. J., & Conway, J. P. (2004). Hate crimes and disability in America. *Rehabilitation Counseling Bulletin, 47*(2), 66–75.

Merscham, C., Van Leeuwen, J. M., & McGuire, M. (2009). Mental health and substance abuse indictors among homeless youth in Denver, Colorado. *Child Welfare, 88*(2), 93–110.

Miranda v. Arizona, 384 U.S. 436 (1966).

National Alliance on Mental Illness (NAMI). (2011). *What is mental illness:* Mental illness facts. Retrieved from http://www.nami.org/Content/NavigationMenu/Inform_Yourself/About_Mental_Illness/About_Mental_Illness.htm.

National Center on Elder Abuse. (1997). *Trends in elder abuse in domestic settings.* Retrieved from www.ncea.aoa.gov/ncearoot/main_site/pdf/basics/fact2.pdf.

National Center on Elder Abuse. (2010). Frequently asked questions, What is elder abuse? Retrieved from http://www.ncea.aoa.gov/NCEAroot/Main_Site/FAQ/Questions.aspx.

National Center on Family Homelessness. (2009). *State report card on child homelessness: America's youngest outcasts.* Retrieved from http://www.homelesschildrenamerica.org.

National Coalition for the Homeless. (2010, August). *Hate crimes against the homeless: America's growing tide of violence.* Washington, DC: Author.

National Crime Prevention Council. (2011). Hate crime. Retrieved from http://www.ncpc.org/topics/hate-crime.

National Resource and Training Center on Homelessness and Mental Illness. (2003). Get the facts. Retrieved from www.nrchmi.samhsa.gov.

Payne, B. K. (2005). *Crime and elder abuse: An integrated perspective.* Springfield, IL: Charles C. Thomas.

Perron, B. E., Alexander-Eitzman, B., Gillespie, D. F., & Pollio, D. (2008). Modeling the mental health effects of victimization among homeless persons. *Social Science & Medicine, 67*(9), 1475–1479. doi:10.1016/j.socscimed.2008.07.012

Ruiz, J., & Miller, C. (2004). An exploratory study of Pennsylvania police officers' perceptions of dangerousness and their ability to manage persons with mental illness. *Police Quarterly, 7*(3), 359–371.

Silver, E. (2002). Mental disorder and violent victimization: The mediating role of involvement in conflicted social relationships. *Criminology, 40*(1), 191–212.

Silver, E., Arseneault, L., Langley, J., Caspi, A., & Moffitt, T. E. (2005). Mental disorder and violent victimization in a total birth cohort. *American Journal of Public Health, 95*(11), 2015–2021. doi:10.2105/AJPH.2003.021436

Southern Poverty Law Center (2011). Who we are. What we do. Retrieved from http://www.splcenter.org.

Steinberg, A., Brooks, J., & Remtulla, T. (2003). Youth hate crimes: Identification, prevention, and intervention. *American Journal of Psychiatry, 160*(5), 979–989.

Teplin, L. A., McClelland, G. M., Abram, K. M., & Weiner, D. A. (2005). Crime victimization in adults with severe mental illness. *Archives of General Psychiatry, 62*, 911–921.

Tyler, K. A., & Johnson, K. A. (2004). Victims and offenders: Accounts of paybacks, invulnerability, and financial gain among homeless youth. *Deviant Behavior, 25*, 427–449. doi:10.1080/01639620490468561

Tyler, K. A., Whitbeck, L. B., Hoyt, D. R., & Cauce, A. M. (2004). Risk factors for sexual victimization among male and female homeless and runaway youth. *Journal of Interpersonal Violence, 19*(5), 503–520. doi:10.1177/0886260504262961

U.S. Department of Justice—Federal Bureau of Investigation. (2009). *About hate crime statistics, 2009*. Retrieved from http://www2.fbi.gov/ucr/hc2009/index.html.

Wallace, H. (2007). *Victimology: Legal, psychological, and social perspectives* (2nd ed.). Boston, MA: Pearson Education.

Walsh, S. M., & Donaldson, R. E. (2010). Invited commentary: National safe place: Meeting the immediate needs of runway and homeless youth. *Journal of Youth and Adolescence, 39*(5), 437–445. doi:10.1007/s10964-010-9522-9

Wenzel, S. L., Koegel, P., & Gelberg, L. (2000). Antecedents of physical and sexual victimization among homeless women: A comparison to homeless men. *American Journal of Community Psychology, 28*(3), 367–390.

Wenzel, S. L., Leake, B. D., & Gelberg, L. (2001). Risk factors for major violence among homeless women. *Journal of Interpersonal Violence, 16*(8), 739–752.

Wessler, S. (2000). *Addressing hate crimes: Six initiatives that are enhancing the efforts of criminal justice practitioners* (NCJ 179559). Washington, DC: U.S. Department of Justice, Office of Justice Programs. Retrieved from http://www.ncjrs.gov/pdffiles1/bja/179559.pdf.

Willis, D. G. (2004). Hate crimes against gay males: An overview. *Issues in Mental Heath Nursing, 25*, 115–132. doi:10.1080/01612840490268090

CHAPTER 17

Introduction to Comparative Issues of Crime Prevention

Timothy Austin
Indiana University of Pennsylvania

Victoria M. Time
Old Dominion University

As shown throughout this book, a study of crime prevention can be approached from a number of viewpoints. One area within the broader scheme of criminal justice and criminology that has gained a strong foothold in the past few decades is the study of comparative justice. All aspects of crime and justice can be viewed from a variety of comparative perspectives. Certainly, crime prevention is no exception.

The following chapter, "Life on the Atoll: Singapore Ecology as a Neglected Dimension of Social Order," considers crime prevention strategies in a Southeast Asian nation. At least six perspectives of comparative justice emerge when considering crime prevention in Singapore, some presented within the chapter in more detail than others.

First, consider the "temporal" dimension of comparative justice. Here one may compare how social or cultural features of a region may have changed over time. In a historical or evolutionary sense, society changes from one decade to the next, and often the way crime is managed follows suit. In Singapore this is illustrated as people were uprooted in a massive urban renewal plan from cohesive but inefficient and unhealthy conditions to reside in high-rise housing blocks. This upheaval of the nation's population mandated that social control agencies, including the police, learn new ways to maintain order. Consequently, one can observe how crime prevention altered from one decade to the next.

Second, and perhaps the most common perspective of comparative justice, is the "spatial" dimension. Here we are concerned with observing how one geographic or cultural area may compare or contrast with another region or location, such as weighing one nation's cultural standards to another. Given the more than 200 nations in the world, this issue necessarily becomes complex. For instance, an individual accustomed to life in the United States will find that Singapore follows a much more rigorous system of laws and regulations than is found in the Western hemisphere. Customs that may seem acceptable to some, even if unseemly, such as spitting on the sidewalk or chewing gum, result in strong penalties in Singapore. Comparing one region or nation to another is instructive and can provide new insights into one's own system of justice.

A third comparative perspective arises when we contrast subunits within the larger social system. This is reminiscent of the ecological model, which illustrates how any social system is made up of smaller, interconnected zones or parts. In this regard, one might compare a state or a province to the larger nation, or a neighborhood within a city to the larger urban area. How does the justice system operate in a Chinatown compared to the larger system of which it is a part? Although it is not fully developed in the Singapore chapter, Singapore is, in fact, subdivided into various ethnic regions composed of Indian, Malay, and Chinese districts. Each of these regions is further divided into housing blocks that fall under different policing divisions. Each would be worthy of scrutiny.

A fourth comparative perspective pertains to distinctions that persist in varying degrees in many nations of the world in regards to their status as colonial or postcolonial nations. When nations are overrun and occupied by foreign powers, obvious tensions build up, sometimes brewing for generations between the indigenous and imposing forces. Some nations cope better than others. A region that has suffered invasion and occupation invariably results in a mixture of cultures—a blend of languages, local customs, and even government structures and allegiances. In earlier decades, before its independence, Singapore was part of the United Kingdom as well as a part of Malaysia. Whenever criminal justice systems are examined, the cultural history must be kept in mind. Singapore represents a merging of different cultures that have remained relatively peaceful over the years.

As a side note, one should also keep in mind that populations are sometimes dispersed from their homeland (i.e., Diaspora) forming a distinct but separated society. These detached populations are sometimes subject to crude, provisional governments that can themselves become semipermanent or permanent, as in the case of Native Americans or Palestinians. How justice agencies operate in such dispersed populations, or how social order is maintained is a fertile area for future research.

A fifth comparative perspective pertains to how specific or detailed one wishes to be in making justice-related comparisons. In the Singapore case, one can examine at a "microcriminology" level how police carry out their patrols utilizing the elevators of high-rise housing blocks (i.e., vertical patrol). On the other hand, one can focus on the larger social structures ("macrocriminology") that attribute crime generally to such features as proportions of youth, unemployment rates, military obligations, or the prevalence of law and standards of punishments in a society.

Sixth, in almost any region of the world, the comparative criminologist can focus on the degree that the justice system follows either "formal" or "informal" systems of social control. Most nations reflect a blend of both perspectives, and it is generally agreed that lower-crime rate nations emphasize informal social controls by not relying on police for smaller crimes and infractions (see, for instance, Adler, 1983). Singapore is notable for instituting relatively intense governmental formal controls that are superimposed on a vast array of neighborhood-based networks of informal controls. What may on first glance appear to be an oppressive government may actually turn out to be a rather carefully ordered system of citizen-based mechanisms of crime prevention.

A final comment is in order regarding how the Singapore example pertains to traditional criminological or social science theory. Most research projects possess some sort of theoretical context, whether explicit or implicit. Some research involves field work and is more ethnographical in its methodology. In such cases, the researcher may not have specific theoretical orientations in mind and leaves the door completely open for theory to emerge from the data itself. In other cases, a research project may begin with an attempt to test or clarify specific theoretical assumptions or predictions. In the Singapore chapter, these two orientations tend to overlap.

As noted in the chapter on Singapore, these findings are actually a 20-year follow up of a similar study completed by the same researcher in Singapore in the mid-1980s. The theoretical works of sociologist Donald Black proved to be helpful in both the earlier and the more recent study. Black (1976, cf. 1993) outlines in uncomplicated proposition format how law behaves as society changes.

Thus, law will change (become more or less necessary) as fluctuations are seen in a society's culture, organization, stratification, morphology (i.e., degree of social intimacy), and levels of social control. For instance, law becomes increasingly required as a society advances in the complexity of its culture, the degree that its people are more or less split into social classes (stratification), or subdivided into few or many organizations. Law also varies or becomes more or less necessary as people increase or decrease in the degree that they are socially intimate with each other. When people in a neighborhood know each other, law is less necessary. The Singapore chapter will discuss how the need for law or formal intrusion of government changed as the island's population moved from crowded villages to high-rise apartments, thus changing the nature of police patrol and crime prevention.

Other theoretical viewpoints are seen in the case of Singapore. For instance, a "critical theory" perspective is suggested when law may be seen to target some segments of the population more than others. Thus, one could argue that a law against picking fruit from public parks tends to target the homeless or the poor who may suffer hunger and could wind up as lawbreakers more often than the wealthy individual. A discussion of such potentially distorted laws in Singapore is detailed in the earlier report (Austin, 1987).

More fully discussed in the present chapter on Singapore is how life on a crowded island presents interesting ways to view how some kinds of inappropriate behavior that tend to "take care of themselves" or become self-regulating. In a sense, ecological characteristics of life might assist in preventing law-breaking. If people live in high-rise buildings with nearly impossible access from the outside, burglary (at least from the outside) would be less likely.

Singapore becomes a social laboratory for understanding how law and order can be maintained on a crowded island nation. It is only one model, among many, of how a people and government interconnect.

A second chapter in this comparative section looks at the nation of Japan. Japan holds a number of similarities to Singapore since it is also an island nation in the Asian Pacific. However, with Japan, we have an island not the size of the District of Columbia, as is Singapore, but an island about the size of California. Yet, Japan has over three times the population of California. By examining Japan we are also able to draw rough contrasts to other nations, including the United States. In this chapter, Victoria Time reports on her first-hand experience of Japanese life and her in-depth interviews with police officers in both urban and rural areas of Japan. Her work is informative because it explores both the sociocultural features of Japanese society as well as some of the daily work routine of Japanese police officers. In order to best understand aspects of crime prevention in any nation, it is imperative that one look deeper than just the daily operations of police to more clearly understand something of the culture and social organization of the people.

Of critical importance when describing Japan's justice system is the unmistakable overlap between the formal justice system and the Japanese neighborhood. To best comprehend such features as crime rates, courts and prisons, and policing in general, one must begin with how social order is maintained within the community. In this regard, the author discusses how police are an integrated part of the neighborhoods and communities, whether in urban or rural areas. Most social control is, in fact, at the informal level, whereby local citizens themselves maintain order rather than risking losing face by calling upon formal police to resolve sometimes petty problems. Victoria Time brings new data to a discussion on Japan, particularly with her on-site accounts of how Japanese police describe their job duties and satisfactions.

While Japan has always enjoyed an enviable reputation as a country with a low crime rate, in recent years the Japanese police have expressed concern about growing rates of crimes especially those committed by foreign visitors. According to the Japanese police, property offenses are on the rise, and with urban anonymity, the informal guardian that the community provided hitherto has declined. Proactive efforts to minimize the incidence of crime in recent years have included establishing a "crime-tough society" (Police of Japan, 2008, p. 21). Measures that have been put in place to accomplish the goal of a "crime-tough society" include: (1) control of offenses affecting the social order, (2) promotion of voluntary activities in crime prevention, (3) promotion of crime prevention through environmental design, and (4) encouragement of sound growth of community safety industry.

(1) Control of offenses affecting the social order: The rationale here is that when offenders are punished, no matter how minimal their crimes are, this "get tough on crime" stance will deter criminals, and will promote law-abidingness in the people.

(2) Promotion of voluntary activities in crime prevention: Community participation in crime prevention is highly encouraged. It is approximated that there are about 32,000 crime prevention volunteer groups in Japan (Police of Japan, 2008, p. 21). Since police officers consider volunteer groups integral to crime control, such groups are updated with "regional safety information"—they are educated or trained on crime preventative measures.

(3) Promotion of crime prevention through environmental design: The assumption is that proper design of the infrastructure in the community may help repress crime. In this regard, police recommend that public spaces like parks, parking lots, and roads be designed following a standard that conforms to a design recommended by the police referred to as "Crime Prevention Standards on Roads, Parks, Parking Lots for Cars and Bicycles, and Public Bathrooms" (Police of Japan, 208, p. 21).

(4) Encouragement of sound growth of community safety industry: Japanese police assume that if more companies that promote public safety are established, efforts to enhance crime prevention will be greatly advanced. As such, the police encourage more private security businesses, as well as, businesses that deal with installing security devices to be established throughout the country. By seeking the services of private security officers, and by installing security devices in their homes, citizens proactively engage in crime prevention.

Mindful of transnational crimes, Japanese police have instituted joint and exchange programs with several Asian countries to cultivate ways of combating drug and human trafficking, terrorism, weapons smuggling, and other crimes. Overall, the Japanese police operate more from a proactive stance to curb crime.

KEY TERMS

Temporal dimension
Spatial dimension
Ecological
Colonialism
Diaspora
Microcriminology
Macrocriminology
Ethnography
Donald Black's Behavior of Law

DISCUSSION QUESTIONS

1. How can studying comparative justice systems provide insights for crime control in the United States?
2. Contrast social control in Singapore with social control in the United States.
3. What are some examples of comparative study of criminal justice within the United States?

REFERENCES

Adler, F. (1983). *Nations not obsessed with crime*. Littleton, CO: Rothman.

Austin, T. (1987). Crime and custom in an orderly society: The Singapore prototype. *Criminology, 25*, 279–294.

Black, D. (1976). *The behavior of law*. New York, NY: Academic Press.

Black, D. (1993). *The social structure of right and wrong*. New York, NY: Academic Press.

Police of Japan. (2008). National Police Agency 2-1-2 Kasumigaseki, Chiyoda-ku Tokyo, Japan.

CHAPTER 18

Life on the Atoll: Singapore Ecology as a Neglected Dimension of Social Order

Timothy Austin
Indiana University of Pennsylvania

Earlier field research (Austin, 1987, 1989) concluded that the Republic of Singapore, in only 20 years after its independence from Malaysia in 1965, has emerged as a squeaky clean society with its citizenry living in what appeared as near-perfect social harmony. All the usual indicators revealed that this tiny Southeast Asian atoll, barely 20 miles wide and 14 miles north to south, and now with a population of 4.7 million, remains surprisingly successful economically while holding unusually high levels of social order. Measured against Americans, Singaporeans live longer, have lover infant mortality rates, less crime, lower rates of unemployment, and hold approximate annual wages.

Most would agree that life in Singapore is highly regimented. Among numerous other ordinances, residents cannot chew gum, jaywalk, pick flowers or fruit from public parks, flag taxies outside official queuing stations, own a car older than 10 years old, spit on sidewalks or read *Cosmopolitan* magazine. These and numerous similar regulations persist that are formally prohibited and, if resulting in arrest, can lead to substantial fines (e.g., Singapore $350 for spitting). Of course, these more minor infractions are in addition to laws against major acts of violence and property offenses and the highly publicized antidrug regulations (Swensen, 1999; Vreeland, 1977).

Deviations certainly do occur in Singapore in all categories; however, they are few compared to the United States and most other nations. Comparing crime rates between nations is chancy. Yet the numbers are provocative with Singapore reflecting in 2003 an index crime rate per 100,000 residents less than one half that found in rural America. Interpersonal violence is rare with murder (0.5 per 100,000) and rape (3.2 per 100,000) offenses being 10 times lower, and with a robbery rate (22.7 per 100,000) 7 times lower than in the United States. The total number of robberies in Singapore is slightly more than 900 per year. The likelihood of being a victim of burglary (27.7 per 100,000) in Singapore is 30 times less than in the United States. Motor vehicle thefts do occur, but most are of motorcycles. Automobile thefts per capita (4.5 per 100,000) are nearly 100 times less than in the United States.

A question raised in the earlier reports was whether Singapore could retain its image portrayed by one news correspondent (Reiss, 1985) as a nation "scrubbed clean of temptation." Would the

Timothy Austin, International Journal of Offender Therapy and Comparative Criminology, October 1, 2005. Reprinted by Permission of SAGE Publications.

tightly knit society be able to maintain such low rates of deviance and crime when the rest of the world was moving at such a fast pace? Fifty percent of Singaporeans own cell phones, and computer use is strong (Central Intelligence Agency, 2002). Internet usage is high, and cybercafés, along with Starbucks, appear on the street corners and in an endless array of shopping malls. Tourism rates remain high—that also works, along with surfing the Web, to increase the mobility of ideas from the outside. Still, between 1985 and 2003, with only minor fluctuations, the overall crime rate for Singapore actually decreased. This challenges traditional criminological theory that crime rates should rise with increases in population size and density. What explanations help us understand such success in what remains one of the most crowded, urban environments of the world with 17,000 persons per square mile.

Of particular interest is whether several of Donald Black's propositions remain as convincing now as they appeared in the mid-1980s. Black's (1976, 1980, 1993) celebrated work on the behavior of law predicts many relationships between the prevalence of law, or lack of it, and other social variables. For instance, in what ways might a rise in informal or nongovernmental social controls in Singapore be associated with less of a need for law and traditional police operations? Is it possible that Singapore could manage with less of a police presence while its population density has increased? Black also predicted the relationship between the necessity for law and the extent of social intimacy or social distance between people. When people reflect higher levels of social intimacy, the need for the mobilization of formal police control would be less critical (Black, 1976). Or, as the proportion of strangers rises in a region, the level of social intimacy would be reduced, and the reliance on formal police would be greater.

It is true that no single factor best explains Singapore's low crime rate. Rather, a series of variables have been addressed over the years to include government and law (Bartholomew, 1989), formal enforcement strategies (Austin, 1987), and the more indirect or strictly informal controls such as religion, education, and employment (Ling, 1989). A parliamentary democracy allows multiple political parties. However, in the years since national independence of Singapore, the People's Action Party has remained singularly dominant. Political debate is kept to a minimum, and the conflict observed in nations with more evenly competing political systems is avoided. The dominant religion of Buddhism is claimed by more than one half of the citizenry, a religion that accepts "right conduct" as one of the paths to enlightenment. To the extent of such spiritual belief is practiced one must presume a positive impact on overall low crime rates (Ling, 1989; cf., Fenwick, 1982).

However, often overlooked is the impact that island ecology or spatial features have exerted on criminal conduct. Donald Black's predictions on the link between law, social intimacy, and styles of social control are logically couched, in part, in the broader perspective of social ecology of urban locales holds a rich tradition in social science beginning with Park, Burgess, and McKenzie (1925). For more recent reviews see Martin, Mutchnik, and Austin, (1990, particularly chap.5), and Stark (1987; cf., Sacco & Kennedy, 2002).

Singapore, with its millions of citizens squeezed onto a land mass only a few times larger than Washington, D.C., offers an appropriate laboratory to help fill the research void.

PROCEDURES

This article represents a 20-year follow-up to field research conducted in 1985. Two additional field trips were made to Singapore during the summers of 1997 and 2003. Multiple, in-depth interviews were carried out with officers of the Singapore Police force, faculty of the National University of Singapore, government workers, local business owners, tourists, students, and other locals. Friendships were rekindled with researchers at the Institution of Southeast Asian Studies (ISEAS) where the investigator held a visiting research affiliation during the three visits.

Beginning with the respondents in the Singapore Police Force and with researchers at ISEAS, a network or snowball sample was initiated (Berg, 1989; Curran & Renzetti, 1994). At least 20 respondents, most of whom must be considered expert informants, were interviewed in-depth and on multiple occasions. The data were synthesized and collapsed into themes that were reintroduced as topics to some of the same respondents as further checks on validity. Interviews continued until a point of redundancy was reached.

Unlike the first trip to Singapore in 1985, frequent e-mail contact after subsequent field trips allowed a rapid clarification and further inquiry with many of the respondents remaining in Singapore. In addition, more recent ethnographic data benefits from easily accessed Web-based Singaporean newspapers and government documents that can be scrutinized to generate further e-mail inquiry with previous interviewees. Numerous thematic parents emerged from the in-depth interviews pertaining to life on the island with particular emphasis on crime prevention and law enforcement styles.

FINDINGS

Island Ecology and Social Order

Life on the small island restricts movement and influences social control in three fundamental ways. First, in several instances, cooperation among citizens ultimately tends to provide positive rewards over conflict and fosters order maintenance, rather than law enforcement perspectives of police. Second, Singapore's housing problem was solved in a way that directly results in the changes in police-community relations. Third, island containment modifies the way some deviance and crimes are defined and carried out. Each of these themes is considered separately.

Order maintenance perspectives. The limited space associated with diminutive island existence crowds people together and introduces a cloistering effect that can work to generate social order. Although territorial theory does suggest that competition and conflict could escalate with increasing density of population, and opposite effect can be observed with increased population size and density working to increase sociality (Sussan & Chapman, 2004). The Singapore example illustrates how "order-maintenance strategies of police" (Bittner, 1980; cf., Skolnick & Bayley, 1988) provide an advantage over rigid law enforcement. The data support this conclusion in a number of ways.

On a small island, where mobility is highly restricted and citizens are forced into tight community living, dispute resolution through negotiation and mediation makes more common sense than making an arrest and carrying a dispute to trial. A formal trial forces a win-lose scenario that in Singapore would be particularly problematic because the loser in a dispute could not easily leave town to save face. Literally, short of departing the country, there are fewer places to run and hide. Rather, disputing parties are typically compelled to return to the same housing block where the disagreement originated that can provoke further stigma and animosity. It is not surprising that informal controls would naturally emerge in such densely populated locales and that formal mobilization of police would be a last resort. Thus, a proactive police approach whereby an officer patrols the streets looking for lawbreakers, making an arrest and forcing a court hearing can become dysfunctional (Black & Baumgartner, 1980; Bracey, 1989; Wilson, 1968; cf., Black 1980).

Although Singapore is well known for being strict, it appears that beneath the surface, minor illegality is dealt with or without official police intervention. In fact, uniformed police and marked patrol cars are not seen on the streets in heavy numbers. For instance, rarely will one observe police interrupting the steady flow of traffic to stop an errant motorist. Rather, video cameras detect traffic infractions resulting in a citation through the mail. Taxies need to pay a toll to enter certain street zones, and violators have fines withdrawn directly from credit cards monitored through required dashboard sensors. It is well publicized that corporal punishment by a rattan cane (caning) and capital punishments do occur. Yet these punishments appear infrequent even if consistently implemented; that is, a few cases of caning are reported daily in newspapers; however, this is not exceptional in a population approaching five million.

The number of executions is not officially reported; however, interview accounts confirm the perception that they are infrequent and deter drug crimes and crimes involving firearms, both capital offenses. When passing through the customs inspection station upon entering the Changi International Airport, officers are occasionally nowhere to be seen. Especially at late hours, travelers may simply walk through with bags uninspected. At the end of the corridor, large signs warn all passerby of mandatory death to any violators of drug laws. No juries operate in Singapore.

The case of Singapore, as a small island, is analogous to shipboard justice whereby a captain can be strict but must encourage camaraderie and social harmony to keep the ship operational that requires the efforts of all. An efficient ship's captain cannot afford to imprison crew members in the hulk of the ship and, as with tightly controlled island life, strategies or order maintenance prove functional. This is similar to *barangay* (community) justice in individual villages and particularly out islands of the Philippines whereby village captains are quickly available though rarely proactive (Austin, 1999). Singapore police tend to be crime prevention oriented and more apt to follow a reactive format of patrol. The confines of the small island allow a very quick response time thus making the physical presence of the police on the street less necessary.

Living space and security. The ecological dilemma of housing Singapore's citizenry on the small island reflects four periods of transition since the mid-1960s. Each displays a distinctive linkage to police strategies that can be viewed in the context of Donald Black's propositions on the behavior of law.

First prior to 1963, when Singapore was part of Malaysia and under British rule, most citizens lived in metal-roofed huts (*kampongs*) oftentimes elevated on stilts and clustered in what appeared to be a haphazard, disorganized, and disease-ridden aggregate of villages. These villages represented Chinese, Malay, and Indian communities that likely were not as disrupted as they first appeared and, in fact, according to some early reports, reflected extended families and culturally cohesive sociopolitical neighborhoods (Chen & Ling, 1977; Hassan, 1976). Rates of crime were conjectured as being high during this kampong era though the data is sporadic. In addition, it is likely that much of the presumed social deviance during the kampong era was managed locally.

Official crime rates were low and police intervention slight even if behind the scenes high levels of hidden illegalities persisted as reflected by public perceptions and accounts of pre-independence Singapore as a seamy, pirate-infested port city (Clutterbuck, 1985; Colless, 1969). Building on Black's theory, formal mobilization of law and police would be infrequent and less needed during the kampong era when locally coalesced neighborhoods tended to manage their own affairs (Black & Baumgartner, 1980). In addition, police intervention of lower levels of the quantity of organization" (Black, 1976).

A second ecological period is observed during the decades of the 1960s and 1970s when what was reputed to be the world's largest urban renewal project was implemented. The project relocated citizens from kampongs to high-rise housing blocks. This project was motivated by a desire to improve the public health of the port city as well as by a fear that the politically charged cultural enclaves might be potentially volatile. By the end of the 1980s, more than 3,000 high-rise housing blocks were spread over the landscape, each with about 1,000 residents. With the exception of the more well-to-do, who could afford individual houses, the masses of Singaporeans lived out their lives high above the city's horizon. Such an ecological transformation greatly affected police-community relations.

With the newly constructed high-rise blocks, police could more efficiently keep tabs on specific households that remained pigeon holed, layer on layer from the ground level to the top floor. With the buildings reminiscent of some prison designs the police could now visualize precisely where everyone was located in a very structured format. As viewed from the outside, the individual flats look nearly identical in the hotel-like housing blocks that average 20 floors in height. With mathematical precision, police were able to quickly identify on a grid exactly where a particular family resided. A $5,000 fine is levied against a resident who fails to notify authorities of a change in residence. This second transition upset many residents who did not want to be moved in the first place from their culturally based yet crowded and unhygienic kampongs. The early housing block initiative was followed by a spike in official crime rates that was of great concern to government organizers. Apparently, the social cohesion earlier associated with kampong life was lost in the high-rise blocks, resulting in disenchantment among some citizens, many of whom were detached from extended families and work locations. The rise in official crime rates affirms Black's prediction that law and police control increase and become more necessary as the social distance among citizenry increases (Black, 1976; cf., Black, 1993). A sense of social intimacy was lacking in the newly established high-rise blocks that previously in the culturally cohesive kampong villages had worked to pull people together without government intervention.

A third ecological and organizational transition is identified when the Singapore government acted to increase police efficiency and police-community relations by initiating the Japanese *koban* (neighborhood police office) model by strategically positioning small police stations, referred to as Neighborhood Police Posts (NPPs) at the base of selected housing blocks. A police officer's beat could be a single housing block, and a police practice known as vertical patrol was introduced. Officers rode elevators to the top of a housing block and walked each floor, passing in front of individual flats periodically and meeting personally with all residents thereby deepening police-community linkages.

Just as important as the establishment of the NPPs, the government also mandated the development of a nationwide network of citizen groups referred to as Residence Committees (RCs) elected within the housing blocks. An RC, comprising 15 to 20 members, meets to discuss neighborhood issues and problems of the housing block (e.g., sanitation, safety, recreation, security etc.). Coincidently, this provided a location for the airing of some grievances at the most grassroots level and generally without police intervention or even their knowledge. A housing block resident could informally bring a grievance before the RC rather than to the NPP. In addition, some grievances and disputes discovered by police could now be referred to the RCs for possible resolution. Potential police matters could be nipped at the bud and without formal police intervention.

The interplay between the NPP and the RC coincided with, and possibly stimulated, a decrease in official crime rates, much to the relief of the government sponsors of the housing block program. The ecological initiatives followed by lower crime rates tend to validate Black's prediction that a mobilization of law and police would be less necessary with an increase of social intimacy between citizens. Police units in the blocks in the 1980s and 1990s worked to maintain close and positive relationships with RCs. The general rate of crime remained low.

A fourth transition was unexpectedly uncovered during a field visit in 2003. The official crime rate had been reduced even further since 1999 with a surprising change in police patrol techniques. The introduction of sophisticated electronic monitoring was beginning to replace the NPP. In the words of once police administrator, "the NPPs were becoming shells of their former selves." Telephone use, and the modern personal cell phone, many now including video and global positioning systems, are highly prevalent in Singapore. Monitoring by police was apparently not disrupted by the physical absence of police officers at the base of the housing blocks. More to the point, the definition of authentic, face-to-face interaction between police and citizens was becoming blurred now that rapid contact via cell phone, or use of a video-phone box at the ground floor of the housing block, could be linked directly to a police center located nearby but outside the individual housing block. This electronic link provides the same function, in many instances, as the original NPP.

It is significant to note, in the Singapore case, electronic communication appears to provide a viable substitute to direct police contact. The crime rates within the housing blocks actually decreased at the same time that the NPPs were being replaced with sophisticated electronic systems. On several occasions, a police official offhandedly referred to the housing block residents as the "collective." Arguably, housing block residents may be even more comfortable linking up with police electronically than by physically visiting a police department office. A greater sense of privacy and attentiveness may unfold between two callers on a video phone than between a police officer and patron across a desk in a crowded office. In addition, if one is in a hurry, a ringing phone might be given precedence over ongoing physical interaction even if the phone momentarily disrupts other interaction. The definition of what is so-called personal and face-to-face must be reconsidered with two-way video becoming so commonplace in Singapore. If it is true, as appears to be happening, that modern electronic communication networks can substitute for physical interaction, then Black's proposition remains true to the Singapore situation.

That is, the mobilization of law and of police can be expected to decrease, or become less necessary, with an increase in social intimacy (i.e., a decrease in social distance) provided by mobile video phones. Cellular video phones may be undisruptive and may even enhance a sense of social intimacy between police and citizen in the time of crisis or need.

Following Black's prediction, the relationship between law and social distance between people is curvilinear (Black, 1976). Thus, law was less necessary during the kampong era where citizens lived in consolidated neighborhoods, became more necessary when citizens were disrupted and disoriented in high-rise housing blocks, and again law became less necessary with the return to social cohesiveness provided by the RCs and NPPs and later by cellular phone technology.

Island containment and self-regulating activities. Some activities tend to emerge as self-regulating because to act otherwise becomes dysfunctional on a small but crowded island. The data argues for a slight modification of Black's perspective with the following proposition: The more self-regulation that exists, the less the need for law and the less need for police intervention. In this case, self-regulation is not a result of individual reliance on one's own group or neighborhood for social control, as commonly equated with "self-help" (Black & Baumgartner, 1980). Rather, it is an outcome of ecological advantage or situation with lesser attention given to culture and personality issues (see the discussion of "situation" by Bats & Harvey, 1975; cf., Garreau, 1992).

Consider the case of jaywalking as influenced by island ecology. In a rural area or even a small town, there is little need for jaywalking laws. Residents stroll at will on the streets and meander across roadways often jumping between slow moving traffic. Jaywalking becomes more complicated and problematic in larger cities and certainly in Singapore. On the heavily used streets crisscrossing the island, the smooth movement of millions of people by motor vehicle is crucial and illustrates how the citizenry adapted to island life. Jaywalking laws have been traditionally severe in Singapore because the fast moving, bumper-to-bumper traffic cannot be disrupted by the added problem of pedestrians dangerously scurrying across the streets to save a few moments. In recent years, where automobiles are kept moving at relatively high speeds, pedestrians jaywalk only at extreme risk to life and limb. Thus, in Singapore jaywalking becomes self-regulating as motor vehicles speed down the multiple-lane highways with infrequent traffic lights. Traffic is kept at an uninterrupted fast pace while pedestrians are left to follow established and sometimes cumbersome walking routes; refusal to use them can result in heavy penalties (up to Singapore $350).

However, in the shopping districts where traffic often slows to a snail's pace, it is not surprising that jaywalking increases even though it remains illegal. Even so, few arrests are noted here given the large groups of shoppers, locals, and foreigners, bolting en masse between slow moving cars. Shoppers reflected a "power in numbers" that seemed to stymie the Singapore police in the summer of 2003 as they looked away as large crowds of tourists cut across the streets on the side roads in the popular Orchard Boulevard district of the city even though nearby road signs disallowing such activity were in clear sight.

As well, the efficient subway system of Singapore has had an impact on jaywalking. In earlier years when buses were more prevalent, pedestrians could be observed illegally running across the street to catch a bus. Today this practice is rarely seen, likely because the rail transportation is accessible from sidewalk entrances, and waiting periods for the subway trains are no more than 10 minutes. In addition, in earlier years elderly Singaporean shoppers, mostly women, could be seen jaywalking while carrying parcels of groceries from the marketplace. Being aged and without an automobile, they chose not to climb the steep walkway bridges crossing the streets. These relatively feeble shoppers broke the law but out of necessity. The more well-to-do citizens were able to drive to markets and avoid the need to consider jaywalking. Regardless, today fewer elderly grocery shoppers are seen jaywalking on the residential streets, likely also benefiting from the rapid rail system. Jaywalking appears to have become less of a problem during the past several decades.

Public spitting as outlawed behavior in Singapore can also be seen as self-regulations because of the extreme density of the population. It makes common sense, as is publicized by the government on public billboards that sidewalk spitting, for instance, can be unhygienic as well as irritating to the sensibilities. Ecologically, widespread spitting in the most densely populated nation in the world has immediate negative consequences for the citizenry. Spitting could spread disease and also be socially irritating. Refraining from public spitting reaps its own rewards. It is true that public spitting is illegal (technically a style of public littering); however, it is unknown how much of the control of spitting results from deterrence from a high fine or simply that the behavior is at least somewhat self-regulating.

The issue of queuing for a taxi is also a function of ecology. Finding a taxi in a densely populated locale can be a problem and even dangerous. Resulting from a government-imposed regulation, Singapore citizenry must use queuing stations where travelers methodically stand in line for transportation rather than to resorting to open competition and provoking a possible disruption to traffic. In some locales, taxi drivers can be fined for picking up passengers outside queuing stations. With military precision, all travelers are eventually accommodated at the queuing stations. Open rivalry for taxis may have immediate rewards for the few but at the certain risk of irritating the many. Getting along with each other becomes mutually beneficial.

Similarly, in the ultra-sleek subway system one experiences conspicuous order and even unusual calm as patrons move in near lock step to assigned ramp locations, prepared to leisurely enter the trains without pushing or shoving. The queuing scenario of collected composure is observed throughout Singapore in many everyday social activities whether on the sidewalk, streets, or in department store checkout lines, all adding to a heightened sense of orderliness and cooperation.

The confinement of island life also works to regulate the nature of more severe criminal conduct. For example, certain kinds of theft do not make common sense given the difficulty of escape. Auto theft is a good example whereby the thief is compelled to drive in circles on the island in avoidance of police, eventually an exercise in futility. Even the 10,000 taxies in Singapore can be altered by police radio to be on the lookout for specific fugitives. Theft of motorcycles, the target of most motor vehicle theft on the island, is more logical because they can be easily hidden or quickly disassembled for illegal sale. Such situational factors are difficult to assess; however, their consequence is not in doubt.

The impact of island ecology can be extended to other kinds of conduct. For example, burglary rates, as in the case of auto theft, are now given the great advantage to police of being able to track down offenders in the confines of the small island. Only a single roadway to the north takes a fleeing offender off the island across a causeway into Malaysia. All cars can be efficiently scrutinized, an all are scanned by video cameras. The waters surrounding Singapore are continuously patrolled by a marine police unit in high-speed cruisers that travel in opposite directions around the island, scrutinizing any unusual activities and making police available at coastline locations.

In addition, from a purely spatial perspective, Singapore's high-rise housing blocks make burglary difficult to execute in the first place, with each floor posing a neighborhood watch effect and typically being situated where police can be quickly summoned. Security and crime prevention are made more efficient by high-rise block living (Newman, 1973). Windows are typically inaccessible to thieves on the upper decks, and the few main doors can be heavily bolted. Burglary becomes self-regulating in housing blocks, particularly the upper levers, due to the difficulty of successful escape by elevators or stairways by offenders. Many housing blocks have no residences at the ground floor level, and a second floor, designated as a void desk, is reserved for recreational and other community activities. This area works to keep residents, especially children, off the streets. Even though one would think it unnecessary, security guards are seen in an increasing number of housing blocks. A desk clerk is often located at the ground floor, and in some blocks a security guard is positioned at the main entrance. In the more well-to-do blocks, a security guard post is located at the entry to the parking area.

Finally, law itself can be influenced by the spatial distribution of people on the small island. For example, any law legislated by the parliament can be immediately disseminated throughout the island. All citizens can be quickly made aware of a new law, and ignorance of new legislation is less meaningful as in nations with widely dispersed populations. In Singapore, the major news outlets are government controlled, which only adds to the rapid dissemination.

DISCUSSION

Human ecology pertains to how people adapt to their living space. As illustrated here, this can be in regards to a high-rise housing block or to adjustment of a larger population to life on a small island. This article was designed as an ethnographic study of a single island community and stands alone. Yet some may question how other similarly positioned nations may compare to Singapore. Specifically, for instance, why would Hong Kong, a nation with many parallel features, show higher crime rates than its Singapore neighbor to the south?

The data and space limitations do not allow full comparisons; however, several differences stand out. First, Hong Kong represents a densely populated nation with a much older urban history than the youthful Singapore. A brief taxi ride through Hong Kong reveals high-risk block living often in comparatively low-rent districts, reminiscent of project dwellers or working poor and frequently minority populations of some large American cities. In contrast, Singapore's high-risk blocks remain pristine and do not suggest crowdedness as foretold by perspectives of Wilson and Kelling (1982). The rougher street life in Hong Kong appears more conducive to youthful gangs that are borne out by others (Lo, 1992; cf., Choi & Lo, 2004).

Second, Singapore appears to have landed on a pragmatic and mandatory conscription process for military obligation of all male citizens that also includes an option of service with the Singapore Police Force. A further requirement of 10 years of reserve duty following active police service compels many youthful male citizens who commonly reside in the housing blocks to be prepared and duty bound to cooperate with regular police and even to intervene with illegal activity if they are first to arrive on the scene.

Without question, the issues of island ecology represent only a few, although consequential, features that work to segment an already low-crime area as generated by social and cultural patterns. This article provides heretofore neglected attention to the issue of how island confinement in Singapore tends to affect, generally in a positive way, several styles of illegality, and also how police strategies are influences.

Several of the propositions set forth by Black are shown to be useful in guiding ethnographic observations conducted in Singapore in 1997 and 2003. Order maintenance perspectives make common sense as citizens are confined to island life. Police community relations tend toward cooperation and partnership rather than on pure law enforcement. This is observed in the Singapore case even though much attention, and possibly myth, surrounds the presumption of relentless and staunch law enforcement and punitiveness on the small island.

Deterrence and punishment does not persist on the surface but is under-ridden by substantial crime preventiveness and strong police-community relations.

Community policing corresponds with the ways that the Singapore government has relocated its millions of citizens into high-rise housing blocks. Ecologically, life in high-rise flats was necessary with little room for outward migration on the small island. When people are forced into close quarters, the end effect does not necessarily lead to conflict. Social intimacy can generate less law and less need for police as suggested by Black. The nature of certain styles of illegality is shaped, at least in part, by island ecology to include, among other, jaywalking, burglary, and motor vehicle theft. The findings set the stage for future hypothesizing and invite replication and increased ethnographic detail.

KEY TERMS

Singapore
Ecology
Crime
Donald Black

REFERENCES

Austin, W. T. (1987). Crime and custom in an orderly society: The Singapore prototype. *Criminology, 25*, 279–294.

Austin, W. T. (1989). Crime and custom. In K. S. Sandhu & P. Wheatley (Eds.), *Management of Success: The molding of modern Singapore* (pp. 913–927). Singapore: Institute of Southeast Asian Studies.

Austin, W. T. (1999). *Banana justice: field notes on Philippine crime and custom.* Westport, CT: Praeger.

Bartholomew, G. W. (1989). The Singapore legal system. In K. S. Sandhu & P. Wheatley (Eds.), *Management of Success: The molding of modern Singapore* (pp. 601–646). Singapore: Institute of Southeast Asian Studies.

Bates, F. L., & Harvey, C. C. (1975). *The social structure of behavior.* New York, NY: Gardner.

Berg, B. L. (1989). *Qualitative research methods for the social sciences.* Boston, MA: Allyn & Bacon.

Bittner, E. (1980). *The functions of police in modern society.* Cambridge, MA: Delgeschlager, Gunn, and Hain.

Black, D. (1976). *The behavior of law.* New York, NY: Academic Press.

Black, D. (1980). *The manners and customs of the police.* New York, NY: Academic Press.

Black, D. (1993). *The social structure of right and wrong.* New York, NY: Academic Press.

Black, D., & Baumgartner, M. P. (1980). On self help in modern society. In D. Black (Ed.), *The manners and customs of the police* (pp. 193–208). New York, NY: Academic Press.

Bracey, D. H. (1989). Policing the people's republic. In R. J. Troyer, J. P. Clark, & D. G. Rojek (Eds.), *Social control in the People's Republic of China* (pp.159–166). New York, NY: Praeger.

Central Intelligence Agency. (2002). *The world fact book.* Washington, D.C.: U.S. GPO.

Chen, P. S., & Ling, T. C. (1977). *Social ecology of Singapore.* Singapore: Federal Publications.

Choi, A., & Lo, T. W. (2004). *Fighting youth crime: A comparative study of two little dragons in Asia* (2nd ed.). Singapore: Marshall Cavendish, East University Press.

Clutterbuck, R. (1985). *Conflict and violence in Singapore and Malaysia 1945–1983.* Singapore: Graham Brach.

Colless, B. E. (1969). The ancient history of Singapore. *Journal of Southeast Asian History, 10*, 1–11.

Curran, D. J., & Renzetti, C. M. (1994). *Theories of crime.* Boston, MA: Allyn & Bacon.

Fenwick, C. R. (1982). Crime and justice in Japan: Implications for the United States. *International Journal of Comparative and Applied Criminal Justice, 6*(1), 61–71.

Garreau, J. (1992). *Edge city: Life on the new frontier.* New York, NY: Anchor.

Hassan, R. (1976). *Singapore: Society in transition.* Kuala Lumpur, Malaysia: Oxford University Press.

Ling, T. (1989). Religion. In K. S. Sandhu & P. Wheatley (Eds.), *Management of success: the molding of Singapore.* (pp. 693–709). Singapore: Institute of Southeast Asian Studies.

Lo, T. W. (1992). Groupwork with youth gangs in Hong Kong. *Groupwork, 5*, 58–71.

Martin, R., Mutchnick, R., & Austin, T. (1990). *Criminological thought: Pioneers past and present.* New York, NY: Macmillan.

Newman, O. (1973). *Defensible space: Crime prevention through environmental design.* New York, NY: Macmillan.

Park, R. E., Burgess, E. W., & McKenzie, R. D. (1925). *The city.* Chicago, IL: University of Chicago Press.

Reiss, S. (1985). Singapore: A case of growing pains. *Newsweek: The International News Magazine, 11*, 6–11.

Sacco, V. F., & Kennedy, L. W. (2002). *The criminal event: Perspectives in space and time.* Belmont, CA: Wadsworth.

Skolnick, J., & Bayley, D. (1988). Theme and variation in community policing. In M. Tonry & N. Morris (Eds.), *Crime and justice, A review of research.* (pp. 1–38). Chicago, IL: University of Chicago Press.

Stark, R. (1987). Deviant places: A theory of ecology of crime. *Criminology, 25*, 841–862.

Sussman, R. W., & Chapman, A. R. (2004). *The origins and nature of sociality.* New York, NY: Aldine de Gruyter.

Swensen, G. (1999). The drug war Asian style: A study of legal measures adopted to combat illegal drug use in Singapore and China. *Murdoch University Electronic Journal of Law, 6*(1), 1–31.

Vreeland, N. (1977). *Area handbook for Singapore.* Washington, DC: U.S. GPO.

Wilson, J. Q. (1968). *Varieties of police behavior: The management of law and order in eight communities.* Cambridge, MA: Harvard University Press.

Wilson, J. Q., & Kelling, G. (1982, March). Broken windows: The police and neighborhood safety. *Atlantic Monthly. 249*, 29–38.

CHAPTER 19

Lessons Learned About Low Crime Rates in Japan: Field Notes from Interviews with Japanese Police Officers

Victoria M. Time
Old Dominion University

INTRODUCTION

Japanese police have for several decades received positive reviews about their style of policing, which contributes in part to the relatively low crime rates in Japan (Bayley, 1976, 1991; Fenwick, 1982; Terrill, 1999; Fairchild & Dammer, 2001; Reichel, 2008). As Albanese (2000) notes, "one commonly used indicator of police performance is the crime rate," although he adds that this may not be a fair method of assessing police performance. More importantly, as he suggests "the manner in which police enforce the law is the key to evaluating their performance in controlling crime" (p. 206).

Literature regarding the topic reveals that respect for Japanese police officers and the low crime rate in Japan are credited in part to the Japanese style of policing, and in part to a deep-seated Japanese culture of respect for seniors and those in authority (Bayley, 1976, 1991; Langworthy & Travis, 1994). Steinhoff (1993), however, maintains that studies that dwell on cultural explanations in discussing Japanese policing may be failing to include other missing pieces that together better inform about low crime rates in the country. Others, like Alarid & Wang (1997), suggest that "individual responsibility and decentralization" (p. 604) are central to successful Japanese policing. Individual responsibility, as Alarid and Wang contend, relates to both the officer and the citizenry taking over their community, while decentralization lends itself to assignment of responsibility from the highest to lowest ranking officers. This latter assertion is not unique to Japanese policing because delegating responsibility and duties is also a visible feature of American policing. In their study, Harper et al. (1999) determine that culture plays a role in police personality and that while some personality traits are common across cultures, some are derived from occupational socialization, and others are culturally influenced. Thus, when a culture emphasizes respect and civility, those aspects of socialization are inculcated into one's personality and eventually become evident in one's job performance.

In the current study, the author addresses the way that Japanese law enforcement officials carry out their law enforcement duties. Such research is useful for several reasons. At the broadest level, given the interactions between culture and policing, comparative research on policing helps in generating understanding about both areas: cultural issues and law enforcement issues. On more specific levels, the research is also important for empirical, subcultural, theoretical, and practical reasons. In terms of an empirical justification for this research, most policing research continues to focus on American and European models of policing. A need exists to continue to increase understanding about Asian models.

Such research is also useful for theoretical reasons. Most prominent criminological and criminal justice theories are American and European based. It is not entirely clear if these theories would be as relevant to other cultures. Consider routine activities theory, which assumes that crime occurs when: (1) a motivated offender is present, (2) a vulnerable target exists, and (3) a capable guardian is not present (Cohen & Felson, 1979). Presumably, law enforcement officers are "capable guardians." Such an assumption, however, is based on American perceptions of law enforcement. If law enforcement officers in other cultures have different functions, one must question the degree to which American and European criminological theories have utility for these other cultures. In this study, the strength of routine activity theory is examined in light of the Japanese situation.

Focusing on Japanese policing also has implications for policy and practice. Identifying practices and strategies that promote successful law enforcement will help to expand the ideals of "evidence-based" policing. Typically, evidenced-based policing strategies are defined with a narrow lens that excludes and ignores cross-cultural influence. In this changing globally interconnected world, it is useful to more broadly approach evidence-based policing strategies and identify practices and strategies that would be useful for all police officers.

REVIEW OF THE LITERATURE

Studies relating to Japanese policing style and low crime rates have hinged on the following primary factors: cultural–structural, and criminal justice.

Cultural and Structural Factors

After analyzing crime and justice issues in Tokyo, Japan, the Citizens Crime Commission of Philadelphia (1975) noted:

> *Fear of "loss of face" contributes measurably to the low crime rate in Japan. By committing a crime, a Japanese not only loses face for himself but also for a senior, whether parent or employer. An action which brings loss of face inevitably results in expulsion from the social structure of which the individual is so essentially a part. (p. 13)*

Several researchers have since made similar findings. Bayley (1976), for instance, observed that in Japanese culture one's identity and self-assessment are closely tied to the conventional system to which one belongs: school, family, work, neighborhood, and other groups. Individuals grow up with an inextricable sensitivity to these social bonds and the fear of shame that deviating from collective norms would bring not only to the person but to the entire family. Disrespect for seniors and of those in authority brings shame and further ramifications that may include ostracism from a community or social group. This is the case in both rural and urban settings, and as Christiansen (1976) observes, not even the growth and robust industrialization of Japan have done much to change the way of life of the Japanese. One would imagine that migration to the larger cities would weaken not only social bonds but more importantly, the "loss of face" that assails one so profoundly in the local community. Clifford (1976), however, notes that some social bonds may be lost upon migration to larger cities, but no sooner are the migrants settled in their new locales than those lost bonds are replaced by other social groups that act as controls.

In discussing retribution as a goal of punishment, Reichel (2008) concludes that the Japanese achieve this goal through "disgrace" or "reintegrative shaming" (p. 382). Reichel goes on to explain that while shaming is effective in Japan because of group consciousness, it is less likely to be effective in several Western societies that are heterogeneous, as is the case in the United States.

Further, as a homogeneous society, it is less cumbersome to deal with the Japanese population. On the contrary, in the United States the population is a hodge-podge of people with a kaleidoscope of values. This makes police work, which entails insisting on people abiding by a single set of rules, exceedingly difficult. Jiao (2001) and Zhang et al. (1996), have pointed out that success in problem solving is easily attained in homogeneous societies with shared values, in contrast to heterogeneous societies where there is constantly a clash in values among different social, racial, and ethnic groups. Further, as they state, the ease and efficacy by which officers do their jobs is fostered by how cohesive a society is in terms of customs and values. A key component of Japanese culture is group or collective work, with each facet of the community looking out for the greater good of the entire community (Yamagishi et al., 1998). Alarid and Wang (1997) explain group work or "groupism" as relating to *ie* or *mura*, with *ie* meaning "household or family," and *mura* "a wider community" (p. 603). This outlook on society permeates all works of life, including Japanese policing. Jiao (2001) notes that, on the contrary, in "the United States, people are more self-centered, more open and forthright in expressing themselves, often with anticipation of conflicts and confrontations" (pp. 161–162). When individuals are egoistic and worry more about their individual selves rather than collective good, then social institutions like law enforcement should not be entirely accountable for peoples' behavior and therefore for the crime rates.

One Japanese respondent acknowledged that while Japan has been a homogeneous society for a long time, things are changing with an increase in the number of immigrants. In one of the pamphlets on Japanese police, concern was expressed about an "increased frequency of crimes committed by foreign visitors, street crimes, and break-in crimes" (*Police of Japan* 2008, p. 21). With an influx of transients and migrants, Japanese police officers may have to contend with a higher volume of crime such as that witnessed by their American counterparts. The prefecture of Kokura, where this study was conducted, is still very homogeneous—with foreigners like the researcher, visiting for a brief time and departing. Potential troublemakers and active offenders are typically already known to police.

The fact that the Japanese are more group oriented than individualistic has been extensively covered (see Reichel, 2008; Alarid & Wang, 1997; Fenwick, 1982; Bayley, 1976, Christiansen, 1976; Clifford, 1976). Group cohesiveness, collective responsibility, and group consciousness combine with a sense of order to compel cooperative relationships among most segments of the Japanese community and their justice agencies (Reichel, 2008, p. 381). These traits make them less susceptible to breaking community norms (Clifford, 1976) and stay with them even when they relocate to a new society, as revealed in a comparative study of group consciousness between Japanese-American managers and Caucasian-American managers (Alarid & Wang, 1997). Some criminologists argue that most people are self-centered and thus more apt to care for their individual well-being first; and that much self-control has to be exercised for people to be empathetic towards others (see Gottfredson & Hirschi, 1990). According to Gottfredson & Hirschi, self-control is not an innate trait. People are socialized to understand the consequences of their actions and when this is done very early in life, it acts as a restraint to criminal behavior. Early introduction of self-control in life more likely stays the life course and, with other reinforcements like school and work, puts negative temptations in abeyance (see also Miller et al., 2008).

Besides its homogeneity, Japan's religious leanings, which include Confucianism, Buddhism, and Japanese-Shintoism, emphasize deep meditation and place much emphasis on respect for seniors as well as for the social order. These religions thus act as restraints to deviant behavior, more so than those religious doctrines practiced in the United States (see Fenwick, 1982, p. 65; Citizens Crime Commission, 1975, p. 51). According to Reichel (2008, p. 381), ridding their society of crime and maintaining and upholding high standards of morality take priority over the protection of "each individual rights" in Japan. Lippman (2007, p.25), however, reasons that in the United States individual rights are considered inalienable and can only be compromised to preserve social order, and at times as he notes, more emphasis is placed on the protection of individual rights.

Criminal Justice Factors

Fenwick (1982, p. 66) outlines a number of justice factors, including the "police, public participation, the courts, the prisons, gun control, and drug enforcement policies" that are responsible for controlling crime in Japan.

The Police

Japanese police engage in automobile patrolling sparingly. For the most part they rely on fixed police boxes/posts—the *kobans* (in urban areas) and the *chuzaishos* (in rural areas) (Bayley, 1976, 1991; Ames, 1976, 1981). Reichel (2008) attributes the reliance on fixed police posts rather than on automobile patrolling to two factors: the use of fixed boxes maintains community solidarity, and given that limited land space is available for roads, limiting the number of cars that traverse the streets is a matter of convenience. The presence of police boxes throughout the cities and in rural environs increases citizens/police officers' interactions, and such interactions are instrumental to a sound esprit de corps in the community and increased respect for the police (Reichel, 2008; Ames, 1976, 1981). The officials in the *kobans* provide a wide array of community services and crime control services in urban areas typical of the common understanding of what community policing is (Police of Japan, 2008, pp. 18–21).

A *koban* is a police station/post or more correctly "box" in urban areas. *Kobans* are different in architectural style and size, but an identification fixture is the sign "KOBAN," as well as a red lamp above the entrance. The officer at the *koban* patrols his sphere of work as well as making visits to residences in the area where he works. The *chuzai-sans* perform similar duties in rural areas. *Chuzaishos* are rural residential police boxes. The officer working in the *chuzaisho* is known as *chuzai-san*. The *chuzaisho* serves as both a police station and a residence. The front of the building is the police office, and the back rooms are the officer's residence. The officer plays both a proactive and reactive role. With regard to proactive policing, the *chusai-san* makes two visits annually to each household to familiarize himself with people in his community, as well as any problems that exist in the community; he also patrols the neighborhood. In regards to reactive policing, he responds to calls made or complaints made to him at the station. His wife and children assist him with little duties like answering phones, mingling with residents and listening to their complaint, as well as to gossip about troublemakers. Officers at both the *kobans* and *chuzaishos* have radio-equipped patrol cars that they sometimes use for patrolling, but more importantly for rapid response to crisis. American police officers on the other hand have been criticized for too heavily relying on automobile patrol (Samaha, 2006; Reiss, 1992). According to Samaha (2006), "Vehicle patrol has serious drawbacks. It contributes to poor police-community relations, especially in poor neighborhoods, where many residents think of police as a hostile occupational force" (p. 188).

Public Participation with the Justice System

The interdependence between the community and Japanese police officers is considered to be a huge contributory factor in crime prevention and control (Reichel, 2008; Bayley, 1991; Fenwick, 1982). The biannual visits that Japanese officers make to each household, the Crime Prevention Association composed of civilian volunteers, and the myriad services that Japanese police officers selflessly render to members of the community perhaps account for the low crime rates. Bayley (1991, p. 86) makes the following analogy: "An American policeman is like a fireman—he responds when he must. A Japanese policeman is more like a postman—he has a daily round of low-key activities that relate him to the lives of the people among whom he works."

Courts and Prisons

Although the court system throughout Japan is well coordinated, the majority of misdemeanors and petty offenses are disposed of informally, particularly since informal controls such as shame and disgrace that lawbreakers bring onto themselves seem more effective than penal sanctions (Reichel, 2008; Fenwick, 1982). Certainly, harsh penal sanctions are administered based on the level of egregiousness of the crime. The retributive stance coupled with those aspects of shame and embarrassment act as a deterrent to criminality.

Gun Control

Compared to the United States, gun control laws are extremely strict in Japan (Fenwick, 1982, Police of Japan, 2008). Indeed, possessing firearms and swords is highly restricted in Japan, and the lower incidence of firearm-related crime is attributed to such controls (Police of Japan, 2008, p. 36). In 2006, only 325 crimes involved the use of firearms in the country. Besides placing restrictions on gun ownership, in 2006 Japanese law enforcement officers seized 458 handguns, many of them from the *Boryokudan* (an organized crime group). This is deemed significant because of the 325 firearms crimes in 2006, 182 involved the use of handguns (see Police of Japan, 2008, p. 36). It is noteworthy that there has been a decline in gun-related crimes in Japan since 2002. Managing the gun problem also entails identifying the sources for gun purchases or smuggling operations and establishing domestic and international networks to intercept weapons.

Drug Enforcement Policies

Drug crimes and drug-related crimes are on the rise in Japan, and in 2006 the country witnessed its highest number of arrests for cannabis offenses (Police of Japan, 2008, p. 38). However, Yamamoto (2006) holds that compared to other countries and regions, drug abuse in Japan is low. Japan has implemented active antidrug measures domestically and in consort with other countries to counter drug abuse, including drastic measures to disrupt drug trafficking by striving to eliminate drug supply and curtail drug demand. It is in part due to these measures that the police contend that "smuggling of cocaine, heroin and opium is insignificant" (Police of Japan, 2008, p. 38).

The purpose of this study was to find out from the Japanese police officers the factors that contribute to the relatively low crime rates in Japan. A secondary focus was to learn from the officers the extent to which culture and police presence influence the high level of social order in that country.

SETTING AND PROCEDURES

The data for this study derive from research conducted in the summer and fall of 2008 in the prefecture of Kokura, comprising the cities of Kitakyushu and Fukuoka. This setting was chosen out of convenience since the researcher was at the time teaching a class at a local Japanese university. The host university was instrumental in arranging the interviews and visits to the police stations. The setting consists of an urban area with a population approximating 2 million people (True Knowledge, 2010).

The data collected in this study were based on interviews with nine law enforcement officers in three different settings. The methodological preference was dictated in part by the officers and in part by the nature of the inquiry. Both a standardized interview and face-to-face interviews were used. First, interviews were completed with four off-duty officers, two of whom were detectives. Weeks before leaving for Japan from the United States, a set of questions was sent to the officers in compliance with their request. In essence, this may be classified as a standardized interview since the questions were predetermined, and the officers' responses prepared (see Berg, 2007). Upon arrival in Kokura, the officers and the researcher met in an office at the local university for a face-to-face interview that also included a review of their prepared responses to the questions sent in advance. The prepared responses were read aloud by one of the officers who was an interpreter and fluent in English. Subsequently, conversations were held that blended open-ended discussions with probing questions regarding some of the prepared responses. Discussions spanned hours until a point of redundancy was reached.

Further, visits to two different police posts were made. These visits were crucial as they involved interviews with on-duty officers, and their responses were relevant in corroborating initial interview outcomes with the off-duty officers. Visits to two different police posts were necessary for several reasons: (1) One of the police posts was in the heart of the city representing an area with more intense police activity. (2) At the *koban* there were four police officers on duty. This was especially important as comments by one officer were reinforced or rebutted by another, or at least comments by one jogged the memory of another, or sparked an issue or response to a question. Preferring this type of group interview over one-on-one interviews, Berg (1995) states, "A far larger number of ideas, issues, topics, and even solutions to a problem can be generated through group discussion than through individual conversations" (p. 69). (3) Also, at the *koban* it was interesting to hear the viewpoint of a female officer, especially since there are not many female officers in the Japanese police force. (4) A visit to the *chuzaisho* was necessary as this police post was in the suburb of about 4,700 residents mostly comprising middle- to upper-middle-class homes. This area is mostly uneventful, and for the several hours spent at the post not a single phone call was received. (5) The *chuzaisho* is unique in that the police officer lives in the building, which serves as both the police office and his home. Here, besides interviewing the officer, the researcher had the opportunity to converse with the officer's spouse and children who also assisted around the office.

Field notes taken from the interviews and the prepared responses by the officers were later transcribed, and some of what the officers revealed was confirmed from observations during a police ride-along. Pamphlets were also compiled by the police in the prefecture of Kokura, which are then distributed to residents, and those published by the National Police Agency were enlightening. Data gathering techniques used in this study are in line with those traditionally used by field researchers involved in comparative or international studies (see Austin, 1987, 1995, 2005; Gerber et al., 1994).

DATA ANALYSIS AND DISCUSSION

Five themes formed the basis of the interviews with the police officers. The themes included: (1) factors that lead to low crime rates in Japan, (2) job responsibilities and impact on crime rates, (3) high points of the job, (4) challenges of the job, and (5) other job-related issues. Each of these themes will be discussed in the following sections.

Factors that Lead to Low Crime Rates in Japan

The officers at the *koban* credited their limited crime rates to their training and to citizens' respect for authority. With regard to their training, which emphasizes "poise and calmness even in the face of profound adversity," the officers stressed that this does not only enhance rapport with citizens, it limits violent confrontations. This sentiment was reiterated by the *chusai-san*, who stated, "Japanese police officers are very careful when and how to use force, because fairness to others, and proper behavior is emphasized at training, and indeed respect for other humans, fosters peace." In summary, the *chusai-san* stated that "What makes the Japanese system of policing efficient is that Japanese believe in respect for others, and the respect you give is the respect you get." In essence, their management style, which includes their ability to be level-headed, creates an atmosphere that limits tension, and even the urge to deviate from social norms.

In their prepared response to this question, the off-duty officers responded as follows: "Police officers need residents' cooperation; and for many years have tried to establish trust with the residents. Maintaining trust with residents facilitates the police officers' on-the-job efficiency. The respect officers receive is a token of the rapport developed with residents."

Given that existing literature supports the fact that the cultural notion of fear of "loss of face" is self-regulating, more so than police presence, it follows that Cohen and Felson's proposition remains true in the Japanese situation. That is, fear of loss of face eliminates to a large extent the urge to deviate, to disrespect seniors and those in authority, and provides some disincentive (guardianship) to commit crimes. The co-existence of fear of loss of face and the constant presence of the police in Japan arguably validates the central premise of routine activity theory even more. It is noteworthy that one of the detectives who participated in the interview had a slightly different take with regard to the role of custom in order maintenance. He stated that "tradition may have a role in instilling values, but people break laws. What is important is that officers try to establish trust with the people because when there is cooperation between the police and citizens the police are better placed to serve the people, and the people are more appreciative of the work of the police."

Whether officer composure and performance is correlated with training and education has not positively been determined (see Rydberg & Terrill, 2010; Truxillo et al., 1998; Sherman, 1980). If, as the on-duty Japanese officers contend that being placid regardless of the situation is emphasized during training, then one wonders how much training is required to achieve that level of discipline. The detectives who submitted prepared responses to questions and who participated in the ride-along had college degrees and had attended the National Police Academy in Tokyo. The *chusai-san*, on the other hand, had received only 21 months of training as a police officer upon graduating from high school, but his views on solving social problems and conducting himself as an officer were no different from those of the detectives. It follows that being civil and courteous to others is not something that one necessarily acquires from training or from extensive education, but instead is part of an officer's own innate characteristics, and how an officer chooses to approach the job is instrumental to how the officer handles encounters with citizens. Indeed the detectives in their prepared responses emphasized that "to citizens, our motto is kindness and sincerity; that's how we treat ordinary people. Community police officers are responsible to seek and maintain order. We make a pledge to do so. We work to maintain peace in communities to which we are assigned by grounding ourselves and winning the trust of the people, and thus gaining tranquility." The ideals expressed here by the Japanese officers are not unique to them; this is a commitment held by police officers involved in community policing in several countries including Singapore, the United States, and the United Kingdom, among others (Fairchild and Dammer, 2001). As Austin (2005) explains, a deep link between the police and the community exists in Singapore to an extent reminiscent of what transpires in Japan due to the officers' constant presence in residential areas and frequent meetings with residents.

Job Responsibilities and Impact on Crime Rates

Their job responsibilities, as the officers recounted them, included "patrolling their beats, criminal investigations, apprehending suspects, maintaining order, providing counseling services, helping distressed people, and helping the community in any way [they] can."

The *chusai-san* indicated that he works seven days a week even though he is allowed to take time off. As he added, the fact that he lives in the police station makes taking time off unrealistic since he still attends to people who stop by or who make phone calls. He was quick to point out that his constant presence reduced fear of crime, and more importantly, helped quell little disputes before they got out of hand. With regard to his responsibilities, the *chusai-san* indicated that his jurisdiction comprises 2,400 homes with 4,700 residents. He walks the beat and stops by people's homes to ask about their well-being, and if they are getting along with neighbors. If he sees any untoward behavior, he assumes the position of "a parent scolding a child so the child makes no further mistakes." He counsels residents on just about any issue, even those for which he has no expertise—such as financial matters. Police officers inquiring into one's financial viability is a cultural mold unique to the Japanese, and that in some societies particularly in the United States may be deemed an encroachment on citizens' privacy rights (see Reichel, 2008). The *chusai-san* contended that it is relevant to note that such consultations are increasing, and that he thinks that they are useful "because when people complain severely about financial issues, it is good to listen and provide advice, as well as to refer them to agencies that might assist them." Little steps like that, as the officer explained, help curb bigger problems in the future, and "when residents know I care, mutual trust is established with residents." The officer hastened to add that even though he runs into circumstances where people are in dire need, given his training, he is able to detach emotionally from the job. With regard to the crime fighting effort, in their prepared responses the detectives noted that "officers work as a team with residents to fight crime. Cooperation is the key for low crime in Japan. Working closely with the community contributes to the high efficiency of Japanese law enforcement. Further, we take a tough-on-crime approach, and we do not hesitate to seek justice if anyone breaks the law."

When asked about any big incidents that he had encountered in the nearly 1 year he had been at that post, the *chusai-san* stated that "I haven't had any. All I get are little disturbances." He noted that "in the event of a major issue, were it to occur, I can immediately alert officers in a nearby *koban* to assist me."

The detectives added that "community police officers patrol the streets and deal with accidents and incidents, and render residents crime prevention and safety guidance. They also deal with annoyances and nuisances." They informed the researcher that a one- or two-page newsletter on how to establish peace and tranquility in the community is sent out to each household. Each police box is required to contribute to this report. Officers go to people's homes to ask questions on a variety of issues. In the event of a felony, police officers get some tips from television; they then issue newsletters and visit residences in efforts to seek out the truth. In the summer, they tell residents to be careful at beaches; they give information on lost-and-found items, and they assist elderly persons who have lost their belongings. Officers organize meetings, and they use this opportunity to ask about the health and well-being of residents.

High Points of the Job

As to the uplifting aspect of their job, the officers at the *koban* indicated that "letters of appreciation from the community are always most gratifying." In response to what he liked about his job, the *chusai-san* volunteered that "citizens' appreciation and the fact that I am offered a home at the post are the top incentives of my job." The fact that he lives at the police post as he noted helps him save money. The officers also indicated that when no serious incidents occur, they feel satisfied that they are doing their job well, and that the community is reciprocating by maintaining order.

The question relating to family participation in police work was posed only to the *chusai-san* because it is only at the *chuzaisho* that the family is required to assist in small police duties. Asked about who mans the post when he is patrolling, he responded "My wife answers the phones, and responds to anyone who stops at the station. In the event of an emergency situation, or if my wife happens not to be at home when I am patrolling, calls are directed automatically to the headquarters, and the headquarters would then alert me and I will speed to the scene." The *chusai-san* is assisted by his family, who also create a rapport with members in the community. While their role is primarily to be supportive, the wife gets a small allowance for the assistance she gives—an allowance that the *chusai-san* acknowledges helps.

Challenges of the Job

The most challenging aspects of their jobs, as the officers at the *koban* indicated, concerned "the decision to treat an act as a crime or to simply regard it as something that could be dismissed with just a reprimand." More difficult even, is if the act was committed by a juvenile. Accusing a juvenile of a crime is particularly disconcerting "because if the juvenile is found guilty, the stigma of being a criminal stays with the child throughout his or her life." This is a legitimate concern especially since unlike in the United States, the records of juveniles are not subject to expungement.

When and how police officers use informal justice varies based upon the circumstances and on the personality of the officers, and at times when they prioritize arrests based on the severity of the offense, such selective enforcement of the law may be administratively ordered. However, police discretion that ignores arrests of habitual offenders or felons may constitute "dereliction of duty" (see LaGrange, 1998, p. 193). The officers at the *koban* noted that while they are sympathetic towards errant youths, when the crime is egregious the youth has to be arrested.

LaGrange (1998) poses a question regarding the impact that an arrest will have on an otherwise decent teenager who, based upon a lack of sound judgment, decides to break a window of a school building. This is the essence of the dilemma that the Japanese police officers expressed. The use of discretion in policing is not unique to the Japanese; informal processes, especially as they relate to juveniles, are utilized extensively especially for minor offenses in the United States unless there is an administrative policy that requires limited use of discretion (see McCluskey et al., 2004), and that is the case in Canada (see Schulenberg & Warren, 2009), and Australia as well (see Parker & Sarre, 2008).

To help minimize juvenile delinquency, the Japanese officers indicated that they have instituted several measures, which include: juvenile support centers that are instrumental in detecting troubled kids early on; monitoring them in hotspots; organizing networks among families of the juveniles, school administrators, and police volunteers; organizing drug prevention campaigns; engaging in sex education and establishing "cyber-control" with efforts to decrease sexually loaded material from reaching juveniles; and engaging juveniles in community events such as "clean–up campaigns" and sporting events.

Asked if she had experiences or issues different from those of her male colleagues, the lone female officer on duty at the *koban* responded that she felt at ease working with the men, and that even though there are few female officers in the police force, interest among female officers had sparked within the last few years, and recruitment of female officers had also increased to about 12,700 of the approximately 282,300 prefectural officers in 2007. She stated that she performs the same types of activities as her male colleagues, gets equal respect and is increasingly called upon to provide counsel to victims of domestic, sexual, and child abuse.

Martin (1989) had long since dispelled the myth that female officers might not be of comparable competence to their male counterparts. After nine surveys spanning different police departments in the United States, the findings in Martin's study revealed that performance evaluations of women vis-à-vis their male colleagues was similar, and that women were more inclined to resign or were fired in just about the same proportion as male officers.

In reference to what he disliked about his job, the *chusai-san* stated that he did not have off-duty time. "I work twenty-four hours each day, and even though, in theory, I may take time off, but because I live at the police station I still have to attend to residents who call or stop by the office with complaints. I must say that living at the post has its drawback since I virtually work all day long, each day of the year." It is to relieve the *chusai-sans* from such demands of the job that they are moved to different police positions after a year or two. Sometimes as the officer indicated, moving the *chusai-san* every other year is disruptive to children's education and also to friendships that the children may have made.

Other Job-Related Issues

When asked about what would constitute corruption, the officers at the *koban* remarked that "taking little gifts such as food is not corruption; it is simply a token of friendship and appreciation." They went on to say that gifts that are taken in exchange for some favor "like not filing a report against a person would constitute corruption;" and to curb corruption, officers are reshuffled every year or two. This is not to suggest that Japanese police officers are free of corruption; they too have been criticized for misusing their powers to extend favors to bureaucrats and other businessmen (see Takeshi, 2000; Hiromitsu, 2000).

What constitutes police corruption varies from country to country, but the Law Enforcement Code of Ethics and the International Association of Chiefs of Police ban officers from taking any gratuities. While it is not by itself a crime to accept things freely given, many police departments in the United States restrict officers from accepting any type of gratuity because of its apparent import (LaGrange, 1998). If the practice is allowed, as LaGrange explains, officers assume that givers expect some favor from the police, and this constitutes corruption. This is exactly what happens regularly in several African countries, especially Cameroon, Nigeria, Ghana (Transparency International, 2005).

Interestingly, the Japanese officers did not see taking little gifts as corruption unless the officer's intent was to circumvent the law in favor of the citizen. The *chusai-san* echoed the sentiments of the officers at the *koban* when asked about what acts would constitute corruption. He added that he avoids any gestures of impropriety, but "welcomes simple acts of kindness and appreciation." In order to minimize corruption, *chusai-sans* get rotated to other communities. However, residents can request an extension of the officer's stay in a community if they like the way the officer is doing his job. Ames (1981) gave an account of a visit that lasted over 3 hours that he and a *chusai-san* made to the home of a burglary victim. The victim provided food and drinks as they watched television. Fairchild and Dammer (2001, p. 108) commented that a practice like this opened up "room for corruption." When asked about how they would handle violations and other acts of impropriety by one of them, one of the detectives responded that "we shall not hesitate to expose any wrongdoing by one of us because what one person does is a poor reflection on the rest of us." Whether the Japanese officers engage in a code of silence and if they do, the extent to which they do, could not be gauged from the officers' responses. Following findings by the National Institute of Ethics in the United States (2000), 79% of the officers in one study indicated "that a law enforcement Code of Silence exists and is fairly common throughout the nation" (Samaha 2006, p. 173).

When asked about violence perpetrated on officers by criminals, the detectives indicated "that very rarely does a community police officer receive an on-the-job injury in Japan. Such is rare." Guns are highly regulated and likely limited to mobsters. Even the police are reluctant to openly carry firearms. No permits are issued for handguns, and only hunting permits are considered appropriate. Even daggers are prohibited, including swords. Interviews and conversations with on-duty officers at the *koban* and the *chuzaisho*, as well as with an archival analysis, strongly corroborated the detectives' response.

CONCLUSION

A quarter century has elapsed since Fenwick (1982, p. 70) analyzed why Japan experienced lower crime problems than the United States. He recommended, among other things, that the United States should "better integrate marginalized groups into the society, and focus attention on the fact that the primary responsibility for generalized social control lies with the community." The thrust of his recommendations rested on the fact that with education and employment extended to the majority of the population, crime should decrease; and when the community is involved in crime control, the police would be more effective in curbing crime. Community involvement in crime control in Japan has been documented as an effective and indispensable alliance, and this was confirmed by the nine Japanese officers interviewed in this study. It is noteworthy that as of 2008, there were about 32,000 volunteer community groups involved in crime prevention duties in Japan (Police of Japan, 2008, p. 21). The officers also stressed the necessity for officers to generate trust and respect with the citizenry since trust is a management tool that not only eases tension but facilitates the resolution of problems.

As Cohen and Felson (1979) explain, offenders are less likely to commit crimes when there is a presence of guardianship, and such guardianship is not only limited to the police or cameras; it includes members of the community. The importance of ordinary members in the community in crime prevention works well in Japan since it is based on long-standing cultural practices of shaming and ostracizing lawbreakers. Felson revisited his and Cohen's routine activity theory and amplified the significance of informal guardianship as the "quiet and natural method by which people prevent crime in the course of daily life. This control occurs as people interact and bring out the best in one another" (1994, pp. xii–xiii). The propositions put forth by both Cohen and Felson have thus proved to be beneficial in this study.

Many police departments in the United States are encouraging their officers to pursue college education, or at least some training relating to interpersonal skills. As an example, Samaha (2006) discusses what is going on in Peoria, Illinois where Chief of police Allen H. Andrews, Jr. says that "society is more complicated now. Society and I expect officers not just to be law enforcers but to be the grease on the wheels of solving social conflicts." In order to prepare officers for this duty, Chief Andrews "sends all recruits to special courses on courtesy and body language so they can read people's movements and focus on their own attitudes and intentions" (p. 166). On the other hand, several studies reveal no causal link between better/higher education and superior relationship with members of the community (see Worden, 1990, 1995; Truxillo et al., 1998). However, overlooked here is the corresponding attitude of people in the community. After all, how a lawbreaker or a would-be lawbreaker responds to a police officer is not entirely dependent on the officer's disposition.

As discussed above, a number of factors including cultural, structural, and criminal justice factors contribute to the low crime rate in Japan, and the majority of studies emphasize cultural factors and police presence as the most dominant. Studies on Japan are replete with accounts that confirm the impact of culture on just about every facet of life in Japan. Sherman (1998) suggests that evidence-based policing by itself is not sufficient; what is germane is an amalgamation of research that deals with an issue in order to come up with "evidence-based guidelines." Without such guidelines the assumption can easily be made that what works for Japan may work elsewhere, but as the Japanese officers stated: "Japanese police officers are not to make recommendations to U.S. officers. American police officers are certainly doing the best to keep peace just like the Japanese officers and remember we have different histories."

The interviews with the police officers in the study did not cover police subculture. Future research on Japanese policing should delve into this aspect. By focusing on the policing subculture in one culture, in this case the Japanese culture, information about the police subculture in general will follow. For example, much research has talked about the police subculture as a monolithic structure characterized by a commitment to the police organization, adherence to police values, and protection of the code of silence. However, it is not entirely clear whether such a subculture exists in all cultures. Expanding research on police subcultures across cultures will help to determine the degree to which the police subculture is influenced by: (1) the nature of police work and (2) the cultural influences guiding human behavior.

KEY TERMS

Routine activity theory
Reintegrative shaming
Groupism
Kobans
Chuzaishos
Evidence-based policing
Loss of face
Group consciousness
Chuzai-san

DISCUSSION QUESTIONS

1. You have read about the *koban*, now search online for additional information, and in a paragraph or two explain your impressions of it.
2. The *chusai-san* and family live in the *chuzaisho*, and the family is required to assist with petty police duties and to inform the *chusai-san* of any crime-related gossip. Do you think that this is a good policing strategy? Explain your response.
3. One of the explanations given about the low crime rates in Japan is the rigid gun laws and limited number of guns in circulation. On the other hand, some contend that much of the violent crime in the United States is a result of the high prevalence of guns. Summarize an argument to support or refute this contention.
4. Do you think that long-standing cultural orientation is the key to low crime rates in Japan?
5. What would you recommend to a heterogeneous society like the United States of America to do to curb crime?
6. Using the Internet, search for an example of a homogeneous society other than Japan. Is the crime rate in that society lower or higher than that of Japan? Explain any similarities and differences.
7. Explain how the *koban* and *chuzaisho* systems contribute to low crime rates in Japan.
8. Do you think that if the United States were to emulate in a complete fashion the *koban* and *chuziasho* systems that: (1) such systems would thrive? (2) that such systems will help curb crime?
9. The Japanese officers in this study explained their dilemma in pressing charges against juveniles. As a crime preventive measure Japanese police officers have instituted a number of programs listed in the discussion above to help curb juvenile crimes. The U.S. has similar programs in place. To what extent do you think these programs help deter juvenile crimes?

REFERENCES

Alarid, L., & Wang, H. (1997). Japanese management and policing in the context of Japanese culture. *Policing: An International Journal of Police Strategies and Management, 20*(4), 600–608.

Albanese, J. (2000). *Criminal justice.* (2000 update), Boston: Allyn and Bacon.

Ames, W. (1976). *Police and community in Japan* (Unpublished dissertation). University of Michigan, Ann Arbor, MI.

Ames, W. (1981). *Police and community in Japan*. Berkeley, CA: University of California Press.

Austin, W. T. (1987). Crime and custom in an orderly society: The Singapore prototype. *Criminology, 25*(2), 279–294.

Austin, W. T. (1995). Filipino self-help and peacemaking strategies: A view from the Mindanao hinterland. *Human and Organization, 54*(1), 10–19.

Austin, W. T. (2005). Life on the atoll: Singapore ecology as a neglected dimension of social disorder. *International Journal of Offender Therapy and Comparative Criminology, 49*(5), 478–490.

Bayley, D. (1976). *Forces of order—Police behavior in Japan and the United States*. Berkeley, CA: University of California Press.

Bayley, D. (1991). *Forces of order: Policing modern Japan*. Berkeley, CA: University of California Press.

Berg, B. (1995). *Qualitative research methods for the social sciences* (2nd ed.). Boston, MA: Allyn and Bacon.

Berg, B. (2007). *Qualitative research methods for the social sciences* (6th ed.). Boston, MA: Allyn and Bacon.

Christiansen, K. (1976). Industrialization, urbanization and crime. In *Crime and industrialization*. Stockholm, Sweden: Scandinavian Research Council for Criminology.

Citizens Crime Commission of Philadelphia. (1975). *Tokyo: One city where crime doesn't pay*. Philadelphia, PA: The Citizens Crime Commission of Philadelphia.

Clifford, W. (1976). *Crime control in Japan*. Lexington, MA: Lexington Books.

Cohen, L., & Felson, M. (1979). Social change and crime rate trends: A routine activity approach. *American Sociological Review, 44*, 588–608.

Dammer H., & Albanese, J. (2010). *Comparative criminal justice systems* (4th ed.). Belmont, CA: Wadsworth/ Thomson.

Fairchild, E., & Dammer, H. (2001). *Comparative criminal justice systems* (2nd ed.). Belmont, CA: Wadsworth/ Thomson Learning.

Felson, M. (1994). *Crime and everday life: Insight and implications for society*. Thousand Oaks, CA: Pine Forge Press.

Fenwick, C. (1982). Crime and justice in Japan: Implications for the United States. *International Journal of Comparative and Applied Criminal Justice, VI,* 1.

Gerber, J., Weeks, S., & Denq, F. (1994). Tea ceremony and tatami mat making: Gender difference in access to educational programs in Japanese prisons. *The Prison Journal, 74*(4), 462–473.

Gottfredson, M., & Hirschi, T. (1990). *A general theory of crime*. Palo Alto, CA: Stanford University Press.

Harper, H., Evans, R., Thornton, M., Sullenberger, T., & Kelly, C. (1999). Cross-cultural comparison of police personality. *International Journal of Comparative and Applied Criminal Justice, 23*(1), 1–15.

Hiromitsu, O. (2000). Who polices the police? *Japan Quarterly, 47*(2), 50–58.

Jiao, A. (2001). Police and culture: A comparison between China and the United States. *Police Quarterly, 4*(2), 156–185.

LaGrange, R. (1998). *Policing American society* (2nd ed.). Chicago, IL: Nelson-Hall Publishers.

Langworthy, R., & Travis, L. (1994). *Policing in America: A balance of forces*. New York, NY: Macmillan.

Lippman, M. (2007). *Contemporary criminal law: Concepts, cases, and controversies*. Thousand Oaks, CA: Sage Publications, Inc.

Martin, S. (1989). Women on the move? A status report on women in policing. In R. G. Dunham & G. P. Alpert (Eds.), *Critical issues in policing*. Prospect Heights, IL: Waveland Press.

McClusky, J., Varano, S., Huebner, B., & Bynum, T. (2004). Why do you refer? The effects of a policy change on juvenile referrals. *Criminal Justice Review, 15*(4),437–461.

Miller, M., Schreck, C., & Tewksbury, R. (2008). *Criminological theory: A brief introduction* (2nd ed.). Boston, MA: Pearson/Alyn and Bacon.

National Institute of Ethics. (2000). Police Code of Ethics facts revealed. International Association of Chiefs of Police Conference. Retrieved from http://www.aele.org/loscode2000.html.

Parker, A., & Sarre, R. (2008). Policing young offenders: What role discretion? *International Journal of Police Science & Management, 10*(4), 474–485.

Police of Japan (2008). Tokyo, Japan: National Police Agency 2-1-2 Kasumigaseki, Chiyoda-ku.

Reichel, P. (2008). *Comparative criminal justice systems: A topical approach* (5th ed.). Upper Saddle River, NJ: Pearson/Prentice Hall.

Reiss, A. (1992). Police organization. In M. Tonry, & N. Morris (Eds.), *Modern policing*. Chicago: IL: University of Chicago Press.

Rydberg, J., & Terrill, W. (2010). The effect of higher education on police behavior. *Police Quarterly*, *13*(1), 92–120.

Samaha, J. (2006). *Criminal justice* (7th ed.). Belmont, CA: Thomsom/Wadsworth.

Schulenberg, J., & Warren, D., (2009). Police discretion with apprehended youth: Assessing the impact of juvenile specialization. *Police Practice and Research*, *10*(1), 3–16.

Sherman, L. (1980). Causes of police behavior: The current state of quantitative research. *Journal of Research in Crime and Delinquency*, *17*, 71.

Sherman, L. (1998). *Evidence-based policing*. Retrieved from http://www.policefoundation.org/pdf/Sherman.pdf.

Steinhoff, P. (1993). Review: Pursuing the Japanese police. *Law and Society Review*, *27*(4), 827–850.

Takeshi, T. (2000). Light and shadow in Japan's police system. *Japan Quarterly*, *47*(2), 41–49.

Terrill, R. (1999). *World criminal justice systems: A survey* (4th ed.). Cincinnati, OH: Anderson Publishing.

Transparency International. (2005). Retrieved from www.transparency.org/policy_research/surveys_indices/cpi/2005/in_depth.

True Knowledge (2010). Population of Kitakyushu, Japan 2010. Retrieved from http://www.trueknowledge.com/q/population_of_kitakyushu_japan_2010.

Truxillo, D., Bennet, S., & Collins, M. (1998). College education and police job performance: A ten year study. *Public Personnel Management*, *27*(2), 269.

Worden, R. (1990). A badge and a baccalaureate: Policies, hypothesis, and further evidence. *Justice Quarterly*, 7, 565.

Worden, R. (1995). The causes of police brutality. In W. A. Geller & H. Toch (Eds.), *And justice for all*: *Understanding and controlling police use of force*. Washington, DC: Police Executive Research Forum.

Yamagishi, T., Cook, K. S., & Watabe, M. (1998). Uncertainty, trust, commitment formation in the United States and Japan. *American Journal of Sociology*, *104*, 165–194.

Yamamoto, J. (2006). Recent trends of drug abuse in Japan. *Annals of the New York Academy of Sciences*, *1025*, 430–438.

Zhang, L., Zhou, D., Messner, S. F., Liska, A. E., Krohn, M., Liu, J., & Lu, Z. (1996). Crime prevention in a communitarian society: Bang-Jiao and Tiao-Jie in the People's Republic of China. *Justice Quarterly*, *13*, 199–222.

CHAPTER 20

Nash in Najaf: Game Theory and Its Applicability to the Iraqi Conflict

Dr. Hank J. Brightman
United States Naval War College

"You, the Iraqi army and police forces, don't walk alongside the occupiers, because they are your archenemy."[1] This call for solidarity amongst indigenous security forces (ISF) and domestic insurgents (DI) by Shiite cleric and leader Muqtada al-Sadr in April 2007 is simply the latest evidence in support of this researcher's three years of applying game theory to the Iraqi conflict. Although other studies have examined Operation Iraqi Freedom from perspectives such as democratic nation building in an area of the world where such forms of government historically have not been the norm, this article represents the first known effort to apply the game-theory concepts of "Pareto improved" and "Paretooptimal" strategies (named after Italian economist Vilfredo Pareto) as well as "Nash" and "preferred" equilibriums (the former named after American mathematician John Nash) to the Iraqi conflict.

Specifically, this article examines how, through application of game theory to this model, U.S. and coalition forces will ultimately suffer casualties at an increasing rate the longer they remain in Iraq. This will occur because both DIs and ISFs will turn away from attacking each other towards a point of mathematical corruption. At this theoretical point, American and coalition troops will become the target of broad based DI attacks, with intelligence frequently provided by ISFs. For the purposes of this article, *ISF* refers to the Iraqi military as well as state and local police, and *DI* refers to the various domestic insurgent groups within Iraq.

In order to fully understand how two seemingly disparate entities—ISFs and DIs—will ultimately work together in an effort to improve both of their respective positions, one must examine the basics of game theory and the associated concepts of bargaining and equilibrium. In the following discussion, such terms as *player, improved, optimal, corruption, preferred,* and so forth, are used in their mathematical rather than their usual sense.

Hank J. Brightman (2007). Nash in Najaf: Game Theory and Its Applicability to the Iraqi Conflict. Air & Space Power Journal, Fall. Reprinted by permission of Air & Space Power.

FLASHBACK TO LOGIC 101: THE PRISONER'S DILEMMA

Developed by Merrill Flood and Melvin Dresher at the RAND Corporation in 1950, the "prisoner's dilemma"—an activity often played out in college logic, mathematics, and economics classes—demonstrates that if two players, suspect A and suspect B, act only in their own self-interest, both will suffer dire consequences.[2] For example, if each suspect is held in a separate interrogation room and told that by either confessing to the crime or "ratting out" his or her accomplice, each can receive a reduced sentence, then both suspects will either implicate the other or confess to the crime. This is commonly referred to as a zero-sum game because one prisoner's gain becomes the other's loss. If each condemns the other, then both will incur the maximum penalty. However, if both confess independently, each will incur some penalty—albeit likely a lesser one because they have shown they are willing to "cooperate" with the authorities.

Lastly, if the two suspects work together and adopt the common strategy that would appear at first blush to benefit each one less (remaining silent), the benefit to both will actually increase—because the State, lacking a confession or statement of the other's guilt, will likely charge each with a lesser offense. The lesson learned from the prisoner's dilemma and similar scenarios is that players in competition with each other sometimes gain more by conspiring than by attempting to combat each other to the last.

GAME THEORY 101: A PRIMER

Mathematicians refer to scenarios such as the prisoner's dilemma as simple form games (SFG)—also referred to as normal form games—which commonly have two players, each of whom strives to receive the highest payoff at the end of a simultaneous move (i.e., by seeking what is referred to in economics as a Pareto optimal position). One determines payoffs—outcomes with real value to each player—through a process called quantification, conducted by primary stakeholders who have a direct, vested interest in the outcome of the game. In the Iraqi conflict, the two players within the SFG are the ISFs and DIs. The United States and coalition forces are not considered players in this game (explained later in this article).

Additionally, in extensive form games (EFG)—which feature two or more players engaged in multiple move-for-move exchanges—players generally worry less about intermediate payoffs than the ultimate payoff at the conclusion of the game. Obviously, quantification of the EFG is far more complex than in the SFG because one must consider both short-term and long-term payoff values. Moreover, as mathematicians John von Neumann and Oskar Morgenstern discovered, EFGs are frequently not zero-sum games (i.e., one player's loss does not always perfectly correlate with another player's gain, depending on the complexity of the rules); therefore, predicting the outcome based solely on the payoffs proves difficult at best.[3] Because EFGs are distinguished by multiple moves, players must possess an overall broad strategy (as they would in the SFG) as well as smaller substrategies to counter the other players' moves throughout the game.

In the EFG, as time progresses, the model becomes susceptible to influence from outside forces, termed "strange attractors." Because payoffs in the EFG are not as readily apparent and the rules are generally more complex than in the SFG, these strange attractors affect the players' willingness to adhere to previously stated rules and therefore decrease the overall stability of the game.

ACHIEVING EQUILIBRIUM: "CAN'T WE ALL JUST GET ALONG?" _____

As time elapses, both SFGs and EFGs become less stable due to player frustration (and, in some cases, physical fatigue). Accordingly, each player will begin to reduce his or her expectations for the ultimate payoff. Consider the gambler who feeds quarters into a slot machine for an hour. This is essentially a two-player SFG (the gambler and the house), consisting of a single turn, with the focus on an immediate payoff. Ultimately, the gambler will likely walk away from the "one-armed bandit" down $25 after 45 minutes without winning the jackpot—an especially likely outcome if the player is down to her last dollar (limited resources), has agreed to meet her sister-in-law in an hour to catch a Las Vegas show (time constraints), and is feeling pangs of hunger because she has not yet eaten lunch (player fatigue). Similarly, the professional poker player may be willing to cut his losses at five-card stud (an EFG because it involves multiple turns, players, payoffs, strategies, and substrategies) and accept a smaller pot rather than play through to the end and face a new dealer later in the game (a strange attractor) who clearly knows the fine art of dealing.

As players' expectations for the ultimate payoff start to fade with the passing of time (in the case of the EFG, with the destabilizing influence of strange attractors), each player begins to think about how, by negotiating with the opponent, he or she might end the game without suffering additional losses. One refers to the point at which players start to work cooperatively towards agreement as bargaining towards equilibrium (or, in economics, Pareto improvement).When both players have reached a point at which they can achieve the highest aggregate payoff, the game ends in preferred equilibrium.

However, the influence of strange attractors in a model that will become increasingly unstable (bifurcated) over time often induces players to hasten their desire for a Pareto improved position instead of a superior (Pareto optimal) position—even though doing so may lessen their ultimate payoff because they did not play through to the end of the game. One refers to the point at which both players reach Pareto improvement, despite the fact that they may have received a greater payoff had they waited, as Nash equilibrium. First theorized by Princeton University professor John Nash, this equilibrium is sometimes described as an inchoate or interrupted equilibrium because the players reach a point of compromise prior to the conclusion of the game's ultimate payoff.[4] Several Nash equilibriums may exist at various points prior to achieving preferred equilibrium. Most SFGs and EFGs do not start out with players seeking to work cooperatively (i.e., striving for Pareto improvement). However, as each player's "winner take all" strategy clearly becomes less viable with the passing of time, both players realize that the longer it takes to come to consensus and the more resources they expend in their individual quest for dominance, the smaller the ultimate payoff should they emerge victorious (an economic concept known as Rubinstein Bargaining).[5] Ultimately, players strive to reach consensus if for no other reason than they wish to lessen their losses.

In applying Nash equilibrium to the prisoner's dilemma, one sees that this equilibrium point (both players confessing to the crime) will preempt the preferred equilibrium (both players remaining silent). This is especially true with the passing of time (prisoners do not like being left alone in interrogation rooms) and, in the case of an EFG, if strange attractors are introduced into the model (e.g., so-called eyewitnesses, purported new evidence, etc.). Thus, the passing of time and the influence of strange attractors preempt achieving the preferred equilibrium and instead yield the inchoate or Nash equilibrium. The presence of U.S. and coalition forces in Iraq, especially over time, may actually hasten a Nash response between ISFs and DIs.

CORRUPTION BETWEEN PLAYERS: THE SIMPLE FORM GAME AND THE IRAQI CONFLICT

Equipped with a working knowledge of SFGs, EFGs, Pareto improvement, Pareto optimal, and Nash and preferred equilibriums, one can not only examine each player's prospective payoffs but also predict the point at which both the inchoate (Nash) and preferred equilibriums will occur in the Iraqi conflict. In order to identify these points, the remainder of this article assumes a two-player game, namely with ISFs and DIs. Admittedly, attempting to contain the myriad of security entities under the ISF umbrella will likely prove as much of a generalization as placing the many native terrorist organizations that exist in Iraq within the DI grouping. The many law-enforcement and military organizations that comprise them ISF category, along with numerous hegemonic entities that make up the DI set, represent a variety of heterogeneous cultures, values, beliefs, and often competing interests.

Figure 20-1 provides a summary of payoffs quantified for both players in the simple-form, zero-sum game for the Iraqi conflict as well as each player's Pareto optimal strategy (point value equals four). It also identifies the respective quadrants in which the Nash and preferred equilibriums will occur.

In Figure 20-1's SFG, the payoffs for both players are based on varying degrees of remaining active or passive. Each player hopes that the other will not move (i.e., will remain passive), thus achieving a Pareto optimal position for himself or herself. However, if this one-move SFG is repeated over and over again, it becomes clear to both players that neither is willing to remain passive. Over time, as player frustration increases, resources begin to dwindle, and fatigue sets in, the players will begin bargaining towards equilibrium (i.e., seeking Pareto improvement as opposed to Pareto optimal).

As illustrated, one would attain the preferred equilibrium in this SFG at the "3, 3" quadrant because the highest aggregate payoff occurs at this point in the game. One must remember that

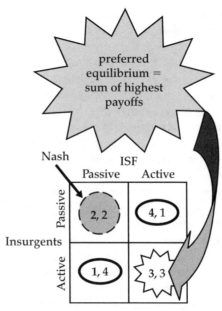

FIGURE 20-1. Iraqi conflict as a simple form game.

preferred equilibrium has no connection to the player's Pareto optimal strategy; rather, it is simply a mathematical expression for the point at which one can derive the greatest quantified payoff value.

As both players continue bargaining, the game moves from a competitive to a cooperative mode, leading to increased communication, which in turn yields further bargaining between players. Inflexible rules and intransigent positions become more elastic, and the players proffer side payments to hasten agreement. At this point, the game is said to have become mathematically corrupted because the players are no longer following the rules established prior to initial play. They have also moved from focusing on Pareto optimal positions to Pareto improved positions. Therefore, the inchoate or Nash equilibrium will inevitably occur at the "2, 2" quadrant.

When one applies these concepts to the SFG for the Iraqi conflict, the challenges faced by U.S. and coalition forces in Iraq become readily apparent. Ultimately, the model will become mathematically corrupted. Both players will move from seeking Pareto optimal to Pareto improved positions (i.e., ISFs and DIs will lessen their expectations, hastening equilibrium). Moreover, for reasons already discussed, Nash equilibrium will preempt the two players from attaining the preferred equilibrium (the quadrant in which equilibrium at the highest aggregate payoff value in the model will occur) wherein DIs continue to carry out attacks with improvised explosive devices throughout Iraq, and ISFs continue to arrest or kill terrorists.

It is important to understand that one can think of all equilibriums (Nash and preferred) as solutions. One can use software such as the publicly available Gambit application (originally developed by Theodore Turocy and Andrew McLennan in 1994 and now in its 11th release) to test the probability and frequency of these solutions occurring within the parameters of the model.[6] Repeated test runs of the zero-sum Iraqi conflict SFG yield the same result: a Nash response in which ISFs and DIs are willing to "sacrifice" U.S. and allied forces to achieve Pareto improvement is inevitable. Evidence already exists to suggest that bargaining between players has begun, such as Prime Minister Nouri al-Maliki's proposed National Reconciliation Plan, which would afford partial amnesty to some DIs.[7]

U.S. INTERESTS IN IRAQ: THE EXTENSIVE FORM GAME _____

Mathematically speaking, neither the United States nor its coalition forces can be considered players in the Iraqi conflict SFG because the United States cannot quantify payoffs. This also holds true in the EFG because America's citizenry does not have a direct, primary stakeholder interest in the conflict (i.e., they are not part of the quantification process). Only the Iraqi people—represented in this game by the two primary players (ISFs and DIs)—are fundamentally and intimately affected by the payoffs at each turn within the EFG, as well as by the ultimate payoff at the conclusion of the game.

Indeed, from a game-theory perspective, one finds very few conflicts in American history wherein U.S. forces have had the ability to participate in the quantification process as a primary player, save for the colonists in the American Revolutionary War, Union and Confederate forces in the Civil War, and servicemen in the U.S. intervention during World War II after the Japanese attack at Pearl Harbor. No one should ever dismiss the brave and noble actions of U.S. forces in other conflicts, but from an EFG perspective, one can mathematically consider the United States a player only when America directly involves itself in the quantification of payoffs.

For a party to assume this role, its stakeholder interest must have value equal to that of the other players. This is not to suggest that U.S. and coalition forces do not affect the model or its two players (ISFs and DIs) in the Iraqi conflict EFG. Indeed, those forces function as strange attractors. For the purposes of the current situation in Iraq, U.S. and coalition forces, multinational business interests, third-party foreign-terrorist organizations, and other interested parties would all be considered strange attractors whose predominant role involves hastening the model towards equilibrium. As time progresses and the model continues to bifurcate, the EFG becomes inherently less stable; thus, strange attractors play a greater role in moving the players towards cooperative bargaining (Pareto improvement). As was the case in the SFG presented earlier, the EFG becomes corrupt. Players begin working in cooperation (bargaining towards equilibrium) rather than competing for a Pareto optimal position.

In the Iraqi conflict, bargaining towards equilibrium entails emergent conspiracies between the two players—ISFs and DIs—as the game becomes less stable. Police officers begin tipping off insurgents as to where raids will take place in exchange for protection from future attacks, and terrorists provide bribes to Iraqi soldiers in exchange for overlooking caches of household weapons. The revelation that the late terrorist leader Abu Musab al-Zarqawi's cell phone contained telephone numbers for some of Iraq's senior Interior Ministry officials and lawmakers provides further evidence that Pareto improvement may have already commenced between ISFs and DIs.[8] In March 2006, Sgt Paul E. Cortez, Pfc Jesse Spielman, SPC James Barker, and Pvt Stephen D. Green raped and murdered 14-year-old Abeer Qassim al-Janabi and then killed her family.[9] Subsequently, in September 2006, insurgents killed three U.S. soldiers simply because they served in the same unit as the four former soldiers who carried out this heinous crime. Iraqi Interior Ministry officials refused to condemn the killing of the U.S. soldiers, which Iraqis widely regarded as an "honor killing."[10] The insurgents' ability to capture and kill U.S. service members suggests a level of access to operational-security plans for U.S. forces previously unavailable to terrorist entities.[11]

Using the Gambit software application, we can model the EFG for the Iraqi conflict from the perspective of DIs: player one in the dominant strategy position (i.e., DIs make the first move). The results (**Fig. 20-2**) appear similar to those for the SFG (Fig. 20-1).

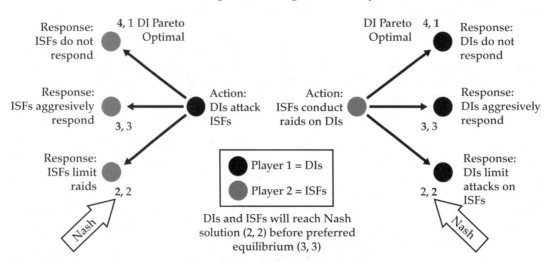

Domestic Insurgents and Indigenous Security Forces

FIGURE 20-2.   Iraqi conflict as an extensive form game.

CONCLUSIONS: WHERE DO WE GO FROM HERE?

As both the SFG and EFG models show when applied to the Iraqi conflict, both players (ISFs and DIs) will ultimately abandon their Pareto optimal strategies and instead begin bargaining towards equilibrium. When this happens, the model will become corrupted, and a Nash solution will pre-empt the preferred equilibrium. In the EFG, the presence of strange attractors such as U.S. and co-alition forces, foreign-terrorist entities, and other third-party interests may serve only to hasten this process in an increasingly bifurcating model. Release of *The Iraq Study Group Report* of December 2006, which specifically cites that "violence is increasing in scope and lethality," coupled with in-creasingly nonlinear attacks against U.S. and coalition forces (e.g., improvised chlorine chemical attacks, use of women as suicide bombers, etc.) suggests that the model explored in this article continues to destabilize.[12] Moreover, additional conflicts between Israeli forces and the Lebanese Hezbollah Party may introduce additional strange attractors into the model, further hastening the "2, 2" Nash payoff even more quickly than initially predicted using the Gambit software application.

It is possible for the United States to assume a player role in Iraq rather than serve as a strange attractor. However, to do so, stakes for Americans would need to equal those of the Iraqi people in order for the quantification process to occur. The United States would have to commit hundreds of thousands—if not millions—of military and civilian personnel to Iraq for decades, which it could accomplish in the short term only by fully mobilizing all reserve-component forces and initiating a military draft to meet future needs. U.S. and Iraqi culture and values would need to become inex-tricably linked. Each American would have to feel a stakeholder interest in Iraq, evidenced through personal sacrifice in the form of military or civilian service in support of Iraqi Freedom or the ra-tioning of U.S. goods to support the Iraqi people (comparable to rationing during World War II). Only then could America effectively participate in the quantification process. It is highly unlikely that present-day Americans or their elected representatives would be willing to commit to personal sacrifices, such as a military draft, war taxes, or the rationing of food and supplies. Accordingly, it is not mathematically possible for America to achieve player status in Iraq.

One must note that U.S. policy decisions take into account elements beyond the theoretical constructs of the SFG or EFG. Even if America cannot obtain player status, excellent reasons may exist for the United States and coalition forces to remain in Iraq, such as nation-building and hu-manitarian purposes.

However, American policy makers and the public must be prepared to accept the fact that if U.S. forces remain in Iraq, the soldiers, sailors, airmen, and marines bravely serving there will re-main a strange attractor in a mathematical model that is destabilizing over time. Within this game, DIs and ISFs will eventually arrive at Nash equilibrium.

NOTES

1. Associated Press, "Radical Cleric Calls on Iraqis to Halt Cooperation with U.S. Military," *FOXNews.com*, 8 April 2007, http://www.foxnews.com/story/0,2933,264814,00.html (ac-cessed 10 April 2007).
2. Following World War II, private and quasigovernmental think tanks such as the RAND Corporation were established as a means to further research in areas such as war gaming and hostile-action contingency planning. Flood and Dresher were among the first of this new breed of mathematicians focusing on multiplayer simulations. Douglas Hofstadter

expanded upon and clarified much of their original research in this area. See Douglas R. Hofstadter, *Metamagical Themas: Questing for the Essence of Mind and Pattern* (New York: Basic Books, 1985).

3. In 1944 Princeton University professors John von Neumann and Oskar Morgenstern authored their landmark economic paper "Expected Utility Theory," which focused exclusively on the application of strategic game theory to social problems. Their technique was subsequently used to examine virtually every social-organizational problem imaginable, from settling antitrust disputes to the U.S.-USSR arms race during the Cold War. "The von Neumann–Morgenstern Expected Utility Theory," *The History of Economic Thought*, Bernard Schwartz Center for Economic Policy Analysis, http://cepa.newschool.edu/het/essays/uncert/vnmaxioms.htm (accessed 10 April 2007).

4. See Carlo C. Jaeger et al., "Decision Analysis and Rational Action," working papers, chap. 3, http://www.pik potsdam.de/~cjaeger/working_papers/v3chap03.pdf (accessed 10 April 2007).

5. Ariel Rubinstein's theory of 1982 states that in an alternating bargaining game in which one player makes an offer followed by the other, the ultimate value of the payoff will decrease the longer the game is played. Ultimately, the players will be willing to settle for a lesser payoff simply to end the game. See Lucy White, "Prudence in Bargaining: The Effect of Uncertainty on Bargaining Outcomes," Harvard Business School, 9 December 2003, http://www.people.hbs.edu/lwhite/pdf/newfiles/prudence%20in%20bargaining.pdf (accessed 10 April 2007).

6. The *Gambit Software Application for Game Theory* has been used extensively in mathematical modeling and simulation since its inception in 1994. The current version of the software, developed by Richard McKelvey, Andrew McLennan, and Theodore Turocy, allows the user to explore player strategies, contingencies, and outcomes for Nash equilibrium as well as for several other game theory models. The current version of the Gambit software application is available free of charge at "Software Tools for Game Theory," *Gambit*, http://econweb.tamu.edu/gambit/support.html (accessed 10 April 2007).

7. Prime Minister Nouri al-Maliki unveiled the National Reconciliation Plan on 6 June 2006 for the purpose of relieving tension between various religious and ethnic elements vying for power in Parliament. Under the terms of this plan, approximately 2,500 Iraqi detainees held in U.S. and allied custody would be released without prejudice or further governmental action. Jaime Jansen, "Iraq Government to Release 2,500 Detainees in Reconciliation Bid," *Jurist: Legal News and Research*, http://jurist.law.pitt.edu/paperchase/2006/06/iraq-government-to-release-2500.php (accessed 10 April 2007).

8. Killed in a targeted bombing north of Baghdad by U.S. and coalition forces on 8 June 2006, Abu Musab al-Zarqawi was considered the leading figure behind many of the bombings and kidnappings in Iraq, from the 2003 invasion up until his death. Al-Zarqawi was credited with implementing a complex terror-cell structure comparable to al-Qaeda's other operations around the world. Ellen Knickmeyer and Jonathan Finer, "Insurgent Leader Al-Zarqawi Killed in Iraq," *washingtonpost.com*, 8 June 2006, http://www.washingtonpost.com/wp-dyn/content/article/2006/06/08/AR2006060800114.html (accessed 10 April 2007).

9. In February 2007, Sergeant Cortez accepted a plea bargain and will be eligible for parole in 10 years. Specialist Barker was sentenced to 90 years in a military prison, and Private Green was dishonorably discharged. "U.S. Soldier Sentenced to 100 Years for Iraq Rape, Killing," *Aljazeera.com*, 23 February 2007, http://www.aljazeera.com/me.asp?service_ID=13000 (accessed 10 April 2007).

10. See Associated Press, "Group: Soldiers Killed over Rape-Slaying," *USA Today*, 11 July 2006, http://www.usatoday.com/news/world/iraq/2006-07-10-group-claim_x.htm (accessed 10 April 2007).

11. DI access to the operations data of U.S. and coalition forces appears to be growing in Iraq. In addition to knowing the details with respect to where and when U.S. forces would be located on the day this ambush took place, *The Iraq Study Group Report* notes that the alliance between insurgent groups and government officials in some cases has compromised operational security. James A. Baker III et al., *The Iraq Study Group Report* (New York: Vintage Books, 2006), 5, http://permanent.access.gpo.gov/lps76748/iraq_study_group_report.pdf (accessed 10 April 2007). Lastly an attack in Karbala on 22 January 2007, which left 27 people dead, including two marines, went undetected because the terrorists had U.S. and Iraqi military uniforms and passes. Damien Cave, "Troops Killed by 'Insurgents' Wearing U.S. Army Uniforms," *Infowars.com*, 22 January 2007, http://www.infowars.com/ articles/iraq/ troops_killed_by_insurgents_wearing_us_army_uniforms.htm (accessed 10 April 2007).

12. Baker et al., *Iraq Study Group Report*, xiii.

Name Index

Subject Index

NOTE: Page numbers followed by *f* refer to figures; page numbers followed by *t* refer to tables.